The Best and Wurst of German Dining: A Guide to Eating Auf Deutsch

German	Pronunciation	English	German	Pronunciation	English
Condiments			**Implements**		
Pfeffer	*fef*-fer	Pepper	**Serviette**	sare-vee-*et*-uh	Napkin
Senf	zenf	Mustard	**Löffel**	*leu*-ful	Spoon
Salz	saltz	Salt	**Teller**	*tel*-ler	Plate
Zucker	*zoo*-ker	Sugar	**Mealtimes**		
Courses			**Abendessen**	*ah*-bent-essen	Dinner
Hauptgerichte	*howpt*-guh-rick-tuh	Main courses	**Mahlzeit**	*mall*-site	Mealtime
			Frühstück	*froo*-shtook	Breakfast
Vorspeisen	*for*-shpeye-zen	Appetizers	**Mittagessen**	*mit*-tog-essen	Lunch
Nachspeisen	*nock*-shpeye-zen	Desserts	**Places to Eat and Drink**		
Drinks			**Biergarten**	*beer*-gar-ten	Outdoor area, serving beer and food
Apfelschörle	*ap*-full-shor-luh	Half apple juice, half sparkling water	**Lokal**	lo-*call*	Local bar
			Bierhalle	*beer*-hall	Large room, serving beer and traditional meals
Saft	zoft	Juice			
Bier	beer	Beer			
Sekt	sect	Sparkling wine, champagne	**Ratskeller**	*rats*-keller	Restaurant in the basement of a town hall
Coke	*co*-ca	Coca-Cola	**Hofbräuhaus**	*hofe*-brow-howse	Beer hall, serving its own brand of beer
Sprudelwasser	*shproodel*-vahs-sir	Sparkling water			
Getränke	geh-*trenk*-kuh	Drinks			
Tee	tay	Tea	**Stube**	*shtu*-buh	A room, literally; also a cozy restaurant
Kaffee	caff-*ay*	Coffee			
Wasser	*vahs*-sir	Water			
Milch	miltsch	Milk	**Imbiss**	*im*-bis	Snack bar; also a snack
Wein	vine	Wine			
Implements			**Weinstube**	*vine*-shtu-buh	Small restaurant where wine is the specialty
Gabel	*gah*-bull	Fork			
Messer	*mes*-sir	Knife			
Glas	glahss	Glass	**Kneipe**	*kni*-puh	Cozy neighborhood bar
Schale	*shawl*-uh	Bowl			
Karte	*car*-tuh	Menu			

German	Pronunciation	English	German	Pronunciation	English
Food Items			**Food Items**		
Ananas	ah-na-*nas*	Banana	**Sauerbraten**	*sour*-bra-ten	Marinated beef oven- or pot- roasted
Kartoffelsalat	car-*toff*-el-saw-lot	Potato salad			
Apfel	*ahp*-fell	Apple			
Kirschen	*keer*-shen	Cherries	**Fleisch**	flysch	Meat
Auflauf	*owf*-lowf	Casserole	**Sauerkraut**	*sour*-kraut	Shredded cabbage cooked in vinegar
Knödel	kuh-*no*-del	Dumplings			
Beilagen	*bie*-loggen	Side dishes			
Kochwurst	*coke*-wurst	Boiled sausages	**Fleischsteak**	*flysch*-shtake	Beefsteak
			Schokolade	shock-oh-*laud*-uh	Chocolate
Birne	*beer*-na	Pear	**Gans**	gahnz	Goose
Kuchen	*koo*-kin	Cake	**Schnitzel**	*shnit*-sul	Seasoned pork cutlet
Blaukohl	*blau*-krout	Red cabbage			
Lebkuchen	*layb*-koo-kin	Spice-and-honey cake	**Geflügel**	guh-*flew*-gull	Chicken (see also Hühnchen)
Braten	*braw*-ten	Roast, grill, fry	**Schweinefleisch**	schwine-uh-flysch	Pork
Mandeln	*mon*-deln	Almonds	**Gemüse**	guh-*muse*-uh	Vegetables
Bratwurst/ Bockwurst	*brawt/bock*-vurst	Partly cooked sausages heated before served	**Spätzle**	*shpay*-tzell	A potato-based pasta
			Gulasch	*goo*-losh	Stew
Nudeln	*noo*-deln	Noodles	**Strudel**	*shtrew*-del	Flaky pastry wrapped around a fruit filling
Brötchen	*bro*-chen	Chewy white breakfast rolls			
Pfannkuchen	*fon*-koo-kin	Pancake	**Hühnchen**	*hen*-shen	Chicken (see also Geflügel)
Ei	eye	Egg			
Quark	qvark	Creamy dairy product, similar to yogurt	**Suppe**	*zoo*-pa	Soup
			Kalbfleisch	*callb*-flysch	Veal
Eis	ice	Ice cream	**Wiener Schnitzel**	*vee*-ner shnit-sul	"Viennese" style, breaded cutlet
Rindfleisch	*rint*-flysch	Beef			
Ente	*en*-tuh	Duck			
Salat	sa-*lot*	Salad			
Fisch	fish	Fish	**Kartoffel**	car-toff-el	Potato
			Wurst	voorst	Any sausage

Wiley, the Wiley Publishing logo, For Dummies, the Dummies Man logo, the For Dummies Bestselling Book Series logo and all related trade dress are trademarks or registered trademarks of Wiley Publishing, Inc. All other trademarks are property of their respective owners.

Copyright © 2005 Wiley Publishing, Inc. All rights reserved.
Item 7823-5.
For more information about Wiley Publishing, call 1-800-762-2974.

Plan your trip

with

For Dummies

Covering the most popular destinations in North America and Europe, *For Dummies* travel guides are the ultimate user-friendly trip planners. Available wherever books are sold or go to www.dummies.com

And book it with our online partner, Frommers.com

- ✔ Book airfare, hotels and packages
- ✔ Find the hottest deals
- ✔ Get breaking travel news
- ✔ Enter to win vacations
- ✔ Share trip photos and stories
- ✔ And much more

Frommers.com, rated the #1 Travel Web Site by PC Magazine

FOR DUMMIES®

The fun and easy way™ to travel!

U.S.A.

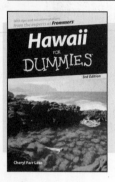

Hawaii For Dummies, 3rd Edition — Cheryl Farr Leas

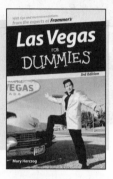

Las Vegas For Dummies, 3rd Edition — Mary Herczog

Also available:
Alaska For Dummies
Arizona For Dummies
Boston For Dummies
California For Dummies
Chicago For Dummies
Colorado & the Rockies For Dummies
Florida For Dummies
Los Angeles & Disneyland For Dummies
Maui For Dummies
National Parks of the American West For Dummies

New Orleans For Dummies
New York City For Dummies
San Francisco For Dummies
Seattle & the Olympic Peninsula For Dummies
Washington, D.C. For Dummies
RV Vacations For Dummies
Walt Disney World & Orlando For Dummies

EUROPE

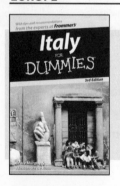

Italy For Dummies, 3rd Edition — Mike Murphy & Alessandra de Rossi

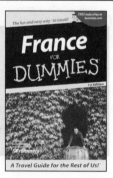

France For Dummies, 1st Edition — A Travel Guide for the Rest of Us!

Also available:
England For Dummies
Europe For Dummies
Germany For Dummies
Ireland For Dummies
London For Dummies

Paris For Dummies
Scotland For Dummies
Spain For Dummies

OTHER DESTINATIONS

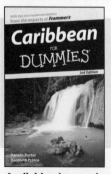

Caribbean For Dummies, 3rd Edition — Darwin Porter & Danforth Prince

Cruise Vacations For Dummies, 2005 — Fran Wenograd Golden & Jerry Brown

Also available:
Bahamas For Dummies
Cancun & the Yucatan For Dummies
Costa Rica For Dummies
Mexico's Beach Resorts For Dummies
Montreal & Quebec City For Dummies
Vancouver & Victoria For Dummies

Available wherever books are sold.
Go to www.dummies.com or call 1-877-762-2974 to order direct.

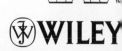

WILEY

Germany
FOR
DUMMIES®
2ND EDITION

by Donald Olson

WILEY

Wiley Publishing, Inc.

Germany For Dummies,® 2nd Edition

Published by
Wiley Publishing, Inc.
111 River St.
Hoboken, NJ 07030-5774
www.wiley.com

Copyright © 2005 by Wiley Publishing, Inc., Indianapolis, Indiana

Published simultaneously in Canada

No part of this publication may be reproduced, stored in a retrieval system, or transmitted in any form or by any means, electronic, mechanical, photocopying, recording, scanning, or otherwise, except as permitted under Sections 107 or 108 of the 1976 United States Copyright Act, without either the prior written permission of the Publisher, or authorization through payment of the appropriate per-copy fee to the Copyright Clearance Center, 222 Rosewood Drive, Danvers, MA 01923, 978-750-8400, fax 978-646-8600. Requests to the Publisher for permission should be addressed to the Legal Department, Wiley Publishing, Inc., 10475 Crosspoint Blvd., Indianapolis, IN 46256, 317-572-3447, fax 317-572-4355, or online at http://www.wiley.com/go/permissions.

Trademarks: Wiley, the Wiley Publishing logo, For Dummies, the Dummies Man logo, A Reference for the Rest of Us!, The Dummies Way, Dummies Daily, The Fun and Easy Way, Dummies.com and related trade dress are trademarks or registered trademarks of John Wiley & Sons, Inc., and/or its affiliates in the United States and other countries, and may not be used without written permission. Frommer's is a trademark or registered trademark of Arthur Frommer. Used under license. Post-it is a registered trademark of 3M Company. All other trademarks are the property of their respective owners. Wiley Publishing, Inc., is not associated with any product or vendor mentioned in this book.

LIMIT OF LIABILITY/DISCLAIMER OF WARRANTY: THE PUBLISHER AND THE AUTHOR MAKE NO REPRESENTATIONS OR WARRANTIES WITH RESPECT TO THE ACCURACY OR COMPLETENESS OF THE CONTENTS OF THIS WORK AND SPECIFICALLY DISCLAIM ALL WARRANTIES, INCLUDING WITHOUT LIMITATION WARRANTIES OF FITNESS FOR A PARTICULAR PURPOSE. NO WARRANTY MAY BE CREATED OR EXTENDED BY SALES OR PROMOTIONAL MATERIALS. THE ADVICE AND STRATEGIES CONTAINED HEREIN MAY NOT BE SUITABLE FOR EVERY SITUATION. THIS WORK IS SOLD WITH THE UNDERSTANDING THAT THE PUBLISHER IS NOT ENGAGED IN RENDERING LEGAL, ACCOUNTING, OR OTHER PROFESSIONAL SERVICES. IF PROFESSIONAL ASSISTANCE IS REQUIRED, THE SERVICES OF A COMPETENT PROFESSIONAL PERSON SHOULD BE SOUGHT. NEITHER THE PUBLISHER NOR THE AUTHOR SHALL BE LIABLE FOR DAMAGES ARISING HEREFROM. THE FACT THAT AN ORGANIZATION OR WEBSITE IS REFERRED TO IN THIS WORK AS A CITATION AND/OR A POTENTIAL SOURCE OF FURTHER INFORMATION DOES NOT MEAN THAT THE AUTHOR OR THE PUBLISHER ENDORSES THE INFORMATION THE ORGANIZATION OR WEB SITE MAY PROVIDE OR RECOMMENDATIONS IT MAY MAKE. FURTHER, READERS SHOULD BE AWARE THAT INTERNET WEB SITES LISTED IN THIS WORK MAY HAVE CHANGED OR DISAPPEARED BETWEEN WHEN THIS WORK WAS WRITTEN AND WHEN IT IS READ. PLEASE BE ADVISED THAT TRAVEL INFORMATION IS SUBJECT TO CHANGE AT ANY TIME AND THIS IS ESPECIALLY TRUE OF PRICES. WE THEREFORE SUGGEST THAT READERS WRITE OR CALL AHEAD FOR CONFIRMATION WHEN MAKING TRAVEL PLANS. THE AUTHOR AND THE PUBLISHER CANNOT BE HELD RESPONSIBLE FOR THE EXPERIENCES OF READERS WHILE TRAVELING.

For general information on our other products and services, please contact our Customer Care Department within the U.S. at 800-762-2974, outside the U.S. at 317-572-3993, or fax 317-572-4002.

For technical support, please visit www.wiley.com/techsupport.

Wiley also publishes its books in a variety of electronic formats. Some content that appears in print may not be available in electronic books.

Library of Congress Control Number: 2005923415

ISBN-13: 978-0-7645-7823-6

ISBN-10: 0-7645-7823-5

Manufactured in the United States of America

10 9 8 7 6 5 4 3 2

2B/QZ/QV/QV/IN

WILEY

About the Author

Novelist, playwright, and travel writer **Donald Olson** is the author of the award-winning *England For Dummies, London For Dummies, Frommer's Best Day Trips from London,* and *Frommer's Vancouver & Victoria 2005.* His novel *The Confessions of Aubrey Beardsley* will be published in the U.S. in 2006 by the University of Wisconsin Press. Under the pen name Swan Adamson he has written the novels *My Three Husbands* – now translated into four languages – and *Confessions of a Pregnant Princess,* both published by Kensington. Donald Olson's travel stories have appeared in the *New York Times*, National Geographic Books, and many other publications.

Dedication

To Gary Larson and Stephen Brewer, with thanks for their help in Germany.

Author's Acknowledgments

I would like to thank RailEurope for its expert assistance.

Publisher's Acknowledgments

We're proud of this book; please send us your comments through our Dummies online registration form located at www.dummies.com/register/.

Some of the people who helped bring this book to market include the following:

Acquisitions, Editorial, and Media Development

Project Editor: Sherri Cullison Pfouts

Development Editor: Paul Prince

Copy Editor: E. Neil Johnson

Cartographer: Elizabeth Puhl

Editorial Manager: Christine Meloy Beck

Editorial Assistant: Melissa S. Bennett

Senior Photo Editor: Richard Fox

Front Cover Photo: Neuschwanstein Castle, Bavaria, © Doug Armand/ Getty Images

Back Cover Photo: Oktoberfest, Munich, © Ulli Seer/Getty Images

Cartoons: Rich Tennant (www.the5thwave.com)

Composition Services

Project Coordinator: Michael Kruzil

Layout and Graphics: Clint Lahnen, Barry Offringa, Lynsey Osborn, Melanee Prendergast, Heather Ryan

Proofreaders: Jessica Kramer, Joe Niesen, Carl William Pierce, Charles Spencer, TECHBOOKS Production Services

Indexer: TECHBOOKS Production Services

Publishing and Editorial for Consumer Dummies

Diane Graves Steele, Vice President and Publisher, Consumer Dummies

Joyce Pepple, Acquisitions Director, Consumer Dummies

Kristin A. Cocks, Product Development Director, Consumer Dummies

Michael Spring, Vice President and Publisher, Travel

Kelly Regan, Editorial Director, Travel

Publishing for Technology Dummies

Andy Cummings, Vice President and Publisher, Dummies Technology/ General User

Composition Services

Gerry Fahey, Vice President of Production Services

Debbie Stailey, Director of Composition Services

Contents at a Glance

Maps at a Glance

Table of Contents

Introduction

So you're going to Germany. *Wunderbar!* But what parts of Deutschland (Germany) do you want to visit? Because of this country's many offerings, answering that question isn't always easy. Germany isn't a huge country — on a superfast train you can buzz from Berlin in the north to Munich in the south in about seven hours — but exciting cities and scenic sightseeing possibilities pack the terrain.

Situated in the very heart of Europe, Germany stretches from the Alps in the south to Denmark and the Baltic and North seas in the north. France bounds Germany to the southwest, with Luxembourg, Belgium, and the Netherlands to the west and the Czech Republic and Poland to the east.

Dramatic regional differences exist in the German landscape. The sunny southwest is where you find the Bodensee, one of the largest lakes in Europe, and the forested hills of the scenic Schwarzwald (Black Forest). In the west, every crag in the Rhine Valley seems to have its own romantic legend — or carefully tended vineyard. Drive or take the train a couple of hours east and you're in the Bavarian Alps, where the peaks are tipped with snow until May. In the far north, the location of the country's great ports, you find a flat maritime landscape.

Regional differences also extend to food and architecture. The sober brick architecture that predominates in the far north gives way to exuberant baroque churches and palaces in the south. In the southwest, which shares a border with France, French cuisine is a major part of the dining scene. In the north, near Germany's coastline, the emphasis is on fresh seafood. Every city or region has its own version of sausage and its favorite local wines and beers. Discovering the special regional differences within Germany will help to deepen your understanding and experiences of the country.

So what cities or regions or specific attractions do you want to see? Berlin, the exciting new capital of a newly reunified republic? Elegant, fun-loving Munich, the city where most Germans would live if they could? The great port city of Hamburg? The romantic university town of Heidelberg? Are there specific landscapes you want to see, such as the Bavarian Alps or the Rhine Valley? Did you know that one of the most beautiful scenic drives in Europe is along Germany's aptly named Romantic Road? What castles and cathedrals would you like to visit? The fairy-tale castles built by King Ludwig of Bavaria are the most famous and popular attractions in Germany. The sheer size of Cologne cathedral, the largest church north of the Alps, will dazzle your senses, too. And how about other historic sites? Do you want to visit Weimar, where Goethe lived, or Leipzig, where Bach conducted? Do you want to stroll down Frankfurt's Zeil, the busiest shopping street in Germany? Are

---

Dummies Post-it® Flags

As you're reading this book, you'll find information that you'll want to reference as you plan or enjoy your trip — whether it be a new hotel, a must-see attraction, or a must-try walking tour. Mark these pages with the handy Post-it® Flags that are included in this book to help make your trip planning easier!

---

you interested in seeing eastern Germany now that the border is open between east and west? The eastern city of Dresden, after all, is one of the great art cities of Europe.

Germany, as you can see, has an embarrassment of riches. In this book, I help you choose from among its many highlights to create the best trip for you. Together you and *Germany For Dummies,* 2nd Edition, can plan a *wunderschöne Reise* (wonderful journey).

About This Book

This is a selective guidebook to Germany. From an enormous list of possibilities, I chose only what I consider to be the best and most essential places for visitors. If you're new to this part of the world, this guidebook is for you.

I exclude places that other, more exhaustive guidebooks routinely include. Germany has so much that is really worth seeing that you don't need to waste your time with the second-rate, the overrated, or the boring. In this guide, I bypass places that are difficult to reach or of interest only to a scholar or specialist.

Use *Germany For Dummies,* 2nd Edition, as a reference guide. You can, of course, start at the first page and read all the way through to the end. But, if you've already been to Germany and know the basics of international travel, you can flip to the specific part you need or home in on one specific chapter.

Please be advised that travel information is subject to change at any time — and this is especially true of prices. I therefore suggest that you write or call ahead for confirmation when making your travel plans. The author, editors, and publisher cannot be held responsible for the experiences of readers while traveling. Your safety is important to us, however, so we encourage you to stay alert and be aware of your surroundings. Keep a close eye on your cameras, purses, and wallets, all favorite targets of thieves and pickpockets.

Conventions Used in This Book

I recently tried to extract some information from a guidebook and felt that I needed training in hieroglyphics to interpret all the different symbols. I'm happy to report that the user-friendly *Germany For Dummies,* 2nd Edition, is not like that. The use of symbols and abbreviations is kept to a minimum.

I include abbreviations for commonly accepted credit cards. Take a look at the following list for an explanation of each:

> AE: American Express
>
> DC: Diners Club
>
> DISC: Discover
>
> MC: MasterCard
>
> V: Visa

I also include some general pricing information to help you decide where to unpack your bags or dine on the local cuisine. In addition to giving you exact prices, I employ a system of dollar signs ($) to show a range of costs for one night in a hotel (double room, year-round) or a meal at a restaurant (appetizer, entree, and dessert). Check out the following table to decipher the dollar signs:

Cost	*Hotel*	*Restaurant*
$	$125 and less	$20 and less
$$	$126 to $175	$21 to $30
$$$	$176 to $225	$31 to $40
$$$$	$226 and more	$41 and more

Prices in this guide for hotels, restaurants, attractions, and services are given in euros (€), the currency that replaced the deutsche mark in 2002, and then converted into dollars. The exchange rate used throughout is €1 = $1.25.

I first give the name of a sight in German, followed by an English translation. If the word is one that you might be using, I also provide a phonetic pronunciation.

Foolish Assumptions

I made some assumptions about you, *lieber Leser* (dear reader), including:

> ✔ You may be an experienced traveler who hasn't had much time to explore Germany and wants expert advice when you finally do get a chance to enjoy that particular locale.

✔ You may be an inexperienced traveler (but you're definitely not a *Dummkopf*) looking for guidance when determining whether to take a trip to Germany and how to plan for it.

✔ You're not looking for a book that provides all the information available about Germany or that lists every hotel, restaurant, or attraction available to you. Instead, you're looking for a book that focuses on the places that will give you the best or most unique experience in Germany.

If you fit any of these criteria, then *Germany For Dummies,* 2nd Edition, gives you the information you're looking for!

How This Book Is Organized

The book is broken down into five parts. The first two parts deal with trip planning and organization. They provide information, advice, and suggestions that can help you map out a wonderful holiday. The next two parts of the book are devoted to the major sights and cities within northern and eastern Germany and western and southern Germany. All of the parts can be read independently, so if you want to zero in on a specific city or area — Munich, say, or the Romantic Road — you can turn right to that part.

Part I: Introducing Germany

This first part introduces Germany and gives you some excellent reasons for going there. This overview gives you the big picture. The individual chapters help you decide when to visit and what to see. I help you to understand and deepen your knowledge of the culture; tell you about German food, wine, and beer; provide a calendar of events; and present you with some possible itineraries.

Part II: Planning Your Trip to Germany

This part helps take some of the wrinkles out of the trip-planning stage. I talk about handling money and give you some sound advice on planning a realistic budget; lay out your options for airlines and how to get the best airfares and book money-saving package tours; and explain the kinds of guided tours that are available. This part helps you to decide what form of transportation (train, rental car) to use to get around the country and explains what kind of accommodations you can expect for your money. I provide special tips for Germany-bound travelers who may have special needs or interests: families, seniors, travelers with disabilities, gay and lesbian travelers, and Jewish travelers. Pretrip loose ends, from passports to buying medical insurance, are also dealt with.

Part III: Northern & Eastern Germany

All you need to know about **Berlin,** Germany's capital and most exciting city, is contained in this part. Along with providing a basic orientation, I point out the best hotels and restaurants and the top attractions to the east and west and all around this remarkable city, including the palace of Sanssouci in Potsdam. Northern Germany, bordering on the North Sea and the Baltic, is also where you find **Hamburg,** Germany's largest port city. I hit the Hamburg highlights, from the mighty harbor to the lurid Reeperbahn (where *un*coverage might better describe the sights). Then I tell you about side-trip options from Hamburg: **Lübeck,** a picturesque city of Gothic church spires and ancient brick buildings, and **Bremen,** a bustling city that offers an array of historic sights.

In this part, I also visit the great eastern German cities of **Dresden, Leipzig,** and **Weimar.** Difficult to visit during the Communist years, these remarkable showcases of art and culture are now "open for business." From Dresden, I tell you how to take a boat trip into a scenic region called **Saxon Switzerland.** I also include a description of the memorial at **Buchenwald** concentration camp near Weimar and an overview of touring options in the Thuringian Forest.

Part IV: Southern & Western Germany

Munich, Germany's "secret capital" and most popular big city, gets a big chapter of its own. I provide information on how to get there, how to get around, and what to see, plus a selection of great hotels and special restaurants. I also include an easy trip to **Nymphenburg Palace** and the moving memorial at **Dachau.** The next chapter goes beyond Munich but stays in Bavaria. Here I describe the principle cities and attractions found along the **Romantic Road,** a scenic driving tour that begins in **Würzburg** and ends at **Neuschwanstein,** King Ludwig of Bavaria's fairy-tale castle in the Bavarian Alps. I also introduce you to the Bavarian towns of **Garmisch-Partenkirchen** and **Oberammergau,** with an additional side trip to **Linderhof,** another castle-fantasy of King Ludwig.

Staying south but moving west, I cover three important cities in south-western Germany: **Heidelberg,** with the oldest university in Germany and the brooding ruins of a mighty castle; **Stuttgart,** the region's cultural capital; and **Nuremberg,** one of Germany's most attractive cities. From the southwest I head farther north, to the lively Rhineside city of **Cologne,** with its world-famous cathedral and array of first-class museums. Side-trip options from Cologne include boat rides down the mighty **Rhine,** with its castles and vineyards, and down the equally picturesque **Mosel River,** one of Germany's principle winegrowing areas. **Frankfurt,** with the busiest international airport in Germany, gets a chapter of its own. You find plenty to see and enjoy in "Mainhattan," as Frankfurt is known, from designer skyscrapers and great museums to distinctive apple-wine taverns.

Part V: The Part of Tens

The Part of Tens enables me to focus a little more attention on extraspecial places, topics, and sights I want you to know about. My "tens" include ten lessons on the German language, ten great hotels, and ten outstanding museums.

You also find two other elements near the back of this book. I include an appendix with an A to Z list of fast facts, like how the telephone system works and what numbers to call in an emergency. You also find a list of toll-free telephone numbers and Web sites for airlines, car-rental agencies, and hotel chains serving Germany, and resources for locating additional information on specific cities or areas. All of this is followed by a few helpful worksheets to help make your trip planning easier.

Icons Used in This Book

In the margins, you find six different icons, little pictures that point out helpful trip-planning details or items that are just for fun.

 Bargain Alert is my favorite icon, and I suspect it may be yours, too. I'm not cheap, but I love to save money. You see this icon every time I tell you about something that can save you money.

 The Best of the Best icon highlights the best the destination has to offer in all categories — hotels, restaurants, attractions, activities, shopping, and nightlife.

 This icon points out tidbits about German culture, personalities, and places of special interest.

 I'm not an alarmist, so you won't find too many of these icons. If you do see one, I want you to be aware of something such as a scam that can cost you money or a hazardous situation.

 Traveling with children? Keep your eyes peeled for this icon, which points out hotels, restaurants, or attractions that welcome children or that kids actually enjoy.

 The Tip icon highlights useful bits of information that can save you time or enhance your travel experience. A Tip icon alerts you to something that you may not otherwise consider or even know about.

Where to Go from Here

To Germany, of course. How you want to use this guide is up to you. You can start at the beginning and read the book straight through to the end. Or you can start anywhere in between and extract information as you want or need it. I hope you'll think of me as your guide or companion on this journey to Germany, which is sure to be *wunderbar*.

Part I
Introducing Germany

The 5th Wave   By Rich Tennant

"...and remember, no more German tongue twisters until you know the language better."

In this part . . .

*W*here to begin? This part lays the groundwork for your trip to Germany. Chapter 1 introduces you to the best Germany has to offer — the most exciting cities, the most scenic landscapes, and the most interesting attractions. Chapter 2 helps you to understand the country and its culture by giving an overview of its history, an introduction to its architecture and cuisine, and a list of recommended books and movies. In Chapter 3, I tell you more about the places included in the book and discuss scheduling your trip so you can decide where and when to go. In Chapter 4, I present four possible itineraries for visitors who want to sample a wide range of sights.

Chapter 1

Discovering the Best of Germany

. . . .

In This Chapter

▶ Experiencing the greatest cities

▶ Exploring romantic landscapes

▶ Discovering legendary castles and palaces

▶ Visiting smaller towns and cities

▶ Enjoying world-class classical music, opera, and ballet

. . . .

Germany holds a special fascination for travelers. This land of contrasting cities, landscapes, and moods appeals to visitors for many different reasons. Perhaps you, like millions of others, have German ancestors, and you want to explore their home turf. Or perhaps you have an image of Germany in your mind — a castle on a hilltop, a palace in a landscaped garden, or a giant beer hall with an oom-pah-pah band — and you want to check it out for yourself. Then there's the culture: Every midsize-to-large German city has at least one art museum, a symphony orchestra, and an opera house, making a visit to Germany a feast for those who enjoy world-class art and music. (See Chapter 23 for my list of the ten best German museums.) Clubbers, too, will find that the club/bar/disco scene in Germany is hot, not only in large cities like Berlin and Munich but also in smaller university towns like Cologne, Leipzig, and Heidelberg. Some visitors come for the chance to drink full-bodied German beer; others come to enjoy a cosmopolitan cafe culture where coffee and cake are afternoon staples. And don't forget the retail: Great shopping opportunities abound year-round in Berlin, Munich, Hamburg, and Cologne. During the Christmas season, the main squares in Germany's smaller cities glitter and glow with the lights, food, and gift stalls of Christmas markets, a tradition that dates back hundreds of years. You'll find as many different reasons to visit Germany as there are tourists who arrive daily, by the thousands, at the airports in Frankfurt, Munich, or Berlin.

This chapter is designed as an at-a-glance reference to the absolute best — the Best of the Best — that Germany has to offer. In the categories that I outline, you'll find some of the things that make traveling in Germany such a fascinating experience. I discuss each of these places and experiences in detail later in this book; you can find them in their indicated chapters, marked with — what else? — a "Best of the Best" icon.

Discovering the Best Big German Cities

Germany's top cities offer a wealth of diversions, as simple or as sophisticated as you want. You'll find world-class museums, music, cuisine of all kinds, great shopping, and plenty of nightlife. You'll also find elegant boulevards, riverside promenades, enormous parks and green spaces, bustling pedestrian-only quarters, fascinating architecture, and plenty of picturesque corners just waiting to be discovered. And thanks to Germany's excellent public transportation systems, you can easily reach it all by subway, streetcar, or bus.

✔ With its endlessly dramatic history and cache of cultural and artistic riches, **Berlin** (Chapters 11 and 12) always has a major-league buzz. But since 1989, when the Wall separating East Germany and West Germany came down, Germany's largest city and new capital has become an international superstar. The pulse of Berlin is felt throughout Europe, and when you're walking down Berlin's two most famous avenues, the Kurfürstendamm and Unter den Linden, you'll feel it, too.

✔ **Munich** (Chapter 15) is a southern German city where the urban pleasures are as soft and sweet as *Schlagsahne* (whipped cream) on a rich slab of cake or as exuberant as an oom-pah-pah band in a giant beer hall during Oktoberfest. The capital of Bavaria is sensuous, sophisticated, and fun-loving, with countless cultural diversions and a kind of urban magic that snares the hearts of millions of visitors each year.

✔ **Hamburg** (Chapter 13), Germany's third-largest city after Berlin and Munich, has the liveliness and lustiness of a big port. The "Queen of the North" presides over a beautiful setting on the Alster Lake but is notorious for her erotically charged entertainment district called the Reeperbahn.

✔ **Dresden** (Chapter 14) reigns as the treasure house of eastern Germany. The old capital of Saxony is where you find the world-famous Zwinger palace/museum complex, the riches of the Green Vaults, and the reconstructed Frauenkirche, Germany's most amazing architectural reconstruction effort.

✔ **Cologne** (Chapter 19), with its soaring cathedral, first-rate museums, and Rhine-side setting, is one of the most attractive and intriguing cities in western Germany. Cologne's carnival is the biggest and brashest in the country, and its vibrant contemporary arts scene gives it a hefty dose of sophistication.

✔ **Frankfurt** (Chapter 20), with its bevy of designer skyscrapers, yields plenty of pleasant surprises, including a fine lineup of museums and great shopping on Germany's busiest shopping street, the Zeil.

Witnessing the Most Romantic Landscapes

Landscapes of fabled beauty and scenic splendor are found throughout Germany, and views of them are accessible by train, boat, and car. From the majesty of the Bavarian Alps in the south to the sandy beaches of the Baltic Sea in the north and from the winegrowing Rhine Valley in the west to the high, rocky cliffs along the Elbe in the east, Germany offers a wealth of sightseeing possibilities.

- ✓ From Dresden you can easily explore a scenic region called **Saxon Switzerland** (Chapter 14), where rocky cliffs rise dramatically above the Elbe River.

- ✓ The **Romantic Road** (Chapter 16) is the most romantic byway of all, offering a remarkable medley of small medieval towns set within a gorgeous Bavarian landscape of river valley and mountain meadow.

- ✓ Perhaps the most dramatic of all German landscapes is the Bavarian Alps. The country's highest mountain, the Zugspitze, towers above the alpine resort town of **Garmisch-Partenkirchen** (Chapter 16).

- ✓ Sophisticated health spas and recreational activities abound in the forest-clad mountains of the **Black Forest** (Chapter 17), where you can find lakes, hiking trails, and scenic lookouts.

- ✓ The **Bodensee** (Chapter 17), an enormous lake near Germany's sunny southwestern border, is like a bit of the Mediterranean, with semitropical gardens and an almost Italian languor.

- ✓ Cruises down the mighty **River Rhine** (Chapter 19) take you past castle-crowned crags and legendary sights, such as Lorelei rock.

- ✓ The **Mosel Valley** (Chapter 19), between Trier and Koblenz, is a scenic winegrowing region encompassing thousands of acres of vineyards, Roman ruins, medieval castles, and riverside towns with cobbled streets and half-timbered houses.

- ✓ With its fruit trees and vineyards growing on sunny, sheltered slopes, the **Rhine Valley** (Chapter 19) from Koblenz south to Alsace is like a northern extension of Italy.

- ✓ The **Rheingau wine district** (Chapter 19), found along a lovely 45km (27-mile) stretch of the Rhine, west of Mainz and Wiesbaden, has been a wine-producing region for upward of 2,000 years.

Marveling over the Best Castles and Palaces

At one time, Germany was a conglomeration of regional kingdoms, duchies, and vast estates, ruled over by an assortment of kings, dukes, princes, and prince-bishops. As a result, Germany is loaded with a fascinating collection of castles and palaces, both great and small, many of them full of art treasures, and all of them open to the public.

✔ **Charlottenburg Palace** in Berlin (Chapter 12) is home to several museums and staterooms that can be visited on guided tours.

✔ **Sanssouci** (Chapter 12), Frederick the Great's 18th-century rococo palace in Potsdam, is remarkable, in part, because it suffered almost no damage during World War II (WWII). Sanssouci and its beautiful grounds can be easily visited on a day trip from Berlin.

✔ Carefully reconstructed after WWII, the amazing **Zwinger** palace in Dresden (Chapter 14) is now an unparalleled showcase for Old Master paintings and porcelain treasures.

✔ **Nymphenburg Palace** on the outskirts of Munich is another king-size showplace and so is the gigantic **Residenz,** right in the heart of the city (see both in Chapter 15). With their precious paintings, porcelains, and furniture, these stately homes reveal aspects of German life and the monarchy that lasted up until 1918.

✔ For sheer, over-the-top opulence, nothing can compare to the fairy-tale castles built in the 19th century by Ludwig II of Bavaria. **Neuschwanstein** and **Linderhof** (see both in Chapter 16) are pre-served almost exactly as they were during Ludwig's lifetime.

✔ Used by the powerful prince-bishops until 1806, the **Residenz** in Wümurzburg (Chapter 16) is famed for its superb ceiling frescos by Tiepolo.

✔ A palace that doubled as a fortress, the Marienburg crowns the vineyard-covered slopes above Wümurzburg and today houses the **Mainfrankisches Museum** (Chapter 16), featuring brilliant Renaissance-era woodcarvings by Tilman Riemenschneider.

✔ Perched on its crag high above Heidelberg, **Heidelberg Castle** (Chapter 18) suffered from war and fire, but it remains an impressive sight even in its semiruined state.

✔ For many visitors, the quintessential image associated with Germany is a castle on a hilltop. You do indeed find castles scattered throughout the country. Ruined castles dot the landscape of the **Rhine** (Chapter 19) and enhance its romantic appeal.

Exploring the Best Small Towns and Cities

Germany is remarkable for its attractive smaller towns and cities, scattered like gemstones around the country. In these historic hamlets, many of them located less than an hour's train ride from a major metropolis, you'll find a very different Germany. Brimming with the flavors of the past, they can easily be savored as day trips.

✔ An easy day trip from Hamburg, lovely **Lübeck** (Chapter 13) epitomizes the maritime culture and red-brick architecture of northern Germany. So many architectural gems are located here that the entire Old Town is a UNESCO World Heritage Site — a place judged to be of exceptional cultural value, according to the United Nations agency that promotes education and the arts.

✔ **Weimar** (Chapter 14), in eastern Germany, was a cradle of the German Enlightenment of the late-18th and early-19th centuries. This small, unspoiled hamlet was home to Goethe and Schiller, among others, and provides a glimpse into 18th-century German life and culture.

✔ **Rothenburg ob der Tauber** (Chapter 16), a major highlight along the Romantic Road, is a walled medieval city loaded with picturesque charm. You can walk along the old city walls of this perfectly preserved gem and stroll down streets that haven't changed much in hundreds of years.

✔ A stop on the Romantic Road or an easy day trip from Munich, **Augsburg** (Chapter 16) is full of historic panache and architectural surprises, including Renaissance-era palaces and the oldest almshouse in Germany.

✔ Located in the Bavarian Alps near Neuschwanstein castle, **Fümussen** (Chapter 16) invites you to stroll along its cobblestone streets past stone houses and a rushing mountain river.

✔ **Lindau** (Chapter 17), a marvelous little island-city in the Bodensee (Lake Constance), has a sunny, flower-filled charm that's perfect for lazing away a day or two. The garden-island of Mainau is a short ferry ride away.

✔ One of the most sophisticated spa towns in Europe, **Baden-Baden** (Chapter 17) offers an extraordinary range of spa treatments during the day and elegant gaming rooms at night.

✔ **Heidelberg** (Chapter 18), an old university town on the Neckar River, enchants visitors with its romantic setting, historic streets, and enormous castle.

✔ **Stuttgart** (Chapter 18), a 40-minute train ride from Heidelberg, is the arts and culture capital of southwestern Germany, with major art collections, intriguing architecture, and the second-largest beer festival after Munich.

✔ **Nuremberg** (Chapter 18) is an important center of the German Renaissance that later became an infamous locale for huge, Nazi-era rallies. Remnants and reminders from both eras are plentiful in Nuremberg, one of the most attractive midsize German cities.

Enjoying the Best in Classical Music, Opera, and Ballet

Lovers of classical music, opera, and ballet will find that Germany is a gold mine. Tickets for musical events, including grand opera, are reasonably priced, and the quality of musical performance is extraordinarily high.

✔ **Berlin** (Chapter 12) is home to three major symphony orchestras, including the famed **Berlin Philharmonic,** conducted by Sir Simon Rattle, and three opera houses that share their stages with resident ballet companies.

✔ A visit to **Dresden** (Chapter 14) can be made even more memorable by an evening at the **Semperoper** (Semper Opera House), one of the world's great opera houses, or hearing a concert by the **Dresden Philharmonic.**

✔ The city of **Leipzig** (Chapter 14) is home to the world-renowned Gewandhaus Orchestra and the acclaimed **Leipzieger Oper** (Leipzig Opera). Leipzig celebrates its most famous citizen — the composer Johann Sebastian Bach, who lived and worked in the city for more than 40 years — with the yearly **Bachfest.**

✔ Up north, **Hamburg** (Chapter 13) plays host to the **Hamburgische Staatsoper** (Hamburg State Opera), the **Hamburg Ballet,** and three highly-regarded orchestras.

✔ In **Munich** (Chapter 15), one of the great cultural centers of Germany, the brilliant **Bayerischen Staatsoper** (Bavarian State Opera) shares the National Theater stage with its ballet company, while the magnificent **Münchner Philharmoniker** (Munich Philharmonic Orchestra) performs in the Philharmonic Hall.

✔ The **Stuttgart Ballet** in **Stuttgart** (Chapter 18) hit international stardom in the 1970s when John Cranko took over the company. Cranko is gone, but the company still performs at the State Theater, and so does the **Staatsoper** (State Opera).

✔ For a city of its size, **Cologne** (Chapter 19) has an amazing array of musical offerings. Major artists appear at the **Kölner Philharmonie** (Cologne Opera), the Rhineland's leading opera house, and two fine orchestras — the **Gürzenich Kölner Philharmoniker** (Cologne Philharmonic) and the **Westdeutscher Rundfunk Orchestra** (West German Radio Orchestra) — perform in the **Kölner Philharmonie** (Philharmonic concert hall).

✔ **Opera Frankfurt/Ballet Frankfurt** give a big musical boost to **Frankfurt** (Chapter 20), and so does the **Frankfurt Philharmonic.**

Chapter 2

Digging Deeper into Germany

● ●

In This Chapter

▶ Perusing the main events in Germany's history

▶ Recognizing Germany's architectural heritage

▶ Learning about German food, beer, and wine

▶ Discovering books and movies about Germany

● ●

*T*his chapter helps you find out more about Germany and deepens your experience of the country. I distill the essence of Germany's complicated and tumultuous past so you can get a clear, quick sense of the major epochs. I highlight the main architectural trends, whet your appetite with a primer on German food and drink, and recommend some excellent books and movies about Germany.

The Main Events: Tracking Germany's History

Germany's long and tumultuous history remains clouded by the horrors of World War II (WWII). How a civilized European nation slipped into a state of barbaric inhumanity that existed during Nazism's rise and WWII is a question that continues to occupy historians and survivors and haunt the Germans themselves. The list that follows highlights the main trends in German history:

> ✔ **Early History:** Prehistoric humans hunted in the Rhine and Neckar valleys of present-day Germany. By the first century A.D., the Roman sphere of influence extended well into the borders of present-day Germany, with garrisons established at Cologne (see Chapter 19), Koblenz, Mainz, and Trier. Following the Roman withdrawal from Germany in A.D. 400, the empire of the Franks represented the transition from a loose conglomeration of German tribes into what eventually would become the German Empire. **Charlemagne** (Karl der Grosse, 768 to 814) was responsible for the earliest large-scale attempt to unite the lands of Germany under one ruler.

✔ **The Middle Ages:** The power struggles and invasions of the Middle Ages continually disrupted the unity hammered out by Charlemagne. Because of the weakness of central authority, various German tribal duchies sought to build their own autonomy, and until the demise of the Holy Roman Empire in 1806, Germany remained a collection of small principalities and free cities. An upswing in international commerce from the 11th to 13th centuries led to the foundation of "Free Imperial Cities" like Hamburg and Lübeck (see Chapter 13).

✔ **The Reformation, the Enlightenment, and Napoleon:** The 16th century was a time of social unrest and religious upheaval throughout Germany. **Martin Luther** (1483 to 1546) battled against the excesses of the Catholic Church, and his work had far-reaching implications. As Protestant Reformation spread, the Catholic Church launched a Counter-Reformation that culminated in the bloody **Thirty Years' War** (1618 to 1648), pitting Protestant north against the Catholic south and affecting the whole of Europe. Under **Frederick the Great** (Friedrich der Grosse, 1740 to 1786), Prussia gained status as a great European power. During this period, the works of German artists, writers, composers, and philosophers ushered in the **Age of Enlightenment.** After defeating the Austrian and Prussian armies, Napoleon occupied several German cities and abolished the Holy Roman Empire in 1806. In 1813, Prussian, Austrian, and Russian armies fought the French emperor in Leipzig, which was followed by the decisive Battle of Waterloo.

✔ **Revolution and the Reich:** Following Napoleon's defeat, the country's military and political rulers were determined to return to a system of absolute monarchy. The question of independence and national unity finally came to a head in the 1848 revolution. When that effort failed, the Austrian Hapsburg monarchy reimposed its sovereignty over Prussia and other parts of Germany. Prussian statesman **Otto von Bismarck** (1815 to 1898) advocated consolidation of the German people under Prussian leadership. After triumphs in the **Franco-Prussian War** (1870 to 1871), Bismarck succeeded in winning over southern German states and, in 1871, became first chancellor of the German Empire (Reich).

✔ **World War I and Weimar:** For many observers, the **Great War** (1914 to 1918) represented a German attempt to dominate Europe. Military conflict on the eastern front resulted in the defeat of Russia, while fighting on the western front ultimately led to German defeat and the abdication of Kaiser Wilhelm II. Although the war wasn't fought on German soil, it resulted in severe food shortages throughout the country and intensified political unrest. In its attempt to establish a democratic and republican government, the so-called **Weimar government** (1919 to 1934) represented a break in dominant traditions of German history. Residual issues from war and hostility from conservative groups conflicted with reformist and radical impulses of the left and cultural avant-garde. During the **"Golden Twenties,"** Berlin — capital of the republic — blossomed into Germany's economic and cultural center.

✔ **The Rise of Nazism and World War II:** Economic crisis in Germany was a major factor in the rise of the Nazi movement, but old authoritarian, nationalistic, and imperialistic attitudes also provided a ripe environment for the National Socialist party to take control. As the brutal anti-Semitic political agenda of **Adolf Hitler** (1889 to 1945) became apparent, thousands of German Jews, including many prominent artists, scientists, and politicians, fled the country to escape persecution. Millions of Jews and other "undesirable" minorities throughout Germany and the rest of Nazi-occupied Europe were systematically exterminated in one of the most horrifying chapters in world history. At the end of the war, with its major cities in smoldering ruins, Germany ceased to exist as an independent state.

✔ **The two Germanys:** Intending at first to govern conquered Germany as one unit, the war's victors divided it into two states as the Cold War intensified. The **Federal Republic of Germany** in the western half of the country had its capital in Bonn, and the Soviet-ruled **German Democratic Republic** (GDR) in the eastern half had its capital in East Berlin. Two Germanys developed with highly different political, economic, and social systems. In 1948, West German recovery got under way with U.S. assistance in the form of the Marshall Plan. The Soviet blockade of West Berlin resulted in the Anglo-American **Berlin airlift,** which continued until 1949. In 1961, the **Berlin Wall** was constructed, sealing off East Berlin from West Berlin.

✔ **Germany Reunited:** The opening of the Berlin Wall in 1989 marked for East Germany the culmination of a wave of previously suppressed revolutionary sentiment across central and eastern Europe. Reforms by U.S.S.R. leader Mikhail Gorbachev and underground, grassroots communication between citizens in East Germany led to massive demonstrations against the repressive, Stalinist government of the GDR. In 1991, with East and West Germany united under one government, Berlin was made the nation's new capital.

Remembering the Nazi-era past

Germany's Nazi-era past and the enormity of crimes committed during World War II are facts that can't be glossed over or overlooked. The most wrenching memorials of that gruesome chapter of German history are the concentration camps **Buchenwald** (Chapter 14), near the eastern German town of Weimar, and **Dachau** (Chapter 15), northwest of Munich. **Berlin** (Chapter 12) is particularly rich in memorials commemorating the hundreds of thousands of Jews, gays, gypsies (*Sinta,* in German), and other groups that were murdered by the National Socialists between 1933 and 1945. In Berlin, you find walking tours that take visitors past Nazi-era buildings and exhibits that interpret Nazi methods. Germany's Jewish past is the subject of Berlin's remarkable **Jüdisches Museum** (Jewish Museum), the most comprehensive of its kind. See Chapter 12 for information on walking tours that focus on Berlin's Nazi and Jewish histories.

Building Blocks: Lauding Local Architecture

Buildings that you can visit on a trip to Germany span some 1,200 years of architectural history and were created in a number of different styles. Bombing raids in WWII left much of the country's rich architectural heritage in ruins. Some areas escaped damage, such as the medieval towns along the Romantic Road (see Chapter 16), but the overall devastation affected nearly the entire country. Many historic buildings are painstaking postwar reconstructions. Here are examples from around Germany of the major architectural trends:

✔ **Romanesque** (10th to 12th centuries): Simple, clear forms, thick walls, and rounded arches signal Romanesque architecture, a building style adapted from much earlier Roman models. Many interesting examples of Romanesque architecture are found in western Germany, particularly in **Cologne** (Chapter 19). The **Dom St. Kilian** in Würzburg (Chapter 16), built from 1045 to 1188, is one of the largest Romanesque churches in Germany.

✔ **Gothic** (13th to 16th centuries): **Cologne cathedral** (see Chapter 19) is Germany's greatest example of Gothic architecture. Compared with Romanesque, this style is slender and daring, with pointed arches, soaring vaults and spires, and enormous windows. A simpler and more monumental kind of Gothic architecture, built of brick, predominates in northern Germany in cities such as **Lübeck** (see Chapter 14).

✔ **Renaissance** (late 15th to 17th centuries): **Augsburg** (Chapter 16) is one of the best cities in Germany to see Renaissance architecture, a style characterized by calm precision, orderly repeating lines, and classical decoration over windows and doors. Renaissance architecture was imported from Italy into southern Germany.

✔ **Baroque** (17th to 18th centuries): A decorative exuberance in curvy baroque architecture sets it apart from the more sober Renaissance style. The baroque flourished in Catholic, Counter-Reformation areas in the south of Germany. The **Residenz** in Würzburg (see Chapter 16) and **Sanssouci Palace** in Potsdam (see Chapter 12) are two of the best examples of baroque architecture in Germany. **Munich** (see Chapter 16) abounds in the baroque.

✔ **Rococo** (18th century): Notch up the elements of baroque and you have rococo, exemplified by curving walls and staggering amounts of gilded and stucco decoration. One of the most famous examples of flamboyant rococo architecture in Germany is the **Wieskirche** (see Chapter 16) in Bavaria.

✔ **Neoclassical/Neo-Gothic** (mid-18th to 19th centuries). The neoclassical style was meant to be a rebuke to the excesses of baroque and rococo, and it was most popular in **Berlin** (see Chapter 12), where the architect Schinkel created a whole neoclassical avenue (**Unter den Linden**) and island of museums. As the century wore on, neoclassicism gave way to the more ponderous Neo-Gothic style. This faux-medievalism is what Ludwig's **Neuschwanstein** (Chapter 16) is all about.

✔ **Jugendstil** (early 20th century). Jugendstil is the German name for Art Nouveau, an early-20th-century European movement that emphasized flowing, asymmetrical, organic shapes. The famous **Mädler-Passage** arcade in Leipzig (see Chapter 14) shows Jugendstil influence, and so do many houses in the Schwabing district of **Munich** (see Chapter 15).

✔ **Bauhaus** (1913 to 1933): A rigorously modern style, free of frills and unnecessary decoration, Bauhaus was championed by Walter Gropius (1883 to 1969), who founded the Bauhaus school to create functional buildings and furnishings. The Bauhaus style predominates in the **Weissenhofsiedlung** area of Stuttgart (see Chapter 18), created for a 1927 building exhibition. Bauhaus museums are in **Weimar** (see Chapter 14) and **Berlin** (see Chapter 12). The school was banned by the Nazis because it didn't promote "German-looking" architecture.

✔ **Modernism** (1948 onward): A major housing shortage and rebuilding effort in bombed cities in Germany followed the devastation of WWII. If you walk down the streets or pedestrian zones in just about any major German city, you'll see modernist buildings all around you. It's a simple, functional style with straight lines and square windows.

✔ **Postmodernism** (1980s). Postmodernism is a style practiced by architects who plunder the past and apply old styles to the buildings of today. James Stirling's **Neue Staatsgalerie** in Stuttgart (see Chapter 18) is a reminder of just how clunky, uninspired, and unappealing most postmodern buildings are.

Essen und Trinken: Eating and Drinking in Germany

German cooking tends to be hearty and filling, with many regional variations and specialties. Seasonal specialties include ***Spargel*** (white asparagus) in May and June, ***Matjes*** (white herring) in June and July, ***Erdbeeren*** (strawberries) in spring, ***Forelle*** (trout) in the summer, and ***Reh*** (venison) in the fall. In the country as a whole, you can taste about 150 different types of sausage; Berlin, Munich, and Nuremberg all have their own special kinds. When it comes to baked goods — bread and pastries — Germany has more variety than any country in the world, with about 300 different types of bread and 1,200 varieties of biscuits and cakes.

Ratskellers, traditional cellar restaurants beneath a city's *Rathaus* (Town Hall), always serve good and fairly inexpensive traditional food, beer, and wine.

Sampling German beer

Bier (pronounced *beer*) remains a vital part of German culture, so much so that the right to drink beer is written into some labor contracts, and a beer with lunch in the factory cafeteria is taken for granted. The traditional *Biergarten* (beer garden), with tables set outdoors under trees or trellises, still is very popular, especially in southern Germany. A *Bräuhaus* (*broy*-house) serves its own brew along with local food.

When you order a beer in Germany, you have many choices. The range of beer varieties includes *Altbier, Bockbier, Export, Kölsch, Lager, Malzbier, Märzbier, Pils, Vollbier,* and *Weizenbier*. The ratio of ingredients, brewing temperature and technique, alcoholic content, aging time, color, and taste all contribute to a German beer's unique qualities. A German law adopted in 1516 dictates that German beer may contain no ingredients other than hops, malt (barley), yeast, and water.

Dark and sweet *Malzbier* (*malltz*-beer; malt beer) contains hardly any alcohol. *Vollbier* (*foal*-beer, or standard beer) has 4 percent alcohol, *Export* has 5 percent, and *Bockbier* has 6 percent. *Pils,* or *Pilsener,* beers are light and contain more hops. *Weizenbier* (*vitsen*-beer), made from wheat, is a Bavarian white beer. *Märzbier* (*maertz*-beer), or "March beer," is dark and strong. The most popular beer in Germany is *Pils,* followed by *Export.*

To order a beer, decide whether you want a **dunkles Bier** (dark beer, brewed with darkly roasted malt fermented for a long period of time) or a **helles Bier** (light beer, brewed from malt dried and baked by the local brewery). You ask for ein Grosses (ine grow-ses), for a large, or ein Kleines (ine *kly*-nis), for a small, and tell the waiter or tavernkeeper whether you want ein Bier vom Fass (fum fahss; from the barrel) or in a Flasche (*flah*-shuh, or bottle). The beer always is served cold, but not too cold, in an appropriate beer glass or mug, with a long-lasting head of white foam. A proper draft beer, according to the Germans, can't be poured in less than seven minutes to achieve the proper head.

Although not kind to the waistline, the German tradition of afternoon *Kaffee und Kuchen* (coffee and cake) is alive and well. Look out for regional specialties, too. **Lübeck** (Chapter 13), for example, is the capital of marzipan (almond paste), and **Nuremberg** (Chapter 18) is famous for its *Lebkuchen* (spice cakes). German wines (Chapter 24), mostly from grapes grown in the scenic Rhine and Mosel valleys (Chapter 19), provide excellent accompaniments to any meal. And German beers are legendary. Each city has its favorites, brewed right in the area.

Background Check: Finding Germany in Books and Movies

The book and movie lists that follow attempt to provide a broad overview of Germany from many different perspectives and historical epochs.

Books (fiction and nonfiction)

The number of books written about Germany, and in particular, about WWII and the Holocaust, has increased dramatically during the past two decades. The books I've selected include many great German authors, past and present, that can help you gain a better understanding of German history, personalities, and politics.

- ✔ *A Tramp Abroad* by Mark Twain. Twain's account of his travels in Germany is as fresh today as when it first was published in 1899.

- ✔ *Before the Deluge: A Portrait of Berlin in the 1920s* by Otto Friedrich. A fascinating portrait of the political, cultural, and social life of Berlin between the wars.

- ✔ *Berlin Journal 1989–1990* by Robert Darnton. An eyewitness account of the events that led to the opening of the Berlin Wall and the collapse of East Germany's Communist regime.

- ✔ *Billiards at Half-Past Nine* by Heinrich Böll. A compelling novel by one of Germany's best-known writers about the compromises made by a rich German family during the Hitler years.

- ✔ *Bismarck* by Edward Crankshaw. An objective and highly readable life of the first chancellor of the German Empire and a seminal figure in Germany's Prussian past.

- ✔ *Buddenbrooks* by Thomas Mann. A classic of German literature, this novel deals with the transition of a merchant family in Lübeck from 19th-century stability to 20th-century uncertainty.

- ✔ *Conversations with Goethe* by Johann Peter Eckermann. Early 19th-century Germany from the viewpoint of the most renowned German figure of the Enlightenment.

- ✔ *Frederick the Great* by Nancy Mitford. Frederick, statesman, scholar, musician, and patron of the arts, sketched with wit and humor.

- ✔ *German Family Research Made Easy* by J. Konrad. If you're interested in tracing your German roots, this easy-to-follow guide makes the task easier.

- ✔ *Germany 1866–1945* by Gordon Craig. One of the best single accounts of the turbulent political, cultural, and economic life in Germany from the foundation of the German Reich through the end of the Third Reich.

- ✔ *Here I Stand: A Life of Martin Luther* by Roland Bainton. A fascinating and meticulously researched account of the Protestant reformer.

- ✔ *Hitler 1936–1945 Nemesis* by Ian Kershaw. Several good biographies about Hitler have been written, including works by Robert Payne, Joachim Fest, and John Toland, but Kershaw's is one of the best.

- ✔ *My Life in Politics* by Willy Brandt. The political memoirs of Willy Brandt (1913 to 1992), winner of the Nobel Peace Prize in 1971, mayor of cold-war West Berlin (1957 to 1966), and chancellor of West Germany (1969 to 1974).

✔ *The German Lesson* by Siegfried Lenz. A bestseller when it first appeared in 1971, this powerful novel explores Nazism and its aftermath in the north German provinces.

✔ *The Germans* by Gordon Craig. A highly readable and knowledgeable portrait of postwar Germany.

✔ *The Last Jews in Berlin* by Leonard Gross. Gripping, true stories of a handful of Jews who managed to remain in Berlin during WWII by hiding out in the homes of non-Jewish German friends.

✔ *The Tin Drum* by Günter Grass. Perhaps the most famous novel about life in post-WWII Germany.

✔ *The Unmasterable Past: History, Holocaust, and German National Identity* by Charles S. Maier. A study of German attempts to come to terms with the Holocaust and the recent controversy surrounding conservative attempts to downplay the historical uniqueness of the German genocide against Jews and other minorities.

✔ *When in Germany, Do as the Germans Do* by Hyde Flippo. A short, entertaining crash course in German culture, customs, and heritage.

Movies

As with literature, WWII and the Holocaust have dominated the subject matter of recent films about Germany — so much so that German-made films about contemporary German life rarely get a showing outside of Germany unless they win a top prize at a film festival. My recommended list includes a selection of German and Germany-themed films available on tape or DVD.

✔ *A Foreign Affair* (1948). Billy Wilder's cynically hilarious look at postwar, occupied Berlin, starring Marlene Dietrich as an amoral cabaret singer and Jean Arthur as a self-righteous American senator.

✔ *Bent* (1997). Movie adaptation of Martin Sherman's powerful play about Max, a gay man sent to Dachau concentration camp under the Nazi regime.

✔ *Berlin Alexanderplatz* (1980). Rainer Werner Fassbinder's 15-part television adaptation of the novel by Alfred Döblin follows the life of a man released from prison between the two world wars.

✔ *The Blue Angel* (1930). The film that shot Marlene Dietrich to international stardom remains stark, startling, and provocative.

✔ *Cabaret* (1972). A musical based on Christopher Isherwood's *Berlin Stories* and set in Berlin at the brink of WWII.

✔ *The Cabinet of Doctor Caligari* (1921). One of the earliest horror films, this classic German silent movie used Expressionist sets to create a tale of murder and madness.

✔ *Goodbye, Lenin!* (2004). A wry comedy about a young man in East Berlin who tries to keep his bed-ridden mother, a loyal Communist, from learning that the Wall has come down and Germany has been reunited.

✔ *Ludwig* (1972). Visconti's turgid epic about the last king of Bavaria, the one who built Neuschwanstein.

✔ *The Marriage of Maria Braun* (1979). Hanna Schygulla stars as a woman married to a soldier in the waning days of WWII.

✔ *Metropolis* (1927). Fritz Lang directed this classic of German cinema, in which The Workers plan a revolt against the aloof Thinkers that dominate them in a future dystopia.

✔ *Olympiad* (1936). Leni Riefenstahl's super-Aryan take on the 1936 Olympic Games in Berlin.

✔ *Run, Lola, Run* (1999). Fast-paced twists and turns as Lola races desperately through Berlin seeking 100,000 deutsche marks to save her boyfriend from being rubbed out by a gangster.

✔ *Triumph of the Will* (1934). Leni Riefenstahl filmed the gigantic 1934 Nazi conference and rally in Nuremberg as "image-control" propaganda for the Third Reich.

✔ *Wings of Desire* (1988). An angel roaming the streets of Berlin and recording the angst and joy of ordinary life falls in love with a mortal.

Chapter 3

Deciding Where and When to Go

*W*hat do you want to see when you visit Germany, and when do you want to go? In this chapter, I help you to narrow your focus so you can start planning your trip in earnest. This chapter points out highlights of each region and gives you the lowdown on the weather so you can determine the best destinations and time of year for your visit. You also find a calendar of events so you can time your trip to coincide with, or avoid, special festivals and events.

Going Where You Want to Be

Germany For Dummies, 2nd Edition, is a selective guidebook, geared to savvy travelers who want to know more about Germany's leading sights. I don't cover every state, region, and city in Deutschland, only the essential highlights. My aim in this book is to introduce you to the best cities, historic towns, special sights, and scenic regions that Germany has to offer. To figure out which regions to visit during your trip, check out the following thumbnail sketches and find details of the best places Germany has to offer in Chapters 1 and 2. For locations, see "The Regions in Brief" map in this chapter.

Discovering northern Germany

Northern Germany is a different world from southern Germany. Architecturally, the north's sober red-brick Gothic churches and buildings lack the ornate baroque decorations found in the Catholic south. The food is plainer, too, with an emphasis on fish. The climate in the

The Regions in Brief

north, which is influenced by the North and Baltic seas, often is wet or misty, but some people believe the maritime atmosphere is part of its overall appeal.

After Berlin and Munich (in the south), **Hamburg** is the third-largest city in Germany, and its **harbor,** one of the biggest in the world, is a major tourist attraction, and so are the breezy **Alster Lakes** in the center of the city. In Hamburg, you can also explore beautiful 19th-century neighborhoods, such as **Altona,** now a lively area with restaurants, cafes, and bars, and visit the **Hamburger Kunsthalle (Fine Arts Museum),** which houses an outstanding, multifaceted collection of art. **Lübeck,** an easy day trip from Hamburg, has so many medieval brick buildings that UNESCO designated it a World Heritage Site — a place judged to be of exceptional cultural value, according to the United Nations' agency that promotes education and the arts. In the **Altstadt,** you see examples of its 900-year-old history everywhere you turn, from the Gothic *Rathaus* (Town Hall) to the church spires that dominate the skyline. In **Bremen,** another easy day trip from Hamburg, you find a historic center with a day's worth of sightseeing possibilities. For the scoop on Hamburg, Lübeck, and Bremen, turn to Chapter 13.

Exploring eastern Germany

Now that Germany is reunited, you have an opportunity to visit sections of **eastern Germany** that for 45 years were inaccessible, or at least difficult to visit, under the Communist regime of the former German Democratic Republic (GDR). **Dresden,** on the Elbe River and only two hours from Berlin by train, has treasures beyond measure in the **Zwinger Palace,** the **Albertinum** museum, and the **Residenzschloss. Leipzig,** on the other hand, has been less interested in restoring its past than looking toward the future. The peaceful revolution of 1989 began there, and the city seems to be working overtime to shake off its GDR legacy: The **Museum in der Runden Ecke** is devoted to the role the Stasi, East Germany's secret police, played in the lives of citizens. Similarly, the new **Zeitgeschichtliches Museum (Contemporary History Museum)** chronicles the history and artifacts of the GDR years. The **Bach Museum** is of interest to classical music lovers, and the new **Museum of Fine Arts,** with a rich collection of Old Masters, is scheduled to open in 2005.

Big, brash **Berlin** was the capital of the old German Reich for 70 years before it was divided into two cities — one capitalist, one Communist — after World War II (WWII). It has stitched itself back together to become the capital (and largest city) of a reunified Germany and now reigns as one of the most fascinating cities in the world. Does the *Berliner Luft* (Berlin air) account for Berlin's endless and ongoing fizz of excitement, as some people claim? With world-class museums, top performing arts venues, historic reverberations, and striking new architecture, Berlin is where all is happening in Germany right now. You find comprehensive coverage of Berlin — including a day trip to Frederick the Great's charming, 18th-century **Sanssouci Palace** in Potsdam — in Chapters 11 and 12.

The small, quiet eastern town of **Weimar** is in a category of its own. It suffered little damaged during the war and was the home of Germany's greatest writer, the poet and dramatist Johann Wolfgang von Goethe (1749 to 1832), and to the playwright Friedrich Schiller (1759 to 1805). The homes of these two literary giants are Weimar's most popular tourist attractions. The small **Bauhaus Museum** exhibits paintings, textiles, pottery, furniture, and drawings from the Bauhaus school, which began here in 1919. A visit to the **Buchenwald Memorial,** the site of a Nazi-run concentration camp just outside of Weimar where at least

56,000 people died, can be an intense and profoundly moving experience. You find complete coverage of Dresden, Leipzig, and Weimar in Chapter 14.

Savoring southern Germany

Southern Germany is worlds apart from the north. **Bavaria,** Germany's largest and most prosperous *Land* (state), is a place that's unmistakably tailor-made for tourists. **Munich,** the capital, is cultured and elegant, with an upscale chic, but it's also boisterous, even raucous: Millions pour into the city during **Oktoberfest** to experience Munich's renowned giant **beer halls** and **beer gardens.** Ranking right up there with the offerings of Berlin are Munich's museums, crammed with Old Masters, 19th-century greats, and major 20th-century artists. The city's most popular museum is the **Deutsches Museum,** the largest science and technology museum in the world. In the center of town sits an enormous palace, the **Residenz,** used by the rulers of Bavaria from the 14th century up to 1918. You also find lovely **churches** with sober Gothic and exuberant baroque interiors. Munich's musical life is the envy of many cities, with year-round opera, symphony, and concerts of all kinds. Chapter 15 is devoted to the many delights of Munich.

Bavaria is full of scenic splendor and picturesque charm. You'll find plenty of both along the **Romantic Road,** the most beautiful driving tour in Germany. This enchanting route winds south from **Würzburg** to **Neuschwanstein,** Ludwig's fairy-tale castle in the Bavarian Alps, with stops at several perfectly preserved medieval towns along the way. From Munich, the day trip to the mountain resort town of **Garmisch-Partenkirchen** is an easy one, and it's close to the **Zugspitze,** Germany's highest peak, which is accessible by cable car. This alpine region, where cowbells clang in the meadows and classic chalets nestle in picturesque valleys, also is where you find **Oberammergau,** a town that's famous for its wood carvers and for the Passion Play performed there every ten years — a tradition dating back to the 17th century. The Romantic Road and day trips in Bavaria are covered in Chapter 16.

Southern Germany also includes the **Bodensee** (also called **Lake Constance**), and the famous **Schwarzwald,** or **Black Forest.** Both areas offer great natural beauty and plenty of recreational opportunities. Germany's largest lake, the Bodensee, sits in a sun-drenched basin with a view of the Alps to the south; semitropical gardens flourish on **Mainau,** an island in the lake, and vineyards and fruit trees grow around its shoreline. **Lindau,** an island-city connected to the mainland by a causeway, is the best spot to stay. In the Black Forest, the lively and lovely city of **Freiburg** is a delight. From there you can explore the surrounding forest or hunt for a cuckoo clock, one of the traditional industries of the Black Forest region. Farther north is the city of **Baden-Baden,** with its famous mineral baths and glamorous casino. Details about the Bodensee and the Black Forest are found in Chapter 17.

Wending through western Germany

Western Germany is a densely populated area with an ancient history and cities with vibrant personalities all their own. **Heidelberg** is for many people the quintessential romantic German town. Sitting on the Neckar River amid green hills, Heidelberg's enormous ruined castle oversees its picturesque **Altstadt (Old Town).** Stuttgart, only 40 minutes by train from Heidelberg, reigns as the cultural capital of southwestern Germany, with major painting collections and the fabulous **Neue Galerie** (slated to open in 2005), an art museum housed in a striking glass cube offering a panoramic view of Stuttgart. Little more than a pile of smoldering rubble at the end of WWII, **Nürnberg** (or **Nuremberg** as it's known in English) was rebuilt in a style that evokes the medieval era when it was one of the most important cities in Germany. Nuremberg has as many romantic corners as Heidelberg, in addition to the country's largest museum of art and culture, the **Germanisches Nationalmuseum (German National Museum),** and a delightful **Spielzeugmuseum (Toy Museum).** Nuremberg's **Christmas Market** is the oldest in Germany; Stuttgart's is one of the largest. Heidelberg, Stuttgart, and Nuremberg are covered in Chapter 18.

Köln, or **Cologne** (as it's known in English), occupies a prime spot on the Rhine River, which comes as a wonderful surprise to many visitors. This lively, sophisticated, and good-natured town offers more than enough to keep you busy for a couple of days. Its chief glory is its awe-inspiring **Dom (Cathedral),** the largest Gothic structure north of the Alps. Cologne was an important Roman town during a period that is wonderfully interpreted in the **Romisch-Germanisches Museum (Roman-Germanic Museum).** By contrast, Cologne also is one of the contemporary art capitals of Germany. Chief among its many outstanding museums are the **Wallraf-Richartz Museum,** one of Germany's best for art from the Middle Ages to the 19th century, and the **Museum Ludwig,** one of the top modern-art museums in Europe.

The **Rhine** and **Mosel valleys** in western Germany form one of Europe's top wine-producing areas. River cruises originating in Cologne and many other cities in the area take you through valleys of neatly clipped vineyards soaking up sunlight on steep hillsides. You can also visit many wine towns by train. For more on Cologne and side trips into Germany's **wine country,** see Chapter 19.

Frankfurt probably is the best-known metropolis in western Germany, in part because it's the point of entry for most visitors who fly into the country. The banking capital of Germany and the European Union, Frankfurt has a modern, business-oriented buzz and a skyline pierced by designer skyscrapers. Among its many cultural offerings are several important museums, all described in Chapter 20.

Scheduling Your Time

If you're flying into the country from outside of Europe, your airport choices are **Frankfurt, Munich,** and **Berlin,** the latter of which has a new Delta direct flight from New York.

Frankfurt airport has its own train station, so it's possible to hop on a fast train at the airport and arrive almost anywhere in Germany within five hours or less. If a driving tour along the **Romantic Road** is part of your itinerary, rent a car at Frankfurt airport and drive to the beginning of the scenic route in Würzburg, an easy hour-and-a-half drive away (see Chapter 16 for more details).

If you want to explore all parts of the country, consider centering your itineraries in Berlin, Hamburg, Munich, and Cologne.

- ✔ From **Berlin,** you have easy access to the cities of **Dresden, Leipzig,** and **Weimar** in eastern Germany.

- ✔ From **Hamburg**, the northern German cities of **Lübeck** and **Bremen** are a short train ride away.

- ✔ From **Munich,** you can easily reach places in the Bavarian Alps, including **Neuschwanstein, Füssen, Garmisch-Partenkirchen,** and **Oberammergau,** in addition to **Augsburg, Nuremberg,** and **Lindau** on Lake Constance.

- ✔ From **Cologne,** all the major cities of western Germany — **Heidelberg, Stuttgart,** and **Baden-Baden** — are never more than three hours away by train. You can also arrange for boat trips on the **Rhine** and visit the **winegrowing regions** by car or train.

Keep German holidays in mind when scheduling your trip. Many museums and attractions close during the following **public holidays:** January 1 (New Year's Day), Easter (including Good Friday and Easter Monday), May 1 (Labor Day), Ascension Day (ten days before Pentecost/Whitsunday, the seventh Sunday after Easter), Whitmonday (day after Pentecost/Whitsunday), October 3 (Day of German Unity), November 17 (Day of Prayer and Repentance), and December 25 to 26 (Christmas). In addition, the following holidays are observed in some German states: January 6 (Epiphany), Corpus Christi (ten days after Pentecost), August 15 (Assumption), and November 1 (All Saints' Day).

Revealing the Secret of the Seasons

How do you decide what time of year to travel to Germany? This section presents the pros and cons of each season, so you can choose the best time for your visit.

Traveling during high and low seasons

Roughly speaking, the high season for travel in Germany is from Easter to the end of September with another peak in December. The country is most crowded during the months of May and June. July and August may be less expensive because that's when Germans take off on their own holidays, and many hotels consequently offer lower summer rates. October and November and January through March are the low seasons.

In general, crowds and prices tend to rise during big **trade fairs.** Nearly all large German cities have a *Messe,* or convention center/fairground, with a year-round schedule of major trade shows in all industries. These trade fairs can put a real squeeze on hotel rooms.

In the winter months, generally from October through March, museums, castles, and tourist offices have shorter hours and may be closed certain days of the week. Most castles and palaces can be visited daily year-round, but from April through September, the lines for major attractions, like Neuschwanstein and Linderhof castles in Bavaria, or the Reichstag dome in Berlin, may be more than two hours long.

Watching those unpredictable skies

Before I write about the weather in Germany, I think a disclaimer is in order. As in many parts of the world, the weather in Germany has become less predictable than in the past. In northern Germany, for instance, some locals claim that they now receive less snow and more rain than in decades past. In southern Germany, some report a hotter and drier climate. So, although I can give you a very broad overview of general weather patterns in Germany, be prepared for variations.

Overall, Germany has a predominantly mild, temperate climate. Average summer temperatures range from 72°F to 80°F (20°C to 30°C). The average winter temperature hovers around 32°F (0°C). That said, bear in mind that the climate is constantly affected by colliding continental and maritime air masses from the Baltic and North seas, resulting in plenty of unpredictable weather, especially in the north. For average temperatures and rainfalls, see Table 3-1 for Berlin in the north and Table 3-2 for Frankfurt in the south.

Table 3-1 Berlin's Average Daytime Temperature and Rainfall

	Jan	Feb	Mar	Apr	May	June	July	Aug	Sep	Oct	Nov	Dec
Temp °F	30	32	40	48	53	60	64	62	56	49	40	34
Temp °C	-1	0	4	9	12	16	18	17	13	9	4	1
Rainfall (in.)	2.2	1.6	1.2	1.6	2.3	2.9	3.2	2.7	2.2	1.6	2.4	1.9

Table 3-2	Frankfurt's Average Daytime Temperature and Rainfall											
	Jan	Feb	Mar	Apr	May	June	July	Aug	Sep	Oct	Nov	Dec
Temp °F	34	36	42	49	57	63	66	66	58	50	41	35
Temp °C	1	2	6	9	14	17	19	19	14	10	5	2
Rainfall (in.)	6.5	5.1	5.6	5.7	5.9	5.5	5.0	5.1	4.2	4.8	6.5	6

If your trip includes northern Germany, consider visiting in April and May, the months that are least cloudy. Even with clear skies, though, the weather up north can remain, shall we say, *invigorating*. In the interior of Germany, the least gray months usually are June and September.

Blossoming in spring

Spring comes earliest in the south and in the Rhine Valley. The *Föhn*, a dry south wind from the Alps, heralds the approach of spring around the giant Bodensee (Lake Constance) and in the river valleys of the Black Forest and throughout southwestern Germany.

Here are some of the season's highlights:

- The warmth of springtime sun coaxes out the new vines in Germany's Rhineland wine country.

- Blossoms appear on the fruit trees grown around the Bodensee and the Rhine.

- In towns around Bodensee, such as Lindau, an early spring means that tables are set up in sunny squares and life begins to move outdoors.

- The carefully tended parks and gardens in German cities show off their first spring flowers.

- May and June is *Spargel* (white asparagus) season throughout Germany; you find asparagus specialties on menus everywhere.

But keep in mind these springtime pitfalls:

- Cold, rainy weather can last well into early summer in Berlin and other northern cities.

- The snow in the Alps usually melts by April, leaving May as an "in-between" off-month: The weather in the Alps tends to be soggy and foggy at this time.

- During school holidays, especially around Easter, major attractions in cities throughout Germany tend to be more crowded.

Shining (and raining) in summer

From April through September, you can generally count on warm, mild weather in southern Germany. However, around Cologne and even as far north as Berlin, mid- and late-summer days can become hot, humid, and thundery, which also can be the case in Dresden, Leipzig, and the land-locked eastern portion of the country. Summer weather in the Bavarian Alps is extremely variable and changes according to altitude, local winds, and the orientation of individual valleys to the sun. Summer in the north comes later and remains variable because of maritime influences from the North and Baltic seas.

Some summer perks to consider:

- ✔ Prices for hotels often are lower in July and August.

- ✔ Warm summer nights stay light much longer, until 10 p.m. or sometimes later.

- ✔ Outdoor musical performances and street fairs take place in many cities and regions.

- ✔ Lakes in the Alps, the Black Forest, and Berlin, become more inviting as warm weather settles in.

- ✔ Many attractions are open longer hours.

- ✔ You can dine alfresco (outdoors) in most German cities.

But keep in mind:

- ✔ Airfare tends to be higher during summer months.

- ✔ In traffic-jammed cities like Berlin, Munich, and Frankfurt, gasoline and diesel exhaust can create air pollution on hot, windless days.

- ✔ Heat and humidity can make for sticky sightseeing throughout central and southern Germany.

- ✔ Air-conditioning is not common in Germany; hotels and concert halls can be broiling.

- ✔ Getting into top attractions like Neuschwanstein and Linderhof castles can take two hours or more.

Glowing in autumn

Fall is one of the best times to visit Germany. Autumn days are beautiful in scenic Bavaria, making this a perfect time to explore the Romantic Road. The deciduous trees in the Black and Thuringian forests and along the Rhine, Neckar, and other river valleys turn golden as the days grow shorter. In southern and western Germany, after the grape harvest, vines turn yellow. Indian summer, or what the Germans call *Altweibersommer* (old women's summer), frequently makes a welcome appearance during October and November. In the north, autumn is likely to be rainy and blustery, heralding gray, wet winters.

A few advantages of autumn:

- ✔ Summer crowds have thinned out by the end of September.
- ✔ Airfares usually drop.
- ✔ Germany's cultural calendar of opera, symphony, and other events swings into high gear.
- ✔ Scenic areas like the Black Forest, the Bavarian Alps, and the Rhineland glow with autumn hues.
- ✔ Giant beer festivals transform Munich and Stuttgart.
- ✔ The smell of new wine fills the old streets of winegrowing towns.
- ✔ Towns in winegrowing areas celebrate with wine festivals.

 This season has only one real drawback: Autumn may be gray and rainy, especially in the north.

Welcoming winter

Snow can fall anywhere in Germany, lending a special air to the country's many Christmas markets. But with winter temperatures hovering right around freezing, snow doesn't stay on the ground for long, and often turns into sleet. This story is different in the Bavarian Alps and the Black Forest, where the winter weather is colder and snow adds to the beauty of the mountain and forest landscapes. Both the Alps and the Black Forest are known for their fine skiing and winter sports.

Winter can be wonderful because:

- ✔ In December, cities throughout the country set up magical outdoor Christmas markets where you find tree ornaments, handcrafted goods, and baked delights.
- ✔ When the snow starts to fall in the Alps and the Black Forest, skiers head for the slopes and cross-country trails.
- ✔ In the weeks before Lent, Cologne and Munich celebrate with city-wide carnivals *(Fasching)*.

 But winter has its downside:

- ✔ Brrr. The cold can be raw, numbing, and seemingly endless, especially in the north.
- ✔ Daylight drops dramatically: Darkness falls as early as 3:30 or 4 p.m.
- ✔ Although you'll be comfortable in your hotel, Germans tend to underheat rather than overheat their spaces.
- ✔ Almost everything shuts down on December 25 and 26 and New Year's Day.

Perusing a Calendar of Events

Germany hums year-round with festivals and special events of all kinds. Verifying dates beforehand with the German National Tourist Board is a good idea. Check its Web site (www.germany-tourism.de), or call or write for a free calendar of events. See the appendix for the tourist board's contact addresses and phone numbers.

January

New Year's Day International Ski Jumping, in Garmisch-Partenkirchen (☎ 08821/180-700; www.garmisch-partenkirchen.de), is one of Europe's major winter sporting events. January 1.

February

The well-respected **Berlin International Film Festival** (☎ 030/25920; www.berlinale.de) lasts for a week and showcases the work of international film directors in addition to the latest German films. February 10 to 20.

Fasching (Carnival) festivals take place in Catholic cities throughout Germany, reaching their peak on the Tuesday (Mardi Gras) before Ash Wednesday. Celebrations in Cologne (☎ 0221/9433; www.koeln.de) and Munich (☎ 089/233-0300; www.muenchen-tourist.de) are particularly famous. A week in February.

May

Hamburg Summer is a summer-long series of cultural events, including concerts, plays, festivals, and special exhibitions. For information, contact **Tourismus-Zentrale Hamburg** (☎ 040/3005-1201; www.hamburg.de). May through July.

During the **Historisches Festspiel (Historic Festival),** Rothenburg ob der Tauber celebrates the story of how a brave citizen saved the town from destruction by drinking a huge tankard of wine (an event called **Der Meistertrunk**). Events take place twice a year. For information, contact **Tourist Information** (☎ 09861/40492; www.rothenburg.de). Third week in May, first week of September.

The renowned **Bachfest/Bach Festival** (☎ 0341/913-7333; www.bach-leipzig.de) in Leipzig features performances of Johann Sebastian Bach's work in the famous Thomaskirche, where he was choirmaster, and in other churches and concert halls. May 23 to June 1.

On special Saturday nights during **Rhein im Feuerzauber (Rhine in Flames),** various towns along the Rhine (between Bonn and Linz, Koblenz and Braubach, Bingen and Rüdesheim, and St. Goar and St. Goarshausen) illuminate their castles and set off fireworks. The best vantage point is from a riverboat on the Rhine. For details, contact the

German National Tourist Office (see the appendix for its addressees and phone numbers). May through September.

June

Fireworks enliven the sky in the romantic university city of Heidelberg during the **Floodlighting of the Castle.** For more information, contact **Heidelberg Tourist-Information,** Pavillon (☎ **06221/19433;** www. heidelberg.de). Early June, mid-July, and early September.

Berlin and Cologne have the largest **Gay Pride** festivals, featuring parades, performances, and street fairs. For events in Berlin, log on to www.berlin.gay-web.de; for events in Cologne, log on to www.koeln.gay-web.de. Berlin, last weekend in June; Cologne, first weekend in June.

During the **Schleswig-Holstein Music Festival** (☎ **0800/7463-2002;** www. shmf.de), one of the best music festivals in Germany, classical concerts take place in venues in and around the lovely old city of Lübeck. June through August.

Enjoy vintages from the surrounding Black Forest area during Freiburg im Breisgau's **Public Wine Tasting.** Events take place in the Münsterplatz surrounding Freiburg's magnificent cathedral. For information, contact **Freiburg Tourist Information** (☎ **0761/388-1880;** www.freiburg.de). Last weekend in June.

July

One of Europe's major opera events, the **Richard Wagner Festival** (☎ **0921/78780;** www.festspiele.de) in Bayreuth, takes place in the composer's famous Festspielhaus (opera house). Unfortunately, opera tickets must be booked *years* in advance. Late July to late August.

August

During **Weinkost (Food and Wine Fair)** in Freiburg im Breisgau, local residents and visitors enjoy the first vintages from grapes grown in the Black Forest district and regional food specialties. For information, contact **Freiburg Tourist Information** (☎ **0761/388-1880;** www.freiburg. de). Mid-August.

The **Traditional Rüdesheim Wine Festival,** in Rüdesheim am Rhein, takes place in the Rhine village most famous for red wines. For information, contact the **Rüdesheim Tourist Bureau** (☎ **06722/19433**). Mid-August.

Nürnberger Herbsfest (Fall Festival), a big Frankish folk festival in Nuremberg (☎ **0911/468-600;** www.volksfest-nuernberg.de), features folk music, jazz concerts, and events for the whole family. August 27 to September 12.

Arts and pleasure abound during Hamburg's **Alstervergnügen (Alster Pleasures)**. Events, which take place around Binnenalster Lake, include food stalls, fireworks, and shows. For information, contact **Tourismus-Zentrale** (☎ 040/3005-1201; www.hamburg.de). Last weekend in August.

At the **Stuttgart Wine Festival**, wine lovers converge on Schillerplatz to taste a selection of more than 350 Württemberg wines and sample regional food specialties. Contact the **Tourist Information Office** (☎ 0711/222-8259; www.stuttgart-tourist.de) for more details. Last week in August.

September

Munich's **Oktoberfest** (www.oktoberfest.de), Germany's most famous festival, happens mostly in September, not October. Millions show up, and visitors pack hotels. Most activities occur at Theresienwiese, where local breweries sponsor gigantic tents that can hold up to 6,000 beer drinkers. Mid-September to the first Sunday in October.

Dating back to 1818, the 16-day **Stuttgart Beer Festival,** the second largest in Germany after Munich's Oktoberfest, begins with a grand procession of horse-drawn beer wagons and people in traditional costumes and features food, rides, and tents for beer drinkers. For more information, contact the **Stuttgart Tourist Information Office** (☎ 0711/222-8259; www.stuttgart-tourist.de). Late September.

One of the high points on the cultural calendar of Germany, the **Berliner Festwochen (Berlin Festival)** brings an international roster of performing artists to Berlin for opera, symphony, and theatrical presentations. Contact **Berlin Tourist Information** (☎ 0190/016-316; www.berlin.de). September 1 to October 11.

October

The largest book fair in Europe, the **Frankfurt Book Fair** (☎ 069/21010; www.frankfurt-book-fair.com) is a major event in the world of international book publishing. Mid-October.

November

The annual **Jazz-Fest Berlin,** staged at the Philharmonie, attracts some of the world's finest jazz artists. Contact **Berlin Tourist Information** (☎ 0190/016-316; www.berlin.de) for information. November 1 to 4.

Hamburger Dom (also called Winter Dom), an annual amusement fair at Hamburg's Heiligengeistfeld, is the biggest public event in northern Germany. For information, contact **Tourismus-Zentrale Hamburg** (☎ 040/3005-1201; www.hamburg.de). November 9 to December 9.

December

Christmas Markets, generally called a *Weihnachtsmarkt* (*Weihnachten* means Christmas) or a *Christkindlmarkt* (literally, "Christ Child Market"), take place in town squares throughout Germany. You find them in Cologne, Dresden, Frankfurt, Leipzig, Munich, Nuremberg, Rothenburg ob der Tauber, and Stuttgart, among other cities. Contact the individual tourist offices of each city, or the German National Tourist Board, for details (see the appendix for contact information). Late November or early December until Christmas.

Chapter 4

Following an Itinerary: Four Great Options

In This Chapter

▶ Seeing Germany's top attractions in one or two weeks
▶ Discovering Germany with your kids
▶ Planning trips for wine aficionados

*P*utting together a good itinerary is one of the hardest parts of any trip. If you haven't visited a destination before, how do you know what's worth seeing and what isn't? In this chapter, I lay out some suggested travel itineraries for those with limited time or with special interests. (See Chapter 1 for some preliminary information on what the country offers.)

Although you can reach all of the destinations in this chapter by train or public transportation, some of these itineraries are more enjoyable if you have a car. For details on getting around the country, see Chapter 7.

Just the Highlights: Germany in One Week

This seven-day itinerary, beginning in Munich and ending in Berlin, shows you the contrasts between southern Germany and northern Germany and introduces you to the country's two greatest cities. I include two of King Ludwig II's castles and a brief stop in Cologne, on the Rhine. For more information about the sights that I mention, see Chapter 15 for Munich, Chapter 16 for the Bavarian Alps and its castles, Chapter 19 for Cologne, and Chapter 12 for Berlin.

Spend **Day 1** in marvelous **Munich.** Shake out your plane-cramped legs by taking to the streets for some general exploration. Head first for **Marienplatz,** the city's main square. You can go up to the top of the **Rathaus** tower for a bird's-eye view, watch the **Glockenspiel,** and visit the nearby **Frauenkirche,** Munich's largest church. Then walk over to the adjacent **Viktualienmarkt,** one of the greatest food markets in Europe. Browse around and find a place for lunch from among the dozens of possibilities in the area. Afterward, make your way to the **Asamkirche** for a glimpse of the baroque ornamentation for which southern Germany is famous. In the afternoon, choose a museum to visit. If you're an art lover, you may want to see the priceless collection of Old Masters at the **Alte Pinakotheke.** If you're interested in science and technology, make your way to the famous **Deutsches Museum.** If you're in the mood for oom-pah-pah, have dinner at the fun-loving **Hofbräuhaus.** Munich is one of Germany's top cultural capitals, so you may want to end your evening at a concert or the opera.

Start **Day 2** in a palace. You need the entire morning to wander through the enormous **Residenz** in central Munich. Or make an easy excursion to beautiful **Schloss Nymphenburg,** which you can reach by streetcar. If you choose Nymphenburg, allow some extra time to wander through the gardens, and be sure to visit the collection of carriages, which includes the bizarrely ornate sleighs and coaches used by King Ludwig II of Bavaria, creator of Linderhof and Neuschwanstein castles. Have lunch near Marienplatz. In the afternoon, choose another museum to visit. Three possibilities are the **Neue Pinakothek,** a showcase for 19th-century German and European art; the brand-new **Pinakothek Moderne Kunst,** which displays an international collection of 20th-century masterpieces; and the **Bayerisches Nationalmuseum,** the location for Bavaria's greatest historic and artistic treasures. At some point, fit in a stroll in the bucolic **Englisher Garten,** Munich's largest and prettiest park. You can bring a picnic or order a meal at the park's famous beer garden.

On **Day 3,** head to the Bavarian Alps, just south of Munich. If you rent a car, you can easily explore some of the sights along the **Romantische Strasse (Romantic Road).** Or you can take a train to **Garmisch-Partenkirchen** and ascend the **Zugspitze,** Germany's highest peak, for a spectacular view of the Alps. Special cog railways and cable cars can take you up and bring you back down. From Garmisch, the trip is only 40 minutes by train or car to **Oberammergau,** the closest town to Linderhof castle. Wander through this small Bavarian town, which is famous for its woodcarvers, whose wares you may want to purchase. If you're without wheels, take a bus from Oberammergau to **Schloss Linderhof,** Ludwig II's French-inspired castle. Spend the night in Garmisch, Oberammergau, or Füssen.

On **Day 4,** make your way to **Füssen,** the town closest to Neuschwanstein and Hohenschwangau castles. Make Neuschwanstein your top priority; as Germany's most popular tourist attraction, this castle quickly fills up with tourists as the day wears on. By train from Oberammergau, the trip takes a little more than an hour. If you're without a car, you can easily get a bus from Füssen for the 6.5-km (4-mile) trip to the castle. Tours of King Ludwig II's fairy-tale castle take about one hour. You can dine near the parking area below Neuschwanstein. Then, if you're still in a "royal" mood, visit adjacent **Hohenschwangau** castle, Ludwig's childhood home. Spend the night in Füssen, and be sure to take time to stroll around the lovely historic district of town. If you're driving, you can make an easy excursion to the **Wieskirche (Church in the Meadow),** a beautiful baroque masterpiece located just a few miles north of Füssen.

If you have your car for a two-day rental, you may be able to return the vehicle in Füssen, or you can drive back to Munich and return it there. From either city, hop on the train and make your way to **Köln (Cologne)** for **Day 5.** (By fast train, the trip from Cologne takes about 5½ hours; the fastest train from Füssen takes about 7 hours.) You'll see Cologne's greatest sight — the enormous Gothic **Dom** (cathedral) — as you step out of the train station. Enjoy the afternoon in this lively Rhine-side city by visiting the cathedral and one or two of its many fine museums, such as the **Römisch-Germanisches Museum (Roman-Germanic Museum),** dedicated to the Romans who made Cologne one of their strategic forts nearly 2,000 years ago; the **Wallraf-Richartz Museum,** displaying Old and Modern Masters; and **Museum Ludwig,** entirely devoted to 20th-century and contemporary art. You can also take a sightseeing **boat ride** along the Rhine. Stay overnight in Cologne and have dinner at one of the city's famous beer halls (be sure to sample Kölsch, Cologne's delicious beer). The city has an excellent music scene, too, so you may want to see an opera or attend a concert.

On the morning of **Day 6,** take one of the sleek, superfast trains to **Berlin** (the trains depart from the Cologne Hauptbahnhof; for train information and schedules, call **German Rail** at ☎ **11861**). The trip from Cologne is under 4½ hours. Huge, sophisticated Berlin has endless things to do. Settle into your hotel and then take one of the sightseeing **bus tours** of the city — otherwise you'll see only a fraction of this enormous metropolis. To book a bus tour, contact **Severin+Kühn,** Kurfürstendamm 216 (☎ **030/880-4190;** www.severin-kuehn-berlin.de). After your tour, make your way over to **Potsdamer Platz,** the new quarter where the Berlin Wall once stood. From Potsdamer Platz, you can walk to the **Brandenburg Gate,** the symbol of the city, and the **Reichstag,** the country's parliamentary headquarters. Take the elevator up to the new dome on top of the Reichstag — the dome is open late, so come back later if the line is long. Then walk east down **Unter den Linden** to **Museumsinsel (Museum Island),** and stop in at the **Pergamon Museum** with its fantastic collection of antiquities. Berlin is famed for its nightlife, so when darkness falls you may want to attend an opera, a concert, or a cabaret.

Here's hoping your flight home departs sometime in the afternoon on **Day 7,** so you can take advantage of the morning by going over to the **Ägyptisches Museum (Egyptian Museum)** to see the world-famous bust of Egyptian queen Nefertiti. Then stroll down the Ku-Damm, western Berlin's renowned boulevard, before making your way to the airport.

East Side, West Side: Germany in Two Weeks

What a treat — two weeks to take in the sights. This suggested itinerary makes a clockwise circuit of Germany. For detailed information on the cities and sights that I mention, check out Chapter 12 for Berlin and

Potsdam, Chapter 14 for Dresden, Leipzig, and Weimar; Chapter 15 for Munich; Chapter 16 for Bavaria and its castles; Chapter 17 for the Black Forest and the Bodensee; and Chapter 18 for Heidelberg and Nuremberg.

Berlin, Germany's capital and largest city, is the starting point on **Day 1** of your two-week tour of Deutschland. Berlin is an enormous city, so start the morning by taking one of the sightseeing **bus tours** (to book one, contact **Severin+Kühn,** Kurfürstendamm 216 (☎ **030/880-4190;** www.severin-kuehn-berlin.de). Devote your afternoon to exploring eastern Berlin, the most historic part of the city. Start at **Potsdamer Platz,** then head over to the **Reichstag** and take the elevator up to the new dome for a view of the city. Afterward, walk to the **Brandenburg Gate** and head east down **Unter den Linden,** the most famous boulevard in this part of the city. Eastern Berlin has numerous attractions: Make sure that you stop at the **Gendarmenmarkt,** a beautiful neoclassical square, and wander into the **Nikolaiviertel (Nicholas' Quarter)** before you head up to the **Museumsinsel (Museum Island)** to visit the **Pergamon Museum.** From Museumsinsel, you can walk to **Friedrichstrasse,** the upscale shopping street, or take the S-Bahn (the city's system of elevated trains) to **Hackescher Markt,** a pre–World War I quarter that now features several smart cafes and shops.

Spend **Day 2** on the western side of the city. Head over to the Charlottenburg neighborhood for a tour of **Schloss (Palace) Charlottenburg** and a stroll through the palace gardens. Several museums are in and around the palace; the most famous is the **Ägyptisches Museum (Egyptian Museum),** which displays the stunning bust of Egyptian Queen Nefertiti. Head back to the **Kurfürstendamm** (known as Ku-Damm), the most famous boulevard in western Berlin, for lunch or to find a cafe for *Kaffee und Kuchen* (coffee and cake). Stop by the **Kaiser-Wilhelm-Gedächtniskirche (Kaiser Wilhelm Memorial Church),** left as a colossal ruin after the devastation of World War II, then spend a while strolling in the **Tiergarten,** Berlin's most famous park. Have something fun lined up for the evening: Berlin has three opera houses, three major symphony orchestras, cabarets, variety shows, and, of course, countless bars and clubs.

Spend the morning of **Day 3** at **Schloss Sanssouci** in **Potsdam,** an easy trip from Berlin by S-Bahn. You want to give yourself at least four hours for this excursion, which includes a tour of Frederick the Great's rococo palace and a walk through the landscaped grounds. You can eat near the palace or back in Berlin. In the afternoon, visit one of Berlin's great museums, such as the **Gemäldegalerie (Painting Gallery)** or the new **Jüdisches Museum (Jewish Museum).** Plenty of entertainment options exist for the evening.

On **Day 4,** you see a different side of Germany (literally) in the eastern cities of the former German Democratic Republic (GDR), which was ruled by the Communists until 1990. **Dresden,** on the Elbe River about two hours south of Berlin by train, is one of the great art cities of Germany. In

Dresden, you want to focus your attention on the **Albertinum,** a vast collection of treasures accrued by Saxon rulers; the **Residenzschloss,** the new home of the famed treasury known as the Green Vaults; and the **Zwinger,** a restored royal palace that is home to four museums, the most important being the **Gemäldegalerie Alte Meister (Old Masters Gallery).** Make it a point to see the **Frauenkirche (Church of Our Lady),** which is being painstakingly restored after destruction during the war. If you're an opera lover, you won't want to miss seeing a performance at the **Semper Opera House.** Spend the night in Dresden.

From Dresden on **Day 5,** you may want to take an excursion boat along the Elbe into the area known as **Saxon Switzerland.** From April through September, 3- to 4½-hour trips take place daily. Otherwise (or afterward), hop on a train for **Leipzig,** only an hour away. Leipzig is a busy, bustling city with a long musical tradition. Johann Sebastian Bach was the choirmaster of the famous **Thomaskirche (St. Thomas Church),** where he is buried, and the **Bach-Museum** is dedicated to his life and works. If you love symphonic music, be sure to reserve a seat to hear the world-famous **Gewandhaus Orchestra.**

The city has two unusual museums that shed light on the GDR era: The **Museum in der Runden Ecke** documents the methods of the dreaded Stasi, East Germany's secret police, and the **Zeitgeschichtliches Forum Leipzig (Contemporary History Forum)** examines all aspects of life in the GDR from 1945 to 1989. By 2005, the **Museum der Bildenden Künste (Museum of Fine Arts)** is scheduled to move into a brand-new building close to **Marktplatz,** the town's liveliest square. Enjoy a dinner of regional food in the famous **Auerbachs Keller,** a vaulted underground restaurant.

From Leipzig, fast trains take less than an hour to reach **Weimar,** your destination for **Day 6.** This small, pretty city, filled with leafy parks and neoclassical buildings, is one of Germany's literary meccas. Johann Wolfgang von Goethe and his friend, the great German dramatist Friedrich Schiller, lived here. **Goethes Wohnhaus (Goethe's House),** portions of which have been left much as they were in his lifetime, is the town's most visited site. Weimar was one of Germany's great centers of art and culture during the late 18th and early 19th centuries. Visit the scene of Duchess Anna Amalia's glittering salons in the **Wittumspalais,** a "city palace" near Goethe's house. In the early 20th century, the Bauhaus School of Art and Design operated in Weimar; today, you can visit the small **Bauhaus Museum.** Weimar has its dark side, too. Not far from the city center, on the site of a Nazi-era concentration camp, is the **Gedenkstätte Buchenwald (Buchenwald Memorial).** Stay overnight in Weimar, or take the train to Munich, the next stop on this itinerary; the journey takes about five hours.

Your destination for **Day 7** is delightful **Munich,** Germany's "secret capital." With only two days, you have to make some decisions about what to see. Start your explorations at **Marienplatz,** the city's main square, and then head over to the adjacent **Viktualienmarkt** to wander through this wonderland of an outdoor market. Choose a museum you'd especially like to visit: Most visitors make the **Alte Pinakothek (Old Masters Gallery)** their top priority, but the **Deutsches Museum,** devoted to science and industry, is one of the most popular museums in the country. Stay overnight in Munich. You have innumerable ways to spend the evening in this cultural mecca: opera, symphony, pop concerts, theater, beer halls, beer gardens, and clubs.

Start **Day 8** with a self-guided tour of the **Residenz,** Munich's gigantic "in town" palace. You need at least two hours to visit the entire complex. After lunch near Marienplatz, take in another museum. Then, if the afternoon is fine, stroll in the lovely **Englisher Garten** and stop for a drink or a meal at the park's famous beer garden. At night, sample one of the city's many entertainment options. Stay overnight in Munich.

On **Day 9,** you may want to consider renting a car for the next four days, but doing so is not essential. By car or train, from Munich make your way to **Füssen,** 6.5km (4 miles) from the most famous tourist attraction in all of Germany: Ludwig II's **Neuschwanstein** castle. Give yourself some leeway with time because the crowds can be dense. You can also visit neighboring **Hohenschwangau** castle, where Ludwig spent his childhood. If you have a car, visit the nearby **Wieskirche (Church in the Meadow),** a world-famous baroque masterpiece. If you're without a car, stay overnight in Füssen or return to Munich. But first, enjoy a stroll through Füssen's lovely historic quarter. If you have a car, you can continue on to Lindau, exploring the Bavarian Alps along the **Deutsche Alpenstrasse (German Alpine Road).** Some small Bavarian village with a cozy *Gasthaus* (guesthouse) may catch your fancy.

From Munich or Füssen, the trip to **Lindau** for **Day 10** is about three hours by train. Even if you're driving from Füssen, travel time is about the same. Germany's sunny southwestern corner comes as a surprise to many visitors. Here you find the **Bodensee,** or **Lake Constance,** the country's largest lake and one of the largest bodies of water in Europe. Spend the day strolling in the sun (hopefully), sitting under an umbrella at a cafe, swimming, or taking a boat ride on the lake to the garden island of **Mainau.** Lindau's sunny charms are reminiscent of Italy. The area has no important museums, so just take it easy.

You've no doubt heard about the **Schwarzwald,** or **Black Forest,** your destination on **Day 11.** This scenic area of forested hills, valleys, and mountains in the southwestern corner of Germany is famed for its health resorts, its hiking and recreational sports facilities, and its cuckoo clocks. Take your pick of cities to stay in. The charming and lively university town of **Freiburg** is about three hours by train from Lindau. In Freiburg, you can happily spend a few hours strolling through old streets lined by *Bächle* (little streams). Freiburg's lovely **Münster (cathedral)** and its surrounding square constitute the main sights in town. This wine town has vineyards nearby and yearly wine festivals. **Baden-Baden,** about 1½ hours farther north by train, is one of Germany's premier spa towns. This upscale, resort-oriented town offers fine hotels and restaurants, many expensive shops, and a famous **casino.** If you opt for Baden-Baden, be sure to "take the waters" at **Friedrichsbad,** a 125-year-old mineral-bath establishment; the experience takes about 3½ hours.

On **Day 12,** make your way to **Heidelberg,** which is less than an hour by train from Baden-Baden or 2½ to 3 hours from Freiburg. Everyone seems to love this ancient university town on the Neckar River. The **Altstadt (Old Town)** is where you want to stay and where you want to wander. Hike or take the funicular train up the hillside to the famed **Heidelberg Castle** for a stunning view of the town and the river valley. The castle is mostly in ruins, but you can take a tour of some restored rooms. Then take a relaxing **boat ride** down the Neckar. Stop in at the **Kurpfälzisches Museum (Museum of the Palatinate)** for a look at Tilman Riemenschneider's powerfully carved altarpiece. The museum's restaurant is one of the nicest places to dine in Heidelberg, especially on a warm evening when your table is in the courtyard near the fountain.

On **Day 13,** hop on the *Bahn* (train) in Heidelberg and in 3½ to 4 hours, you're in **Nürnberg** (or **Nuremberg,** as it's known in English), one of the most attractive towns in Germany. As in many German cities, the entire **Altstadt** is a pedestrian zone. You find squares with lovely fountains, a picturesque area alongside the Pegnitz River, the **Kaiserburg (Imperial Castle),** and fine Gothic churches. Give yourself at least two hours to visit the marvelous **Germanisches Nationalmuseum (German National Museum),** which covers the entire spectrum of German fine arts from its prehistoric beginnings to the present day. And then, if you're in the mood, stop at the **Spielzeugmuseum (Toy Museum)** for a glimpse of the toys for which this city has long been famous.

On **Day 14,** head back to **Berlin,** where your tour began, to catch your flight home. The train ride from Nuremberg is about 5½ hours. (Alternatively, you can fly home from Frankfurt, a little more than two hours by train from Nuremberg, or from Munich, under two hours from Nuremberg.) Sit back and enjoy the scenery. If you have time in any of these cities before your flight departs, just wander around without an itinerary. Find a cafe to sit and people-watch while you plan your next trip to Germany.

Discovering Germany with Kids

Face it: Traveling with kids isn't easy. You face difficulties in the basic areas of food choices and sightseeing options. No kid I know wants to spend two hours wandering around a museum admiring Old Master paintings, or seated in a quiet, formal restaurant awaiting the main course. Luckily, some aspects of traveling in Germany appeal to kids just because of the novelty (taking a train, for example, or visiting a castle). I slant this very general itinerary toward outdoor activities and give other options only when they seem relevant. Some hotels let children stay for free in their parents' room; at the ones that don't, you can pay a few euros more and request an extra bed. When it comes time to eat, look for casual bistros, cafes, or even outdoor food stands (yes, you'll also find American-style fast-food restaurants in all midsize and large cities). Public transportation is a priority in every German city, with easy access and reduced rates for kids. Just remember one thing: Well-behaved children are smiled upon in Germany; the other kind are not.

Spend **Day 1** in **Munich.** The entire inner city is a car-free pedestrian zone where you and your kids can stroll with ease. You can find plenty of outdoor cafes around **Marienplatz,** the city's main square; while there, be sure to catch the **glockenspiel** show at 11 a.m. on the spire of the Rathaus. Right next to Marienplatz is the **Viktualienmarkt,** the best outdoor market in Germany and a great place to have a casual lunch. Later, you may want to take a train or subway over to the **Englisher Garten (English Garden),** one of the largest and most beautiful city parks in Europe, where you can wander along the tree-shaded walks, dance in the meadows, or sit in the famous beer garden (nonalcoholic refreshments available for the kids). Alternatively, head over to the kid-friendly **Deutsche Museum,** the largest science and technology museum in the world. It's loaded with interesting stuff for kids and adults.

On **Day 2, Schloss Nymphenburg** is on the top of your list. The *Schloss* (palace) is a breeze to get to (it's right in the city on the streetcar line), and 500-acre **Nymphenburg Park** is grand and inviting, with formal, French-style gardens behind the palace and an English-style park with quiet meadows, forested paths, and some intriguing buildings, including an 18th-century swimming pool and a baroque hunting lodge. If you didn't make it to the Deutsches Museum the day before, you can head over there in the afternoon.

On **Day 3,** you can rent a car or take the train to **Garmisch-Partenkirchen** in the Bavarian Alps south of Munich. Here you're going to ascend the **Zugspitze,** Germany's highest peak (2,960m/9,720 ft.). A cog railway and a cable car take you up and bring you back — a fascinating treat for kids. The view from the summit is — what else? — *spectacular.* If you're a dedicated hiker, the area around Garmisch-Partenkirchen is magnificent hiking country. Most hikes take an energetic four to five hours, but some of them are shorter and easy enough for children. Stay overnight in Garmisch (good skiing and ice-skating are available all winter).

Drive or take the train to **Füssen** on **Day 4,** and then drive or take a bus to **Neuschwanstein,** "Mad" Ludwig's fairy-tale castle. Germany's most-visited tourist attraction perches on a rocky spur that requires a good uphill hike to reach. You also can reach the castle by bus or horse-drawn cab. The forested hills all around Neuschwanstein and neighboring **Hohenschwangau** castle are full of excellent hiking paths. Stay overnight in Füssen and explore the charming old town on foot.

Bodensee (Lake Constance) is your destination for **Day 5.** By car or train make your way to **Lindau,** a sunny flower-filled resort town that sits on its own small island in the Bodensee. Lindau is virtually car-free, so you and the kids can easily walk everywhere. The area around Bodensee is Germany's sunniest corner, and the lake is clean enough for swimming. You can bike along the shore or relax on an excursion boat ride to the island of **Mainau,** a plant-lover's paradise. Spend the night in Lindau.

Ride the train or drive north to **Freiburg,** your headquarters in the **Schwarzwald (Black Forest)** on **Day 6.** If you're traveling by train, I suggest that you rent a car for just one day. From Freiburg you can make an easy 145km (90-mile) circuit through a scenic part of the Schwarzwald, with stops for short hikes and cable-car rides to the top of the **Belchen,** a famous mile-high peak with spectacular views of the Rhine plain, and to the 1,450m (4,750-ft.) summit of a peak called **Seebuck.** On this drive, you can stop at two Black Forest lakes, the **Schluchsee** and **Titisee.**

On **Day 7** make your way back to Frankfurt or Munich for the trip home. How about that — the kids actually had a good time!

Prosit! Germany for Wine Lovers

When you raise a glass of wine in Germany, the toast often is a simple "*Prosit!*" (pronounced *prohst*). This itinerary takes you to the wine regions in western Germany. The trip begins and ends in Frankfurt. You may want to incorporate this four-day itinerary into a longer trip. For more information, see Chapter 17 for the Black Forest and the Bodensee and Chapter 19 for Cologne and sights along the Rhine.

From Frankfurt airport, you can hop on a train on **Day 1** and be in **Freiburg** in about two hours. Or you may want to rent a car in Frankfurt for the duration of the trip. Freiburg, a lively university town in the Black Forest, is surrounded by 1,600 acres of vineyards, more than any other city in Germany. On the last weekend in June, the city celebrates with a **four-day wine festival** that includes public tastings. **Weinkost** is another wine-tasting event in mid-August. Most of the grapes grow on the warm lower slopes of the nearby **Kaiserstühl (Emperor's Throne),** a volcanic massif. The young, light Silvaner wine is an ideal accompaniment to *Spargel* (white asparagus) in May. For a great meal with regional wines, dine at **Zum Roten Bären,** the oldest inn in Freiburg.

Head to Cologne on the River Rhine for **Day 2.** The train trip from Freiburg takes about four hours. From Cologne, by car or boat, you can explore the neighboring wine country. In the **Rheingau wine district,** a 45km (27-mile) stretch of the Rhine between the towns of **Biebrich** and **Bingen,** wine has been produced since Roman times. Rheingau Rieslings rank among the best white wines made anywhere. You can drive through this area on a day trip from Cologne. Or you can take a Rhine cruise between Koblenz and Mainz, a scenic winegrowing region.

The **Mosel Valley,** southwest of Cologne, is another scenic winegrowing region and your destination on **Day 3.** The valley follows the course of the Mosel River for more than 160km (100 miles) between **Trier** and **Koblenz.** Beautiful scenery and fine wines make this a prime area for leisurely exploration. The easiest way to enjoy a **cruise** down the Mosel River is to take a train to Koblenz. Between late April and the third week in October, cruises depart daily from Koblenz to **Cochem,** a picturesque wine village surrounded by vineyards and a popular spot for wine tastings and festivals. **Mosel-Wein-Woche (Mosel Wine Week),** which takes place the first week in June, celebrates the region's wines with tasting booths and a street fair; **Weinfest** takes place the last weekend of August. The half-timbered **Alte Thorschenke** in Cochem, both a hotel and a wine restaurant, is one of the oldest and best-known establishments along the Mosel.

From Cochem, Cologne, or Freiburg, make your way back to **Frankfurt** on **Day 4.** If you have a few more days, you can continue your tasting tour of Germany. Wherever you go, look for the local *Weinstube* (wine tavern), a convivial spot to sample Germany's many fine vintages.

Part II

Planning Your Trip to Germany

The 5th Wave   By Rich Tennant

"I think we should arrange to be there for the 'Sauerbraten-Bratwurst-Sauerkraut Week', and then shoot over to the 'Antacid-Breathmint-Festival.'"

In this part . . .

This part helps you with the practical details of planning your trip to Germany. In Chapter 5, I get into the nitty-gritty of *Geld* — that is, money — so you have an approximate idea of what things cost and how to use ATMs, credit cards, or travelers checks. Chapter 6, I go over the transportation options for getting you to Germany, including information on which airlines fly into Germany, guided and package tours, and how to get the best fare. In Chapter 7, I tell you about traveling through Germany by train, car, plane, and boat. In Chapter 8, I discuss all the various accommodation options, outlining the kinds of hotels and guesthouses that you'll find, explaining what hotel rack rates are, and offering suggestions for landing the best room at the best price. In Chapter 9, I offer advice and tips for visitors with special needs and interests: families traveling with children, seniors, gay and lesbian travelers, and Jewish travelers. I load Chapter 10 with information about getting a passport, buying travel and medical insurance, using cellphones and staying connected with e-mail in Germany, and adhering to airport security measures.

Chapter 5

Managing Your Money

. . . .

In This Chapter

▶ Planning a realistic budget for your trip

▶ Changing your dollars into euros

▶ Using ATMs, traveler's checks, and credit cards

▶ Dealing with theft and loss

▶ Paying and recouping German sales tax

▶ Knowing when — and how — to tip

. . . .

So, you want to go to Germany. You're excited and eager to pack. But can you really afford the trip? At this point, a financial reality check is in order. This chapter is all about *Geld* (pronounced *gelt,* meaning money). You may have heard that Germany is an expensive country — but just how expensive? What does a hotel in Munich cost? How much does a train ticket cost for travel from Berlin down to Bavaria, for instance? And how much is a meal in a nice restaurant after you get there? This chapter points you toward all the answers.

 Although you may think a trip to Germany is prohibitively expensive because of the transatlantic flight, you often can find bargain airfares to Frankfurt and Munich, the two German airports with several direct international flights. Adding everything up, your trip to Germany — even if you visit Munich and/or Berlin, the two most expensive German cities — can actually cost less than a trip to New York, San Francisco, or Los Angeles.

Planning Your Budget

Planning a budget for your trip to Germany isn't as difficult as you may think. To come up with a workable figure, you need to break your trip down into its various components: airfare, transportation while there, hotels, meals, entertainment, and so on. In the sections that follow, I provide vital clues on how to create a realistic budget that works for you.

Transportation costs

Your first big outlay is going to be for **airfare.** In Chapter 6, I tell you about flying to Germany and help you with some strategies for finding the cheapest airline fares. Based on my own experience, I can tell you that finding a nonstop, round-trip fare from a major city on the West Coast of the U.S. to Frankfurt is possible for about $600 to $900 during low season and $800 to $1,200 during high season. From New York or Boston, you probably can find flights for $400 to $800 in low season and $700 to $1,000 in high season. Please note that these are ballpark figures for economy-class seats found by using every cost-saving trick in the book, including advance purchase. Finding flights that cost less is quite possible, but so is finding flights that cost a whole lot more.

The next transportation expense to consider is dependent upon how you plan to travel around Germany after you arrive.

Here's some good news: You won't need to rent a car in any German city because public transportation is so good. That saves you a bundle. You can also tour by train throughout the whole of Germany without ever renting a car. Keep in mind, however, that in some areas, such as Bavaria and the Black Forest, having a car makes exploration of the countryside much easier.

Berlin, Munich, Frankfurt, Hamburg, and Cologne all have subway systems called the *U-Bahn* (short for *Untergrundbahn,* or underground train). U-Bahns are fast, convenient, and easy to use. The same cities also have light-rail or aboveground trains called the *S-Bahn* and a system of trams or streetcars and buses. Special reduced-price transportation passes are good for a full day *(Tageskarten)* or longer on all forms of public transportation. The passes make getting around German cities fairly inexpensive (approximately $6 to $8 per day). Many larger cities have special passes that include public transportation and free or reduced-price admission to various attractions. I mention these money-saving cards in the city sections of this guide whenever they're available and worthwhile.

In smaller towns and cities of Germany, you can walk almost every-where, because city centers are so compact and close to the train stations. The historic inner-city area of German cities nearly always is called the *Altstadt,* or Old Town. If you don't want to walk, you can hop on a bus or tram. If you're traveling by train and want to see some of Germany's great castles, such as Neuschwanstein in Bavaria, you may need to take a local bus or taxi from the nearest town (Füssen, for Neuschwanstein) to the castle.

If you're planning to travel around Germany by train, you can save money by buying a **German Rail Pass** before you leave home. I talk more about these cost-cutting train passes and the popular **Eurailpass** in Chapter 7. You can order them through a travel agent or by calling **Rail Europe** at ☎ **888-382-7245** in the United States, 800-361-7245 in Canada, or by going online at www.raileurope.com.

Lodging expenses

A large piece of your budget will be the cost of your hotel or other accommodations. That cost will be higher in Munich and Berlin than anywhere else in Germany.

Nearly all hotels throughout Germany (except for boutique or five-star luxury hotels) include a buffet breakfast as part of the room rate.

As a general rule, you can always find a double room in a good hotel in Germany for less than €150 ($188) a night and sometimes for less than €100 ($125) a night. But because rates vary from one hotel to the next, depending on their respective government-appointed categories (one-star, two-star, and so on), giving a reliable average is difficult. For the recommendations in this guide, however, the rates at inexpensive hotels in Munich or Berlin, the major cities, generally are less than €125 ($156), moderate hotels run from €126 to €175 ($158 to $218), and expensive hotels cost from €176 to €225 ($220 to $281). After that, you hit the high end of €226 ($282) and up. See Chapter 8 for information on what to expect in each price range and for a discussion of your lodging options and how to get the best rate.

Outside of Munich and Berlin, hotel rates are lower, generally from €80 to €150 ($100 to $188) per double room per night, including breakfast. But you can still find plenty of opportunities to drop a king's ransom for a hotel, especially in some of the truly elegant five-star properties. Make sure to ask about special deals wherever you stay. Many hotels in the Bavarian countryside, for instance, offer bed, breakfast, lunch, and a full dinner at bargain prices. Throughout the country, hotels offer special price breaks for weekends *(Wochenende)* and during the summer (generally July and August). In some cases, the price drops so dramatically that you can stay in a double room at a five-star luxury hotel for less than €175 ($219) per night.

Food in Germany often is characterized as heavy. Although that may be true, traditional German food also is *ganz schmackhaftig* (very tasty). In nearly every town and village throughout Germany, you can find a **Ratskeller** (restaurant beneath a town hall), a beer hall, a **Weinstube** (restaurant where wine is the primary beverage served), or some other kind of nonfancy restaurant where you can dine inexpensively and well and where you can enjoy your meal among the locals. Traditional food, however, isn't the only cuisine you'll find in Germany. In recent years, large cities like Berlin and Munich have emerged as international food capitals. Of course, eating at top restaurants, no matter where you are, is going to cost, but you'll find that many of the best restaurants in Berlin, Munich, and elsewhere offer special fixed-price meals that can be real bargains.

As with hotels, food is more expensive in big cities like Berlin and Munich. When eating lunch and dinner at moderately priced restaurants in Berlin, you can expect to pay from €35 to €50 ($44 to $62) per person per day (assuming your hotel rate includes breakfast), and that doesn't include beer or wine. Outside of Berlin or Munich, unless you splurge on really high-priced restaurants, expect your daily food cost to be about €25 to €40 ($31 to $50).

If you eat breakfast at a cafe instead of your hotel, and you're content with coffee and a roll at a stand-up counter (or a Starbucks), expect to pay about €3.50 to €6 ($4.40 to $7.50) anywhere in the country. But remember, a buffet breakfast nearly always is included in your hotel cost. Only at luxury hotels do you have to pay extra for breakfast — usually €17 to €22 ($21 to $27) — but the buffet breakfast invariably is fabulous. Afternoon *Kaffee und Kuchen* (coffee and cake) sets you back about €6 or €7 ($7.50 or $8.75) anywhere in Germany.

Sightseeing expenses

Your budget for admission fees depends, of course, on what you want to see. Fortunately, sightseeing in Germany is fairly inexpensive. Finding a museum that costs more than €7 ($8.75) is rare. And some of the top sights — such as the Reichstag in Berlin or the Frauenkirche and Englisher Garten in Munich — are free. Admission to Neuschwanstein, the Bavarian castle that is Germany's top attraction, costs only €8 ($10). In addition, if you're a senior or a student, you can often get a reduced-price admission.

Strolling down Berlin's great avenues, Kurfürstendamm or Unter den Linden, or viewing the Brandenburg Gate, is *kostenlos* (free). In fact, exploring by foot in almost any German town is a good way to soak up the local culture free of charge.

As a general rule, expect to pay from €2 to €4 ($2.50 to $5) for admission to museums and local attractions outside of the big cities. In some locations, the top attraction is a cable car that can whisk you to the top of a famous peak for a spectacular view. The most expensive ride is to the top of the Zugspitze, Germany's highest mountain, and back again; the cost for adults is €43 ($54). Most cable cars cost much less, generally around €5 ($6.25) round-trip. Sightseeing boat excursions typically are between €8 and €15 ($10 and $19), depending on the duration of the trip. City sightseeing tours by bus cost from €10 to €24 ($12 to $30).

Shopping and nightlife costs

Shopping and entertainment are the most flexible parts of your budget. You don't have to buy anything at all, and you can hit the sack right after dinner instead of going to a concert or dancing at a club. You know what you want. Flip through the shopping and nightlife options of each destination chapter. If anything strikes you as something you can't do without, budget accordingly. (Keep in mind that a small beer sets you back about €2.50 ($3.10), a glass of good German wine about €5 ($6.25), and an opera ticket in either Berlin or Munich anywhere from €10 to €80 ($12 to $100). Berlin, especially, is a late-night city, so you may want to check out the club scene while you're there; cover charges rarely are more than €5 ($6.25), but drinks other than beer can be pricey.

Tables 5-1 and 5-2 give you an idea of what things typically cost in Berlin and the rest of the country.

Table 5-1	What Things Cost in Berlin
Item	*Cost in Euros (Dollars)*
Transportation from Tegel airport to central Berlin by bus	€2 ($2.50)
Transportation from Tegel airport to central Berlin by taxi	€20 ($25)
One-way U-Bahn (subway) fare within central Berlin	€2 ($2.50)
Tageskarte one-day public transportation pass for two zones	€5.60 ($7)
Double room without breakfast at Hotel Adlon Kempinski ($$$$)	€330–€490 ($412–$612)
Double room with breakfast at Brandenburger Hof ($$$$)	€245–€285 ($306–$336)
Double room with breakfast at Sorat Art'otel ($$$)	€165–€180 ($206–$225)
Double room with breakfast at Arco Hotel ($–$$)	€75–€102 ($94–$127)
Dinner for one excluding wine at Die Quadriga ($$$$)	€60 ($75)
Dinner for one excluding wine at Marjellchen ($$–$$$)	€30 ($37)
Meal for one excluding wine at La Riva ($$)	€23 ($29)
Cafe meal for one at Café Silberstein ($)	€8 ($10)
Sausage at a stand-up snack stand ($)	€3 ($3.75)
Kaffee und Kuchen at a café or stand-up coffee shop ($)	€6–€8 ($7.50–$10)
Large glass of beer at a café, bar, or tavern	€3.50 ($4.40)
Admission to the Gemäldegalerie (Painting Gallery)	€6 ($7.50)
Admission to the Pergamon Museum	€6 ($7.50)
Admission to Charlottenburg Palace	€8 ($10)
Opera ticket	€10–€90 ($12–$112)

Table 5-2   What Things Cost outside Berlin

Item	*Cost in Euros (Dollars)*
First-class/second-class one-way train ticket Berlin–Dresden	€49 ($61)/€27 ($34)
First-class/second-class one-way train ticket Berlin–Munich	€167 ($209)/€111 ($139)
Double room with breakfast at Der Kleine Prinz, Baden-Baden ($$$–$$$$)	€165–€185 ($206–$231)
Double room with breakfast at Burg Hotel, Rothenburg ob der Tauber ($–$$$)	€100–€170 ($125–$212)
Double room with breakfast at Hotel-Garni Brugger, Lindau ($)	€86–€92 ($107–$115)
Double room with breakfast at Eden-Hotel-Wolf, Munich ($$$–$$$$)	€172–€282 ($215–$352)
Fixed-price dinner for one excluding wine at Der Kleine Prinz, Baden-Baden ($$$$)	€52–€70 ($65–$87)
Lunch for one excluding beer at Café Schinkelwache, Dresden ($)	€10 ($12)
Fixed-price dinner for one excluding wine at Zum Röten Bären, Freiburg ($$$)	€35–€43 ($44–$54)
Dinner for one including one glass of beer at Hofbräuhaus, Munich ($)	€20 ($25)
Admission to Neuschwanstein Castle, Bavaria	€8 ($10)
Admission to Zwinger Palace (all museums), Dresden	€10 ($12)
Admission to Alte Pinakothek (Old Masters Gallery), Munich	€5 ($6.25)
Adult/child admission to Deutsches Museum (Science and Industry), Munich	€7.50 ($9.50)/€3 ($3.75)
Opera ticket, Semper Opera House, Dresden	€10–€80 ($12–$100)
Complete bath and massage treatment at Friedrichsbad, Baden-Baden	€29 ($36)
Average losses at gambling tables, Baden-Baden	€5,000 ($6,250)
Tank of unleaded gas, economy car	€60 ($75)

Cutting Costs — But Not the Fun

 Throughout this book, Bargain Alert icons (like the one in the left margin) highlight money-saving tips and/or great deals. Here are some additional cost-cutting strategies:

✔ **Go during the off season.** If you can travel at off-season times (October, November, and January through March), you'll find hotel prices are as much as 20 percent less than during peak months. The same is true for July and August, which are peak travel months for Germans but often a time of lower hotel prices. Sound odd? Not really. Germans tend to travel outside of Germany on their holidays, which means more beds are available in German hotels. Because more rooms are available, prices go down.

✔ **Travel on off days of the week.** Generalizing about airfares is difficult because the entire industry is changing all the time. In general, airfares vary depending on the day of the week and even the hour you fly. If you can travel on a Tuesday, Wednesday, or Thursday, you may find cheaper flights to Frankfurt, Munich, or Berlin. When you inquire about airfares, be sure to ask whether you can obtain a cheaper rate by flying on a specific day.

✔ **Try a package tour.** For popular destinations like Frankfurt and Munich, you can book airfare, hotel, ground transportation, and even some sightseeing by making just one call to a travel agent, airline, or packager — and you'll pay much less than if you tried to put the trip together yourself (see Chapter 6).

✔ **Always ask for discount rates.** Membership in AAA, frequent-flier plans, AARP, or other groups may qualify you for discounts on plane tickets, hotel rooms, car rentals, and guided tours booked before you go. Attractions within Germany usually offer a lower admission rate for seniors, children, and students with ID.

✔ **Ask if your kids can stay in your room with you.** A room with two double beds usually doesn't cost any more than one with a queen-size bed. And many hotels won't charge you the additional person rate when that person is pint-size and related to you. Even if you have to pay a few extra euros for a rollaway bed, you save a bundle by not taking two rooms.

✔ **Ask about weekend, midweek, and off-season special offers.** To encourage year-round tourism, many hotels in Germany offer special price breaks on weekends or midweek during the off season. Sometimes these special rates are offered as romantic getaway packages and include dinner and a glass of wine. Surfing the Web is the best way to find out about special packages at specific hotels. (See Chapter 8 for some recommended Web sites.)

✔ **Try expensive restaurants at lunch rather than dinner.** At most top restaurants in Berlin and Munich, prices at lunch are lower than those at dinner, and the menu often includes many of the dinnertime specialties. Regardless of where you travel in Germany, always look for value-added fixed-price menus.

✔ **Travel second class.** First-class train tickets generally cost about one-third more than standard second-class tickets.

✔ **Know the advantages and disadvantages of buying a rail pass before you leave home.** The amount of money you save with a rail pass depends on how often you use it and how far you go. If you are headquartering in one city and making side trips to nearby towns, buying your local train tickets in Germany is cheaper.

✔ **Walk a lot.** That's what the Germans do. Most German cities are compact and eminently walkable. Each usually has a historic *Altstadt,* or Old Town, that contains most of the attractions and is within walking distance of the train station. A good pair of walking shoes can save you money on taxis and other local transportation. As a bonus, you get to know the city and its inhabitants more intimately, and you can explore at a slower pace.

✔ **Skip the souvenirs.** Your photographs and memories make the best mementos of your trip. If you're worried about your budget, do without the T-shirts, key chains, beer steins, cuckoo clocks, Bavarian hats, and the trinkets sold at major tourist attractions.

Handling Money

In January 2002, Germany's unit of currency changed from the deutsche mark to the **euro** (€). One euro is divided into *100 cents.* Coins come in denominations of 1¢, 2¢, 5¢, 10¢, 20¢, 50¢, €1, and €2. Notes are available in €5, €10, €20, €50, €100, €200, and €500 denominations. As with any unfamiliar currency, euros take a bit of getting used to. The coins have different sizes, shapes, and weights according to value. Each banknote denomination has its own color.

The *exchange rate,* which fluctuates daily, is the rate you get when you use your own currency to buy euros. In general, **1€ = $1.25.** I use this *approximate* exchange rate for prices in this book. (If the U.S. price is less than $10, I round it off to the nearest dime; if more than $10, to the nearest dollar.)

When you're about to leave on your trip, check with your bank or look in the newspaper to find out the current rate. You also can check currency conversions online at www.xe.com.

Using ATMs and carrying cash

The easiest and best way to get cash away from home is from an ATM (automated teller machine). In German cities, you find 24-hour ATMs in airports, train stations, and outside banks. **Cirrus** (☎ 800-424-7787; www.mastercard.com) and **PLUS** (☎ 800-843-7587; www.visa.com) are

the most popular networks; check the back of your ATM card for the
network to which your bank belongs, then call or check online for ATM
locations at your destination.

 Make sure you know your **personal identification number (PIN)** before
you leave home, and be sure to find out your daily withdrawal limit
before you depart. At some banks, the amount you can withdraw must
be in a checking (not a savings) account. Also keep in mind that many
banks impose a fee every time your card is used at a different bank's
ATM, and that fee can be higher for international transactions (up to $5
or more) than for domestic ones. In addition, the bank from which you
withdraw cash may charge its own ATM fee.

Charging ahead with credit cards

Credit cards are a safe way to carry money: They also provide a convenient record of all your expenses, and they generally offer relatively good
exchange rates. You also can withdraw cash advances from your credit
cards at banks or ATMs, provided you know your PIN. If you've forgotten
yours, or didn't even know you had one, call the number on the back of
your credit card and ask the bank to send it to you. It usually takes five
to seven business days, though some banks provide the number over
the phone if you tell them your mother's maiden name or some other
personal information.

 Keep in mind that when you use your credit card abroad, most
banks assess a 2 percent fee above the 1 percent fee charged by Visa,
MasterCard, or American Express for currency conversion on credit
charges. But credit cards still may be the smart way to go when you
factor in things like high ATM fees and higher traveler's check exchange
rates and service fees.

 Some credit-card companies recommend that you notify them of any
impending trip abroad so that they don't become suspicious when the
card is used numerous times in a foreign destination and block your
charges. Even if you don't call your credit-card company in advance,
you can always call the card's toll-free emergency number if a charge is
refused — a good reason to carry the phone number with you. But perhaps the most important lesson here is to carry more than one card with
you on your trip; a card may not work for any number of reasons, so
having a backup is the smart way to go.

 In smaller German towns and villages, many pensions (B&Bs) with one to
three guest rooms operate on a cash-only basis, as do some restaurants.

Toting traveler's checks

These days, traveler's checks are less necessary because most cities
have 24-hour ATMs that enable you to withdraw (usually for a fee) small
amounts of cash as needed. Cashing traveler's checks is more time con-
suming and can end up costing more because you must go to a bank or
money-exchange service and pay a check-cashing fee.

Changing your currency in Germany

You can easily change cash or traveler's checks by using a currency-exchange service called a *Geldwechsel* or *bureau de change*. These services are available in German airports, any branch of a major bank, all major rail stations, post offices countrywide, many tourist information offices, and American Express offices. Currency-exchange windows in airports and rail stations generally are open daily from 6 a.m. to 10 p.m. Banks generally are open weekdays from 8:30 a.m. to 1 p.m. and 2:30 p.m. to 4 p.m.

You can get traveler's checks at almost any bank. **American Express** offers denominations of $20, $50, $100, $500, and (for cardholders only) $1,000. You pay a service charge ranging from 1 percent to 4 percent. You can also get American Express traveler's checks over the phone by calling ☎ **800-221-7282**; Amex gold and platinum cardholders who use this number are exempt from the 1 percent fee.

Visa offers traveler's checks at Citibank locations nationwide and at several other banks. The service charge ranges between 1.5 percent and 2 percent; checks come in denominations of $20, $50, $100, $500, and $1,000. Call ☎ **800-732-1322** for information. AAA members can obtain Visa checks without a fee at most AAA offices or by calling ☎ **866-339-3378**. **MasterCard** also offers traveler's checks. Call ☎ **800-223-9920** for a location near you.

 If you choose to carry traveler's checks, be sure to keep a record of their serial numbers separate from your checks in the event that they are stolen or lost. You'll get a refund faster if you know the numbers.

 You can avoid paying a second commission fee by using **American Express** traveler's checks and cashing them at an American Express office. American Express has offices in Berlin, Cologne, Dresden, Frankfurt am Main, Hamburg, Heidelberg, Leipzig, Munich, and Nuremberg, among other cities. You find addresses for American Express offices throughout Germany at www.americanexpress.com.

 Citibank customers using ATMs at German branches of Citibank don't pay additional withdrawal fees. Find Citibank branches in Berlin, Cologne, Frankfurt, Hamburg, Leipzig, and Munich. For addresses of Citibanks in Germany, go online to www.citibank.com.

Dealing with a lost or stolen wallet

Be sure to contact all of your credit-card companies the minute you discover your wallet has been lost or stolen, and file a report at the nearest police precinct. Your credit-card company or insurer may require a police report number or record of the loss. Most credit-card companies have an emergency toll-free number to call if your card is lost or stolen; they may be able to wire you a cash advance immediately or deliver an emergency credit card in a day or two. If your credit card gets lost or stolen while you're in Germany, call the following numbers:

- ✔ **American Express** ☎ **954-503-8850** (collect)

- ✔ **MasterCard** ☎ **0800/819-1040** (toll-free)

- ✔ **Visa** ☎ **0800/811-8440** (toll-free) or 417-581-9994 (collect)

For other credit cards, call the toll-free number directory at ☎ **800-555-1212.**

If you need emergency cash during the weekend, when all banks and American Express offices are closed, you can have money wired to you via **Western Union** (☎ **800-325-6000;** www.westernunion.com).

Identity theft and fraud are potential complications of losing your wallet, especially if you've lost your driver's license along with your cash and credit cards. Notify the major credit-reporting bureaus immediately; placing a fraud alert on your records may protect you against liability for criminal activity. The three major U.S. credit-reporting agencies are **Equifax** (☎ **800-766-0008;** www.equifax.com), **Experian** (☎ **888-397-3742;** www.experian.com), and **TransUnion** (☎ **800-680-7289;** www.transunion.com). Finally, if you've lost all forms of photo ID, call your airline and explain the situation; the airline may allow you to board the plane if you have a copy of your passport or birth certificate and a copy of the police report you've filed.

Taking Taxes into Account

Germany's version of a sales tax, called the *Mehrwertsteuer* (abbreviated MWST) or **value-added tax** (abbreviated VAT), amounts to 16 percent. This hefty percentage already is figured into the total prices of consumer goods and hotel and restaurant bills. (The general hotel and restaurant prices in this book include VAT.) This tax isn't a hidden expense, and you can't avoid paying it.

If you're not a resident of the European Union, you can get a VAT refund on purchases made in Germany (excluding hotel and restaurant bills). To receive a refund, shop at stores displaying a **Tax-Free Shopping** sign. Most stores have a minimum amount that you must spend to qualify for the refund. When you make a qualifying purchase, you receive a **tax-free voucher,** which must be completed by the store and must have a copy of your sales receipt attached to it.

Before checking your luggage upon your departure from Germany, have the voucher stamped by German customs to confirm that the goods have been exported. Then, redeem the voucher for cash (euros or dollars) at a **Europe Tax-Free Shopping** window, located at all major airports, border crossings, ferry ports, and railroad stations.

A Tip about Tipping

As a general rule, Germany isn't a country where you must tip excessively, unless, of course, you're staying in an expensive hotel with porters who carry your bags (€1/$1.25 per bag carried) and doormen who hail you a cab (€1/$1.25 per successful hail). Otherwise, service charges are included in the bill. In restaurants, if the service has been very good, you can add 5 percent to 10 percent to your bill, or round up to the next euro.

Chapter 6

Getting to Germany

● ●

In This Chapter

▶ Deciding which German city to fly into

▶ Saving on airfare and booking online

▶ Arriving in Germany by train or boat

▶ Joining an escorted tour

▶ Finding out how a package tour can save you money

● ●

*N*ow that you've decided to visit Deutschland (Germany, that is), you're going to need to find a way to hop across that little puddle called the Atlantic. In this chapter, I discuss getting you to Germany. What are your options for direct, nonstop flights? How can you save money on your flight (and your hotel)? What are the pros and cons of taking an escorted tour? You'll find answers to your basic travel questions here.

Finding Out Which Airlines Fly Where

In Germany, an airport is called a *Flughafen* (*floog*-haf-en). Germany has several airports, but direct flights from the United States fly only into Frankfurt, Munich, Berlin (one flight only), and Düsseldorf. You also can fly to Cologne, Stuttgart, Nuremberg, and other cities in Germany, but if you're coming from the United States, these routes require a change of planes — usually in Frankfurt, Amsterdam, Copenhagen, Paris, or London. See the appendix at the back of this book for a list of the main international carriers with direct flights into Germany from the United States, Canada, the United Kingdom, and Australia.

Flying into Frankfurt

Frankfurt airport, called **Flughafen Frankfurt Main,** is Germany's main international hub. The airlines below offer direct flights:

> ✔ **Lufthansa,** Germany's national carrier (now partnered with United Airlines and Air Canada), has direct flights to Frankfurt from Atlanta, Boston, Chicago, Dallas/Fort Worth, Detroit, Houston, Los Angeles, Miami, Newark, New York JFK, Philadelphia, Portland, San Francisco, and Washington, D.C., and from Toronto and Vancouver, B.C.

✔ **American Airlines** has nonstop service to Frankfurt from Dallas/ Fort Worth, Chicago, and Miami.

✔ **Delta Air Lines** has daily nonstops from Newark and Atlanta.

✔ **Northwest Airlines** (partnered with KLM Royal Dutch Airlines) flies nonstop to Frankfurt from Boston, Chicago, Minneapolis/St. Paul, and Washington, D.C.

✔ **United Airlines** offers nonstop service to Frankfurt from Chicago and Washington, D.C.

✔ **British Airways** flies direct to Frankfurt from London.

✔ **Qantas** flies to Frankfurt from Melbourne and Sydney, Australia.

Flights to other cities in Germany from Frankfurt rarely take more than 1½ hours. The airport has its own train station, so you can fly in, hop on a train, and be off to your first destination. For more information on the Frankfurt airport, see Chapter 20.

Flying into other German airports

Here's a brief rundown of other major airports in Germany and some of the airlines that fly into them. In each city section of this guide, I give you more specific information about how to get into the city from the airport.

✔ **Munich: Franz Josef Strauss International Airport,** located 29km (18 miles) northeast of the city center, is Germany's second-largest airport. Opened in 1992, this airport is among the most modern and efficient in the world (completely accessible for the disabled). **Lufthansa** flies nonstop to Munich from Newark, JFK, Boston, Chicago, and San Francisco; **Delta** flies nonstop from Atlanta; and **British Airways** flies nonstop from London. See Chapter 15 for more about flying into Munich.

✔ **Berlin:** Berlin has two airports, but you probably will fly into **Tegel,** which is quite small but has easy public transportation into central Berlin. From Berlin, you can easily reach other cities in eastern Germany by train, especially Dresden, Leipzig, and Weimar (see all in Chapter 14), and you're close to Hamburg and the northern Hanseatic cities (see Chapter 13). **Delta** currently is the only airline that flies direct to Berlin from New York; service is to begin in May 2005. See Chapter 11 for a complete description of Berlin's airports.

✔ **Cologne: Konrad-Adenauer-Flughafen Köln/Bonn** is a good spot to land whenever you're planning to tour western Germany and the Rhineland wine country. Excursion boats leave from Cologne for trips on the Rhine and other German rivers (see Chapter 19). Although no direct flights are scheduled from the U.S., **British Airways** and **British Midland** fly direct to Cologne from the United Kingdom. Direct flights also are scheduled from most major European cities.

✔ **Düsseldorf:** Although I don't cover Düsseldorf in this guidebook (the closest city that I cover is Cologne in Chapter 19), you nevertheless can use the airport in Düsseldorf as an alternative to Cologne. From Düsseldorf, reaching the Rhine Valley is easy. **Lufthansa** and **Continental** offer direct flights from Newark. **Aer Lingus** flies non-stop from Dublin. **British Midland** has flights from London.

✔ **Hamburg:** Direct flights to **Flughafen Hamburg-Fuhlsbüttel** are scheduled from most major European cities, but none arrive directly from the United States. **Delta** offers service from Atlanta via Paris.

Getting the best airfare

Competition among the major U.S. airlines is unlike that of any other industry. Every airline offers virtually the same product (basically, a coach seat is a coach seat is a . . .), and yet prices can vary by hundreds of dollars.

Business travelers who need the flexibility of being able to buy their tickets at the last minute and changing their itineraries at a moment's notice — and who want to get home before the weekend — pay (or at least their companies pay) a premium rate, known as the *full fare.*

If you can book your ticket far in advance, stay overnight Saturday, and you're willing to travel midweek (Tuesday, Wednesday, or Thursday), you can qualify for the least expensive price — usually a fraction of the full fare. Obviously, planning ahead pays.

The airlines also periodically hold sales in which they lower the prices on their most popular routes, such as Frankfurt and Munich. These fares have advance-purchase requirements and date-of-travel restrictions, but you can't beat the prices. As you plan your vacation, keep your eyes open for these sales, which tend to take place in seasons of low travel volume: October, November, and January through March in Germany.

Consolidators, which also are known as bucket shops, are great sources for international tickets, but they often can't beat the Internet. Start by looking in Sunday newspaper travel sections.

Bucket shop tickets usually are nonrefundable or rigged with stiff cancellation penalties, often as high as 50 percent to 75 percent of the ticket price, and some put you on charter airlines with questionable safety records.

Several reliable consolidators are worldwide and available on the Net. **STA Travel** (☎ **800-781-4040;** www.statravel.com), the world's leader in student travel, offers good fares for travelers of all ages. **ELTExpress** (☎ **800-TRAV-800** (800-872-8800); www.flights.com) started in Europe and has excellent fares worldwide, especially on flights to that continent. Flights.com also has local Web sites in 12 countries. **FlyCheap** (☎ **800-FLY-CHEAP** (800-359-2432); www.1800flycheap.com) is owned by package-holiday megalith MyTravel and has especially good access to fares for sunny destinations. **Air Tickets Direct** (☎ **800-778-3447**; www.airticketsdirect.com) is based in Montreal and leverages the currently weak Canadian dollar for low fares.

Booking your flight online

The "big three" online travel agencies, **Expedia** (www.expedia.com), **Travelocity** (www.travelocity.com), and **Orbitz** (www.orbitz.com), sell most air tickets bought on the Internet. (Canadian travelers need to try www.expedia.ca and www.travelocity.ca; U.K. residents can go for expedia.co.uk and opodo.co.uk.) Each has different business deals with the airlines and may offer different fares on the same flights, so shopping around is wise. Expedia and Travelocity also will send you an **e-mail notification** whenever a cheap fare to your favorite destination becomes available. Of the smaller travel agency Web sites, **SideStep** (www.sidestep.com) receives good reviews from users. It's a browser add-on that purports to "search 140 sites at once," but in reality beats competitors' fares as often as other sites do.

Great **last-minute deals** are available through free weekly e-mail services provided directly by the airlines. Most of these deals are announced on Tuesday or Wednesday and must be purchased online. Most are valid for travel only that weekend, but some can be booked weeks or months in advance. Sign up for weekly e-mail alerts at airline Web sites or check megasites that compile comprehensive lists of last-minute specials, such as **Smarter Living** (smarterliving.com). For last-minute trips, www.site59.com in the U.S. and www.lastminute.com in Europe often have better deals than the major-label sites.

If you're willing to give up some control over your flight details, use an *opaque fare service* like **Priceline** (www.priceline.com) or **Hotwire** (www.hotwire.com). Both offer rock-bottom prices in exchange for traveling on a mystery airline at a mysterious time of day, often with a mysterious change of planes en route. The mystery airlines all are major, well-known carriers — and the possibility of being sent from New York to Frankfurt via Detroit is remote. But your chances of getting a 6 a.m. or 11 p.m. flight are pretty high. Hotwire tells you flight prices before you buy; Priceline usually has better deals than Hotwire, but you have to play their "name our price" game.

 In 2004, Priceline added nonopaque service to its roster. For a flight more to your liking, pick exact flights, times, and airlines from a list of offers — or opt to bid on opaque fares as before.

Arriving by Other Means

Germany is accessible by land and sea, and from all directions, so it's easy to include Germany as part of a larger European trip.

Traveling by train

Germany is extremely well connected by train to the rest of Europe. Perhaps you're flying into Paris and from there going on to Berlin or Heidelberg as part of your European dream vacation. Have no fear. You can reach all major German cities by train with ease. Trains are very much a part of the German (and European) travel ethic. **EuroCity** (EC) trains connect Germany with neighboring countries, and sleek, high-speed **Thalys** trains link Cologne and Düsseldorf with Paris and Brussels. When you're traveling between countries, border formalities, such as passport checks, are taken care of onboard the train. Major cities, such as Berlin and Hamburg, have more than one station, but you almost always find one main or central inner-city station called a *Hauptbahnhof* (*howpt*-bahn-hof). In every city section of this guide, I tell you how to get into the city center from the train station, which usually is conveniently located.

In Chapter 7, I discuss traveling around Germany by train and the various rail passes that can cut down on transportation costs. For more information about trains in Europe, contact **Rail Europe** (☎ **888-382-7245** in the U.S., 800-361-7245 in Canada; www.raileurope.com). Its Web site provides useful trip-planning information on train schedules and travel times, promotional offers, fares, and rail pass prices.

Arriving by boat

Germany's northern coast lies along the North Sea and the Baltic Sea. International ferry services are available from the United Kingdom, Denmark, Norway, Sweden, Finland, Poland, Russia, Latvia, and Estonia. **DFDS Seaways** (☎ **800-533-3755 ext. 114** in the U.S. and Canada; www.seaeurope.com) provides ferry service from Harwich, England, to Hamburg; the journey takes 20 hours. **Silja Lines** (same telephone and Web site as above) sails from Helsinki across the Baltic to Rostock in northern Germany.

Joining an Escorted Tour

You may be one of many people who love escorted tours. The tour company takes care of all the details and tells you what to expect on each leg of your journey. You know your costs upfront, so you don't encounter many surprises. Escorted tours can take you to the maximum number of sights in the minimum amount of time with the least amount of hassle.

If you decide to go with an escorted tour, I strongly recommend purchasing travel insurance, especially when the tour operator asks you to pay upfront. But don't buy insurance from the tour operator! If the tour operator doesn't fulfill its obligation to provide you with the vacation you paid for, you have no reason to think that the tour operator will fulfill its insurance obligations either. Get travel insurance through an independent agency. (I tell you more about travel insurance in Chapter 10.)

When choosing an escorted tour, along with finding out whether you have to put down a deposit and when final payment is due, ask a few simple questions before you buy:

✔ **What is the cancellation policy?** How late can you cancel if you can't go? Do you get a refund if you cancel? Do you get a refund if the operator cancels?

✔ **How jampacked is the schedule?** Does the tour schedule try to fit 25 hours into a 24-hour day, or does it give you ample time to relax or shop? If getting up at 7 a.m. every day and not returning to your hotel until 6 or 7 p.m. sounds like a grind, certain escorted tours may not be for you.

✔ **How big is the group?** The smaller the group, the less time you spend waiting for people to get on and off the bus. Tour operators may be evasive about providing this fact, because they may not know the exact size of the group until everybody has made their reservations, but they should be able to give you a rough estimate.

✔ **Does the tour require a minimum group size?** Some tour operators require a minimum group size and may cancel the tour when they don't book enough people. If a quota exists, find out what it is and how close they are to reaching it. Again, tour operators may be evasive with their answers, but the information can help you select a tour that's sure to take place.

✔ **What exactly is included?** Don't assume anything. You may be required to get yourself to and from the airports at your own expense. A box lunch may be included in an excursion, but drinks may be extra. Beer may be included but not wine. How much flexibility does the tour offer? Can you opt out of certain activities, or does the bus leave once a day, with no exceptions? Are all your meals planned in advance? Can you choose your entree at dinner, or does everybody get the same chicken cutlet?

Tour operators in the United States

Several companies offer escorted tours to Berlin, Munich, and destinations in the rest of Germany (or include Germany in a Europe-wide tour). Many escorted-tour companies cater to special interests, such as castles on the Rhine for history buffs, while others are more general. A good travel agent can help you find a tour that suits your particular interests. The following companies offer escorted tours to Germany:

✔ **Brendan Tours** (☎ 800-421-8446; www.brendantours.com) offers escorted itineraries in Berlin and Munich and a river cruise in western Germany.

✔ **Contiki Holidays** (☎ 866-CONTIKI; www.contiki.com) provides escorted tours for 18- to 35-year-olds and has offices in the United States, Canada, Australia, and the United Kingdom. Its 12-day European Horizon tour (from $889 per person double occupancy without airfare) and its 11-day, 8-country European Magic tour (from $1,039 per person double occupancy without airfare) include stops in the Rhine Valley and Munich. Contiki also offers an escorted eight-day Berlin–Prague trip.

✔ **Globus** (www.globusjourneys.com) offers "German Romance," a seven-day tour that includes a Rhine cruise, visits to vineyards, and trips to Cologne and Heidelberg.

✔ **Maupintour** (www.maupintour.com) has an eight-day escorted tour of German Christmas Market Towns from $2,549, not including airfare; an eight-day Bavaria and Bodensee tour with stops in Munich, Neuschwanstein and Oberammergau, and Mainau (from $2,959 without airfare); and a nine-day Berlin to Bohemia tour that takes you to Berlin, Potsdam, Dresden, Meissen, and Prague (from $2,469 without airfare).

Choosing a package tour

For many destinations, package tours can be a smart way to go. In many cases, a package tour that includes airfare, hotel, and transportation to and from the airport costs less than the hotel alone on a tour you book yourself. That's because packages are sold in bulk to tour operators, who then resell them to the public.

Every package tour is different. Some offer a better class of hotels than others; some provide the same hotels for lower prices; and many let you choose the hotel category you want. Some book flights on scheduled airlines; others sell charters. In some packages, your choice of accommodations and travel days may be limited. Some let you choose between escorted vacations and independent vacations; others allow you to add on just a few excursions or escorted day trips (also at discounted prices) without booking an entirely escorted tour.

Locating airline and hotel packages

To find package tours, check out the travel section of your local Sunday newspaper or the ads in the back of national travel magazines, such as *Travel & Leisure, National Geographic Traveler,* and *Condé Nast Traveler.* **Liberty Travel** (call ☎ 888-271-1584 to find the store nearest you; www.libertytravel.com) is one of the biggest packagers in the Northeast and usually boasts a full-page ad in Sunday papers.

Several big **online travel agencies** — Expedia, Travelocity, Orbitz, Site59, and Lastminute.com — also do a brisk business in packages. If you're unsure about the pedigree of a smaller packager, check with the Better Business Bureau in the city where the company is based, or go online at www.bbb.org.

If a packager won't tell you where it's based, don't fly with them.

Other good sources of package deals are the airlines. The following U.S. airlines offer packages to Germany from the United States in 2005:

✔ **American Airlines Vacations** (☎ 800-321-2121; www.aavacations. com) offers an air/hotel package to Frankfurt and Munich. In Frankfurt, the hotel portion, double occupancy, ranges from $62 to $140 per night per person; in Munich, the average hotel price is $71 per night, double occupancy (minimum three- to five-night stays are required for these rates). Sightseeing add-ons are not available.

✔ **Continental Airlines Vacations** (☎ 800-301-3800; www.co vacations.com) has a hotel/airfare package to Frankfurt from a number of U.S. departure cities. From Los Angeles, for example, round-trip airfare and three nights in a Frankfurt hotel cost between $1,686 and $2,001, per person, double occupancy, during the low season.

✔ **Delta Vacations** (☎ 800-221-6666; www.deltavacations.com) offers flight and hotel packages to Frankfurt and Munich. Prices depend on your departure city. A seven-day package from New York to Frankfurt costs $1,842; to Munich, $1,983, per person, based on double occupancy.

✔ **Northwest Airlines World Vacations** (☎ 800-800-1504; www. nwaworldvacations.com) has air/hotel packages to Frankfurt, Munich, and Berlin, and an array of sightseeing and transportation add-ons, including Frankfurt and Munich city tours, a half-day tour of Heidelberg, a day tour of the Rhine, a daylong Black Forest tour, a day tour of Rothenburg ob der Tauber, and a day tour of Neuschwanstein and Linderhof castles. You also can rent a car or buy a Eurailpass for train travel.

✔ **United Vacations** (☎ 800-800-1504; www.unitedvacations.com) has air/hotel packages to Berlin, Munich, and Frankfurt. Add-ons include a Munich city tour, a daylong Rhine tour from Frankfurt, and a day tour of Neuschwanstein and Linderhof castles.

Airline packages don't always include airport taxes and surcharges, which typically amount to about $80.

Chapter 7

Getting around Germany

• •

In This Chapter

▶ Traveling through Germany by train
▶ Touring the sites by car
▶ Cruising the rivers of Germany
▶ Flying from city to city

• •

*I*n this chapter, you find out more about your travel options within Germany — that is, the mode of travel best suited to your needs and itinerary. Compared with the United States, Australia, and Canada, Germany is a fairly small country. With the area added by reunification, Germany (356,734 sq. km/137,735 sq. miles) is smaller than the state of Montana (but with more than 80 million people). By fast train or car, you can get from Berlin, in the north, to Munich, in the south, in about seven or eight hours. Many historic towns and castles in Germany are manageable day trips from larger cities.

If you want to get a feel for the country, consider exploring at least a portion of Germany that has nothing to do with huge urban Berlin or Munich. When you get out of the cities and into the countryside, where you can sip wine in a small Rhineland village or explore a scenic region like Bavaria, the atmospheric charms of Germany are most strongly felt. You'll notice fascinating differences in culture, customs, food, and language as you travel from one part of Germany to another.

Weighing the Options: Train or Car?

Because of Germany's *comparatively* small size and easy-access train and road networks, the country is a snap to explore. From Berlin you can reach Dresden or Leipzig in about two hours. The train trip between Hamburg and Lübeck is less than an hour. From Munich, the trip to Garmisch-Partenkirchen in the Bavarian Alps is only an hour by car and less than 90 minutes by train. The cities in western Germany — Cologne, Heidelberg, Stuttgart, Nuremberg — usually are no more than two or three hours apart by car or train.

So should you rent a car or take the train? In almost all cases, I recommend train travel for its convenience, speed, and fun. However, having a car in scenic areas, such as the Black Forest (see Chapter 17) or the Romantic Road in Bavaria (see Chapter 16), enables you to explore the countryside more easily.

Taking the Train: The Easy Way to Go

In Germany, a train is called an *Eisenbahn* (*eye*-sen-bawn) or a *Zug* (zoog). I recommend traveling by train above all other forms of transportation — especially if you're a first-time visitor to Germany. Traveling by train is fast, fun, and convenient.

The railway system in Germany is operated by **Deutsche Bahn (DB,** **German Rail** in English). If you need any kind of train-related information while you're in Germany — from timetables to fares and special services — call DB's general information number at ☎ **11861**. Someone who speaks English will be available to help you. You also can access train information online, in English, at DB's Web site, www.bahn.de.

Following basic training

Throughout Germany, long-distance and local train timetables are coordinated to minimize waiting for connections. And, yes, German trains almost always run on time.

Train types

The federally owned and operated Deutsche Bahn has been modernizing and upgrading its trains steadily while integrating two different systems (Deutsche Bundesbahn in western Germany and Deutsche Reichsbahn in eastern Germany) into one. You may be surprised by the bright-red, high-tech look of the newest trains. What follows is a rundown of the trains that you find within Germany:

- ✔ **InterCity (IC)** passenger trains offer express service between all major German cities at intervals of one or two hours. IC trains have adjustable cushioned seats, individual reading lights, and telephone service. Dining cars (*Speisewagen,* pronounced *shpy*-zuh-vahg-en) and cafe or bistro cars (for lighter snacks) are on all trains. On IC trains, you can choose whether to sit in a compartment with six seats or in an open saloon coach.

- ✔ **InterCity Express (ICE)** trains, which connect major cities on heavily traveled routes, are among the fastest in Europe, reaching speeds of 265 kmph (165 mph). ICE trains run from Hamburg to Munich, from Frankfurt to Munich, and from Berlin to Munich. Each train makes stops at cities along the way. ICE significantly reduces travel time, enabling passengers to cross the entire country in only a few hours. ICE trains have telephones, a restaurant, and a high standard of comfort in both first and second classes.

✔ The **CityNightLine (CNL)** is one of the most comfortable night trains in Europe. This train operates between Berlin and Zürich (stopping at Frankfurt, Baden-Baden, and Freiburg, among other towns), Berlin and Dresden, Hamburg and Zürich, and Dortmund and Vienna. The CNL offers four different categories. Sleeping accommodations in **Deluxe** include compartments with a shower and toilet, key cards, phones for wake-up service, and a panoramic window with blinds. **Comfort Single** or **Double** gives you a single- or double-bed compartment with washing facilities. **Economy** provides a four-bed compartment with washing facilities (you can book this class as a single or double). The *Ruhesessel* (sleeper chair) category offers open saloon seating with reclining seats. The CNL includes a restaurant and cafe car. Advance reservations are mandatory for all sleeping accommodations. Eurail and GermanRail pass holders are accepted on this train but have to pay for the seat or sleeper reservation.

✔ **DB Nachtzug (Night Train)** service is available between many cities in Germany and continues on to Amsterdam, Brussels, Paris, Prague, and Copenhagen. The night trains have comfortable couchettes (basic sleeping compartments) and some more deluxe sleeping compartments with showers.

✔ For shorter local trips, usually within a suburban area around a large town, **S-Bahn (urban light-rail)** trains are used. For some out-of-the-way places, you may need to transfer to a **RegionalBahn (RB)** train to reach your destination. **RegionalExpress (RE)** trains link rural areas to the long-distance rail network.

An announcement is made before the train arrives at each station. Station stops are short, so have your luggage in hand and be ready to disembark when the train comes to a halt. In new high-speed trains, you find a well-marked button that automatically opens the door. In other trains, you may need to open the door by pulling up on a handle.

 All German trains are divided into **smoking** (*rauchen,* pronounced *rau*-kin) and **nonsmoking** (*nicht rauchen,* pronounced nickt *rau*-kin) sections. You can specify your preference when reserving your seat.

Ticket classes

German trains have a two-tiered ticket system: **first class** *(Erste Klasse)* and **second class** *(Zweite Klasse),* which now sometimes is called *standard class.* First-class tickets cost about one-third more than second class. The first-class cars have roomier seats, fewer passengers, and a more luxurious feel. But you can travel quite comfortably in second class. You may appreciate the difference on long-distance journeys — from Berlin to Munich, say, when you're onboard the train for seven hours or more.

First-class service on InterCity Express (ICE) trains includes a higher standard of personal service; you can order beverages and snacks that are brought to your seat. First- and second-class passengers otherwise use the same dining cars and cafe cars for buying sandwiches and drinks. On some trains, an employee comes through both first- and second-class cars with a food-and-beverage trolley. Local and commuter trains don't have food service.

Auto trains

If you want to avoid long-distance driving but need a car after you arrive at your destination, you can take yourself and your car on an overnight car-sleeper **Auto Train**. You ride in a sleeper compartment on the train, while your automobile, stowed elsewhere, comes along for the ride. When you reach your destination, you can pick up your car and go. Although less common, daytime automobile trains also operate.

Heading to the Hauptbahnhof

A German city's **Hauptbahnhof** (howpt-*bahn*-hof), or main train station, rarely is more than a few minutes' walk from the historic town center and all the main attractions. The station always is a main link in the city's public transportation system, so you can continue your local explorations by subway, light-rail, tram, or bus from there.

German train stations in major cities offer all kinds of services, including currency exchange, food and beverages, newsstands, and usually a tourist information office. Hotels are always close at hand. If you're arriving in a city for sightseeing only, and not spending the night, you can check your luggage (*Gepäck,* pronounced geh-*peck*) at a luggage checkroom. At larger stations, porters (recognized by their red or blue uniforms) can transport your luggage, or you can use self-service luggage trolleys available for €1 ($1.25).

 In many German train stations, you can take an elevator to the track level. But in others, you must climb stairs, which sometimes have a ramp for luggage trolleys and baby carriages. If you're loaded down with several large, heavy bags, getting to your track without help may be difficult. (Just another way of saying: Don't overpack.)

Getting off on the right track

After arriving at the station, you need to find the right track (*Gleis,* pronounced *glice*) for your departing train. In large cities, prominently placed departure and arrival boards list train numbers, arrival or departure times, final destinations, and track numbers. This information also is posted as a printed schedule in the station. The German word for **arrival** is **Ankunft** (*on*-koonft); **departure** is **Abfahrt** (*ob*-fahrt).

 Like other European trains, the German train system works on a **24-hour clock.** Midnight always is listed as 0:00 hours and noon is 12:00. Therefore, train times can be 13:00 (1 p.m.), 14:00 (2 p.m.), 15:00 (3 p.m.), and so on, up to 23:59 (11:59 p.m.). If your train leaves at 4:20 p.m., the time on the schedule reads 16:20.

If you have a reserved seat, your ticket lists the car and seat number. Trains can be very long, so you want to be near the appropriate area for boarding when your train pulls into the station. Diagrams posted on the platform show the layout of first-class, second-class, and restaurant cars. Each car, or *Wagen* (*vah*-ghen), is numbered. The *Wagen* numbers correspond with numbers or letters on the platform, usually 1 to 6 or A to G. Check the diagram and then make your way to the appropriate area of the platform before the train arrives. If you have a Eurailpass, and you're risking a journey without a seat reservation, make your way to the platform areas where the first- or second-class cars will stop.

Reserving your seat

When traveling for any distance in Germany, reserving your seat in advance, even if you have a Eurailpass or German Rail Pass, is always a good idea. Otherwise, the only free seat you find may be in the smoking area or out in the hallway (I speak from experience).

You can make a seat (*Platz,* pronounced plotz) reservation and buy train tickets (*Fahrkarten,* or *far*-karten) at any train station. In larger stations, look for the **Reisezentrum (travel center)**. In smaller stations, make your booking at the ticket counter. In larger stations, the staff usually speaks English and can answer any questions you have. If you have a German Rail Pass or a Eurailpass (see the next section), the seat reservation costs €3 ($3.75). You're issued a ticket that lists the *Wagen* (car) number and the *Platz* (seat) number.

Saving time and euros with rail passes

Rail passes are tickets that enable you to travel for a certain number of days without buying a ticket for each leg of your journey. They help you save time (ticket lines can be long) and, usually, money. Most rail passes must be purchased before you leave home; they can't be purchased after you arrive in Germany or the rest of Europe.

Before you buy a rail pass, do a little research to find out whether it's going to save you money. At Rail Europe's Web site, www.raileurope. com, you can click on "Fares and Schedules" and get an estimated cost (in U.S. or Canadian dollars) of fares between destinations within Germany. You can also find fares on Deutsche Bahn's Web site, www.bahn.de.

Travel agents throughout the United States and Canada sell all the rail passes described later in this section, but the biggest supplier is **Rail Europe** (☎ **888/382-7545** in the U.S., or 800/361-7245 in Canada; www.raileurope.com), which allows you to order online.

Many different rail passes are available in the United Kingdom for travel in Germany and continental Europe. You can check out passes and prices at Rail Europe's U.K. Web site: www.raileurope.co.uk. Or stop in at the **International Rail Centre,** Victoria Station, London SW1V 1JY (☎ **0990/848848** in the U.K., or 020/7834-2345). Some of the most popular passes, including Inter-Rail and Euro Youth, are available only to travelers younger than 26 years of age; these passes allow unlimited second-class travel through most European countries.

German rail passes: For Deutschland only

The **German Rail Pass** allows for four to ten nonconsecutive days of travel in one month within Germany. A four-day pass costs $260 first class or $180 second class; each additional day costs $34 first class, $24 second class.

A **German Rail Youth Pass** is valid only for persons younger than 26 years of age and is available only in second class (for four to ten days of travel in one month). Sample prices: $142 for four days, each additional day $13.

An even bigger bargain is the **German Rail Twinpass,** for two adults (they do not have to be married and can be of the same sex) traveling together in first or second class. The second pass represents a 50 percent savings over single prices. Sample prices *per person:* $195 for four days first class or $135 for second class.

German Rail Passes for kids ages 6 to 11 are half the adult price. Children younger than 6 travel free.

A German Rail Pass also entitles the bearer to free or discounted travel on selected bus routes operated by Deutsche Touring/Europabus, including destinations not serviced by trains, and free travel on **KD German Line steamers** (day trips only) along the Rhine, Main, and Mosel rivers.

German Rail Passes are most conveniently available from **Rail Europe** (☎ **888-382-7245** in the U.S., or 800-361-7245 in Canada); you can purchase the passes online at www.raileurope.com. Rail Europe also provides cost-effective **"Rail 'n Drive" packages** that combine a certain number of days on the train with a certain number of days in a rental car. For instance, you can ride the train from Frankfurt to Munich, spend three days exploring the city, and then rent a car for a two-day excursion into the Bavarian Alps to see Ludwig's castles.

Eurailpass: For travel throughout Europe

The **Eurailpass** is one of Europe's best bargains. With a Eurailpass you can enjoy unlimited first-class rail travel in 17 countries, including Germany. Passes are for periods as short as 15 days or as long as 3 months. These passes are for *consecutive* days of travel. The 15-day Eurailpass costs $588.

If you're younger than 26, you can purchase a **Eurailpass Youth,** entitling you to unlimited second-class travel for $414 for 15 days, $534 for 21 days, $664 for 1 month, $938 for 2 months, and $1,160 for 3 months.

Eurailpasses can be bought and used only by non-European residents. Seat reservations are required on some trains. The night trains have couchettes (sleeping cars), which cost extra. Eurailpass holders also are entitled to considerable reductions on certain buses and ferries.

A host of different Eurailpass options are available, including the **Eurail Pass Flexi,** good for first-class travel for 10 or 15 days in a 2-month period; **Eurailpass Saver** for two to five persons traveling together; and **Eurail Selectpass,** allowing travelers to select three, four, or five countries linked by rail or ferry. Buy your Eurailpass before you leave home, from a travel agent or from **Rail Europe** (☎ **888/382-7245** in the U.S., or 800-361-7245 in Canada; www.raileurope.com).

Touring by Car: Autobahns, Tankstellen, and Benzin

I'm a *Zug* (train) nut. To me, nothing is more pleasant than sitting in a train and watching the countryside roll by. However, Germany has scenic regions — the Romantic Road, the Bodensee, and the Black Forest, for example — where even I succumb to car rental to explore the countryside.

If you're going to tour Germany by car, you may want to pick up a copy of *Frommer's Germany's Best-Loved Driving Tours* (Wiley).

Renting a car in Germany

Renting a car is fairly easy in Germany. Drivers from the United States, Canada, Australia, and other non–European Union countries must have a valid driver's license, but no other special license is required. I recommend that you make all the arrangements *before* you leave home. You can pick up your car at most airports and major train stations, or at an office within German cities. You can often rent a car in one German city and return the vehicle in another city for no additional charge.

Prepaying rentals in dollars before leaving the United States offers some advantages. You get an easy-to-understand net price (which you have to prepay by credit card at least 14 days before departure), the rental process is more streamlined, and you can avoid unpleasant surprises caused by sudden unfavorable changes in currency exchange rates. Remember, however, that if you opt to prepay and your plans change, you have to go through some rather complicated paperwork (and, in some cases, have to pay a penalty of around $25) for changing or canceling a prepaid contract. Whenever you rent, keep in mind that you may get a better rate if you reserve the car at least seven days in advance.

Several **international car-rental firms** rent cars in Germany. See the appendix for a list of names and contact information.

You can also rent a car through **Rail Europe** (☎ **888-382-7245** in the U.S., or 800-361-7245 in Canada; www.raileurope.com) at the same time you book your German Rail Pass or Eurailpass (see "Saving time and euros with rail passes," earlier in this chapter). They offer a **German Rail 'n Drive** option that gives you two days of unlimited train travel (first or second class) and two days of Hertz car rental within one month. You can purchase extra days for both train travel and car rental.

If you rent a car in Germany, I recommend that you purchase all the optional insurance coverage. A *Collision-Damage Waiver* **(CDW)** is an optional insurance policy that can be purchased when you sign a rental agreement. If you don't have a CDW and have an accident, you'll pay for all damages up to the cost of actually replacing the vehicle.

Some credit cards (especially platinum and gold cards) cover the CDW, so call your company to check on these benefits before you spend the extra money on additional insurance. Neither the CDW nor credit-card companies cover liability if you injure yourself, another passenger, or someone else, so if your own car insurance doesn't cover you abroad, consider taking out *Personal Accident Insurance* **(PAI)** for extra liability coverage.

Taking the roads less traveled

The roads that make up the *Autobahn* (pronounced *otto*-bahn) form Germany's main long-distance highway network. In theory, the Autobahn does not have a speed limit (in the left, fast lane), but many drivers going too fast report that they've been stopped by police and fined on the spot. So exercise reasonable caution. A German driver on the Autobahn can be like one possessed, so you may prefer the slower, right lane. The government recommends an Autobahn speed limit of 130 kmph (80 mph).

The *Bundesstrassen* (state roads) vary in quality from region to region. The Bundesstrassen in the major touring areas of the Romantic Road in Bavaria, the Rhine Valley, and the Black Forest are smoothly paved and kept in good repair. In eastern Germany, some secondary and local roads are not in good shape.

Michelin publishes the best regional **maps,** which are available at all major bookstores throughout Germany. Hallweg also produces good road maps. However, in general, finding your way by looking for directional signs rather than highway number signs is easier. In this book, individual Autobahns are indicated by the letter *A* followed by a number, and Bundesstrassen, by the letter *B* (examples: A96, B31). Germany's **road signs** are standard international signs. See Table 7-1 for a few important words that you should know.

Table 7-1	German Road Signs
German	**English Translation**
Anfang	Start, or beginning
Ausfahrt	Exit
Baustelle	Building site, or roadworks
Einbahnstrasse	One-way street
Einfahrt	Entrance
Ende	End
Gefahr	Danger
Links einbiegen	Turn left
Rechts einbiegen	Turn right
Verengte Fahrbahn	Road narrows
Vorsicht	Attention! Look out!

Following the rules of the road

If you're going to drive in Germany, you need to know a few general facts:

✔ Signs show distances and speed limits in **kilometers** (km) and **kilometers per hour** (kmph). A kilometer is 0.62 of a mile, and a mile is 1.62km.

✔ Unless posted differently, **speed limits** are

- 50 kmph (30 mph) in towns
- 100 kmph (60 mph) on regular highways
- 130 kmph (78 mph) on Autobahns

✔ On Autobahns, the **left lane** is the fast lane. And I mean fast. Do not drive in this lane unless you are passing another car.

✔ You can **pass** other vehicles only **on the left.** German motorists generally flash their lights if they want you to move over so they can pass.

✔ The law requires that all passengers wear **seat belts.** Children younger than 12 must sit on booster seats in the back so that regular seat belts can be used safely. Children younger than 4 must ride in a car seat.

✔ You must use **low-beam headlights** at night and during fog, heavy rain, and snowfalls.

✔ **Parking** in the center of most big towns is difficult, expensive, or just plain impossible, because most historic town centers are for pedestrians only. Look for parking lots and parking garages outside the center. They are always identified by a large *P;* in some larger cities, signs on the way into town indicate how much space is available in various lots or parking garages. Most parking lots use an automated ticket system. You insert coins (or credit cards) to purchase a certain amount of time.

✔ You must stop for pedestrians in **crosswalks.** They have the right of way.

✔ **Driving while intoxicated** and drinking while driving are very serious offenses in Germany. If you've had more than a glass of wine or beer, don't risk driving.

Handling a roadside emergency

The major automobile club in Germany is **Allgemeiner Deutscher Automobile Club (ADAC),** Am Westpark 8, 81373 München (☎ **089/ 76760**). If you have a breakdown on the Autobahn, you can call ADAC from an emergency phone. On the Autobahn, you find emergency phones every 2km (about 1¼ miles); the point of the black triangle on posts alongside the road indicates the direction of the nearest phone. If you don't belong to an auto club, call ADAC's breakdown service at ☎ **01802/222-222.** In English, ask for "road service assistance" *(Strassenwachthilfe).* Emergency assistance is free, but you pay for parts and materials.

Fill 'er up, bitte (please)

Gasoline, called *Benzin* (ben-*seen*), is readily available throughout Germany, and gas stations, called *Tankstelle* (*tonk*-shtel-leh) appear frequently along the Autobahns. The cheapest gasoline is at stations marked SB-TANKEN (*Selbstbedienung,* or self-service). But remember that gas is always much more expensive than in the United States. In 2004, a liter (about a fourth of a gallon) of regular unleaded gas cost about €1 ($1.25). Filling up the tank of a medium-size car cost about €50 ($62).

The self-service process is basically the same as that of the United States. You fill your tank and pay inside at the counter. The types of gasoline are *Normal Bleifrei* (regular unleaded), *Super Bleifrei* (super unleaded), *Super Plus Bleifrei* (supreme unleaded), and diesel.

Sailing through Germany: River Cruises

Germany's major river is the **Rhine,** which flows through the heart of Europe from the Alps to the North Sea. Through the centuries, more castles were built in the Rhine Valley than in any other valley in the world. This area has great appeal to visitors. The **Main** flows from the Danube, past Frankfurt, and enters the Rhine at the city of Mainz. The **Elbe,** which begins in the Czech Republic, cuts through Germany's eastern border in a beautiful area called Saxon Switzerland (see Chapter 14), flows past the great art city of Dresden, and continues northeastward; situated on tributaries of the Elbe are Berlin and Hamburg.

Viking KD River Cruises and Peter Deilman EuropAmerica Cruises offer several cruises along these three great waterways. Itineraries range from 2 to 20 nights, mostly between April and October but with some in December. If you're looking for an unusual and relaxing way to see Germany, you may want to consider this option. For more information, contact **Viking KD River Cruises of Europe,** 21820 Burbank Blvd., Woodland Hills, CA 91367 (☎ **877/66VIKING (845464)** or 818/277-234; www.rivercruises.com), or **Peter Deilmann EuropAmerica Cruises,** 1800 Diagonal Rd., Suite 170, Alexandria, VA 22314 (☎ **800/348-8287;** www.deilmann-cruises.com).

In the city and regional chapters of this guidebook, I tell you about river excursions along the Mosel and Neckar rivers and local sightseeing cruises in Berlin, Cologne, Dresden, Frankfurt, and Heidelberg.

Flying around Germany: A Good Idea?

Flying from city to city within Germany makes sense if you're traveling from, say, Hamburg or Berlin in the north to Munich in the south, or from Cologne in the west to Leipzig in the east. A trip that would take seven or eight hours by train or car takes about an hour by plane. The downside is that you won't see the countryside.

Flying doesn't make much sense if you're traveling short distances between cities that are connected by high-speed trains. The train from Frankfurt to Stuttgart, for example, takes 1 hour and 20 minutes. You can fly this route, but when you factor in time spent getting to the airport, going through security, waiting for your departure, and then getting into the city after your plane lands . . . you can already be there, in the city center, by train.

Lufthansa (☎ **800/645-3880** in the U.S. and Canada, 9639-6499 in Australia, 01803/803-803 in Germany; www.lufthansa.com or www.lufthansa.de) offers the most extensive and frequent flights within the country, but other European carriers are increasing their German domestic routes.

Chapter 8

Booking Your Accommodations

● ●

In This Chapter

▶ Checking out the options

▶ Getting the best room for the best rate

▶ Surfing for cyberdeals

▶ Landing a room without a reservation

● ●

*T*his chapter deals with that age-old question asked by every traveler going to an unfamiliar country or city: Where should I spend the night? Everyone travels differently, and every country offers its own lodging possibilities. In the following pages you find out about German hotels — how to find them, what to expect in each category, how to book a room online, and how to get the best deal for your money.

In Germany, booking your hotel room ahead is essential in large cities like Berlin and Munich — especially if you're going to be in Munich during Oktoberfest. Throughout the year, Berlin, Munich, Frankfurt, Cologne, and other cities throughout the country play host to large trade fairs and special events that make hotel rooms scarce. From April through September, and again in December (the period that constitutes *high season*), hotels in the inexpensive-to-moderate range always are first to be snapped up.

Booking ahead isn't as important in the rest of Germany, but I still recommend doing so — particularly when you're going to be spending a Friday or Saturday night in a major tourist spot like Dresden or Füssen, near Ludwig's castles. Hotels in popular tourist areas, such as the Black Forest, the Rhine and Mosel valleys, and the Bodensee (Lake Constance), also fill up quickly during high season. During *off season,* especially in the middle of winter, you won't have a problem booking a room on the spot, wherever you are. In a small village, finding a room may be as simple as spotting a sign in a house window that reads *Zimmer frei* (room available).

Tourist information centers, located in or near the main train stations in all German cities and towns, can help you find a room. Charges for this service vary. Some places charge nothing; others charge a small fixed fee (usually no more than €3/$3.75); and others charge 10 percent of the first night's hotel rate, but you get that back at the hotel, so the service ends up costing nothing. Most tourist information centers also have a free directory of local accommodations.

Finding the Place That's Right for You

Germany has very high standards for hotels and inns. You find all types of lodging, from luxury Old World palaces and super-high-tech showoffs to hip boutique hotels, small family-run hotels, cozy inns, chain hotels, rustic guesthouses, and simple rooms in private homes and apartments. You won't find a speck of *Schmutz* (dirt) in any of them. Hotel associations, regional tourist associations, and local tourist boards control standards in all categories of accommodations. Even the smallest pension (bed-and-breakfast, or B&B) must open its doors for inspection to be able to list and rent rooms.

These same state agencies and tourist boards rate hotels according to a **star system.** The system isn't used to recommend hotels but rather simply to categorize them according to their amenities. A one-star hotel is basic and inexpensive. A five-star hotel is a luxury property with an on-site spa or pool and a rate at the top end of the price spectrum. I don't use that star-rating system in this book, but instead, I try to give you the best options in different price categories.

Breakfast *(Frühstück)* always is included in the price of a room, except at some boutique and high-end luxury hotels. In a pension (B&B), breakfast may be coffee, a roll with butter and jam, an egg, and some cold cuts. At hotels, depending on the size and degree of luxury, breakfast is more likely to be a self-serve buffet with juice, cereal, yogurt, fruit, pastries, fresh bread, eggs, cold cuts, and smoked fish or pickled herring.

Smoke-free rooms and **smoke-free floors** finally are catching on in Germany. You're most likely to find them in midrange to high-end hotels. But remember that Europeans in general are not as committed to smoke-free environments as are Americans. The term for "no smoking" is *nicht rauchen* (nickt *rau*-kin).

In all accommodation types in Germany, you find a *Decke* (*deck*-uh) on the bed. If two beds are joined to make a double, you find a Decke on each side. A Decke is what Americans call a comforter or duvet. This light, feather-filled covering, buttoned within a sheet, takes the place of blankets.

In Germany, you have several different kinds of hotels and accommodations from which to choose. In the following sections, I describe each type, beginning with the most expensive.

Luxury hotels

Public spaces in luxury hotels are sophisticated and elegant. The staff is unusually welcoming and the service impeccable. Porters are available to take your luggage up to your room (tip €1/$1.25 per bag). The rooms themselves are generally spacious and beautifully furnished with amenities such as a minibar, a couple of phones, cable and satellite TV, high-speed and wireless Internet access, and bathrobes. Bathrooms are large and well equipped with magnifying mirrors, tubs (often with whirlpools) and showers, and high-quality toiletries. Your bed is turned down at night, 24-hour room service is available, and the property has an on-site health club, usually with a sauna and pool. The hotel has at least two fine gourmet restaurants, which often are the best restaurants in town. What you don't get is a free breakfast. Charges for the (fabulous) breakfast buffet are anywhere from €17 to €22 ($21 to $27). Some brand-name hotel chains — Hyatt, Kempinski, Le Meridien, and Steigenberger, in particular — have properties in this luxury category; the Hotel Excelsion Ernst in Cologne (see Chapter 19) and the Hotel Adlon in Berlin (see Chapter 11) are two of the most luxurious luxury hotels. Expect to pay €175 ($219) and up, but also look for special weekend rates on the hotels' Web sites, which you can find in the appendix.

Boutique hotels

Think of them as small luxury hotels. Boutique hotels generally have fewer than 70 rooms and offer a unique ambience and high level of personalized service. Each one has its own personality. The Bleubtreu in Berlin (see Chapter 11) is big on hip, contemporary design; Hotel Brandenburger Hof in Berlin (see Chapter 11) emphasizes a sleek, classic Bauhaus style; Der Kleine Prinz in Baden-Baden (see Chapter 17) is built around old-fashioned luxury. These establishments often are part of hotel associations, such as Relais & Châteaux, Small Luxury Hotels, and Romantic Hotels. Rooms and bathrooms are not always large, but they are beautifully fitted out. Boutique hotels always have a fine-dining restaurant and a bar. Amenities typically include brand-name toiletries, a minibar, telephone, high-speed and wireless Internet access, satellite TV, and bathrobes. Breakfast may or may not be included. Most boutique hotels are too small to have a pool or health club but may have an arrangement with a nearby facility. Pricewise, they generally cost €150 ($188) and up.

Chain hotels

Holiday Inn, Radisson SAS, Sheraton, Best Western, Ramada — names you probably know — all have hotels in Germany. German, European, and international chains include Accor, InterCity Hotels (always near train stations), Inter-Continental, Mercure, Mövenpick, Park Plaza/Art'otel, Ringhotels, Swissôtel, Travel Charme, and Treff Hotels. For the most part, chain hotels offer brand-name familiarity and dependable service.

They also tend to be newish, enormous, and somewhat anonymous.
Tour packagers and convention planners often house their groups in
chain hotels.

The rooms are smaller and have a more standardized décor than rooms
in luxury hotels. Amenities include a telephone, cable TV, and sometimes a minibar. Bathrooms are smaller and less glamorous than the
ones a luxury property. Room service is available, and the hotel often
has an on-site pool or health club with sauna. You generally find different room categories, some with breakfast included. Prices vary greatly
for chain hotels, depending on the time of year and the presence of
trade shows or conventions. In general, expect to pay anywhere from
€110 to €175 ($137 to $219). Shopping around on the Web may net you
some big savings.

Smaller independent hotels

Many small and medium-size hotels in Germany are family owned and
operated. Properties like Hotel Jedermann in Munich (see Chapter 15) or
Garni-Hotel Brugger in Lindau (see Chapter 17) offer basic, comfortable
rooms without much personality but at hard-to-beat prices. In these
hotels, which typically are given a two- or three-star rating by the local
tourist authority, you find a telephone and cable TV. Rates at small and
midsize properties always include a buffet breakfast. Prices for a small
to midsize independent hotel range from €85 to €175 ($106 to $219).

Garni, a word sometimes attached to a hotel's name, means that breakfast is the only meal the hotel serves.

Guesthouses

A guesthouse, called a **Gasthaus** (*gahst*-house) or a **Gasthof** (*gahst*-
hofe), is basically an inn with a restaurant that serves breakfast, lunch,
and dinner to hotel guests and outside patrons. You're more likely to
find guesthouses in small towns, medium-size cities, or in the country
than in large cities. The ambience tends to be rustic and cozy, and many
of the properties are older and located in the oldest and most picturesque quarters of the city. The restaurant occupies the main or first
floor, and the upper floors, usually no more than three total, have just a
few rooms. Most guesthouses don't have an elevator. Some rooms have
small private bathrooms with showers or bathtubs; other rooms have
sinks but share bathrooms and showers in the hallway. The rooms themselves often are charming — what you'd typically expect in an Old World
inn. You probably won't find a telephone in your room or too many
amenities, but your rate will include breakfast. The inn may also offer a
special rate for dinner or lunch and dinner. The Greifensteiner Hof in
Wümurzburg and Feriengasthof Helmer in Schwangau (see Chapter 16
for both) are examples of this kind of accommodation. Rates are typically from €55 to €110 ($69 to $137).

Pensions

The **pension** (pronounced pen-see-*own* in Germany) has long been the backbone of budget travel in Germany. A pension is the same as a B&B (bed-and-breakfast): a room in a private home or apartment, with breakfast included in the price. Some half a million beds are available in private homes across the country, often advertised with a simple sign: *Zimmer frei* (room available). You may luck out and find a place with a private bathroom, or you may have to share the bathroom. Breakfast always is included in the price, and in some cases, you can also use the kitchen. Amenities vary from place to place, so you may or may not have a TV, but you generally won't have a phone. In smaller towns, rooms start around €30 ($37) per person per night; prices are higher in large cities. Pension Niebuhr in Berlin (see Chapter 11) is a good big-city pension. Keep in mind that many pensions operate on a cash-only basis.

Finding the Best Room at the Best Rate

The **rack rate** is the maximum rate a hotel charges for a room. It's the rate you get if you walk in off the street and ask for a room for the night. You sometimes see these rates printed on the fire/emergency exit diagrams posted on the back of your door.

Hotels are happy to charge you the rack rate, but you can almost always do better. Perhaps the best way to avoid paying the rack rate is surprisingly simple: Just ask for a cheaper or discounted rate. You may be pleasantly surprised. Prices aren't negotiable at smaller hotels, pensions, and guesthouses, although some of these properties do offer special rates for longer stays.

In all but the smallest accommodations, the rate you pay for a room depends on many factors — chief among them being how you make your reservation. A travel agent may be able to negotiate a better price with certain hotels than you can get by yourself. (That's because the hotel often gives the agent a discount in exchange for steering his or her business toward that hotel.)

Reserving a room through the hotel's toll-free number also may result in a lower rate than calling the hotel directly. On the other hand, the central reservations number may not know about discount rates at specific locations. Your best bet is to call both the local number and the toll-free number and see which one gives you a better deal.

Room rates (even rack rates) change with the season, as occupancy rates rise and fall. If you travel in the high season (April through June, September, and December), you'll probably pay more. In Germany, hotel rates usually go down in July and August, considered high season elsewhere in Europe. (See Chapter 3 for more information on Germany's different seasons.) But even within a given season, room prices are subject to change without notice, so the rates quoted in this book may be different from the actual rate you receive when you make your reservation.

 Be sure to mention membership in AAA, AARP, frequent-flier programs, and any corporate rewards programs you can think of when you call to book. You never know when the affiliation may be worth a few euros off your room rate.

For more tips about how to get the best room rate, see the information about choosing a tour package in Chapter 6.

Surfing the Web for hotel deals

Shopping online for hotels generally is done one of two ways: by booking through the hotel's own Web site or through an independent booking agency (or a fare-service agency like Priceline). These Internet hotel agencies have multiplied in mind-boggling numbers of late, competing for the business of millions of consumers surfing for accommodations around the world. This competitiveness can be a boon to consumers who have the patience and time to shop for and compare the online sites for good deals — but shop they must, because prices can vary considerably from site to site. And keep in mind that hotels at the top of a site's listing may be there for no other reason than that they paid money to get the placement.

Of the "big three" sites, **Expedia** offers a long list of special deals and virtual tours or photos of available rooms so you can see what you're paying for. **Travelocity** posts unvarnished customer reviews and ranks its properties according to the AAA rating system. Also reliable are **Hotels. com** and **Quikbook.com**. An excellent free program, **TravelAxe** (www. travelaxe.net), can help you search multiple hotel sites at once — even ones you may never have heard of — and conveniently lists the total price of the room, including the taxes and service charges.

Another booking site, **Travelweb** (www.travelweb.com), is partly owned by the hotels it represents (including the Hilton, Hyatt, and Starwood chains) and is therefore plugged directly into the hotels' reservations systems — unlike independent online agencies that have to fax or e-mail reservation requests to the hotel, a good portion of which get misplaced in the shuffle. More than once, travelers have arrived at the hotel only to be told that they have no reservation. To be fair, many of the major sites are undergoing improvements in service and ease of use, and Expedia soon will be able to plug directly into the reservations systems of many hotel chains. In the meantime, **getting a confirmation number** and **making a printout** of any online booking transactions are good practices.

In the opaque Web site category, **Priceline** is even better for booking hotels than it is for booking flights; you're allowed to pick the neighborhood and quality level of your hotel before offering up your money. Priceline is much better at getting five-star lodging for three-star prices than at finding anything at the bottom of the scale. On the down side, many hotels stick Priceline guests in their least desirable rooms. Be sure to go to the BiddingForTravel.com Web site (www.biddingfortravel. com) before bidding on a hotel room on Priceline; it features a fairly up-to-date list of hotels that Priceline uses in major cities. For Priceline, you pay upfront, and the fee is nonrefundable. *Note:* Some hotels don't provide loyalty program credits or points or other frequent-stay amenities when you book a room through opaque online services.

Although the major travel booking sites (Frommer's, Travelocity, Expedia, and Orbitz) offer hotel booking, you may be better off using a site devoted primarily to lodging. You often find properties not listed with more general online travel agencies. Some lodging sites specialize in a particular type of accommodation, such as B&Bs, which you won't find on the more mainstream booking services. The following list includes sites that enable you to make online reservations at hotels throughout Germany:

- ✔ **Hotel Discount.com** (www.180096hotel.com) lists bargain rates at hotels throughout Germany. Because the site prebooks blocks of rooms, it sometimes has rooms at hotels that are sold out. Call its toll-free number (☎ **800/364-0801**) if you want more options than the Web site lists online.

- ✔ **Hotel Online** (www.hotelonline.de) is a site that you may want to use if you can read German. It features independent hotels throughout Germany and northern Europe that are a good value for your money.

- ✔ **InnSite** (www.innsite.com) provides B&B listings for inns in dozens of countries around the globe, including Germany. You can find a B&B in Berlin or the Black Forest, look at images of the rooms, check prices and availability, and then e-mail the innkeeper if you have questions.

- ✔ **Landidyll** (www.landidyll.de), another good site if you can read German, focuses on family hotels all across Germany that are managed according to ecological principles and have gastronomic flair.

- ✔ **SRS-Worldhotels** (www.srs-worldhotels.com) has about 450 hotels worldwide, including first-class and resort hotels throughout Germany. You can check for special discounted and weekend rates at many great German hotels.

- ✔ **TravelWeb** (www.travelweb.com) lists more than 16,000 hotels worldwide, including Germany, and focuses on chains such as Hyatt and Hilton. You can book almost 90 percent of these accommodations online. Its Click-It Weekends, updated each Monday, offer weekend deals at many leading chains.

Reserving the best room

 After you make your reservation, asking one or two more pointed questions can go a long way toward making sure you get the best room in the house. Always ask for a corner room. They're usually larger, quieter, and have more windows and light than standard rooms, and they don't always cost more. And ask whether the hotel is renovating; if it is, request a room away from the renovation work. Inquire, too, about the location of the restaurants, bars, and discos in the hotel — all sources of annoying noise. And if you aren't happy with your room when you arrive, talk to the front desk. If they have another room, they should be happy to accommodate you, within reason.

Chapter 9

Catering to Special Needs or Interests

● ●

In This Chapter

▶ Traveling with your kids
▶ Discovering discounts and special tours for seniors
▶ Locating wheelchair-accessible attractions
▶ Finding lesbigay communities and special events
▶ Tracing Germany's Jewish history

● ●

Many of today's travelers have special interests or needs. Parents may want to take their children along on trips. Seniors may like to take advantage of discounts or tours designed especially for them. People with disabilities need to ensure that sites on their itineraries are barrier-free. Gays and lesbians may want to know about welcoming places and events. Jewish visitors may want to visit Holocaust memorials and worship in a synagogue.

In this chapter, I offer advice and resources for all of these travelers.

Traveling with the Brood: Advice for Families

Germany is a pretty kid-friendly country, but traveling anywhere with *Kinder* (pronounced *kin*-der, meaning children), from toddlers to teens, is a challenge — no doubt about it. If you have enough trouble getting your kids out of the house in the morning, dragging them thousands of miles away to a country where a different language is spoken may seem like an insurmountable challenge. But family travel can be immensely rewarding, giving you new ways of seeing the world through smaller pairs of eyes.

Familyhostel (☎ 800-733-9753; www.learn.unh.edu/familyhostel) takes the whole family, including kids ages 8 to 15, on moderately priced domestic and international learning vacations. A team of academics guides lectures, field trips, and sightseeing.

You can find good family-oriented vacation advice on the Internet from sites like the **Family Travel Forum** (www.familytravelforum.com), a comprehensive site that offers customized trip planning; **Family Travel Network** (www.familytravelnetwork.com), an award-winning site that offers travel features, deals, and tips; **Traveling Internationally with Your Kids** (www.travelwithyourkids.com), a comprehensive site that offers customized trip planning; and **Family Travel Files** (www.the familytravelfiles.com), which offers an online magazine and a directory of off-the-beaten-path tours and tour operators for families.

For information on passport requirements for children, see Chapter 10.

Look for the Kid Friendly icon as you flip through this book. I use it to highlight hotels, restaurants, and attractions that are particularly family friendly. Zeroing in on these places can help you plan your trip more quickly and easily.

Admission prices for attractions throughout Germany are reduced for children ages 6 to 14. Kids younger than 6 almost always get in for free. If you're traveling with children, always check to see whether the attraction offers a money-saving **family ticket,** which considerably reduces the admission price for a group of two adults and two or more children. The same is true for public transportation: Low-priced family or group tickets usually are available. On trains, children ages 6 to 11 pay half the adult fare, and children younger than 6 travel free.

Locating family-friendly businesses

Most German hotels happily accommodate your family if you reserve your rooms in advance and make the staff aware that you're traveling with kids. The establishment may bring in an extra cot or let you share a larger room; these types of arrangements are common. Smaller pensions, or bed-and-breakfasts (B&Bs), may present problems, such as cramped rooms and shared toilet facilities. Ask questions before you reserve.

Berlin, Munich, and midsize German cities have American-style fast-food places, including **Burger King** and **McDonald's.** You won't, however, find these food chains in smaller villages and towns. Younger teens traveling in Berlin and Munich may want to check out the **Hard Rock Café** in those cities. In larger cities, you can keep costs down by eating at low-key, local restaurants.

Expensive, high-toned restaurants in Germany are not particularly welcoming toward young children. The menus aren't geared to the tastes of U.S. youngsters, and the staff can be less than welcoming to children who are not well behaved. In fact, in Germany you don't see many families dining in expensive restaurants even when the place welcomes kids.

The best of the Wurst

Your time in Germany may be a good opportunity to introduce your kids to some dishes that they've never tried. Germany's ever-present *Wurst* (pronounced *voorst,* and meaning sausage) is 100 percent meat with no filler. For something more familiar, kids can choose from a selection of cereals at most buffet breakfasts in hotels; however, the selection may not include as many presweetened varieties as in the United States.

When considering museums, bear in mind that most German museums do not translate their signage and texts into English. Therefore, a trip to a museum may try the patience of those children who can't understand what they're reading. However, don't relent, many of the top museums offer audio guides in English.

You can spur your kids' interest (and your own) by buying a German language tape or checking one out from the library. In the evening, everyone can spend an hour together, listening to the tape, and familiarizing themselves with the sounds of the German language and learning at least a few words.

Hiring a baby sitter in Germany

What you really need is an exciting evening at the opera and a romantic late dinner with a glass of fine German wine. But you can't take Junior along on this special evening. What are your options? Ask your hotel staff whether they can recommend a local baby-sitting service. Most of the hotels marked with a Kid Friendly icon in this book can help arrange baby-sitting.

Making Age Work for You: Tips for Seniors

Germany won't present any problems for you if you're a senior who gets around easily. If not, when you plan your trip, be aware that not all hotels — particularly smaller, less-expensive pensions and guesthouses — have elevators. The staircases in some places are a test for *anyone* with luggage. When you reserve a hotel, ask whether you'll have access to an elevator or a *Fahrstuhl* (*far*-shtool), as they're called in Germany.

Being a senior may entitle you to some terrific travel bargains, such as lower prices for German Rail Passes and reduced admission at museums and other attractions. Always ask, even if the reduction isn't posted. Carrying an ID with proof of age can pay off in all these situations. ***Note:*** In Germany, you may find that some discounts are available only for German or EU (European Union) residents.

The sources in the list that follows can provide information about discounts and other benefits for seniors:

- ✔ **AARP** (formlerly known as the American Association of Retired Persons; 601 E St. NW, Washington, DC 20049; ☎ **866-687-2277**; www.aarp.org) offers member discounts on car rentals and hotels. With a $12.50 annual membership (anyone 50 or older can join), AARP offers members a wide range of benefits, including discounts on U.S. Airways flights to Frankfurt and Munich from several U.S. cities and discounts on escorted tours from Globus and Cosmos, major tour operators offering trips to Germany.

- ✔ **Elderhostel** (75 Federal St., Boston, MA 02110-1941; ☎ **877-426-8056**) offers people 55 and older a variety of university-based education programs in Berlin and throughout Germany. These courses are value-packed, hassle-free ways to learn while traveling. The price includes airfare, accommodations, meals, tuition, tips, and insurance. And you'll be glad to know that you won't be graded. Popular Germany offerings have included "Opera in Berlin" and "Bavaria to Bauhaus."

- ✔ **Grand Circle Travel** (347 Congress St., Boston, MA 02210; ☎ **800-221-2610** or 617/350-7500; www.gct.com) offers package deals for the 50-plus market, mostly of the tour-bus variety, with free trips thrown in for those who organize groups of ten or more.

Accessing Germany: Advice for People with Disabilities

The German word for disabled is *behindert* (bee-*hin*-dert). A disability needn't stop anybody from traveling, because more options and resources are available than ever before. In fact, Germany is one of the more advanced countries in Europe when it comes to accessibility for disabled travelers.

Locating resources

The German National Tourist Office's Web site (www.visits-to-germany.com), with its section on travel for the disabled, is a good place to begin researching your trip. Here are some other helpful resources in the United States:

- ✔ **The Moss Rehab Hospital** (www.mossresourcenet.org) provides general information on accessible travel.

- ✔ **The Society for Accessile Travel and Hospitality** (☎ 212-447-7284; fax: 212-725-8253; www.sath.org) offers a wealth of travel resources for all types of disabilities and informed recommendations on destinations, access guides, travel agents, tour operators, vehicle rentals, and companion services.

✔ **Mobility International USA** (☎ 541-343-1284; www.miusa.org) publishes *A World of Options,* a 658-page book of resources that covers everything from biking trips to scuba outfitters, and a newsletter, *Over the Rainbow.*

✔ **The American Foundation for the Blind** (☎ 800-232-5463; www.afb.org) provides information on traveling with Seeing Eye dogs.

British travelers with disabilities may want to contact **RADAR** (Royal Association for Disability and Rehabilitation, 12 City Forum, 250 City Rd., London EC1V 8AF; ☎ 020/7250-3222; fax: 020/7250-0212; www.radar.org), which publishes vacation "fact packs," containing information on trip planning, travel insurance, specialized accommodations, and transportation abroad.

If you can read German, you may want to use one of these resources:

✔ **Nationale Koordinationsstelle Tourismus für Alle** (NatKo; national Tourism Coordination Agency for All People, Kötherhofstrasse 4, 55116 Mainz; ☎ 06131/250-410; fax: 0631/214-848; www.natko.de) is the central organization in the country for all inquiries concerning barrier-free travel. On the Web site, under "*Wer hilft*" (Who is helping?), you can find special offers and a list of German tour operators offering special tours and travel opportunities.

✔ The Web site **You-Too** (www.you-too.net) has information on the accessibility of public buildings throughout Germany, accessible accommodations, and accessible activities.

Several organizations offer tours designed to meet the needs of travelers with disabilities. Tour operators with trips to Germany include:

✔ **Accessible Journeys** (☎ 800-846-4537 or 610-521-0339; www.disabilitytravel.com)

✔ **S E Unlimited Travel** (☎ 800-552-9798 in the U.S. and Canada, or 605-366-0202; fax: 605-334-0000; www.seunlimitedtravel.com)

Touring in a Rollstuhl (wheelchair)

Traveling in a wheelchair (called a *Rollstuhl,* pronounced *roll*-shtool) presents unique challenges. For many wheelchair-bound travelers, an escorted tour is a necessity. But others want the adventures of being on their own. Thanks to its comprehensive accessibility, Germany offers both options.

The international airports in Munich and Frankfurt are wheelchair accessible.

Deutsche Bahn (German Rail) offers transportation service for the disabled. Some 385 train stations throughout the country have lifting aids or mobile ramps. You can reserve your seat in advance and obtain information about traveling with a disability by calling the special **Deutsche**

Bahn number for disabled travelers at ☎ **01805/512-512.** You can also find information (in English) for disabled travelers on its Web site, www. bahn.de (click on "Service" and *"Mobilitätseingeschränkte"*).

Not all U-Bahn (subway) stations have wheelchair access. However, in larger cities, public buses are generally wheelchair accessible.

Many hotels in Berlin, Munich, and the rest of Germany (more in the western part than the east) have rooms for the disabled (these tend to be in larger, more modern hotels). Most of the older and less expensive pensions and guesthouses don't have elevators, or they may not be wide enough for a wheelchair. Ask about this issue before you reserve, or use one of the travel agencies that specializes in travel for people with disabilities (see "Locating resources," earlier in this section).

Although not all restaurants provide wheelchair ramps, most restaurants are happy to accommodate people with disabilities.

Most of the top sights in the country are wheelchair accessible, although calling ahead to make arrangements and getting directions to special entrances and/or elevators always is a good idea. Larger theaters and performing-arts venues are often wheelchair accessible, too (again, call first). Also keep in mind that in older, historical areas, you have to deal with cobblestones.

If you're interested in gliding down the Rhine and Mosel rivers, looking at vineyards and castles, the **Köln-Düsseldorfer (KD) line** has wheelchair-accessible boats (see Chapter 19 for more about KD and Rhine journeys).

Following the Rainbow: Resources for Gays and Lesbians

Germany is one of the most "developed" countries in the world when it comes to gay pride, gay culture, and gay tourism. If you are *schwul* (pronounced *shwool,* and meaning gay) or *lesbisch* (*lez*-bish; lesbian), you'll find plenty to do in Deutschland. Berlin, Munich, Hamburg, Frankfurt, and Cologne all have large gay communities, but gay life flourishes outside the big cities, too. A network of gay or gay-friendly restaurants, cafes, stores, bars, dance clubs, and community centers exists throughout the country, in small towns and large.

Gay and lesbian couples (or friends) qualify for family tickets on public transportation in many Germany cities. With most family, or *Gruppen* (group) tickets, all that matters is that two (or more) individuals travel together.

Pride and politics

Perhaps some of the openness of gay life in Germany today has to do with the murderous antihomosexual policies of the Nazis, leading up to and during World War II. Between 1933 and 1945, untold thousands of homosexuals were arrested and sent to their deaths in labor camps. That may explain why German gays and lesbians today are so politically active and determined not to tolerate discrimination. At Europride 2002, the huge Europe-wide Gay Pride celebration that took place in Cologne (the location of the annual event changes each year), the featured speaker was German Foreign Minister Joschka Fischer.

Celebrating Gay Pride in Germany

Every summer, parades and special events celebrate Gay Pride. Lesbigay travelers may want to time their visits to coincide with these big festivals:

- ✔ **Berlin** holds its annual **Gay & Lesbian Street Festival** in mid-June, celebrates its **Christopher Street Day and Parade** around the third weekend in June, and stages its famous **Loveparade** in mid-July (this event was canceled in 2004 but may return in 2005). Find information on the Web at www.berlin.de.

- ✔ **Munich** celebrates **Christopher Street Day** in mid-July.

- ✔ **Hamburg** celebrates with a **Gay Pride Parade and Festival** around June 8 to 10.

- ✔ **Cologne's Christopher Street Weekend** usually is the first weekend in June.

- ✔ **Frankfurt's Christopher Street Weekend** takes place around the third weekend in July.

Finding gay-friendly travel agents and tour operators

If you want to keep your hard-earned travel money pink, you can use a gay travel service. The **International Gay and Lesbian Travel Association** (**IGLTA**) maintains a worldwide network of gay and lesbian travel-agent professionals who can help you plan your trip. For information on the nearest IGLTA travel agent and gay-friendly resources in Germany, contact **IGLTA** (☎ **800-448-8550;** www.IGLTA.org).

Unfortunately, Germany seems to fall below the radar screen of most gay tour operators (too bad, because Berlin is such a great destination for gay tours).

Researching German lesbigay life on the Web

The following are just a few of the Web sites you may want to check out as you begin to plan your trip to Germany:

- ✔ www.pinkpassport.com. This site is a destination service provider for international gay travelers. You can select a city in Germany and find out pertinent travel-related information.

- ✔ www.stadt.gay-web.de. One of the best all-purpose gay sites for lesbigay travelers planning a trip to Germany, this site enables you to access a lesbigay guide for each city you want to visit. (By the way, *Stadt* means "city.")

- ✔ **Specific city Web sites.** Try the following Web sites for information on specific cities: www.berlin.gay-web.de, www.munich.gay-web. de, www.hamburg.gay-web.de, www.frankfurt.gay-web.de, and www.koeln.gay-web.de or www.gaykoeln.com.

Beloved Berlin — lesbigayest of all German cities

You find plenty of gay life in all large German cities, but Berlin is something special. Statistics claim that out of a population of 3.5 million, 300,000 gays and lesbians call Berlin home! The openness of the city, lasting from the start of the 20th century and up to the Nazi era, made Berlin a travel destination for gays and lesbians. More happens in Berlin for the gay and lesbian traveler than in any other city in Germany.

Gay life goes on all across Berlin, but gay bars and cafes abound in three main areas. In western Berlin, the oldest gay neighborhood extends from **Nollendorfplatz** to **Wittenbergplatz. Kreuzberg,** long known for its healthy mix of alternative lifestyles, is pretty homo-geneous, too. In eastern Berlin, the new gay beehive is **Prenzlauer Berg,** especially on and around Schönhauser Allee.

A great way to acquaint yourself with Berlin's incredible gay past is by taking the **gay sightseeing tour** called "Von der Kaiserzeit zum Nationalsozialismus" ("From the Kaisers to the Nazis"). From April to October, the tour departs from Lutherkirche Dennewitzplatz (U-/S-Bahn: Yorkstrasse) at 3 p.m. on Saturday and Sunday and lasts about 90 minutes. Call **Movin' Queer Berlin,** Liegnitzer Strasse 5 (☎ 030/618-6955) for current price information and to verify times. **Frauen-Touren Unterwegs (Women's Tours),** Potsdamer Strasse 139 (☎ 030/215-1022), offers tours with gender-specific themes like "Women in the Middle Ages" and "Jewish Women"; you also can request lesbian themes. If you don't speak any German, check to make sure that an English-speaking guide is available.

Mann-o-Meter, the gay community center at Bülowstrasse 106 (☎ 030/216-8008), provides free information on what's going on in this gayest of German cities and has an English-speaking staff. See Chapter 12 in this guide for lesbigay places to visit in Berlin.

Remembering the Past: Resources for Jewish Travelers in Germany

In this guidebook, I can't even begin to scratch the surface of this huge and sensitive issue. Jewish life in Germany dates back hundreds of years. Throughout the centuries, Jews from all levels of society contributed to German culture. Large Jewish communities flourished in cities throughout Germany until the Nazi era, when systematic persecution, banishment, seizure of property and assets, and extermination policies created horrors that are almost beyond comprehension. Today, with a number of around 70,000, Germany's Jewish population is third largest in Western Europe and one of the few that's actually growing, in large part because many Jewish people from the former Soviet Union are choosing to live in Germany.

Special and very emotional issues confront Jewish visitors to Germany. The Germany you visit today is a democratic federal republic sensitive to the past. Several places are dedicated to remembering the Jewish experience in this country. One of the most remarkable is the new **Jüdisches Museum (Jewish Museum)** in Berlin (see Chapter 12). Another is the Holocaust memorial, the largest in Europe, to be completed in Berlin in 2005 between the Brandenburg Gate and Potsdamer Platz. Throughout the country, synagogues have been restored, and memorials erected. The most moving memorials are at **Dachau** (see Chapter 15), near Munich, and **Buchenwald** (see Chapter 14), near Weimar.

For assistance in planning your itinerary, contact the German National Tourist Office (see the appendix for the address and phone number) and request a copy of *Germany for the Jewish Traveler*. This free booklet presents an overview of Jewish history and lists recommended places to visit and what to see.

Chapter 10

Taking Care of the Remaining Details

●●●

In This Chapter

▶ Obtaining a passport
▶ Taking care of your health: Travel and medical insurance
▶ Communicating via cellphone and e-mail
▶ Dealing with airline security measures

●●●

Do you have an up-to-date passport? Have you taken steps to meet your health needs while on your trip? Are you wondering how to use a cellphone or access e-mail while in Germany? This chapter gives you the information you need.

Getting a Passport

A valid passport is the only legal form of identification accepted around the world. You can't cross an international border without one. If you're a citizen of the United States, Australia, or Canada, you must have a valid passport to enter Germany. Getting a passport is easy, but the process takes some time. For an up-to-date country-by-country listing of passport requirements around the world, go to the "Foreign Entry Requirement" Web page of the U.S. State Department at `travel.state.gov/foreignentryreqs.html`.

Applying for a U.S. passport

If you're applying for a first-time passport, follow these steps:

1. **Complete a** *passport application* **in person at a U.S. passport office; a federal, state, or probate court; or a major post office.**

   To find your regional passport office, either check the **U.S. State Department** passport Web site, `travel.state.gov/passport/index.html`, or call the **National Passport Information Center** (☎ 877-487-2778) for automated information.

2. **Present a *certified birth certificate* as proof of citizenship.**

    Bringing along your driver's license, state or military ID, or Social Security card also is a good idea.

3. **Submit *two identical passport-size photos,* measuring 2 inches by 2 inches in size.**

    You often find businesses that take these photos near a passport office. *Note:* You can't use a strip from a photo-vending machine because the pictures aren't identical. You may submit digital photos that have been printed on your printer at home, but they must meet the same requirements for all passport photographs. In addition, the digital photographs must have a continuous tone image that looks very photolike; grainy-looking photos composed of visible dots are not acceptable.

4. **Pay the fee.**

    For people 16 and older, a passport is valid for ten years and costs $85. For those 15 and younger, a passport is valid for five years and costs $70.

Allow plenty of time before your trip to apply for a passport; processing normally takes three weeks, but it can take longer during busy periods (especially spring).

If you have a passport in your current name that was issued within the past 15 years and you were older than 16 when it was issued, you can renew the passport by mail for $55. Whether you're applying in person or by mail, you can download passport applications from the U.S. State Department passport Web site at travel.state.gov/passport/index.html. For general information, call the **National Passport Agency** (☎ 202-647-0518).

American Passport Express (☎ 800-455-5166; www.americanpassport.com) is a service that can expedite the processing of your first-time passport application. Using this service, and paying the appropriate fees, you can receive your passport in as little as 24 hours.

Applying for other passports

The following list offers more information for citizens of Australia, Canada, New Zealand, and the United Kingdom:

- ✔ **Australians** can visit a local post office or passport office, call the **Australia State Passport Office** (☎ 131-232 toll-free from Australia), or log on to www.passports.gov.au for details on how and where to apply. Forms can be completed and printed online at the Web site, but applications must be submitted in person.

- ✔ **Canadians** can pick up applications at passport offices throughout Canada, at post offices, and from the central **Passport Office,**

Department of Foreign Affairs and International Trade, Ottawa, Ont. K1A 0G3 (☎ **800-567-6868;** www.ppt.gc.ca). You also can download an application form from the Passport Office Web site. Applications must be accompanied by two identical passport-size photographs and proof of Canadian citizenship. Processing takes five to ten days if you apply in person, or about three weeks by mail.

✔ **New Zealanders** can pick up a passport application at any New Zealand Passports Office or download it from the Passports Office Web site. For information, contact the **Passports Office** at ☎ **0800-225-050** in New Zealand or 04-474-8100, or log on to www.passports.govt.nz.

✔ **United Kingdom** residents, as a member of the European Union, need only an identity card, not a passport, to travel to other EU countries, such as Germany. However, if you already possess a passport, carrying the document with you is a good idea. For more information, contact the **United Kingdom Passport Service** (☎ **0870-521-0410;** www.ukpa.gov.uk).

Playing It Safe with Travel and Medical Insurance

Three kinds of travel insurance are available: trip-cancellation insurance, medical insurance, and lost-luggage insurance. The cost of travel insurance varies widely, depending on the cost and length of your trip, your age and health, and the type of trip you're taking, but expect to pay between 5 percent and 8 percent of the vacation itself. Here is my advice on all three:

✔ **Trip-cancellation insurance** helps you get your money back if you have to back out of a trip, if you have to go home early, or if your travel supplier goes bankrupt. Allowed reasons for cancellation can range from sickness to natural disasters to the State Department declaring your destination unsafe for travel. (Insurers usually won't cover vague fears, though, as many travelers discovered who tried to cancel their trips in October 2001 because they were wary of flying.)

A good resource is **"Travel Guard Alerts,"** a list of companies considered high-risk by Travel Guard International (www.travelinsured.com). Protect yourself further by paying for the insurance with a credit card — by law, consumers can get their money back on goods and services not received if they report the loss within 60 days after the charge is listed on their credit-card statement.

Note: Many tour operators include insurance in the cost of the trip or can arrange insurance policies through a partnering provider, a convenient and often cost-effective way for the traveler to obtain insurance. Make sure, however, that the tour company is a reputable one. Some experts suggest you avoid buying insurance from the tour or cruise company you're traveling with, saying it's better to buy from a third-party insurer than to put all your money in one place.

For travel overseas, most health plans (including Medicare and Medicaid) do not provide coverage, and the ones that do often require you to pay for services upfront before reimbursing you only after you return home. Even if your plan covers overseas treatment, most out-of-country hospitals make you pay your bills upfront and send you a refund only after you've returned home and filed the necessary paperwork with your insurance company. As a safety net, you may want to buy travel medical insurance. If you require additional medical insurance, try **MEDEX Assistance** (☎ **410-453-6300;** www.medexassist.com) or **Travel Assistance International (TAI)** (☎ **800-821-2828;** www.travelassistance. com; for general information on TAI's services, contact TAI's service provider, Worldwide Assistance Services (☎ **800-777-8710;** www. worldwideassistance.com).

✔ **Lost-luggage insurance** is not necessary for most travelers. On domestic flights, checked baggage is covered for up to $2,500 per ticketed passenger. On international flights (including U.S. portions of international trips), baggage coverage is limited to approximately $9.07 per pound, up to approximately $635 per checked bag. If you plan to check items more valuable than the standard liability, find out whether your valuables are covered by your homeowner's policy, get baggage insurance as part of your comprehensive travel-insurance package, or buy the "BagTrak" product from Travel Guard (☎ **800-826-4919;** www.travelguard.com). Don't buy insurance at the airport, because it's usually overpriced. Be sure to take any valuables or irreplaceable items with you in your carry-on luggage, because many valuables (including books, money, and electronics) aren't covered by airline policies.

If your luggage is lost, immediately file a lost-luggage claim at the airport, detailing the luggage contents. For most airlines, you must report delayed, damaged, or lost baggage within four hours of arrival. The airlines are required to deliver luggage, once found, directly to your house or destination free of charge.

For more information, contact one of the following recommended insurers: **Access America** (☎ 866-807-3982; www.accessamerica. com); **Travel Guard International** (☎ 800-826-4919; www.travel guard.com); **Travel Insured International** (☎ 800-243-3174; www. travelinsured.com); and **Travelex Insurance Services** (☎ 888-457-4602; www.travelex-insurance.com).

Staying Healthy When You Travel

Getting sick will ruin your vacation, so I *strongly* advise against it (of course, last time I checked, the bugs weren't listening to me any more than they probably listen to you).

For domestic trips, most reliable health-care plans provide coverage if you get sick away from home. For travel abroad, you may have to pay all medical costs upfront and be reimbursed later. For information on purchasing additional medical insurance for your trip, see the previous section.

If you have a serious and/or chronic illness, talk to your doctor before leaving on a trip. For conditions such as epilepsy, diabetes, or heart problems, wear a **MedicAlert identification tag** (☎ **888-633-4298;** www. medicalert.org), which immediately alerts doctors to your condition and gives them access to your records through Medic Alert's 24-hour hotline. Contact the **International Association for Medical Assistance to Travelers (IAMAT)** (☎ **716-754-4883** or, in Canada, 416-652-0137; www. iamat.org) for tips about travel and health concerns in the countries you're visiting and lists of local English-speaking doctors. The United States **Centers for Disease Control and Prevention** (☎ **800-311-3435;** www.cdc.gov) provides up-to-date information on health hazards by region or country and offers tips on food safety.

Bring all your medications with you, and prescriptions for more (in generic, not brand-name, form) if you worry that you'll run out. A pharmacy in Germany is called an *Apotheke* (pronounced ah-po-*tay*-kuh). Pharmacies are open regular shopping hours, and they take turns staying open all night and on weekends. If you have an emergency and need a prescription filled after hours or on weekends, go to any pharmacy. A notice will be posted in the window providing the address and telephone number of the closest on-duty pharmacy.

Avoiding "economy-class syndrome"

Deep-vein thrombosis, or as it's know in the world of flying, "economy-class syndrome," is a blood clot that develops in a deep vein. It's a potentially deadly condition that can be caused by sitting in cramped conditions — such as an airplane cabin — for too long. During a flight (especially a long-haul flight), get up, walk around, and stretch your legs every 60 to 90 minutes to keep your blood flowing. Other preventative measures include frequent flexing of the legs while sitting, drinking lots of water, and avoiding alcohol and sleeping pills. If you have a history of deep-vein thrombosis, heart disease, or another condition that puts you at high risk, some experts recommend wearing compression stockings or taking anticoagulants when you fly; always ask your physician about the best course for you. Symptoms of deep-vein thrombosis include leg pain or swelling, or even shortness of breath.

If you fall ill while traveling, ask the concierge or hotelkeeper to recommend a local doctor. (*Arzt,* pronounced *artst,* is the German word for a medical doctor.) At night and on weekends, you can call the **Ärtzlicher Notdienst** (Medical Emergency Service) listed in the telephone directory. In a life-threatening situation, dial ☎ **112** (free call anywhere in Germany), the number for general emergencies. The word for hospital is *Krankenhaus* (pronounced *kronk*-in-house).

Staying Connected by Cellphone or E-mail

The cheapest and easiest way to call home from Germany, I've found, is to use a prepaid phone card and the hotel phone. If you're accustomed to using a cellphone, keep in mind that your U.S. phone won't work in Germany without a special chip, and renting a phone in Germany, although possible, costs a lot. Collecting e-mail is fairly easy in Germany: If you can't do it at your hotel, the staff will be able to direct you to the nearest cybercafe. Below you'll find general information on using cellphones and sending or receiving e-mail in Germany.

Using a cellphone outside the U.S.

The three letters that define much of the world's wireless capabilities are **GSM** (Global System for Mobiles), a big, seamless network that makes for easy cross-border cellphone use throughout Europe and dozens of other countries worldwide. In the U.S., T-Mobile, AT&T Wireless, and Cingular use this quasi-universal system; in Canada, Microcell and some Rogers customers are GSM, and all Europeans and most Australians use GSM.

If your cellphone is on a GSM system, and you have a world-capable multiband phone — many Sony Ericsson, Motorola, or Samsung models are so equipped — you can make and receive calls across civilized areas on much of the globe, from Andorra to Uganda. Just call your wireless operator and ask for "international roaming" to be activated on your account. Unfortunately, per-minute charges can be high — usually $1 to $1.50 in western Europe.

That's why it's important to buy an "unlocked" world phone from the get-go. Many cellphone operators sell "locked" phones that restrict you from using any removable computer memory phone chip (called a **SIM card**) other than the ones they supply. Having an unlocked phone enables you to install a cheap, prepaid SIM card (found at a local retailer) in Germany. (Show your phone to the salesperson; not all phones work on all networks.) You'll get a local phone number — and much, much lower calling rates. Getting an already-locked phone unlocked can be a complicated process, but it can be done; just call your cellular operator and say you'll be going abroad for several months and want to use the phone with a local provider.

If you have an unlocked phone, you can purchase a prepaid German SIM card with call credit already incorporated and easily add more talk time to the SIM card if needed. However, if you want to purchase a German SIM card in Germany, you'll be asked for proof of residency. For that reason, you either need to have a friend or relative in Germany purchase the card for you or buy one in North America before your departure.

For many, **renting** a phone is a good idea. Although you can rent a phone from any number of German sites, including kiosks at airports and at car-rental agencies, we suggest renting the phone before you leave home. That way you can give loved ones and business associates your new number, make sure the phone works, and take the phone wherever you go — especially helpful for overseas trips through several countries, where local phone-rental agencies often bill in local currency and may not let you take the phone to another country.

Phone rental isn't cheap. You'll usually pay $40 to $50 per week, plus airtime fees of at least a dollar a minute. If you're traveling to Europe, though, local rental companies often offer free incoming calls within their home countries, which can save you big bucks. The bottom line: Shop around.

In Germany, a mobile phone is called a *Handy* (pronounced as it's spelled).

Two good wireless rental companies are **InTouch USA** (☎ 800-872-7626; www.intouchglobal.com) and **RoadPost** (☎ 888-290-1606 or 905-272-5665; www.roadpost.com). Give them your itinerary, and they'll tell you what wireless products you need. InTouch also will advise you for free on whether your existing phone will work overseas; simply call ☎ 703-222-7161 between 9 a.m. and 4 p.m. EST, or go to intouchglobal.com/travel.htm.

Accessing the Internet away from home

Travelers have any number of ways to check their e-mail and access the Internet on the road. Of course, using your own laptop — or even a PDA (personal digital assistant) or electronic organizer with a modem — gives you the most flexibility. But even if you don't have a computer, you still can access your e-mail and even your office computer from cybercafes.

Finding a city in Germany that *doesn't* have a few cybercafes is hard to do. Although no definitive directory exists for cybercafes — they are, after all, independent businesses — two places to start looking are at www.cybercaptive.com and www.cybercafe.com.

Aside from formal cybercafes, most **youth hostels** nowadays have at least one computer with Internet access. And most **public libraries** across the world offer Internet access free or for a small charge. Some **business centers** in large luxury hotels are free for guests, but others charge high rates to go online.

Most major airports now have **Internet kiosks** scattered throughout their gates. These kiosks, which you'll also see in shopping malls, hotel lobbies, and tourist information offices around the world, give you basic Web access for a per-minute fee that's usually higher than cybercafe prices. The kiosks' clunkiness and high price mean they need to be avoided whenever possible.

To retrieve your e-mail, ask your **Internet service provider (ISP)** whether it has a Web-based interface tied to your existing e-mail account. If your ISP doesn't have such an interface, you can use the free **mail2web** service (www.mail2web.com) to view and reply to your home e-mail. For more flexibility, you may want to open a free, Web-based e-mail account with **Yahoo! Mail** (mail.yahoo.com). (Microsoft's Hotmail is another popular option, but Hotmail has severe spam problems.) Your home ISP may be able to forward your e-mail to the Web-based account automatically.

If you need to access files on your office computer, look into a service called **GoToMyPC** (www.gotomypc.com). The service provides a Web-based interface for you to access and manipulate a distant PC from anywhere — even a cybercafe — provided your target PC is on and has an always-on connection to the Internet (such as with Road Runner cable). The service offers top-quality security, but if you're worried about hackers, use your own laptop rather than a cybercafe computer to access the GoToMyPC system.

Wi-Fi: Wireless Networks

If you're bringing your own computer, the buzzword in computer access to familiarize yourself with is **Wi-Fi** (wireless fidelity), and more and more hotels, cafes, and retailers are signing on as wireless hotspots where you can get high-speed connection without cable wires, networking hardware, or a phone line. Many laptops sold during the last year have built-in Wi-Fi capability (an 802.11b wireless Ethernet connection). Mac owners have their own networking technology called Apple AirPort. For those with older computers, an 802.11b/**Wi-Fi card** (around $50) can be plugged into your laptop. You sign up for wireless access service much as you do cellphone service, through a plan offered by one of several commercial companies that have made wireless service available in airports, hotel lobbies, and coffee shops, primarily in the U.S. (followed by the U.K. and Japan). **T-Mobile Hotspot** (www.t-mobile.com/hotspot) serves up wireless connections at more than 1,000 Starbucks coffee shops nationwide. **Boingo** (www.boingo.com) and **Wayport** (www.wayport.com) have set up networks in airports and high-class hotel lobbies. **IPass** (www.ipass.com) providers also give you access to a few hundred wireless hotel lobby setups. Best of all, you don't need to be staying at the Four Seasons to use the hotel's network; just set yourself up on a nice couch in the lobby. The companies' pricing policies can be byzantine, with a variety of monthly, per-connection, and per-minute plans, but in general you pay around $30 a month for limited access — and as more and more companies jump on the wireless bandwagon, prices are likely to get even more competitive.

Plugging Into Germany

You can't plug a laptop or appliance from the United States or Canada into a German outlet. North American current runs 110V; the standard voltage throughout Germany is 220V. You need an electric converter or transformer to bring the voltage down and an adapter plug to fit North American plugs into the two-pronged, round, German wall sockets. Plug adapters and converters are available at most travel, luggage, electronics, and hardware stores. Most contemporary laptop computers and electric razors automatically sense the current and adapt accordingly, but check first or you may fry your equipment. The standard voltages and wall plugs in Australia, New Zealand, and the United Kingdom also are different from those in Germany. If you're coming from one of those countries, you'll need to bring an electric converter and a plug adaptor with you.

Some places also provide **free wireless networks** in cities around the world. To locate these free hotspots, go to www.personaltelco.net/index.cgi/WirelessCommunities.

If Wi-Fi isn't available, most business-class hotels throughout the world offer dataports for laptop modems, and many hotels in Germany now offer free high-speed Internet access using an Ethernet network cable. **Call your hotel in advance** to see what your options are.

In addition, major Internet service providers (ISPs) have **local access numbers** around the world, enabling you to go online by simply placing a local call. Check your ISP's Web site or call its toll-free number and ask how you can use your current account away from home, and how much it will cost. If you're traveling outside the reach of your ISP, the **iPass** network has dial-up numbers in most of the world's countries. You'll have to sign up with an iPass provider, which then tells you how to set up your computer for your destination. For a list of iPass providers, go to www.ipass.com and click on "Individual Purchase." One solid provider is **i2roam** (☎ **866-811-6209** or 920-235-0475; www.i2roam.com).

Wherever you go, bring a **connection kit** of the right power and phone adapters, a spare phone cord, and a spare Ethernet network cable — or find out whether your hotel supplies them to guests.

Keeping Up with Airline Security

With the federalization of airport security, security procedures at U.S. airports are more stable and consistent than ever. Generally, you'll be fine as long as you arrive at the airport **one hour** before a domestic flight and **two hours** before an international flight; if you show up late, tell an airline employee and she'll probably whisk you to the front of the line.

Bring a **current, government-issued photo ID** such as a driver's license or passport. Keep your ID at the ready to show at check-in, the security checkpoint, and sometimes even the gate. (Children younger than 18 do not need government-issued photo IDs for domestic flights, but they do for international flights to most countries.)

In 2003, the TSA phased out **gate check-in** at all U.S. airports. And **e-tickets** have made paper tickets nearly obsolete. Passengers with E-tickets can beat the ticket-counter lines by using airport **electronic kiosks** or even **online check-in** from your home computer. Online check-in involves logging on to your airlines' Web site, accessing your reservation, and printing out your boarding pass — and the airline may even offer you bonus miles to do so. If you're using a kiosk at the airport, bring the credit card you used to book the ticket or your frequent-flier card. Print out your boarding pass from the kiosk and simply proceed to the security checkpoint with your pass and a photo ID. If you're checking bags or looking to snag an exit-row seat, you'll be able to do so using most airline kiosks. Even the smaller airlines are employing the kiosk system, but always call your airline to make sure these alternatives are available. **Curbside check-in** also is a good way to avoid lines; however, a few airlines still ban curbside check-in; call before you go.

Security checkpoint lines are getting shorter, but some doozies remain. If you have trouble standing for long periods of time, tell an airline employee; the airline will provide a wheelchair. Speed up security by **not wearing metal objects** such as big belt buckles. If you've got metallic body parts, a note from your doctor can prevent a long chat with the security screeners. Keep in mind that only **ticketed passengers** are allowed past security, except for folks escorting disabled passengers or children.

Federalization has stabilized **what you can carry on** and **what you can't.** The general rule is that sharp things are out, nail clippers are okay, and food and beverages must be passed through the X-ray machine — but security screeners can't make you drink from your coffee cup. Bring food in your carryon rather than checking it, because explosive-detection machines used on checked luggage have been known to mistake food (especially chocolate, for some reason) for bombs. Travelers in the U.S. are allowed one carry-on bag, plus a "personal item" such as a purse, briefcase, or laptop bag. Carry-on hoarders can stuff all sorts of things into a laptop bag; as long as it has a laptop in it, it's still considered a personal item. The Transportation Security Administration (TSA) has issued a list of restricted items; check its Web site (www.tsa.gov/public/index.jsp) for details.

Airport screeners may decide that your checked luggage needs to be searched by hand. You can now purchase luggage locks that enable screeners to open and relock a checked bag if hand-searching is necessary. Look for Travel Sentry–certified locks at luggage or travel shops and Brookstone stores (you can buy them online at www.brookstone.com). These locks are approved by the TSA and can be opened by luggage inspectors with a special code or key. For more information on the locks, visit www.travelsentry.org. If you use something other than TSA-approved locks, your lock will be cut off your suitcase if a TSA agent needs to hand-search your luggage.

Part III

Northern & Eastern Germany

The 5th Wave   By Rich Tennant

"After visiting a Neo–Gothic church, a Neo–Gothic warehouse, and a Neo–Gothic museum, I'm ready to take out my Neo–Gothic shoe inserts and rest awhile."

In this part . . .

*H*istory has left its mark throughout northern and eastern Germany, and nowhere more so than in **Berlin,** the country's "new" capital. I devote two chapters to Berlin. Chapter 11 fills you in on all the Berlin basics: getting there, getting around, and finding the best hotels and restaurants. I devote Chapter 12 to exploring the largest and most exciting city in Germany.

Northern Germany, bordering the Baltic and the North Sea, is the focus of Chapter 13. I tell you all about **Hamburg,** the region's largest city and greatest port. From Hamburg you can make an easy side trip to beautiful **Lübeck,** with so many historic buildings that UNESCO recognizes the city as a World Heritage Site, or **Bremen**, full of proud reminders of its seafaring past. All three of these cities were members of the powerful Hanseatic League that ruled the seas and dominated trade in northern Europe for hundreds of years.

Since reunification in 1990, eastern Germany has been in the midst of a major building and rebuilding boom. In Chapter 14, I introduce you to the best places to visit in this newly opened region: **Dresden,** with its superb museums, historic panache, and location on the Elbe river; **Leipzig,** a busy business city where the "peaceful revolution" began; and **Weimar,** city of Goethe and one of Germany's cultural jewels. In Chapter 14, I also tell you about visiting the **Thuringian Forest** and taking a boat trip into the scenic region known as **Saxon Switzerland.**

Chapter 11

Settling into Berlin

*B*erlin is, for my money, the most exciting city in Europe. You feel a sense of immediacy here because everything is happening at once — past, present, and future meet and meld all over the place. You can dive into Berlin on many levels, even if you don't speak German. Your experiences can be as sophisticated, cultured, or raunchy as you want them to be.

Berlin has a kind of inexhaustible energy, a fizz and a flair and a drive that you find nowhere else in Germany. Berliners, perhaps because they've been through so much, both triumph and tragedy, have always been a breed apart. Their cosmopolitan live-and-let-live attitude, laced with sharp-edged humor and sarcastic irreverence, gives the city an added bite. When you're in Berlin, you see a city in transition, part of the reason why a visit here is so intriguing.

But, even as the city reinvents itself yet again, *"Berlin bleibt doch Berlin."* That old song lyric meaning "Berlin always remains Berlin" still holds true. This city has seen it all — Prussian power, artistic brilliance, endless political upheaval, and Nazi terror — and survived to tell the tale. By the end of World War II (WWII), much of Berlin was reduced to smoldering rubble. The city then was divided into American, British, and Russian sectors. Later, during the Berlin Airlift of 1948, food and supplies had to be flown in because the Soviets blockaded the city. The Wall went up in 1961, and for almost 30 years, Berlin was split in two, physically and politically. Now, with the Wall down and Deutschland reunited, Berlin once again is the capital of the Federal Republic of Germany. In many ways it's a new city — and yet, *"Berlin bleibt doch Berlin."*

Getting There

You can arrive in Germany's capital and largest city by plane, train, or car.

By plane

In May 2005, Delta is expected to begin offering direct flights from New York to Berlin, inaugurating the only direct flights to Berlin from anywhere within the United States. Otherwise, if you fly from the United States, you have to change planes in Frankfurt or another European city, depending on what airline you use. Berlin has two airports, both with easy public transportation connections to the city at standard public fares.

Arriving at Berlin-Tegel

Tegel (TXL) airport (☎ 0180/5000-186), Berlin's main and most convenient airport, is on the outskirts of central Berlin in Reinickedorf. The facility recently was revamped to make it more passenger-friendly. Inside the terminal, you find currency-exchange windows and a small branch of the **Tourist Information Center** (no phone; open daily 7:30 a.m.– 7 p.m.) where you can pick up free city transit maps and general-interest brochures and buy a bus ticket into town.

To get into central Berlin from Tegel, you can take a bus or taxi. Buses arrive outside the airport terminal, where you also find the taxi stand. On the bus, use euro coins (no bills) to buy your ticket from the driver. Four buses run from the airport into central Berlin; tickets for each of them cost €2 ($2.50), the regular two-zone A/B fare. (For information on public transportation, see "Getting around Berlin," later in this chapter.)

- ✔ **JetExpress Bus TXL** runs about every ten minutes between the airport and Potsdamer Platz, Friedrichstrasse, and Unter den Linden in Mitte, the "new" center of Berlin.

- ✔ **Bus X9**, an express bus, connects to the Jakob-Kaiser-Platz *U-Bahn* (underground train) station. From there you can change to the subway and reach any destination. **The X9** also goes to the Bahnhof Zoologischer Garten (Zoo Station), the central train station in the western part of the city near Kurfürstendamm. The X9 takes about 20 minutes to reach Zoo Station. Another bus that goes to Zoo Station is **Bus 109,** which travels down Kurfürstendamm and takes about 30 minutes. At the train station, you can connect to the U-Bahn or the *S-Bahn* (elevated train). Berlin's main Tourist Information Center is at the nearby Europa Center (see "Finding Information After You Arrive" later in this chapter).

- ✔ A **taxi** ride to central Berlin (east or west) costs €15 to €20 ($19 to $25) and takes about 20 minutes.

A tale of three airports

Tempelhof, built in the 1920s, was Berlin's main airport during the Third Reich. The airport also was the base for the Berlin Airlift in 1948, when U.S. and other Allied forces brought food and supplies to the city during the Soviet blockade. During the Cold War, the U.S.–built **Tegel** airport served West Berlin, while another airport, **Schönefeld,** served travelers to the city's Communist, eastern sector.

As part of a new plan for Berlin airports, Templehof was closed in October 2004 and a massive $4 billion expansion of Schönefeld airport now is underway. When the project is completed, a few years from now, Tegel also will close. All air traffic then will be consolidated into a single hub called Berlin Brandenburg International Airport.

Arriving at Berlin-Schönefeld

Schönefeld (SXF) (☎ **01805/000-186**), located about 24km (15 miles) southeast of the city, is the old East Berlin airport, now mostly used for European charter flights. The easiest way to get into town from this airport is by **Airport Express,** an S-Bahn that leaves the Flughafen Berlin-Schönefeld station about every 20 minutes for central Berlin, stopping at Alexanderplatz and Fredrichstrasse in Berlin Mitte (eastern Berlin), and Bahnhof Zoo (about a 30-minute journey) in the western center of Berlin. The S-Bahn station is a ten-minute walk from the airport terminal, or you can take **Bus 171,** a shuttle service that runs from the airport to the S-Bahn station and the **Rudow U-Bahn station.** From the U-Bahn station, you can take the U7 subway to Bahnhof Zoo in about 50 minutes. Bus, U-Bahn, or S-Bahn fare is €2 ($2.50).

A **taxi** ride to the Alexanderplatz area in Mitte takes about 45 to 60 minutes and costs about €45 ($56). Taxis wait outside the terminal.

By train

You can reach Berlin by train from everywhere in Europe. Two main train stations currently handle all long-distance trains. The railway stations are connected to public buses, subways, and elevated trains.

By 2006, all high-speed Europewide trains will arrive at or depart from Berlin at one central station, **Lehrter Bahnhof.** When that happens, for the first time in its history, Berlin will have one train station that dominates all others. Until then, two main stations continue to operate: Bahnhof Zoologischer Garten (Zoo Station) and Ostbahnhof (East Station).

For 24-hour train information, call the **Deutsche Bahn** (☎ **11861**).

Arriving at Bahnhof Zoologischer Garten (Zoo Station)

Usually called **Bahnhof Zoo** (Zoo Station; Hardenbergplatz 11, ☎ 01805/
996-633), this busy station is centrally located close to Kurfürstendamm,
the main artery in western Berlin. Zoo Station is the point of arrival from
western destinations, including Hamburg and Amsterdam. In addition to
long-distance trains, U-Bahn and S-Bahn trains converge at this station.
Inside the station, the train travel office **Reisezentrum Bahnhof Zoo**
(☎ 030/19419) is open daily from 6 a.m. to 11 p.m. to handle train tickets
and information. At the **BVG-Pavilion** outside the station, you can buy
tickets and special passes for buses, underground trains (U-Bahn), and
elevated trains (S-Bahn); the pavilion is open daily from 6 a.m. to 10 p.m.

Arriving at Ostbahnhof (East Station)

Ostbahnhof (☎ 01805/996-633), in the eastern neighborhood of
Friedrichshain, currently is Berlin's second main station. Trains entering
and departing Berlin for destinations in Bavaria and eastern Germany
usually stop here and at Zoo Station. Unless you're staying in the eastern
section of Berlin, you probably won't use Ostbahnhof. The U5 U-Bahn
line connects the station to Alexanderplatz and Zoo Station.

Arriving at Bahnhof Lichtenberg

Some trains from eastern European destinations arrive at **Bahnhof
Lichtenberg,** Weitlinger Strasse 22 (☎ 01805/996-633), in eastern Berlin.
You may arrive at Lichtenberg if you're coming from a destination such
as Prague or Budapest. The station is on the U5 U-Bahn line, which runs
to Alexanderplatz and Zoo Station.

By car

Four *Autobahn* (freeway) routes enter Berlin from western Germany;
three enter from the east. The drive from Frankfurt or Munich takes about
eight hours, depending on traffic. Once you're in Berlin, however, a car is
a nuisance. In fact, you'll want to keep the car parked at your hotel or in
a garage. Unless you know this huge city well, getting around by public
transportation is far easier than by car. See "Driving a car" later in this
chapter for general driving tips in the city.

Finding Information After You Arrive

At a **Tourist Info Center,** you can find information or book a hotel room
(for a fee of €3/$3.75). You can also buy the CityTourCard (see "Trans-
portation basics" later in this chapter), the SchauLUST museum pass
(described in Chapter 12), or bus and subway tickets. Berlin has three
walk-in Tourist Info Centers:

✔ The main office in western Berlin is in the **Europa-Center,** Budapester Strasse 45, close to Bahnhof Zoo (U-/S-Bahn: Zoologischer Garten). The office is open Monday through Saturday from 10 a.m. to 7 p.m., Sunday from 10 a.m. to 6 p.m.

✔ The eastern Berlin branch is in the south wing of the **Brandenburg Gate** (U-/S-Bahn: Unter den Linden). The office is open daily from 10 a.m. to 6 p.m.

✔ A Tourist Info Café is located under the **Fernsehturm** (Television Tower) at Alexanderplatz. This center is open daily from 10 a.m. to 6 p.m.

The three Tourist Info Centers operate one **information line** (☎ 030/25-00-25), which costs a minimum of €0.40 (50¢) per minute.

Orienting Yourself in Berlin

Covering some 60 square miles, Berlin is one of the world's largest cities. For first-time visitors, getting a handle on this sprawling, complex metropolis can be difficult. Even though the Wall has been down since 1989, the first and simplest way to understand Berlin is still to think in terms of the old political boundaries of West and East. (See the "Berlin Neighborhoods" map in this chapter.)

Introducing western Berlin

From 1961 to 1989, West Berlin was an island of capitalism inside Communist East Germany. West Berlin was richer, showier, and wilder than its drab eastern counterpart. The city's main attractions now are spread almost evenly across the whole city.

West Berlin's glitziest artery was — and remains — the 4km-long (2½-mile) boulevard known as **Kurfürstendamm,** or the **Ku-Damm** for short. The train station **Bahnhof Zoologischer Garten,** or **Bahnhof Zoo** for short, near the Ku-Damm, is the major transportation hub on the western side of the city and a good landmark for orienting yourself. The zoo itself is part of the **Tiergarten,** a beautiful park stretching east and ending at the cultural center known as the **Kulturforum,** near Potsdamer Platz.

Charlottenburg

The district known as Charlottenburg is the wealthiest and most commercialized in western Berlin. Along the famous **Ku-Damm,** which runs through it, you find the best concentration of hotels, restaurants, theaters, cafes, nightclubs, shops, and department stores. The 22-story **Europa Center,** a shopping center and entertainment complex, rises just across

Berlin Neighborhoods

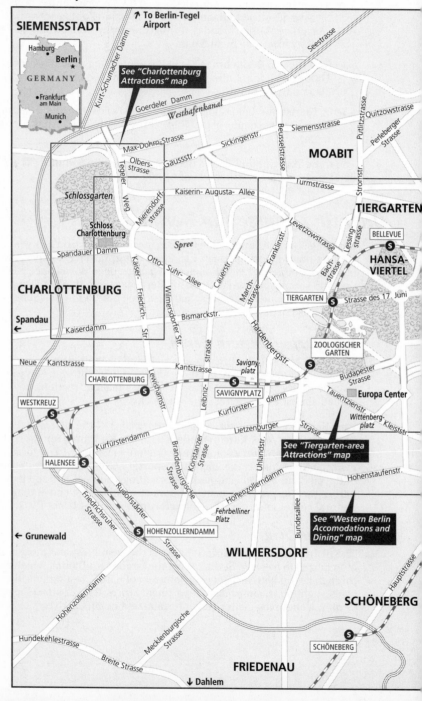

SIEMENSSTADT

To Berlin-Tegel Airport

Hamburg
Berlin ★
GERMANY
Frankfurt am Main
Munich

See "Charlottenburg Attractions" map

Kurt-Schumacher Damm

Goerdeler Damm

Westhafenkanal

Seestrasse

Max-Dohrn-Strasse

Sickingenstr.

Beusselstrasse

Siemensstrasse

Siemensstrasse

Putlitzstrasse

Quitzowstrasse

Perleberger Strasse

MOABIT

Olbers-strasse

Gaussstr.

Tegeler Weg

Turmstrasse

Stromstr.

Schlossgarten

Mierendorff-strasse

Kaiserin- Augusta- Allee

TIERGARTEN

Levetzowstrasse

Lessing-strasse

BELLEVUE
Ⓢ

Schloss Charlottenburg

Spandauer Damm

Kaiser- Friedrich-

Otto- Suhr- Allee

Spree

Franklinstr.

Bach-strasse

HANSA-VIERTEL

Wilmersdorfer Str.

Cauerstr.

March-strasse

CHARLOTTENBURG

Bismarckstr.

Hardenbergstr.

TIERGARTEN
Ⓢ

Strasse des 17. Juni

Spandau ←

Kaiserdamm

Str.

ZOOLOGISCHER GARTEN
Ⓢ

Neue / Kantstrasse

Kantstrasse

Leibniz-strasse

Savigny-platz

Budapester Strasse

CHARLOTTENBURG
Ⓢ

Lewishamstr.

Kantstrasse

SAVIGNYPLATZ
Ⓢ

damm

Tauentzienstr.

Europa Center

WESTKREUZ
Ⓢ

Kurfürsten-

Wittenberg-platz

Kleiststr.

Lietzenburger

Strasse

See "Tiergarten-area Attractions" map

Kurfürstendamm

Brandenburgische Strasse

Konstanzer Strasse

Uhlandstr.

Hohenstaufenstr.

HALENSEE
Ⓢ

Rudolfstädter

Hohenzollerndamm

See "Western Berlin Accomodations and Dining" map

← Grunewald

Friedrichsruher Strasse

Fehrbelliner Platz

HOHENZOLLERNDAMM
Ⓢ

Bundesallee

WILMERSDORF

Hohenzollerndamm

Strasse

Hauptstrasse

SCHÖNEBERG

Hundekehlestrasse

Mecklenburgische Strasse

SCHÖNEBERG
Ⓢ

Breite Strasse

FRIEDENAU

↓ Dahlem

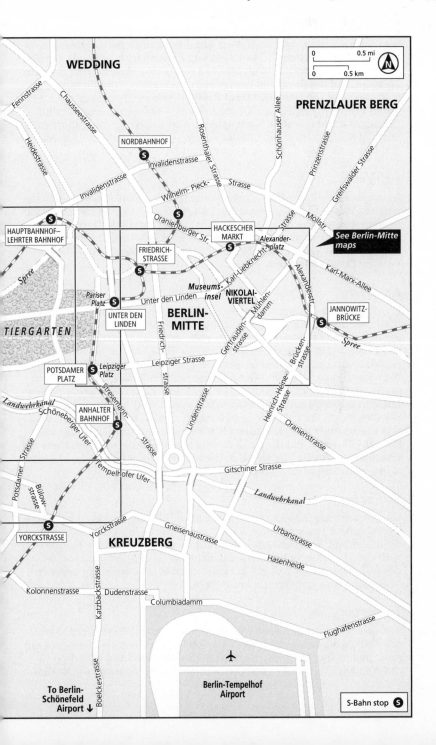

the plaza from the **Kaiser-Wilhelm-Gedächtnis Kirche** (Memorial Church) near the Ku-Damm and Zoo Station. Charlottenburg's regal centerpiece is **Schloss Charlottenburg** (Charlottenburg Palace), with its lovely gardens and nearby museums: the **Ägyptisches** (Egyptian) **Museum,** the **Bröham Museum,** and the **Bergruen Sammlung** (Collection). Charlottenburg also is the home of the **Deutsche Oper Berlin** (German Opera House), one of Berlin's three opera houses. Upscale shops, restaurants, and cafes fill the neighborhood around **Savignyplatz,** a tree-lined square a short walk north of Kurfürstendamm. Charlottenburg, which has plenty of hotels and pensions (B&Bs), makes a convenient base for visitors.

Dahlem

Now the university district, Dahlem originally was established as an independent village to the southwest of Berlin's center. Up until reunification, Dahlem was the site of western Berlin's major museums; however, most of them have now moved farther into the city. This neighborhood no longer is a convenient place to stay, but you may want to come here to visit the **Brücke Museum.**

Kreuzberg

Filled with 19th-century tenement buildings (called *Hinterhof,* because they have an interior courtyard) constructed for the workers of a rapidly industrializing Prussia, Kreuzberg traditionally has been the poorest and most crowded of western Berlin's districts. Today, about 35 percent of its population is composed of *Gastarbeiter* ("guest workers") from Turkey, the former Yugoslavia, and Greece, many of whom have now lived here for 30 years or more. Starting in the 1960s and 1970s, the district became home to the city's artistic countercultural scene. Although gentrification is taking place, the neighborhood remains funky around the edges, with lots of bars and clubs. Kreuzberg is where you find the new **Jüdisches** (Jewish) **Museum** and the small museum called **Mauermuseum Haus am Checkpoint Charlie,** dedicated to the history of divided Berlin. The area is more residential than hotel-oriented.

Schöneberg

Like Kreuzberg, Schöneberg developed in the 19th century as an independent suburb for workers. After WWII, the area was rebuilt as a middle-class neighborhood. The borough is centrally located, close to the Ku-Damm, with good U-Bahn connections and many hotels and pensions. Berlin's densest concentration of gay bars and clubs is in Schöneberg between Nollendorfplatz and Victoria-Luise-Platz.

Tiergarten

The name Tiergarten means "Animal Garden," and it refers both to western Berlin's massive urban park and a business-residential district of the same name. The Tiergarten park, originally intended as a backdrop to the grand avenues laid out by the German kaisers, contains the **Berlin**

Zoo in its southwest corner. The **Hansaviertel** (Hans Quarter), occupying the northwest section of Tiergarten, contains a series of residential buildings designed in the late 1950s by different architects, including Le Co busier, Walter Gropes, and Alva Alto. The Tiergarten neighborhood also contains the **Kulturforum,** home of the **Philharmonic** (Philharmonic Hall), the famed **Gemäldegalerie** (Painting Gallery), the **Neue Nationalgalerie** (New National Gallery), and other museums. Tiergarten also is where you find the **Brandenburg Gate** and the **Reichstag** (Parliament) building. Tiergarten is one of the best areas in Berlin for hotels and restaurants.

Wilmersdorf

The huge park called the **Grünewald** (*groo*-nuh-vald) takes up the western portion of this borough. This 38 sq. km (15 sq. mile) lake-filled forest begins just beyond the western edge of the Kurfürstendamm and is Berlin's largest uninterrupted wooded area. **Wannsee** is the most popular lake for swimming and boating. Closer in, toward the Ku-Damm, Wilmersdorf is a quiet residential neighborhood filled with an excellent assortment of hotels and pensions and plenty of low-key restaurants and cafes. All in all, Wilmersdorf is a very pleasant borough in which to stay.

Introducing Berlin-Mitte (Berlin Center)

Berlin-Mitte, also called **Stadtmitte** (City Center) or just plain **Mitte** (Center), is the new name of the central section of former East Berlin. Before the war and the division of the city, this area was, in fact, the center of Berlin. The oldest and most historic part of Berlin, Berlin-Mitte has numerous attractions. I recommend giving this fascinating area at least a full day of your time.

Berlin-Mitte symbolically begins at **Potsdamer Platz** and the **Brandenburg Gate,** on the east side of Tiergarten park. Both areas formerly stood behind the Berlin Wall and now are full of new buildings and ongoing construction. The grand boulevard called **Unter den Linden,** which starts at the Brandenburg Gate and extends east, is lined with 18th- and 19th-century palaces and monuments. The **Staatsoper Unter den Linden** is the main opera house in eastern Berlin. (The **Komische Oper,** Berlin's third opera house, also is in Berlin-Mitte.) The beautiful neoclassical square called **Gendarmenmarkt,** just off Unter den Linden, is where you find the magnificently restored early 19th-century Schauspielhaus (theater), now called **Konzerthaus am Gendarmenmarkt** and used for concerts. At the eastern end of Unter den Linden, you find the marvelous **Museumsinsel** (Museum Island), site of four major museums.

Friedrichstrasse, which intersects Unter den Linden, is regaining its prewar reputation as Berlin's preeminent shopping street. Luxury boutiques and department stores crowd the street. U-Bahn and S-Bahn lines converge at **Friedrichstrasse train station,** the transportation hub of Berlin-Mitte.

Alexanderplatz, a square named for Russian Czar Alexander I, was the center of activity in the Soviet era. Surrounded by dreary buildings from that time, the square is still pretty grim, although the opening of small markets is bringing new life. The 368m (1,207-ft.) **Fernsehturm** (TV tower) on Alexanderplatz is one of the highest structures in Europe and has an observation platform.

The **Nikolaiviertel** (Nicholas Quarter), just south of Alexanderplatz along the Spree River, is a charming area restored to look as it did in Berlin's medieval and baroque eras. Period taverns and riverside restaurants make this quarter ideal for a leisurely and picturesque stroll.

Prenzlauer Berg, northeast of Mitte, is now the hippest neighborhood in eastern Berlin. Except to check out the ongoing gentrification, short-term travelers find little of interest. Gay and lesbian visitors may want to explore Prenzlauer Berg's burgeoning gay cafe and club scene.

Getting around Berlin

Berlin is a huge city, and even dedicated walkers won't be able to cover it entirely on foot. Luckily, Berlin has a comprehensive public transportation system. The following sections describe the various options you have for getting from place to place.

Going public: U-Bahn, S-Bahn, bus, and Strassenbahn

Berlin's excellent public transportation system makes getting around fast, convenient, safe, and relatively inexpensive. The system consists of the **U-Bahn** (underground train), the **S-Bahn** (surface or elevated train), **buses, ferries** on the lakes, and a few *Strassenbahnen* (streetcars) that still operate in eastern Berlin only. This well-integrated public transport system is run by BVG, Berlin's Transport Authority. For a map of Berlin's U-Bahn and S-Bahn, see the inside back cover of this book.

Transportation basics

You can **buy your ticket** at any U-Bahn station (at windows or machines that have English translations) or from a bus driver. You can also buy tickets and passes (and receive a free transportation map) at the **BVG-Pavillion** on Hardenbergplatz, directly outside Zoo Station; the office is open daily from 6 a.m. to 10 p.m.

The fare is based on **three zones** (A, B, and C). One ticket enables you to change from U-Bahn to S-Bahn and to the bus during a two-hour period. All of your sightseeing within the Berlin city limits will be in zones A and B. Zone C extends far beyond the city's borders.

A regular *Normaltarif* or *Einzelfahrscheine* (one-way fare), good for
two hours in zones A and B is €2 ($2.50).

For short hops (three consecutive U- or S-Bahn stops or six stops on a
bus or streetcar), you can get a *Kurzstrecke* (short-stretch) ticket for
€1.20 ($1.50).

When purchasing tickets for public transportation, you also have three
money-saving options:

   ✔ A **Tageskarte** (day ticket) is good on all forms of transportation
     from validation until 3 a.m. the following day and costs €5.60 ($7)
     for zones A and B.

   ✔ If you're in Berlin for two or three days, consider the **CityTourCard**,
     which costs €14.50 ($18) for 48 hours or €18.90 ($24) for 72 hours.
     The card is good for all public transportation in central Berlin and
     provides price reductions of up to 50 percent at many tourist attrac-
     tions in Berlin.

   ✔ The **7-Tage-Karte** (seven-day ticket) costs €24.30 ($30) for zones A
     and B.

The entire transportation system runs on an honor system — you won't
find turnstiles or ticket collectors. You must **validate your ticket** by stick-
ing it into one of the validation boxes on all U-Bahn and S-Bahn platforms
or inside buses and streetcars. Long-term tickets are validated only
once, before your first trip. Ticket inspectors may suddenly appear to
check everyone's ticket. If yours hasn't been validated, you're guilty of
Schwarzfahren (black travel) and fined €50 ($62) on the spot.

U-Bahn (underground train)

The subway in Berlin is called the U-Bahn. Nine lines crisscross the city
in all directions and extend to the far reaches of Brandenburg. A large
U in a blue box identifies each station, and the routes are clearly marked
in all stations and in the trains. Service is fast and efficient, but after
midnight only two lines, U9 and U2, run on a limited schedule; they intersect at Bahnhof Zoo. In each car, you find a map of the stops, which are
announced. For general **U-Bahn information,** call ☎ **030/19449** (daily
6 a.m. to 11 p.m.).

S-Bahn (elevated train)

The venerable elevated train system in Berlin is called the S-Bahn. Thirteen
lines cover most of central Berlin; each car contains a map of the stops,
which are announced. A large *S* in a green circle identifies each station.
S-Bahn and U-Bahn stations sometimes overlap, so you can change from
one to the other. Service is basically nonexistent after midnight.

The S-Bahn is particularly handy if you're going from Bahnhof Zoo east to the Friedrichstrasse/Unter den Linden area or southwest to Grünewald and the lakes.

Bus

Riding atop one of Berlin's double-decker buses (single-deckers also operate) is a fun way to see the city. A green *H* (for *Haltstelle,* or stop) in a yellow circle identifies each stop. Regular service begins about 5 a.m. and ends about midnight. Night buses (designated with an *N*) leave every half-hour, going west and east, from Bahnhof Zoo and Bahnhof Hackescher Markt (near Alexanderplatz in eastern Berlin).

 One of the best and cheapest sightseeing routes is on **Bus 100,** which leaves from Bahnhof Zoo and travels through the Tiergarten, passing Bellevue Palace (the Berlin residence of the German president), the Reichstag, and the Victory Column all the way to the Brandenburg Gate, Unter den Linden, Museum Island, and Alexanderplatz.

Strassenbahn (streetcar)

Streetcars, called **Strassenbahnen,** run in eastern Berlin only. Because you can get practically everywhere on the U-Bahn or S-Bahn, you probably won't be using the streetcar. Ticket prices are the same as for the U-Bahn, S-Bahn, and buses.

Taking a taxi

Thousands of ivory-colored taxis cruise Berlin's main streets. Hailing one during the day is easier than at night. The fare starts at €2.50 ($3.10) and costs €1.53 ($1.90) per kilometer (½ mile). To order a taxi, call ☎ 210-101. Tip taxi drivers by rounding up to the nearest euro.

Driving a car

I don't recommend renting *ein Auto* in Berlin. Local drivers tend to be aggressive, and the street system itself can be fiendishly difficult to navigate. The public transport system gets you everywhere you want at a fraction of the cost. If you're out very late, you can grab a cab to get back to your hotel. The only time a car may come in useful is when you want to explore the surrounding countryside. The offices for **Hertz** (Budapester Strasse 37, ☎ 030/262-1053) and **Avis** (Budapester Strasse 43, ☎ 030/230-9370) are close to Bahnhof Zoo.

 If you drive in town, be aware that the right lanes in inner-city areas are often reserved for buses, taxis, and bicycles *only*. When turning right, you must give way to any vehicle (including bikes) in that lane. Some right-hand lanes are reserved for buses at stated times and otherwise can be used by cars. Also remember that in Germany, using a mobile phone while driving is against the law.

In Berlin and throughout Germany, cars can park only on the right side of the road. In most inner-city areas, you must obtain a parking ticket at one of the street-side ticket machines to display on your dashboard. The police quickly tow cars that violate these laws. If that happens, you can go to any police station to find out where your car is. The whole process costs more than €150 ($187) — and a great deal of time. Parking garages are more expensive than street parking, but they save you the potential hassle of getting towed.

Staying in Style

Finding a hotel room in Berlin is easy, unless a big trade fair or soccer match is happening in town. Prices generally are lower than in other major European cities. (You can find a good hotel in Berlin for less than €150/$187 a night.) I do, however, strongly recommend that you reserve your room before you arrive.

 If you arrive in Berlin without a hotel room, you can go to the main **Tourist Information Center** in the Europa Center, close to Bahnhof Zoo (entrance on Budapester Strasse; U-/S-Bahn: Zoologischer Garten). For €3 ($3.75), the center's staff will find you a room. The office is open Monday through Saturday 10 a.m. to 7 p.m. and Sunday 10 a.m. to 6 p.m. You can also book hotels by calling ☎ 030/25-00-25.

For locations of the hotels in this chapter, see the maps "Western Berlin Accommodations and Dining" and "Berlin-Mitte Accommodations and Dining."

The top hotels

For details on two of the city's best hotels, **Hotel Adlon Kempinski** ($$$$) and **Hotel Brandenburger Hof** ($$$$), see Chapter 22.

Alsterhof Ringhotel Berlin
$–$$$$ Wilmersdorf

Location — just a few minutes walk from Bahnhof Zoo and the Ku-Damm — is this hotel's greatest asset. If you're in Berlin on business and need a full-service hotel in a central location, this place fits the bill. The 195 rooms are comfortable and quiet, and have plenty of extra amenities (trouser press, safe, minibar, hair dryer), although they aren't particularly stylish. You find a pool and sauna on the sixth floor. The breakfast buffet costs €16 ($20).

See map p. 126. Augsburger Strasse 5, 10789 Berlin. ☎ *030/212-420. Fax: 030/218-3949.* www.alsterhof.com. *U-Bahn: Kurfürstendamm (then a 5-minute walk east across Joachimstaler Platz and east on Augsburger Strasse). Rack rates: €74–€289 ($92–$361) double. AE, DC, MC, V.*

Western Berlin Accommodations and Dining

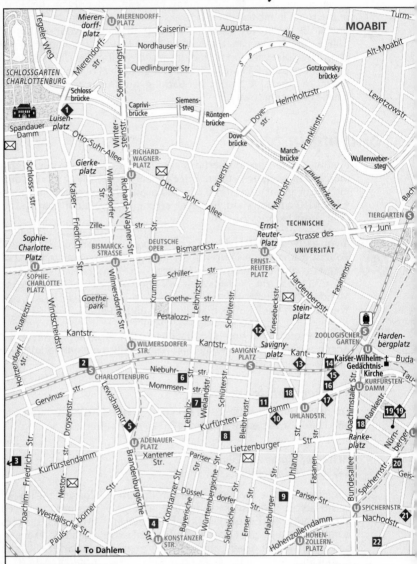

ACCOMMODATIONS ■

Alsterhof Ringhotel Berlin **24**
Ambassador Berlin **27**
Arco Hotel **23**
Artemisia **4**
Art-Hotel Charlottenburger
  Hof **2**
Bleibtreu Hotel **8**
Grand Hotel Esplanade **28**

Grand Hyatt Berlin **29**
Hecker's Hotel **11**
Hotel Art Nouveau **7**
Hotel Brandenburger Hof **19**
Hotel Domus **9**
Hotel Wilmersdorf **20**
Kempinski Hotel Bristol **16**
Kü Damm 101 **3**
Pension München **22**

Pension Niebuhr **6**
Pension Nürnberger Eck **25**
Ritz-Carlton **30**
Savoy Hotel **14**
Sorat Art'otel Berlin **18**

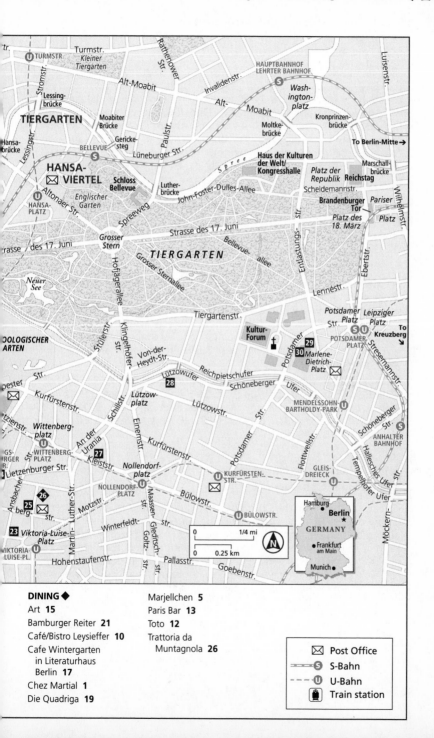

DINING ◆

Art **15**

Bamburger Reiter **21**

Café/Bistro Leysieffer **10**

Cafe Wintergarten
  in Literaturhaus
  Berlin **17**

Chez Martial **1**

Die Quadriga **19**

Marjellchen **5**

Paris Bar **13**

Toto **12**

Trattoria da
  Muntagnola **26**

⊠ Post Office

Ⓢ S-Bahn

Ⓤ U-Bahn

🚆 Train station

Arco Hotel
$–$$ Schöneberg

This small, gay-friendly hotel is housed in a four-story turn-of-the-century building on a quiet street near the Ku-Damm. Most of the 21, fairly large rooms have high windows and modern furniture. Private bathrooms, all with showers, are on the small side. One of the nicest features is the airy breakfast room, which looks out on a courtyard garden (you can eat outside in warm weather). The English-speaking staff is friendly and helpful. One potential drawback: no elevator.

See map p. 126. Geisbergstrasse 30, 10777 Berlin. ☎ *030/218-8065. Fax: 030/2147-5178.* www.arco-hotel.de. *U-Bahn: Wittenbergplatz (then a 5-minute walk south on Ansbacher Strasse and west on Geisbergstrasse). Rack rates: €75–€102 ($94–$127) double. Rates include breakfast. AE, DC, MC, V.*

Artemisia
$ Charlottenburg

Located on the top floors of a large apartment building, Artemisia is an excellent hotel for women only. The rooms are large, light, and free of frou-frou but still have a warm ambience heightened by splashes of color. Ten of the 12 rooms have toilets and small showers. You can save money by renting one of the two rooms that share a toilet and shower. A private roof terrace with wonderful views over Berlin becomes a gathering spot on warm afternoons and evenings.

See map p. 126. Brandenburgischestrasse 18, 10707 Berlin. ☎ *030/873-8905. Fax: 030/ 861-8653.* www.frauenhotel-berlin.de. *U-Bahn: Blissestrasse (then a 3-minute walk northwest on Brandenburgischestrasse). Rack rates: €97–€115 ($121–$144) double with bathroom, €82–€89 ($102–$111) double without bathroom. Rate includes breakfast. AE, DC, MC, V.*

Art-Hotel Charlottenburger Hof
$–$$ Charlottenburg

Located across from the Charlottenburg S-Bahn station, this budget hotel is one of the best and brightest in Berlin. This inexpensive property is unusually well decorated for its price range and offers several amenities, such as in-room safes, hair dryers, and laundry facilities. Primary colors of blue, yellow, red, and white brighten some of the 45 contemporary-style rooms, a few of which have balconies. Rooms and bathrooms, which have showers, are fairly small. All guest rooms are equipped with computers that provide free Internet access. The breakfast buffet costs an additional €8 ($10).

See map p. 126. Stuttgarter Platz 14, 10627 Berlin. ☎ *030/329-070. Fax: 030/332-3723.* www.charlottenburger-hof.de. *S-Bahn: Charlottenburg (the hotel is north of the station). Rack rates: €60–€120 ($75–$150) double. AE, MC, V.*

Berlin-Mitte Accommodations and Dining

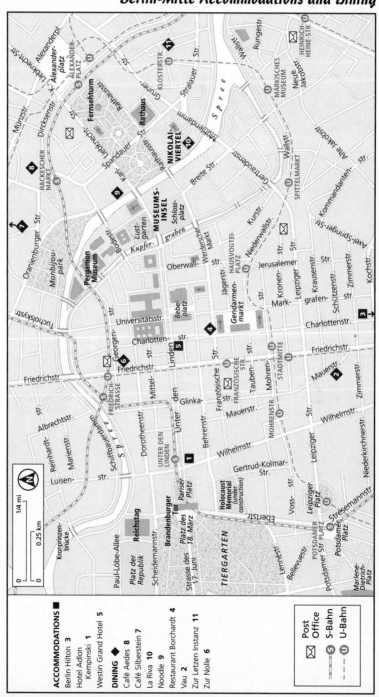

ACCOMMODATIONS ■
Berlin Hilton **3**
Hotel Adlon
Kempinski **1**
Westin Grand Hotel **5**

DINING ◆
Café Aedes **8**
Café Silberstein **7**
La Riva **10**
Noodle **9**
Restaurant Borchardt **4**
Vau **2**
Zur Letzten Instanz **11**
Zur Nolle **6**

⊠ Post
  Office
Ⓢ S-Bahn
Ⓤ U-Bahn

Bleibtreu Hotel
$$$–$$$$ Charlottenburg

If you're looking for chic, central, contemporary digs near the Ku-Damm, this 60-room boutique hotel is *the* place for you. The rooms aren't particularly large but are artfully designed and furnished. The furniture coverings are hypoallergenic, and no chemicals of any kind are used for cleaning. The small, stylish bathrooms have sinks of carved stone. Other features include remote-control-operated lights, wireless phones, fax machines in every suite, and electric awnings over street-facing windows. The hotel has a Wellness Center where you can take a pore-cleansing sauna. Restaurant 31, near the small lobby, lays out a healthy breakfast buffet (an extra €15/$19); the bar is lively at night.

See map p. 126. Bleibtreustrasse 31, 10707 Berlin. ☎ **030/884-740.** *Fax: 030/8847-4444.* www.bleibtreu.com. *S-Bahn: Savignyplatz (then a 5-minute walk south on Bleibtreustrasse). Rack rates: €152–€232 ($190–$240) double. AE, DC, MC, V.*

Grand Hyatt Berlin
$$$$ Tiergarten

The Grand Hyatt Berlin, right smack-dab in the center of all the action in the new Potsdamer Platz area, is one of the coolest places to stay. This big hotel, built in 1998 with 342 rooms, is sleek and glamorous throughout. Rooms are large and have beautiful wood finishes and wonderful bathrooms set up with Japanese-style soaking tubs. Restaurants include Vox, for Eurasian cuisine and sushi; Tizian, for international classics; and Bistro Dietrich, for casual cafe-style food. The staff can arrange baby-sitting.

See map p. 126. Marlene-Dietrich-Platz 2, 10785 Berlin. ☎ **030/2553-1234.** *Fax: 030/2553-1235.* www.berlin.grand.hyatt.com. *U-Bahn: Potsdamer Platz (then a 5-minute walk west to Marlene-Dietrich-Platz). Rack rates: €210–€355 ($262–$444) double. AE, DC, MC, V.*

Hotel Domus
$$–$$$ Wilmersdorf

Set in an unusually pretty section of Wilmersdorf, down the street from St. Ludwig's Church and within walking distance of the Ku-Damm, this modern 73-room hotel has a calm, appealing simplicity. The spacious rooms are quiet (thanks to soundproof windows) and tastefully decorated with high-quality contemporary furniture (lots of light-colored wood). Rooms face the inner courtyard or the street. The bathrooms are unusually large and have either a shower or a tub. Breakfast is served in a lovely dining room.

See map on p. 126. Uhlandstrasse 49, 10719 Berlin. ☎ **030/880-3440.** *Fax: 030/8803-4444.* www.hotel-domus-berlin.de. *U-Bahn: Spichernstrasse (then a 5-minute walk west on Hohenzollerndamm and north on Uhlandstrasse). Rack rates: €115–€145 ($144–$181) double. Rate includes breakfast. AE, DC, MC, V.*

Kempinski Hotel Bristol
$$$$ Charlottenburg

One of Berlin's most famous luxury hotels, the 301-room Kempinski is right in the thick of things on the Ku-Damm. This place possesses high-toned classic styling. Every room is unique, but the general color scheme favors dark blues and greens enlivened by lustrous wood finishes. The bathrooms are large and have double sinks. The public rooms are predictably grand, with amenities such as a business center, a fitness center, a pool, and 24-hour room service. Children younger than 12 stay free in their parents' room, and the staff can arrange baby-sitting. The only thing you don't get is breakfast (it costs an addition €15/$19), but if you can afford to stay here, that probably doesn't matter.

See map on p. 126. Kurfürstendamm 27, 10719 Berlin. ☎ *800/426-3135 in the U.S. or 030/884-340. Fax: 030/883-6075.* www.kempinski-bristol.de. *U-Bahn: Kurfürstendamm (then a 2-minute walk west on Kurfürstendamm). Rack rates: €294–€354 ($367–$442) double. AE, DC, MC, V.*

Pension Niebuhr
$ Charlottenburg

This pleasant, gay-friendly pension in Charlottenburg is one of the best deals in Berlin. The 12 rooms, all on the second floor of a turn-of-the-century apartment building (no elevator), have a fresh, modest flair. The furnishings and color schemes are bright and cheerful. Three street-facing rooms have balconies; the rooms facing the courtyard *(Hinterhof)* can be a bit dark, but they're very quiet. One bonus: Breakfast is brought up to your room.

See map p. 126. Niebuhrstrasse 74, 10629 Berlin. ☎ *030/324-9595. Fax: 030/881-4707.* www.pension-niebuhr.de. *S-Bahn: Savignyplatz (then a 5-minute walk west on Niebuhrstrasse). Rack rates: €55 ($69) double without bathroom, €75 ($94) double with bathroom. Rate includes breakfast. AE, MC, V.*

Pension Nürnberger Eck
$ Charlottenburg

If you're seeking an atmospheric old-fashioned pension, try this one on the second floor of a building near the Europa Center, a shopping and entertainment complex. High-ceilinged rooms with heavy doors open off a long, dark hallway. Although the eight rooms are stylistically something of a mish-mash, with patterned wallpaper, Oriental rugs, and big pieces of furniture, the pension does convey an Old Berlin charm. The bathrooms are a decent size, and the breakfast room is pleasant.

See map p. 126. Nürnberger Strasse 24a, 10789 Berlin. ☎ *030/235-1780. Fax: 030/ 2351-7899. U-Bahn: Wittenbergplatz (then a 5-minute walk west on Tauentzienstrasse and south on Nürnberger Strasse). Rack rates: €87–€92 ($108–$115) double. Rates include breakfast. MC, V.*

Savoy Hotel
$$$–$$$$ **Charlottenburg**

The quietly elegant Savoy, which opened in 1930, has played host to more than a few celebrities through the years. You can't beat the location, just a skip from the Ku-Damm. The lobby is a luxe version of neoclassical styling. All 125 rooms are individually decorated and provide spacious and comfortable accommodations, with unusually large bathrooms. Public areas include a fitness room with a sauna and solarium.

See map p. 126. Fasanenstrasse 9–10, 10623 Berlin. ☎ **800/223-5652** *U.S. or 030/311-030. Fax: 030/3110-3333.* www.savoy-hotels.com. *U-Bahn: Zoologischer Garten (then a 5-minute walk west on Kantstrasse and north on Fasanenstrasse). Rack rates: €152–€232 ($190–$290) double. AE, DC, MC, V.*

Sorat Art'otel Berlin
$$–$$$$ **Charlottenburg**

So-called Art hotels are springing up all across Germany, but the Sorat Art'otel Berlin was the first. Designed by artist Wolf Vostell, the Sorat features a modern European design aesthetic in its public spaces, art installations set into the corridors, and original artwork in all 133 rooms. The rooms aren't particularly large, but they're all comfortable and well designed. The filling breakfast buffet, included in the room rate, is served in a large, light-filled room with contemporary furniture. The convenient location is close to the Ku-Damm.

See map p. 126. Joachimstalerstrasse 29, 10719 Berlin. ☎ **030/884-470.** www.sorat-hotels.com. *U-Bahn: Kurfürstendamm (then a 5-minute walk south on Joachimstalerstrasse). Rack rates: €146–€261 ($183–$326) double. Rates include breakfast. AE, DC, MC, V.*

The big splurge

If you're looking for top-of-the-line luxury, here are a few more $$$$ suggestions:

- ✔ **Berlin Hilton,** Mohrenstrasse 30, 10117 Berlin. ☎ **800/445-8667** in the U.S. and Canada, or 030/20230. Fax: 030/2023-4269. www.hilton.com. U-Bahn: Stadtmitte.

- ✔ **Grand Hotel Esplanade,** Lützowufer 15, 10785 Berlin. ☎ **030/254-780.** Fax: 030/265-1171. www.esplanade.de. U-Bahn: Zoologischer Garten. See map p. 126.

- ✔ **Ritz-Carlton,** Potsdamer Platz 3, 10785 Berlin. ☎ **800/241-3333** in the U.S. and Canada, or 030/33-77-77. Fax: 030/777-5555. www.ritz-carlton.com. U-Bahn: Potsdamer Platz. See map p. 126.

- ✔ **Westin Grand Hotel,** Friedrichstrasse 158–164, 10117 Berlin. ☎ **800/937-8461** in the U.S., or 030/20270. Fax: 030/2027-3362. www.westin-grand.com. U-Bahn: Stadtmitte. See map p. 129.

Runner-up hotels

Ambassador Berlin

$$ Schöneberg Kids love the swimming pool in this well-maintained family-friendly hotel. *See map p. 126. Bayreutherstrasse 42–43, 10787 Berlin.* ☎ *030/ 219-020. Fax: 030/2190-2380.* www.sorat-hotels.com. *U-Bahn: Wittenbergplatz.*

Hecker's Hotel

$$–$$$ Charlottenburg The streamlined rooms in this small, trendy hotel may look a bit sterile to some, but the place is conveniently located and impeccably maintained. *See map p. 126. Grolmanstrasse 35, 10623 Berlin.* ☎ *030/88900. Fax: 030/889-0260.* www.heckershotel.com. *S-Bahn: Savignyplatz.*

Hotel Art Nouveau

$–$$ Charlottenburg This small, atmospheric hotel is on the fourth-floor of an Art Nouveau apartment house. *See map p. 126. Leibnizstrasse 59, 10629 Berlin.* ☎ *030/327-7440. Fax: 030/327-7440.* www.hotelartnouveau.de. *S-Bahn: Savignyplatz.*

Hotel Wilmersdorf

$ Wilmsersdorf This no-fuss pension is large, clean, and comfortable, and offers a buffet breakfast overlooking the rooftops of Berlin. *See map p. 126. Schaperstrasse 36, 10719 Berlin.* ☎ *030/2177-07476. Fax: 030/217-7077. U-Bahn: Spichernstrasse.*

Ku'Damm 101

$$ Wilmersdorf A minimalist aesthetic and a bit of off-putting "I'm so cool" attitude characterize this interesting new hotel. *See map p. 126. Kurfürstendamm 101, 10711 Berlin.* ☎ *030/520-0550. Fax: 030/2005-5555.* www.kudamm101.com. *U-Bahn: Adenauerplatz.*

Pension München

$ Wilmersdorf You find simple, modern decor and plenty of nice touches in this third-floor pension. *See map p. 126. Günzelstrasse 62, 10717 Berlin.* ☎ *030/ 857-9120. Fax: 030/8579-1222.* www.hotel-pension-muenchen-in-berlin. de. *U-Bahn: Günzelstrasse.*

Dining Out

Berlin offers every kind of international cuisine. The local culinary tradition is fairly basic and very filling. Typical Berlin dishes include grilled or pickled herring with onions, fried potatoes, and bacon; pickled or roast pork *(Schweinefleisch)* or pork knuckles *(Eisbein)* with red cabbage and dumplings; meatballs *(Buletten)* with boiled potatoes; and pea soup *(Erbsensuppe)*. A plate with various cold meats is called a *Schlachteplatte* *(schlock-*tuh-plaht-tuh*)*. Game like venison, duck, and wild boar appears seasonally; carp and trout often are available. Fancier restaurants often serve what's called *neue Deutsche Küche* (New German Cuisine), which uses the old standbys as a starting point but dolls them up with unusual ingredients and international touches.

Restaurant and cafe bills include the service charge and value-added tax (MWST), but rounding out the total bill with an extra amount as a gratuity is standard practice. If the bill is €6.30, for example, round the total up to €7 and add another euro or two if the service was good.

Scattered all around town are vendors selling Berlin's classic fast-food snacks: *Currywurst* (sausage with a glob of "curry" sauce) or fried bratwurst. Grabbing a wurst or eating at the stand-up counters of the fast-food snack shops (look for signs that read "IMBISS" or "SCHNELL-IMBISS") is a good way to save time and money.

You can always get an inexpensive meal (soup, sandwiches, and lighter dishes) at one of Berlin's plentiful cafes. And speaking of cafes: Don't forget that in Germany, afternoon *Kaffee und Kuchen* (coffee and cake) is a time-honored tradition. I list some good cafe choices at the end of this chapter.

For a few recommended brewpubs, places to enjoy a casual meal with a freshly drawn beer, see Chapter 12.

For locations of the restaurants in this chapter, see the maps "Western Berlin Accommodations and Dining" and "Berlin-Mitte Accommodations and Dining" earlier in this chapter.

The top restaurants

Art
$–$$ Charlottenburg   GERMAN/INTERNATIONAL

A restaurant, bar, and cafe rolled into one, Art is tucked beneath the S-Bahn track at Fasanenstrasse. Come to this great, gay-friendly place for an English breakfast (bacon, eggs, and beans). For lunch, try a bowl of potato soup with sausage or one of the many salads. Dinner choices include homemade pasta, duck with cassis sauce, chicken, fish, and a vegetarian *Maultaschen* (stuffed pasta). The staff is friendly and outdoor seating is available in good weather.

See map p. 126. Fasanenstrasse 81A. ☎ *030/313-2625. U-Bahn: Zoologischer Garten (then a 5-minute walk west on Hardenberg Strasse and south on Fasanenstrasse). Reservations recommended for dinner. Main courses: €9–€17 ($11–$21). AE, DC, MC, V. Open: Mon–Fri 11 a.m.–2 a.m., Sat–Sun 10 a.m.–2 a.m. (winter Sat–Sun 12:30 p.m.–2 a.m.)*

Bamburger Reiter
$$$$ Schöneberg   AUSTRIAN

Housed in a 100-year-old wine tavern at the corner of Regensburger Strasse and Bamburger Strasse, Bamburger Reiter is small (maximum 35 diners) and rustic, with parquet floors, flowers, and plenty of antiques. For many years, this was a temple of *neue Deutsche Küche* (New German Cuisine), but the place now serves mostly Austrian dishes. The menu changes monthly and may include cream of mushroom soup, roast quail, *wiener schnitzel* (breaded veal cutlets), marinated boiled beef with chive cream, or smoked-fish pie. The restaurant has a leafy outdoor arbor for summertime dining.

See map p. 126. Regensburgerstrasse 7. ☎ *030/218-4282. U-Bahn: Spichernstrasse (then a 10-minute walk east on Regensburgerstrasse). Reservations required. Main courses: €22–€39 ($27–$49). No credit cards. Open: Tues–Sat 5:30–11:30 p.m.*

Chez Martial
$$ Charlottenburg FRENCH

Top-quality products and good cooking have helped establish Chez Martial as one of Berlin's most popular French restaurants. Every dish is freshly prepared, so be ready to wait (while savoring a bottle of good French wine). The menu changes daily and offers about 15 main courses, including fresh fish, poultry, lamb, beef, and couscous. The fish soup, cooked in a broth of fish and shellfish that's whipped into a foam, is wonderful. For dessert, try the pumpernickel mousse.

See map p. 126. Otto-Suhr-Allee 144. ☎ *030/341-1033. U-Bahn: Richard-Wagner-Platz (then a 5-minute walk north on Richard-Wagner-Strasse and west on Otto-Suhr-Allee). Reservations recommended. Main courses: €15–€17 ($19–$21). MC, V. Open: Tues–Sun 6–11:30 p.m.*

Die Quadriga
$$$$ Wilmersdorf FRENCH

Die Quadriga, the one-star Michelin restaurant (in Michelin's guides, one star means very good) in the beautiful Brandenburger Hof Hotel, offers a truly memorable dining experience, but you need to reserve well in advance because the elegant restaurant seats only 28 diners. Everything is of the finest quality. Dishes are classically French and seasonally fresh. The wonderful wine list includes several wines available by the half-bottle or by the carafe.

See map p. 126. In Hotel Brandenburger Hof, Eislebener Strasse 14. ☎ *030/214-050. U-Bahn: Kurfürstendamm (then a 2-minute walk south on Eislebener Strasse). Reservations required. Main courses: €24–€34 ($30–$42); fixed-price menu €80–€90 ($100–$112). AE, D, MC, V. Open: Mon–Fri 7–11 p.m. Closed July 17–Aug 20.*

La Riva
$$ Mitte ITALIAN/SEAFOOD

One of the prettiest buildings in the restored Nikolaiviertel (Nicholas Quarter), just south of Alexanderplatz, is the Ephraim-Palais, a richly ornamented 1765 mansion. Part of the building is a museum, while another section contains this Italian-influenced restaurant, which sits right next to the Spree River. You'll want a table outside if the weather is fine. And you'll probably want to order fish, because that's what this place does best. Choices include salmon with white-wine sauce; grilled trout; swordfish with fresh tomatoes, onions, and basil; and grilled or baked crayfish. Pasta is made fresh daily, and the good pizzas are kid-pleasing. The restaurant also has a well-stocked wine cellar.

See map p. 129. Spreeufer 2. ☎ 030/242-5183. U-Bahn: Klosterstrasse (then a 5-minute walk southwest on Mühlendamm to Spreeufer, the pedestrian street along the river). Reservations recommended. Main courses: €13–€19 ($16–$23). AE, MC, V. Open: Daily 11 a.m. to midnight.

Marjellchen
$$–$$$ Charlottenburg EAST PRUSSIAN

Old East Prussian recipes prepared by the owner's grandmother inspired the dishes that are served at this popular restaurant, which celebrates its 20th anniversary in 2005. For an appetizer, try homemade aspic, smoked Pomeranian goose, or fried chicken legs. Other starters include *Beetenbartsch,* a delicious red-beet soup with beef strips and sour cream, and a tasty potato soup with shrimp and bacon. Main courses are something of an adventure: stewed pickled beef with green dumplings and stewed cabbage, smoked ham in cream sauce, pork kidneys in sweet-and-sour cream sauce, or roast of elk with chanterelle mushrooms. You also find vegetarian dishes, such as broccoli soufflé.

See map p. 126. Mommsenstrasse 9. ☎ 030/883-2676. U-Bahn: Uhlandstrasse (then a 3-minute walk west on Mommsenstrasse). Reservations recommended. Main courses: €11–€21 ($14–$26). AE, DC, MC, V. Open: Mon–Sat 5 p.m. to midnight.

Noodle
$–$$ Mitte JAPANESE/ASIAN

Located right beside the Spree River, across from the giant Berlin cathedral, this new Japanese-inspired noodle house offers a good, reasonably priced selection of sushi, sashimi, and satays (skewers with meat or fish), plus noodle soups, fried noodles, and other specialties. Everything on the menu is listed in English; diners mark what they want and hand it to the server. The dining room has long communal tables, or you can dine outside in nice weather.

See map p. 129. Spreepromenade beside Liebknecht Bridge. ☎ 030/2328-3464. U-Bahn: Uhlandstrasse (then a 3-minute walk west on Mommsenstrasse). Reservations recommended. Main courses: €5–€10 ($6.25–$12). AE, MC, V. Open: Daily noon to 11 p.m.

Paris Bar
$$–$$$ Charlottenburg FRENCH/AUSTRIAN/MEDITERRANEAN

Since the end of WWII, the Paris Bar, between Savignyplatz and the Memorial Church, has been a Berlin institution. In the past couple of years, the restaurant has expanded its classic French bistro menu to include more upscale Austrian and Mediterranean-inspired dishes. Main courses change often. You may find asparagus with hollandaise sauce, ham, and new potatoes; risotto with porcini mushrooms; wiener schnitzel; fresh fish; or grilled foie gras.

See map p. 126. Kantstrasse 152. ☎ *030/313-8052. U-Bahn: Zoologischer Garten (then a 5-minute walk west on Kantstrasse). Reservations recommended. Main courses: €10–€25 ($12–$31). No credit cards. Open: Daily noon to 2 a.m.*

Restaurant Borchardt
$$–$$$ Mitte   FRENCH/INTERNATIONAL

You can recognize Borchardt, directly across from the Gendarmenmarkt, by its blood-colored awning and red sandstone facade. Inside, the restaurant is large, spare, and elegant, with marble, gilding, and a bit of French attitude. If you like it rich, go for the foie gras fillet with caramelized onions. Menu offerings typically include baked tuna fish with Asian vegetables, glazed duck breast, saddle of veal with lemon butter, and suckling pig. The best bet for lunch is one of the fixed-price specials.

See map p. 129. Französische Strasse 47. ☎ *030/2038-87110. U-Bahn: Französische Strasse (then a 3-minute walk east on Französische Strasse). Reservations recommended. Main courses: €16–€26 ($20–$32); lunch specials €12 ($15). AE, MC, V. Open: Daily 11:30 a.m. to midnight.*

Toto
$–$$ Charlottenburg   ITALIAN

Toto is a good place to sit outside on a warm Berlin afternoon and have a good, inexpensive lunch. The restaurant's interior, with wooden tables and benches, is nothing fancy. But the Italian chef knows his stuff. You can get a good plate of spaghetti or a good salad. The bean soup is filling. Fresh fish, available every Tuesday and Friday (market days), includes grilled salmon with butter and lemon and grilled crayfish cooked in olive oil. The menu includes a nice selection of Italian wines and aperitifs. The casual atmosphere makes Toto a good place to bring kids.

See map p. 126. Bleibtreustrasse 55. ☎ *030/312-5449. S-Bahn: Savignyplatz (then a 5-minute walk south on Bleibtreustrasse). Main courses: €8–€20 ($10–$25). No credit cards. Open: Daily noon to 2 a.m.*

Trattoria da Muntagnola
$–$$ Wilmersdorf   ITALIAN

This popular Italian place is casually rustic, with braids of garlic hanging from the beamed ceiling. The menu is huge and the cooking is reliable, not remarkable; however, the menu has several items that kids generally like. Some of the pastas are made on the premises. The lasagna is worth trying. All kinds of meat dishes and some good seafood (calamari and scampi grilled or cooked with radicchio and rosemary in white-wine sauce) round out the menu. The pizzas are good, too, particularly the Pizza della Mamma with bacon and Parma ham. *Note:* The restaurant can be a bit smoky.

Fuggerstrasse 27. ☎ *030/211-6642. U-Bahn: Nollendorfplatz (then a 5-minute walk west on Motzstrasse, north on Luther Strasse, and west on Fuggerstrasse). Reservations recommended. Main courses: €5–€20 ($6.25–$25). AE, DC, MC, V. Open: Daily 6 p.m. to midnight.*

Vau
$$$$ Mitte INTERNATIONAL

This sleek and unabashedly upscale gastronomic showcase, which opened near the Gendarmenmarkt in early 1997, has earned a Michelin star for its refined cooking. Vau is a very dress-up kind of place for a superfancy lunch or dinner with impeccable service. The menu choices are deftly prepared and can be surprisingly unfussy: venison with artichokes and mushrooms, roast duck breast with herbs and carrots, classic wiener schnitzel, and various fish choices. In this long, rather narrow room with an arched ceiling, everything is very precise, very modern, and very beautiful.

See map p. 129. Jägerstrasse 54–55. ☎ *030/202-9730. U-Bahn: Stadtmitte (then a 5-minute walk east across Gendarmenmarkt). Reservations required. Main courses: €18–€38 ($22–$47); fixed-price dinner €78–€115 ($97–$144). AE, DC, MC, V. Open: Mon–Sat noon to 2:30 p.m. and 7–11:30 p.m.*

Zur Letzten Instanz
$–$$ Mitte BERLINER

The former East Berlin now has several trendy new restaurants, but I still recommend this place, which happens to be Berlin's oldest restaurant, dating from 1525. The restaurant occupies two floors of a much-restored baroque building in the Nikolaiviertel (Nicholas Quarter), and the menu is as traditional and atmospheric as can be. Main courses include Old Berlin staples like grilled herring, meatballs, and braised lamb knuckles with green beans and dumplings. For dessert, try the chocolate-covered pancakes filled with blueberries, vanilla ice cream, and whipped cream.

See map p. 129. Waisenstrasse 14–16. ☎ *030/242-5528. U-Bahn: Klosterstrasse (then a 3-minute walk south on Waisenstrasse). Main courses: €9–€13 ($11–$16). AE, DC, MC, V. Open: Mon–Sat noon to 1 a.m., Sun noon to 11 p.m.*

Zur Nolle
$ Mitte GERMAN

A hundred years ago, Zur Nolle was a busy working-class beer hall. The place closed in 1968 (GDR years) but reopened in 1993, as a sign of post-reunification nostalgia for a bit of Old Berlin. The menu is unpretentious and the portions hearty. Try the jacket potatoes with herring, yogurt, apple, or onion fillings. Vegetarian offerings include vegetable lasagna and roasted broccoli with cheese served on pasta. For old time's sake, I recommend the homemade *Bulette* (meatballs), which come with a variety of sauces, spices, and additions (fried egg, bacon, onions, or mushrooms), or the roast bratwurst. Wash everything down with a cold, foamy *Bier von Fass* (beer from the tap).

See map p. 129. Beneath the arches of Friedrichstrasse S-Bahn station (S-Bahnbogen 30). ☎ *030/208-2655. U-/S-Bahn: Friedrichstrasse (then a 1-minute walk east along the street below the tracks). Main courses: €7–€10 ($8.75–$12). AE, DC, MC, V. Open: Mon–Sat 11:30 a.m. to midnight, Sun 11:30 a.m.–6 p.m.*

The best cafes

Berlin is a city filled with cafes. These are places to go for breakfast, a cup of coffee and a piece of *Kuchen* (cake), or a light meal or snack. The cafes likewise are bars, so you also can get a beer or a glass of wine. Bleibtreustrasse (U-Bahn: Savignyplatz), between Savignyplatz and the Ku-Damm, is particularly rich in cafes.

✔ **Café Aedes,** Rosenthaler Strasse 40–41 (see map p. 129; ☎ **030/285-8278;** U-Bahn: Weinmeisterstrasse), is trendy, convivial, and very hip. The menu usually has dishes like tortellini with cheese sauce, soups, and vegetarian salads. Meals range from €7 to €9 ($8.75 to $11). The cafe is open daily from 10 a.m. to midnight.

✔ **Café/Bistro Leysieffer,** Kurfürstendamm 218 (see map p. 126; ☎ **030/885-7480;** U-Bahn: Kurfürstendamm), has a pastry and candy shop at street level; upstairs, you find an old-fashioned cafe with a balcony overlooking the busy Ku-Damm. This place is a good one for having an elegant breakfast or light lunch. Meals range from €10 to €16 ($12 to $20). The cafe is open daily from 10 a.m. to 7 p.m.

✔ **Café Silberstein,** Oranienburger Strasse 27 (see map p. 129; ☎ **030/281-2095;** S-Bahn: Oranienburger Tor), is one of the best places to see the "new" eastern Berlin in all its up-to-the-nanosecond trendiness. The cafe is housed in a long, tall, narrow room with original 1920s wall paintings and modern furniture. On the menu, you find sushi, salads, miso soup with noodles, and an all-day breakfast. A meal costs around €7 ($8.75). The cafe is open Monday to Friday from 10 a.m. to 4 a.m., Saturday and Sunday from 10 a.m. to 5 a.m.

✔ **Cafe Wintergarten in Literaturhaus Berlin,** Fasanenstrasse 23 (see map p. 126; ☎ **030/882-5414;** U-Bahn: Hohenzollernplatz), occupies two modern-looking rooms in a 19th-century villa one block south of the Ku-Damm. The menu includes pastas, soups, salads, and vegetarian curries. Main courses range from €7 to €18 ($8.75 to $22). The cafe is open daily from 9:30 a.m. to 1 a.m.

Chapter 12

Exploring Berlin

In This Chapter

▶ Visiting Berlin's top attractions

▶ Choosing a tour that's right for you

▶ Finding the hot shopping spots

▶ Discovering Berlin's performing arts and nightlife

▶ Taking a side trip to Potsdam and Sanssouci Palace

*B*erlin overflows with sightseeing options and diversions. The city is particularly rich in museums, although you also find picturesque parks and lakes, famous avenues, and historic architecture. Plus, thanks to rebuilding in Potsdamer Platz and portions of eastern Berlin, this city has more new buildings than any other city in the world.

Sightseeing in Berlin

Where do you begin? Do want to spend all your time in Berlin's fabulous museums? Saunter and shop your way down famous avenues like Unter den Linden or the Ku-Damm? See historic buildings like the Reichstag? Check out the "new" Berlin at Potsdamer Platz? You have to make some decisions because the possibilities for sightseeing in Berlin are almost endless. The places described in this section are my roster of the most important Berlin attractions. For locations, see the "Tiergarten-Area Attractions," "Charlottenburg Attractions," and "Berlin-Mitte Attractions" maps in this chapter. *Note:* The ages for children's tickets always are 6 to 14, except where otherwise indicated below. In addition, kids younger than 6 generally get in for free.

Remember: Nearly all Berlin museums are **closed Mondays** throughout the year. They're also closed January 1; December 24, 25, and 31; and the Tuesday after Easter.

Saving money with a museum pass

SchauLUST Museen Berlin is a money-saving three-day museum pass that gets you into 50 top Berlin museums and collections for €12 ($15) adults, €6 ($7.50) seniors and children. The pass gains you admittance into all the museums described in the next section, "Discovering the top attractions from A to Z." You can purchase the SchauLUST museum pass at the three Berlin Tourist Info Centers (Europa Center, Brandenburg Gate, Television Tower; for addresses, see Chapter 11).

An admission ticket purchased at any one of the state museums is good for the rest of the day at any of the other state museums operated by **Staatliche Museen zu Berlin.** Included within this group are museums on Museum Island in Berlin Mitte, in the Kulturforum, and at Charlottenburg Palace.

Discovering the top attractions from A to Z

Ägyptisches Museum (Egyptian Museum)
Charlottenburg

The greatest treasure of the Egyptian Museum is the famous and fabulous **bust of Queen Nefertiti,** dating from around 1350 B.C. The piece occupies a small room of its own and is worth a trip to the museum. Other collection highlights include the small, expressive head of Queen Tiy, the world-famous head of a priest in green stone, and the monumental Kalabasha Gateway, built by Emperor Augustus around 30 B.C. If you're interested in Egyptian antiquities, you'll find enough here to make you linger for at least an hour.

See map p. 145. Schlossstrasse 70. ☎ *030/3435-7311. U-Bahn: Sophie-Charlotte-Platz (then a 5-minute walk north on Schlossstrasse). Admission: €6 ($7.50) adults, €3 ($3.75) children. Open: Daily 10 a.m.–6 p.m.*

Alte Nationalgalerie (Old National Gallery)
Museum Island, Mitte

Behind the Altes Museum is the Alte Nationalgalerie, which looks like a Corinthian temple and contains a collection of 19th-century painting and sculpture, including works by van Gogh, Manet, Monet, Renoir, and Cézanne. Give yourself at least an hour just for the highlights of this rich collection. A free audio tour in English is available.

See map p. 147. Bodestrasse 1–3. ☎ *030/2090-5801. U-/S-Bahn: Friedrichstrasse (then a 5-minute walk east on Georgenstrasse to Museum Island). Admission: €8 ($10) adults, €4 ($5) children. Open: Tues–Sun 10 a.m.–6 p.m. (Thurs until 10 p.m.).*

Berlin Wall
Mitte

The Wall that separated Berlin and Germany from 1961 to 1989 is no more, but the fragments that remain are grimly essential pieces of Berlin's history. By 1990, most of the concrete barrier that divided this city into two political entities had been razed. Only two portions of the Wall (*Mauer* in German, pronounced *Mao*-er) are left.

The **East Side Gallery** is a half-mile-long section on Mühlenstrasse on the banks of the Spree River in the former East Berlin. An international group of artists painted murals on this section in 1990.

The other remaining section of the Wall, known as the **Gedenkstätte und Dokumentationzentrum Berliner Mauer (Berlin Wall Memorial and Documentation Center)** lies between Bernauer Strasse and Invalidenstrasse. The 70km-long (230-ft.) memorial consists of two walls that include fragments of the original wall (much of which was bulldozed away or carried off by souvenir hunters), a chapel of reconciliation, and a documentation center with photographs and a history of the Wall. The mirrorlike stainless steel surfaces of the memorial have slits through which visitors can peer. A plaque reads: "In memory of the division of the city from 13 August 1961 to 9 November 1989." This place is the only one in Berlin where you still can see a complete border area.

See map p. 147. East Side Gallery: Mühlenstrasse along the Spree River; U-/S-Bahn: Warschauer Strasse. Gedenkstätte Berliner Mauer: between Bernauer Strasse and Invalidenstrasse; U-Bahn: Bernauer Strasse.

Touring by neighborhood

You can save a lot of time by clustering your museum and other sightseeing visits geographically. The main museum areas in Berlin are as follows:

✔ **Charlottenburg:** Across from Charlottenburg Palace are three museums worth visiting: The Ägyptisches Museum (with the famous bust of Nefertiti), the Sammlung Bergruen (with Picassos), and the Bröhan Museum (with Art Nouveau and Art Deco furniture). Charlottenburg Palace also has museums, which you can visit before or after a guided palace tour, and historic buildings in the palace gardens.

✔ **Tiergarten:** In or near the Tiergarten, Berlin's great city park, you find the Bauhaus-Archiv, the Hamburger Bahnhof Museum für Gegenwart (with contemporary art), and the Reichstag (House of Parliament). On the eastern edge of the Tiergarten, close to Potsdamer Platz, is a group of buildings known as the Kulturforum (Culture Forum), home to the Gemäldegalerie (Painting Gallery), the Neue Nationalgalerie (with 20th-century art), and the Kunstgewerbe (with applied and decorative arts). The Kulturforum area is within walking distance of Potsdamer Platz, the newest area of Berlin, where you find the new Filmmuseum Berlin.

✔ **Museum Island (Museumsinsel):** Museum Island in eastern Berlin has four of the city's oldest museums, but only two of them currently are open. They include the Altes Museum (closed for renovation), the Alte Nationalgalerie (with 19th-century art), the Pergamon Museum (with the Pergamon altar and Middle Eastern antiquities), and the Bode Museum (closed until 2006). In this same vicinity, you can visit the Brandenburg Gate; Unter den Linden, a grand boulevard; Gendarmenmarkt, a baroque square; and the Nikolaiviertel (Nicholas Quarter), a restored historic neighborhood.

Tiergarten-Area Attractions

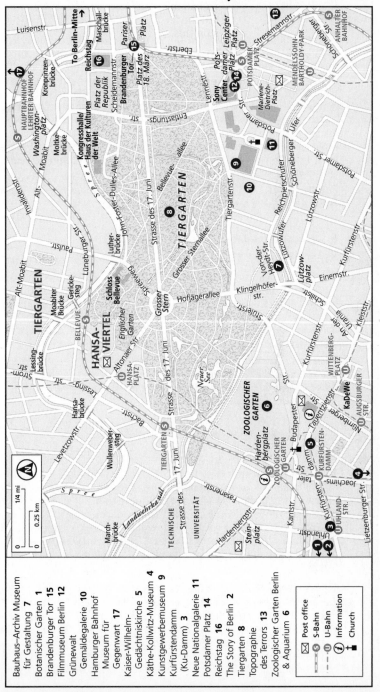

Bauhaus-Archiv Museum
für Gestaltung 7
Botanischer Garten 1
Brandenburger Tor 15
Filmmuseum Berlin 12
Grünewalt
Gemäldegalerie 10
Hamburger Bahnhof
Museum für
Gegenwart 17
Kaiser-Wilhelm-
Gedächtniskirche 5
Käthe-Kollwitz-Museum 4
Kunstgewerbemuseum 9
Kurfürstendamm
(Ku-Damm) 3
Neue Nationalgalerie 11
Potsdamer Platz 14
Reichstag 16
The Story of Berlin 2
Tiergarten 8
Topographie
des Terrors 13
Zoologischer Garten Berlin
& Aquarium 6

⊠ Post office
S S-Bahn
U U-Bahn
i Information
✝ ■ Church

Brandenburger Tor (Brandenburg Gate)
Mitte

If you watched the televised fall of the Communist German Democratic Republic (GDR) in 1989, you saw this historic monument, one of Berlin's most potent symbols, in every news clip. When the Wall came down, hundreds of thousands of East Germans walked freely through the gate into West Berlin for the first time since 1961. A neoclassical triumphal arch completed in 1791, the gate is crowned by the famous **Quadriga,** a four-horse copper chariot drawn by the goddess Victoria. The revolutionary events of 1848 and 1918, such as those in 1989, saw the gate used as a symbolic gathering place. In the Room of Silence (open daily 11 a.m.–6 p.m.), built into one of the guardhouses, visitors still gather to meditate and reflect on Germany's past.

See map p. 143. Pariser Platz. U-/S-Bahn: Unter den Linden (you see the gate to the west). Admission: Free.

Grünewalt Gemäldegalerie (Painting Gallery)
Kulturforum, Tiergarten

The Gemäldegalerie houses Berlin's greatest collection of European painting, with an emphasis on medieval German and Dutch art and 16th-century Italian and 17th-century Dutch painting. Several Italian masterpieces are on display, including Raphael's *Virgin and Child with the Infant St. John* and Bronzino's *Portrait of Ugolino Martelli.* The gallery contains one of the world's largest collections of Rembrandts.

See map p. 143. Matthäiskirchplatz. ☎ 030/2090-5555. U-/S-Bahn: Potsdamer Platz (then a 5-minute walk west on Potsdamer Strasse and Margaretenstrasse). Admission: €6 ($7.50) adults, €3 ($3.75) children; free Thurs 6–10 p.m. Open: Tues–Sun 10 a.m.–6 p.m. (Thurs until 10 p.m.).

Gendarmenmarkt
Mitte

Twin churches inspired by Rome's Piazza del Popolo flank this monumentally graceful baroque square — one of the most beautiful architectural ensembles in Berlin. Looking at the square today, it's hard to imagine that by the end of World War II (WWII), the Gendarmenmarkt had been reduced to a pile of smoldering rubble and remained in ruins until 1977, when East Berlin finally began its reconstruction. The square was named for the Gens d'Armes regiment, which had its guardhouse and stables here from 1738 to 1782.

The centerpiece of the square is Friedrich Schinkel's beautiful neoclassical **Schauspielhaus,** or theater (now also called the Konzerthaus, or Concert House), completed in 1821. On the north side of the square is the **Französicher Dom** (French Cathedral; ☎ 030/229-1760; open daily 9 a.m.–7 p.m.), built for the influx of French Huguenots (Protestants) who settled in Berlin after being forced to flee Catholic France in 1685. Facing this church like a mirror image on the south side is the **Deutscher Dom** (German

Charlottenburg Attractions

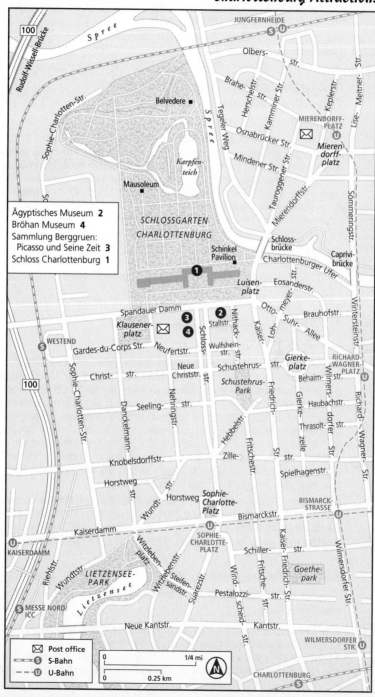

Ägyptisches Museum **2**
Bröhan Museum **4**
Sammlung Berggruen:
 Picasso und Seine Zeit **3**
Schloss Charlottenburg **1**

Post office
S-Bahn
U-Bahn

0   1/4 mi
0   0.25 km

Cathedral; ☎ 030/202-2690; open Tues–Sun 10 a.m.–6 p.m.). Surrounding the square is a bevy of chic new restaurants. *See map p. 147. U-Bahn: Französische Strasse (then a 2-minute walk east on Taubenstrasse).*

Hamburger Bahnhof Museum für Gegenwart (Museum of Contemporary Art)
Tiergarten

This showcase of contemporary art opened in 1996 in the 19th-century Hamburger Bahnhof, the oldest train station in Berlin. The building still retains traces of its former use, including the high roof designed for steam engines. The modern art on display dates from the second half of the 20th century and includes everything from Andy Warhol's now legendary *Mao* to an audio-visual Joseph Beuys archive. You also find a major collection of works by Cy Twombly, Robert Rauschenberg, and Roy Lichtenstein together with changing exhibitions. You can see everything in about an hour. *See map p. 143. Invalidenstrasse 50–51. ☎ 030/397-8342. S-Bahn: Lehrter Stadtbahnhof (then a 3-minute walk northeast on Invalidenstrasse). Admission: €6 ($7.50) adults, €3 ($3.75) children; free Thurs 2–6 p.m. Open: Tues–Fri 10 a.m.–6 p.m., Sat–Sun 11 a.m.– 6 p.m.*

Jüdisches Museum (Jewish Museum)
Kreuzberg

One of the newest and most talked-about museums in Europe is located in Kreuzberg, just south of Berlin-Mitte. Designed by American architect Daniel Libeskind, now the masterplan architect for the World Trade Center site in New York City, the building is shaped like a stretched-out Star of David and houses Europe's largest Jewish museum. Items on display include ceremonial objects, portraits of prominent Jewish figures, historical objects, works of Jewish artists, documents, photos, and memorabilia. You follow a chronological pathway occasionally interrupted by deliberately disorienting memorial spaces. This museum has plenty to see. I recommend that you give yourself at least three hours. *See map p. 147. Lindenstrasse 9–14. ☎ 030/2599-3300. U-Bahn: Hallesches Tor (then a 5-minute walk east on Gitschiner Strasse and north on Lindenstrasse). Admission: €5 ($6.25) adults, €2.50 ($3.75) students and children, €10 ($13) family ticket (2 adults, 2 children). Open: Daily 10 a.m.–8 p.m. (Mon until 10 p.m.). Closed on Jewish holy days.*

Kaiser-Wilhelm-Gedächtniskirche (Emperor William Memorial Church)
Charlottenburg

One of Berlin's most famous landmarks, the Gedächtniskirche (Memorial Church) is a ponderous neo-Romanesque structure from the late 19th century. Built to commemorate the 1871 establishment of the German Empire, the church later was blasted by a bomb in WWII, and the ruined shell was

Berlin-Mitte Attractions

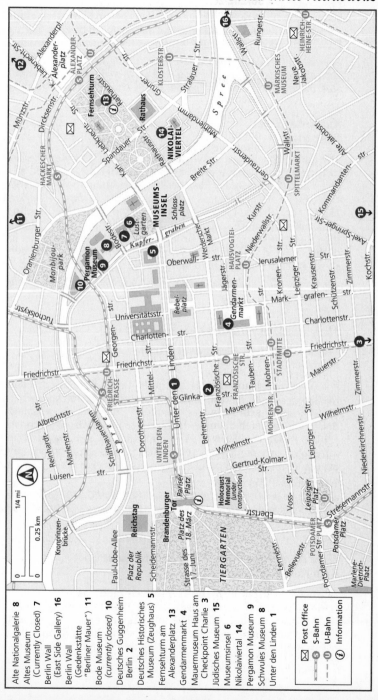

Alte Nationalgalerie **8**
Altes Museum
(Currently Closed) **7**
Berlin Wall
(East Side Gallery) **16**
Berlin Wall
(Gedenkstätte
"Berliner Mauer") **11**
Bode Museum
(currently closed) **10**
Deutsches Guggenheim
Berlin **2**
Deutsches Historisches
Museum (Zeughaus) **5**
Fernsehturm am
Alexanderplatz **13**
Gendarmenmarkt **4**
Mauermuseum Haus am
Checkpoint Charlie **3**
Jüdisches Museum **15**
Museumsinsel **6**
Nikolaiviertel **14**
Pergamon Museum **9**
Schwules Museum **8**
Unter den Linden **1**

⊠ Post Office
Ⓢ S-Bahn
Ⓤ U-Bahn
ⓘ Information

preserved as a symbol of the ravages of war. You probably won't want to spend more than a few minutes inside. The small modern church beside the Gedächtniskirche is an octagonal hall designed by Egon Eierman in 1961. Free organ concerts take place there every Saturday year-round at 6 p.m.

See map on p. 143. Kurfürstendamm at Breitscheidplatz. ☎ *030/218-5023. U-/S-Bahn: Zoologischer Garten (then a 5-minute walk south on Budapester Strasse). Admission: Free. Open: Memorial church Mon–Sat 10 a.m.–4 p.m.; new church daily 9 a.m.–7 p.m.*

Kurfürstendamm
Tiergarten

The famous boulevard known as the Ku-Damm is western Berlin's answer to Paris's Champs-Elysées. For years the Ku-Damm hogged all the city's glamour because dreary East Berlin had nothing to rival it. Today's busy commercial artery began as nothing more than a humble log road, built in 1542 for the Prince-Electors *(Kurfürsten)* to reach their hunting lodge in the Grünewald more easily. From the start of the 20th century until WWII, the Ku-Damm was the most brilliant, lively, and elegant street in this part of Berlin, filled with legendary cafes and renowned for its nightlife. The street still is a good place to shop, stroll, sit, and people-watch.

See map p. 143. U-Bahn: Kurfürstendamm (you on are the Ku-Damm when you exit the station).

Mauermuseum Haus am Checkpoint Charlie (Wall Museum at Checkpoint Charlie)
Kreuzberg

If you're interested in the history of the Berlin Wall, this small museum in Kreuzberg is well worth an hour of your time. Located near what once was Checkpoint Charlie, the most frequently used traffic crossing into East Berlin, the museum documents the Wall's history from its construction in 1961 to its fall in 1989–1990. The photographs, newspaper clippings, and attempted escape devices (chairlifts, false passports, hot-air balloons, even a minisub) used by East Germans may give you a new take on the meaning of freedom.

See map on p. 147. Friedrichstrasse 43–45. ☎ *030/253-7250. U-Bahn: Kochstrasse (then a 5-minute walk north on Friedrichstrasse). Admission: €9 ($11.25) adults, €4.50 ($5.75) children and students. Open: Daily 9 a.m.–10 p.m.*

Neue Nationalgalerie (New National Gallery)
Kulturforum, Tiergarten

The only old structure in the aggressively modern Kulturforum complex is the New National Gallery, designed in 1968 by famed German architect Ludwig Mies van der Rohe. The museum, an enormous expanse of glass windows and simple symmetry, contains a small but impressive collection of international 20th-century painting and sculpture, including works by de Chirico, Dalí, Miró, Mark Rothko, and Frank Stella. Of special interest are the paintings by early- to mid-20th-century German artists Max Beckmann, Max Ernst, and Otto Dix, and two bitter and brilliant oils by George Grosz that capture the decadent despair of the Weimar years in the 1920s. The gallery also is used for special traveling exhibitions.

See map on p. 143. Potsdamer Strasse 50. ☎ *030/266-2951. U-/S-Bahn: Potsdamer Platz (then a 5-minute walk south on Potsdamer Strasse). Admission: €6 ($7.50) adults, €3 ($3.75) children and students; free Thurs 6–10 p.m. Open: Tues–Fri 10 a.m.–6 p.m. (Thurs until 10 p.m.), Sat–Sun 11 a.m.–6 p.m.*

Pergamon Museum
Museum Island, Mitte

Of all the museums on Museum Island, the renowned Pergamon Museum is the one must-see. And what you must see is the **Pergamon Altar,** considered one of the Seven Wonders of the ancient world and still holding its own today. Part of the enormous Temple of Zeus and Athena, dating from 180 to 160 B.C., the altar was discovered in 1876 in western Turkey. Another showpiece is the ornate two-storied Market Gate of Miletus, a Roman building facade from the time of Emperor Marcus Aurelius (around A.D. 165).

The **Near East Museum** in the museum's south wing contains one of the largest collections anywhere of antiquities from ancient Babylonia, Persia, and Assyria.

See map p. 147. Am Kupfergraben. ☎ *030/2090-5577. U-/S-Bahn: Friedrichstrasse (then a 5-minute walk east on Georgenstrasse to the Museum Island). Admission: €8 ($10) adults, €4 ($5) students and children; free admission 1st Sun of each month. Open: Tues–Sun 10 a.m.–6 p.m. (Thurs until 10 p.m.).*

Potsdamer Platz
Tiergarten

Before WWII, Potsdamer Platz was the busiest spot in Berlin. In 1961, the square was cut off from the western sector by the Wall and became an ugly strip of mined no-man's-land. After reunification, corporations like Sony and Mercedes-Benz rushed in and bought the entire area. Today, Potsdamer Platz is a brand-new, supermodern showcase of corporate glitz, government offices, upscale housing, and entertainment. To experience the area, stroll along The Potsdamer Platz Arcades, where 140 stores, restaurants, and cafes invite you to shop and relax. One of the most visited attractions is the **Sony Center am Potsdamer Platz** (☎ 030/2094-5400), which has two movie theaters and a viewing area from which you can look out over the Philharmonie, the Kulturforum, and the Tiergarten. Around newly created **Marlene-Dietrich-Platz,** you find the Berlin IMAX-Theater, the Stella Musical-Theater, the Grand Hyatt Hotel, the Madison City Suites, the Berlin Casino, and the Cine-Max cinema center.

See map p. 143. U-Bahn: Potsdamer Platz (you are on Potsdamer Platz as you exit the station).

Reichstag (House of Parliament)
Tiergarten

The Reichstag is the seat of the reunified German Parliament. Built in a pompous high-Renaissance style between 1884 and 1894, the building was partially destroyed by a fire in 1933 that probably was set by the Nazis, who, blaming the fire on the Communists, used the incident as an opportunity to seize power. Allied bombs destroyed part of the Reichstag in WWII. Today, a new glass dome designed by British architect Sir Norman Foster crowns the building. After a security check, you take an elevator up to the dome, where a sweeping vista of Berlin opens out before you. The dome also has an outdoor observation area and a rooftop restaurant with so-so food (reservations ☎ 030/226-2990). I recommend that you arrive as early as possible; otherwise, you may have to stand in line for up to three hours before getting in.

See map p. 143. Platz der Republik. ☎ 030/2273-2131. U-/S-Bahn: Friedrichstrasse (then a 5-minute walk west along the Reichstagufer, the street that follows the river). Admission: Free. Open: Dome daily 8 a.m.–10 p.m.

Schloss Charlottenburg (Charlottenburg Palace)
Charlottenburg

The oldest section of this lovely, yellow baroque palace was built in 1695 as a breezy summer abode for Sophie Charlotte, the wife of Friedrich I. Its present form dates from 1790. Much of the palace was destroyed in WWII and painstakingly reconstructed.

You can see the palace only on a tour, and to take that tour you have to don huge felt slippers (so you're effectively polishing the wood floors as you slide around after the guide). The tour is given only in German (you can buy an English-language guidebook at the ticket counter) and includes the **historical rooms,** the living quarters of Friedrich I and Sophie Charlotte, the eye-catching **porcelain room,** and the **royal chapel.** With a combined ticket, you can, on your own, additionally visit the **Galerie der Romantik,** with its fine collection of paintings from the neoclassical, Romantic, and Biedermeier periods, and the beautifully landscaped **Schlossgarten** (palace gardens). In the Schlossgarten, you find the charming **Schinkel Pavilion,** an Italianate summer house designed by Karl Friedrich Schinkel, the leading architect of the day, in 1825. At the far end of the Schlossgarten, close to the Spree River, is the **Belvedere.** This former royal teahouse contains exquisite Berlin porcelain, much of it from the 1700s. To see the palace and museums, you need at least four to five hours.

The **Museum für Vor- und Frühgeschichte** (Museum of Prehistory and Early History), in the Langhansbau wing, displays the famous Schliemann collection of antiquities from Troy. You must pay a separate admission of €6 ($7.50) adults, €3 ($3.75) children for this museum, which is open Tuesday through Friday from 9 a.m. to 5 p.m., and Saturday and Sunday from 10 a.m. to 5 p.m.

See map p. 145. Luisenplatz. ☎ *0331/969-4202. U-Bahn: Sophie-Charlotte-Platz (then a 5-minute walk north on Schlossstrasse). Admission: Combination ticket for historical rooms, Galerie der Romantik, and Schlossgarten €8 ($10) adults, €5 ($6.25) children. Open: Palace and museums Tues–Fri 9 a.m.–5 p.m.; Sat–Sun 10 a.m.–5 p.m. (last tour at 4 p.m.).*

Tiergarten
Tiergarten

The popular Tiergarten (literally, "animal garden") covers almost 2.5 sq. km (1 sq. mile) and is the most popular green space in central Berlin. Tiergarten also is the name of Berlin's smallest neighborhood. With its lawns, canals, leafy trees, and more than 23km (14 miles) of meandering paths, the Tiergarten park is a great place to stroll and relax. The Tiergarten originally was laid out by Peter Josef Lenné, one of the great landscape architects of the early 19th century, as a private park for the electors of Prussia. The park was devastated during and just after WWII, when desperate citizens chopped down the trees for fuel. Beginning in 1955, trees were replanted and walkways, ponds, and flower beds restored to their original patterns. The Berlin Zoo, which is described in the "Zoologischer Garten Berlin & Aquarium (Berlin Zoo-Aquarium)" section later in this chapter, occupies the park's southwestern corner. In the northwestern corner, you find the Hansaviertel (Hansa Quarter), a residential area where architects were invited to build projects in the 1950s, and pretty **Schloss (Palace) Bellevue** (S-Bahn: Bellevue), the residence of Germany's president. If you just want to stroll, give yourself a couple of hours.

The **Siegessäule** (Victory Column), a golden goddess of victory perched high atop a red-granite pedestal, is the most famous of the Tiergarten's many monuments. The column stands in the center of the Strasse des 17 Juni, a wide boulevard that bisects the Tiergarten and is the western extension of Unter den Linden. The column's 48m-high (157-ft.) observation platform, reached by climbing up a 290-step spiral staircase, is open daily from 9:30 a.m. to 6:30 p.m. Admission is €1 ($1.25) for adults, free for children younger than 12.

See map p. 143. Bounded on the west by Bahnhof Zoo and the Europa Center, on the east by Berlin-Mitte, the Brandenburg Gate, and Potsdamer Platz. U-Bahn: Zoologischer Garten or Hansaplatz. S-Bahn: Tiergarten or Bellevue. Bus: 100.

Unter den Linden
Mitte

Laid out in 1647 and extending a bit more than a kilometer (¾ mile) east from the Brandenburg Gate, Unter den Linden is one of Berlin's most famous and historically significant streets. The name, which means "under the lindens," came from the linden trees that were originally planted along the street. This boulevard is the oldest and royalest in central Berlin, with several monumental buildings from the 18th and 19th centuries.

Museumsinsel (Museum Island): Art by decree

Four museums on an island in the River Spree form the oldest museum complex in Berlin and are listed as a UNESCO World Heritage Site. UNESCO is the United Nations Educational, Scientific and Cultural Organization. The buildings, some dating back to the early and mid 19th century, were constructed after Frederick William III issued a decree stipulating that the privately owned artwork of the royal family needed to be made accessible to the public. The museums were the main attractions in old East Berlin. After reunification, a complicated process of restoring the buildings and reuniting various collections from the East and West began. The domed neo-baroque **Bode Museum** at the far northern end of the island and the **Altes Museum** with its antiquities collection will be closed until 2006, so I don't include them in this guide, but you can visit the other two museums on Museum Island: the Alte Nationalgalerie and the Pergamon Museum.

Friedrich Schinkel's 1818 **Neue Wache** (New Watch) served as headquarters for the King's Guard and now contains the Tomb of the Unknown Soldier and the Tomb of the Unknown Resistance Fighter. The **Zeughaus** (Armory), Berlin's largest baroque building and the first (1706) major building to be constructed on Unter den Linden, houses the Deutsches Museum (see the later section on "Finding more cool things to see and do"). The giant **Berliner Dom** (Berlin Cathedral; Lustgarten; open daily 9 a.m. to 8 p.m.) squats at the end of Unter den Linden.

See map p. 147. U-/S-Bahn: Unter den Linden (you are on the avenue as you exit the station).

Zoologischer Garten Berlin & Aquarium (Berlin Zoo-Aquarium)
Tiergarten

Founded in 1844, Germany's oldest and Europe's largest zoo occupies almost the entire southwest corner of the Tiergarten. More than 13,000 animals live here, many of them in open habitats. The most popular residents are the giant pandas. The zoo also has a modern aviary, with more than 550 species of birds. The aquarium is home to more than 9,000 fish, reptiles, amphibians, insects, and other creatures. The hippoquarium is a new attraction. With kids in tow you can easily spend half a day in the zoo and aquarium.

See map p. 143. Hardenbergplatz 8. ☎ 030/254-010. U-/S-Bahn: Zoologischer Garten (the entrance is a 3-minute walk east on Budapester Strasse). Admission: Zoo €10 ($12.50) adults, €5 ($6.25) children; aquarium €10 ($10.25) adults, €5 ($6.25) children; combined ticket €15 ($19) adults, €7.50 ($9.50) children. Open: Zoo Apr–Oct daily 9 a.m.–6:30 p.m.; Nov–Mar daily 9 a.m.–5 p.m.; aquarium year-round daily 9 a.m.–6 p.m.

Finding more cool things to see and do

✔ The **Bauhaus–Archiv Museum für Gestaltung** (Bauhaus Design Museum), Klingelhöferstrasse 14 (☎ 030/254-0020; U-Bahn: Nollendorfplatz), is dedicated to the Bauhaus school, which sought to combine art, design, and technology. The Bauhaus was founded in 1919 at Weimar, moved to Dessau, and finally settled in Berlin, before the Nazis forced the school to disband in 1933. The museum, completed in 1979, is one of the last works of the great Berlin-born architect Walter Gropius. English-language texts describing the exhibits are available. You need at least an hour to peruse the exhibits. The museum, near the Tiergarten, is open Wednesday through Monday from 10 a.m. to 5 p.m. Admission is €4 ($5) adults, €2 ($2.50) children younger than 12.

✔ Berlin's **Botanischer Garten** (Botanical Garden), Königin-Luise-Strasse 6–8 (☎ 030/8385-0100; S-Bahn: Botanischer Garten; U-Bahn: Dahlem–Dorf), located near the Dahlem Museums on the outskirts of Berlin, contains vast collections of European and exotic plants. The Palm House is one of the largest in the world. You also find an extensive arboretum and several special collections, including a garden for blind visitors and another with water plants. A small botanical museum (open daily 10 a.m. to 6 p.m), of more interest to dedicated gardeners than the general public, is also on the premises. Give yourself an hour or so to stroll through the garden itself. Admission is €5 ($6.25) for adults, €2.50 ($3) for children. The garden is open daily April through August from 9 a.m. to 8 p.m.; September through March, the garden opens at 9 a.m. and closes at dusk.

✔ The **Bröhan Museum**, Schlossstrasse 1A (☎ 030/3269-0600; U-Bahn: Sophie-Charlotte-Platz), houses one of the world's finest collections of Jugendstil (Art Nouveau) and Art Deco furniture, painting, sculpture, glass, silverware, and crafts, all from 1889 to 1939. A must-see is the **Suite Emile-Jacques Ruhlman,** a completely decorated set of rooms from a luxurious private residence of the 1920s and 1930s. The museum is small enough that you can see everything in an hour. Admission is €4 ($5); free for children 11 and younger. Hours are Tuesday through Sunday 10 a.m. to 6 p.m.

✔ The **Fernsehturm am Alexanderplatz** (Television Tower), Panoramastrasse 1a, Alexanderplatz (☎ 030/242-3333; U-/S-Bahn: Alexanderplatz), is a weird-looking television tower built by the Communists back in the 1960s. Berliners call it "the onion" because of its shape. An elevator whisks you up to the top for a stunning panorama. You find a revolving restaurant up there, too. The tower is open daily March through October from 9 a.m. to 1 a.m., and daily November through February from 10 a.m. to midnight. The elevator to the top costs €6 ($7.50) for adults and €2.50 ($3) for children.

✔ The **Filmmuseum Berlin,** Sony Center in Potsdamerstrasse 2 (☎ 030/300-9030; U-/S-Bahn: Potsdamer Platz), appeals to anyone who has an interest in German film or film in general. The entire history of German cinema is documented in rare film clips from the silent era up to the present. One wing is devoted to the legendary Marlene Dietrich, a native Berliner who catapulted to international fame in 1930 in Josef von Sternberg's *Der Blaue Engel (The Blue Angel)* and went on to become Germany's only major star in Hollywood. The fascinating Marlene memorabilia includes photos, costumes, props, letters, and documents. You need at least an hour here. Admission is €6 ($7.50) for adults, and €4 ($5) for students, children, and senior citizens. The museum is open Tuesday through Sunday from 10 a.m. to 6 p.m. (Thursday until 8 p.m.).

✔ The **Grünewald** (S-Bahn: Grünewald), a 39 sq. km (15 sq. mile) forest that begins just beyond the western edge of the Kurfürstendamm, is Berlin's largest uninterrupted wooded area. From Heerstrasse, the forest stretches some 10km (6 miles) south to the popular **Wannsee** lake. Havelchausee, the forest's western border, winds past several picturesque bays and beaches along the Havel River, while the eastern border is roughly marked off by four lakes: **Schlachtensee, Krumme Lanke, Grünewaldsee,** and **Schildhorn.** Loaded with wooded paths and sandy beaches, the Grünewald (Green Forest) is a good place to get away from the urban jungle, although on weekends you have plenty of company.

✔ The **Käthe-Kollwitz-Museum,** Fasanenstrasse 24 (☎ 030/882-5210; U-Bahn: Uhlandstrasse), is devoted to the powerful works of Berlin-born artist Käthe Kollwitz (1867–1945). The first woman ever elected to the Prussian Academy of the Arts, Kollwitz resigned her position in 1933 to protest Hitler's rise to power. The Nazis later banned her works. Many of Kollwitz's works express the sorrow, loss, and deprivations of wartime and have a stark, grieving quality. The lower floors of the museum display woodcuts and lithographs; the upper floors contain sculptures. Admission is €5 ($6.25) for adults, €3 ($3.75) for children and students. The museum is open Wednesday through Monday from 11 a.m. to 6 p.m.

✔ **Kunstgewerbemuseum** (Arts and Crafts Museum), Matthäiskirchplatz, Kulturforum (☎ 030/2090-5555; U-/S-Bahn: Mendelssohn–Bartholdy–Park), opposite the Philharmonie in the Kulturforum, displays applied arts and crafts from the Middle Ages through the present day. The Guelph Treasure, its most dazzling exhibit, is a collection of medieval church articles in gold and silver. The basement rooms display contemporary design from the German Bauhaus school to American Charles Eames and the Memphis design group. You also find a nice cafeteria, open from 10 a.m. to 4:30 p.m. Admission is €6 ($7.50) for adults, €3 ($3.75) for children. The museum is open Tuesday through Friday from 10 a.m. to 6 p.m., Saturday and Sunday 11 a.m. to 6 p.m.

✔ **Nikolaiviertel** (Nicholas Quarter; U-Bahn: Klosterstrasse), not far from the Gendarmenmarkt in Berlin Mitte, is a historic riverside quarter restored to resemble its medieval and baroque heyday (with a few modern design touches). Reconstructed palaces, period taverns, and old churches make this quarter ideal for a leisurely and picturesque ramble along the Spree River, down narrow streets illuminated by gas lanterns. Named for Berlin's oldest church, the Nikolaikirche (Church of St. Nicholas; Nikolaikirchplatz; ☎ 030/ 2472-4529; open Tues–Sun 10 a.m.–6 p.m.), the quarter was the last major reconstruction project of the German Democratic Party that ruled former East Germany; the church was restored in time for the city's 750th anniversary in 1987.

✔ **Sammlung Berggruen: Picasso und Seine Zeit** (Berggruen Collection: Picasso and His Times), Schlossstrasse 1 (☎ 030/3269-5819; U-Bahn: Sophie-Charlotte-Platz), a small museum located across from the Egyptian Museum in Charlottenburg, showcases several important paintings by Picasso and works by Klee, Matisse, Braque, and Giacometti. You can see the collection in about half an hour. Admission is €6 ($7.50) for adults, and €3 ($3.75) for students and children. The museum is open Tuesday through Sunday from 10 a.m. to 6 p.m.

✔ **The Story of Berlin,** Ku'damm-Karree, Kurfürstendamm 207–208 (☎ 030/8872-0100; U-Bahn: Uhlandstrasse), is an enjoyable multimedia museum that uses films, photos, sounds, and colorful displays to tell about eight centuries of life in Berlin. Beginning with the city's founding in 1237, the themed exhibits chronicle all the major historical events, including the reign of Frederick the Great, the Industrial Revolution, the Golden 1920s, WWII and its aftermath, divided Berlin during the Cold War, and the fall of the Wall. At the end of the tour, a guide takes you down to visit an underground nuclear bomb shelter built in the 1970s. Allow at least two hours to see everything. This attraction is a good overall introduction to Berlin that teens may enjoy. Admission is €9.30 ($12) for adults, € 7.50 ($9) for students, €3.50 ($4.50) for children, and €21 ($26) for families (2 adults, 2 children). The museum is open daily from 10 a.m. to 8 p.m. (last admission 6 p.m.).

✔ **Topographie des Terrors** (Topography of Terror), Niederkirchnerstrasse 8 (☎ 030/2548-6703; U-/S-Bahn: Potsdamer Platz), located in what once was part of the Nazi SS and Gestapo headquarters, is an exhibit detailing how the Nazis came to power and the crimes against humanity they committed under the leadership of *der Führer,* Adolf Hitler. The exhibit is open daily from 10 a.m. to 6 p.m. (until 8 p.m. May–Sept). Admission is free.

Gay and lesbian Berlin

Berlin has a century-old gay and lesbian history, and the city remains a mecca for international gay and lesbian travelers. The city's gay information center is **Man-o-Meter,** Bülowstrasse 106 (☎ **030/216-8008;** www.mann-o-meter.de; U-Bahn: Nollendorfplatz). The center is open Monday through Friday from 5 to 10 p.m., and Saturday and Sunday from 4 to 10 p.m. Another good source for information is **Eisenherz,** Lietzenburger Strasse 9a (☎ **030/313-9936;** www.prinz-eisenherz.com; S-Bahn: Wittenbergplatz), one of the world's oldest gay and lesbian bookstores. The store stocks a vast array of new and rare fiction, nonfiction, art books, and magazines in German, English, and other languages. The staff is extremely knowledgeable and helpful.

Berlin is the only city in the world with a gay museum. The **Schwules Museum** (Gay Museum), Mehringdamm 61 (☎ **030/693-1172;** U-Bahn: Mehringdamm), is a large gallery-like space in Kreuzberg with changing exhibitions on gay life in Germany and around the world. The museum is open Wednesday through Monday from 2 to 6 p.m., Saturday until 5 p.m. Admission is €5 ($6.25).

Traditionally, lesbian and gay life has centered around **Nollendorfplatz** (U-Bahn: Nollendorfplatz), the so-called Pink (or Gay) Village. A **memorial plaque** mounted on the outside south wall of the Nollendorfplatz subway station, in the heart of what has been for decades the gay heart of Berlin, reads: *Totgeschlagen-Totgeschiegen. Den Homosexuellen Opfern des National Socialismus* ("Killed and Forgotten. The homosexual victims of National Socialism"). The plaque serves as a poignant reminder that the Nazis exterminated thousands of homosexuals in addition to millions of Jews, Gypsies, and other political victims.

In mid-June, Nollendorfplaz is the site of the **Lesbisch-Schwules Stadtfest** (Lesbian–Gay Street Fair). The **Christopher Street Day** parade is an even larger citywide gay event that takes place the last week in June; up to 500,000 people congregate for this Gay Pride festival. **Love Parade/Love Week** in early July attracts thousands to a huge gay party scene (canceled in 2004, but may return in 2005).

The gay scene is more international in the area around **Nollendorfplatz,** which has had gay bars since the 1920s. **Kreuzberg** is another gay-friendly borough with a big selection of bars. In the eastern part of the city, **Prenzlauer Berg** has become the new gay area. For my recommended gay and lesbian nightspots, see "Checking out the dance clubs and bars," later in this chapter. More information on gay life in Berlin is available on the Web site www.berlin.gay-web.de.

Seeing Berlin by Guided Tour

Taking a guided sightseeing tour *(Stadtrundfahrt)* can help you to see parts of this huge city that you may otherwise miss. You can tour Germany's capital with an experienced guide by bus, on foot, or by boat.

Bus tours

Severin+Kühn, Kurfürstendamm 216 (☎ **030/880-4190;** www.severin-kuehn-berlin.de; U-Bahn: Kurfürstendamm), offers a two-hour "City Circle Tour" that departs daily every half-hour from 10 a.m. to 4 p.m. (Nov–March until 3 p.m.). Tickets cost €18 ($22) per person. The tour passes 14 important stops in Berlin, including the Europa Center, the Brandenburg Gate, and Potsdamer Platz. You can get on and off the bus at any point during the hour. The same company's three-hour "Big Berlin Tour" departs at 10 a.m. and 2 p.m. daily, costs €21.50 ($27) per person, and covers more sites. All tours include a guide who delivers commentaries in German and English, making them accessible and enjoyable for kids and adults. From May through September, Severin+Kühn also conducts an interesting tour of Potsdam, site of Sanssouci Palace, former residence of Frederick the Great (see "Day-tripping to Potsdam and Sanssouci Palace" later in this chapter). The price is €35 ($44) per person. Departures are Tuesday through Sunday at 10 a.m. From April through October, Severin+Kühn operates additional Saturday and Sunday tours at 2:15 p.m.

Although you don't get a guide, the cheapest bus tour of Berlin is **public bus 100,** which leaves from Bahnhof Zoo and passes most of the major sites in western and eastern Berlin. You can catch the bus in front of Bahnhof Zoologischer Garten (Zoo Station).

Walking tours

For an excellent introduction to Berlin and its history, try one of the walking tours offered by **Berlin Walks** (☎ **030/301-9194;** www.berlinwalks.com). "Discover Berlin" is a three-hour introductory tour that takes you past the Reichstag and the Brandenburg Gate, among other major sites. This walk starts daily at 10 a.m. and 2:30 p.m. (in winter at 10 a.m. only). "Infamous Third Reich Sites" focuses on the sites of major Nazi buildings in central Berlin, such as Goebbels's Propaganda Ministry and Hitler's New Reichschancellery; this tour, available April through October, starts at 10 a.m. on Saturday, Sunday, Wednesday, and Thursday (Saturday and Sunday only in April and October). "Jewish Life in Berlin" takes you through the prewar Jewish community; the tour starts at 10 a.m. Monday and Friday. You don't need advance reservations for any of the tours. You meet the guide, who wears a Berlin Walks badge, outside the main entrance to Bahnhof Zoologischer Garten (Zoo Station), in front of the taxi stand. Tours last from 2½ to 3 hours and cost €12 ($15) for adults, €9 ($11) for those younger than 26, free for children younger than 14.

Boat tours

A boat tour is the most unusual way to see portions of Berlin. Local waterways include the Spree and Havel rivers — ranging in size from narrow channels to large lakes — in addition to the many canals created in the 19th century. **Stern- und Kreisschiffahrt,** Pushkinallee 60–70 (☎ **030/536-3600;** www.sternundkreis.de), the city's best-known boat operator, offers boat trips from April through October. Be aware, though, that all of its tours are given only in German (on most tours, you can request an English translation). From April through October, one-, two-, three-, and four-hour tours depart daily from Jannowitzbrücke in Berlin-Mitte. These trips offer good views of the Reichstag, the Pergamon Museum, the Königliche Bibliothek (Royal Library), and the monumental heart of the former East Berlin. A one-hour tour costs €8 ($10) per person; two-hour tours cost €10 ($12.50); four-hour tours cost €15.50 ($19). The same company offers other boat tours from Schlossbrücke near Charlottenburg Palace. Several other companies offer boat tours; just walk along the Spreepromenade behind the Berlin cathedral, and you'll find several landing docks with waiting boats.

Following an Itinerary

Every visitor to Berlin faces one problem: how to see as much as possible in a limited amount of time. What do you see if you have only one, two, or three days at your disposal? The itineraries in this section are common-sense, limited-time suggestions that include the top Berlin sights. For descriptions of most of the stops, see "Discovering the top attractions from A to Z" earlier in this chapter.

If you have one day in Berlin

Start early. First visit the **Reichstag,** where the new dome provides a marvelous view out over the city. From there you can walk to the **Brandenburg Gate,** symbol of Berlin, then walk down **Unter den Linden,** exploring the nearby **Gendarmenmarkt** and paying a brief visit to the **Pergamon Museum** to see the Pergamon Altar. Return to Potsdamer Platz to see the newest section of Berlin, and then go on to **Schloss Charlottenburg** (Charlottenburg Palace) for a palace tour. Afterward, stop in at the **Ägyptisches Museum** (Egyptian Museum) for a look at the celebrated bust of Queen Nefertiti. In the evening, walk along the Kurfürstendamm and dine in a local restaurant.

If you have two days in Berlin

On the second day, visit the **Gemäldegalerie** (Painting Gallery) in the Kulturforum. Afterward, head over to the **Jüdisches Museum** in Freuzberg or **The Story of Berlin** multimedia show (see "Finding more cool things to see and do" earlier in this chapter). In the evening, enjoy an opera, a concert, or a cabaret/variety show.

If you have three days in Berlin

Spend half of the third day in **Potsdam,** visiting **Sanssouci Palace** and grounds (see "Day-tripping to Potsdam and Sanssouci Palace" later in this chapter). In the afternoon, stop in at **Mauermuseum Haus am Checkpoint Charlie,** with its Cold War museum, and end with a stroll through the **Tiergarten.**

Shopping for Local Treasures

You can buy just about anything you want in Berlin, a great shopping city. But keep in mind that you'll pay less for goods made in Germany and the European Union than for goods imported to Germany from the United States. German porcelain, china, and cutlery, for example, are prized for their quality, and their prices are lower here than in the United States.

Most stores in Berlin are open Monday through Friday from 9 or 10 a.m. to 6 or 6:30 p.m. Many stay open late on Thursday evenings, often to 8:30 p.m. Saturday hours usually are from 9 or 10 a.m. to 2 p.m.

Don't expect a lot of "deals" in Berlin, except on the sales racks in the department stores. For the two major *Trödelmarkts* (flea markets), see the "Berlin flea markets" sidebar.

Shopping in western Berlin

Throughout the decades when the Wall divided Berlin, the only decent shopping was in western Berlin, which remains the best place for all-purpose, all-around shopping.

Neighborhoods and malls

The main shopping boulevard in the western part of Berlin is the famous **Ku-Damm,** short for Kurfürstendamm (U-Bahn: Kurfürstendamm). Quality stores, in addition to stores carrying cheap souvenirs and T-shirts, line the street. The specialty stores on the side streets around the Ku-Damm, especially between **Breitscheidplatz** and **Olivaer Platz,** are good shopping grounds.

Berlin flea markets

A flea market in Germany is called a *Trödelmarkt* or a *Flohmarkt.* **Antik & Flohmarkt** (☎ 030/208-2645; U-/S-Bahn: Friedrichstrasse), a daily flea market from 9 a.m. to 4 p.m. in the Friedrichstrasse S-Bahn station, has some 60 vendors selling all manner of bric-a-brac, including brassware and World War II (WWII) mementos. The **Berliner Trödelmarkt** (☎ 030/2655-0096; S-Bahn: Tiergarten), adjacent to the Tiergarten S-Bahn station near the corner of the Bachstrasse and Strasse des 17 Juni, is the favorite weekend shopping spot for countless Berliners, who come to find pieces of kitsch, nostalgia, sort-of-antiques, and used clothing. The market is open every Saturday and Sunday from 10 a.m. to 5 p.m.

Another good shopping street in western Berlin, close to Ku-Damm, is **Tauentzienstrasse** (U-/S-Bahn: Zoologischer Garten) and its intersecting streets: **Marburger Strasse, Ranke Strasse,** and **Nürnberger Strasse.** This area offers a wide array of stores, many specializing in German fashions for women. Stores here often are cheaper than on the fancier Ku-Damm. Berlin's first shopping mall, the **Europa Center** (☎ 030/348-0088), is on Tauentzienstrasse (U-/S-Bahn: Zoologischer Garten); here you find around 75 shops joined by restaurants and cafes.

The **Uhland-Passage,** at Uhlandstrasse 170 (U-Bahn: Uhlandstrasse), has some of the best boutiques and big-name stores in Berlin. Shoppers interested in quality at any price need to head to **Kempinski Plaza,** Uhlandstrasse 181–183 (U-Bahn: Uhlandstrasse), home to some of the most exclusive boutiques in the city, including haute-couture women's clothing. You find trendier boutiques along **Bleibtreustrasse.**

The new **Potsdamer Platz Arkaden** (U-/S-Bahn: Potsdamer Platz), one of the most comprehensive shopping malls in Berlin, contains about 100 shops, with more being added all the time, scattered over three levels. Some of the stores offer cost-cutting clothing and housewares.

Department stores

Kaufhaus des Westens (called KaDeWe [ka-day-vay] for short), Tauentzien 21 (☎ 030/21210; U-Bahn: Zoologischer Garten), is a huge department store, known for its six floors of upscale merchandise and sixth-floor food department. **Wertheim,** Kurfürstendamm 231 (☎ 030/880-030; U-Bahn: Kurfürstendamm), is good for travel aids and general basics: perfumes, clothing for the entire family, jewelry, electrical devices, household goods, photography supplies, and souvenirs. Wertheim has a large restaurant with a view over half the city.

Berlin's newest old shopping neighborhood: Scheuneviertel

The newest shopping, arts, and happening neighborhood area is eastern Berlin's Scheuneviertel, or "barn district" (S-Bahn: Hackescher Markt), named for the hay barns that once stood here. The area later became Berlin's Jewish quarter, and, amazingly, some of its oldest buildings survived the World War II (WWII) bombing raids that reduced most of Berlin to rubble. A grand pre–World War I shopping arcade with interconnected courtyards *(Hinterhöfe)* occupies most of the block formed by Oranienburger Strasse, Rosenthaler Strasse, Grosse Hamburger Strasse, and Sophienstrasse. The spaces within the courtyards have now been turned into a series of galleries, studios, and theaters. Cutting-edge shops line the streets around the arcade.

Fashion

Bleibgrün, Bleibtreustrasse 30 (☎ **030/885-0080;** S-Bahn: Savignyplatz), a small, fashionable women's clothing store with a helpful staff, sells Paul Smith, Marithé François Girbaud, and a handful of other fashionable trendsetters. **Bogner Zenker-Berlin,** Kurfürstendamm 45 (☎ **030/881-1000;** S-Bahn: Savignyplatz), is a long-established shop for women's clothing made in Germany, Austria, and Italy. **Chapeaux Hutmode Berlin,** Bleibtreustrasse 51 (☎ **030/312-0913;** S-Bahn: Savignyplatz), is a couture hatmaker inspired by vintage fashion magazines and glamorous movies from the 1930s. **Modenhaus Horn,** Kurfürstendamm 213 (☎ **030/881-4055;** U-Bahn: Kurfürstendamm), sells whatever is *au courant* for chic Berlin women. **Treykorn,** Savignyplatz 13 Passage (☎ **030/312-4275;** S-Bahn: Savignyplatz), carries the most avant-garde jewelry in Berlin, showcasing more than three dozen of the boldest jewelry artisans in the city.

Perfumes

Harry Lehmann, Kantstrasse 106 (☎ **030/324-3582;** U-Bahn: Wilmersdorferstrasse), is a wonderfully old-fashioned parfumerie where most of the scents come from old family recipes, distilled from flowers, grasses, and leaves. The prices are amazingly reasonable for the quality of the perfumes.

Porcelain and china

Königliche Porzellan-Manufaktur (KPM; Royal Porcelain Factory), Kurfürstendamm 27 in Kempinski Hotel Bristol (☎ **030/8867-2110;** U-Bahn: Kurfürstendamm), sells porcelain pieces hand-painted and hand-decorated with patterns based on traditional 18th- and 19th-century KPM designs. **Meissener Porzellan,** Kurfürstendamm 26A (☎ **030/8868-3530;** U-Bahn Kurfürstendamm), one of the most famous porcelain manufacturers in Europe, offers an array of Meissen dinner plates, sculptures, and chandeliers. **Rosenthal,** Kurfürstendamm 226 (☎ **030/885-6340;** U-Bahn: Kurfürstendamm), is the place to go for contemporary Rosenthal porcelain and china from Bavaria.

Shopping in eastern Berlin

The eastern part of the city has undergone major changes in the retail sector since reunification more than a decade ago. The main street, **Friedrichstrasse** (U-/S-Bahn: Friedrichstrasse), now offers some of Berlin's most elegant shopping, with upmarket boutiques selling everything from women's fashions to Meissen porcelain. The largest shopping mall in eastern Berlin, offering a little bit of everything, is at the **Berliner Markthalle,** at the corner of Rosa-Luxemburg-Strasse and Karl-Liebknecht-Strasse (U-/S-Bahn: Alexanderplatz).

For more shopping in the eastern part, see this chapter's sidebar, "Berlin's newest old shopping neighborhood: Scheuneviertel."

Discovering Nightlife in Berlin

You find more going on in Berlin than in any other city in Germany. The performing arts scene is jammed with opera, dance, classical-music concerts, and theater performances every night of the week. Berlin's nightlife is legendary, with hundreds of bars, clubs, and cabarets appealing to every taste.

Finding out what's happening

Check the listings in *Zitty* (www.zitty.de) or *Berlin Programm*, available at all newsstands, for the latest schedules of what's going on where. An excellent online source is www.berlin-tourist-information.de; click "Events/Tickets" to access a complete list of events in any category for the specific dates of your visit.

Getting tickets

You can buy tickets at the venue's box office (the box office is called a *Kasse*, pronounced *kah*-suh). Tickets can usually be purchased right up to curtain time. Alternatively, you can buy tickets from ticket agencies, which charge a commission. **Theater Konzertkasse**, Kurfürstendamm 16 (☎ 030/852-4080; U-Bahn: Kurfürstendamm), is one of the most centrally located agencies.

For some of the larger opera, ballet, and classical-music venues, you can buy tickets online. If the venue doesn't have its own Web site, you may be able to order tickets online at www.berlin-tourist-information.de.

 Unsold tickets for more than 100 venues, including opera, classical concerts, and cabarets, are available for up to 50 percent off at **Hekticket** (www.hekticket.de), with outlets at Hardenbergstrasse 29 (☎ **030/ 230-9930**; U-Bahn: Zoologischer Garter) and Karl-Liebknecht-Strasse 12, on the S-Bahn bridge at Alexanderplatz (☎ **030/230-9930**; U-/S-Bahn: Alexanderplatz); both are open Monday through Friday from 10 a.m. to 6 p.m.

Raising the curtain on performing arts and music

Good news for culture vultures: With three major symphony orchestras, three opera houses, ballet companies, and dozens of theaters and cabarets, you won't be lacking for things to do. The newest trend is to start performances as early as 6 p.m., so everyone can get home at a reasonable hour. Whenever possible, I include Web sites in this section so you can check performance schedules and ticket information before you arrive in Berlin.

Opera and ballet

In Charlottenburg, the **Deutsche Oper Berlin,** Bismarckstrasse 35 (☎ **030/341-0249** for recorded information or 030/343-8401; www. deutscheoperberlin.de; U-Bahn: Deutsche Oper), is the 1950s-era opera house that served the former West Berlin. You can see both opera and ballet here; some tickets bought on the day of performance are 25 percent off. The box office is open Monday through Saturday from 11 a.m. up to the time of performance and on Sunday from 10 a.m. to 2 p.m. You also can buy tickets online. Ticket prices range from €15 to €100 ($19 to $125).

The **Staatsoper Unter den Linden,** Unter den Linden 7 (☎ **030/20-35-40;** www.staatsoper-berlin.org; U-Bahn: Unter den Linden), is housed in a historic building in Berlin-Mitte. The programs feature opera and ballet performances. The box office is open Monday through Friday from 10 a.m. to 8 p.m. and Saturday and Sunday from 2 to 8 p.m. You can buy tickets online. Tickets range from about €16 to €120 ($20 to $150).

Berlin's **Komische Oper,** Behrenstrasse 55–57 (☎ **030/4799-7400;** www. komische-oper-berlin.de; U-/S-Bahn: Unter den Linden), is a famous and well-respected East Berlin house with a unique artistic identity, but performances don't include internationally known stars, and every opera is sung in German. The box office is open Monday through Saturday from 11 a.m. to 7 p.m. and Sunday from 1 p.m. to the time of performance. Prices ranges from about €18 to €75 ($22 to $94).

Symphony orchestras and classical music

In the Kulturforum complex, the renowned **Berlin Philharmonic Orchestra** under the direction of Sir Simon Rattle plays in the acoustically outstanding **Philharmonie,** Matthäikirchstrasse 1 (box office ☎ **030/ 2548-8999;** www.berlin-philharmonic.com; U-Bahn: Potsdamer Platz). Chamber music concerts are given at the adjoining **Kammermusiksaal.** The box office is open Monday through Friday from 3 to 6 p.m., Saturday and Sunday from 11 a.m. to 2 p.m., and one hour before performances. Ticket prices range from about €7 ($8.75) for standing room to €110 ($137). You can order tickets online.

The historic Schauspielhaus in the former East Berlin has undergone a stunning transformation and is now the **Konzerthaus am Gendarmenmarkt,** Gendarmenmarkt (☎ **030/203-090;** S-Bahn: Unter den Linden). The **Berlin Symphony Orchestra** and other orchestras and classical music groups perform in this glittering, pitch-perfect hall. Different ticket prices apply for each event. You can buy tickets at the Konzerthaus box office, which is open daily noon to 6 p.m. and an hour before performances.

The city's third major orchestra, the **Berlin Symphony,** performs at both the Philharmonie and the Konzerthaus am Gendarmenmarkt. Tickets are available at the box offices of both venues.

Theater

Berlin's theater scene is outstanding, but, of course, most of the plays are performed in German. The Web site www.berlin-tourist-information.de has a useful listing of plays and films in English.

The **Berliner Grundtheater** (☎ 030/7800-1497; www.thebgt.de) performs English-language plays in different venues around the city. If you don't speak the language but want to experience German theater, I recommend going to see a production by the famous **Berliner Ensemble,** Bertolt-Brecht-Platz 1 (☎ 030/2840-8155; www.berliner-ensemble.de; U-Bahn: Friedrichstrasse). Playwright Bertolt Brecht formed this group with his wife, Helene Weigel, and many theater fans enjoy seeing Brecht's plays performed in "his" theater. The box office is open Monday through Friday from 8 a.m. to 6 p.m., Saturday and Sunday from 11 a.m. to 6 p.m., and one hour before performances. Ticket prices range from about €5 to €30 ($6.25 to $37).

Cabarets and variety shows

Berlin has long been famous for its cabarets and variety shows, and spending an evening in one can be enjoyable even if you don't speak a word of German.

Chez Nous Travestie-Theater, Marburgerstrasse 14 (☎ 030/213-1810; U-Bahn: Wittenbergplatz), is a famous little cabaret where all the performers are in drag and most of the audience is heterosexual. Believing that these glamorous ladies are really gentlemen sometimes is difficult. Nightly shows start at 8:30 and 11 p.m. Cover is €30 ($37).

Die Stachelschweine (The Porcupine), Europa Center, Tauentzienstrasse and Budapester Strasse (☎ 030/261-4795; U-Bahn: Kurfürstendamm), is a cabaret that's been poking fun at the German and American political scenes for many years now. Part of the performance usually involves a selection of popular songs. Shows take place Tuesday through Friday at 7:30 p.m. and Saturday at 6 p.m. and 9:15 p.m. The cover charge is €13 to €22 ($16 to $27). This cabaret is closed in July.

Friedrichstadt-Palast, Friedrichstrasse 107 (☎ 030/2326-2326; www.friedrichstadtpalast.de; U-/S-Bahn: Friedrichstrasse), in Mitte, is a big theater that features variety acts from around the world. Shows and showtimes vary, but most nights (except Monday, when the theater's closed) the performances begin at 8 p.m., with 4 p.m. matinees on Saturday and Sunday. Ticket prices range from €15 to €60 ($19 to $75).

Wintergarten Variété, Potsdamer Strasse 96 (☎ 030/2500-8888; www.wintergarten-variete.de; U-Bahn: Kurfürstenstrasse), is the largest and most nostalgic Berlin cabaret, with a nightly variety show featuring magicians, clowns, jugglers, acrobats, and live music. The most expensive seats are on stage level; balconies have conventional theater seats (but drinks are sold there, too). Shows begin at 8 p.m. Monday through Friday, and Saturday at 6 and 10 p.m. Cover is about €38 to €51 ($48 to $64).

Checking out the dance clubs and bars

If you're into nightlife, you can find something to do all across the city.
This section includes just a few of the bars and dance clubs in Berlin.
For more listings, visit www.berlin-tourist-information.de.

 Bars and clubs don't generally get going until midnight. Many bars now
have an open-ended closing policy. An empty club may choose to close at
2 a.m., but a packed club can stay open until 6 a.m. Please keep in mind
that new bars open and bars close all the time. This section includes
places that are likely to be around for years to come.

Dance clubs

Big Eden, Kurfürstendamm 202 (☎ **030/882-6120;** U-Bahn Uhlandstrasse),
holds 1,000 dancers on its huge dance floor. DJs play the latest international hits with impressive light effects and sound equipment. Cover,
which includes one drink, is €7 to €9 ($8.75 to 11), depending on the
night. The club is open Sunday through Thursday from 9 p.m. to 5 a.m.,
Friday and Saturday until 6 a.m.

Chip, Berlin Hilton, Mohrenstrasse 30 (☎ **030/20230;** U-Bahn: Stadtmitte),
is a glossy and popular dance club with a great lighting system, video
clips, and fog machine. Club hours are Wednesday through Saturday
from 10 p.m. to 4 a.m. Cover is €5.50 ($7).

Far Out, Kurfürstendamm 156 (☎ **030/3200-0717;** U-Bahn:
Adenauerplatz), is a large, industrial-looking late-night disco that plays
mostly high-energy retro rock for a crowd that includes lots of students.
The club is open Tuesday through Sunday from 10 p.m. to 4 a.m. The
cover ranges from €3 to €8 ($3.75 to $10).

Metropole, Nollendorfplatz 5 (☎ **030/217-3680;** U-Bahn: Nollendorfplatz),
housed in an old theater with an Egyptian temple interior, draws a young
20-something crowd. The club is open Friday and Saturday nights from
9:30 p.m. to 5 a.m. Cover is €10 to €16 ($12 to $19).

SO36, Oranienstrasse 190 (☎ **030/6140-1306;** U-Bahn: Prinzenstrasse),
in trendy Kreuzberg, has two very large rooms, a stage for floor shows,
and highly danceable music; the crowd is a hip mixture of gay and straight.
The club is open most nights from 10:30 p.m. to 4 a.m.; call first to verify.
Cover usually is about€5 ($6.25).

Live music

A Trane, Pestalozzistrasse 105 (☎ **030/313-2550;** U-Bahn: Savignyplatz),
is a small, smoky jazz club featuring musicians from around the world.
The club is open Monday through Thursday from 8 p.m. to 4 a.m., Friday
and Saturday from 9 p.m. to 4 a.m. Cover is €8 to €13 ($10 to $16),
depending on the night and who's playing.

Sampling fresh beer at brewpubs

The first *Bierhaus* (brewpub, or microbrewery) in Berlin, **Gasthaus Luisenbräu,** Luisenplatz 1 (☎ 030/341-9388; U-Bahn: Richard-Wagner-Platz), opened in 1987 across the street from Charlottenburg Palace. The house beer is a pale, blond, unfiltered, top-fermented beer. You can order beer in a smallish 6-ounce (0.2-liter) glass (€1.60/$2) or in an 11-ounce (0.4-liter) serving (€3.20/$4). The smoky interior of this brewpub is comfortably Old Berlin, even though the building is relatively new. You can order hearty portions of German food (meat, sauerkraut, dumplings, and salads) to accompany your beer. The brewpub is open Sunday to Thursday from 10 a.m. to 12:30 a.m., Friday and Saturday 10 a.m. to 2 a.m.

Gasthaus Georgenbräu, Spreeufer 4 (☎ 030/242-4244; U-Bahn: Klostergasse), a brewpub in the Nikolaiviertel beside the River Spree, is named after the statue of St. George right outside. You can choose between beers brewed on-premises; the *helles* (light) is top-fermented, blond, and unfiltered. The *dunkles* (dark), also unfiltered and top- fermented, has a darkish amber color, a yeasty aroma, and a nice balance of hop bitterness and malt flavor. You can also order plates of hearty German food; main courses go for €8.50 to €12 ($11 to $14). The Gasthof is open daily from 10 a.m. to midnight.

Knaack-Klub, Greifswalderstrasse 224 (☎ 030/442-7060; U-Bahn: Alexanderplatz), in happening Prenzlauer Berg, is a four-story club with live rock shows four nights a week featuring German and international touring bands. Show days vary, so call first. You always find dancing on Wednesday, Friday, and Saturday nights. Hours are Monday to Friday 10 p.m. to 4 a.m., Saturday and Sunday until 7 a.m. Cover is €3 to €8 ($3.75 to $10), depending on the band.

Quasimodo, Kantstrasse 12A (☎ 030/312-8086; U-Bahn: Zoologischer Garten), is Berlin's top jazz club, where you encounter many different styles of music, including rock and Latin jazz. The club is open Tuesday through Saturday from 9 p.m. to 2 a.m. Admission is free on Tuesday and Wednesday when local musicians perform, otherwise €13 ($16).

Wild at Heart, Wienerstrasse 20 (☎ 030/611-7010; U-Bahn: Görlitzer Bahnhof), is dedicated to hard-core punk, rock, and rockabilly, with bands from Germany and elsewhere playing Wednesday through Saturday nights. The club is open Monday through Friday from 8 p.m. to 4 a.m., Saturday and Sunday from 8 p.m. to 10 a.m. Admission is about €4 ($5) for concerts, otherwise free.

Popular bars

Later is better if you want to go out barhopping and see what's happening in Berlin. Expect to pay at least €6 ($7.50) for a straightforward drink, more for anything exotic, less for a glass of beer.

The following bars currently are popular. These places tend to be fashion-conscious, so you may feel out of place if you show up in blue jeans and sneakers.

Bar am Lützowplatz, Lützowplatz 7 (☎ 030/262-6807; U-Bahn: Nollendorfplatz), one of the longest and narrowest bars in Berlin, is hip and fun. The bar is open daily from 3 p.m. until 4 a.m.

Harry's New York Bar, Lützowufer 15 in Grand Hotel Esplanade (☎ 030/2547-8821; U-Bahn: Nollendorfplatz), with minimalist décor, pop art, and photographs of American presidents, has a menu listing almost 200 drinks and a limited selection of food. Harry's is open daily from noon to 2 a.m.

Lore Berlin, Neue Schönhauser Strasse 20 (☎ 030/2804-5134; U-Bahn: Rosenthaler Platz), features cutting-edge design, great dance music, and an intriguing mix of people hanging around a long and narrow bar with theatrical lighting that makes almost everyone look attractive. Lore Berlin is open nightly until 3 a.m.

Reingold, 11 Novalistrasse (☎ 030/2838-7676; U-Bahn: Friedrichstrasse), is chic and elegant, geared toward a very late-night glamour crowd. The place is open nightly until 4 a.m.

Times Bar, Savoy Hotel, Fasanenstrasse 9 (☎ 030/311-030; U-/S-Bahn: Zoologischer Garten), quiet, cozy, and intimate, is reminiscent of a wood-paneled private club in London. The Times Bar isn't a late-night-scene bar, but rather a place where you can relax in a big leather chair and read *The Times* of London. Times Bar is open daily from 11 a.m. to 2 a.m.

Neighborhood bars: Kneipes and Lokals

Do you want to find a casual, unpretentious spot for a plain old glass of *Bier vom Fass* (beer on tap)? What you need is a *Kneipe* (ka-*nigh*-puh), a cozy place similar to a neighborhood pub in the United Kingdom. A small bar like this sometimes is called a *Lokal* (low-*call*). Many Berliners have a favorite Kneipe where they stop in after work or later in the evening for a beer and a chat with their friends. Brewpubs also are good places to sample beer, and they offer meals. See this chapter's sidebar "Sampling fresh beer at brewpubs."

Berlin is home to hundreds of Kneipes and Lokals. A famous one is **Gaststätte Hoeck,** Wilmersdorferstrasse 149 (☎ 030/341-8174; U-Bahn: Bismarckstrasse). Dating from 1892, Gaststätte Hoeck is the oldest Kneipe in Charlottenburg and still has its original wood panels with inlaid glass on the walls. The bar can be loud, smoky, and raucous. Bartenders pour more than a dozen kinds of beer and serve wine by the glass. Hours are 8 a.m. to midnight. Traditional food is served in an adjacent room Monday through Saturday from 11 a.m. to 10:30 p.m.; main courses run from €5.50 to €13 ($6.90 to $16).

Day-tripping to Potsdam and Sanssouci Palace

Frederick the Great's **Schloss Sanssouci** (Sanssouci Palace) in Potsdam is the architectural signature of one of Germany's most dominating personalities. Allow yourself at least half a day to visit this remarkable palace and its beautiful grounds. Potsdam, 24km (15 miles) southwest of Berlin, a former garrison town on the Havel River, is now the capital of the state of Brandenburg. The town celebrated its 1,000th anniversary in 1993 and has historic sites of its own, but be sure to make Sanssouci Palace your top priority. (See the "Potsdam" map in this chapter.)

Getting there

To get to Sanssouci, you must first get to Potsdam. The trip couldn't be easier: From Berlin, **S-Bahn** line **S7** stops at the **Potsdam Hauptbahnhof** station. Hop on **bus No. 695** in front of the station and ride nine stops to the Schloss Sanssouci stop. The bus fare is €1.40 ($1.75). Cross the road, turn left, and you'll almost immediately come to a flight of stairs leading up to the palace. If you don't want to hassle with anything, you can take one of the **Potsdam–Sanssouci bus tours** offered by the sightseeing bus companies on Ku-Damm (see "Bus tours" earlier in this chapter); the cost is generally about €35 ($44) for a half-day fast-track tour.

Finding tourist information

Maps, brochures, and inexpensive guidebooks for both the town and the palace are available at the **Potsdam Tourist Information** office in the Hauptbahnhof (☎ **0331/270-9051**), open daily from 9 a.m. to 8 p.m. You find another tourist office at Friedrich-Ebert-Strasse 5 (☎ **0331/275-580**), open Monday through Friday from 9 a.m. to 6 p.m. (Apr–Oct until 7 p.m.) and on Saturday and Sunday from 10 a.m. to 2 p.m. (in summer, Sat until 6 p.m. and Sun until 4 p.m.)

Discovering the top attractions

Potsdam didn't gain true importance until the "Great Elector" Friedrich Wilhelm (1620–1688) chose the lovely, leafy, lakey area to be his second seat of residence outside Berlin. From then on, Potsdam was a royal hangout. To escape the rigors of Berlin court life, Friedrich II (called Frederick the Great; 1712–1786) built in Potsdam a "small" country palace where he could retire "*sans souci*" (without a care) and indulge his passions for music, poetry, and philosophy.

Schloss (Palace) **Sanssouci** (☎ **0331/969-4190**) is open Tuesday through Sunday from 9 a.m. to 5 p.m. (Nov–Mar to 4 p.m.). You can see the palace only on a guided tour costing €8 ($10) for adults, and €5 ($6.25) for children and students. Your tour time is printed on your ticket. Before setting

Potsdam

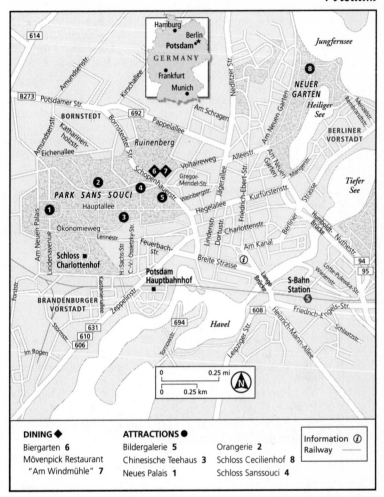

DINING ◆
Biergarten **6**
Mövenpick Restaurant
"Am Windmühle" **7**

ATTRACTIONS ●
Bildergalerie **5**
Chinesische Teehaus **3**
Neues Palais **1**

Orangerie **2**
Schloss Cecilienhof **8**
Schloss Sanssouci **4**

Information *ⓘ*
Railway ------

off on the tour, you're required to don huge felt slippers so you don't scuff the floors. The tour is given only in German, but information sheets in English are available from the guide, and you must ask for them.

A timed-entry system is in effect at Sanssouci. Your ticket tells you what time you can enter the palace to begin your guided tour. If you don't arrive early, you may have to wait for a much later tour. Waits in summer months can be up to three hours long.

One of the greatest and most beautiful examples of European rococo, Sanssouci was built between 1745 and 1747 as Frederick's summerhouse, a place where he could let his wig down, discuss weighty matters with French philosopher Voltaire, and make music with composer Carl Philip Emanuel Bach. In short, Sanssouci was a summer resort for an enlightened monarch. All kinds of rococo treasures fill the palace, which you see on a tour that lasts about 45 minutes.

Either before or after your tour, spend some time wandering through the magnificent landscaped **gardens** with their bevy of historic buildings. Fred the Great created the original design for the grounds, and his planning still is evident in the restored vineyard terraces and the area immediately around the palace. All the buildings listed here are signposted so you won't get lost on the grounds.

✔ The **Bildergalerie** (Picture Gallery; ☎ 0331/969-4181), on the eastern side of the palace grounds, was completed in 1763 and displays a collection of works from the Italian Renaissance and baroque eras. The gallery is open Tuesday through Sunday from 9 a.m. to 5 p.m. (Nov–Mar until 4 p.m.). Admission is €2 ($2.50).

✔ The **Chinesische Teehaus** (Chinese Teahouse) is a little gem of a rococo building resembling a pagoda. Ornamental "Oriental" buildings like this were all the rage in 18th-century Europe. The privileged classes would retire here to drink a new beverage called tea. This building is not open to the public.

✔ The **Neues Palais** (New Palace; ☎ 0331/969-4255), the largest building in Sanssouci park, was completed in 1769 and used by the Hohenzollern royal family. Inside you see rococo rooms filled with paintings and antiques. The palace is open Saturday through Thursday from 9 a.m. to 5 p.m. (Nov–Mar until 4 p.m.). Admission is €4 ($5).

✔ The mid-19th-century **Orangerie** (☎ 0331/969-4280), west of the palace, contains copies of paintings by Raphael and features ornately decorated salons. The Orangerie is open mid-May to mid-October, 10 a.m. to 5 p.m. (closed Thursday). Admission is €3 ($3.75).

✔ Built to look like an English country manor, **Schloss Cecilienhof** (Cecilienhof Palace; ☎ 0331/969-4200) was a royal residence from 1917 until 1945. At the end of WWII, the palace was used as headquarters for the Potsdam Conference attended by the heads of the Allied powers, including U.S. President Harry Truman, British Prime Minister Winston Churchill, and Russian dictator Joseph Stalin. Now the palace serves as a hotel and conference center. On a guided tour, you can visit the private rooms used by Crown Prince Wilhelm and Princess Cecelie. More interesting are the rooms used for the Potsdam Conference. The palace is open Tuesday through Sunday from 9 a.m. to 5 p.m. (Nov–Mar until 4 p.m.). Admission for the guided tour is €8 ($10).

Dining at Sanssouci

From May through September, you can grab a quick, inexpensive bite at the **Biergarten** kiosk (no phone; open May–Sept daily 10 a.m. to 5 p.m.) across the road behind Sanssouci Palace. The food is basic wursts with *Kartoffelsalat* (potato salad). You can eat for under €4 ($5) and sit at outdoor tables. In the adjacent Pavillon, you find the fancier **Mövenpick Restaurant "Am Windmühle,"** where you can order a complete meal (open year-round daily 10 a.m. to 6 p.m.).

Fast Facts: Berlin

American Express

American Express has two main offices: Bayreutherstrasse 37–38 (☎ 030/214-9830; U-Bahn: Wittenbergplatz), open Monday through Friday 9 a.m. to 7 p.m. and Saturday 10 a.m. to 1 p.m.; and Friedrichstrasse 172 (☎ 030/201-7400; U-bahn: Friedrichstrasse), open Monday through Friday 9 a.m. to 7 p.m and Saturday 10 a.m. to 2 p.m.

ATMs

You find ATMs all across Berlin. Two convenient bank branches with 24-hour ATM service are Deutsche Bank at Wittenbergplatz (U-Bahn: Wittenbergplatz) and Dresdner Bank at Kurfürstendamm 237 (U-Bahn: Kurfürstendamm).

Business Hours

Most banks are open Monday through Friday 9 a.m. to 1 or 3 p.m. Most other businesses and stores are open Monday through Friday from 9 or 10 a.m. to 6 or 6:30 p.m. and Saturday from 9 a.m. to 2 p.m. On *langer Samstag* (longer Saturday), the first Saturday of the month, shops stay open until 4 or 6 p.m. Some stores stay open late on Thursday (usually until 8:30 p.m.). Stores are not open on Sunday.

Country Code and City Code

The city code for Berlin is **30.** Use 30 whenever you're calling Berlin from outside Germany. If you're within Germany but not in Berlin, use 030. If you're calling within Berlin, leave off the city code and dial only the regular phone number. Berlin phone numbers may have from five to eight digits. See also "Telephones" later in this list and in the appendix.

Currency Exchange

The currency exchange office in Bahnhof Zoo is open Monday through Saturday from 8 a.m. to 9 p.m. and on Sunday from 10 a.m. to 6 p.m. You can also exchange money at American Express (see the beginning of this list for addresses).

Dentists and Doctors

The Berlin tourist office in the Europa Center (U-Bahn: Wittenbergplatz) keeps a list of English-speaking dentists and doctors in Berlin. For an emergency doctor, call ☎ **030/304-505** (24 hours); for an emergency dentist, call ☎ **030/8900-4333.**

Embassies and Consulates

See the appendix for the addresses of the Australian, Canadian, Irish, South African, U.K., and U.S. embassies and consulates.

Emergencies

To call the police, dial ☎ **110.** To report a fire or to summon an ambulance, dial ☎ **112.**

Hospitals

Hotel employees are familiar with the location of the nearest hospital emergency room. In an emergency, call ☎ 112 for an ambulance.

Information

The main tourist information centers are located close to the Europa Center (U-/S-Bahn: Zoologischer Garten) in the south wing of the Brandenburg Gate (U-/S-Bahn: Potsdamer Platz or Unter den Linden) and under the Fernsehturm (Television Tower) at Alexanderplatz. For hours and other information about each office, see Chapter 11.

Internet Access

Berlin's largest Internet cafe is Website, Joachimstaler Strasse 41 (☎ 030/886-79630; U-/S-Bahn: Zoologischer Garten), offering 30 terminals that rent for €4 ($5) per hour.

Maps

The most detailed Berlin map with a complete street index is the fold-out Falk plan, available at most newsstands.

Newspapers/Magazines

Newsstands carry *Zitty* and *Berlin-Programm,* which list events around the city. For more, see the appendix.

Pharmacies

If you need a pharmacy (*Apotheke,* pronounced ah-po-*tay*-kuh) at night, go to the nearest one and look for a sign in the window giving the address of the nearest pharmacy with nighttime hours (such postings are required by law). For a centrally located pharmacy, go to Europa–Apotheke, Tauentzienstrasse 9–12 (☎ 030/261-4142; U-Bahn: Wittenbergplatz), located near the Europa Center. In Mitte, a few steps from Unter den Linden, is the Dorotheenstadtische Apotheke, Friedrichstrasse 154 (☎ 030/204-4817; U-Bahn: Friedrichstrasse).

Police

To call the police, dial ☎ 110.

Post Office

The main post office at Joachimstaler Strasse 7 (☎ 030/8870-8611; U-/S-Bahn: Zoologischer Garten) is open Monday through Saturday from 8 a.m. to midnight, Sunday and holidays from 10 a.m. to midnight. Regular post office hours are Monday through Friday 8 a.m. to 6 p.m., Saturday 8 a.m. until noon.

Restrooms

You find public facilities throughout Berlin and at all train terminals.

Safety

One unfortunate side effect of reunification has been an increase in muggings, hate crimes, and car break-ins. But Berlin still is safer than most large American cities. As in any large metropolis, use common sense and caution when you're in a crowded public area. Single women need to avoid the dimly lit streets in Kreuzberg at night.

Taxes

See the appendix for details.

Taxis

You can hail taxis along Berlin's major streets. Taxis with illuminated roof signs are available. For more about fares and where to call for a taxi, check out Chapter 11.

Telephones

Finding a coin-operated telephone in Berlin is now rare; most accept only *Telefonkarte* (telephone cards), which you can purchase in €6 and €25 ($7.50 and $31) denominations at any post office. Many phones also accept Visa cards. To make an international call, use a call box marked *Inlands und Auslandsgespräche.* Most have instructions in English. You can also make long-distance calls from post offices.

Transit Assistance

The Transit Authority (BVG; www.bvg.de) provides U-Bahn information (☎ 030/19449) and S-Bahn information (☎ 030/2974-3333) daily from 6 a.m. to 11 p.m. The same hours apply to the BVG information kiosk outside Bahnhof Zoo, where you can buy tickets and obtain a free transit map.

Weather

You can check the weather online before you go at www.zitty.de.

Web Sites

The best overall Web sites for tourist information on Berlin are www.berlin.de, www.berlin-tourist-information.de, and www.berlin-tourism.de. At these sites, you find information in English about events, nightlife, shopping, restaurants, and more.

Chapter 13

Hamburg, Bremen, and Lübeck: Hanseatic Cities of the North

In This Chapter

▶ Discovering the port city of Hamburg
▶ Touring the ancient city of Bremen
▶ Exploring medieval Lübeck

This chapter covers three cities in northern Germany with long histories of seafaring, trade, and commerce. In medieval times, Hamburg, Lübeck, and Bremen were important members of the Hanseatic League, the most powerful commercial network in Europe. Hansa cities formed trade affiliations that linked northern Germany to the eastern Baltic regions and Scandinavia. In fact, Hamburg and Lübeck still retain the term *Hansestadt* (Hanseatic City) in their official titles.

 Don't expect warm, sunny weather in northern Germany at any time of the year. If you're traveling in the north, even during the summer, an umbrella, raincoat, and sweater probably will come in handy.

Hamburg: Germany's Gateway to the World

 Hamburg, located on the Elbe River about 100km (62 miles) from the North Sea, has a flat, watery landscape that spreads out over 754 sq. km (294 sq. miles). (See the "Hamburg" map in this chapter.) The terrain is characteristic of northern Germany: low, windswept, often gray and misty, but also densely green and filled with marshlands and lakes. A sense of the vast northern seas permeates the city.

Everyone carries away a different impression of this bustling, prosperous city, which also is one of Germany's 16 federal states. Some find Hamburg to be a bit smug, even haughty, a city of "high culture" and elegance and obsessed with making money. For others, Hamburg is sin-city incarnate, land of the lurid Reeperbahn, a street where sex is sold over-the-counter, not under. Hamburg has a huge, bustling, horn-blaring port and sedate late-19th-century neighborhoods. Although much of the city was destroyed during World War II (WWII), you find historic buildings standing side by side with steel-and-glass structures. Because of the Elbe and two enormous inner-city lakes, you're as much aware of water as land — Hamburg has more bridges than Venice and Amsterdam combined.

Intriguing Hamburg is worth a day or two of your time. If you want to explore northern Germany, this city makes a good headquarters. With its giant port and strongly international flair, Germans often call it the "gateway to the world."

Getting there

Hamburg is the largest city in northern Germany and is easy to reach by train, plane, and car.

By plane

Eight kilometers (5 miles) north of the city center is Hamburg's airport, **Flughafen Hamburg-Fuhlsbüttel,** Paul-Baumer-Platz 1–3 (☎ **040/50750**). Most major European cities have direct flights to Hamburg. The terminal contains a **Tourist-Information** office (☎ **3005-1300**) in the arrivals area of Terminal 4 (open daily 6 a.m. to 11 p.m.), an array of easily identified banks with currency-exchange windows, and other independent currency-exchange services and ATMs.

The easiest way to get into the city is by the **Airport Express bus,** which stops in front of Terminals 1 and 4. The bus runs every 15 to 20 minutes (5 a.m. to 9:20 p.m.) to the city's Hauptbahnhof (main train station); the journey takes about 25 minutes. The one-way fare is €4.60 ($5.75) for adults and €2.50 ($3.10) for children younger than 12. A **taxi** from the airport to the city costs about €17 ($21) and takes about 30 minutes, depending on traffic. Taxi stands are in front of all the terminals.

By train

Hamburg has two major rail stations. Most trains arrive at the centrally located **Hamburg Hauptbahnhof,** Hachmannplatz 10 (☎ **040/3918-3046**), and then make a second stop at **Hamburg-Altona** (☎ **040/3918-2387**) in the western part of the city. An S-Bahn line connects the two stations. Hamburg has train connections with all major German and European cities. From Berlin, the trip time is 2½ hours. For train information, call **Deutsche Bahn** (German Rail) at ☎ **01805/11861.**

By car

The **A1** Autobahn reaches Hamburg from the south and west, the **A7** from the north and south, the **A23** from the northwest, and the **A24** from the east. *A word to the wise:* Park your car and use public transportation in this busy city.

Hamburg

ACCOMMODATIONS ■
Aussen Alster **29**
Hamburg Marriott **15**
Hotel Hafen Hamburg **6**
Hotel Prem **30**
Hotel Side **14**
Kempinski Hotel Atlantic
  Hamburg **27**
Park Hyatt Hamburg **23**
Pension Helga Schmidt **26**
Wedina **28**

DINING ◆
Apples Restaurant **23**
Cremon Weinkeller **18**
Die Rösterei **24**
Eisenstein **3**
Fischküche Karin Brahm **19**
Le Paquebot **22**
Ratsweinkeller Hamburg **20**
Voltaire Bistro **2**
Zum Alten Rathaus **17**

ATTRACTIONS ●
Alster Lake **31**
Erotic Art Museum **4**
Hafen Harbor **5**
Hamburger Kunsthalle **25**
Museum für Hamburgische
  Geschichte **9**
Rathaus **16**
Reeperbahn **8**
St. Jacobikirche **21**
St. Michaelis **7**
Tierpark Hagenbeck **1**
Wallringpark
  Alter Botanischer Garten **13**
  Grosse Wallanlagen **10**
  Kleine Wallanlagen **11**
  Planten und Blomen **12**

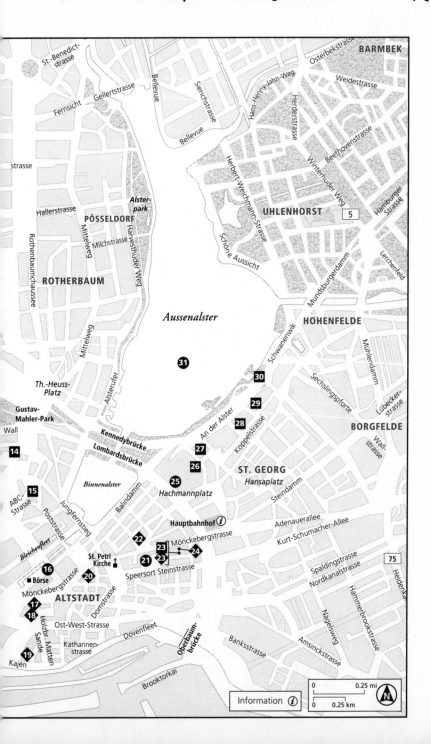

BARMBEK

St.-Benedict-strasse

Osterbekstrasse

Weidestrasse

Bellevue

Sierichstrasse

Gellertstrasse

Fernsicht

Bellevue

Hans-Henny-Jahn-Weg

Herderstrasse

Beethovenstrasse

Herbert-Weichmann-Strasse

UHLENHORST

5

Winterhuder Weg

Hamburger Strasse

strasse

Alster-park

Hallerstrasse

PÖSSELDORF

Milchstrasse

Harvesthuder Weg

Mittelweg

ROTHERBAUM

Rothenbaumchaussee

Schöne Aussicht

Lerchenfeld

Aussenalster

HOHENFELDE

Mundsburgerdamm

Schwanenwik

Mühlendamm

Sechslingspforte

Th.-Heuss-Platz

Mittelweg

Alsteruler

31

30

Lübecker-strasse

Gustav-Mahler-Park

29

An der Alster

28

BORGFELDE

Wall

14

Kennedybrücke

Lombardsbrücke

27

Koppelstrasse

Wall-strasse

26

ST. GEORG

Binnenalster

Balindamm

25

Hachmannplatz

Hansaplatz

15

ABC-Strasse

Jungfernstieg

Poststrasse

Steindamm

Adenauerallee

Kurt-Schumacher-Allee

Hauptbahnhof (i)

22

Mönckebergstrasse

Bleichenfleet

23

23

24

Spaldingstrasse

Nordkanalstrasse

75

16

Börse

20

St. Petri Kirche

21

Speersort Steinstrasse

Heidenka

Mönckebergstrasse

ALTSTADT

Domstrasse

Hammerbrookstrasse

17

Ost-West-Strasse

Nagelsweg

18

Holzbr. Matten

Sande

Dovenfleet

Oberbaum-brücke

Banksstrasse

Amsinckstrasse

19

Kajen

Katharinen-strasse

Brooktorkai

0   0.25 mi
0   0.25 km

Information (i)

N

Finding information

Tourismus-Zentrale Hamburg operates the **Tourist Information** office
(☎ 040/3005-1300; www.hamburg.de) in the main train station near the
main entrance. The office is open daily from 7 a.m. to 10 p.m. and can
book a hotel room for you for a €4 ($5) fee. In the harbor area, you find
Tourist Information (☎ 040/3005-1300) at the St.-Pauli-Landungsbrücken
between Piers 4 and 5. This office is open April through September daily
from 8 a.m. to 6 p.m., October through March 10 a.m. to 5:30 p.m.

Taking a bus tour

A guided bus tour is the best way to get a feel for Hamburg and its various neighborhoods and special areas. Daily tours on double-decker
buses operated by **Hamburger Stadtrundfahrten** (☎ 040/792-8979)
leave from the main train station, Kirchenallee entrance. The 90-minute
Top Tour departs every 30 minutes beginning at 9:30 a.m. (tours at 11
a.m. and 3 p.m. only in winter). Cost is €13 ($16) for adults, €7 ($8.75)
for children up to 14. The Elbe Tour, which lasts 2 hours and 30 minutes
and includes towns along the Elbe River, departs Saturday and Sunday
from April through October at 2 p.m. from the St.-Pauli-Landungsbrüucken.
Cost is €18 ($22) for adults, €6 ($7.50) for children. The three-hour
"Lights of Hamburg" tour starts at 8 p.m. from April through October and
includes a visit to the St. Pauli Reeperbahn district. Cost, including a drink,
is €30 ($37). Tickets for all tours are available on the bus. All tours have
live commentary in English.

Orienting yourself

The Hauptbahnhof is located on the eastern fringe of **central Hamburg,**
the city's commercial and shopping district. Central Hamburg surrounds
the **Alster,** a lake rimmed by Hamburg's most significant buildings. Two
bridges, the Lombardsbrücke and the Kennedybrücke, divide the Alster
into the **Binnenalster** (Inner Alster) and the larger **Aussenalster** (Outer
Alster). **Pösseldorf,** northwest of Aussenalster, is a tree-filled residential
district with many fine 19th-century villas and Jugendstil (Art Nouveau)
buildings.

Flanking the Binnenalster on the south is the **Jungfernstieg,** Hamburg's
most vital artery and shopping district. Two canals, **Alsterfleet** and
Bleichenfleet, run south from Binnenalster, channeling water from the
Alster to the Elbe. Many of Hamburg's finest hotels and restaurants cluster around the Binnenalster and the Rathaus (City Hall), a short distance
to the south.

The **Port** *(Hafen)* **of Hamburg,** the world's seventh-largest harbor,
stretches for nearly 40km (25 miles) along the Elbe River, south of
Central Hamburg and the Alster. The **St. Pauli** district, the old sailor's
quarter that became the center of Hamburg nightlife, is located northwest of the river. The **Reeperbahn,** a famous neon-lit boulevard with
cafes, sex shows, bars, discos, and music halls, bisects St. Pauli.

The western district of **Altona,** formerly a city in its own right, now integrated into Greater Hamburg, is the scene of Hamburg's famous *Fischmarkt* (fish market), which takes place at dawn every Sunday. The Altona neighborhood is a great place to explore or have dinner.

Getting around Hamburg

Hamburg is not a compact city and can't be easily covered on foot. To see everything of interest, you have to depend on public transportation or taxis. **Hamburger Verkehrsverbund (HVV; ☎ 040/19449;** www.hvv. com) operates the **U-Bahn** (subway), **S-Bahn** (light rail), **A-Bahn** (commuter rail), buses, and harbor ferries.

The **HamburgCard** is good for travel on all public transport, admission to 11 Hamburg museums, and discounts on city tours, guided tours of the port, and lake cruises. A one-day card costs €7.30 ($9.10) for one adult, €13.50 ($17) for a group ticket, known as a *Gruppenkarte,* which is good for two or more people traveling together. A three-day card costs €15 ($19) for one adult, €23.90 ($30) for a group ticket. You can buy the card at the Tourist Information offices (see "Finding information," earlier in this chapter).

The U-Bahn (subway) and buses

Hamburg's **U-Bahn** serves the entire central area and connects with the **S-Bahn** light-rail trains in the suburbs. The U-Bahn is the fastest means of getting around, but **buses** offer a good alternative and enable you to see more of the city. The fare, which is the same for both U-Bahn and bus, depends on how far you travel.

A **single one-way fare** for both U-Bahn and bus costs €2.40 ($3) within Greater Hamburg. Buy your ticket from the bus driver or from automatic vending machines at U-Bahn stations and bus stops. A **Tageskarte** (day ticket) for unlimited use of public transportation costs €5.50 ($6.90) for an adult and includes fare for up to three children traveling with an adult.

Taxis

For a taxi, call ☎ **040/441-011** or 040/666-666. Taxi meters begin at €2 ($2.50) and rise €1.55 ($1.90) per kilometer.

Staying in Hamburg

Hamburg is an expensive city with plenty of first-class hotels and a limited number of budget accommodations, especially in the center of the city. If you arrive without a room, Hamburg's **Tourist Information** office in the main train station can help you find accommodations (see "Finding information," earlier in this chapter). You also find hotel-booking desks at the airport.

See Chapter 22 for details on the **Kempinski Hotel Atlantic Hamburg** ($$$$).

Aussen Alster
$$–$$$ Central Hamburg

This small, stylish hotel in a late-19th-century building sits on a quiet residential street near the Aussenalster lake. The 27 midsize rooms are minimalist in terms of décor but very comfortable and meticulously maintained. The bathrooms are small with shower-tub combinations. You find an on-site sauna and solarium. The hotel can arrange baby-sitting.

See map p. 176. Schmilinskystrasse 11, 20099 Hamburg. ☎ 040/241-557. Fax: 040/280-3231. www.aussen-alster.de. *U-Bahn: Hauptbahnhof (then a 5-minute walk east on Steindamm and west on Stiftstrasse, which becomes Schmilinskystrasse). Rack rates: €129–€155 ($161–$194) double. Rates include buffet breakfast. AE, DC, MC, V.*

Hamburg Marriott
$$$–$$$$ Central Hamburg

This large, traditionally styled hotel is near the Hanse Viertel, a fashionable area filled with boutiques, wine bars, shops, and restaurants. Geared toward business travelers, this hotel features an array of business-oriented in-room amenities. The 227 rooms are priced according to size and degree of luxury. The well-done bathrooms have shower-tub combinations. The hotel has a fitness center with pool and sauna and can arrange baby-sitting.

See map p. 176. ABC Strasse 52, 20354 Hamburg. ☎ 800/228-9290 in the U.S. or 040/35050. Fax: 040/3505-1777. www.marriott-hotels.com. *U-Bahn: Gänsemarkt (then a 3-minute walk south on ABC Strasse). Rack rates: €135–€245 ($169–$306) double. Rates include breakfast. AE, DC, MC, V.*

Hotel Hafen Hamburg
$$–$$$ St. Pauli/Harbor area

This Hamburg landmark, originally built in the mid–19th century as a home for sailors, offers rooms with panoramic views of the river and harbor. The building was restored and converted into a hotel in 1979, and today consists of three adjacent buildings with a total of 255 rooms. The rooms vary in size, but most are large with updated modern furnishings; all have well-equipped bathrooms with a shower-tub combination. The third and fourth floors are nonsmoking. The neighboring ship-shaped **Hotel Residenz,** the Hafen's modern sister hotel, was built in 1995.

See map p. 176. Seewartenstrasse 9, 20459 Hamburg. ☎ 040/311-130. Fax: 040/3111-3755. www.hotel-hamburg.de. *U-/S-Bahn: St.-Pauli-Landungsbrücken (then a 7-minute walk north through the small park outside the station to Seewartenstrasse). Rack rates: Hafen €80–€125 ($100–$156) double; Residenz €130–€160 ($162–$200). Breakfast: €13 ($16). AE, DC, MC, V.*

Hotel Prem
$$–$$$$ Central Hamburg

Called the "white house on the Alster," the facade of this centrally located mansion-hotel overlooks the Aussenalster, and the rear faces a quiet garden.

Hamburg U-Bahn and S-Bahn

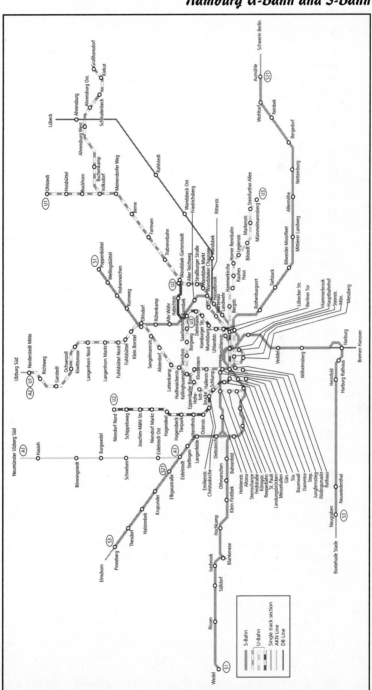

Each of the 53 rooms is individually decorated, some with French antiques, others with a contemporary flair. Although not large, rooms are comfortable; if you want quiet, ask for a room facing the garden. Half the bathrooms are well-equipped with big mirrors, marble tubs, and showers; the rest have shower stalls only.

See map p. 176. An der Alster 9, 20099 Hamburg. ☎ *040/2483-4040. Fax: 040/280-3851.* www.hotel-prem.de. *U-Bahn: Lohmülen Strasse (then a 5-minute walk northwest on Bülaustrasse to An der Alster). Rack rates: €115–€200 ($144–$250) double. Breakfast: €15 ($19). AE, DC, MC, V.*

Hotel Side
$$$–$$$$ Central Hamburg

Hamburg's newest hotel, which opened in the spring of 2001, takes high design to new heights. A stark white and steel high-tech minimalism is offset by dramatic, glowing colors and contemporary furniture placed as carefully as sculptures. Built around a central atrium, the 178 good-size rooms are quiet and comfortable. The luxurious bathrooms have a tub-shower combination. A terrace on the eighth floor opens onto panoramic views of Hamburg. Amenities include a health club with pool. You may find a bit of attitude, but staying here is definitely a memorable experience.

See map p. 176. Drehbahn 49, 20354 Hamburg. ☎ *40/309-990. Fax: 40/3099-9399.* www.side-hamburg.de. *U-Bahn: Gänsemarkt (then a 3-minute walk north on Dammtorstrasse and west on Drehbahn). Rack rates: €180–€280 ($225–$350). Breakfast: €18 ($22). AE, DC, MC, V.*

Park Hyatt Hamburg
$$$–$$$$ Central Hamburg

One of the most beautifully designed hotels in Hamburg, the Hyatt occupies a former trading house from 1912 that was transformed into a hotel in 1998. Lots of wood and warm-toned fabrics adorn the 252 spacious rooms. The large bathrooms have a separate area for Japanese-style soaking tubs. This full-service hotel has virtually every amenity you can imagine, the largest pool in Hamburg, and a fine-dining restaurant called **Apples** (see "Dining in Hamburg," later in this chapter).

See map p. 176. Bugenhagenstrasse 8, 20095 Hamburg. ☎ *040/3332-1234. Fax: 40/3332-1235.* www.hamburg.hyatt.de. *U-Bahn: Hauptbahnhof (then a 5-minute walk west across Steintor Wall to Bugenhagenstrasse). Rack rates: €170–€250 ($212–$312) double. Breakfast: €22 ($27). Special weekend and summer rates. AE, DC, MC, V.*

Pension Helga Schmidt
$ Central Hamburg

This small, traditional, 17-room pension sits right across the street from the superdeluxe Kempinski Hotel Atlantic Hamburg (see Chapter 22) and costs a fraction of the price. You won't find anything fancy here. But the double rooms are of a decent size and have an old-fashioned comfort of their own. The rooms have private bathrooms with showers. Breakfast costs extra, but you can eat in your room.

See map p. 176. Holzdamm 14, 20099 Hamburg. ☎ *040/280-83-90. Fax: 040/243-705.* www.t-online.de/home/Pension-Schmidt. *U-Bahn: Hauptbahnhof (then a 5-minute walk north on Holzdamm). Rack rates: €55 ($69) double without bathroom; €65 ($81) double with bathroom. Breakfast: €6 ($7.50). AE, DC, V.*

Wedina
$$–$$$ Central Hamburg

This recently remodeled hotel is in three different buildings painted three different colors (red, blue, and yellow). Most of the 42 rooms open onto a small, Tuscan-style garden. They range in size from small to medium and are individually decorated with modern furnishings. The smallish bathrooms have a shower-tub combination. The hotel doesn't have an elevator, and to reach rooms on the third floor, you have to climb 55 steps. The place is hip without being pretentious.

See map p. 176. Gurlittstrasse 23, 20099 Hamburg. ☎ *040/280-8900. Fax: 040/280-3894.* www.wedina.de. *U-Bahn: Hauptbahnhof (then a 5-minute walk north along Koppel Strasse to Gurlittstrasse). Rack rates: €105–€150 ($131–$187) double. Rates include buffet breakfast. AE, DC, MC, V.*

Dining in Hamburg

It shouldn't come as any surprise that most of Hamburg's traditional cuisine comes from the sea. On the menus of the city's many fish restaurants, you usually find lobster, shrimp, turbot, plaice, salmon, sole, fresh oysters, and eel (*Aalsuppe,* or eel soup, is a famous Hamburg dish). Traditional meat dishes include *Stubenküchen* (hamburger steak) and *Labskaus* — made with beer, onions, corned beef, potatoes, herring, and pickle — which is a hearty, protein-packed dish that sailors and dockworkers order. Pancakes *(Pfannkuchen)* with cranberries or other fruit toppings are popular. *Rote Grütze,* a local dessert specialty, is a compote of red fruits served with vanilla ice cream or cream.

Apples Restaurant
$$$–$$$$ Central Hamburg   INTERNATIONAL

Centered around an open kitchen and wood-fired oven, Apples is the showcase restaurant of the Park Hyatt Hamburg. The menu, which changes according to seasonal availability, features fresh, organically grown produce. Appetizers may include wok-fried squid with spring vegetables and black bean sauce or asparagus with black truffle vinaigrette. As a main course, you may find grilled lobster, chargrilled turbot and peppers, rack of lamb, or oven-roasted duck. Fresh specials of the day also are available. Come here for an elegant evening out.

See map p. 176. In the Park Hyatt Hamburg, Bugenhagenstrasse 8. ☎ *040/3332-1234.* U-Bahn: Hauptbahnhof (then a 5-minute walk west across Steintor Wall to Bugenhagenstrasse). Reservations required. Main courses: €18–€33 ($22–$41). AE, DC, MC, V. Open: 6:30 a.m.–2:30 p.m. and 6–11 p.m.

Cremon Weinkeller
$ **Harbor area NORTH GERMAN**

If you want to eat lunch with the locals, with a minimum of fuss, this bar-restaurant is a good place to try. From the below-street-level location, you can see the Nikolaifleet canal from the windows. The restaurant serves four or five hot dishes of fish and meat buffet-style at lunchtime; a cold buffet is available in the evening. Typical offerings include goulash with noodles, salmon, jacket potatoes with sour cream and crab or other fillings, and the Cremonteller, a platter with crab, meat, cheese, and bread and butter.

See map p. 176. Cremon 33–34. ☎ *040/362-190.* U-Bahn: Baumwall (then a 10-minute walk east on Kajen and north on Cremons). Main courses: €5–€7.50 ($6.25–$9.50) per dish. MC, V. Open: Mon–Fri 11 a.m.–10 p.m.

Die Rösterei
$ **Central Hamburg LIGHT MEALS/BREAKFAST/DESSERTS**

Located in the shopping arcade attached to the Park Hyatt hotel, this casual cafe is a good place to stop for breakfast, a light lunch, or afternoon coffee. For breakfast, you can order eggs, sausages, cold cuts, and croissants. Luncheon offerings usually include chicken and fish dishes plus daily specials and several different salads. The cafe roasts its own coffee beans, so you can get a cappuccino with your afternoon *Kuchen* (cake). You can eat on the balcony overlooking the shops or in the wood-paneled dining room.

See map p. 176. Mönckebergstrasse 7. ☎ *040/3039-3735.* U-Bahn: Mönckebergstrasse (then a 2-minute walk east on Mönckebergstrasse). Breakfast: €3.50–€9 ($4.40–$11). Main courses: €9–€12 ($11–15). No credit cards. Open: Mon–Sat 9 a.m.–9 p.m., Sun 10 a.m.–9 p.m.

Eisenstein
$$–$$$ **Altona INTERNATIONAL**

The menu in this hip Altona restaurant, housed in a former tram station, includes specialties from Thailand, Japan (including sushi and sashimi), southern France, and Italy, and fresh, traditional versions of North German cuisine, particularly fresh Atlantic fish. Popular offerings include breast of duck with caramelized cherries, homemade pastas, and saltimbocca.

See map p. 176. Friedensallee 9. ☎ *040/3904-606.* S-Bahn: Altona (then a 10-minute walk west on Hauptstrasse and northwest on Bahrenstrasse, which becomes Friedensallee). Reservations recommended. Main courses: €8–€26 ($10–$32); fixed-price lunch €14 ($17), fixed-price dinner €26 ($32). No credit cards. Open: Daily noon to 3 p.m. and 6 p.m. to midnight..

Fischküche Karin Brahm
$$–$$$ Harbor area   SEAFOOD

This pleasant fish restaurant in a modern building has a bright dining room and outdoor tables. The food is robust, and the service is no-nonsense. The menu changes all the time, depending on the catch of the day. Choices may include different kinds of clear or creamy fish soup, herring filets on black bread with onions, a mixed fish platter, flounder with spaghetti and lemon-butter sauce, or codfish with potatoes and onion.

See map p. 176. Kajen 12. ☎ 040/365-631. U-Bahn: Baumwall (then a 3-minute walk west to Kajen). Reservations recommended. Main courses: €17–€25 ($21–$31). AE, DC, MC, V. Open: Mon–Fri noon to midnight, Sat 6 p.m. to midnight..

Le Paquebot
$$ Central Hamburg   INTERNATIONAL

In warm weather, you can sit outside on the square and enjoy a good meal at this quietly stylish restaurant and bar. (Indoor dining is available year-round.) The menu, an international mix of French and modern German, changes daily. For starters, you may try the avocado salad with herring or some crostini. Main courses typically include offerings such as cannelloni stuffed with mushrooms and ricotta, salmon filet, and breast of chicken with basil and mushrooms. The young wait staff usually speak English.

See map p. 176. Gerhart-Hauptmann-Platz 70. ☎ 040/326-519. U-Bahn: Möncke-bergstrasse (then a 2-minute walk across Gerhart-Hauptmann-Platz). Main courses: €7–€16 ($8.75–$20). AE, MC, V. Open: Mon–Sat 11 a.m.–2 a.m., Sun 5:30 p.m.–2 a.m.

Ratsweinkeller Hamburg
$$–$$$ Central Hamburg   HAMBURG/INTERNATIONAL

In business since 1896, the Ratsweinkeller Hamburg has high, vaulted ceilings, wood-paneled columns, and large stained-glass windows. Don't bother with appetizers; the main courses are more than enough. Try the halibut steak in curry sauce, the fresh sole, or the Hamburg crab soup. Or, step up to the herring buffet featuring many different condiments and sauces. If you don't like fish, you can choose from other dishes such as chicken breast in a green rice crust or turkey curry.

See map p. 176. Grosse Johannisstrasse 2. ☎ 040/364-153. U-Bahn: Rathaus (then a 3-minute walk south on Grosse Johannisstrasse). Reservations recommended. Main courses: €11–€31 ($14–$39); fixed-price menus €30–€45 ($37–$56). AE, DC, MC, V. Open: Mon–Sat 11 a.m.–10:30 p.m., Sun 11 a.m.–4 p.m. Closed holidays.

Voltaire Bistro
$$ Altona   INTERNATIONAL

This pleasant, reasonably priced restaurant is across from Eisenstein (see the listing earlier in this section) in the popular Altona area. The dining room is a high-ceilinged brick-walled room with big windows and a bistrolike atmosphere. The menu borrows from French, Italian, and German cuisine, with coq au vin and spaghetti with mushroom sauce available every day. You also find many different salad choices. Meat and fish dishes typically include entrecôte (boned rib steak) with mustard sauce, rabbit with sweet-and-sour sauce, wild duck with plum sauce, scampi, and herring. Voltaire also has a good wine list and live jazz on most evenings.

See map p. 176. Friedensalle 14–16. ☎ *040/397-004. S-Bahn: Altona (then a 10-minute walk west on Hauptstrasse and north on Bahrenstrasse, which becomes Friedensallee). Main courses: €9–€14 ($11–$17). No credit cards. Open: Daily 6 p.m.–1 a.m.*

Zum Alten Rathaus
$–$$ Altstadt   NORTH GERMAN

This restaurant occupies a mid-19th-century building in the most historic part of the Altstadt (Old Town). A good lunch spot popular with local workers, Alten Rathaus offers different specials every day of the week. Popular staples include homemade *Sauerfleisch* (stewed, marinated meat in aspic), a fish dish of zander and salmon in a mustard sauce, and herring filets with potatoes. You can also get *Labskaus,* turkey steak, or simple pasta dishes.

See map p. 176. Börsenbrücke 10. ☎ *040/3751-8908. U-Bahn: Rathaus (then a 5-minute walk southwest on Johannis-Mönckebergstrasse to Börsenbrücke). Main courses: €5–€10 ($6.25–$12) No credit cards. Open: Mon–Fri 11:30 a.m.–8 p.m.*

Exploring Hamburg

Surprisingly enough, Hamburg is not a city with many world-class cultural attractions. Sightseeing usually centers on the giant harbor and picturesque Alster Lake.

Alster Lake

Sailboats, excursion ferries, windsurfers, and canoes ply the waters of this lake that forms the watery heart of central Hamburg. The Alster consists of the **Binnenalster,** a smaller, inner lake with canals running south to the Elbe, and the **Aussenalster,** a larger body of water ringed by fine villas. Damming the meandering Alster River created the lake in 1235. Walking paths and parkland surround the 7km (4 miles) of shoreline. **Alsterpark,** which covers 175 acres on the northwest banks, features beautiful trees, flower gardens, and panoramic views of the Hamburg skyline.

See map p. 176. U-Bahn: Hallerstrasse (then a 10-minute walk east on Hallerstrasse to the park).

Hafen (Harbor)

Hamburg is probably most famous for its busy harbor, one of the largest in the world. Its official history dates back to 1189, when the emperor Friedrich Barbarossa issued an edict granting free-trading privileges to Hamburg. The city still commemorates the event every year in early May with three days of huge harborside celebrations, including a windjammer parade, fireworks, and hundreds of booths.

Seeing the Alster by boat

You can tour both inner *(Binnen)* and outer *(Ausser)* Alster by boat. **ATG-Alster-Touristik,** Am Anleger Jungfernstieg (☎ 040/357-4240), offers daily 50-minute trips that depart about every half-hour, April through September, from 10 a.m. to 6 p.m.; from November through March, tours depart daily at 10:30 a.m., noon, and 1:30 and 3 p.m. The ships leave from the Jungfernstieg quayside (U-Bahn: Jungfernstieg). The cost for the tour is €9.50 ($12) for adults and €4.50 ($5.50) for children younger than 16. A brochure and cassettes with a description of the tour in English are available at no additional cost. The same company offers boat tours of Hamburg's canals and along the Elbe.

The harbor is an open tidal port, in which the North Sea tides influence the water level of the Elbe River. Just southeast of Hamburg, where the Elbe splits into two arms, there is a giant network of quays, warehouses, and drydocks.

Tourist activity centers around the **St.-Pauli-Landungsbrücken,** a long, floating landing stage where you can embark on boat tours of the harbor. Docked just east of the landing stage at Pier 1 is the **Rickmer Rickmers** (☎ 040/319-5959), a 19th-century clipper ship, now a museum of maritime history. This former East Indies windjammer is open daily from 10 a.m. to 5:30 p.m. Admission is €3 ($3.75) for adults, €2.50 ($3.10) for children ages 4 to 12.

 The best way to see the port and all its activity is by taking a **guided harbor tour.** Excursion boats operated by **HADAG** (☎ 040/311-7070) leave from St.-Pauli-Landungsbrücken, Piers 1 through 9. Tours depart from April through October daily every hour from 10 a.m. to 6 p.m.; from November through March, Saturday and Sunday only from 10:30 a.m. to 3:30 p.m. From March through November, an English-language tour departs daily from Pier 1 at noon. The 75-minute trip costs €9 ($11) for adults, €5 ($6.25) for children.

See map p. 176. U-Bahn: St.-Pauli-Landungsbrücken (the harbor is right across the street).

 Hamburger Kunsthalle (Fine Arts Museum)

Northern Germany's leading art museum displays works from the medieval era to the present day. The museum has an outstanding collection of 19th-century German Romantic paintings, including works by Philipp Otto Runge and Caspar David Friedrich. You can also see dazzling works by German impressionists Max Liebermann and Lovis Corinth, and late-19th-early-20th-century artists Edvard Munch, Leon Kirchner, Otto Dix, Max Beckmann, Paul Kandinsky, and Paul Klee. The new **Galerie der Gegenwart** (Contemporary Gallery) wing displays art created since 1960. Allow yourself at least two hours to see everything on view.

See map p. 176. Glockengiesserwall 1. ☎ 040/2854-2612. U-Bahn: Hauptbahnhof (exit at Hauptbahnhof Nord, then a 2-minute walk north on An der Kunsthalle). Admission: €8.50 ($11) adults, €5 ($6.25) children. Open: Tues–Sun 10 a.m.–6 p.m. (Thurs until 9 p.m.).

Museum für Hamburgische Geschichte (Hamburg History Museum)

This museum provides a portrait of Hamburg from the 8th through 20th centuries. Scale models show the changing face of the port, and reconstructed period rooms — from the hall of a 17th-century merchant's house to an air-raid shelter from WWII — illustrate the different eras in Hamburg's history. Give yourself about an hour to browse through the exhibits.

See map p. 176. Holstenwall 24. ☎ 040/4284-12360. U-Bahn: St. Pauli (then a 2-minute walk east across Millentordamm). Admission: €7.50 ($9.50) adults, €1 ($1.25) children. Open: Tues–Sat 10 a.m.–5 p.m., Sun 10 a.m.–6 p.m.

Rathaus (Town Hall)

Hamburg's Rathaus, built in the late 19th century on a foundation of oak pilings, is the largest of the old buildings in the Altstadt. You can visit the interior of this Renaissance-style structure with its 647 rooms on a guided tour. The Rathaus's 49m-tall (160-ft.) clock tower overlooks Rathausmarkt and the **Alsterfleet,** the city's largest canal. The **Alsterarkaden,** across the canal, is an arched passageway with upscale clothing shops, jewelry stores, and boutiques. You can combine a visit to the Rathaus with a stop at the 16th-century **Börse** (Stock Exchange), Adolphsplatz 1 (☎ 040/361-3020), which stands back to back with the Rathaus. Guides conduct free tours of the Börse on Tuesday and Thursday at 11 a.m. and noon. Tours of the Rathaus and the Börse last about 30 to 45 minutes.

See map p. 176. Rathausplatz. ☎ 040/4283-12063. U-Bahn: Rathaus. Admission: Rathaus tour €1 ($1.25) adults, €0.50 (65¢) children. Tours (in English): Mon–Fri hourly 10 a.m.–3 p.m., Sat–Sun 10 a.m.–1 p.m.

St. Jacobikirche (St. James's Church)

WWII bombings almost completely destroyed the 13th-century Gothic Jacobikirche. The rebuilt church contains several medieval altars, pictures, and sculptures, in addition to one of Hamburg's musical treasures, a baroque organ built in 1693 by Arp Schnitger, a master craftsman whose instruments were played by Johann Sebastian Bach. The 60-register organ at St. James's is one of only two surviving Schnitger organs in Germany.

See map p. 176. Jakobikirchhof 22, entrance on Steinstrasse. ☎ 040/327-744. U-Bahn: Mönckebergstrasse (then a 2-minute walk south to Jakobikirchhof). Admission: Free. Open: Mon–Sat 10 a.m.–5 p.m., Sun 10 a.m. to noon.

St. Michaelis (St. Michael's Church)

Constructed of brick, like so many other buildings in Hamburg, St. Michael's, completed in 1762, is one of the finest baroque churches in northern Germany. The tower, with its hammered-copper roof, is a famous Hamburg landmark and the principal reason to visit. Take the elevator or climb the

449 steps to enjoy the sweeping view from the top. The crypt, one of the largest in Europe, contains the tomb of composer Carl Philipp Emanuel Bach. Give yourself about 15 minutes to visit the church and tower. One block to the south of the church are the **Krameramtswohnungen,** Hamburg's last remaining 17th-century brick-and-timber almshouses, which have been made into art galleries.

See map p. 176. Krayenkamp 4C, Michaeliskirchplatz. ☎ *040/3767-8100. S-Bahn: Stadthausbrücke (then a 10-minute walk west on Michaelisstrasse). Admission: Church free; tower €2.50 ($3.10) adults, €1.25 ($1.60) children. Open: Daily Apr–Sept 9 a.m.–6 p.m., Oct–Mar 10 a.m.–5 p.m.*

Tierpark Hagenbeck (Zoo)

Founded in 1848, Hamburg's zoo is home to about 2,500 animals. This zoo in the northwest suburbs offers sea-lion and dolphin shows, elephant and camel rides, a train ride through a fairyland, and a spacious children's playground. A restaurant serves fixed-price meals for €9.50 to €14 ($12 to $17) from 11:30 a.m. to closing.

See map p. 176. Hagenbeckallee at Steilingen. ☎ *040/540-0010. U-Bahn: Hagenbeck's Tierpark. Admission: €14.50 ($18) adults, €8.50 ($11) children ages 7 to 16, children younger than 6 free. Open: Daily 9 a.m.–5 p.m. (until 4:30 p.m. in winter).*

Wallringpark

Four beautifully maintained parks and gardens comprise this greenbelt area west of the Altstadt and Alster Lake. **Planten und Blomen** (Plants and Flowers), laid out in 1936, contains the largest Japanese garden in Europe, with rock gardens, flowering plants, miniature trees, and winding pathways. The **Alter Botanischer Garten** (Old Botanical Garden), south of Planten and Blomen, is known for its rare plant specimens and greenhouses filled with tropical flora. The **Kleine** (small) and **Grosse** (large) **Wallanlagen** parks contain many recreational facilities, including a roller-skating rink, playgrounds, restaurants, and an ice-skating rink in winter. A miniature railway connects all four parks.

See map p. 176. U-Bahn: Dammtor (the station is at the southeastern corner of the park). Admission: Free.

Tracing your German ancestry

The **Museum für Hamburgische Geschichte** (see the listing in this chapter) is especially worth a visit if you have German ancestors and want to do genealogical research. The museum's office of historic emigration contains passenger lists of all the people who shipped out of Hamburg from the 1850s to about 1930. On record are hundreds of thousands of emigrants' names including the names of the cities and towns in which they originated. To use the service, you need to bring records with you that indicate the approximate date that your ancestors left Germany.

Shopping in Hamburg

Hamburg is a big shopping city, but don't expect to find many bargains, or any kind of local specialty or handicraft. Stores are generally open Monday through Friday from 9 a.m. to 6:30 p.m. (some until 8 p.m. on Thursday) and on Saturday from 9 a.m. to 2 p.m. (until 4 or 6 p.m. on *langer Samstag,* the first Saturday of the month).

From the Hauptbahnhof, two major shopping streets fan out in a south-westerly direction toward the Rathaus: the pedestrian-only **Spitalerstrasse** and **Mönckebergstrasse.** These streets contain some of the city's less expensive stores. Two of the city's oldest and most prestigious shopping streets, **Grosse Bleichen** and **Neuer Wall,** run parallel to the canals, connected transversely by **Jungfernstieg** and **Ufer Strasse** on the Binnenalster.

Karstadt, Mönckebergstrasse 16 (☎ **040/30940**), is part of a department-store chain that carries many of the same brands and items as the other leading department stores. Less expensive is **Kaufhof,** Mönckebergstrasse 3 (☎ **040/333-070**), which offers better deals on merchandise markdowns. **Alsterhaus,** Jungfernstieg 22 (☎ **040/359-011**), carries more-fashionable merchandise.

Living it up after dark in Hamburg

To find out what's happening in Hamburg, pick up a copy of the monthly *Hamburger Vorschau* for €1.20 ($1.50), available at tourist offices, hotels, and newsstands. You can obtain tickets at venue box offices, at tourist offices, or through the service **Theaterkasse Central,** Gerhart-Hauptmann-Platz 48, Landesbank-Galerie (☎ **040/337-124;** U-Bahn: Mönckebergstrasse).

The performing arts

Hamburgische Staatsoper (Hamburg State Opera), Dammtorstrasse 28 (☎ **040/35-68-68;** www.hamburgische-staatsoper.de; S-Bahn: Dammtor), one of the world's leading opera houses, is the home of the **Hamburg State Opera** and the **Hamburg Ballet.** Ticket prices range from €5 to €146 ($6.25 to $182). The ticket office is at Grosstheaterstrasse 34.

The famous Hamburg Fischmarkt

The Hamburg **Fischmarkt (fish market),** between Hexenberg and Grosse Elbstrasse (U-Bahn: St.-Pauli-Landungsbrücken), takes place every Sunday from 5 a.m. in summer or from 7 a.m. the rest of the year. Besides fish, you can buy flowers, fruit, vegetables, plants, and pets at this traditional market, in existence since 1703. The nearby taverns are open to serve Fischmarkt visitors and vendors.

The **Musikhalle,** Johannes-Brahms-Platz (☎ 040/35-68-68; U-Bahn: Messehallen), plays host to concerts by the **Hamburg Symphony,** the **Hamburg Philharmonic,** and the **NDR Symphony,** in addition to performances by choirs, chamber orchestras, and guest artists. Ticket prices vary from program to program.

Hamburg has dozens of theaters, but you need to understand German to enjoy the productions. One exception is the **English Theatre of Hamburg,** Lerchenfeld 14 (☎ 040/227-7089; U-Bahn: Mundsburg), the only English-speaking theater in the northern part of Germany. Tickets range from €7 to €25 ($8.75 to $31).

The club, bar, and music scenes

Hamburg is famous for its nightlife. The following list gives a small sampling of bars, beer halls, nightclubs, dance clubs, and live-music venues:

- ✔ **After Shave,** Spielbudenplatz 7 (☎ 040/319-3215; S-Bahn: Reeperbahn), a dance club for 20- to 30-year-olds, features funk, soul, jazz, and fusion. The club is open from 11 p.m. to 4 a.m. Thursday, to 5 a.m. Friday, and to 6 a.m. Saturday. Cover is €5 to €8 ($6.25 to $10); free admission for women Fri–Sat after midnight.

- ✔ **Bayrisch Zell,** Reeperbahn 10 (☎ 040/314-281; S-Bahn: Reeperbahn), a giant beer hall, is one of the most popular places in the St. Pauli district, attracting singles and couples young and old. If someone catches your fancy, you can call him or her from the phone on your table. The food is okay, too, with meals ranging from €5 to €12 ($6.25 to $15). The hall is open daily from 7 p.m. to 3 a.m.

- ✔ **Club Grosse Freiheit,** Grosse Freiheit 36 (☎ 040/317-7711; S-Bahn: Reeperbahn), in St. Pauli, is where the Beatles performed in their earliest days. Today this cultural institution is a free-for-all venue with acts that change nightly. Cover is €4.50 to €22 ($5.75 to $27).

- ✔ **Cotton Club,** Alter Steinweg 10 (☎ 040/343-878; S-Bahn: Stadthausbrücke), the oldest and best established of the Hamburg jazz clubs, features jazz and Dixieland bands from throughout Europe and the U.S. The club is open year-round Monday through Saturday from 8 p.m. to midnight; from September to April, it's also open Sunday from 11 a.m. to 3 p.m. Cover charge is €4 to €15 ($5 to $19), depending on the band.

- ✔ **Molotow,** Spielbudenplatz 5(☎ 040/31-08-45; S-Bahn: Reeperbahn), is one of the hottest dance clubs in Hamburg, especially if you're into funk. The club opens at 9 p.m. Wednesday and Sunday and at 11 p.m. Thursday to Sunday from 11 p.m and has no set closing time. Cover is €2 to €12 ($2.50 to $15).

St. Pauli and the Reeperbahn: For adults only

Commercialized sex is a major tourist attraction in Hamburg. The place where it all hangs out is the St. Pauli district, just west of the center, along a half-mile thoroughfare called the **Reeperbahn** (pronounced *ray*-per-bahn; S-Bahn: Reeperbahn). The name literally translates as "rope street" and refers to the nautical rope produced there during the 18th and 19th centuries. By the mid-1800s, St. Pauli, which is close to Hamburg's great harbor, had become a hangout for sailors and prostitutes, who set up shop with the legal sanction of municipal authorities. Many of the prostitutes who work there today are licensed and must submit to a medical examination every two weeks.

St. Pauli is a place to visit at night. The area is not exclusively devoted to sex, and you do find all kinds of theaters (mostly for musicals and comedies), cabarets, bars, discos, and restaurants (although I wouldn't recommend dining in this area). The district's sex-related bars and theaters are up and running by 8 p.m. Between midnight and 5 a.m., thousands of "working girls" strut their stuff along the Reeperbahn and through St. Pauli's streets. The most famous street besides the Reeperbahn itself is **Herbertstrasse,** where bordel-los line both sides of the street, and the women display themselves behind plate-glass windows. Herbertstrasse is open only to men older than 18; metal gates block each end of the street. Please note that women are not welcome on Herbertstrasse, and may even be doused with a bucket of water if they enter.

Grosse Freiheit, a street whose name appropriately translates as "Great Freedom," is known for its erotic theaters. Municipal regulations forbid prostitution, or overt solicita-tion, inside erotic theaters. The district also contains the **Erotic Art Museum,** Nobistor 10A (☎ 040/3178-4126), at the corner of Reeperbahn and Groose Freiheit. Open to those older than 16, the museum presents its displays and changing exhibits in a way that's both academic and titillating. The museum is open Sunday through Thursday from 10 a.m. to midnight, Friday and Saturday from 10 a.m. to 2 a.m.; admission is €8 ($10).

Gay and lesbian clubs

Hamburg, like Berlin, is one of the major gay centers of Europe, with a dense concentration of gay shops, bars, and cafes along **Lange Reihe** just northeast of the train station (U-Bahn: Hauptbahnhof). The free magazine ***Dorn Rosa,*** distributed at most gay and lesbian bars, lists the city's many gay and lesbian clubs, restaurants, bars, and events.

A Side Trip: Bremen

Bremen, 120km (75 miles) southwest of Hamburg, has a history that dates back some 1,200 years. (See the "Bremen" map in this chapter.) Located on the Weser River, which flows to the North Sea, it already was a significant port when it was made an episcopal see in 787. During the Middle Ages, Bremen was one of the strongest members of the Hanseatic League, and in 1646, it became a Free Imperial City. Silting of the Weser led to the establishment of Bremerhaven, Bremen's deep-water port at the mouth of the Weser, in 1827. With a population of about half a million

Bremen

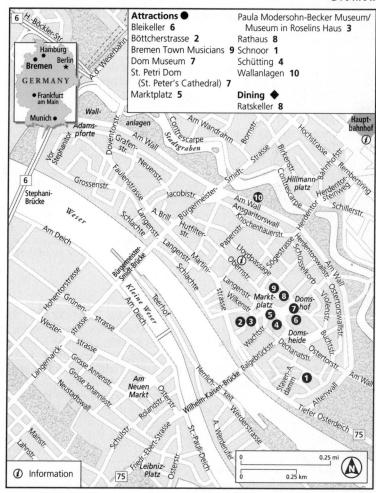

Attractions ●
Bleikeller **6**
Böttcherstrasse **2**
Bremen Town Musicians **9**
Dom Museum **7**
St. Petri Dom
  (St. Peter's Cathedral) **7**
Marktplatz **5**

Paula Modersohn-Becker Museum/
  Museum in Roselins Haus **3**
Rathaus **8**
Schnoor **1**
Schütting **4**
Wallanlagen **10**

Dining ◆
Ratskeller **8**

people, Bremen is the second most important foreign trade location in the Federal Republic, after Hamburg. Although it's mostly an industrial city that was badly damaged in WWII, enough remains in old Bremen to make for an intriguing day trip from Hamburg.

Getting to Bremen

By **train**, the trip time from Hamburg is less than an hour. For train information and schedules, call **Deutsche Bahn** (☎ **11861**). If you're **driving**, Bremen is a major junction on the **A1** Autobahn between Hamburg and the Rhineland. **Bremen Flughafen** (**Airport**; ☎ **0421/55-950**) has flights from major cities in Germany and Europe.

Finding information and taking a tour

Bremer-Touristik-Zentrale (☎ **01805/10-10-30;** www.bremen.de) operates **Tourist Information** offices at the **Hauptbahnhof** (main train station; open Monday to Friday 8 a.m.–8 p.m., Saturday and Sunday 9:30 a.m.–6 p.m.). A second branch at **Obernstrasse/Liebfrauenkirchhof** also is open daily. If you decide to stay overnight in Bremen, this office will help you find a hotel or pension. A second branch at **Obernstrasse/Liebfrauenkirchhof** is also open daily.

Guided bus tours, conducted in German and English, depart Tuesday through Sunday year-round at 10:30 a.m. from the Central Coach Station (Rank M) just behind the Tourist Information Office at the main train station. The tour lasts two hours and costs €15 ($19) for adults and €9.50 ($12) for children younger than 13. **Guided walking tours,** with English-speaking guides, depart daily at 2 p.m. from mid-May to early October, and Saturdays at 11 a.m. in January and February, from the Tourist Information Office at the main train station. They last two hours, and cost €6.50 ($8), free for children younger than 13. Buy your tickets at the tourist office. If you decide to stay overnight in Bremen, this office will help you find a hotel or pension. A second branch at **Obernstrasse/Liebfrauenkirchhof** also is open daily.

Dining in Bremen

The **Ratskeller** below Bremen's Rathaus, Am Markt (☎ **0421/32-16-76),** is a wonderfully atmospheric place to try North German regional specialties such as *Bremer Festtagsuppe* (a beef consomme with meatballs, noodles, and vegetables), *Bremer Fischtopf* (diced salmon, haddock, and red snapper in a vegetable stock), herring with sour cream and roasted potatoes, and *Flammkuchen,* a pizzalike dish with mushrooms, herbs, and cheese. There's also an adjoining restaurant called **Vor dem Bacchus** that serves fresh fish. Main courses go for €9.50 to €19 ($12 to $23). The restaurants are open daily from noon to 2:30 p.m. and 7 to 10:30 p.m. All major credit cards are accepted. See map p. 193.

Exploring Bremen

Bremen's main sights are in the Altstadt, clustered around **Marktplatz** (**Market Square**), the center of Bremen life for more than a millennium. Most of the compact oval Altstadt, with the Weser River along the south side and the Stadtgraben canal on the north, is a pedestrian zone and can easily be explored on foot. Recent restoration work has brightened up the center and its many historic buildings.

From Bahnhofsplatz in front of the train station, head south to Herdentor and the bridge that crosses the Stadtgraben canal. To your right, in the **Wallanlagen,** the pretty parkland along the canal (formerly the city wall stood here), you'll see a large Dutch-style windmill. At one time, more than a dozen windmills operated in this area.

Chocolate lovers take note

Hachez, a famous Bremen chocolatier founded in 1890, occupies a charming 18th-century patrician house near the Rathaus. The shop, Stoevesandt-Diele, Am Markt 1 (€ 0421/50-90-00), is a chocolate-lover's emporium where you can find sweet specialties such as chocolate champagne truffles.

At the beginning of Sümogestrasse (Sow Street), a bronze swineherd and a herd of bronze sows and piglets commemorates the street where medieval butchers kept their pigs. A short walk south brings you to the **Marktplatz,** where a 15th-century sandstone **statue of Knight Roland,** the city's protector, stands guard beside the Rathaus.

Bremen's impressive three-story **Rathaus** (Town Hall; ☎ 0421/36-10) has been standing on the Marktplatz for 600 years and was untouched by the bombing raids of WWII. The main Gothic structure was built in 1405, but in 1612 the upper section of the façade was redone in what is known as Weser Renaissance style. (Weser Renaissance, a term applied to architecture created in and around the Weser River valley between 1520 and 1620, is characterized by ornate decoration on classically proportioned buildings.) Inside, the upper hall with its beautifully carved early 17th-century oak staircase and mural of *The Judgment of Solomon* (1537), was used as council chamber and courtroom. You can visit the Rathaus on 45-minute guided tours Monday through Saturday at 11 a.m., noon, 3 and 4 p.m., and on Sunday at 11 a.m. and noon. Admission is €4 ($5) adults, €2 ($2.50) children and students. You can dine in the historic Ratskeller beneath the building (see "Dining in Bremen" earlier in this section).

Walk around to the west end of the Rathaus to see Bremen's most famous characters, the **Bremen Town Musicians** from the Grimm's fairy tale of the same name. Local artist Gerhard Marcks created the bronze sculpture of a donkey, dog, cat, and cock in 1951.

Directly opposite the Rathaus stands the **Schütting,** a 16th-century guild hall today used by the chamber of commerce (not open to the public). Adding a modern architectural touch to the ancient square is the **Haus der Bürgerschaft,** constructed in 1966 and home of Bremen's Parliament. Free 20-minute tours of the building are given Monday to Friday at 2 p.m.

At the southeast end of the Marktplatz, towering majestically over the entire Altstadt, is **St. Petri-Dom (St. Peter's Cathedral),** Sandstrasse 10–12 (☎ 0421/36-50-40), originally constructed in 1043 as the archbishop's church and rebuilt in the 16th and 19th centuries. There's a 12th-century bronze baptismal font in one of the Romanesque crypts, but otherwise not much of exceptional interest within the cathedral, which is open Monday to Friday 10 a.m. to 5 p.m., Saturday 10 a.m. to 2 p.m., and Sunday 2 to 5 p.m. From Easter through October you can climb to the top of the cathedral towers for a panoramic view of the Altstadt. The **Dom Museum (Cathedral Museum; ☎ 0421/365-04-41)** displays artifacts discovered during a restoration of the cathedral in the early 1970s, including vestments found in archbishops' graves and 15th-century wall paintings by Lucas Cranach the Elder. More interesting than the museum is the **Bleikeller (Lead Cellar),** reached by going outside and around to the side of the cathedral. It contains a bizarre collection of mummified corpses — 16th- and 17th-century lords, ladies, students, and soldiers, plus a cat and monkey — whose leathery bodies were found in graves beneath and around the cathedral. Admission for the cathedral museum and the Lead Cellar is €1.20 ($1.50) for adults, €1 ($1.25) for students and children; both are open the same hours as the cathedral, but the Lead Cellar is closed November to Easter.

The **Paula Modersohn-Becker Museum**, Böttcherstrasse 6–10 (**☎ 0421/ 336-5077**), is dedicated to Bremen's outstanding painter (1876 to 1907) and contains many of her best works, including paintings, drawings, and prints. The museum is open Tuesday through Sunday 11 a.m. to 6 p.m. Admission is €5 ($6.25) for adults and €3 ($3.75) for children. With the same ticket you can visit the nearby **Museum im Roselius Haus** (same address, phone, and hours), a 16th-century merchant's home filled with Ludwig Roselius's collection of medieval art and furniture.

Böttcherstrasse leads to the **Schlachte** embankment along the Weser River. The riverside promenade is lined with taverns and restaurants and is the locale of the Weserfloshmarket (Weser Flea Market), open every Saturday from 8 a.m. to 5 p.m. The Schlachte embankment also is where you find **guided boat trips** (in German only) around the harbor. Boats depart from the landing in front of the Martinikirche (St. Martin's Church) every day from April through October at 11:45 a.m., 1:30 p.m., and 3:15 p.m. on a voyage that lasts about 75 minutes. The cost is €8 ($10) for adults and €4.50 ($5.60) for children.

Bells are ringing on Böttcher Street

Böttcherstrasse, running from Marktplatz to the Weser River, is one of the most architecturally intriguing streets in Germany and one of Bremen's most noteworthy attractions. Ludwig Roselius, a rich Bremen merchant who invented decaffeinated coffee, paid for the construction of the red-brick buildings that line the street, which was dedicated in 1926 and rebuilt after World War II (WWII). Part of the narrow brick-paved street was built in an avant-garde German Expressionist style; the other part was meant to look more traditionally medieval. The street is lined with shops, crafts workshops, restaurants, two museums, and galleries. Time your visit to hear the carillon of bells made of Meissen porcelain. Every hour between noon and 6 p.m. (January through April at noon, 3, and 6 p.m.), they play a tune for a full 15 minutes as a sequence of woodcarved panels in a revolving tower tells the story of transatlantic aviators.

A five-minute walk southeast from the Schlachte brings you to the charming albeit touristy **Schnoor** district, Bremen's oldest surviving quarter. The 16th- and 17th-century cottages in the Schnoor once were the homes of simple fishermen. In an effort to revive old arts and crafts, they're now rented to artists and artisans. Sightseers visit not only for the atmosphere but also for the unusual restaurants, shops, and art galleries.

Lübeck: In a (Hanseatic) League of Its Own

Seven Gothic church spires rise above the picturesque town of Lübeck, located 66km (41 miles) northeast of Hamburg in the state of Schleswig-Holstein. (See the "Lübeck" map in this chapter.) Along the ancient streets of its Altstadt, you find more buildings from the 13th to the 15th centuries than in any other city in northern Germany. Most of the buildings, including the churches, are fine examples of the red-brick architecture so characteristic of northern Germany. The city's architectural heritage is so rich that the United Nations Educational, Scientific and Cultural Organization (UNESCO) placed Lübeck on its World Heritage list of international monuments. UNESCO bestows World Heritage status to places judged to have exceptional cultural value.

From the 13th century on, Lübeck was capital of the Hanseatic League, the powerful association of merchants that controlled trade along the Baltic as far as Russia. The town still retains the name *Hansestadt Lübeck.*

Lübeck makes a rewarding day trip from Hamburg, less than an hour away by train, but its charms may beguile you to stay overnight. With its enormous churches, high-gabled houses, massive gates, and historic buildings at every turn, Lübeck is a delightful city to explore.

Getting there

By train, you can reach Lübeck from anywhere in Germany or Europe. Dozens of trains arrive daily from Hamburg, only 40 minutes away. For train schedules and information, call **German Rail (☎ 11861).**

By boat, you can take a passenger or car ferry service between Denmark (the port of Rødbyhaven) and Lübeck (the port of Puttgarden). **ScandLines** (☎ 04371/865-161; www.scandlines.com) offers daily departures. **TT Saga Line (☎ 04502/80181; www.ttline.de)** operates between the German port of Travemünde and the Swedish port of Trelleborg.

By car, you can reach Lübeck via the **A1** Autobahn north and south.

Finding information

In the train station, **Touristinformation Hauptbahnhof (☎ 0451/864-675)** is open Monday through Saturday from 9 a.m. until 1 p.m. and 3 to 6 p.m. The **Lübeck und Travemünde Tourist Service,** Breite Strasse 62

(☎ 01805/882-233, €0.12 (15¢) per minute; www.luebeck-tourismus.
de), behind the Rathaus, is open January through May and October
through November, Monday through Friday from 9:30 a.m. to 6 p.m. and
Saturday from 10 a.m. to 3 p.m.; June through September and December,
hours are Monday through Friday from 9:30 a.m. to 7 p.m., Saturday from
10 a.m. to 3 p.m., and Sunday from 10 a.m. to 2 p.m. This office can help
you with hotel reservations.

Orienting yourself

The Trave and Wakenitz rivers and other waterways encircle Lübeck's
Altstadt, an oval-shaped island a little more than a mile long and less
than a mile wide. Eight bridges connect the old town with greater Lübeck
on the mainland. Only about 12,000 residents (out of about 225,000) live
on the island, which is where all the major attractions are located.

Getting around Lübeck

The Altstadt and all the major attractions can be reached on foot from
the train station. You also can take Buses 5, 6, 7, 11, 14, or 16 from the
train station into the Altstadt. The fare is €2 ($2.50).

A fun and relaxing way to see Lübeck is by water. Excursion boats operated by **MAAK-Linie** (☎ 0451/706-3859; www.maak-linie.de) leave
from docks on the Trave River just north of the Holstentor. In summer,
departures are hourly between 10 a.m. and 6 p.m. (between 11 a.m. and
4 p.m. the rest of the year). The trip (commentary in German with English
text available) lasts one hour and encircles the entire Altstadt. Cost is
€7 ($8.75) for adults, €5.50 ($7) for seniors, and €3 ($3.75) for children.

Lübeck's Nobel sons

Lübeck has had several famous sons, notably Thomas Mann and Willy Brandt. As a young
man, Brandt (1913 to 1992), who later became West German chancellor and won the
Nobel Peace Prize in 1971, opposed the Nazis so vehemently that he had to flee on a
boat to Norway. The writer Thomas Mann (1875 to 1955) used his hometown of Lübeck
as the setting for his novel *Buddenbrooks,* which catapulted the 27-year-old author to
international fame in 1902. In 1929, Mann won the Nobel Prize for literature. Günter
Grass, author of *The Tin Drum,* won the Nobel Prize for literature in 1999. Although he
was not born in Lübeck, he lives nearby. The relationship between Grass's literary
output and his artwork is explored in the permanent exhibits at the **Günther Grass
House,** Glockengiesserstrasse 21 (☎ 0451/122-4231), which opened in 2002. Here you
can see some of Grass's paintings, drawings, and sculptures. The museum is open
daily April through October from 10 a.m. to 6 p.m, November through March 11 a.m. to
4 p.m. Admission is €4 ($5) for adults, €2.20 ($2.75) students and children.

Lübeck

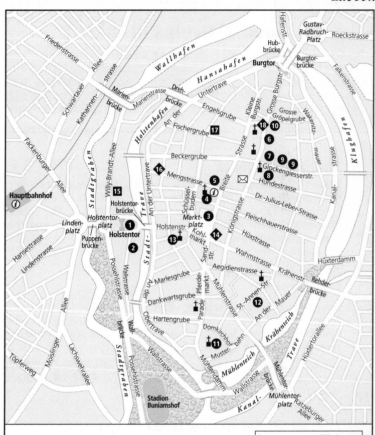

ACCOMMODATIONS ■

Klassik Altstadt Hotel **17**

Radisson SAS Senator
Hotel Lübeck **15**

DINING ◆

Cafe Niederegger **14**

Historischer Weinkeller **18**

Schabbelhaus **16**

ATTRACTIONS ●

Museum Holstentor **1**

Salzspeicher **2**

Rathaus **3**

Marienkirche **4**

Buddenbrookhaus **5**

Museen Behnhaus/Drägerhaus **6**

Füchtingshof **7**

Günther Grass House **8**

Glandorps-Gang/Glandorps-Hof **9**

Heiligen-Geist-Hospital **10**

Dom **11**

St.-Annen-Museum **12**

Petrikirche **13**

| 0 | | 0.25 mi |
| 0 | 0.25 km | |

Church ✝

Information ⓘ

Post Office ✉

Railway —

Special events in Lübeck

The **Schleswig-Holstein Music Festival,** one of the best music festivals in Germany, occurs in Lübeck (which has a famed music school) with performances from early July until the end of August every year. For more information, call ☎ **0800/7463-2002** or log on to www.shmf.de. A **Christmas market** featuring handmade wares from all across northwestern Germany takes place during the three weeks preceding Christmas.

Staying in Lübeck

Lübeck offers a full range of hotel options, from small inns and pensions to modern facilities. To enjoy the ancient, atmospheric charms of Lübeck, I recommend that you choose a hotel in the Altstadt. The Lübeck and Travemünde Tourist Service (see "Finding information" earlier in this chapter) also can help you find a room.

Klassik Altstadt Hotel
$–$$ **Altstadt**

If you want to stay in a smaller, older hotel in the Altstadt, Klassik Altstadt Hotel is a good choice. The 28 individually decorated rooms, all named for famous Lübeckers, have a pleasant, traditional style. Most of the bathrooms have showers, a few have tubs.

See map p. 199. Fischergrube 52, 23552 Lübeck. ☎ *0451/702980. Fax: 0451/73778.* www. klassik-altstadt-hotel.de. *Rack rates: €75–€112 ($94–$140) double. Rates include buffet breakfast. AE, MC, V.*

Radisson SAS Senator Hotel Lübeck
$$$–$$$$ **Altstadt**

If you want a modern, full-service hotel, the Radisson is the best place to stay. A pedestrian bridge connects the hotel from its riverside location to the Altstadt. The 231 medium-size rooms are attractively furnished. Bathrooms have shower-tub combinations. Amenities include an on-site health club with pool, sauna, and steam rooms, and a computer in the lobby that enables you to check your e-mail. Children up to age 12 stay for free in their parents' room.

See map p. 199. Willy-Brandt-Allee 6, 23554 Lübeck. ☎ *800/333-3333 in the U.S. or 0451/1420. Fax: 0451/142-2222.* www.senatorhotel.de. *Rack rates: €155–€195 ($194–$244). AE, MC, V.*

Dining in Lübeck

As you may have guessed, fresh seafood from the North and Baltic seas is featured on the menus of many restaurants in Lübeck. Below are two good restaurants where you can dine well in historic surroundings.

Historischer Weinkeller
$$-$$$ **Altstadt**

The Historischer Weinkeller, located beneath the 13th-century Heiligen-Geist-Hospital (see the "Walking through Lübeck" section next), is an excellent and atmospheric restaurant with an international menu. You can choose from several different fixed-priced menus. You may begin with smoked Norwegian salmon, goose-liver pâté, or a fish-based soup. Entrees range from filet of cod with sauerkraut and poached haddock in a mustard sauce to meat dishes and vegetarian choices.

See map p. 199. Koberg 8. ☎ *0451/76234. Fixed-price menu €25–€40 ($31–$50). AE, MC, V. Open: Daily noon to midnight.*

Schabbelhaus
$$-$$$ **Altstadt**

Occupying two elegant town houses on a lovely medieval street, Schabbelhaus serves North German and Italian cuisine. The atmospheric dining room overlooks a small garden. Try the crab soup, if available, followed by fresh fish from the Baltic Sea. You also can get pasta dishes such as tagliatelle with fresh mushrooms or with salmon and lemon. The service is attentive, and the wine list is excellent.

See map p. 199. Mengstrasse 48–52. ☎ *0451/72011. Main courses: €11–€20 ($13–$25); fixed-price menus €38–€45 ($47–$56). AE, MC, V. Open: Mon–Sat noon to 2:30 p.m. and 6–11 p.m.*

Walking through Lübeck

Concentrate your sightseeing in Lübeck's remarkable **Altstadt,** surrounded by the Trave River and its canals. About one-fifth of the Altstadt was destroyed in a 1942 bombing, but approximately 1,000 medieval buildings still stand within a 5-sq.-km (2-sq.-mile) area around the Marktplatz. Builders used brick as the predominant material for houses, churches, shops, and guild halls. The city mandated the use of brick after fires in the 13th century destroyed many wooden structures.

The sweet side of Lübeck

Lübeck is the world capital of marzipan, a sweet almond paste. According to legend, Lübeckers ran out of flour during a long siege and started grinding almonds to make bread. They were so pleased with the sweet results that they've been making marzipan ever since. To sample Lübeck's famous marzipan, stop in at **Cafe Niederegger,** Breitestrasse 98 (☎ 0451/53010), located right across from the main entrance to the Rathaus since 1806. On the ground floor, you can purchase bars and boxes of marzipan to take away (an excellent gift idea), or you can go upstairs to the pleasant cafe for dessert and coffee. Niederegger's is open daily from 9 a.m. to 6 p.m.

What follows are the stops on a **walking tour** of the Altstadt that begins at the **Hauptbahnhof** (train station). The entire walk, with stops at museums, takes about four to five hours. From the train station, cross the **Puppenbrücke** (Dolls' Bridge) and head east into the Altstadt. The bridge got its irreverent name from the seven statues of classical gods and goddesses that stand on its stone railings.

1. After you enter the Altstadt, directly in front of you is the 15th-century **Holstentor** (Holsten Gate), once the main town entrance. The **Museum Holstentor** (☎ 0451/122-4129), a small local history museum housed within the gate, contains a model of Lübeck as the town appeared in the mid-17th century, models of Hanseatic *Kogge* (cogs, or single-sail vessels), and medieval torture instruments.

   The museum is open Tuesday through Sunday from 10 a.m. to 5 p.m. in summer and until 4 p.m. in winter. Admission is €4 ($5) for adults, €1 ($1.25) for students and children under 18. You can see everything inside 30 minutes.

2. Just south, across the street from the Holstentor, stand the **Salzspeicher** (Salt Lofts), a group of six gabled Renaissance buildings; the oldest dates from 1579, the newest from 1745.

   Merchants stored salt (considered "white gold") from nearby Lüneburg in these buildings before shipping it to Scandinavia, where the salt was used to preserve fish.

3. Continuing a few blocks east on Holstenstrasse, you reach Lübeck's **Rathaus,** Rathausplatz (☎ 0451/122-1005), one of the oldest and most beautiful city halls in Germany.

   The Rathaus was rebuilt several times since the first foundation stone was laid in 1230. The present building, topped by slender turrets, is a mixture of Gothic and Renaissance styles. Black glazed-brick *courses* (horizontal lines) and round panels emblazoned with coats of arms adorn the red-brick walls. The building sits on brick arcades that allow easy access to the main entrance on Breite Strasse. You can see the interior on a guided tour (in German) Monday through Friday at 11 a.m., noon, and 3 p.m.; the cost is €2.60 ($3.25) for adults and €0.50 (60¢) for children and students.

4. The Rathaus stands on the north and east sides of the **Marktplatz,** a large square filled with meat, fruit, and vegetable stalls every Monday and Thursday. In December, the Markt is the site of Lübeck's Christmas Market.

   Towering above the Markt and the Rathaus is one of Northern Germany's most outstanding examples of the brick Gothic style, the twin-towered **Marienkirche** (St. Mary's Church), Schüsselbuden 13 (☎ 0451/397-700). The Marienkirche served as a model for many other churches built in the Baltic region. Its central nave, 36m

(120 feet) high, has the highest brick vaulting in the world. During a WWII bombing attack, the tower bells crashed down into the church and embedded themselves in the stone floor. They still are there, left as a reminder and warning of the horrors of war. Organ concerts take place during the summer and fall, carrying on a tradition established by St. Mary's best-known organist and composer, Dietrich Buxtehude (1637 to 1707).

5. If you're a fan of the great German writer Thomas Mann, whose works include *Death in Venice, The Magic Mountain,* and *Buddenbrooks,* plan to spend at least half an hour at **Buddenbrookhaus,** Mengstrasse 4 (☎ 0451/122-4192), just north of the Marienkirche.

This big, solid stone house with a gabled roof belonged to Mann's grandparents and was the model for the family home Mann wrote about in *Buddenbrooks.* Inside, you find a comprehensive collection of photographs, letters, and documents chronicling Mann's life, and that of his family, from birth to death. Mann's brother, Heinrich Mann (1871 to 1950), was the author of *Professor Unrat,* the source of the movie *The Blue Angel.* On the second floor are period rooms and artifacts. The house is open daily April through October from 10 a.m. to 6 p.m., the rest of the year from 11 a.m. to 4 p.m.; admission is €8 ($10) for adults, €2.60 ($3.25) for students.

6. An outstanding collection of German Romantic and German Impressionist paintings is on view at **Museen Behnhaus/Drägerhaus,** Königstrasse 9–11 (☎ 0451/122-4148), a few blocks north of the Rathaus.

The museum, formed from two 18th-century town houses, also displays major 20th-century artists such as Leon Kirchner, Max Beckmann, and Ernst Barlach, and has exhibits relating to the city's cultural life in the 18th and 19th centuries. The museum is open Tuesday through Sunday from 10 a.m. to 5 p.m. (until 4 p.m. Oct–Mar). Admission is €4 ($5) for adults, €1 ($1.25) for students and children 6 to 18.

7. At Glockengiesserstrasse 23, just to the south of the Museen Behnhaus/Drägerhaus, is the **Füchtingshof,** an almshouse built in the 17th century for the widows of seamen and merchants. Step through the ornamented baroque portal and you enter a tranquil courtyard with houses still occupied by widows.

8. Across the street, at Glockengiesser 21, you find the new **Günther Grass Haus** museum; for information, see the sidebar "Lübeck's Nobel sons" earlier in this chapter.

9. The **Glandorps-Gang,** at No. 41, and the **Glandorps-Hof,** at Nos. 49–51, are the city's oldest almshouses, dating from 1612 and built for the widows of merchants and craftsmen.

10. A short distance to the north stands the **Heiligen-Geist-Hospital** (Hospital of the Holy Spirit), Am Koburg (☎ 0451/122-2040).

    This building, with its belfry and four turreted spires, is one of the oldest social-welfare institutions in Europe, and one of the most important monumental buildings of the Middle Ages. Philanthropic local citizens founded the hospital in 1230. In the early 19th century, when the building was converted to a shelter for elderly men and women, 130 tiny wooden cabins without ceilings were built within its enormous main hall. The cabins remain intact, and you can poke your head inside them (no admission charge).

11. On the south side of town, you find Lübeck's **Dom,** Mühlendamm 2–6 (☎ 0451/74704). Construction on this massive edifice began in 1173.

    The church was destroyed in WWII and later rebuilt. Except for its size, the church itself isn't that interesting. The building is open daily from 10 a.m. to 6 p.m.

12. Two blocks northeast of the Dom, you find the **St.-Annen-Museum,** St.-Annen-Strasse 15 (☎ 0451/122-4137). Housed in a 16th-century Augustinian convent that was later used as an almshouse and a prison, the museum has a noteworthy collection of medieval and Renaissance altarpieces, including a work by Hans Memling.

    You can see everything in about half an hour. The museum is open Tuesday through Sunday from 10 a.m. to 5 p.m. Admission is € 3 ($3.75) for adults, €0.50 (60¢) for students and children 6 to 18.

13. To round off your tour of Lübeck, head over to the 750-year-old **Petrikirche** (St. Peter's Church), Schmiedestrasse (☎ 0451/397-330), and take the elevator up to the top of its tower for a memorable view of Lübeck and its port.

    From March through September, the church is open daily from 9 a.m. to 7 p.m. Admission is €3 ($3.75) for adults, €1.50 ($2.10) for students and children.

Chapter 14

Dresden, Leipzig, and Weimar: Jewels of the East

In This Chapter

▶ Visiting Dresden and its famous museums
▶ Discovering old and new Leipzig
▶ Enjoying the beautiful town of Weimar
▶ Remembering the past at Buchenwald

Saxony and **Thuringia** (Thüringen in German) are side-by-side *Länder* (states) in eastern Germany that are well worth visiting. (See the "Saxony and Thuringia" map in this chapter.) The cities of **Dresden** and **Leipzig,** with their outstanding museums, historic buildings, and musical heritage, are the largest cities in Saxony. **Weimar,** associated with Goethe (Germany's greatest writer, author of *Faust*) and the German Enlightenment of the late 18th and early 19th centuries, is the cultural jewel in Thuringia's crown.

Both states are rich in sightseeing possibilities. In Saxony, the mighty Elbe River flows through an area near Dresden known as **Saxon Switzerland,** famed for its river scenery. Thuringia is considered the "green heart" of Germany because the **Thüringer Wald** (Thuringian Forest) covers much of its southern portion. Narrow, winding roads lead through spruce-covered hills to unspoiled villages that waft you back to the Middle Ages.

Dresden: Florence on the Elbe

Dresden, located 198km (123 miles) south of Berlin and 111km (69 miles) southeast of Leipzig, celebrates its 800th anniversary in 2006. One of the most important celebratory events is the reopening of the famous domed Frauenkirche (Church of Our Lady), destroyed in the bombings of World War II (WWII). The Frauenkirche is a symbol of what Dresden once was — a city known as "Florence on the Elbe," and renowned for its architecture and art treasures — and hopes to become again. Dresden became the most important city in Saxony when the ruling Wettin Dynasty decided to make the city its capital in the late 15th century. Under the rule of Elector Augustus the Strong — the preeminent personality in the town's history — Dresden flourished as one of the great cultural centers of Europe.

Then came the night of February 13, 1945, when Allied firebombs destroyed three-quarters of Dresden's *Altstadt,* the beautiful old core of the city. Historic buildings have been rebuilt, but the work has taken decades. The reconstruction of the Frauenkirche, using original plans and even some of the original stone (bombed pieces of which were found in the Elbe), is the most ambitious reconstruction effort in the entire country and marks an important stage in Dresden's recovery.

After reunification, Dresden emerged as the top contender for tourists in the former East Germany. Many visitors come just to visit the museums in the Zwinger Palace, the Albertinum, and the newly reopened portion of the Residenzschloss (palace).

Getting there

Getting to Dresden is easy. This major city has an airport, frequent train service, and a good road network.

By plane

Flughafen Dresden, the city airport, lies 9km (5½ miles) north of the city center. Lufthansa and other international carriers provide regularly scheduled service between Dresden and cities throughout Germany and Europe. For flight information, call ☎ **0351/881-3360.** The easiest and least expensive way to get into the city center is by the **Flughafen S-Bahn** (airport train), which runs from the airport to the two main train stations. The trip takes about 20 minutes and costs €1.60 ($2). You can buy your ticket at the S-Bahn window in the underground station beneath the new terminal. A **taxi** from the airport to the center of Dresden costs about €20 ($25).

By train

Dresden has two main rail stations. All long-distance trains pull into the **Hauptbahnhof** (main train station), on Wiener Platz on the south side of the Elbe. Within easy walking distance of Altstadt (Old Town), getting to the station currently is a bit confusing because of construction, but around it you find nearly all of Dresden's major attractions. **Dresden-Neustadt,** the station on the north side of the river, at Schlesischer Park, is used more for regional trains, although some trains, including the Airport S-Bahn, stop at both stations.

Getting to Dresden by train from anywhere in Germany or Europe is easy. More than a dozen trains make the daily trip from Berlin (2–2½ hours) and Frankfurt (4½ hours). For rail information and schedules, call ☎ **11861.**

Saxony and Thuringia

By car

The **A13** Autobahn connects Dresden to Berlin. The **A4** comes in from Leipzig and Bavaria (eventually the A4 will connect Dresden to Prague). The highways run along the west side of the city. Four exits (Altstadt, Neustadt, Hellerau, and Wilder Mann) lead into the center. Trying to find a parking spot in the center of Dresden isn't easy. I recommend that you park on the outskirts and travel to the city center by bus or tram.

Finding information

At the **Information Center,** Prager Strasse (☎ **0351/491-920** information line), near the main train station, you can book a hotel room and purchase a map of Dresden and information booklets in English. You also can buy theater, opera, or concert tickets. The same services are available at the Information Center located in the **Schinkelwache** (Old City Guard House), at Theaterplatz Square. The hours for both are Monday through Friday 10 a.m. to 6 p.m., Saturday 10 a.m. to 4 p.m., and Sunday (Schinkelwache only) 10 a.m. to 4 p.m.

The **Dresden Card** is good for 48 hours on all trams, busses, and ferries in Dresden and admission to all of the top museums, including those in the Zwinger and the Albertinum. You also get reduced prices for other museums, city tours, and boat tours in the Dresden area. The cost is €18 ($22). You can buy the Dresden Card at the tourist information centers.

Orienting yourself

The Elbe River divides Dresden more or less in half. On the south side, between the main train station (Hauptbahnhof) and the river, you find all the major cultural attractions, including art museums, churches in the **Altmarkt** (Old Market) and **Neumarkt** (New Market) squares, the Zwinger Palace museums, and the Semper Opera House. **Prager Strasse,** a wide pedestrian street lined with shops, hotels, and restaurants, is the main thoroughfare (and site of the main tourist information office).

On the north side of the river is **Dresden-Neustadt.** Pretty 19th-century houses reconstructed to hold shops, apartments, and restaurants line **Hauptstrasse** and **Königstrasse,** its main streets. Germany's reunification triggered a real estate and reconstruction boom in this picturesque neighborhood of art galleries, boutiques, and cafes.

Getting around Dresden

If you plan to visit only the historic center of Dresden, you can easily get around on foot. The city's transport authority, **Dresdner Verkehrsbetriebe** (DVB; ☎ **0351/857-1011;** www.dvbag.de), maintains an extensive system of **bus** and **tram** lines within the city and far out into the suburbs. Service is limited after midnight, but the major lines continue to operate every hour.

Dresden

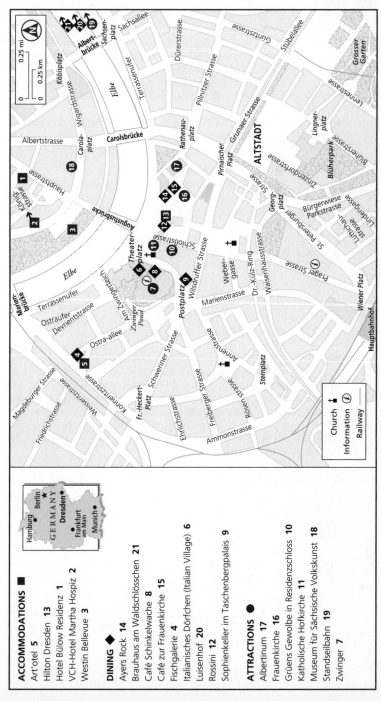

ACCOMMODATIONS
Art'otel **5**
Hilton Dresden **13**
Hotel Bülow Residenz **1**
VCH-Hotel Martha Hospiz **2**
Westin Bellevue **3**

DINING
Ayers Rock **14**
Brauhaus am Waldschlösschen **21**
Café Schinkelwache **8**
Café zur Frauenkirche **15**
Fischgalerie **4**
Italianisches Dörfchen (Italian Village) **6**
Luisenhof **20**
Rossini **12**
Sophienkeller im Taschenbergpalais **9**

ATTRACTIONS
Albertinum **17**
Frauenkirche **16**
Grünes Gewölbe im Residenzschloss **10**
Katholische Hofkirche **11**
Museum für Sächsische Volkskunst **18**
Standseilbahn **19**
Zwinger **7**

The city is divided into fare zones; unless you're visiting the outskirts of Dresden, you only need a one-zone ticket. Purchase your tickets and a transportation map from the vending machines (marked "Fahrkarten") outside the train stations, or at DVB service centers inside the Hauptbahnhof or at Postplatz; both are open Monday through Friday from 7 a.m. to 7 p.m., and Saturday and Sunday from 8 a.m. to 6 p.m. A single ticket for the bus or tram costs €1.60 ($2) for a one-hour ride anywhere in Zone 1. A one-day *Tageskarte* (day pass) costs €4 ($5). A *Familientageskarte* (family day ticket), good for two adults and up to four children in one zone, costs €5 ($6.25). Validate your ticket (by stamping the ticket in a machine) upon entering the bus or tram.

Seeing Dresden by guided tour

Stadtrundfahrt Dresden (☎ 0351/899-5650; www.stadtrundfahrt.com), offers a daily 90-minute Super Dresden Tour *(Grosse Stadtrundfahrt)*, a guided (audio headsets for English translations) bus tour that leaves from Schlossplatz, adjacent to the Augustusbrücke (Augustus Bridge) and covers both sides of the Elbe, including the lovely Loschwitz neighborhood. Buses leave every half-hour from 10 a.m. to 3 p.m. You can hop on or off the bus at any of 18 points along the way. The price is €18 ($22) for adults, free for children 14 and younger. **DVB** (☎ 0351/857-1011; www.dvbag.de) offers a one-hour Historical City Tour *(Historischer Stadtrundgang)*, a walk through the city's historic center. This tour departs from Postplatz daily at 11 a.m. and costs €7 ($8.75). Buy your tickets on the bus or at a tourist Information Center.

Sächsische Dampfschiffahrt (☎ 0351/866-090) offers daily 90-minute boat trips along the Elbe from May into October at 11 a.m., 1 p.m., 3 p.m., and 5 p.m. An English-speaking guide accompanies the 1 and 3 p.m. tours from Thursday through Sunday. The paddle-wheel steamers depart from the Terrassenufer quay below the Brühlsche Terrasse (embankment) along the south bank of the river and travel upstream to Loschwitz and back again. The cost is €10 ($12) for adults, €5 ($6.25) for children. Buy your tickets at the kiosk on the quay.

Staying in Dresden

Since reunification and the amazing increase in tourism, Dresden's hotel prices have soared, and so has the demand for rooms. If you want to stay here, book your room ahead of time.

Art'otel
$$$–$$$$ **Altstadt**

The six floors of this dramatic postmodern hotel, located a bit out of the center of the Altstadt, are the "artiest" of any hotel in Dresden. The 174 good-size bedrooms are stylish and comfortably chic without being pretentious.

Double rooms have bathrooms with stainless-steel sinks and a shower. You find a small gym and sauna on the premises. The hotel opened in 1995.

See map p. 209. Ostra-Allee 33, 01067 Dresden. ☎ *0351/49220. Fax: 0351/492-2777.* www. artotel.de. *Tram: 11 to Haus der Presse. Rack rates: €160–€215 ($200–$269) double. Rates include buffet breakfast. AE, DC, MC, V.*

Hilton Dresden
$$–$$$$ Altstadt

This 333-room hotel across from the Frauenkirche is one of the best (and largest) in eastern Germany. Rooms are midsize and somewhat short on style but well-maintained. Bathrooms have shower-tub combinations. You find a pool, fitness club, and sauna on the premises, and the staff can arrange baby-sitting. Breakfast is an additional €19 ($24).

See map p. 209. An der Frauenkirche 5, 01067 Dresden. ☎ *800/445-8667 in the U.S. and Canada, or 0351/86420. Fax: 0351/864-2725.* www.dresden.hilton.com. *Tram: 4 or 8 to Theaterplatz. Rack rates: €130–€240 ($162–$300) double. AE, DC, MC, V.*

Hotel Bülow Residenz
$$$$ Neustadt

One of the finest restorations in Neustadt, on the north bank of the Elbe River, this luxury boutique hotel is housed in a building that dates from 1730. Each of the 30 spacious rooms is laid out differently and furnished with modern designer and reproduction Biedermeier pieces. The large marble-tiled bathrooms have shower-tub combinations. The hotel's elegant, expensive, Michelin-starred Carousel Restaurant serves fresh French cuisine with a Mediterranean influence (main courses from €25–€35/$31–$44). The staff is unusually friendly and helpful. Baby-sitting can be arranged. Breakfast is an additional €17 ($21).

See map p. 209. Rähnitzgasse 19, 01097 Dresden. ☎ *0351/80030. Fax: 0351/800-3100.* www.buelow-residenz.de. *Tram: 4 or 9 to Palaisplatz. Rack rates: €220 ($275) double. AE, DC, MC, V.*

VCH-Hotel Martha Hospiz
$$ Neustadt

Managed by the Association of Christian Hoteliers (VCH), this simple but comfortable four-story hotel is a 15-minute walk from the heart of Dresden's Altstadt. The 50 rooms have a simple, modern décor and are well-maintained. Bathrooms, each with a shower, are on the small side.

See map p. 209. Nieritzstrasse 11, 01097 Dresden. ☎ *0351/81760. Fax: 0351/817-6222.* marthahospiz.dresden.vch.de. *Tram: 4 or 9 to Palaisplatz. Rack rates: €102–€118 ($127–$147) double. Rates include buffet breakfast. AE, MC, V.*

Westin Bellevue
$$$$ Neustadt

The 339-room Westin Bellevue is located near the most attractive part of the Elbe River, and many of the rooms have lovely river and Altstadt views. The rooms are large, if not spacious, well-appointed, and comfortable. The bathrooms have shower units or shower-tub combinations. You find an on-site pool and health club, and the staff can arrange baby-sitting. A green, grassy, riverside park stretches behind the hotel; you can walk across the river to the Altstadt in ten minutes. Children younger than 18 stay for free in their parents' room.

See map p. 209. Grosse Meissner Strasse 15, 01097 Dresden. ☎ *800/937-8461 in the U.S. and Canada, or 0351/805-1733. Fax: 0351/805-1749.* www.westin.com. *Tram: 9 from the Hauptbahnhof stops in front of the hotel at Neustädter Markt. Rack rates: €251–€307 ($314–$384) double. AE, DC, MC, V.*

Dining in Dresden

Dresden is bursting with new restaurants of every kind. For a sample of the city's culinary offerings, wander down Münzgasse, the narrow lane that runs north from the Frauenkirche to the river.

Ayers Rock
$–$$ Altstadt   AUSTRALIAN

This likable Australian restaurant with outdoor tables is famous for its cocktails but also serves German and Aussie beer on tap. Menu items include kangaroo rump steak, grilled lamb cutlets, ostrich steak, grilled salmon, and salads. As the night wears on, the bar area becomes a crowded singles scene.

See map p. 209. Münzgasse 8. ☎ *0351/490-1188. Tram 4 or 8 to Theaterplatz. Main courses: €8.50–€17 ($11–$21). AE, DC, MC, V. Open: Daily 10 a.m.–3 a.m.*

Brauhaus am Waldschlösschen
$–$$ Neustadt   GERMAN

Some 250 diners can fit into the dining rooms in this newly built replica of an old-fashioned beer hall, and another 800 can be accommodated within the sprawling beer garden (open Apr–Oct). The menu features heaping plates of traditional favorites such as roast pork shank, sautéed fish with parsley and onions, *schnitzels* (breaded veal cutlets), soups, sausages, and roasts. Waldschlösschen beer is brewed on the premises. On Saturday and Sunday afternoons, you can eat and drink to the sounds of an oompah-pah band.

See map p. 209. Am Brauhaus 8B, Neustadt (5km/3 miles northeast of city center). ☎ *0351/811-990. Tram: 11 to Brauhaus am Waldschlösschen. Main courses: €8–€14 ($10–$17). Fixed-price meals: €13–€20 ($16–$25). AE, DC, MC, V. Open: Daily 11 a.m.–1 a.m.*

Dinner with a view

For a fun, easy, and memorable dining experience, take one of Dresden's old funiculars (mountain railways) up to the top of a hill in the suburb of Loschwitz and dine in a pleasant restaurant overlooking the city. First, take Tram 8 to Schillerplatz and walk across the famous Blaue Wunder bridge. On the other side, at Trachtenbergerstrasse 40, you'll see the **Standseilbahn,** a funicular that began operation in 1895. The funicular runs from 6 a.m. to 9 p.m. and costs €3 ($3.75) round-trip. Take the funicular to the top, a residential area called Weisser Hirsch. Across the street from the station is **Luisenhof,** Bergbahnstrasse 8 (☎ **0351/214-9960**), a restaurant with an outdoor terrace offering wonderful panoramic views of the Elbe River and Dresden in the distance. The German/Saxon menu features traditional dishes such as potato soup with sausages, and *Sauerbraten* with cabbage and dumplings. Main courses go for €8 to €17 ($10 to $22). The service can be slow, but relax with a glass of beer or wine and enjoy the view of Dresden's spires. The restaurant is open Monday through Saturday from 11 a.m. to 1 a.m., Sunday from 10 a.m. to midnight (brunch 10 a.m.–2 p.m.). The restaurant accepts MasterCard and Visa.

Café Schinkelwache
$–$$ **Altstadt   CONTINENTAL**

This sandstone structure in the center of Theaterplatz was built in 1832 by architect Karl Friedrich Schinkel to house soldiers and guards. In 1995, the building was rebuilt and reconfigured into an intimate cafe with outdoor tables on the terrace (you find a Tourist Information center around the other side). Menu selections include pastries, meal-size salads, soups, crepes with mushrooms and chicken, and veal stew. You can also sit and enjoy wine, beer, or coffee.

See map p. 209. Sophienstrasse am Theaterplatz. Tram: 1, 2, 4, 7, 8, 11, 12, 14, or 17. ☎ *0351/490-3909. Tram: 4 or 8 to Theaterplatz. Pastries: €2–€5 ($2.50–$6.25). Main courses: €6.50–€12 ($8–$15). Fixed-price meals: €13–€20 ($16–$25). AE, MC, V. Open: Daily 9 a.m. to midnight.*

Café zur Frauenkirche
$–$$ **Altstadt   GERMAN/INTERNATIONAL**

This streetside corner cafe, located directly across from the Frauenkirche, is a good place to sit outside and eat or have a drink. The menu typically has dishes such as grilled lamb cutlet with asparagus and sauce bearnaise; pastas such as rigatoni with chicken breast; and pork goulash with cabbage and dumplings. For dessert try the homemade *Quarkkeutchen,* a baked dumpling filled with cheese and raisins.

See map p. 209. An der Frauenkirche 5. ☎ *0351/498-9836. Tram: 4 or 8 to Theaterplatz. Main courses: €5.50–€18 ($6.75–$23). AE, MC, V. Open: Daily 10 a.m.–2 a.m.*

Fischgalerie

$$–$$$ Altstadt   SEAFOOD

The interior of Dresden's best fish restaurant is a sophisticated affair with an open-view kitchen, dramatic lighting, minimalist design, and a blue-black color scheme. The menu changes every week. Fresh seafood dishes may include salmon with champagne sauce, scampi and white fish served with tomato-flavored *spaghettini,* or bouillabaisse with North Sea fish. Fresh oysters and marinated herring, served with black bread, are good appetizers. Fresh sushi is available on Wednesday and Friday nights.

See map p. 209. Maxstrasse 2. ☎ *0351/490-3506. Reservations recommended. Tram: 11 to Haus der Presse. Main courses: €14–€24 ($17–$30). AE, MC, V. Open: Tues–Fri noon to 3 p.m., Tues–Sat 6–11 p.m.*

Italianisches Dörfchen (Italian Village)

$$ Altstadt   ITALIAN/INTERNATIONAL

This quartet of restaurants in a neoclassical building, erected on the site of a cluster of cottages ("the Italian Village"), once housed Italian workers. Each of the four restaurants has a different theme. The **Bierkeller** (beer hall) with a painted ceiling serves traditional dishes such as *Sauerbraten* (pot- or oven-roasted marinated beef), as does the formal, red-walled **Weinzimmer** (wine room). **Bellotto,** an upscale Italian eatery on the top floor with an outdoor balcony overlooking Theaterplatz, serves dishes such as risotto with artichokes and radicchio and veal scaloppini. The **Café,** a graceful-looking room with windows that overlook the river, is a good place for *Kaffee und Kuchen* (coffee and cake).

See map p. 209. Theaterplatz. ☎ *0351/498-160. Tram: 4 or 8 to Theaterplatz. Pastries: €4–6.50 ($5–$8). Main courses: €10–€20 ($12–$25). AE, DC, MC, V. Open: Daily 10 a.m. to midnight.*

Rossini

$$$ Altstadt   ITALIAN

Rossini offers fine Italian cuisine in a stylish, dress-up setting, one floor above the lobby of the Dresden Hilton. Menu items may include homemade gnocchi with asparagus and Parma ham in cream sauce; veal in thyme sauce with tomato fettuccine; or risotto with spring vegetables. For dessert try the *cassata* (tart) made with ricotta cheese and candied fruit or a *granita* (sorbet) of oranges and lemons floating on white wine.

See map p. 209. An der Frauenkirche 5 (in the Dresden Hilton). ☎ *0351/864-2855. Tram: 4 or 8 to Theaterplatz. Main courses: €19–€24 ($24–$30). AE, DC, MC, V. Open: Daily 6–11:30 p.m.*

Sophienkeller im Taschenbergpalais
$$ Altstadt GERMAN

The food in this famous cellar restaurant is a modern approximation of a medieval feast. Flickering candles set beneath vaulted ceilings provide suitable atmosphere, and so do the waitresses in their traditional German dresses, called *dirndls*. You can order dishes such as grilled rabbit with thyme or trout fried in butter, or you may want to try the famous house specialty, "August's Hunting Trophy": roasted medallions of venison, wild boar, and juniper sauce, served with asparagus and roast potatoes. The restaurant has a menu in English to help you make up your mind.

See map p. 209. Taschenberg 3. ☎ 0351/497-260. Reservations recommended. Tram: 4 or 8 to Theaterplatz. Main courses: €11–€18 ($14–$22). AE, DC, MC, V. Open: Daily 11 a.m.–1 a.m.

Exploring Dresden

The amount of restoration work going on throughout Dresden is tremendous. Despite the rebuilding, you still encounter wartime ruins as you walk through the relatively compact **Altstadt,** the historic center where you find Dresden's major attractions. The cleanup work necessary after a major flood in 2002 has been completed.

The **Neustadt** quarter on the north bank of the Elbe also is an area you may want to visit. Although you won't find the museum attractions of the Altstadt here, the Neustadt quarter has Germany's largest concentration of houses from the Gründerzeit (Biedermeier; early 19th century) period.

Separate admission prices apply for the six museums in the Albertinum, Residenzschloss, and the Zwinger complex. A money-saving **Tageskarte** (day ticket) gets you into all six and the Museum für Sächsische Volkskunst (also described later), for €10 ($12) adults, €4 ($5) children and senior citizens. For more information on all of Dresden's major museums, visit the Web site of the Staatliche Kunstsammlungen Dresden (State Art Collections), www.skd-dresden.de.

Albertinum
Altstadt

Between 1884 and 1887, the Saxon king Albert converted this former royal arsenal into a home for his vast collection of art and precious jewelry. The **Gemäldegalerie Neue Meister** (New Masters Gallery), taking up two floors, is a rich collection of 19th- and 20th-century art. The collection concentrates on German art, starting with moody works by Caspar David Friedrich, the great German Romantic artist, and going up to the brilliant works of Dresden-born Otto Dix (1891 to 1969), a brilliant painter who ran afoul of the Nazis. Allot at least an hour to see the highlights.

See map p. 209. Brühl Terrace. ☎ *0351/491-4619*. Tram: 3, 7, or 8 to Rathenau Platz. Admission: €4 ($5) adults, €2.50 ($3.10) children and students. Open: Wed–Mon 10 a.m.–6 p.m. Closed 2 weeks in Jan.

Frauenkirche (Church of Our Lady)
Altstadt

Built between 1726 and 1743, the Frauenkirche on the southeast side of Neumarkt (New Market Square) was the most important Protestant church in Germany and had one of the most famous domes in Europe. The 1945 Allied bombing of Dresden destroyed 80 percent of the city, including the Frauenkirche. After the war, the East German government let the charred ruin remain as a memorial. Since 1993, however, a major restoration project has been underway, and today the Frauenkirche is the biggest rebuilding job in Germany. In 2004, a huge crowd gathered to watch as a giant golden cross, an exact replica of the 18th-century original, was hoisted to the top of the church. The new cross, as it turned out, was built by the son of a British bomber pilot who took part in the original bombing raid. The church expected to reopen late in 2005.

Neumarkt. Tram: 4 or 8 to Theaterplatz.

Grünes Gewolbe (Green Vaults)
Altstadt

The fabulous assortment of treasures displayed in the Residenzschloss formerly was housed in the Albertinum, but it was moved to this new location in September 2004. Known as the **Grünes Gewölbe** (Green Vaults), the collection consists of 16th- to 18th-century objects, including rococo chests, ivory carvings, gold jewelry, bronze statuettes, intricately designed mirrors, and priceless porcelain. Allow yourself at least an hour to browse this treasure-trove.

Residenzschloss, Taschenberg 2. ☎ *0351/491-4619*. Tram: 4 or 8 to Theaterplatz. Admission: €6 ($7.50) adults, €3.50 ($4.50) children and students. Open: Daily 10 a.m.–6 p.m.

Katholische Hofkirche (Catholic Court Church)
Altstadt

The restored Hofkirche, also known as the Cathedral of St. Trinitas, is the largest church in Saxony. Built by the son of Augustus the Strong, Frederick Augustus II (ruled 1733 to 1763), the church was constructed in a lavish Italian baroque style with a curving facade and 86m (282-ft.) bell tower decorated with statues of saints and apostles. Inside, you can see the crypt with the tombs of 49 kings and princes of Saxony. You need about 15 minutes to look around.

Schlossplatz. ☎ *0351/495-1133*. Tram: 4 or 8 to Theaterplatz. Admission: Free. Open: Mon–Fri 9 a.m.–4:30 p.m., Sat 10 a.m.–4 p.m., Sun noon to 4 p.m.

Museum für Sächsische Volkskunst
(Museum of Saxon Arts and Crafts)
Neustadt

The oldest Renaissance building in Dresden, the 16th-century Jägerhof (Hunters Court) houses this fine collection of regional folk art. What you see are everyday objects used by the common folk — a far cry from the gem-encrusted treasures in the Albertinum. On display are pieces of painted furniture, handwoven baskets, pottery, tableware, and folk costumes. Also shown are toys, carvings, and Christmas decorations from the nearby Erzgebirge region.

Jägerhof, Kopckestrasse 1. ☎ *0351/803-0817. Tram: 3, 5, 7, 8, or 51 to Carolaplatz. Admission: €3 ($3.75) adults, €2 ($2.50) seniors and children. Open: Tues–Sun 10 a.m.–6 p.m.*

 ## Zwinger
Altstadt

Augustus the Strong, elector of Saxony and king of Poland, built this magnificent baroque palace in 1719. He wanted the Zwinger to be his Versailles and a place where he could show off his incredible art collections. The architect, M. D. Pöppelmann (1662 to 1736), designed a series of galleries and domed pavilions to enclose a large rectangular courtyard with formal gardens, fountains, and promenades. The semicircular **Wallpavilion** at the west end and the adjacent **Nymphenbad** (Bath of Nymphs), with its graceful fountains and mythological figures, are notable buildings that rely on the exuberant sculptures of the Bavarian artist Balthasar Permoser (1651 to 1732). On the northeast side is the **Semper Gallery,** a Renaissance-style two-story pavilion linked by one-story galleries; Gottfried Semper added the pavilion in 1846. Today, this entire complex of buildings contains a stunning collection of museums. They all are open the same hours but charge separate admission prices.

The most important museum is the **Gemäldegalerie Alte Meister** (Old Masters Gallery) in the Semper Gallery (entrance at Theaterplatz 1). Admission is €3.50 ($4.50) adults, €2 ($2.50) children and senior citizens. This gallery, one of the best in the world, has as its showpiece Raphael's *Sistine Madonna.* The collection also includes Flemish, Dutch, and German paintings by van Dyck, Vermeer, Dürer, Rubens, and Rembrandt. In Galleries two through four, you find a series of detailed townscapes of Dresden painted by Canaletto in the mid–18th century. Canaletto's views of Dresden are so true to life that they were used as reference works during the post–WWII reconstruction of the city. Allow at least two hours for unhurried browsing. Admission is €6 ($7.50) adults, €3.50 ($4.50) children and seniors.

In the **Rüstkammer** (Armory), a separate section of the Semper Gallery, you can see a small but superlative collection of armor and weapons from the 15th to 18th centuries. Give yourself about 15 minutes to wander through. Admission is €3 ($3.75) for adults, €2 ($2.50) for children and senior citizens; the entrance is directly across from the entrance to the Gemäldegalerie Alte Meister.

The **Porzellansammlung** (Porcelain Collection), with its entrance in the Glockenspiel (carillon) Pavillon, displays Japanese, Chinese, and Meissen porcelain from the 18th and 19th centuries. The "giant animal room" on the second floor has a collection of 18th-century Meissen animals. Depending on your interest, you can see everything in under half an hour. Admission is €5 ($6.25) adults, €5 ($6.25) children and seniors. This collection is closed on Monday.

On the west side of the Zwinger, to the left of the Wallpavillon, you find the **Mathematische-Physikalischer Salon** (Salon of Mathematics and Physics), with all manner of clocks and scientific instruments of the 16th to 19th centuries. Again, depending on your interest level, you can spend 15 minutes or an hour. Admission is €3 ($3.75) for adults, €2 ($2.50) for children and senior citizens.

Theaterplatz 1. ☎ *0351/491-4622. Tram: 2, 4, or 8 to Postplatz. Open: daily 10 a.m.–6 p.m.*

Shopping in Dresden

Dresden's main shopping streets are **Prager Strasse,** where you find department stores, **Wilsdruffer Strasse,** and **Altmarkt.** More-exclusive shops reside in Neustadt on the north side of the river on **Königstrasse** and **Hauptstrasse.**

In Neustadt, you find many high-quality antiques dealers lining both sides of a lane called **Am Goldenen Reiter,** accessible via Hauptstrasse 17–19 (Tram: 9).

A **Trödelmarkt** (flea market) is open Saturdays from 9 a.m. to 3 p.m. beneath the Albertbrücke (bridge) (Tram: 1 or 4).

The best shops

Weihnachtsland am Zwinger, Kleine Brüdergasse 5 (☎ 0351/862-1230; Tram: 4 or 8), in the Altstadt, is the best-stocked and most interesting gift shop in Dresden, selling handmade Christmas, New Year's, and Easter ornaments from the nearby Erzgebirge region.

The oldest manufacturer of porcelain in Dresden is **Wehsener Porzellan,** 5km (3 miles) southeast of the center at Donaustrasse 72 (☎ 0351/470-7340; Tram: 13; Bus: 72 or 76). Its hand-painted objects are the most charming and interesting in Dresden. Anything you buy can be shipped. You can also take a free tour of the studios and factory.

The famous Christmas market

Dresden's **Weihnachtsmarkt** (also called the **Striezelmarkt**) is the oldest Christmas market in Germany. This December event, which began in 1434, takes place in the Altmarkt and features handmade regional crafts and gift items and homemade foods. Look for woodcarvings from the Erzgebirge Mountains, indigo-printed cloth and pottery from Lusatia, gingerbread from Pulsnitz, filigree lace from Plauen, Advent stars from Hermhut, and blown-glass tree decorations from Lauscha.

The Zwinger

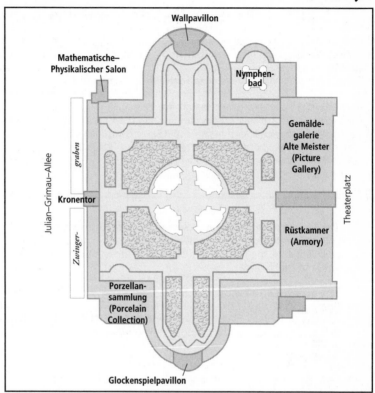

Discovering nightlife in Dresden

Dresden is the cultural center of Saxony, so many and varied nightlife options always are available. Depending on your tastes, you can find classical concerts, rock shows, discos, or just a good place to drink.

 Tickets for classical concerts, dance, and opera are available from the **Tourist Information centers** on Prager Strasse and Theaterplatz.

Opera and classical concerts

 The **Semperoper** (Semper Opera House), Theaterplatz 2 (☎ 0351/491-1705; www.semperoper.de; Tram: 4 or 8), is one of the world's great opera houses. Several operas by Richard Wagner and Richard Strauss had their premieres in this house, which was built in the mid-19th century and twice rebuilt after that. If you're an opera buff, seeing a performance by the resident company, the **Sächsisches Oper** (Saxon Opera), can be a highlight of your trip. The opera and ballet season lasts from September to mid-July. Ticket prices range from €8 to €62 ($10 to $77).

Sailing through Saxon Switzerland

If you have the time, I recommend that you take a boat trip along the Elbe River. The **Sächsische Dampfschiffahrtsgesellschaft** (Saxon Excursion Boat Company; ☎ 0351/866-090) runs several trips on historic paddle-wheelers and modern boats through a scenic region known as **Sächsiches Schweiz** (Saxon Switzerland), where you see castle-crowned hilltops, giant rocks, deep gorges, and sheer sandstone cliffs. Other routes travel to Meissen and through Bohemia. Elbe cruises leave from the dock below Brühl Terrace, the esplanade that runs along the south bank of the river. From May into October, daily excursions depart for the Saxon Switzerland route. The round-trip cost is €17 ($21) per person. The trips take from 3 to 4½ hours. Food and drink are for sale onboard. You can check out all the Elbe excursions, in English, online at www.saechsische-dampfschiffahrt.de.

The **Dresden Philharmonic** performs at the **Kulturpalast,** in the Altmarkt (☎ 0351/48660; www.dresdnerphilharmonie.de; Tram: 3 or 5). Tickets cost €11 to €30 ($14 to $37). Summer concerts take place in the courtyards of the Zwinger.

The main stage for classical theater in the city is the **Schauspielhaus,** Postplatz (☎ 0351/491-350; Tram 1, 2, 4, or 7), where actors perform dramas by Goethe, Schiller, and Shakespeare. Tickets are €10 to €22 ($12 to $27). The theater is closed during August.

Bars and clubs

Café Hieronymous, Louisenstrasse 10 (☎ 0351/801-1739; Tram: 7 or 8), a small, low-key bar without intrusive music, is open daily from 7 p.m. to 2 a.m. **Die 100,** Alaunstrasse 100 (☎ 0351/801-3957; Tram: 7, 8, or 11), is a trendy drinking place set in a cellar and popular with students and artists; open daily from 5 p.m. to 3 a.m.

The upstairs cafe at **Planwirtschaft,** Louisenstrasse 20 (☎ 0351/801-3187; Tram: 7 or 8), is open from 9 a.m. to 1 a.m.; the downstairs bar stays open until 3 a.m. on weekends. Although it doesn't look like much, **Raskolnikoff,** Böhmische Strasse 34 (☎ 0351/804-5706; Tram: 3, 5, 7, 8, or 11), is a hip dive with sand-covered floors. The place is open Monday to Friday from 11 a.m. to 2 a.m.; Saturday and Sunday from 10 a.m. to 2 a.m.

A dance club with room for everyone is **DownTown and Groove Station,** Katherinenstrasse 11–13 (☎ 0351/802-8801; Tram: 7 or 8). Monday is gay and lesbian night, and on Sunday you find dinner and dancing. The club is open daily from 9 p.m. until the last person leaves. Cover is €4 ($5).

Leipzig: City of Heroes

Historic Leipzig, located at the confluence of the Weisse Elster and Pleisse rivers, is called a *Heldenstadt*, or "city of heroes," for its role in toppling the former Communist government of East Germany. Visiting Leipzig is worth the trip to see a proud East German city rediscovering and redefining itself after years of Communist rule. (See the "Leipzig" map in this chapter.)

With a population of about 450,000 people, Leipzig is only a little smaller than Dresden. Leipzig has long been a major cultural and commercial force in Saxony, a center of publishing, and home to a famous university with some 20,000 students. For centuries, trade fairs have played an important role in the city's life. Leipzig also is a city with many great musical traditions, including the famed Gewandhaus Orchestra. Johann Sebastian Bach is closely associated with Leipzig, Mozart and Mendelssohn performed here, and Richard Wagner was born in Leipzig in 1813.

Leipzig was heavily bombed by British and American forces in 1943, and much of the city is rebuilt or being rebuilt. You still find some narrow streets and houses dating back to the 16th and 17th centuries, and some Jugendstil (Art Nouveau) buildings and arcades from the early 20th century. But people in Leipzig are much more interested in looking forward than looking back, and its skyscrapers and nightlife give the city a cosmopolitan flair that's unique for this region.

You can easily visit Leipzig as a day trip from Dresden, 111km (68 miles) to the northwest, or you may want to spend the night in this lively Saxon metropolis.

Getting there

Leipzig has all the transportation options of a major city: airport, train station, and a good road network. You can easily get there from anywhere in Germany.

By plane

Several airlines link Leipzig to major German cities, such as Munich and Frankfurt, and to other European destinations. **Leipzig-Halle International Airport** (☎ **0341/224-1155**) lies 11km (7 miles) northwest of the city center. The **Flughafen (Airport) Express** train runs between the airport and the Leipzig Hauptbahnhof (main train station) every 30 minutes from 4:30 a.m. to midnight; trip time is 14 minutes. The fare is €8 ($10). The 25- to 30-minute **taxi** ride to the city center costs about €30 ($37).

By train

The **Leipzig Hauptbahnhof** (main train station), Willy-Brandt-Platz, is the largest on the Continent. Trains arrive daily from Berlin (about 2½ hours), Dresden (about 1½–2 hours), and Frankfurt (5 hours). For information and schedules, call ☎ **11861.** The recently restored Hauptbahnhof is one of the most happening places in Leipzig, a new commercial flash point for cafes, shops, and restaurants.

By car

Leipzig is connected to the **A9** (Berlin–Munich) and the **A14** (Halle–Dresden) Autobahns. A number of federal highways (B2, B6, B87, B95, B181, B184) pass by or skirt Leipzig.

Finding information and taking a tour

Pick up a city map at the **Tourist Information** office, Richard-Wagner-Strasse 1 (☎ **0341/710-4260;** www.leipzig.de), open Monday through Friday from 9 a.m. to 6 p.m., Saturday 9 a.m. to 4 p.m., and Sunday 9 a.m. to 2 p.m. You can also book a hotel room here and purchase tickets for concerts and sightseeing tours.

The tourist office offers a 90-minute city-sightseeing tour daily at 11 a.m. for €12 ($15). The commentary is in German only.

Getting around Leipzig

If you arrive by train for a day trip, you can easily walk from the train station to all the attractions in the Altstadt (Old Town). **LVB** (☎ **0341/ 19449**), the public transit authority, runs the city's tram, S-Bahn (surface trains), and bus network. Fares are based on zones. An *Einzelfahrkarte* (single ticket) in "Zone Leipzig" costs €1.60 ($2). You can purchase tickets from automated machines at the stops.

Staying in Leipzig

Twice a year, usually the first week in September and the second week in March, Leipzig is the site of huge trade fairs that bring in tens of thousands of visitors. If you travel to Leipzig during those periods, booking your room in advance is essential.

Hotel Fürstenhof
$$–$$$$ City Center

Housed in a historic 18th-century building, this hotel has 92 rooms redecorated to reflect the original neoclassical styling. The rejuvenated bathrooms are nicely done and have a combination tub and shower. An on-site health club has a pool and a sauna.

See map p. 223. Tröndlinring 8, 04105 Leipzig. ☎ 800/426-3135 in the U.S. or 0341/ 14-00. Fax: 0341/140-3700. www.arabellasheraton.com. *Tram: 15. Rack rates: €100–€245 ($125–$306) double. AE, DC, MC, V.*

Leipzig

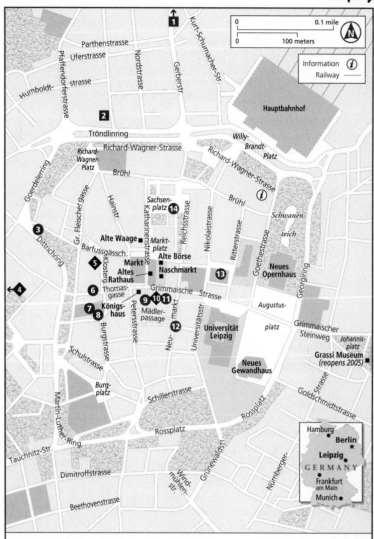

ACCOMMODATIONS ■
Hotel Fürstenhof **2**
The Westin Leipzig **1**

DINING ◆
Apels Garten **4**
Auerbachs Keller **10**
Paulaner Palais **5**

ATTRACTIONS ●
Bach-Museum **6**
Museum der
  Bildenden Künste **14**
Museum für
  Kunsthandwerk **12**
Museum für
  Völkerkunde **9**

Museum in der
  Runden Ecke **3**
Musikinstrumenten-
  Museum **8**
Nikolaikirche **13**
Thomaskirche **7**
Zeitgeschichtliches
  Forum Leipzig **11**

The Westin Leipzig
$$$$ City Center

One of the city's tallest buildings, and one of its finest modern hotels, the 27-story Westin reflects the Leipzig of today. It was an Inter-Continental hotel until 2003, when Westin took over and began redecorating the 447 rooms in a sleek, contemporary style. Not all rooms have been upgraded (the new ones are on the highest floors), but the old ones are comfortably furnished and have good-size bathrooms with shower-tub combinations. This full-service hotel contains a health club, pool, and sauna, and has room service. The restaurant **Brühl** serves traditional German food, while **Yamato** is one of the best places in Leipzig for Japanese food. The hotel is a convenient five-minute walk from the train station, and within easy walking distance of all the sights in the Altstadt.

See map p. 223. Gerberstrasse 15, 04105 Leipzig. ☎ *800/327-0200 in the U.S. and Canada, or 0341/9880. Fax: 0341/988-1229.* www.westin.com/leipzig. *Tram: 4 or 6. Rack rates: €183–€241 ($228–$301) double. AE, DC, MC, V.*

Dining in Leipzig

More restaurants are opening in Leipzig all the time, but this city is not particularly well known for its culinary scene. Regional cooking favors hearty portions and simple, filling ingredients.

Apels Garten
$–$$ GERMAN/SAXON

This restaurant, in a quiet Leipzig neighborhood close to the Altstadt, is known for its home-style German food. Specialties include Saxon potato soup with wurst, roast duck with arugula, and pork steaks. Although more robust than refined, the cuisine is good. The décor is nostalgically old-fashioned. You can dine out on the porch in warm weather. The restaurant is named after one of the old pleasure gardens that used to adorn Leipzig.

See map p. 223. Kolonnadenstrasse 2. ☎ *0341/960-7777. Reservations recommended. Tram: 4, 6, 8, 10, 11, or 13. Main courses: €7.50–€16 ($9.50–$20). AE, MC, V. Open: Mon–Sat 11:30 a.m. to midnight, Sun 10 a.m.–3:30 p.m.*

Auerbachs Keller
$–$$ SAXON/INTERNATIONAL

A group of sculpted bronze characters from Goethe's play *Faust* adorns the staircase leading down to this famous medieval cellar restaurant where Goethe had Faust debate Mephistopheles. Guests have a choice of the Historic Rooms (dinner only) or the Big Room (lunch and dinner), with its painted ceiling. The menu features regional cuisine of Saxony, such as *warmes Bratenneckchen* (roasted pork on brown bread with a pepper dip), along with a selection of international dishes. Kids enjoy the underground atmosphere and usually can find something on the menu to their liking.

Leipzig S-Bahn

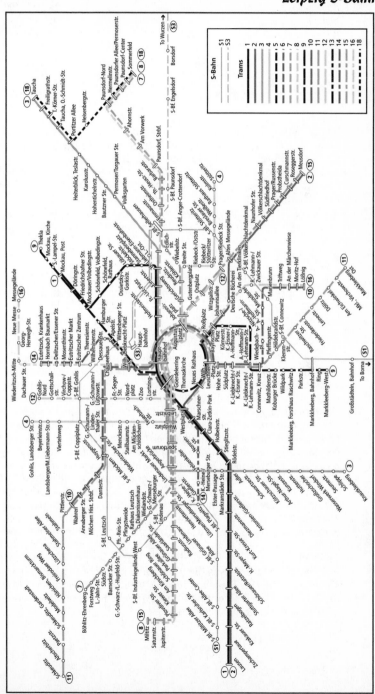

See map p. 223. Mädlerpassage, Grimmaischestrasse 2–4. ☎ *0341/216-100. Reservations recommended for dinner in Historic Rooms. Tram: 4 or 6. Main courses: €8–€19 ($10–$24). AE, MC, V. Open: Historic Rooms Mon–Sat 6 p.m. to midnight; Big Room daily 11:30 a.m. to midnight.*

Paulaner Palais
$ GERMAN/BAVARIAN/AUSTRIAN

This large, popular restaurant, housed in an 18th-century rococo building, has a restaurant and a more casual pub section, each offering the same menu. The summer courtyard within the building is the nicest place to dine. The menu emphasizes boiled meats such as *Tafelspitz* (beef) with heavy sauces, but you can also get Saxon *Sauerbraten, Weisswurst* (steamed pork sausage) from Munich, or *Rostbratwurst* (roasted sausages) from Nuremberg. The only beer they serve is the Munich-brewed Paulaner Bier.

Klostergasse 3–5. ☎ *0341/211-3115. Reservations recommended. Tram: 4 or 6. Main courses: €8–€14 ($10–$17). AE, DC, MC, V. Open: Daily 11 a.m. to midnight.*

Exploring Leipzig

Bombing in 1943 destroyed about one-quarter of Leipzig. The city has placed more of an emphasis on constructing the new than on restoring the old. Most of the old and the new Leipzig that has appeal for visitors is concentrated in the **Zentrum** (City Center), a small, easily walked area south of the Hauptbahnhof (main train station).

Remnants of old Leipzig have been reconstructed around the **Markt,** the city's best-known square. On the east side of the square is the long, gabled, Renaissance **Altes Rathaus.** Reconstructed on the north side of the square is the step-gabled Renaissance **Alte Waage** (Old Weighing House). Across from this house, on the south side of the square, is the **Königshaus** (King's House), once used by the rulers of Saxony as a royal guesthouse. (Peter the Great of Russia and Napoleon also stayed there.) In the neighboring **Naschmarkt,** behind a statue of Goethe as a student, stands the yellow and white **Alte Börse** (Old Produce Exchange), with curving stairs and stucco garlands above the windows; completed in 1687, the Alte Börse was the first baroque building in Leipzig. To the south of Marktplatz is the **Mädlerpassage,** a famous arcade of shops and restaurants, home of Auerbachs Keller (see "Dining in Leipzig" earlier in this chapter). A short walk leads to the pastel baroque houses along **Katharinenstrasse** and the **Brühl.** Just east of the Marktplatz is the 12th-century **Nikolaikirche** (St. Nicholas Church), where demonstrators for democracy gathered in 1989. To the west rises the high-pitched roof of the 1,000-year-old **Thomaskirche** (St. Thomas Church), where Bach served as choirmaster for 27 years. The **Universität Leipzig** (Leipzig University) occupies the area south of Grimmaisch-Strasse.

Augustus-Platz, to the east of the Nikolaikirche and the university, serves as the cultural heart of modern Leipzig. The immense and not very attractive new opera house occupies the north side of the square; the **Neues Gewandhaus** concert hall stands on the south.

Bach-Museum

This reconstructed house standing in the shadow of the Thomaskirche once was home to the Bose family, friends of J. S. Bach's. The house now contains the largest Bach archive in Germany. Many mementos of the composer, including scores and letters, are on display. You can see everything in this small museum in about half an hour; if you love Bach, you'll be tempted to linger. An excellent audio guide in English is included in the price of admission.

See map p. 223. Thomaskirchhof 16. ☎ *0341/964-4133. Tram: 21. Admission: €3 ($3.75) adults, €2 ($2.50) children, €6 ($7.50) family ticket. Open: Daily 10 a.m.–3 p.m. Tours: Guided tours at 11 a.m. and 3 p.m.*

Grassi Museum

Completed in 1929, the Grassi Museum, on Johannis-Platz just east of the Zentrum, houses Leipzig's important arts and crafts, ethnography, and musical instruments collections. After years of restoration, the museum is scheduled to reopen in 2005. In the interim during the restoration, the three museums still are housed in temporary locations, as noted below:

✔ The **Museum für Kunsthandwerk** (Arts and Crafts Museum), Neumarkt 20 (☎ 0341/213-3719), has a wonderful array of handmade objects from the Middle Ages up to the early 20th century. You find beautiful examples of furniture, porcelain, and glassware. Look for the extremely rare, jointed doll dating from 1526. Admission is €2.50 ($3.10) for adults, €2 ($2.50) seniors and students. The museum is open Tuesday through Sunday from 10 a.m. to 6 p.m., Wednesday until 8 p.m.

✔ The **Museum für Völkerkunde** (Museum of Ethnography), Mädlerpassage, Grimmaische Strasse 2–4 (☎ 0341/268-9568), displays highlights from the permanent collection of cultural artifacts relating to the peoples of the world. Admission is €2 ($2.50) adults, €1 ($1.25) seniors and children. The museum is open Tuesday through Friday from 10 a.m. to 5:30 p.m., Saturday and Sunday from 10 a.m. to 5 p.m.

✔ The **Musikinstrumenten-Museum** (Musical Instruments Museum), Thomaskirchhof 20 (☎ 0341/214-2125), considered one of the best of its kind in the world, exhibits Italian, German, and French musical instruments of the 16th to the 19th centuries. Admission is €3 ($3.75) for adults, €1 ($1.25) seniors and children. The museum is open Tuesday through Sunday from 11 a.m. to 5 p.m.

Bach in Leipzig

The composer Johann Sebastian Bach (1685 to 1750) is Leipzig's most famous citizen. He came to Leipzig at the age of 38 to be choirmaster and director of the Thomaskirche's boys' choir and director of music at Leipzig University, and stayed for the rest of his life. In Leipzig, Bach wrote more than 200 cantatas, the *Passion According to St. Matthew*, and the Mass in B Minor. Bach was the father of no fewer than 17 children (4 by his first wife; 13 with his second). Three of his sons, Carl Philipp Emanuel, Johann Christian, and Wilhelm Friedemann, also became composers. Every May, Leipzig celebrates Bach's musical legacy with the famous **Bachfest** (☎ **0341/913-7333**; www.bach-leipzig.de), during which Bach's works are performed in the Thomaskirche and other venues around town.

Museum der Bildenden Künste (Museum of Fine Arts)

In late 2005 or early 2006, this collection — one of Germany's most important art collections with some 2,500 paintings and sculptures including works by Dürer, Rubens, Rembrandt, Rodin, and van Eyck — is scheduled to move to a new museum on Sachsenplatz. Unfortunately, it can't be seen until then. Opening times or admission prices for the new museum were not available for this edition of *Germany For Dummies.*

See map p. 223. Sachsenplatz.

Museum in der Runden Ecke (Stasi Museum)

This chillingly fascinating museum is housed in the building that once was the headquarters of the dreaded Stasi (short for *Staatssicherheit,* or "state security"), the East German Ministry for State Security. An exhibition called "The Power and Banality of the East German Secret Police" documents the meticulous and paranoid methods by which Stasi agents monitored every exchange of information in East Germany, confiscating private letters and listening in on phone conversations. On the nights of December 4 and 5, 1989, local citizens took a giant step toward toppling the government of East Germany when they seized this building. You may want to spend a few minutes here, but be aware that none of the exhibits are translated into English.

See map p. 223. Dittrichring 24. ☎ 0341/961-2443. www.runde-ecke-leipzig.de. Tram: 1, 2, 4, 6, 15, 17, 21, or 24. Admission: Free. Open: Daily 10 a.m.–6 p.m.

Nikolaikirche (St. Nicholas Church)

The present church was built in the 16th century and has a white, neo-classical interior. On this site in 1989, a group of 10,000 demonstrators gathered with candles and began the peaceful revolution that toppled the GDR, East Germany's Communist government. The movement started as a prayer group in the Nikolaikirche in 1982.

See map p. 223. Nikolaikirchhof. ☎ *0341/960-5270. Tram: 4, 6, 15, or 20. Admission: Free. Open: Daily 8 a.m.–5 p.m.*

Thomaskirche (St. Thomas Church)

Leipzig's most famous resident, Johann Sebastian Bach, was choirmaster in this church from 1723 until his death 27 years later. His body was moved here in 1950 on the 200th anniversary of his death and reburied in front of the altar. Bach wrote his great cantatas for the Thomanerchor, the church's famous boys' choir, first organized in the 13th century. Both Mozart and Mendelssohn also performed in the Thomaskirche, and Richard Wagner was christened here in 1813. The church was built on the site of a 13th-century monastery and was heavily restored after WWII and again after reunification. Its high-pitched roof dates from 1496. When it isn't touring, the choir presents concerts every Sunday morning and Friday evening.

See map p. 223. Thomaskirchhof 18 (just off Marktplatz). ☎ *0341/960-2855. Tram: 4, 6, 8, 10, 11, or 13. Admission: Free. Open: Daily 9 a.m.–6 p.m.*

Zeitgeschichtliches Forum Leipzig (Contemporary History Forum)

I recommend that anyone traveling to Leipzig visit this free multimedia exhibition, which opened in 2002. Described as a place of "living remembrance," the exhibit may help you better understand contemporary German history, what life was like in Communist East Germany, and the events that triggered the fall of the GDR. Set up chronologically, the exhibit uses photos, documents, newsreels, audio, and memorabilia to guide you through the tumultuous last half century in eastern Germany. Give yourself at least an hour.

See map p. 223. Grimmaische Strasse 6. ☎ *0341/22200. Tram: 2, 4, 6, or 8. Admission: Free. Open: Tues–Fri 9 a.m.–6 p.m., Sat–Sun 10 a.m.–6 p.m.*

Shopping in Leipzig

Exploring the handsomely restored Art Nouveau **Arkaden** (arcades) that thread through the historic core of Leipzig is fun. **Mädlerpassage** is Leipzig's finest arcade, lined with chic, sophisticated, expensive boutiques.

The **Naschmarkt,** open Monday through Saturday, is a lively, centrally located outdoor market that sells vegetables, plants, cheeses, meats, and a bit of everything.

Leipzig's **Hauptbahnhof** (Central Station) recently was transformed into a giant shopping mall, with about 140 shops and cafes that open between 6:30 and 9 a.m. and close at 10 p.m. on weekdays and 4 p.m. on Saturday.

Open daily in December in front of the Altes Rathaus, **Leipzig's Weihnachtsmarkt** (Christmas Market) is a tradition dating back to 1767. Stalls (open daily 10 a.m.–8 p.m.) sell a variety of craft items and Christmas food and drink. Special organ concerts and performances of Bach's Christmas Oratorio and Handel's Messiah also take place.

Discovering nightlife in Leipzig

Leipzig's active nightlife offers something for everyone, from opera and classical concerts to late-night bars and discos. The area around the Markt is full of bars, cafes, and other entertainment options. For a sampling of lively cafes, walk down **Barfüssergässchen,** just south of the Altes Rathaus.

The **Neues Gewandhaus,** Augustusplatz (☎ **0341/127-0280;** www. gewandhaus.de; Tram: 4, 5, 12, 13, or 15), a concert hall built in 1981, is the home of the world-famous **Gewandhaus Orchestra.** Founded in 1781, the orchestra premiered works by Beethoven, Felix Mendelssohn, Franz Schubert, and Johannes Brahms. Ticket prices range from €10 to €45 ($12 to $56).

The **Leipzieger Oper** (Leipzig Opera) is one of Germany's most acclaimed opera companies. Its home is the **Opernhaus,** Augustusplatz 8 (☎ **0341/ 126-1261;** oper-leipzig.de; Tram: 4, 5, 12, 13, or 15), opposite the Neues Gewandhaus. Ticket prices for opera and ballet range from €9 to €40 ($11 to $50).

Leipzig's main theater, the **Schauspielhaus,** Bosestrasse 1 (☎ **0341/ 12680;** Tram: 1, 2, 4, 6, 15, 17, 21, or 24), is home to several arts companies that stage a mix of theatrical and musical productions in German. Ticket prices range from €10 to €30 ($12 to $37).

Mephisto Bar, Mädlerpassage (☎ **0341/216-100;** Tram: 4 or 6), which honors Goethe and the *Faust* legend, is the hippest bar and cafe in Leipzig, great for people-watching. Live music is performed Thursday through Saturday, beginning around 8 p.m.

Weimar: Capital of the Enlightenment

Beautiful Weimar (*Vi*-mar), a 1,000-year-old town on the edge of the Thuringian Forest that once was a center of the German Enlightenment, is one of Germany's greatest cultural shrines. Some of the country's most revered painters, writers, and composers made their homes in this small Thuringian town on the River Ilm, or spent portions of their creative lives here. Goethe, considered Germany's greatest literary genius, lived and worked in Weimar for 50 years. Weimar also is famous in the history of Germany, because the German national assembly met here in 1919 to draw up the constitution for the ill-fated "Weimar Republic," Germany's first democratic government after World War I (WWI). The town is well known to architecture buffs, because the first Bauhaus School of Art and Design was founded here in 1919. During WWII, the Nazis established the concentration camp Buchenwald on the outskirts of this city.

Weimar is a joy to explore, in part because its old winding streets are sprinkled with the homes (now museums) of famous figures. Unlike Dresden and Leipzig, Weimar was not completely destroyed by bombs in WWII. Enough of old Weimar remains to give you a good sense of what the town was like when Goethe lived there.

Weimar

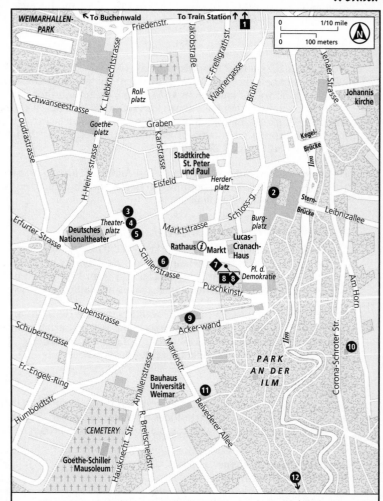

WEIMARHALLEN-PARK

To Buchenwald

To Train Station
1

0   1/10 mile
0   100 meters

Friedenstr.
Jakobstraße
F.-Frelligrathstr.
Wagnergasse
Brühl
Jenaer Strasse
Johannis kirche

K. Liebknechtstrasse
Schwanseestrasse
Roll-platz
Graben
Kegel-Brücke
Ilm

Coudrastrasse
Goethe-platz
Karlstrasse
Stadtkirche St. Peter und Paul
H.-Heine-strasse
Eisfeld
Herder-platz

Erfurter Strasse
Theater-platz **3** **4**
Deutsches Nationaltheater **5**
Marktstrasse
Schloss-g.
Burg-platz
2
Stern-Brücke
Leibnizallee

Schillerstrasse
Rathaus *(i)* Markt
6
Lucas-Cranach-Haus
7
8 **8** Pl. d. Demokratie
Puschkinstr.
Am Horn

Stubenstrasse
Schubertstrasse
Acker-wand **9**
Ilm
10
Corona-Schroter Str.

Fr.-Engels-Ring
Marienstr.
Amalienstrasse
Bauhaus Universität Weimar
Liszt-Haus **11**
PARK AN DER ILM

Humboldtstr.
Hausknecht Str.
R. Breitscheidstr.
Belvederer Allee

CEMETERY
Goethe-Schiller Mausoleum
12

ACCOMMODATIONS ■
Hotel Elephant Weimar **8**
InterCityHotel Weimar **1**

DINING ◆
Hotel Elephant Weimar **8**
Zum Schwarzen Bären **7**

ATTRACTIONS ●
Bauhaus-Museum **3**
Goethes Gartenhaus **10**
Goethes Wohnhaus &
   Goethe Nationalmuseum **9**
Liszt-Haus **11**
Schillers Wohnhaus **6**
Schloss Belvedere **12**
Schlossmuseum **2**
Weimar Haus–
   Das Geschichtserlebnis **4**
Wittumspalais **5**

Berlin ★
GERMANY
Weimar •

Information *(i)*

Weimar is an easy day trip from Leipzig or Dresden, but because Weimar offers plenty to see, you may want to spend the night.

Getting there

Weimar lies 262km (162 miles) southwest of Berlin, 118km (74 miles) southwest of Leipzig, and 215km (134 miles) southwest of Dresden. You find good **train** connections to Weimar's **Hauptbahnhof** (main train station) from throughout Germany. Fast InterCity Express (ICE) trains run from Frankfurt, Leipzig, and Dresden, and Weimar is a stop on the InterRegio express train between Frankfurt and Berlin. For rail information and schedules, call ☎ **11861.**

By **car,** you can reach Weimar via the **A4** Autobahn linking Frankfurt and Dresden, or the **A9** Autobahn between Berlin and Munich, turning off at Hermsdorfer Kreuz for Weimar.

Finding information and taking a tour

Tourist-Information am Markt, Markt 10 (☎ **03643/7450;** www.weimar. de), in the town's central marketplace, is open Monday to Friday from 9:30 a.m. to 6 p.m., and Saturday and Sunday from 10 a.m. to 3 p.m. *Takt,* the local entertainment listings magazine, is available free.

The tourist office offers a two-hour **walking tour** (in German) of Weimar daily at 10 a.m. and 2 p.m. The meeting point is the Tourist Information office; the price is €6 ($7.50) for adults, €4 ($5) for students, children younger than 14 free. Buy tickets at the tourist office.

Staying in Weimar

Since reunification, new hotels have opened throughout Weimar, often in historic buildings. The tourist offices listed earlier under "Finding information and taking a tour" also can help you find a hotel room or pension.

Hotel Elephant Weimar
$$$–$$$$ City Center

The Hotel Elephant is Weimar's most famous hotel, with a past guest roster that includes Bach, Tolstoy, even Adolf Hitler. The elegant late-17th-century facade, fronting Weimar's picturesque marketplace, hides a stylishly contemporary interior. The 99 rooms come in different sizes but are furnished basically the same, with pearwood furniture and Art Deco styling. Bathrooms are large; most have a tub and shower combination. The staff can arrange baby-sitting. Breakfast costs an additional €18 ($22).

See map p. 231. Am Markt 19, 99423 Weimar. ☎ *03643/8020. Fax: 03643/802-610.* www.arabellasheraton.com. *Bus: 10, 11, or 71. Rack rates: €150–€245 ($187–$306) double. AE, DC, MC, V.*

InterCityHotel Weimar
$$ City Center

This good, convenient, moderately priced hotel sits right across the street from the train station. The InterCityHotel chain always is reliable. The 134 rooms are not large or luxurious, but they are fully equipped, comfortable, and very well maintained. Bathrooms are small and have showers only. The staff is friendly, and the buffet breakfast is good. One nice perk: The hotel gives you a free bus pass.

See map p. 231. Carl-August-Allee 17, 99423 Weimar. ☎ *03643/2340. Fax: 03643/234-444.* www.intercityhotel.de. *Rack rates: €109–€114 ($136–$142). Rates include buffet breakfast. MC, V.*

Dining in Weimar

As with Leipzig, Weimar is not a city renowned for its culinary past. Since reunification, however, some new restaurants with savvier cooking and better ingredients have opened.

Hotel Elephant Weimar
$$–$$$ GERMAN/INTERNATIONAL

Weimar's oldest hotel has two restaurants. **Anna Amalia** is modern and airy, a dress-up sort of place with beautifully set tables, a garden terrace, and good service. Its Italian dishes, among the best in the region, make use of local produce and ingredients.

Down one flight of steps is the historic **Elephantenkeller** (Elephant Cellar), a place for casual dining in a rustic atmosphere. In October, when Weimar's famous *Zwiebelmarkt* (onion market) is open (a tradition dating back to 1653), this restaurant serves specialty onion salads. Otherwise, try local specialties such as sweet-and-sour Thuringian pot roast with dumplings or Thuringian-style grilled bratwurst on sauerkraut with pureed peas.

See map p. 231. Am Markt 19. ☎ *03643/802-639. Reservations recommended. Bus: 10, 11, or 71. Main courses: Anna Amalia €15–€22 ($19–$27); Elephantenkeller €4–€16 ($5–$20). AE, DC, MC, V. Open: Anna Amalia daily 6:30–10:30 p.m.; Elephantenkeller Thurs–Tues noon to 3 a.m. and 6 p.m.–11 p.m.*

Zum Schwarzen Bären
$ THURINGIAN

Located next door to the Hotel Elephant, this restaurant is Weimar's oldest. Nothing is fancy about it, but you can get a good, hefty meal for a reasonable cost. Dishes include potato soup with sausage, rumpsteak, schnitzel with potatoes, and pork medallions with Gorgonzola sauce.

See map p. 231. Markt 20. ☎ *03643/853-847. Bus: 10, 11, or 71. Main courses: €7–€15 ($9–$19). MC, V. Open: Daily 11 a.m. to midnight.*

Exploring Weimar

Weimar enjoys a scenic location on the Ilm River, set against the backdrop of the Ettersberg and Vogtland hills. The **Altstadt** (Old City), with its large park, has many historic sights, all of which you can easily see on foot. **Markt,** the town's main square, remains the lively heart of the old city. Surrounding the Altstadt is the newer Weimar, with broad, tree-lined boulevards and many 19th-century buildings.

Bauhaus-Museum

The focus of this museum is the Bauhaus movement, which was founded in Weimar in 1919 and sought to unify arts and crafts within the context of architecture. The collection of Bauhaus memorabilia includes rugs, architectural drawings, furniture, tea sets, and toys collected by the school's director, the architect Walter Gropius. One room showcases the work of Henry van de Velde, an important architect-designer of Art Nouveau. The museum is fairly compact, so you can see everything in about half an hour.

See map p. 231. Theaterplatz. ☎ *03643/564-161. Bus: 1, 2, 3, 5, 6, or 7. Admission: €4 ($5) adults, €3 ($3.75) seniors and students. Open: Apr–Oct Tues–Sun 10 a.m.–6 p.m., Nov–Mar 10 a.m.–4 p.m.*

Goethes Gartenhaus (Goethe's Garden House)

This simple stone cottage with a high-pitched roof, located in the bucolic park on the Ilm River, was Goethe's first residence when he came to Weimar in 1775 as a guest of Duke Karl August. Throughout his life, Goethe used the house as a summer retreat. The structure was built as a garden house in the 16th century, enlarged in the 17th century, and reconstructed in 1996 according to the plans of 1820. You can see the interior, which has a few pieces of period furniture, in less than 15 minutes.

See map p. 231. Im Park an der Ilm. ☎ *03643/545-375. Bus: 1, 10, or 12. Admission: €3 ($3.75) adults, €2 ($2.50) students and children. Open: Wed–Mon Apr–Oct 10 a.m.–6 p.m.; Oct–Mar 10 a.m.–4 p.m.*

Goethes Wohnhaus (Goethe House) & Goethe Nationalmuseum

The large baroque house where Goethe lived from 1782 to 1832 is Weimar's most popular attraction. When Goethe returned from Italy, overflowing with enthusiasm for all things Italian, he replaced the baroque staircase with broad stairs in the style of the Italian Renaissance, filled the house with casts of ancient busts and statues, and designed special cabinets to display his Italian majolica plates. Believing that colors affect mood, Goethe had his dining room painted a sunny yellow, his study a soothing green, and his reception room a calming blue. The house has 14 rooms, some of them pretty much as Goethe and his wife, Christiane, left them. Goethe died in his sparsely furnished bedchamber on March 22, 1832, when he was 82 years old. You need about half an hour to see everything, longer if you're a Goethe fan; an audio guide in English is available.

The house is part of the adjoined Goethe National Museum, but the museum requires a separate admission. In the musuem, you find more Goethe memorabilia.

See map p. 231. Frauenplan 1. ☎ *03643/545-320. Bus: 1, 2, 5, 6, or 8. Admission: House €6 ($7.50) adults, €4.50 ($5.50) students and seniors; museum €2.50 ($3.10). Open: House and museum Tues–Sun April–Oct 9 a.m.–6 p.m., Nov–Mar 9 a.m.–4 p.m. Tours (in German): Tues and Fri at 1 p.m., €2 ($2.50).*

Liszt-Haus

Franz Liszt, the Hungarian composer and most famous pianist of the 19th century, spent the last period of his life in this house located at the west entrance of Park an der Ilm. Liszt gathered young musicians around him in the high-ceilinged, handsomely furnished rooms. Displayed in the red-carpeted salon are one of Liszt's pianos and the portable clavichord he used to exercise his fingers while he was traveling. Letters and other personal and musical mementos also are on view.

See map p. 231. Marienstrasse 17. ☎ *03643/545-388. Bus: 1, 10, or 12. Admission: €2 ($2.50) adults, €1.50 ($2) students and children younger than 12. Open: Tues–Sun Apr–Oct 10 a.m.–1 p.m. and 2–6 p.m.*

Schillers Wohnhaus (Schiller House)

After his friend Goethe, Friedrich von Schiller (1759 to 1805) is the greatest name in German literature. He lived with his family in this house, located just up the street from Goethe's house, from 1802 to 1805. The house is furnished as it would have been in Schiller's day. In the attic rooms, Schiller wrote his last works, including *Wilhelm Tell (William Tell)*. You can wander through the entire house in about 15 minutes.

See map p. 231. Schillerstrasse 12. ☎ *03643/545-350. Bus: 1, 2, 3, 5, 6, 7, or 8. Admission: €3.50 ($4.50) adults, €2.50 ($3.10) seniors, €1 ($1.25) students. Open: Fri–Wed Apr–Oct 9 a.m.–6 p.m.; Nov–Mar 9 a.m.–4 p.m. Tours (in German): Mon 1 p.m., €2 ($2.50).*

Goethe and the court of Weimar

In 1775, Johann Wolfgang von Goethe (1749 to 1832)) was invited to the duchy of Weimar by the teenaged Duke Karl August. Goethe's fame rested on the novel *The Sorrows of Young Werther,* which had become a sensation throughout Europe for its depiction of a suffering, suicidal artist. Duke Karl, Goethe's patron, wanted to surround himself with clever, entertaining people. His mother, Duchess Anna Amalia, set the tone for the salons, which were referred to as the "Court of the Muses." Thanks to Goethe and his friends, particularly the playwright Friedrich Schiller, the little duchy of Weimar gained renown as a center of the German Enlightenment *(Erklärung),* which brought a new, classically inspired rationalism to German art and literature. In Weimar, Goethe wrote the play *Faust,* the work for which he is most famous.

Schloss Belvedere (Belvedere Palace)

A pretty, baroque chateau located 3km (2 miles) south of Weimar, Belvedere Palace was a favorite retreat of Duchess Anna Amalia and her son's "enlightened" Weimar court. The orangerie displays a collection of historical coaches. Inside the chateau, you find a collection of decorative art from the rococo period. The English-style park was laid out between 1814 and 1840. You can visit both in about two hours.

See map p. 231. Belvederer Allee. ☎ *03643/546-162. Bus: 12. Admission: €3.50 ($4.50) adults, €2.50 ($3.10) children. Open: Apr–Oct Tues–Sun 10 a.m.–6 p.m.; Nov–Mar 9 a.m.– 4 p.m.*

Schlossmuseum (Castle Museum)

This neoclassical structure, begun in 1789 and completed in 1803, replaced the royal castle that burned down in 1774. The museum has a series of galleries dedicated to Schiller, Goethe, and other famous names associated with Weimar. Of more general interest are the painting galleries containing important works by Lucas Cranach the Elder (including a portrait of Martin Luther), Flemish and Italian paintings, and Expressionist paintings by Max Beckmann and Max Lieberman. Give yourself about 45 minutes to wander through the galleries.

See map p. 231. Burgplatz 4. ☎ *03643/546-160. Bus: 1, 5, 6, 8, or 10. Admission: €4.50 ($5.75) adults, €3.50 ($4.50) children. Open: Tues–Sun Apr–Oct 10 a.m.–6 p.m.; Nov–Mar 10 a.m.–4 p.m.*

Weimar Haus–Das Geschichtserlebnis (Weimar House–The Weimar Story)

This multimedia attraction provides a good introduction to Weimar's history. Wax figures created by artists who worked for London's Madame Tussaud, theater sets, and videotaped projections help tell Weimar's story from the earliest settlers in 3,000 B.C. through the time of Goethe, Schiller, Luther, and Napoleon. The tour lasts about 30 minutes; audio guides in English are available.

See map p. 231. Schillerstrasse 16–18. ☎ *03643/901-890. Bus: 1, 2, 3, 4, 5, or 6. Admission: €6.50 ($8) adults, €5.50 ($7) seniors, students, and children. Open: daily, winter 10 a.m.–6 p.m., summer 10 a.m.–8 p.m.*

Wittumspalais

A short walk along Schillerstrasse from the Schiller House leads to the elegant Wittumspalais (*vit*-ooms-pa-*lay*). Completed in 1767, the "Widow's Palace" was the residence of the widowed Dowager Duchess Anna Amalia, who presided over a "Court of the Muses," where artists, poets, doctors, and philosophers met to discuss issues of science, thought, and art. The house, devoted to mementos of the German Enlightenment, has an extensive collection of paintings, silhouettes (all the rage back then), and costumes.

See map p. 231. Theaterplatz. ☎ 03643/545-377. Bus: 1, 2, 3, 4, 5, or 6. Admission: €3.50 ($4.50) adults, €2.50 ($3.10) students and children. Open: Tues–Sun Apr–Oct 10 a.m.– 6 p.m., Nov–Mar 10 a.m.–4 p.m.

Exploring the Thuringian Forest

Weimar sits in the northeastern corner of the Thüringer Wald (Thuringian Forest), long extolled by nature lovers for its scenic beauty. Within the forest, spruce-clad mountains rise to about 985m (3,225 ft.), old castles crown the tops of hills, and dozens of picturesque medieval villages dot the narrow, winding roads. **Erfurt,** 22km (14 miles) west of Weimar, is the oldest town in the region and the capital of Thuringia. Just south of Erfurt is picturesque **Arnstadt,** once the home of Johann Sebastian Bach. **Ilmenau,** a lively university town south of Arnstadt, is the starting point of a popular hiking trail known as *Auf Goethes Spuren* (In Goethe's Footsteps), which leads to places associated with the great poet. If you want to explore this picturesque area by car, a 110km (68-mile) scenic road called the **Thuringer Hochstrasse** (Thuringian High Road) runs from Eisenach to Ilmenau.

Buchenwald: Remembering the past

About 10km (6 miles) from Weimar, one of the great cities of German art and culture, in beech woods *(Buchenwald)* where Goethe and Schiller once walked, the Nazis set up one of their nightmare concentration camps. Bus No. 6 from Weimar's main train station makes the trip northwest of town to **Gedenkstätte Buchenwald** (Buchenwald Memorial; ☎ 03643/4300), the site of the camp. The Nazis confined about a quarter of a million Jews, Slavs, Gypsies, homosexuals, political prisoners, prisoners of war, and others in this work camp from 1937 until the camp's liberation by the U.S. Army in 1945. At least 56,000 people died at Buchenwald, and many thousands of others were sent from here to death camps in the east. Later, Soviet occupation forces also used the site as an internment camp. Between 1945 and 1951, the Soviets sent thousands of prisoners here to die. A memorial with a cluster of "larger than life" people, representing victims of fascism, honors the people from 32 nations who lost their lives at Buchenwald. The museum reflects both the Soviet and the Nazi past of the camp. You can visit Buchenwald May through September, Tuesday to Sunday from 9:45 a.m. to 6 p.m.; October through April, Tuesday to Sunday from 8:45 a.m. to 5 p.m. Admission is free. To reach the memorial, take bus No. 6 marked "Buchenwald."

Shopping in Weimar

A visit to Weimar's antiques stores offers a chance to buy porcelain, silver, crystal, and furniture that survived the devastation of WWII. The most interesting shops include **Antikitäten am Palais,** Schillerstrasse 22 (☎ 03643/59625), and its immediate neighbor, **Kaiser Antikitäten,** Schillerstrasse 22 (same phone). Also appealing are **Antikitäten am Schloss,** Obereschlossgasse 2 (☎ 03643/512-993); **Goethe-Antiquariat,** Kaufenstrasse 7 (☎ 03643/402-567), selling books only; and **Thiersch Antikitäten,** Bräuhausgasse 15 (☎ 03643/402-540).

Discovering nightlife in Weimar

Weimar's main performance venue is the **Deutsches Nationaltheater** (German National Theater), Theaterplatz (☎ 03643/755-334), where Franz Liszt and Richard Strauss once conducted. (This building also is where in 1919 the National Congress passed the new democratic constitution that was the basis for the short-lived Weimar Republic.) You can buy tickets for opera, dance, and concerts at the tourist information centers or the theater box office; prices range from €8 to €35 ($10 to $37).

Weimar's bars and outdoor cafes are good places to drink and talk into the night. You find a good selection to choose from along **Schillerstrasse** and around **Theaterplatz.**

Part IV
Southern & Western Germany

The 5th Wave   By Rich Tennant

In this part . . .

Southern Germany is different from other regions in Germany, as you discover in this part. I devote Chapter 15 entirely to **Munich,** the beautiful capital of Bavaria. You find everything you need to know about Germany's secret capital: how to get there and get around, how to find a fine hotel or restaurant, and what to see. Going beyond Munich, in Chapter 16, I describe additional sightseeing possibilities in Bavaria, including the **Romantic Road**, an ideal driving tour loaded with unspoiled medieval towns, bucolic scenery, and must-see attractions such as **Rothenburg ob der Tauber,** Germany's most famous walled medieval city, and **Neuschwanstein,** the most dramatic of Ludwig II's fairy-tale castles. I also tell you about visiting the alpine resort towns of **Garmisch-Partenkirchen** and **Oberammergau**, famed for its woodcarvers. In Chapter 17, I highlight lovely Lake Constance, known as the **Bodensee** in Germany, and the **Schwarzwald,** or Black Forest, one of the most scenically delightful areas in all of Deutschland, home to the cities of **Freiburg** and **Baden-Baden.**

Western Germany includes the popular and populous Rhineland region and many famous cities that are easy to reach and fun to explore. Chapter 18 covers three cities in western and central Germany: **Heidelberg,** the romantic town on the Neckar River; **Stuttgart**, the cultural capital of southwest Germany; and **Nuremberg** (**Nürnberg** in German), with its picturesque corners and Gothic churches. Chapter 19 is all about **Cologne** (**Köln** in German), a lively Rhineside city famous for its spectacular Gothic cathedral. Easy day trips from Cologne include the wine-growing regions of the Mosel Valley and the Rheingau section of the Rhine Valley. In case you're eager to ride the Rhine, I tell you about boat trips through the river's most scenic stretches. Chapter 20 is all about **Frankfurt,** the sophisticated city with the huge international airport that is the German port of entry for many international visitors.

Chapter 15

Munich: Capital of Gemütlichkeit

*M*unich (München, pronounced *Mewn*-shin, in German), the capital of Bavaria, is a town that likes to celebrate. Walk through the *Altstadt* (Old Town) on a warm, sunny day or a balmy night and you see people sitting outside, in every square, drinking, eating, and enjoying life. **Oktoberfest,** which attracts some 7 million revelers, starts in September and lasts for 16 days. Before Lent, from January through February, the city goes into party mode again and celebrates **Fasching** (Carnival), a whirl of colorful parades, masked balls, and revelry. Throughout the year, people gather in the giant beer halls and beer gardens to quaff liters of beer, listen to the oom-pah-pah bands, and have a good time.

Oom-pah-pah aside, Munich also is a rich, elegant, sophisticated city, with an unparalleled array of artistic and cultural treasures. World-class museums, palaces, concert halls, and theaters are part and parcel of life in the Bavarian capital. The city is all about prosperity and good-natured *Gemütlichkeit,* one of those hard-to-translate words that means something like cozy and/or good-natured. Think of *Gemütlichkeit* as a kind of cozy charm and you'll get the picture.

If you believe the polls, Munich is the Germans' first choice as a desirable place to live. Many Germans — especially the 1.5 million people who live in Munich — think of the city as Germany's secret capital. Munich offers so much to visitors that I recommend you give yourself at least three days here.

The little monk of Munich

In the ninth century, a small village located near a Benedictine abbey on the river Isar called itself Mönch, German for "monk." Since that time, Munich's coat of arms has included a figure of the *Münchner Kindl,* or "little monk."

Getting There

As one of Germany's major cities, Munich has no lack of transportation options. Like Frankfurt, Munich has an international airport, so you can fly there directly from the United States. The city is easily accessible from anywhere within Germany or Europe.

By plane

Munich's **Franz Josef Strauss International Airport** (☎ **089/9752-1313** flight information; www.munich-airport.com) is located 29km (18 miles) northeast of the city center. Opened in 1992, the airport is among the most modern and efficient in the world. The S-8 S-Bahn (☎ **089/4142-4344**) train connects the airport with the *Hauptbahnhof* (main railroad station) in downtown Munich. Trains leave from the S-Bahn platform beneath the airport every 20 minutes daily between 4:05 a.m. and 1:05 a.m. The fare for the 40-minute trip is €8 ($10) adults, €.90 ($1.10) children. The Lufthansa Airport Bus (☎ **089/323-040**) also runs between the airport and the main train station in Munich every 20 minutes from 5:10 a.m. to 7:50 p.m. The trip takes about 40 minutes and costs €9.50 ($12) for adults, €4.50 ($5.50) for children. A taxi to the city center costs about €70 ($87) and can take more than an hour if traffic is heavy.

By train

You can easily reach Munich by train from any city in Germany or Europe. Daily trains arrive from Frankfurt (trip time: 3¾ hours) and Berlin (trip time: 7 hours). Munich's **Hauptbahnhof,** on Bahnhofplatz near the city center, is one of Europe's largest train stations, with a hotel, restaurants, shopping, and banking facilities. You find a train information office on the mezzanine level, open daily from 7 a.m. to 8 p.m.; you can also call **Deutsche Bahn** (German Rail; ☎ **11861** for train information and schedules; an English speaker will be available to help you). Connected to the rail station are the city's extensive **S-Bahn** rapid-transit system and the **U-Bahn** (subway) system.

By car

I do not recommend driving in Munich. Most of downtown is a pedestrian-only area — wonderful if you're a walker, a nightmare if you're a driver.

Traffic jams are frequent, and parking spaces are elusive and costly. If you plan on making excursions into the countryside, renting a car in the city center instead of trekking out to the airport is more convenient. Car-rental companies with windows at the main train station include **Avis** (☎ 089/1260-000), **Hertz** (☎ 089/1295-001), and **Sixt Autovermietung** (☎ 089/550-2447).

Finding Information After You Arrive

Munich's tourist office, **Fremdenverkehrsamt München** (☎ 089/233-96500; www.muenchen-tourist.de), operates a **tourist information center** in the main train station (Bahnhofplatz 2, adjacent to the DER Reisebüro/German Rail Travel Office). You can pick up a map of Munich, obtain information on cultural events, and book a hotel room. The center is open Monday through Saturday from 9:30 a.m. to 6:30 p.m. and Sunday from 10 a.m. to 6 p.m. You find another branch of the tourist office in the city center at Marienplatz in the **Neues Rathaus** (New Town Hall); hours are Monday through Friday from 10 a.m. to 8 p.m., Saturday from 10 a.m. to 4 p.m. You can make a hotel reservation by calling ☎ 089/233-30233.

Orienting Yourself in Munich

The **Altstadt,** or Old Town, is an oval-shaped pedestrian-only district on the west bank of the Isar River. (See the "Munich Neighborhoods" map in this chapter.) Munich's **Hauptbahnhof** (main train station) lies just west of the Altstadt. **Marienplatz,** the Altstadt's most important square, is where you find several important churches, the **Residenz** (former royal palace), the **National Theater,** and the **Viktualienmarkt,** a wonderfully lively outdoor market. Between Marienplatz and the Nationaltheater is the **Platzl** quarter, famed for its nightlife, restaurants, and the landmark **Hofbräuhaus,** the most famous beer hall in the world.

Odeonsplatz, to the north of Marienplatz, is Munich's most beautiful square. Running west from Odeonsplatz is Briennerstrasse, a wide shopping avenue that leads to **Königsplatz** (King's Square). Flanking this large square, in an area known as the **Museum Quarter,** are three neoclassical buildings constructed by Ludwig I and housing Munich's antiquities: the **Propyläen,** the **Glyptothek,** and the **Antikensammlungen.** Another triad of world-famous art museums — the **Alte Pinakothek** (Old Masters Gallery), the **Neue Pinakothek** (New Masters Gallery), and the brand-new in 2002 **Pinakothek Moderne Kunst** (Gallery of Modern Art) — also lie in the Museum Quarter, just northeast of Königsplatz.

Ludwigstrasse connects the Altstadt with **Schwabing,** a former artists' quarter located north of the Altstadt and known for its cafes, restaurants, and nightlife. **Olympiapark,** site of the 1972 Olympics, is northwest of Schwabing. The sprawling park known as the **Englischer Garten** is located east of Schwabing. East of the Isar River lie **Bogenhausen** and

Munich Neighborhoods

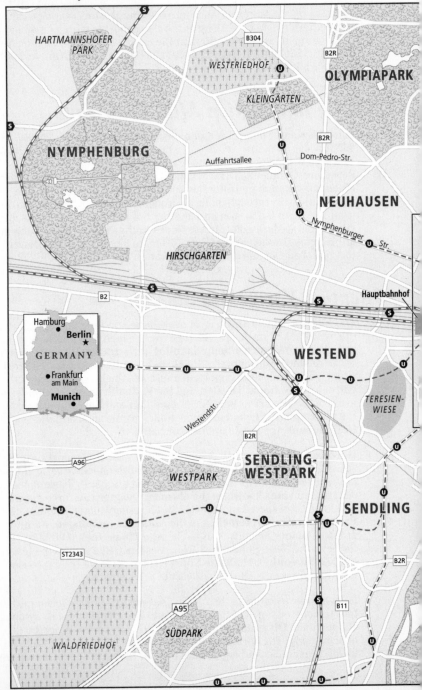

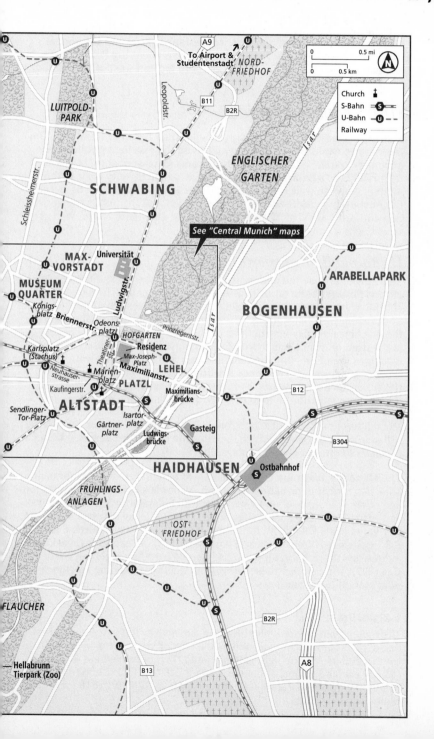

Haidhausen, leafy neighborhoods just outside the city center where you find some hotels and restaurants. **Theresienwiese,** site of the annual Oktoberfest, and **Schloss Nymphenburg** (Nymphenburg Palace), one of Germany's most beautiful palaces, are both located west of the Altstadt.

Getting around Munich

Munich is a large city, only slightly smaller than Berlin or Hamburg. The best way to explore is by walking and using the excellent public transportation system. Subways (U-Bahn), trams (Strassenbahn), buses, and light-rail lines (S-Bahn) make getting anywhere in the city easy. In the Altstadt, you can walk to all the attractions — in fact you have to, because the Altstadt is a car-free zone. For information, call the public transportation authority, **MVV,** at ☎ **089/4142-4344,** or visit them on the Web at www.mvv-muenchen.de.

Using public transportation

You'll probably use the underground **U-Bahn** (subway) and the aboveground **Strassenbahn** (tram) systems most frequently. The same ticket entitles you to ride U-Bahn, S-Bahn, trams, and buses. Purchase tickets from vending machines marked *Fahrkarten* in U-Bahn and S-Bahn stations; the machines display instructions in English. You also can buy tickets in the tram or from a bus driver. Tickets must then be **validated** in the machines found on platforms and in buses and trams; stick your ticket into the machine, which stamps it with the date and time. A validated ticket is valid for two hours. You can transfer as often as you like to any public transportation as long as you travel in the same direction.

Munich has four concentric fare zones. Most, if not all, of your sightseeing will take place in Zone 1, which includes the city center. A **single ticket** *(Einzelfahrkarte)* in Zone 1 costs €2.10 ($2.60).

The **München Welcome Card,** available at either Fremdenverkehrsamt München tourist information center, lets you ride all public transportation and offers discounts of up to 50 percent off on major tourist attractions and city tours. A **Tageskarte** (day ticket) good for a day of travel within the city limits costs €6 ($7.50) for adults, €1.90 ($2.40) for children 6 to 14. A **3-Tageskarte** (three-day ticket) costs €11 ($14). A **Partner 3-Tageskarte,** a three-day ticket good for up to five people traveling together, costs €24 ($29). You can buy these cards from the ticket vending machines or at station ticket windows.

Catching a cab

Taxis are cream-colored, plentiful, and expensive. You can get a taxi at one of the stands located all across the city, or you can hail a cab on the street if its rooftop light is illuminated. Taxi fares begin at €2.50 ($3.10); each additional kilometer costs €1.20 to €1.45 ($1.50 to $1.81), depending on the distance. Call **Taxizentrale** at ☎ **089/21610** for a radio-dispatched taxi.

Munich U-Bahn and S-Bahn

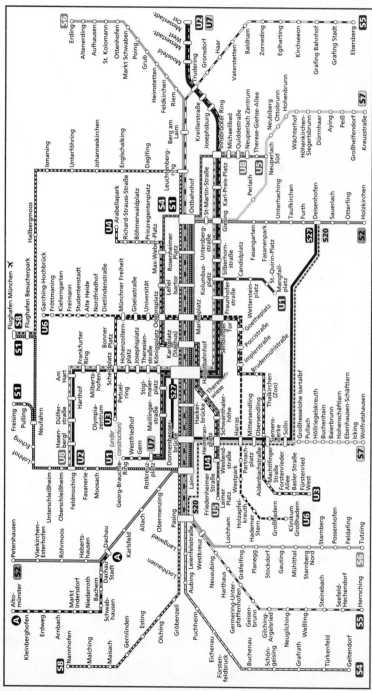

Staying in Style

Hotels in Munich are more expensive than elsewhere in Germany, and rooms can be scarce during Oktoberfest when trade fairs are in town. I strongly recommend that you book your Munich hotel room in advance. I've weighted my choices toward hotels in central Munich.

 The **Fremdenverkehrsamt** (tourist office) in the main train station (see the "Finding Information After You Arrive" section earlier in this chapter) can book a room for you and give you a map with instructions for reaching it. The service is free, but the office collects a 10 percent deposit of the total value of the room; the hotel then deducts this amount from your bill. For direct access to the hotel booking department, call ☎ 089/233-30123.

For locations, see the "Central Munich Accommodations and Dining" map in this chapter.

The top hotels

Here you can find a variety of great hotels. See also the listing for the outstanding **Kempinski Hotel Vier Jahreszeiten München** ($$$$) in Chapter 22.

Advokat Hotel
$$$–$$$$ Altstadt

You don't find frills or frou-frou in this streamlined 50-room hotel in a 1930s apartment building. The Advokat is strictly minimalist in approach and has an understated elegance. The rooms are medium-size, with clean, simple furnishings. Each room comes with a compact bathroom, most with tub and shower.

See map p. 250. Baaderstrasse 1, 80469 München. ☎ *089/21-63-10. Fax: 089/216-3190.* www.hotel-advokat.de. *S-Bahn: Isartor (then a 5-minute walk south on Zweibrücken Strasse and west on Baaderstrasse). Rack rates: €150–€190 ($187–$237) double. Rates include breakfast. MC, V.*

An der Oper
$$$–$$$$ Altstadt

This five-story hotel, dating from 1969, is wonderfully situated for sightseeing and shopping in the Altstadt. The décor is basic modern without being particularly distinguished. The 68 rooms are on the small side but have double-glazed windows and a small sitting area. The bathrooms are small, too, and come with a shower.

See map p. 250. Falkenturmstrasse 11 (just off Maximilianstrasse, near Marienplatz), 80331 München. ☎ *089/290-0270. Fax: 089/2900-2729.* www.hotelanderoper.com. *Tram: 19 to Nationaltheater stop (then a 5-minute walk south on Sparkassen Strasse* *and east on Falkenturmstrasse). Rack rates: €150–€235 ($187–$294) double. Rates include buffet breakfast. AE, MC, V.*

Eden-Hotel-Wolff
$$$–$$$$ **Near train station**

If you want a nice place right across the street from the train station, this is the best. From the outside, this large hotel looks a bit austere, but the interior has been redone with a pleasantly modern look. Most of the 211 rooms are fairly large, and all are decorated in a comfortable, unobtrusive style. Bathrooms are larger than average, with tub and shower. One child younger than age 6 is allowed to stay free in the parents' room; for an additional child, an extra bed can be rented for €42 ($52).

See map p. 250. Arnulfstrasse 4, 80335 München. ☎ **089/551-150.** *Fax: 089/5511-5555.* www.ehw.de. *U-/S-Bahn: Hauptbahnhof (the hotel is opposite the north side of the train station). Rack rates: €172–€282 ($215–$352) double. Rates include buffet breakfast. AE, DC, MC, V.*

Gästehaus Englischer Garten
$–$$ **Schwabing**

This 25-room guesthouse near the Englischer Garten is quiet, charming, and an excellent value. The rooms are small to medium in size and decorated with a homey mixture of antiques, old-fashioned beds, and Oriental rugs. The bathrooms are small, with showers only. You can save a few euros by renting one of the six rooms that share bathrooms. In an annex across the street are 15 small apartments, each with a bathroom and a kitchenette. Breakfast costs an extra €9 ($11); on nice mornings, you can eat outside in the back garden.

See map p. 250. Liebergesellstrasse 8, 80802 München-Schwabing. ☎ **089/383-9410.** *Fax: 089/3839-4133.* www.hotelenglischergarten.de. *U-Bahn: Münchener Freiheit (then a 10-minute walk east on Haimhäuserstrasse to Erninger Platz and east on Liebergesellstrasse). Rack rates: €70–€103 ($87–$129) double without bathroom; €103–€115 ($129–$144) double with bathroom. AE, MC, V.*

Hotel Bristol München
$–$$$ **Altstadt**

Built around 1960 and renovated in 2002, this efficient, modern hotel is a congenial, convenient place to stay in central Munich. The 56 rooms are fairly small, but each has a little balcony. Furnishings are simple, serene, and comfortable. Bathrooms are compact and have showers. For a quieter room, request one that faces the courtyard.

See map p. 250. Pettenkoferstrasse 2, 80336 München. ☎ **089/5999-3902.** *Fax: 089/5999-3994.* www.bristol-muc.com. *U-Bahn: Sendlinger Tor (then a 5-minute walk west on Pettenkoferstrasse). Rack rates: €78–€150 ($97–$187) double. Rates include breakfast. AE, MC, V.*

Central Munich Accommodations and Dining

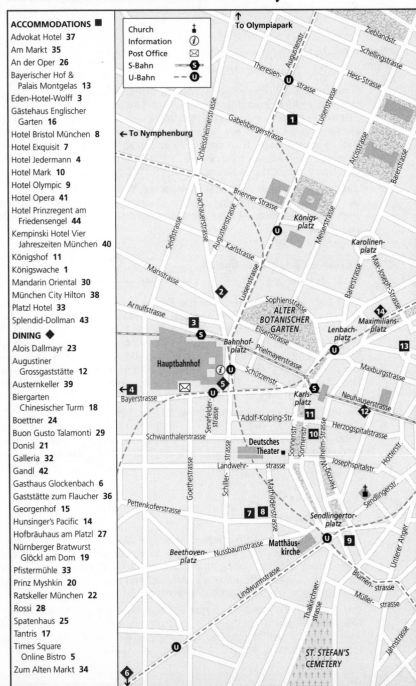

ACCOMMODATIONS ■

Advokat Hotel **37**
Am Markt **35**
An der Oper **26**
Bayerischer Hof & Palais Montgelas **13**
Eden-Hotel-Wolff **3**
Gästehaus Englischer Garten **16**
Hotel Bristol München **8**
Hotel Exquisit **7**
Hotel Jedermann **4**
Hotel Mark **10**
Hotel Olympic **9**
Hotel Opera **41**
Hotel Prinzregent am Friedensengel **44**
Kempinski Hotel Vier Jahreszeiten München **40**
Königshof **11**
Königswache **1**
Mandarin Oriental **30**
München City Hilton **38**
Platzl Hotel **33**
Splendid-Dollman **43**

DINING ◆

Alois Dallmayr **23**
Augustiner Grossgaststätte **12**
Austernkeller **39**
Biergarten Chinesischer Turm **18**
Boettner **24**
Buon Gusto Talamonti **29**
Donisl **21**
Galleria **32**
Gandl **42**
Gasthaus Glockenbach **6**
Gaststätte zum Flaucher **36**
Georgenhof **15**
Hunsinger's Pacific **14**
Hofbräuhaus am Platzl **27**
Nürnberger Bratwurst Glöckl am Dom **19**
Pfistermühle **33**
Prinz Myshkin **20**
Ratskeller München **22**
Rossi **28**
Spatenhaus **25**
Tantris **17**
Times Square Online Bistro **5**
Zum Alten Markt **34**

Church ✝
Information ⓘ
Post Office ✉
S-Bahn Ⓢ
U-Bahn Ⓤ

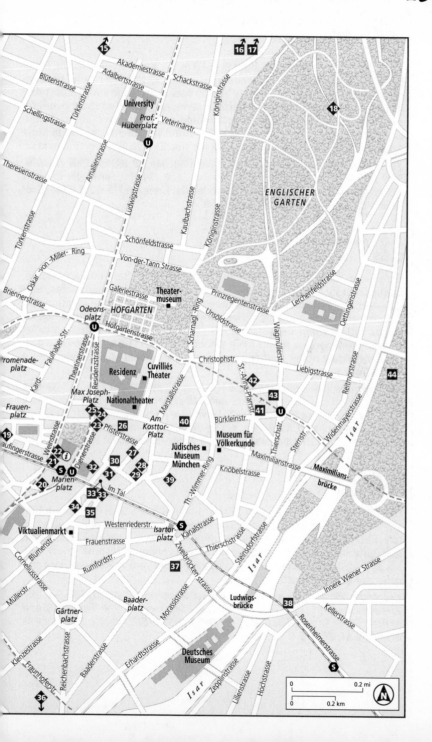

Hotel Exquisit
$$–$$$$ Altstadt

This small, appealing hotel, built in 1988 in the same vicinity as the Hotel Bristol München (see the preceding listing), is located on a quiet residential street in the heart of Munich. The 50 rooms are large and comfortably furnished in an old-fashioned German style. About half of them overlook a pretty garden. The small bathrooms contain tiled showers. The staff here is unusually pleasant and helpful. The hotel is attached to the famous Augustiner beer hall and restaurant (see the "Dining Out" section next).

See map p. 250. Pettenkoferstrasse 3, 80336 München. ☎ 089/551-9900. Fax: 089/ 5519-9499. www.augustiner-restaurant.com. U-Bahn: Sendlinger Tor (then a 3-minute walk west on Pettenkoferstrasse). Rack rates: €115–€205 ($144–$256) double. Rates include breakfast. AE, DC, MC, V.

Hotel Jedermann
$–$$$ Near train station

Jedermann means "everyman," and that translates here into affordable, family-friendly prices (including cribs and cots, adjoining rooms, and baby-sitting). This pleasant, family-run hotel offers a central location and 55 comfortable rooms, most with roomy, shower-only bathrooms. Cheaper rooms with in-room showers but toilets down the hall also are available; 14 newly redecorated rooms have air-conditioning. The hotel serves a generous breakfast buffet, and you can check your e-mail on the computer in the lobby.

See map p. 250. Bayerstrasse 95, 80335 München. ☎ 089/543-240. Fax: 089/5432-4111. www.hotel-jedermann.de. U-/S-Bahn: Hauptbahnhof (then a 10-minute walk west on Bayerstrasse from south exit). Tram: 19 to Herman-Lingg-Strasse (the stop across from the hotel). Rack rates: €49–€74 ($61–$92) double without bathroom; €67–€149 ($84–$186) double with bathroom. Rates include buffet breakfast. MC, V.

Hotel Olympic
$$ Altstadt

Built as a private villa around 1900, this hotel has a high-ceilinged lobby and a large wood-paneled breakfast room that retain much of their original late-19th-century detailing. The 38 rooms, however, are white, minimalist, and modern. Most of the midsize bathrooms come with shower only. The small, stylish hotel is popular with gay travelers, and several gay bars and cafes are located nearby.

See map p. 250. Hans Sachs Strasse 4, 80469 München. ☎ 089/231-890. Fax: 089/ 2318-9199. www.hotel-olympic.de. U-Bahn: Sendlinger Tor, then Tram 18 or 20 east to Hans Sachs Strasse. Rack rates: €140–€180 ($175–$225) double. Rates include breakfast. AE, DC, MC, V.

Hotel Opera
$$$$ Altstadt

An early-20th-century Italianate building with a courtyard and garden houses this small, elegant, boutique hotel. The 25 distinctively decorated rooms have country antiques or a cool, modern look. Some of the rooms have small balconies. Rooms in the rear on the third and fourth floors are quieter but also smaller than those facing the street. The bathrooms have a tub and shower. The hotel is a short walk from chic Maximilianstrasse and several major attractions.

See map p. 250. St.-Anna-Strasse 10, 80538 München. ☎ *089/225-533. Fax: 089/ 2104-0977.* www.hotel-opera.de. *U-Bahn: Lehel (then a 5-minute walk north on St.-Anna-Strasse). Rack rates:* € *185–*€ *245 ($231–$306) double. Rates include breakfast. AE, MC, V.*

Hotel Prinzregent am Friedensengel
$$$–$$$$ Bogenhausen

This quietly charming boutique hotel on the east bank of the Isar has a lobby, breakfast room, and 64 guestrooms nicely decorated in a Bavarian-chalet style with big, comfy beds and lots of wood. The rooms are fairly large and have good bathrooms; some face a garden. The level of service is exceptional. The hotel is a 10-minute walk from Maximilianstrasse and the center of the city.

See map p. 250. Ismaninger Strasse 42–44, 81675 Munich. ☎ *089/416-050. Fax: 089/ 4160-5466.* www.prinzregent.de. *U-Bahn: Prinzregenten-Platz (then a 5-minute walk west on Prinz Regenten Strasse and south on Ismaninger Strasse). Rack rates:* € *169–*€ *200 ($211–$250) double. Rates include buffet breakfast. AE, MC, V.*

Mandarin Oriental
$$$$ Altstadt

The sophisticated, superclassy Mandarin Oriental, located in the historic heart of Munich, occupies an ornate 19th-century building that was turned into a hotel in 1990. Biedermeier-era (early-19th-century) furnishings, fine prints and engravings, and big marble-tiled bathrooms with tub-shower combinations outfit the 73 rooms and suites. Most of the rooms have terraces with panoramic views of the city. The hotel has a heated rooftop swimming pool. The staff at this full-service hotel will arrange baby-sitting.

See map p. 250. Neuturmstrasse 1, 80331 München. ☎ *089/290-980. Fax: 089/222-539.* www.mandarinoriental.com. *Tram: 19 to Nationaltheater (then a 3-minute walk south on Neuturmstrasse). Rack rates:* € *330–*€ *430 ($412–$537) double. AE, DC, MC, V.*

Platzl Hotel
$$$–$$$$ Altstadt

Owned by the Ayinger brewery, this reconstructed "medieval" hotel is located across from the Hofbräuhaus, Munich's famous beer hall. If you're looking for a gulp of old-fashioned Bavarian ambience, this is one of the best choices in Munich. The 167 rooms tend to be small, but they're paneled in chestnut and alderwood and furnished with 19th-century reproduction antiques. Each comes with a compact tiled bathroom, most with a tub and shower combination. The rooftop terrace provides a view of Munich's steeples and spires.

See map p. 250. Sparkassenstrasse 10, 80331 München. ☎ *089/237-030. Fax: 089/2370-3800.* www.platzl.de. *U-Bahn: Marienplatz (then a 5-minute walk north on Sparkassenstrasse). Rack rates: €157–€242 ($196–$302) double. Rates include buffet breakfast. AE, DC, MC, V.*

Splendid-Dollmann
$$ Altstadt

A small, beautifully done boutique hotel, the Splendid-Dollman is in the same league as Hotel Opera down the street, but not quite as chi-chi. The Splendid-Dollmann's owners moved the hotel (formerly located about a block away) to this building in 2003 and completely redid the interior. No two rooms are the same, and some are on the small side, but the overall ambience is hard to beat. Breakfast, an additional €11 ($13), can be enjoyed outside on a patio.

See map p. 250. Thierschstrasse 49, 80538 München. ☎ *089/23-80-80. Fax: 089/2380-8365.* www.splendid-dollmann.de. *U-Bahn: Lehel (then a 3-minute walk east from St.-Anna-Platz to Thierschstrasse). Rack rates: €124–€130 ($155–$162) double. AE, DC, DISC, MC, V.*

Runner-up hotels

Am Markt
$–$$ Altstadt   This popular budget hotel centrally located in the Altstadt has small, neat rooms, many of which share bathrooms. *See map p. 250. Heiliggeiststrasse 6, 80331 München.* ☎ *089/225-014. Fax: 089/224-017. No credit cards. U-/S-Bahn: Marienplatz.*

Bayerischer Hof & Palais Montgelas
$$$$ Altstadt   This full-service luxury hotel dates from 1841 and has individually decorated rooms with large bathrooms, plus a health club with pool and sauna. The staff can arrange baby-sitting. *See map p. 250. Promenadeplatz 2–6, 80333 Munich.* ☎ *800-223-6800 in the U.S. or 089/21200. Fax: 089/212-0906.* www.bayerischerhof.de. *Tram: 19.*

Hotel Mark

$–$$ Near the train station   Although not fancy, this 90-room hotel is convenient, well maintained, and moderately priced. *See map p. 250. Senefelderstrasse 12, 80336 München.* ☎ ***089/559-820.*** *Fax: 089/5598-2333.* www. heh.de. *U-/S-Bahn: Hauptbahnhof.*

Königshof

$$$$ Altstadt   This famous hotel boasts a Michelin-starred restaurant and has lushly decorated rooms with marble bathrooms. *See map p. 250. Karlsplatz 25, 80335 Munich.* ☎ ***089/551-360.*** *Fax: 089/5513-6113. U-/S-Bahn: Karlsplatz/Stachus.*

Königswache

$$ Near Altstadt   This 1960s-era hotel features modern, comfortable rooms with compact tiled bathrooms. *See map p. 250. Steinheilstrasse 7, 80333 München.* ☎ ***089/542-7570.*** *Fax: 089/523-2114.* www.koenigswache.de. *U-Bahn: Theresienstrasse.*

München City Hilton

$$$ Haidhausen   An excellent choice for business travelers and families with children, the München City Hilton lies on the east bank of the river and features well-designed rooms with nice bathrooms. *See map p. 250. Rosenheimerstrasse 15, 81667 München.* ☎ ***800-455-8667*** *in the U.S. and Canada or 089/48-040. Fax: 089/4804-4804.* www.hilton.com. *S-Bahn: Rosenheimer Platz.*

Dining Out

Munich is a city that loves to eat and eat big. Homemade dumplings are a specialty, and so are all kinds of sausages and *Leberkäse,* a large loaf of sausage eaten with freshly baked pretzels and mustard. *Schweinbraten,* a braised loin of pork served with potato dumplings and rich brown gravy, is Bavaria's answer to the north's sauerbraten (pot- or oven-roasted marinated beef). Filling the city are all kinds of fine restaurants, small cafes and bistros, and beer halls that serve food. Inexpensive sausages, soups, and snacks also are sold from outdoor stalls all around the Viktualienmarkt.

If you want a refreshing nonalcoholic drink, served everywhere, ask for *Apfelsaftschorle* (*ap*-fell-saft-shor-luh), apple juice mixed with sparkling water.

If a restaurant bill says *Bedienung,* which means that a service charge already has been added, round up the total to the nearest euro. If service is not included, round up the total to the nearest euro and add another euro. The server takes the tip when you pay the bill; don't leave the tip on the table.

The top restaurants

Alois Dallmayr

$$–$$$ Altstadt DELICATESSEN/CONTINENTAL

In business for almost 300 years, Alois Dallmayr is the most famous delicatessen in Germany, and one of the most elegant. Downstairs you can buy fine food products; upstairs in the dining room you can order a tempting array of dishes, including herring, sausages, smoked fish, and soups. A crowd always fills the restaurant at lunchtime.

See map p. 250. Dienerstrasse 14–15. ☎ *089/213-5100. U-/S-Bahn: Marienplatz (then a 2-minute walk north on Dienerstrasse). Main courses: €14–€36 ($17–$45); fixed-price menus €32–€45 ($40–$56). AE, DC, MC, V. Open: Mon–Wed 11:30 a.m.–7 p.m.; Thurs–Fri 11:30 a.m.–8 p.m.; Sat 9 a.m.–4 p.m.*

Augustiner Grossgastätte

$$ Altstadt BAVARIAN/GERMAN

Located on Munich's main pedestrians-only shopping street, this famous beer hall and restaurant has cavernous rooms and a genuinely *gemütlich* atmosphere. Specialties include dumpling soup and roast duck with red cabbage. The house beer, Augustiner Brau, comes from one of Munich's oldest breweries, which owns the restaurant.

See map p. 250. Neuhauser Strasse 27. ☎ *089/2318-3257. U-Bahn: Karlsplatz/Stachus (then a 5-minute walk east on Neuhauser Strasse). Main courses: €10–€20 ($13–$25). MC, V. Open: Daily 9 a.m. to midnight.*

Austernkeller

$$$$ Altstadt SEAFOOD

At this "oyster cellar," you find the largest selection of oysters in town, served raw or in dishes such as oysters Rockefeller. The shellfish platter with fresh oysters, mussels, clams, scampi, and sea snails is a delicious way to start your meal, so is the fish soup. Menu offerings include fresh fish (salmon in champagne sauce is worth trying), in addition to time-honored favorites such as lobster thermidor and shrimp grilled in the shell. The restaurant is a bit pretentious but the food is excellent.

See map p. 250. Stollbergstrasse 11. ☎ *089/298-787. U-Bahn: Isartor (then a 5-minute walk north on Herrnstrasse and northeast on Stollbergstrasse). Reservations required. Main courses: €20–€35 ($25–$44). AE, DC, MC, V. Open: Daily 6–11 p.m.*

Boettner

$$$$ Altstadt INTERNATIONAL

When this century-old restaurant moved to its new location, in a 16th-century building in the heart of Munich, it brought its wood-paneled interior with it. The cooking is light and refined, with a French influence, but several traditional Bavarian dishes also are on the menu. Special offerings include herb-crusted lamb, beef filet, lobster stew in a cream sauce, and seasonal dishes with white truffles. The desserts are sumptuous.

See map p. 250. Pfisterstrasse 9. ☎ *089/221-210. U-Bahn: Marienplatz (then a 5-minute walk north on Sparkassen Strasse and east on Pfisterstrasse). Reservations required. Main courses: €25–€38 ($31–$47); fixed-price lunch €31 ($39), fixed-price dinner €71 ($89). AE, DC, MC, V. Open: Mon–Sat 11:30 a.m.–3 p.m. and 6 p.m. to midnight.*

Buon Gusto Talamonti
$$ Altstadt   TUSCAN/ITALIAN

This highly regarded Italian restaurant has two dining areas — a simple bistro overlooking an open kitchen and a more formal dining room — with the same menu items and prices. Try the *Tris di pasta* (three pastas with vegetables), pasta with truffles, spaghetti carbonara, ravioli stuffed with mushrooms and herbs, or the roasted lamb with potatoes. The various *risottos* (rice dishes) are especially good. The atmosphere is light-hearted and fun.

See map p. 250. Hochbrückenstrasse 3. ☎ *089/296-383. U-/S-Bahn: Marienplatz (then a 5-minute walk east on Tal and northeast on Hochbrückenstrasse). Reservations recommended. Main courses: €10–€20 ($13–$25). AE, DC, MC, V. Open: Mon–Sat 9 a.m.– 1 a.m.*

Donisl
$ Altstadt   BAVARIAN/INTERNATIONAL

Munich's oldest beer hall dates from 1715 and provides diners and drinkers with a relaxed, comfortable atmosphere. In summer you can dine in the garden area out front. The standard menu offers traditional Bavarian food and weekly specials. *Weisswürste,* the little white sausages famous in Munich, have long been a specialty. The beers come from Munich's Hacker-Pschorr Brewery. An accordion player provides music in the evening.

See map p. 250. Weinstrasse 1. ☎ *089/220-184. U-/S-Bahn: Marienplatz (then a 1-minute walk north on Weinstrasse). Reservations recommended. Main courses: €8–€15 ($10–$19). AE, DC, MC, V. Open: Daily 9 a.m. to midnight.*

Galleria
$$$–$$$$ Altstadt   ITALIAN

The roster of dishes at this appealing Italian restaurant changes seasonally, but you may find main courses such as mushroom tartar, homemade gnocchi with duck and figs, veal with arugula, roast duck with lentils, or braised crab with polenta.

See map p. 250. Sparkassenstrasse 11. ☎ *089/297-995. U-/S-Bahn: Marienplatz (then a 3-minute walk north on Sparkassenstrasse). Reservations recommended. Main courses: €21–€24 ($26–$30) Fixed-price dinner: €48–€54 ($60–$67). AE, DC, MC, V. Open: Mon–Sat noon to 2:30 p.m. and 6:30 p.m. to midnight. Closed Aug 10–30.*

Gandl
$$–$$$ Altstadt ITALIAN/FRENCH

At this attractive and lively neighborhood bistro, the lunch menu leans toward Italian, but at night the booking becomes more traditionally French. The Italian dishes include homemade pastas, such as spaghetti carbonara, gnocchi, and ravioli. Dinner offerings change often, but you'll typically find fare such as entrecote with arugula salad, grilled filet of salmon in saffron sauce, or lamb in red wine sauce. The big gourmet salad with various meats and pates is delicious, too. Eat on the terrace if the weather's nice.

See map p. 250. St.-Anna Platz 1. ☎ 089/2916-2525. U-Bahn: Lehel (the restaurant is less than a block from the St.-Anna Platz exit). Main courses: €8–€18 ($10–$22). Fixed-price menu: €31 ($39). AE, MC, V. Open: Mon–Sat 9 a.m.–1 a.m.

Gasthaus Glockenbach
$$$$ South of train station MODERN EUROPEAN

This elegant but unpretentious restaurant serves imaginative, mostly organic, nouvelle French-German-Bavarian cuisine and has earned a Michelin star. The menu offerings change with the seasons and typically include venison and pheasant in autumn and lamb and veal dishes in spring. The vegetables come from local farms. Wines are mostly from Italy, France, and Austria.

See map p. 250. Kapuzinerstrasse 29. ☎ 089/534-043. U-Bahn: Goetheplatz (then a 10-minute walk south on Lindwurm and east on Kapuzinerstrasse to the corner of Maistrasse). Reservations recommended. Main courses: €23–€30 ($29–$37). Fixed-price menus: €20–€45 ($25–$56) lunch, €35–€70 ($44–$87) dinner. AE, MC, V. Open: Tues–Sat noon to 2 p.m. and 7–10 p.m. Closed 1 week at Christmas.

Georgenhof
$$ Schwabing GERMAN/INTERNATIONAL

This pleasant Schwabing eatery has a comfortably rustic interior with a wood-fired grill, but if the weather is nice, sit outside under the chestnut trees. The menu reflects seasonal specialties *Spargel* (asparagus) in May and June and regional favorites. Bavarian game dishes include *Rehpfeffer* (venison) with egg *spätzle* (German pasta) or tagliatelle with venison ragout. Grilled meats such as lamb and steak are popular. For dessert, try the simple but delicious Bavarian cream with strawberries.

See map p. 250. Fredrichstrasse 1. ☎ 089/39-31-01. U-Bahn: Universität (then a 10-minute walk west on Schelling Strasse and north on Turkenstrasse to the corner of Friedrichstrasse and Georgenstrasse). Main courses: €11–€22 ($14–$27). MC, V. Open: Daily 11 a.m. to midnight.

Hofbräuhaus am Platzl
$$ Altstadt GERMAN

A boisterous atmosphere prevails in Munich's huge and world-famous beer hall. In the *Schwemme* (tap room) on the ground floor, you sit on benches at bare wood tables as a brass band plays; a big courtyard is on this level, too. Upstairs are a number of smaller, quieter dining rooms. The beer is Hofbrau, which is served by the *Mass* equal to about a quart. The food is heavy and hearty with a menu that includes *Weisswürste* and several other sausages, *Schweinbraten* (roasted pork), *Spanferkel* (roast suckling pig), and stuffed cabbage rolls. Everything on the menu is translated into English.

See map p. 250. Am Platzl 9. ☎ *089/290-1360. U-/S-Bahn: Marienplatz (then a 5-minute walk north on Sparkassenstrasse and east on Bräuhausstrasse). Main courses: €8–€15 ($10–$19). No credit cards. Open: Daily 9 a.m. to midnight.*

Hunsinger's Pacific
$$–$$$ Altstadt CONTINENTAL/ASIAN

This restaurant offers good food at reasonable prices. The menu empha-sizes fresh fish prepared according to classic French cooking techniques but using spices from Malaysia (coconut milk), Japan (wasabi), Thailand (lemongrass), and India (curry). The tuna carpaccio with sliced plum, fresh ginger, and lime is a delicious starter. Main courses include bouilla-baisse with aïoli (a fish soup with a spicy mayonnaise), cold melon soup, fried monkfish, and turbot in chili and ginger sauce.

See map p. 250. Maximiliansplatz 5. ☎ *089/5502-9741. U-/S-Bahn: Karlsplatz/Stachus (then a 10-minute walk northeast on Oskar-von-Miller Strasse to the entrance on Max-Joseph-Strasse). Main courses: €19–€40 ($24–$50). AE, MC, V. Open: Daily noon to 2:30 p.m. and 6–10:30 p.m. Closed Aug.*

Nürnberger Bratwurst Glöckl am Dom
$ Altstadt BAVARIAN

A short walk from Marienplatz, across from the cathedral *(Dom)*, this is the coziest and friendliest of Munich's local restaurants. You sit in carved wooden chairs at shared tables. *Nürnberger Schweinwurstl mit Kraut* (pork sausages with cabbage, a specialty from Nuremberg) is the dish to try. Hot dogs will never taste the same again after your kid has tried one of these delectable little sausages.

See map p. 250. Frauenplatz 9. ☎ *089/295-264. U-/S-Bahn: Marienplatz (then a 5-minute walk west on Sporerstrasse to Frauenplatz beside the Frauenkirche). Main courses: €8–€16 ($10–$20). No credit cards. Open: Daily 10 a.m.–1 a.m.*

Brezeln und Bier (Pretzels and Beer)

In Munich, a *Brezel* (*bray*-zuhl; pretzel) is the traditional accompaniment to *"ein Glas helles"* (ine glahss *hel*-les; a glass of light wheat beer). Munich pretzels are delicious, with a golden, chewy, not-too-salty crust and a soft thick interior. In the beer halls, you'll usually find pretzels on the table, but keep in mind that you'll be charged about €1 ($1.25) for every *Brezel* you eat.

Pfistermühle
$$ Altstadt BAVARIAN

This old-fashioned, vine-covered restaurant housed in a converted mill serves hearty portions of traditional Bavarian food in a series of charmingly decorated dining rooms or at outdoor tables. Come for roast meats served with fresh vegetables, fresh trout accompanied by chive-flecked sour cream and a potato pancake, or the fish platter served with ragout and noodles. For dessert try vanilla custard with fresh berry sauce. Toast the end of your Bavarian meal with a glass of wild-cherry schnapps.

See map p. 250. In the Platzl Hotel, Pfistermühle 4. ☎ 089/2370-3800. U-Bahn: Marienplatz (then a 5-minute walk north on Sparkassenstrasse and east on Pfisterstrasse). Reservations recommended. Main courses: €16–€22 ($20–$27). AE, DC, MC, V. Open: Mon–Sat noon to midnight.

Prinz Myshkin
$ Altstadt VEGETARIAN

If sausages and meat dishes are getting to you, you may want to try this popular vegetarian restaurant near Marienplatz. The menu includes freshly made salads, macrobiotic dishes, Asian-inspired vegetarian entrees, and vegetarian *involtini* (stuffed rollups). The casseroles, soups, and pizzas generally are excellent.

See map p. 250. Hackenstrasse 2. ☎ 089/265-596. U-/S-Bahn: Marienplatz (then a 10-minute walk southwest on Rindermarkt and Oberanger and north on Sack Strasse to Hackenstrasse). Reservations recommended. Main courses: €9.50–€16 ($12–$20). AE, MC, V. Open: Daily 11 a.m.–1 a.m.

Ratskeller München
$–$$ Altstadt BAVARIAN

A *Ratskeller* is a cellar restaurant in a *Rathaus* (town hall), where you find good, inexpensive food and wine. Munich's *Ratskeller* has a dark, woody interior with carved wooden chairs and tables and painted ceilings. The menu showcases regional dishes but also includes some vegetarian choices.

See map p. 250. Marienplatz 8, in the Rathaus. ☎ 089/219-9890. U-/S-Bahn: Marienplatz (the Rathaus is on the square). Main courses: €7.50–€21 ($9.50–$26). AE, MC, V. Open: Daily 10 a.m.–11:30 p.m.

Rossi
$$ Altstadt ITALIAN

With its columns, red-tiled floor, and white walls with wood-paneled ceiling, this well-liked Italian restaurant across from the famous Hofbräuhaus is an inviting place to dine. The simply prepared pastas (*Teigwaren* in German) are always good. Try spaghetti *alle pomodoro* (with tomatoes) or *penne ai formaggi* (with cheese). The daily special pasta may be something more exotic, like fettucine with *tartufo* (truffles). You can also get a good pizza, veal piccata with lemon sauce, or grilled steak *(Rindfilet)*.

See map p. 250. Bräuhausstrasse 6. ☎ *089/227-735. U-/S-Bahn: Isartor (then a 5-minute walk west on Tal and northeast on Hochbrücken to Bräuhausstrasse). Main courses: €7.50–€17 ($9.50–$21). AE, MC, V. Open: Mon–Fri 11:30 a.m.–3 p.m. and 6 p.m. to midnight, Sat 6 p.m. to midnight.*

Spatenhaus
$$ Altstadt BAVARIAN/INTERNATIONAL

This well-known beer restaurant with big windows overlooking the opera house serves hearty portions of typical Bavarian food at reasonable prices. The *Bayerische Teller* (Bavarian plate) comes loaded with various meats, including pork and sausages. Wash down your meal with the restaurant's own beer, Spaten-Franziskaner-Bier.

See map p. 250. Residenzstrasse 12. ☎ *089/290-7060. U-Bahn: Marienplatz (then a 10-minute walk north on Diener Strasse and Residenzstrasse). Reservations recommended. Main courses: €14–€26 ($17–$32). AE, MC, V. Open: Daily 9:30 a.m.–12:30 a.m.*

Tantris
$$$$ Schwabing FRENCH/GERMAN/INTERNATIONAL

A famed culinary mecca since 1972, this Michelin-starred restaurant has a red and black interior that reminds some of an airport lounge. The choice of dishes is limited and changes often. You may begin with a terrine of smoked fish served with green cucumber sauce, followed by roast duck on mustard-seed sauce, or perhaps lobster medallions on black noodles.

See map p. 250. Johann-Fichte-Strasse 7, Schwabing. ☎ *089/361-9590. U-Bahn: Dietlindenstrasse (then a 10-minute walk west on Potsdamer Strasse, north on Leopold Strasse, and east on Johan-Fichte-Strasse). Reservations required. Fixed-price lunch: €60–€85 ($75–$106). Fixed-price dinner: €110–€128 ($137–$160). AE, DC, MC, V. Open: Tues–Sat noon to 3 p.m. and 6:30 p.m.–1 a.m. Closed public holidays and annual holidays in Jan and May.*

Times Square Online Bistro
$ Train station CONTINENTAL/SNACKS

A bank of online computers, which you can rent for €2.50 ($3.10) per quarter hour, takes up one side of this bright, high-ceilinged, technobistro in the main train station. The bistro also has a section for noncomputerized dining, where you can order simple dishes such as pork cutlets, baked Camembert, tagliatelle, and spinach strudel. The quality varies here, and I'd recommend it more for a snack between e-mails than a real meal.

See map p. 250. Bayerstrasse 10 A, in the main train station. ☎ *089/550-8800. U-/S-Bahn: Hauptbahnhof. Breakfast: €4–€10 ($5–$12). Main courses: €7–€14 ($9–$17). AE, DC, MC, V. Open: Daily 7:30 a.m.–1 a.m.*

Zum Alten Markt
$$ Altstadt BAVARIAN/INTERNATIONAL

This snug, friendly eatery is located on a tiny square just off the Viktualienmarkt, Munich's big outdoor produce market. In summer, tables are set up outside. You may begin with homemade cream of carrot soup or black-truffle tortellini in cream sauce. The chef makes a great *Tafelspitz* (boiled beef). You can also order classic dishes such as roast duck with apple sauce or roast suckling pig.

Dreifaltigkeitsplatz 3. ☎ *089/299-995. U-/S-Bahn: Marienplatz (then a 5-minute walk south to Dreifaltifkeitsplatz on the east side of the Viktualienmarkt). Main courses: €12–€20 ($15–$25). No credit cards. Open: Mon–Sat noon to midnight (food served until 10 p.m.).*

The best beer gardens

Munich is famed for its beer gardens *(Biergartens)*, where you can sit outdoors, quaff Munich's famous brews, and order hearty Bavarian food at reasonable prices. For a glass or mug of beer, expect to pay €3 to €6.50 ($3.75 to $8), depending on its size. A simple meal generally costs around €10 ($13). Salty pretzels and large white radishes *(Radl)* are traditional accompaniments to the beer. Oom-pah-pah bands, zither players, or accordianists sometimes add to the jovial atmosphere. The food, drink, and atmosphere are much the same in the two places that I recommend.

- ✓ **Biergarten Chinesischer Turm,** Englischer Garten 3 (☎ 089/383-8720; U-Bahn: Giselastrasse), one of Munich's largest and most popular beer gardens, is located in the Englischer Garten at the foot of the *Chinesischer Turm* (Chinese Tower), an easy-to-find landmark. This beer garden is open daily from May to October from 11 a.m. to 1 a.m.

- ✓ **Gaststätte zum Flaucher,** Isarauen 8 (☎ 089/723-2677; Bus: 52), near the zoo, has tables set in a tree-shaded garden overlooking the Isar river. This beer garden is open daily from May to October from 10 a.m. to midnight; November to April, it's open Friday, Saturday, and Sunday from 10 a.m. to 9 p.m.

For two of the best beer halls in Munich, see the listings under "The top restaurants," earlier in this chapter, for the **Hofbräuhaus am Platzl** and **Augustiner Grossgastätte.**

Sightseeing in Munich

Munich is one of the great sightseeing cities in Germany. You can discover several world-class museums with exhaustive collections, many fine churches and historic buildings, and lovely parks and gardens. Visitors on limited schedules have some difficult decisions to make.

For locations, see the "Central Munich Attractions" map in this chapter.

Discovering the top attractions from A to Z

Munich is a city bursting with first-rate museums, fascinating architecture, and beautiful places to stroll. Enjoying Munich is easy, but if your time is limited, you'll have to make some difficult decisions.

Alte Pinakothek (Old Masters Gallery)
Museum Quarter

Pinakothek means "painting gallery," and the nearly 800 paintings on display in this enormous building represent the greatest European artists of the 14th through 18th centuries. The museum is so immense that you could easily spend several days exploring the two floors of exhibits. To make the most of your time here, pick up a museum guide at the information desk, decide which paintings you particularly want to see, and then spend at least two to three hours.

A free audio tour in English is available in the lobby. When you see a painting you want to know more about, punch the corresponding number into your audio guide to hear a full commentary. Free tours highlighting various parts of the vast collection take place on Tuesday at 6:30 p.m. and Friday at 3 p.m.

See map p. 264. Barer Strasse 27. ☎ *089/2380-5216. Tram: 27 to Pinakothek (the museum entrance on Theresienstrasse is across the street). Admission: €5 ($6.25) adults, €3.50 ($4.50) students, free for children 14 and younger; free admission on Sun. Open: Tues–Sun 10 a.m.–5 p.m. (Tues until 10 p.m.). Closed major holidays.*

Bayerisches Nationalmuseum (Bavarian National Museum)
East of Altstadt

This museum contains three vast floors of sculpture, painting, folk art, ceramics, furniture, and textiles, in addition to clocks and scientific instruments. The objects on view are among Bavaria's greatest historic and artistic treasures. A major highlight is the **Riemenschneider Room,** which contains works in wood by the great sculptor Tilman Riemenschneider (1460 to 1531). The museum also contains a famous collection of Christmas Nativity cribs from Bavaria, Tyrol, and southern Italy. Give yourself at least an hour just to cover the highlights.

See map p. 264. Prinzregentenstrasse 3. ☎ *089/211-2401. U-Bahn: Lehel (then a 10-minute walk north on Wagmüllerstrasse and east on Prinzregentenstrasse). Admission: €3 ($3.75) adults, €2 ($2.50) students and seniors, free for children younger than 18; free admission on Sun. Open: Tues–Sun 10 a.m.–5 p.m. (Thurs until 8 p.m.).*

Deutsches Museum (German Museum of Science and Technology)
Museumsinsel

Located on the Museumsinsel, an island in the Isar River, this is the largest science and technology museum in the world and one of the most popular attractions in Germany. Its huge collection of scientific and technological

Central Munich Attractions

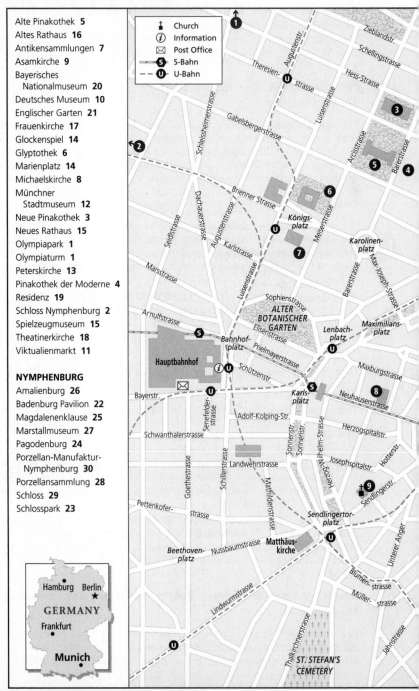

Alte Pinakothek **5**
Altes Rathaus **16**
Antikensammlungen **7**
Asamkirche **9**
Bayerisches
  Nationalmuseum **20**
Deutsches Museum **10**
Englischer Garten **21**
Frauenkirche **17**
Glockenspiel **14**
Glyptothek **6**
Marienplatz **14**
Michaelskirche **8**
Münchner
  Stadtmuseum **12**
Neue Pinakothek **3**
Neues Rathaus **15**
Olympiapark **1**
Olympiaturm **1**
Peterskirche **13**
Pinakothek der Moderne **4**
Residenz **19**
Schloss Nymphenburg **2**
Spielzeugmuseum **15**
Theatinerkirche **18**
Viktualienmarkt **11**

NYMPHENBURG
Amalienburg **26**
Badenburg Pavilion **22**
Magdalenenklause **25**
Marstallmuseum **27**
Pagodenburg **24**
Porzellan-Manufaktur-
  Nymphenburg **30**
Porzellansammlung **28**
Schloss **29**
Schlosspark **23**

Church
Information
Post Office
S-Bahn
U-Bahn

Zieblandstr.
Schellingstrasse
Hess-Strasse
Theresien-
strasse
Augustenstr.
Luisenstrasse
Arcisstrasse
Barerstrasse
Schleissheimerstrasse
Gabelsbergerstrasse
Dachauerstrasse
Augustenstrasse
Brienner Strasse
Königs-
platz
Meiserstrasse
Karolinen-
platz
Seidlstrasse
Karlstrasse
Barerstrasse
Max-Joseph-Strasse
Marsstrasse
Luisenstrasse
Sophienstrasse
ALTER
BOTANISCHER
GARTEN
Arnulfstrasse
Bahnhof-
platz
Elisenstrasse
Lenbach-
platz
Maximilians-
platz
Prielmayerstrasse
Maxburgstrasse
Hauptbahnhof
Schützenstr.
Bayerstr.
Karls-
platz
Neuhauserstrasse
Herzogspitalstr.
Senefelder-
strasse
Adolf-Kolping-Str.
Schwanthalerstrasse
Sonnenstr.
Sonnerstr.
Josephspitalstr.
Hotterstr.
Schillerstrasse
Landwehrstrasse
Goethestrasse
Mathildenstrasse
Herzog-Wilhelm-Strasse
Sendlingerstr.
Pettenkofer-
strasse
Sendlingertor-
platz
Unterer Anger
Beethoven-
platz
Nussbaumstrasse
Matthäus-
kirche
Blumen-
strasse
Müller-
strasse
Lindwurmstrasse
Thalkirchnerstrasse
Jahnstrasse
ST. STEFAN'S
CEMETERY

Hamburg Berlin
GERMANY
Frankfurt
Munich

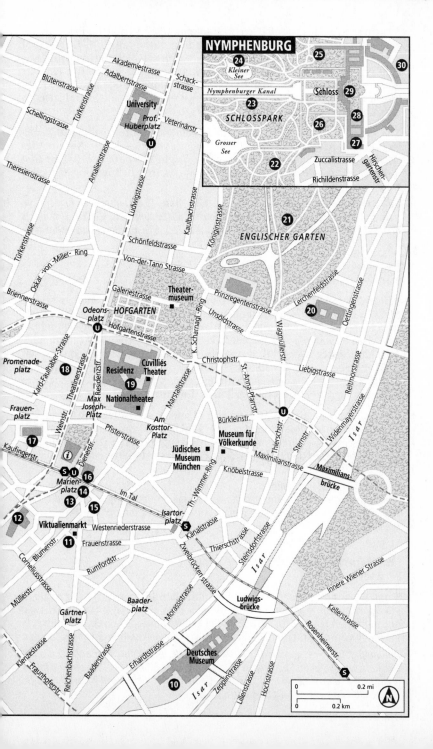

NYMPHENBURG

24 Kleiner See
25
30
Nymphenburger Kanal
Schloss 29
23
SCHLOSSPARK
28
26
Grosser See
27
22
Zuccalistrasse
Richildenstrasse
Hirschen-gartenstr.

Akademiestrasse
Blütenstrasse
Adalbertstrasse
Schackstrasse
Schellingstrasse
Türkenstrasse
University
Prof.-Huberplatz
Veterinärstr.
U
Theresienstrasse
Amalienstrasse
Ludwigstrasse
Kaulbachstrasse
Königinstrasse
Türkenstrasse
Oskar von -Miller- Ring
Schönfeldstrasse
Von-der-Tann Strasse
ENGLISCHER GARTEN
21
Brienerstrasse
Galeriestrasse
Theater-museum
Prinzregentenstrasse
Lerchenfeldstrasse
20
Oettingenstrasse
Odeons-platz
HOFGARTEN
Hofgartenstrasse
Unsöldstrasse
Wagmüllerstr.
K. Schanagl -Ring
Promenade-platz
Kard-Faulhaber-Strasse
18
Theatinerstrasse
Residenz
Cuvilliés Theater
Christophstr.
St.-Anna-Pfarrstr.
Liebigstrasse
Reitmorstrasse
Residenzstr.
19
Max Joseph-Platz
Nationaltheater
Marsallstrasse
U
Thierschstr.
Steinstr.
Widenmayerstrasse
Isar
Frauen-platz
Weinstr.
Pfisterstrasse
Am Kosttor-Platz
Bürkleinstr.
Museum für Völkerkunde
Maximilianstrasse
17
Kaufingerstr.
Diener.str.
Jüdisches Museum München
Knöbelstrasse
Maximilians-brücke
i
S U 16
Marien-platz 14
13
15
Im Tal
Th.-Wimmer-Ring
Isartor-platz
S
Kanalstrasse
12
Viktualienmarkt
Westenriederstrasse
11
Frauenstrasse
Rumfordstr.
Zweibrückenstrasse
Thierschstrasse
Steinsdorfstrasse
Isar
Innere Wiener Strasse
Cornelliusstrasse
Blumenstr.
Müllerstr.
Baader-platz
Morassistrasse
Ludwigs-brücke
Rosenheimerstr.
Kellerstrasse
Gärtner-platz
Klenzestrasse
Reichenbachstrasse
Baaderstrasse
Erhardstrasse
Deutsches Museum
10
Isar
Zeppelinstrasse
Lillenstrasse
Hochstrasse
S
Fraunhoferstr.

0   0.2 mi
0   0.2 km
N

treasures includes the first electric locomotive (1879), the first electric generator (called a *dynamo;* 1866), the first automobile (1886), the first diesel engine (1897), and the laboratory bench at which the atom first was split (1938). This hands-on, kid-friendly museum has interactive exhibits and an English-speaking staff to answer questions and demonstrate glass blowing, papermaking, and how steam engines, pumps, and historical musical instruments work.

The **Automobile** department in the basement is noteworthy, with a collection of luxury Daimler, Opel, and Bugatti vehicles. In the **Aeronautics** section, you see a biplane flown by the Wright brothers in 1908, the first airliner (1919), and an assortment of military aircraft. Spending half a day here is easy.

See map p. 264. Museumsinsel 1. ☎ *089/21791. Tram: 18 to Deutsches Museum (the tram stops outside the museum). Admission: €7.50 ($9.50) adults, €3 ($3.75) students and children 6–16. Open: Daily 9 a.m.–5 p.m. (Wed until 8 p.m.). Closed major holidays.*

Englisher Garten (English Garden)
Northwest of Altstadt

Munich's famous city park is one of the largest (922 acres) and most beautiful city parks in Europe. Established in 1789, the Englisher Garten also is the oldest public park in the world. You can wander for hours along the tree-shaded walks, streams, and lake, and admire the view of Munich's Altstadt from the round, hilltop temple called the **Monopteros,** constructed in the 19th century. The banks of the Eisbach, the stream that runs through the park, are popular nude-sunbathing spots. A giant beer garden occupies the plaza near the **Chinesischer Turm** (Chinese Tower).

 The park is a lovely place to have a picnic. You can pick up expensive picnic goodies at **Alois Dallmayr** (see "Dining Out," earlier in this chapter), or less-expensive fare from the Viktualienmarkt (the produce market described later in this section), or at **Hertie,** the department store across from the Hauptbahnhof.

See map p. 264. Bounded on the south by Von-der-Tann Strasse and Prinzregentenstrasse, on the west by Königinstrasse, on the east by Lerchenfeldstrasse. U-Bahn: Odeonsplatz (then a 10-minute walk northeast through the Hofgarten to the park).

Frauenkirche (Cathedral of Our Lady)
Altstadt

Munich's largest church, completed in the late 15th century, was a pile of smoldering rubble at the end of World War II (WWII). Only its landmark twin onion-domed towers from 1525 remained standing. The rebuilt church is strikingly simple and dignified, and the view from the tower is spectacular.

See map p. 264. Frauenplatz 12. ☎ *089/290-0820. U-/S-Bahn: Marienplatz (then a 5-minute walk west on Sporerstrasse to the church). Admission: Church free; tower €3 ($3.75) adults, €1.50 ($1.90) students. Open: Church Sat–Thurs 7 a.m.–7 p.m.; Fri 7 a.m.–6 p.m.; tower Apr–Oct daily 10 a.m.–5 p.m.*

Deutsches Museum

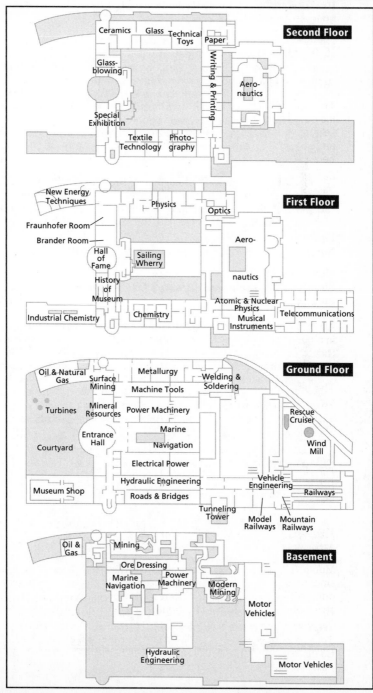

Marienplatz
Altstadt

This large pedestrian-only square in the heart of the Altstadt also is the old heart of Munich. Chances are you'll return here again and again, because many of the city's attractions are clustered in the vicinity. On the north side of Marienplatz is the **Neues Rathaus** (New City Hall), built in 19th-century Gothic style and famous for its Glockenspiel (see the sidebar "Watching the Glockenspiel" in this chapter). You can take an elevator to the top of the Rathaus's tower for a good view of the city center. The tower is open Monday to Friday from 9 a.m. to 7 p.m., Saturday and Sunday from 10 a.m. to 7 p.m. Admission is €1.50 ($1.90) for adults, €.75 (95¢) for children 6 to 18.

To the right of the Neues Rathaus stands the **Altes Rathaus** (Old City Hall), with its plain, 15th-century Gothic tower. Inside is the **Spielzeugmuseum** (☎ **089/294-001**), a historical toy collection, open daily from 10 a.m. to 5:30 p.m. Admission is €2.50 ($3.10) for adults, €.50 (65¢) for children, and €5 ($6.25) for a family.

See map p. 264. In the center of the Altstadt. U-/S-Bahn: Marienplatz.

Münchner Stadtmuseum (Munich City Museum)
Altstadt

This museum chronicles Munich's history and the everyday lives of its residents. The museum's one must-see exhibit is the **Moorish Dancers** *(Moriskentanzer),* featuring ten carved and brightly painted 15th-century wooden figures. The second-floor photo museum traces the early history of the camera back to 1839. Children love the third-floor collection of marionettes and hand puppets from around the world and the gallery of fairground art, which includes the oldest-known carousel horses, dating from 1820. You find a cafeteria in the museum's main courtyard.

See map p. 264. St.-Jakobs-Platz 1. ☎ 089/2332-2370. U-/S-Bahn: Marienplatz (then a 5-minute walk south on Rindermarkt and Oberanger). Admission: €2.50 (3.15) adults, €1.50 ($1.90) students and children 6–15; free on Sun. Open: Tues–Sun 10 a.m.–6 p.m.

Watching the Glockenspiel

The best show on Marienplatz takes place at 11 a.m. and 9 p.m. daily (also at noon and 5 p.m. during the holiday seasons) when the 43-bell Glockenspiel (carillon) on the 280-foot central spire of the Neues Rathaus (New Town Hall) goes through its paces. Brightly painted mechanical figures re-enact two famous events from Munich's history: the knights' tournament during the 1586 wedding feast of Wilhelm V and Renate of Lorraine, and, one level below, the *Schäfflertanz* (Coopers' Dance), first performed in 1683 to express gratitude for the end of the plague.

Neue Pinakothek
Museum Quarter

Housed in a postmodern building from 1981, this museum is a showcase for 19th-century German and European art, starting right around 1800. Not quite as daunting as the nearby Alte Pinakothek, this museum still contains plenty to see. Artists whose works are on view include Thomas Gainsborough, Joshua Reynolds, William Turner, Francesco Goya, Caspar David Friedrich, Vincent van Gogh, and Paul Gauguin, among many others. A tour of the highlights takes a couple of hours; an audio tour in English is free with your admission.

See map p. 264. Barer Strasse 27 (across Theresienstrasse from the Alte Pinakothek). ☎ *089/2380-5195. Tram: 27 to Pinakothek (the museum entrance on Theresienstrasse is across the street). Admission: €5 ($6.25) adults, €3.50 ($4.40) students and seniors; free admission on Sun. Open: Weds–Mon 10 a.m.–5 p.m. (Weds until 10 p.m.). Closed major holidays.*

Peterskirche (St. Peter's Church)
Altstadt

The belltower of this 13th-century Gothic church, remodeled during the baroque era, is known locally as Old Pete. You get a splendid view from the top, but you have to climb (and climb and climb) 306 steps to see it. The interior of the church contains baroque-era sculptures, frescoes, and a bizarre relic in the second chapel (on the left): the gem-studded skeleton of St. Mundita, who stares at you with two false eyes in her skull.

See map p. 264. Rindermarkt 1. ☎ *089/260-4828. U-/S-Bahn: Marienplatz (then a 2-minute walk south on Rindermarkt). Admission: Church free; tower €1.50 ($1.90) adults, €0.75 (95¢) students. Open: Apr–Oct daily 8 a.m.–7 p.m.; Nov–Mar daily 8 a.m.–6 p.m.*

Pinakothek der Moderne (Gallery of Modern Art, Architecture, Design)
Museum Quarter

Munich's newest museum, the Pinakothek der Moderne, opened in September 2002. You find four collections housed inside. The most important is the **Staatsgalerie moderner Kunst** (Gallery of Modern Art), displaying major 20th-century classics by internationally known artists including Matisse, Picasso, Juan Gris, Kandinsky, Kirchner, Max Ernst, Giacometti, and others. The other collections include the **Neue Sammlung** (Craft and Design Collection), the **Museum of Architecture,** and the **Graphische Sammlung** (Graphics Collection).

Barer Strasse 40. ☎ *089/2380-5360. Tram: 27 to Pinakothek (the museums are across the street). Admission: €9 ($11) adults, €5 ($6.25) for students 10–18, free for children younger than 10. Open: Tues–Sun 10 a.m.–5 p.m. (Thurs–Fri until 8 p.m.). Closed major holidays.*

Residenz (Royal Palace)
Altstadt

This magnificent building was the official residence of the Wittelsbach family, the rulers of Bavaria, from 1385 to 1918. Added to and rebuilt through the centuries, the palace is a compendium of various architectural styles, including German and Florentine Renaissance, and Palladian. Artisans painstakingly restored the Rezidenz, which was almost totally destroyed in WWII. The must-sees are the **Residenz Museum,** with arts and furnishings displayed in some 130 rooms; the **Schatzkammer** (Treasury), with three centuries' worth of accumulated treasures; and the **Altes Residenztheater,** a stunning rococo theater. You enter both the Residenz Museum and the Schatzkammer from Max-Joseph-Platz on the south side of the palace. On the north side of the palace is the Italianate **Hofgarten** (Court Garden), laid out between 1613 and 1617.

See map p. 264. Max-Joseph-Platz 3. ☎ *089/290-671. Tram: 19 to Nationaltheater (the palace is on the same square as the theater) or U-Bahn: Odeonsplatz (the palace is southeast across the square). Admission: Combined ticket for Residenz Museum and Schatzkammer €9 ($11) adults, €8 ($10) students, children; Residenztheater €3 ($3.75) adults, €2 ($2.50) students and children. Open: Apr 1–Oct 15 daily 9 a.m.–6 p.m., Oct 16– Mar 30 daily 10 a.m.–4 p.m. Guided tours (in German): Daily at 10 a.m. and 12:30 p.m.*

Schloss Nymphenburg (Nymphenburg Palace)
Nymphenburg

Schloss Nymphenburg, the Wittelsbachs's summer residence, is one of the most sophisticated and beautiful palaces in Europe. The palace was begun in 1664 and took more than 150 years to complete. In 1702, Elector Max Emanuel decided to enlarge the original Italianate villa by adding four large pavilions connected by arcaded passageways. From central Munich, you can easily reach the palace by tram in about 20 minutes. You need at least half a day to explore the buildings and grounds.

Inside, you come first to the **Great Hall,** decorated in a vibrant splash of rococo colors and stuccowork. In the south pavilion, you find Ludwig I's famous **Gallery of Beauties** with paintings by J. Stieler (1827 to 1850). The beauties include Schöne Münchnerin (Lovely Munich Girl) and a portrait of Lola Montez, the raven-haired dancer whose affair with Ludwig caused a scandal.

To the south of the palace buildings, in the rectangular block of low structures that once housed the court stables, is the **Marstallmuseum,** where you find a dazzling collection of ornate, gilded coaches and sleighs, including those used by Ludwig II. The **Porzellansammlung** (Porcelain Collection; entrance across from the Marstallmuseum) contains superb pieces of 18th-century porcelain, including miniature porcelain copies of masterpieces in the Alte Pinakothek.

A factory on the grounds of Schloss Nymphenburg still produces the famous Nymphenburg porcelain. **Porzellan-Manufaktur-Nymphenburg,** Nördliches Schlossrondell 8 (☎ **089/179-1970**), has a sales room and exhibition center open Monday through Friday from 8:30 a.m. to 5 p.m.

The Residenz

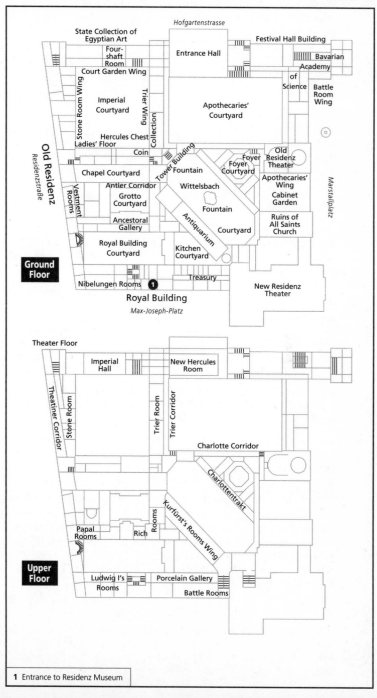

A canal runs through 500-acre **Schlosspark,** stretching all the way to the so-called grand cascade at the far end of the formal, French-style gardens. In the English-style park, full of quiet meadows and forested paths, you find the **Badenburg Pavilion**, with an 18th-century swimming pool; the **Pagodenburg,** decorated in the Chinese style that was all the rage in the 18th century; and the **Magdalenenklause** (Hermitage), meant to be a retreat for prayer and solitude. Prettiest of all the buildings in the park is **Amalienburg,** built in 1734 as a hunting lodge for Electress Amalia; the interior salons are a riot of flamboyant colors, swirling stuccowork, and wall paintings.

See map p. 264. Schloss Nymphenburg 1, 8km (5 miles) northwest of the city center. Tram: 12, 16, or 17 to Romanplatz (then a 10-minute walk west to the palace entrance). ☎ *089/179-080. Admission: Palace grounds free; admission to all attractions €10 ($12.50) adults, €8 ($10) seniors, free for children younger than 7. Open: Oct 16–Mar 30 daily 10 a.m.–4 p.m.; Apr 1–Oct 15 daily 9 a.m.–6 p.m. Badenburg and Magdalenenklause closed Oct 16–Mar 30.*

Theatinerkirche (Church of the Theatines)
Altstadt

Named for the Theatines, a group of Roman Catholic clergy, this church is Munich's finest example of Italian baroque architecture. The church was begun by Italian architects in 1663 and was completed by German court architects about a century later. Fluted columns lining the center aisle support the arched ceiling of the nave. Every surface appears to be loaded with dollops of fanciful white stuccowork. The dome above the transept is decorated with an ornate gallery of large statues. Dark wooden pews and a canopied pulpit provide the only color in the all-white interior.

See map p. 264. Theatinerstrasse 22. ☎ *089/210-6960. U-Bahn: Odeonsplatz (then a 2-minute walk south on Theatinerstrasse). Admission: Free. Open: Mon–Fri 10 a.m.– 1 p.m. and 1:30–4:30 p.m.; Sat 10 a.m.–3 p.m.*

Viktualienmarkt (Produce Market)
Altstadt

Located on the square of the same name, close to Marienplatz, the Viktualienmarkt has been serving Munich residents for nearly 200 years and is a wonderful place to stroll and sniff and take in the scene. In an area the size of a city block, you find two dozen butcher shops, five cheese sellers, a whole section of bakeries stocked with dozens of different kinds of Bavarian breads and rolls, fish sellers, wine merchants, and dozens of produce stalls. Most of the permanent stands open at 6 a.m. and stay open until 6 p.m. weekdays or until 1 p.m. Saturdays.

The Viktualienmarkt has a large beer garden. You can buy food at the market stalls and eat it in the beer garden if you buy a beer, coke, water, or other beverage at the beer-garden drink stand.

At the Viktualienmarkt, and in other outdoor food markets throughout Germany, remember two points: Do not touch the merchandise (doing so is against German food laws) and don't try to bargain for lower prices (prices are not negotiable).

See map p. 264. Bounded by Prälat-Zistl-Strasse on the west, Frauen Strasse to the south, Heiliggeiststrasse on the east, and Tal on the north. U-/S-Bahn: Marienplatz (then a 5-minute walk southeast through the square).

Finding more cool things to see and do

✔ The **Antikensammlungen** (Museum of Antiquities), Königsplatz 1 (☎ 089/598-359; U-Bahn: Königsplatz), is an essential stop for anyone interested in ancient art. The museum's five main-floor halls house more than 650 Greek vases, from a pre-Mycenaean version carved in 3000 B.C. from a mussel shell to large Greek and Etruscan vases. The museum is open Tuesday through Sunday from 10 a.m. to 5 p.m. (until 8 p.m. on Wednesday). Admission is €3 ($3.75) for adults, free for children younger than 14, free for everyone on Sunday. A joint ticket to the Museum of Antiquities and the neighboring Glyptothek (included later in this list) is €6 ($7.50).

✔ Munich has many important churches in addition to those described in the preceding section. Here are two of the more important ones:

- The **Asamkirche,** on Sendlinger Strasse (☎ 089/260-9357; U-/S-Bahn: Sendlinger Tor), is a remarkable rococo church built by the Asam brothers between 1733 and 1746. Multicolored marbles, gold leaf, and silver cover every square inch of this small rectangular church with rounded ends. The church is open daily from 8 a.m. to 5:30 p.m.

- The **Michaelskirche** (St. Michael's Church), Neuhauserstrasse 52 (☎ 089/231-7060; U-/S-Bahn: Marienplatz), is a single-nave church with a barrel-vaulted ceiling completed in 1597, is the largest Renaissance church north of the Alps. The church is open Monday to Saturday from 8:30 a.m. to 7 p.m., Sunday from 6:45 a.m. to 10 p.m.

✔ Located across from the Antikensammlungen (see the first entry in this list), the **Glyptothek,** Königsplatz 3 (☎ 089/286-100; U-Bahn: Königsplatz), exhibits Germany's largest collection of ancient Greek and Roman sculpture. Here you find sixth-century B.C. *kouroi* (statues of youths), a colossal *Sleeping Satyr* from the Hellenistic period, and a haunting collection of Roman portraits. The museum is open Tuesday through Sunday from 10 a.m.–5 p.m. (until 8 p.m. on Thursday). Admission is €3 ($3.75) for adults, €2 ($2.50) for students and seniors, free for children younger than 14.

✔ **Olympiapark** (☎ 089/3067-2414; U-Bahn: Olympiazentrum), site of the 1972 Olympic Games, sits at the northwestern edge of Munich and is a small city unto itself. Various events, including concerts, take place at the colossal 69,000-seat stadium. **Olympiaturm** (☎ 089/3067-2750), the 293m-high (960-ft.) television tower in the center of the park, is open daily from 9 a.m. to midnight. A ticket for a ride to the top costs €3.50 ($4.50) for adults and €2.50 ($3.10) for children younger than 15. The extraordinary view reaches all the way to the Alps.

Seeing Munich by Guided Tour

A good way to familiarize yourself with the city is to take the one-hour Munich Highlights bus tour. **Münchner Stadt-Rundfahrten** (☎ 089/5502-8995) offers the tours, with commentary in English, daily at 10 a.m., 11 a.m., noon, 1 p.m., 2 p.m., 2:30 p.m., 3 p.m., and 4 p.m. (from April through October there are additional tours at 11:30 a.m. and 5 p.m.). Tour cost is €11 ($14) for adults, €6 ($7.50) for children younger than 14. You buy tickets on the bus and don't need to reserve in advance. The company offers many other tours, including a 2½-hour trip to Schloss Nymphenburg (daily at 2:30 p.m.); cost is €19 ($24) for adults, €10 ($12) for children. All tours depart from Bahnhofplatz, in front of the Hertie department store at the main train station plaza.

Dachau: Germany's first concentration camp

In 1933, shortly after Hitler became German chancellor, Himmler ordered the first German concentration camp to be set up in Dachau, 19km (12 miles) northwest of Munich. Between 1933 and 1945, more than 206,000 prisoners arrived (the exact number is unknown), and more than 32,000 died. The first to arrive were political prisoners (Communists and Social Democrats), followed soon after by "beggars," "antisocial elements," homosexuals, Jehovah's Witnesses, and, after 1938, growing numbers of Jews.

In 2002, parts of the **KZ-Gedenkstätte Dachau** (Dachau Concentration Camp Memorial), Alte-Roemer-Strasse 75 (☎ 08131/1741), were redesigned to focus on the fate of the prisoners and to integrate the still-existing historic buildings into the reworked permanent exhibition. Visitors now follow the route of the prisoners, enter rooms in which citizens were stripped of all their belongings and rights, and where, after disinfecting, they were given a striped prison uniform. Inscribed boards show the rooms' original conditions and functions. Captions are in German and English.

Dachau did not have gas chambers. Prisoners died through work, hunger, disease, and mass executions by shooting. The names of many of the dead are not known, but displays showing prisoners' faces and videos of survivor interviews put a very human face on the horrific pain and suffering endured by these ordinary citizens.

To get to the camp, take S-Bahn train S2 from the Hauptbahnhof to Dachau (direction: Petershausen), and then transfer to bus 724 or 726 to the camp. The camp is open Tuesday to Sunday from 9 a.m. to 5 p.m.; admission is free.

Munich Walk Tours (☎ 0171/274-0204; www.munichwalktours.de), conducted in English, are a great way to find out about Munich's history and architecture. The company offers several options; the meeting point for all walks is the New Rathaus directly under the Glockenspiel on Marienplatz. No need to reserve; you pay the guide (identifiable by a yellow sign). The 2¼-hour City Walk Tour starts daily at 10:45 a.m., February through November. Hitler's Munich, lasting about 2½ hours, covers all the important facts and sites that played a role in Munich's Nazi era. The cost for each tour is €10 ($12) for adults, €9 ($11) for those younger than 26, free for children younger than 14.

Shopping for Local Treasures

Munich is the fashion capital of Germany, and when the topic is shopping, Munich ranks right up there with Paris and London. This city is not one in which you're likely to find many bargains, however.

General shopping is less pricey on and around **Marienplatz** and along the main pedestrian streets **Kaufingerstrasse** and **Neuhauser Strasse**. The biggest concentration of shops selling secondhand goods is on **Westenriederstrasse**.

 Sometimes called "the Bloomingdale's of Germany," **Ludwig Beck am Rathauseck,** Marienplatz 11 (☎ 089/236-910; U-/S-Bahn: Marienplatz), is Munich's best department store and a good place to shop for handmade crafts from all across Germany. **Hertie's,** Bahnhofplatz 7 (☎ 089/55120; U-Bahn: Hauptbahnhof), across from the main train station, is a good, all-purpose department store.

The best streets for elegant boutiques and specialty shops are **Briennerstrasse, Maximilianstrasse** (which also has the leading art galleries), **Maffeistrasse,** and **Theatinestrasse.** On these streets, you find branches of all the top European couturiers and Germany's and Munich's own designers: Jil Sander, Joop, Bogner, Max Dietl, and Rudolph Moshammer. Antiques devotees with deep pockets find what they want on **Ottostrasse.**

Marienplatz at Christmas

Marienplatz, the main square of the inner city, is the scene of a famous **Christkindl Markt,** or Christmas Market. From late November through December, the plaza overflows with stalls selling toys, tree ornaments, handicrafts, and a mouth-watering array of traditional snacks and sweets, including gingerbread, sugar-coated almonds, fruitcakes, smoked meats, and piping hot *Glühwein,* a spiced red wine.

Loden-Frey, Maffeistrasse 7–9 (☎ **089/210-390;** U-/S-Bahn: Marienplatz), founded in 1842, is the place for all kinds of high-quality loden (a waterproof wool) wear, such as coats, jackets, and hats. **Dirndl-Ecke,** Am Platzl 1/Sparkassenstrasse 10 (☎ **089/220-163;** U-/S-Bahn: Marienplatz), has a large selection of high-quality Bavarian costumes, dirndls (traditional German dresses), folk art, and handicrafts.

Discovering Nightlife in Munich

Something always is going on in Munich. As southern Germany's cultural capital, Munich is renowned for its opera and symphony concerts and theater. But you can sit back in a leafy beer garden or in a beer hall, have a beer, and enjoy the local scene. (See "The best beer gardens" earlier in this chapter.) You also find plenty of bars and dance clubs for late-night partying.

Raising the curtain on performing arts and music

Few cities in Europe can rival Munich for the sheer number of musical and theatrical events. To find out what's playing, pick up a copy of *Monatsprogramm* (€1.50/$1.90) from one of the tourist offices. The best way to purchase tickets is to go directly to the venue's box office, called a *Kasse,* which generally is open during the day and an hour before the performance.

Altes Residenztheater (Cuvilliés Theater, Residenzstrasse 1 (☎ **089/ 2185-1940;** Tram: 19), the jewel-box rococo theater in the Residenz (see "Discovering the top attractions from A to Z" earlier in this chapter) also is an important performance venue for plays and operas.

Bayerischen Staatsoper (Bavarian State Opera; ☎ **089/2185-1920;** www.bayerische.staatsoper.de) is one of the world's great opera companies. Performances of both opera and ballet take place in the National Theater, Max-Joseph-Platz 2 (Tram 19).

The famous **Münchner Philharmoniker** (Munich Philharmonic Orchestra; www.muenchnerphilharmoniker.de) performs from mid-September to July in the Philharmonic Hall in the Gasteig Kulturzentrum (Cultural Center), Rosenheimerstrasse 5 (☎ **089/5481-8181;** S-Bahn: Rosenheimerplatz).

Checking out bars and clubs

Cafes are quiet in the afternoon but pick up noise and steam as the evening wears on. In a cafe you can sit with a coffee or a drink and order light meals or pastries. Nightclubs in Munich, as in the rest of the world, tend to get going around 11 p.m. or midnight.

Bars and cafes

Café Extrablatt, Leopoldstrasse 7 (☎ 089/333-333; U-Bahn: Universität), is a sprawling, smoke-filled hangout for writers, artists, and the occasional celeb. The cafe is open Monday through Thursday from 8 a.m. to midnight, Friday and Saturday from 9 a.m. to 1 a.m., and Sunday from 9 a.m. to midnight.

Havana Club, Herrnstrasse 30 (☎ 089/291-884; S-Bahn: Isartor), is a lively singles bar fueled by rum-based cocktails. The club hours are Monday through Wednesday from 6 p.m. to 1 a.m. and Thursday through Saturday from 7 p.m. to 2 a.m.

Master's Home, Frauenstrasse 11 (☎ 089/229-909; U-/S-Bahn: Marienplatz), is done up like an Edwardian-era London club and attracts an eclectic assortment of locals and tourists. You find a restaurant on the premises if you get hungry. The club is open nightly from 6 p.m. to 3 a.m.

Nachtcafé, Maximilianplatz 5 (☎ 089/595-900; Tram: 49), is one of the most happening nightspots in Munich, attracting soccer stars, movie stars, writers, and waves of "ordinary" patrons to its bar, restaurant, and stage shows (which begin at 11 p.m.). The décor is updated 1950s; the music is jazz, blues, and soul. There's no cover charge. The place is open daily from 9 p.m. to 6 a.m.

Schumanns American Bar, 36 Maximilianstrasse (☎ 089/229-060; Tram 19), offers expensive cocktails, mixed and/or invented by the owner, Charles Schumann; if you're looking for a chic spot, this is it. The bar is open Sunday through Friday from 5 p.m. to 3 a.m.

Nightclubs

Set within an old factory, **Kunstpark Ost,** Grafingerstrasse 6 (☎ 089/4900-2730; S-Bahn: Ostbahnhof), is a complex of bars, restaurants, and dance clubs. You can move from venue to venue according to your interest. All the bars open by 8 p.m. (don't show up before then); discos start around 10:30 p.m. Cover ranges from €4 to €8 ($5 to $10).

Fast Facts: Munich

American Express

American Express, Promenadeplatz 6 (☎ 089/290-900; Tram: 19), is open for mail pickup and check cashing Monday through Friday from 9 a.m. to 6 p.m. and Saturday from 9:30 a.m. to 12:30 p.m.

Business Hours

See the appendix for details.

City Code

The city code for Munich is **089**. Use 89 if you're calling Munich from outside Germany. If you're within Germany but not in Munich, use 089. If you're calling within Munich, leave off the city code and dial only the regular phone number. See also "Telephone" in the appendix.

Currency Exchange

You can exchange money at the currency exchange in the Hauptbahnhof (main train station) daily from 6 a.m. to 11:30 p.m.

Emergencies

For emergency medical aid, or for the police, call ☎ 110. For the fire department, call ☎ 112.

Internet Access

Times Square Online Bistro in the Hauptbahnhof, Bayerstrasse side (☎ 089/ 5508-8000), has computer workstations, a bistro, and bar, and is open daily from 7:30 a.m. to 1 a.m.

Pharmacies

International Ludwig's Apotheke, Neuhauserstrasse 11 (☎ 089/260-3021; U-/S-Bahn: Marienplatz), a drugstore where English is spoken, is open Monday to Friday from 9 a.m. to 8 p.m. and Saturday from 9 a.m. to 4 p.m.

Post Office

The Postamt München (main post office) is across from the Hauptbahnhof, at Bahnhofplatz 1 (☎ 089/599-0870). The office is open Monday to Friday from 7 a.m. to 8 p.m., Saturday from 8 a.m. to 4 p.m., and Sunday from 9 a.m. to 3 p.m.

Restrooms

You find restrooms in cafes, restaurants, and beer halls throughout the Altstadt.

Safety

Munich, like all big cities, has its share of crime, especially pickpocketing and purse- and camera-snatching. Most robberies occur in the much-frequented tourist areas, such as Marienplatz and the Hauptbahnhof.

Transit Assistance

For information on the U-Bahn and trams, call the public transportation authority, MVV, at ☎ 089/4142-4344.

Web Sites

The tourist office Web site, www. muenchen-tourist.de, is the best site for general information. You find more information on Munich and Bavaria at www.bavaria.com.

Chapter 16

Going Beyond Munich: The Romantic Road and Day Trips in Bavaria

. . . .

In This Chapter

▶ Exploring the medieval towns along the Romantic Road
▶ Discovering Neuschwanstein, the fairy-tale castle of Ludwig II
▶ Visiting the alpine resort of Garmisch-Partenkirchen
▶ Day-tripping to Oberammergau and Schloss Linderhof

. . . .

*A*lthough Bavaria's recorded history dates back some 1,100 years, the region didn't become a kingdom until 1806, by order of Napoleon. Bavaria remained a kingdom until 1918, when a German republic replaced the Bavarian monarchy. Brief as it was, many Bavarians still regard that royal era with nostalgia. When they speak wistfully about "the king," they mean only one: Ludwig II, the legendary "dream king" (or "mad king," depending on your interpretation) whose castles at Linderhof and Neuschwanstein draw millions of visitors. Ludwig's castles mark the end of the **Romantische Strasse,** or Romantic Road, one of Germany's most beautiful scenic drives and one of the best ways to sample the delights of Bavaria. Upper Bavaria (Oberbayern), the southernmost part of Germany, gently rises through foothills covered with verdant pastures, lake-splashed countryside, and groves of evergreens to the dramatic heights of the Alps that divide Germany and western Austria. Visitors find a great deal to enjoy in this mountainous region in addition to Ludwig's castles. Bavaria abounds with romantic villages, rococo churches, houses with fancifully painted façades, historic buildings, world-class ski and winter-sports resorts, and nature on a grand scale. Garmisch-Partenkirchen and Oberammergau, both easy day trips from Munich, will give you a taste of what Bavaria has to offer.

Greetings from Bavaria

In Bavaria, people generally use the greeting *Grüss Gott* (pronounced *grease* got) instead of *Guten Morgen* (good morning) or *Guten Tag* (good day). The saying means, roughly, "God greets you." Goodbye is *für Gott* (for God; *fear* got) or *für dich* (for you; *fear* dikh).

The Romantic Road: Seeing the Best of Bavaria

If I had to recommend only one scenic drive in Germany, it would be Bavaria's Romantische Strasse, or Romantic Road. Driving these 290km (180 miles) of specially marked lanes and secondary roads, winding from the vineyard-clad hills surrounding Würzburg south to the green alpine pastures and craggy forested peaks around Neuschwanstein castle, travelers enjoy an unfolding panorama of surprisingly beautiful rural landscapes interspersed with a host of small medieval cities. In three or four days of very easy driving, you can hit all the highlights. (See "The Romantic Road" map in this chapter.)

If you're arriving in Frankfurt, renting a car at Frankfurt airport (see Chapter 20) is easy. From there, you can drive southeast 119km (74 miles) to Würzburg, the official start of the Romantic Road. From Munich (see Chapter 15) you can drive 119km (74 miles) southwest to Füssen and drive the route in reverse. The major towns for overnight stays are **Würzburg, Rothenburg ob der Tauber, Augsburg,** and **Füssen,** all of which I describe later in this chapter. You also can visit these towns by train as day trips from Munich or Frankfurt. For more information, visit the Romantic Road's Web site, www.romantischestrasse.de.

Würzburg: Franconian Fortress

Würzburg on the river Main is a lovely, lively university town surrounded by miles of vineyards. The charms of this old, graceful river and wine town are most obvious in the **Altstadt,** the old city center with its leafy squares and historic buildings, many of them rebuilt after World War II (WWII).

Though today it's part of Bavaria, Würzburg was in ancient times an important town in the duchy of Franconia, which spread across south-central Germany. The bishops of Würzburg, who took possession of the town in 1050, were also princes of Franconia, and remained so until Napoleon ended the power of the church in 1802. The two sights of most interest to tourists are the Residenz, the baroque palace of the prince-bishops, and the Festung Marienburg, their earlier fortress-castle high on a hill overlooking the town. (See the "Würzburg" map in this chapter.)

The Romantic Road

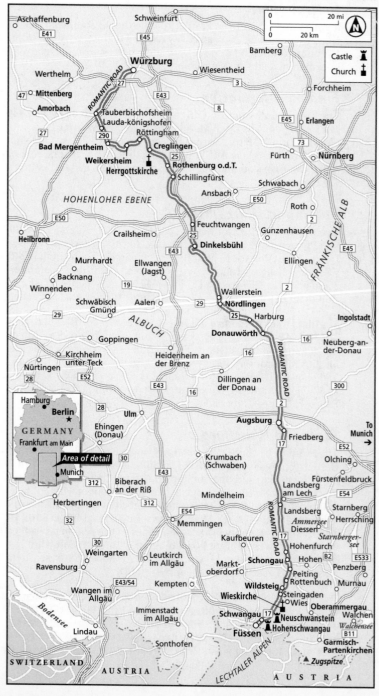

Getting there

If you come **by car** from Frankfurt, take the A3 southeast and follow the signs to Würzburg. You can easily reach Würzburg **by train** from Frankfurt (1½ hours), Munich (2½ hours), or anywhere else in Germany. For train information, call **Deutsche Bahn** (☎ 11861.

Finding information

The **Tourist Information Office,** Marktplatz 9 (☎ 0931/37-23-98; www. wuerzburg.de), is open Monday through Friday from 10 a.m. to 6 p.m. (Jan–Mar until 4 p.m.), Saturday from 10 a.m. to 2 p.m. (Jan–Mar until 1 p.m.), and Sundays April through October from 10 a.m. to 2 p.m. The office can help you find a hotel room and offers general information on the city.

Staying in Würzburg

Greifensteiner Hof, Dettelbachergasse 2, 97070 Würzburg (☎ 0931/35170; www.greifensteiner-hof.de), is a charming 40-room hotel right in the heart of the Altstadt behind the Marienkirche. Each room is different, with nice designer touches and a smallish bathroom. A standard double room goes for €59 to €89 ($74 to $111) per night, breakfast included. American Express, Diners Club, MasterCard, and Visa are accepted.

Maritim Hotel Würzburg, Pleichortorstrasse 5, 97070 Würzburg (☎ 0931/ 30530; www.maritim.de), is a pleasant, modern hotel within easy walking distance of the Altstadt. The medium-size rooms are decorated in an unobtrusive contemporary style and have good-size bathrooms with tub and shower. Rack rates for a double room run from €100 to €210 ($125 to $262), with the big buffet breakfast an additional €15 ($19). American Express, Diners Club, MasterCard, and Visa are accepted.

Dining in Würzburg

The **Fränkische Stuben,** in the Hotel Greifensteiner Hof (described above), Dettelbachergasse 2 (☎ 09861/87809), is a lovely place to sit outside on a warm evening and dine on Franconian specialties of the Würzburg area. Try fresh fish in Riesling wine sauce; herring filets with apples, onions, and pickles in sour cream; roasted meats; or *Zwiebelkuchen* (*zwee*-bel-kook-en; an onion tart). Main courses range from €8 to €16 ($10 to $20). The fresh, light, fruity Franconian wines of the region go well with anything. The restaurant is open Monday through Saturday 11 a.m. to midnight, and Sunday 11 a.m. to 3 p.m. American Express, Diners Club, MasterCard, and Visa are accepted.

Frankish foods with an occasional French twist are served at the atmospheric **Ratskeller Würzburg,** Langgasse 1 (☎ 0931/13021), where main courses range from €6 to €15 ($7.50 to $19). Homemade sausage mixed with fried potatoes and eggs, or roast beef with fried onions and potatoes make for filling feasts. The restaurant, with tables on the square in

Würzburg

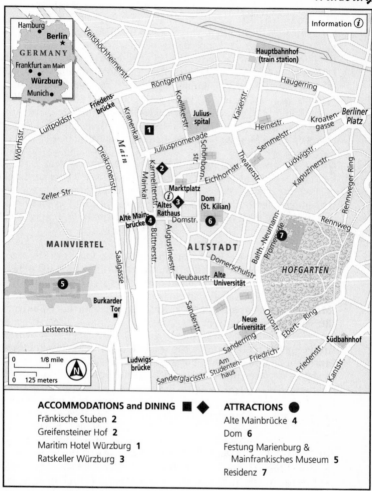

ACCOMMODATIONS and DINING ■ ◆

Fränkische Stuben **2**
Greifensteiner Hof **2**
Maritim Hotel Würzburg **1**
Ratskeller Würzburg **3**

ATTRACTIONS ●

Alte Mainbrücke **4**
Dom **6**
Festung Marienburg &
   Mainfrankisches Museum **5**
Residenz **7**

good weather, is open daily from noon to midnight. American Express, MasterCard, and Visa are accepted.

Exploring Würzburg

The town is compact enough so that you can walk everywhere — except, perhaps, up to the Festung Marienburg, accessible by a scenic footpath up or bus No. 9, which will take you right up to the gate. A single fare on the bus or tram costs €1.50 ($1.90); for local transportation information call ☎ **0931/36-12-52.**

Considered one of the most important palaces in Europe and a master-piece of the baroque era, the 345-room **Residenz,** Residenzplatz 2 (☎ **0931/35-51-70**), was completed in 1744 by architect Balthasar Neuman for Prince-Bishop Johann von Schönborn. The most important areas to visit are the vaulted *Treppenhaus,* or stairway, with a ceiling covered by a huge fresco with mythological allegories painted by Tiepolo; the *Hofkirche,* a court chapel with colored marble columns and two impor-tant altar paintings by Tiepolo; and the *Weisser Saal* (White Hall) and *Gartensaal* (Garden Room), both slathered with a riot of fanciful stucco work. Behind the palace, the formal and elegant *Hofgarten,* or court garden, also is worth visiting. The Residenz is open daily from 9 a.m. to 6 p.m. (November to March 10 a.m. to 4 p.m.); admission is €4 ($5).

One of the annual highlights of Würzburg's cultural year is the **Mozart Festival,** which takes place during the first three weeks in June. Many of the concerts by renowned musicians are performed in the beautiful baroque rooms of the Residenz. For more information on this popular event, call ☎ **0931/37-23-36** or visit the festival's Web site, www.mozart fest-wuerzburg.de.

Following Hofstrasse west from the Residenz, you come to the Romanesque **Dom (Cathedral) St. Kilian,** Domstrasse (☎ **0931/321-1830**), begun in 1040 and rebuilt after extensive damage in WWII. Continuing west on Domstrasse from the cathedral, you come to the **Rathaus,** and, just north of it, the **Marktplatz (Market Square),** the liveliest square in Würzburg.

Crowning the high slope on the west side of the Main is the **Festung Marienburg (Marienburg Fortress; ☎ 09317/20-59-40),** reached by crossing the late-15th-century **Alte Mainbrücke (Old Main Bridge)** and following the marked footpath (you can also take the No. 9 bus from the Residenz). Now a UNESCO World Heritage Site, Marienburg Fortress is a huge complex of buildings that includes within its walls the 8th-century Marienkirche (St. Mary's Church), one of the oldest churches in Germany, and the **Mainfränkisches Museum,** open Tuesday through Sunday from 10 a.m. to 5 p.m. (until 4 p.m. in winter). The one must-see attraction in this local history collection is the room devoted to the carved wooden sculptures of Tilman Riemschneider, the great Gothic master woodcarver.

Driving from Würzburg to Rothenburg

From Würzburg, the Romantic Road leaves the river Main and follows Route 27 in a southwesterly direction to the town of Tauberbischofsheim where you pick up B290 to **Bad Mergentheim,** 47km (29 miles) south of Würzburg. This small, attractive spa town is worth a stop to stroll along its pretty cobbled streets and to have a quick look at the **Deutschordenschloss,** a palace used by the medieval order of Teutonic Knights. Devoted to armor and weaponry, the **Deutschordensmuseum (Teutonic Knights Museum; ☎ 07931/52212),** within the palace complex, is open Tuesday through Sunday 10 a.m. to 5 p.m.; admission is €3.50 ($4.50) adults, €1 ($1.25) for seniors, students, and children 6 to 12.

Tilman Riemenschneider: Würzburg's Master Woodcarver

Tilman Riemenschneider (1460 to 1531), whose incredibly expressive wood sculptures are the highlight of the Mainfränkisches Museum, lived and worked in Würzburg for 48 years, serving as both a councilor and mayor. During the Peasants' Revolt of 1525, this master woodcarver sided with the rebels and incurred the implacable wrath of the prince-bishops. As a result of his political views, Riemenschneider was imprisoned and tortured. He died shortly after being released from prison. You can see more work by this great artist at the Herrgottkirche near Creglingen on the Romantic Road, described in this section.

Another 18km (11 miles) on B19 brings you to **Creglingen,** worth a stop to see the famous carved wooden altar by Tilman Riemenschneider in the **Herrgottskirche,** located on a signposted road about 2km (1½ miles) south of Creglingen in Herrgottstal. The church, dating from 1389, was built where a farmer plowing his fields claimed to have found a sacred host. It quickly became a place of pilgrimage, and between 1505 and 1510, Riemenschneider, the master woodcarver from Würzburg, created an extraordinarily beautiful altar with figures representing the Assumption of the Blessed Virgin framed by scenes from her life. The church is open daily from 9:15 a.m. to 5:30 p.m.; admission is €1.50 ($1.90); you buy your ticket at a machine outside the church. Across the road from the church is the small **Fingerhutmuseum (Thimble Museum; ☎ 07933/370),** the only museum in the world devoted to the history of thimbles. It's interesting . . . if you're into that sort of thing. The museum is open Tuesday through Sunday from 10 a.m. to 12:30 p.m. and 2 to 5 p.m.; admission is €1.50 ($1.90).

Rothenburg ob der Tauber: Medieval Memories

Rothenburg, a completely intact walled medieval city located on a high promontory above the Tauber River, is one of the major highlights along the Romantic Road. The town, just 51km (32 miles) southeast of Würzburg, has been a tourist destination for nearly a century, and from May through September you'll likely encounter hordes of visitors. Don't let that deter you from visiting this remarkable reminder of Germany's medieval past. (See the "Rothenburg ob der Tauber" map in this chapter.)

Getting there

If you're driving the Romantic Road, continue south from Creglingen on B290. You also can reach Rothenburg **by train** from Nuremberg, Heidelberg, or Stuttgart, but you need to transfer at Würzburg or Ansbach and again at Steinach. For train information, call **Deutsche Bahn (☎ 11861).**

Finding information

Tourist Information, Marktplatz (☎ **09861/40492;** www.rothenburg.de),
is open November through April Monday through Friday from 9 a.m. to
noon and 1 to 5 p.m. and Saturday from 10 a.m. to 1 p.m.; May through
October hours are Monday through Friday from 9 a.m. to 6 p.m. and
Saturday from 10 a.m. to 3 p.m. The office can help you find a hotel room
and offers general information about the city.

Staying in Rothenburg

See Chapter 22 for a description of Hotel Eisenhut ($$–$$$$),
Rothenburg's premier hotel.

Everything about the 15-room **Burg Hotel,** Klostergasse 1–3, 91541
Rothenburg ob der Tauber (☎ **09861/94890;** www.burghotel.
rothenburg.de), is picturesque, from its half-timbered façade at the
end of a cobblestone cul-de-sac to its large, prettily decorated rooms
with views out across the Tauber Valley. Boutique hotel standards pre-
vail, but only breakfast is served. Double rooms go for €100 to €170
($125 to $212); parking costs €7.50 ($9.50). American Express, Diners
Club, MasterCard, and Visa are accepted.

Dining in Rothenburg ob der Tauber

Burgerkeller, Herrngasse 24 (☎ **09861/2126**), housed in a 16th-century
cellar (with tables outside in nice weather), is a pleasant spot to dine on
good, basic, local cooking and sample local wines. Standard dishes include
Maultaschensuppe (stuffed pasta in broth) and Nuremberg sausages on
sauerkraut. Expect to pay between €6 and €9 ($7.50 and $11) for a main
course. The restaurant is open daily except Wednesday from 11:30 a.m.
to 2 p.m. and 6 to 9 p.m. MasterCard and Visa are accepted.

Gasthof Marktplatz, Grüner Markt 10 (☎ **09861/6722;** www.gasthof-
marktplatz.de), on the square to the right of the Rathaus, serves hearty,
old-fashioned Swabian dishes, such as *Käsesptzle* (cheese-coated noodles)
cooked with onions, and *Jägerschnitzel,* a pork schnitzel with cream
sauce. It isn't gourmet by any stretch, more like German comfort food.
Main courses range from €8.50 to €14 ($11 to $17). The restaurant is
open Wednesday through Sunday 11 a.m. to 2 p.m. and 6 to 9 p.m. The
Gasthof also rents out simple, inexpensive rooms (€38–€48/$47–$60,
breakfast included), some with a nice view of busy, carless Marktplatz.
No credit cards are accepted.

The **Ratsstube,** Marktplatz 6 (☎ **09861/92411**), in the town hall, has a
tavernlike interior and is a favorite of those who prefer hearty cooking
(including sauerbraten and venison) without a lot of fuss and bother.
American-style breakfasts also are available. Main courses range from €9
to €18 ($11 to $22). The restaurant is open Monday through Saturday from
9 a.m. to 11 p.m., and on Sunday from noon to 6 p.m. (closed Jan–Mar).
MasterCard and Visa are accepted.

Rothenburg ob der Tauber

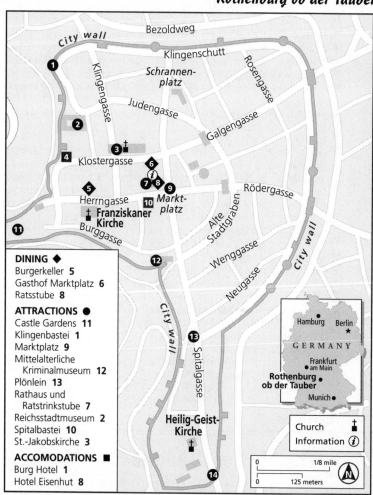

DINING ◆
Burgerkeller **5**
Gasthof Marktplatz **6**
Ratsstube **8**

ATTRACTIONS ●
Castle Gardens **11**
Klingenbastei **1**
Marktplatz **9**
Mittelalterliche
 Kriminalmuseum **12**
Plönlein **13**
Rathaus und
 Ratstrinkstube **7**
Reichsstadtmuseum **2**
Spitalbastei **10**
St.-Jakobskirche **3**

ACCOMODATIONS ■
Burg Hotel **1**
Hotel Eisenhut **8**

Church ✝
Information ⓘ

Exploring Rothenburg ob der Tauber

Medieval walls encircle almost half of Rothenburg; the other half sits on a high ridge above the Tauber River. For an excellent visual introduction, take a walk on a portion of the town ramparts from the massive 16th-century **Spitalbastei** (a medieval tower-gate at the end of the Spitalgasse) to the **Klingenbastei** (another tower-gate). Then just stroll around and soak up the atmosphere in one of Europe's best-preserved medieval cities. As you're walking, look for a Rothenburg specialty called *Schneeballen* (snowballs) — crisp, round pastries covered with powdered sugar. You can buy them in bakeries all across town.

At the center of Rothenburg is the bustling **Marktplatz (Market Square)** dominated by the **Rathaus (☎ 09861/40492)**, part 13th-century Gothic, part 16th-century Renaissance. From the top of its 50m (165-ft.) tower, you get a great view of the town (open Apr–Oct 9:30 a.m.–12:30 p.m. and 1–5 p.m.; admission €1/$1.25). Adjacent to the Rathaus, and now serving as the Tourist Information office, is the **Ratstrinkstube (Councilors' Tavern),** an old inn with three clocks on its gabled façade (now the tourist information office). Windows on either side of the lowest clock open at 11 a.m., noon, and 1, 2, 3, 9, and 10 p.m. to reveal the figures of General Tilly and Herr Nusch, chief protagonists in the drinking bout that saved Rothenburg.

South of the Rathaus, a 14th-century hospital with Rothenburg's only 18th-century baroque façade houses the macabre-minded **Mittelalterliche Kriminalmuseum (Medieval Criminal Museum),** Burggasse 3–5 (☎ 09861/5359). Medieval crime and punishment are the fascinatingly gruesome subjects of the museum's displays. Here's a rare chance to see chastity belts, shame masks, a shame flute for bad musicians, a dunking basket, and an iron maiden. Admission is €3.20 ($4) adults, €2.10 ($2.30) for students and children younger than 13. The museum is open April through October daily from 9:30 a.m. to 6 p.m.; November and January through February daily from 2 to 4 p.m.; December and March daily from 10 a.m. to 4 p.m.

The Gothic **St.-Jakobskirche (Church of St. James),** Klostergasse 15 (☎ 09861/700-620), is worth visiting to see the Heiliges-Blut-Altar (Altar of the Holy Blood), a masterpiece created by the Würzburg sculptor Tilman Riemenschneider. (Riemenschneider's work also is on view in Würzburg and in the Herrgottskirche, described earlier in this section.) The fine painted-glass windows in the church choir date from the late Gothic period. Admission is €1.50 ($1.90) adults, €.50 (65¢) children. The church is open daily from 9 a.m. to 5:30 p.m.

The Master Draught: How Mayor Nusch Saved Rothenburg

In 1631, during the Thirty Years' War, General Tilly, commander of the armies of the Catholic League, captured the Protestant city of Rothenburg and was given, as victor, a 3½-liter (6-pint) tankard of wine. He said he would spare the town from destruction if one of the town burghers could down the huge tankard in one draught. Former mayor Nusch accepted the challenge and succeeded, thus saving Rothenburg and giving himself a three-day hangover. This historical episode was performed as a festival play, called *Die Meistertrunk (The Master Draught),* in 1881. The play forms the centerpiece of a weekend festival that takes place every September in Rothenburg, when hundreds of citizens dress up in period costumes and re-create the period of the Master Draught.

Just northwest of the Jakobskirche is the **Reichsstadtmuseum** (City Museum), Klosterhof 5 (☎ **09861/93-9043**), which is housed in a 700-year-old Dominican nunnery with well-preserved cloisters, convent hall, and kitchen. It displays medieval panel paintings, a collection of gold coins, drinking vessels, armaments, and objects of local interest. Admission to the museum is €3 ($3.75) for adults, €1.50 ($1.90) for children and students. Open hours are April through October daily from 10 a.m. to 5 p.m.; November through March daily from 1 to 4 p.m.

Rothenburg has plenty of picturesque lands, nooks, and crannies to explore. One particularly pretty spot with lovely views over the Tauber Valley is **Castle Gardens,** a park on the site of the imperial castle. Also look for the photogenic corner known as the **Plönlein,** where two streets, an upper and a lower, converge.

Shopping in Rothenburg

Kunstwerke Friese, Grüner Markt (☎ **09861/7166**), specializes in cuckoo clocks and carries Hummel figurines, pewter beer steins, music boxes, and dolls. Every day is Christmas at **Käthe Wohlfahrt's Weinachtsdoft** (Christmas Village), Herrngasse 1 (☎ **09861/4090**), a Christmas-related emporium loaded with thousands upon thousands of Christmas ornaments.

Driving from Rothenburg to Augsburg

The charm of driving along the Romantic Road is enhanced by the bucolic landscapes seen between the villages. North and south of Rothenburg, the drive parallels the lovely, leafy Tauber Valley. Driving along **B25,** on the way to Augsburg, you also pass neatly tended farms and fields. Two walled medieval towns worth a stop and stroll are **Dinkelsbühl** and **Nördlingen.** No must-see sights are in either town, just the picturesque streets, squares, churches, and houses.

Augsburg: Reminders of the Renaissance

Augsburg is a city of pleasant surprises. With a population of about 260,000, it's the largest town along the Romantic Road and serves as a gateway to the Bavarian Alps. The city was founded some 2,000 years ago by the Roman emperor Augustus and reached its cultural zenith during the Renaissance, under the patronage of the enormously wealthy Fugger family. A stroll through Augsburg reveals an attractive urban landscape loaded with historic buildings, charming corners, and the lively ambience of a university town. (See the "Augsburg" map in this chapter.)

Getting there

If you're driving the Romantic Road, continue on **B25** south from Rothenburg to Augsburg. **Trains** from Frankfurt (trip time about three hours) and Munich (trip time about 30 minutes) arrive frequently throughout the day. For train information, call **German Rail** at ☎ **11861.**

Finding information and taking a tour

The **Tourist Information office**, Rathausplatz (☎ **0821/502-0724**; www. augsburg-tourismus.de), open Monday through Friday 9 a.m. to 5 p.m. and Saturday from 10 a.m. to 2 p.m., distributes city maps, dispenses general information, and can help you find a room.

The best way to appreciate Augsburg's architectural and cultural heritage is by taking the **walking tour** (in Germany and English) offered by the tourist office daily at 2 p.m. from May through October, on Saturdays at 2 p.m. the rest of the year (€7/$8.75). The office also offers a two-hour **bus tour** May through October Thursday through Sunday at 10 a.m. (€9/$11). All tours begin at the Rathaus.

Staying in Augsburg

Romantikhotel Augsburger Hof, Auf dem Kreuz 2, 86152 Augsburg (☎ **0821/34-30-50;** www.augsburger-hof.de), is a 36-room boutique-style hotel located just minutes from central Rathausplatz and all Augsburg attractions. Rooms are nicely done with exposed beams in some and small but well-designed bathrooms with showers. Larger (and quieter) rooms face an inner courtyard. Service is friendly and efficient. The hotel's restaurant is one of the best in town. Doubles go for €80 to €130 ($100 to $162) and include a good breakfast buffet. American Express, Diners Club, MasterCard, and Visa are accepted.

The 102-room **Steigenberger Drei Mohren,** Maximilianstrasse 40, 86150 Augsburg (☎ **0821/50360;** www.augsburg.steigenberger.de), on Augsburg's most elegant boulevard, is the town's full-service luxury-oriented hotel, though the rooms vary in size and level of finesse. The best are large and comfortable, with marble-clad bathrooms with big bathtubs. Rack rates for a double room range from €143 to €163 ($179 to $203). American Express, Diners Club, MasterCard, and Visa are accepted.

Dining in Augsburg

For fine food and impeccable service in lovely surroundings, dine at the restaurant in the **Romantikhotel Augsburger Hof,** Auf dem Kreuz 2 (☎ **0821/34-30-50**), where the rear dining room is paneled in pale linden wood. Your best bet here is the reasonably priced three-course daily menu, which offers appetizers such as mixed salad with tuna and capers, and main courses such as bacon-wrapped steak in bechamel sauce or pan-fried rock salmon in tomato sauce. Expect to pay €12 to €25 ($15 to $31) for main courses; fixed-price daily menu €18 ($22). The restaurant is open daily for lunch and dinner.

Fuggerei Stube, Jakoberstrasse 26 (☎ **0821/30870**), an unpretentious local eatery, serves generous portions of Swabian food with a few "international" dishes. Look for potato cream soup with mushrooms; chicken breast with curry and rice; calves liver with apples, onions, and roast potatoes; and vegetarian offerings. Main courses range from €9 to €18

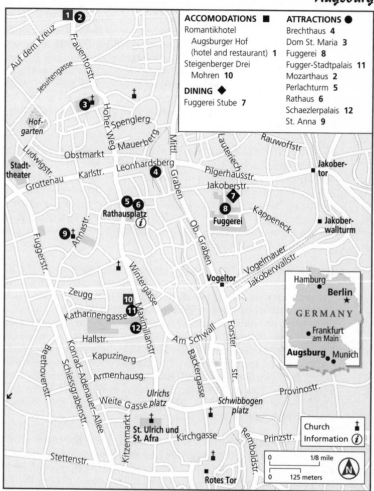

Augsburg

ACCOMODATIONS ■
Romantikhotel
 Augsburger Hof
 (hotel and restaurant) 1
Steigenberger Drei
 Mohren 10

DINING ◆
Fuggerei Stube 7

ATTRACTIONS ●
Brechthaus 4
Dom St. Maria 3
Fuggerei 8
Fugger-Stadtpalais 11
Mozarthaus 2
Perlachturm 5
Rathaus 6
Schaezlerpalais 12
St. Anna 9

($11 to $22); fixed-price menu €19 ($24). American Express, MasterCard, and Visa are accepted. Hours are Tuesday through Saturday 11:30 a.m. to 2 p.m. and 5:30 to 11 p.m., Sunday 11:30 a.m. to 3 p.m.

Exploring Augsburg

Augsburg's main square, **Rathausplatz,** is dominated by two imposing Renaissance-era buildings, both considerably rebuilt after damage in WWII. The **Rathaus,** Am Rathausplatz 2 (☎ **0821/324-9180**), designed by Elias Holl and completed in 1620, is one of the most significant secular buildings of the German Renaissance. The interior is famous for its sumptuous *Goldener Saal* (Golden Hall), which can be visited only as part of a Rathaus tour (daily May through October at 10 a.m. and 3 p.m.; €7/$8.75). The **Augustus fountain** in front of the Rathaus was dedicated on the occasion of the town's 1,600th birthday in 1594. If you climb to the top of the soaring spire of the **Perlachturm** (Perlach Tower), next to the Rathaus, you'll be rewarded with a marvelous view of the old town center. The tower, capped by a distinctive dome called an "Augsburg onion" (you'll see these onion domes on churches all across Augsburg and as you head south into Bavaria), is open May through October from 10 a.m. to 6 p.m.

West of Rathausplatz, on Annahof, stands **St. Anna,** a former Carmelite monastery church dating from 1321. In 1518, Martin Luther stayed in the adjoining monastery when he was called to Augsburg to recant his 95 Theses before a papal emissary. The church, which contains paintings by Lucas Cranach and the chapel of the Fugger family, is open Tuesday through Sunday from 10 a.m. to 6 p.m. Right next to the church, on the Annahof, you find the city market with stalls selling flowers, produce, pastries, and much more.

Maximilianstrasse, ornamented by three large Renaissance-era fountains and lined with shops and fine patrician houses, stretches south from Rathausplatz. As you stroll along Augsburg's most elegant boulevard, duck into the courtyard of Maximilianstrasse 36 to have a look at the *Damenhof,* or Ladies' Court, of what was once the **Fugger-Stadtpalais (Fugger City Palace).** A late-18th-century mansion, the **Schaezlerpalais,** Maximilianstrasse 46 (☎ 0821/324-4125), houses the Bavarian State Gallery, noted for its Old Masters painting collection with works by Dürer, Holbein, and Cranach. The museum is open Tuesday through Sunday from 10 a.m. to 6 p.m.; admission is €3.50 ($4.50). A pair of churches, **St. Ulrich and St. Afra,** both dating from 1500, demarcate the southern end of Maximilianstrasse.

East of Maximilianstrasse, on Jakobsplatz in the old residential quarter of town, you'll find the **Fuggerei,** one of the most important building complexes in Augsburg. The first almshouses in the world, and still in use today, the Fuggerei was built in 1523 by Jacob Fugger the Rich. Surrounded by walls and gates (locked from 10 p.m. to 5 a.m.), the compound looks like a miniature town with 67 identical cottages containing 147 small apartments, a church, a fountain, and a park. Residents pay an annual rent of €1 (equivalent to one old Rhenish guilder) and are expected to pray three times a day for the soul of their benefactor. Tiny but fascinating, the **Fuggerei Museum,** Mittlere Gasse 13 (☎ 0821/319-8810), lets you glimpse the interior of one of the cottages as it looked in centuries past. It's open March through December daily from 10 a.m. to 6 p.m.; admission is €1 ($1.25).

The Wieskirche: Masterpiece in a meadow

On the stretch of B17 from Augsburg to Füssen, the Romantic Road passes through some industrialized areas that aren't particularly appealing, but then the verdant (or snow-covered) pastures of the Bavarian Alps appear. On this segment of the drive, I strongly recommend that you make a short detour to **Wies**, 6km (4 miles) southeast of the town of Steingaden off B17, where you find the **Wieskirche (☎ 08862/501)**, a remarkable pilgrimage church in a beautiful alpine meadow (the name means "church in the meadow"). One of the world's most exuberantly decorated buildings, this rococo masterpiece was created by Dominikus Zimmermann (1685 to 1766), who worked on the church with his brother from 1746 to 1754. Behind a rather sober façade, the light-flooded interior with its enormous cupola shimmers with a superabundance of woodcarvings, gilded stucco, columns, statues, and bright frescoes. The church is open daily from 8 a.m. to 5 p.m. (Apr–Sept until 7 p.m.). Admission is free. To return to the Romantic Road, backtrack to B17 and follow it south to Neuschwantstein, Ludwig II's famous castle in the Bavarian Alps.

Some of the oldest stained-glass windows in Germany, dating from the 12th century, are found in the south transept of Augsburg's cathedral, **Dom St. Maria,** Hoher Weg (☎ **0821/316-6353**). Altered during the centuries, the cathedral features Gothic frescoes, paintings by Hans Holbein the Elder, and a 14th-century bronze door.

 If you're a fan of Mozart, you may want to take a look at the humble **Mozarthaus,** Frauentorstrasse 30 (☎ **0821/324-3984**), where Wolfgang's father, Leopold, was born. Wolfie's great-grandfather Franz Mozart, a master mason reduced to penury, lived in the Fuggerei almshouse at Mittlere Gasse 14. The **Brechthaus,** Auf dem Rain 7 (☎ **0821/324-2779**) was the birthplace of playwright Bertolt Brecht (1898–1956) and today serves as a Brecht memorial. The Mozarthaus and the Brechthaus are open Tuesday to Sunday 10 a.m. to 5 p.m.; admission to each is €1.50 ($2).

Neuschwanstein and Hohenschwangau: Castles in the Air

Located 116km (72 miles) southwest of Munich, the two Bavarian royal castles of Hohenschwangau and Neuschwanstein (and the nearby town of Füssen) mark the end of the Romantic Road. Hohenschwangau, built by Maximilian II in 1836, is the less remarkable and more intimate of the two. Neuschwanstein, the most photographed building in Germany, was the fairy-tale concoction of Maximilian's son, King Ludwig II. (See "The Romantic Road" map earlier in this chapter.)

The royal castles of Hohenschwangau and Neuschwanstein are the most popular tourist attractions in Germany, receiving nearly a million visitors a year. Be prepared for long lines (sometimes up to three hours) in the summer, especially in August. On some days, 25,000 people visit. To save yourself time, try to arrive as soon as the castles open in the morning.

Getting there

If you're **driving** from Augsburg along the Romantic Road, head south along B17 to Schwangau. From there, it's a 7km (4-mile) drive along a signposted road. One parking lot serves both castles; parking costs €4 ($5). Ten **buses** a day (No. 9713) arrive from Füssen, the nearest large town (described later in this section).

Finding information and buying tickets

Information about both castles and the region in general is available in Schwangau at the **Kurverwaltung** (tourist office) in the Rathaus, Münchenerstrasse 2 (☎ 08362/81980), open Monday through Friday from 8 a.m. to 5 p.m., Saturday from 9 a.m. to noon.

A **ticket office** near the parking lot of the castles sells tickets for both Hohenschwangau and Neuschwanstein. You can see the castles only on guided tours, which last about 35 minutes each. Tours in English are available throughout the day. A tour number and entry time are printed on your ticket. A digital sign informs you when your tour is ready. When the time comes, feed your ticket into the turnstile in front of the respective castle. The tour guide will meet you inside.

Exploring Hohenschwangau

The castle was a 600-year-old ruin when Ludwig's father, Maximilian II, then Bavaria's crown prince, bought it in 1832. On the ruins he built the neo-Gothic castle you see today and used it as a summer holiday residence. Ludwig II spent much of his joyless childhood at Hohenschwangau with his strait-laced father and his mother, Queen Maria of Prussia.

The rooms of Hohenschwangau were designed and furnished in a ponderous "Gothic Castle" style that was fashionable in the 1830s and 1840s. The **Hall of the Swan Knight,** named for the wall paintings depicting the saga of Lohengrin (a Germanic hero associated with the swan), is one of the castle's most attractive chambers. The **music room** on the second floor contains copies of letters between Ludwig II and his musical idol, Richard Wagner, and the grand piano on which the two played duets. For many years, the extravagant dream king financed Wagner, who was first invited to Hohenschwangau by a teenaged Ludwig.

Hohenschwangau, Alpseestrasse (☎ 08362/81127), is open daily. March 15 to October 15 hours are 8:30 a.m. to 6 p.m.; October 16 to March 14 hours are 9:30 a.m. to 4 p.m. Admission is €8 ($10) for adults and €7 ($8.75) for students and children 6 to 15.

Exploring Neuschwanstein

Reaching the castle entrance involves a steep 800m (½-mile), 30-minute climb from the parking lot at Hohenschwangau Castle. If you don't want to walk, you can take a **bus** to **Marienbrücke,** a bridge that crosses over the Pöllat Gorge and offers a panoramic view of the castle dramatically perched on its crag above. The bus ride, which starts in front of the Schlosshotel Lisl near the parking lot, costs €1.80 ($2.25). From Marienbrücke, the walk to the castle entrance includes a steep, 170-step stairway and takes about ten minutes. A more picturesque way to reach Neuschwanstein is by horse-drawn **carriage.** The carriage ride, which begins at the ticket office, costs €3.50 ($4.40) for the trip up to the castle entrance and €1.50 ($1.90) for the descent. Be aware that the carriages are sometimes crowded. Buy tickets from the bus driver or at the carriage.

Ludwig watched the construction of his dream palace through a telescope from neighboring Hohenschwangau. Building began in 1869 and continued for some 17 years, stopping only when Ludwig died in 1886. Between 1884 and 1886, the king lived in Neuschwanstein on and off for 170 days. At Neuschwanstein, he received news of his dethronement. Three days later he was dead.

The king's **study** is decorated with painted scenes from the medieval legend of Tannhäuser. Everything from curtains to chair coverings is made of silk embroidered with the gold-and-silver Bavarian coat of arms. The sumptuous ornamentation seen throughout the castle influenced Jugendstil, the German form of Art Nouveau.

Ludwig II: Madman or dreamer?

For some, Ludwig II is "the mad king." For others, he is "the dream king." This strange, self-obsessed monarch has become one of the legendary figures in Bavarian history. Biographies, films, plays, and even a musical have been written about him.

Born in Munich in 1845, Ludwig II was only 18 years old when he was crowned king of Bavaria. Tall, handsome, and blue-eyed, Ludwig grew bored with the affairs of state and eventually became more and more obsessed with acting out his extravagant fantasies. A patron of the composer Richard Wagner, he often had Wagner's operas performed for his own solitary pleasure. At **Linderhof,** the first palace that he built (see "A side trip to Schloss Linderhof: Ludwig's little Versailles," later in this chapter), Ludwig went so far as to reconstruct the Venus grotto from Wagner's opera *Tannhäuser.* The most famous of his design efforts is the turreted castle of **Neuschwanstein,** perched on a crag high above the town of Schwangau. Ludwig's excesses eventually threatened to bankrupt the kingdom, and in 1886, at age 41, he was declared insane. Three days later, he was found drowned in Lake Starnberg on the outskirts of Munich, along with the physician who had declared him insane. Was he murdered or did he commit suicide? No one knows. The crypt of the Michaelskirche (St. Michael's Church) in Munich contains Ludwig's grave and those of other Wittelsbach royals.

The **throne room,** designed to look like a Romanesque basilica with columns of red porphyry and a mosaic floor, was never completed. A stairway of white Carrara marble leads up to the golden apse where the king's throne was to stand. Paintings of Christ looking down on the 12 apostles and 6 canonized kings of Europe decorate the walls and ceiling.

The intricate woodcarving in the **king's bedroom** took 4½ years to complete. Artisans carved wall panels to look like Gothic windows; a mural depicts the legend of the doomed lovers Tristan and Isolde. The ornate bed rests on a raised platform with an elaborately carved canopy. Through the balcony window you can see the 46m-high (150-ft.) waterfall in the Pöllat Gorge, with the mountains in the distance.

Decorated with marble columns and frescoes depicting the life of Parsifal, a mythical medieval knight, the **Sängerhalle** (Singer's Hall) takes up almost the entire fourth floor of the castle. Architects modeled the room, another architectural fantasy, after Wartburg castle in Eisenach, the site of song contests in the Middle Ages.

In September, Wagnerian and other classical music concerts take place in the Singer's Hall. For information and reservations, contact the **Verkehrsamt** (tourist office) in Schwangau (☎ **08362/81980**). Tickets go on sale in early June and always sell out quickly.

After you leave the guided tour, you can make your way down to see the enormous **kitchens** of the castle. A 20-minute film about the life of Ludwig II is shown in an auditorium.

Located at Neuschwansteinstrasse 20 (☎ **08362/81035**), the castle can be visited year-round by guided tour only. From April through September, tours depart every half-hour from 9 a.m. to 6 p.m.; October through March, from 10 a.m. to 4 p.m. Admission is €9 ($11) for adults, €8 ($10) for children and students, free for children ages 6 to 14. Neuschwanstein is closed November 1; December 24, 25, and 31; January 1; and Shrove Tuesday (the Tuesday before Ash Wednesday on the Christian calendar).

Dining near the castles

Neuschwanstein has a pleasant cafe where you can get sandwiches, desserts, and beverages. Otherwise, you encounter no lack of restaurants (or hotels) right around the parking lot near Hohenschwangau. If the weather is fine, you can eat outdoors on the terrace of **Hotel Müller,** where the restaurant serves sandwiches, herring, soup, or larger meals. Main courses go for €8 to €16 ($10 to $20).

Füssen: End of the (Romantic) Road

Situated in foothills of the Bavarian Alps, 119km (74 miles) southwest of Munich and just 3km (2 miles) from Neuschwanstein, the medieval town of Füssen marks the official end (or beginning) of the Romantic Road.

Füssen

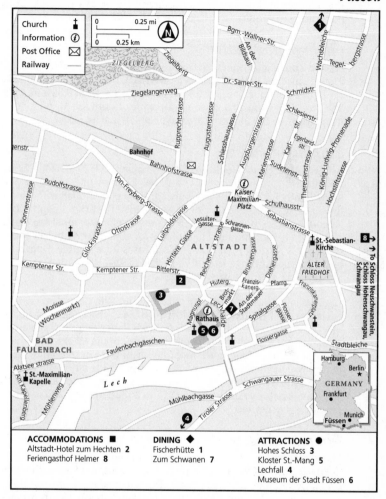

ACCOMMODATIONS ■	DINING ◆	ATTRACTIONS ●
Altstadt-Hotel zum Hechten **2**	Fischerhütte **1**	Hohes Schloss **3**
Feriengasthof Helmer **8**	Zum Schwanen **7**	Kloster St.-Mang **5**
		Lechfall **4**
		Museum der Stadt Füssen **6**

Divided by the Lech River, this town of 15,000 inhabitants has lovely squares and narrow, cobblestone streets flanked by medieval stone houses. Its history dates back to Roman times, when Füssen was a trading station. Füssen is an atmospheric place to headquarter while exploring the castles of Neuschwanstein and Hohenschwangau or other places in the Bavarian Alps. (See the "Füssen" map in this chapter.)

Getting there

If you're driving along the Romantic Road from Augsburg, continue south on B17. From Munich, take the A8 Autobahn west to Landsberg and then head south on B17. **Trains** from Munich (trip time 2½ hours) and Frankfurt (trip time 5 to 5½ hours) arrive frequently throughout the day. For train information, call **German Rail** at ☎ 11861.

Finding information

Füssen Tourismus operates two tourist offices, one at Kaiser-Maximilian-Platz 1, another in the **Rathaus** (town hall), Lechhalde 3 (☎ 08362/93850 for both). Summer hours are Monday to Friday from 8:30 a.m. to 6:30 p.m. and Saturday from 10 a.m. to noon; winter hours are Monday to Friday from 9 a.m. to 5 p.m. and Saturday from 10 a.m. to noon.

Staying in Füssen

Altstadt-Hotel zum Hechten, Ritterstrasse 6, 87629 Füssen (☎ 08362/ 91600; www.hotel-hechten.com), has been owned and operated by the same family for generations. This spotless guesthouse with blooming flower boxes exudes an air of old-fashioned Bavarian hospitality. The 35 comfortable rooms are small to medium in size; most have small shower-only bathrooms. The hotel is located directly below the castle in Füssen's *Altstadt* (Old Town). Rack rates for a double room with buffet breakfast range from €74 to €84 ($92–$105). American Express, MasterCard, and Visa are accepted.

Located in Schwangau, a small village about 4km (2½ miles) east of Füssen, **Feriengasthof Helmer,** Mitteldorf 10, 87645 Schwangau (☎ 08362/9800; www.hotel-helmer.de), is a traditional Bavarian guesthouse with views of the mountains and nearby castles. The rooms all are furnished differently; some have balconies, most have showers in the bathrooms. Stay here if you want old-fashioned atmosphere. Kids enjoy the nearby pool and find plenty of room to play outside. Rack rates for a double room with breakfast are €60 to €106 ($75 to $132). MasterCard is the only credit card accepted.

Dining in Füssen

Fischerhütte, Uferstrasse 16, Hopfen am See (5km/3 miles northwest of Füssen; ☎ 08362/91970), at the edge of a small lake within sight of dramatic mountain scenery, specializes in seafood from around the world. Menu offerings may include Alaskan salmon, North Atlantic lobster, French-style bouillabaisse, fresh local trout, or grilled halibut. A few meat dishes are also available. Diners can enjoy Bavarian specialties during the summer in an outdoor beer garden. Main courses go for €11 to €25 ($14 to $31). The restaurant is open daily from 11:30 a.m. to 2 p.m. and 5:30 to 9:30 p.m. Reservations are recommended. American Express, MasterCard, and Visa are accepted.

Small and old-fashioned, **Zum Schwanen,** Brotmarkt 4 (☎ 08362/6174), serves a flavorful blend of Swabian and Bavarian cuisine. Specialties include homemade sausage, roast pork, lamb, and venison. Service is helpful and attentive, and portions are generous. Main courses range from €7 to €18 ($8.75 to $22). Zum Schwanen is open Tuesday through Saturday from 11:30 a.m. to 2 p.m. and 6:30 to 10 p.m. MasterCard and Visa are accepted.

Exploring Füssen

Füssen's main attraction is the **Hohes Schloss** (High Castle), Magnusplatz (☎ 08362/903-146), reached by a steep lane behind the parish church. The powerful prince-bishops of Augsburg used the Hohes Schloss, one of the finest late-Gothic castles in Bavaria, as a summer residence. Now the castle is the home of the **Staatsgalerie,** where you find a collection of Swabian artwork from the 1400s to the 1700s. The museum is open daily 9 a.m. to 6 p.m. and charges €2.50 ($3.10) for admission.

Immediately below the castle lies the **Kloster St.-Mang** (Monastery of St. Magnus), founded by Benedictine monks in the eighth century on the site where an Irish missionary monk named St. Magnus died in 750. In the early 18th century, Johann-Jakob Herkomer, a local architect, turned the church and monastery into a baroque gem with a strong Venetian influence. The Romansque crypt in front of the high altar contains frescoes painted around A.D. 1000. Access to the secularized church complex is through the **Museum der Stadt Füssen** (City Museum), Lechhalde 3 (☎ 08362/903-145), which occupies the former state apartments of the abbey and displays artifacts relating to the history and culture of the region, including a collection of locally produced violins and lutes. The museum is open Tuesday through Sunday. From April through October, hours are 10 a.m. to 5 p.m., from November through March, 1 to 4 p.m. Admission is €2.50 ($3.10) for adults, children younger than 14 free.

The **Lechfall,** a waterfall less than a kilometer ([bf]1/2 mile) south of town, is a popular walk from Füssen. A pedestrian footbridge spans the falls, located where the Lech River squeezes through a rocky gorge and over a high ledge.

Garmisch-Partenkirchen: Doing the Zugspitze

Located about 97km (60 miles) southwest of Munich, the twin villages of Garmisch and Partenkirchen comprise Germany's top winter-sports resort. (See the "Garmisch-Partenkirchen" map in this chapter.) In 1936, the fourth Winter Olympics took place here, and in 1978, the towns played host the World Alpine Ski Championships. Garmisch-Partenkirchen enjoys a stunning location at the foot of the Wetterstein range. Two giant peaks, the Alpspitze and the Waxensteine, rear up to the south of town, hiding Germany's tallest mountain, the famed **Zugspitze.**

Despite the commercial, touristy air of the towns, you still find charming details: the sound of cowbells in the meadows outside town, and streets and lanes (particularly in Partenkirchen) with a quiet, village atmosphere.

Getting there

Trains run frequently from all directions to Garmisch-Partenkirchen. The trip time from Munich is about 1½ hours. For information and schedules, call **German Rail** at ☎ **11861**. To reach Garmisch-Partenkirchen by **car** from Munich, take the **A95** Autobahn and exit at Eschenlohe; the trip takes about one hour.

Finding information

The **Tourist Information office** at Richard-Strauss-Platz 2 (☎ **08821/180-700;** www.garmisch-partenkirchen.de) is open Monday to Saturday from 8 a.m. to 6 p.m. and Sunday and holidays from 10 a.m. to noon. The office supplies maps and details of area hikes and attractions.

Getting around Garmisch-Partenkirchen

A free municipal bus runs every 15 minutes between the **Bahnhof** (train station) and **Marienplatz,** Garmisch's main square. From Marienplatz, you can walk to all the centrally located hotels. The **Bayerische Zugspitzbahn** at Garmisch (☎ **08821/7970**) provides rail service to the top of the Zugspitze and other local peaks.

Staying in Garmisch-Partenkirchen

Hotel Hilleprandt
$–$$ Garmisch

This chalet, with wooden balconies, a pretty garden, an outdoor terrace, and a backdrop of forest-covered mountains, is an excellent budget choice. The 13 rooms, some with a private balcony, are small but very comfortable. The tiled bathrooms have either showers or tub-shower combinations. The hotel is close to the Zugspitze Bahnhof and the Olympic Ice Stadium. Children younger than 6 stay free in their parents' room.

See map p. 301. Riffelstrasse 17, 82467 Garmisch-Partenkirchen. ☎ *08821/943040. Fax: 08821/74548.* www.hotel-hilleprandt.de. *Rack rates: €76–€106 ($95–$132) double. Rates include buffet breakfast. MC, V.*

Hotel-Gasthof Drei Mohren
$ Partenkirchen

Located in Partenkirchen, the quieter side of town, this family-owned and -operated hotel offers cozy accommodations at moderate prices. The 25 rooms are comfortable without a lot of frills; each has a small bathroom with tub or shower.

See map p. 301. Ludwigstrasse 65, 82467 Garmisch-Partenkirchen. ☎ *08821/9130. Fax: 08821/18974.* www.vierjahreszeiten.cc/DreiMohren. *Rack rates: €56–€89 ($70–$111) double. Rates include buffet breakfast. AE, DC, MC, V.*

Garmisch-Partenkirchen

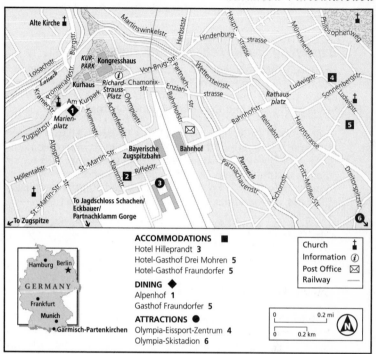

ACCOMMODATIONS ■
Hotel Hilleprandt **3**
Hotel-Gasthof Drei Mohren **5**
Hotel-Gasthof Fraundorfer **5**

DINING ◆
Alpenhof **1**
Gasthof Fraundorfer **5**

ATTRACTIONS ●
Olympia-Eissport-Zentrum **4**
Olympia-Skistadion **6**

Church ✝
Information ⓘ
Post Office ✉
Railway —

Dining in Garmisch-Partenkirchen

Alpenhof
$–$$ Garmisch BAVARIAN

Locals regard the Alpenhof as one of the finest restaurants in Garmisch. Traditional Bavarian specialties are on the menu, and so are fresh trout, grilled salmon, and ragout of venison. For dessert, try a soufflé.

See map p. 301. Am Kurpark 10. ☎ **08821/59055.** *Reservations recommended. Main courses: €10–€19 ($12–$24). MC, V. Open: Daily 11:30 a.m.–2 p.m. and 5:30–9:30 p.m. Closed 3 weeks in Nov.*

Gasthof Fraundorfer
$–$$ Partenkirchen BAVARIAN

Visitors to Garmisch-Partenkirchen enjoy this large restaurant because every evening yodelers, musicians, and dancers provide Bavarian entertainment. The food is hearty and uncomplicated: potato soup with wurst, ham hocks with sauerkraut, pork cutlets, and duck. It's a touristy scene but fun.

See map p. 301. Ludwigstrasse 24. ☎ *08821/9270. Reservations recommended. Main courses: €8–€14 ($10–$17). AE, MC, V. Open: Daily except Tuesday 11–2:30 p.m. and 5–10 p.m.*

Exploring Garmisch-Partenkirchen

Garmisch-Partenkirchen is a center for winter sports, summer hiking, and mountain climbing. The best way to explore this international resort is simply to stroll around the town and its environs, enjoying the panoramic views of the Alps and the colorful buildings that line the side streets.

Built for the 1936 Winter Olympics, the **Olympia-Eissport-Zentrum** (Olympic Ice Stadium; ☎ **08821/753-294**) in Garmisch contains three giant skating rinks with stands for 12,000 spectators. The ice rinks are open to the public daily from July until the middle of May from 10 a.m. to noon (also from 2–4 p.m. on Saturday and Sunday). Admission is €3.80 ($4.75) for adults, €2.20 ($2.75) for children 6 to 15.

On the slopes at the edge of town is the **Olympia-Skistadion** (Olympic Ski Stadium), with two ski jumps and a slalom course. Like the ice stadium, this ski facility opened in 1936 and remains an integral part of winter life in Garmisch. The World Cup Ski Jump takes place here every January 1.

Alpine hiking is a major summertime attraction. People come from around the world to roam the mountain paths (called *Hohenwege*, or "high ways"), enjoy nature, and watch animals in the forest. One hiking destination, 1,688m (5,628 ft.) above Garmisch-Partenkirchen and accessible only by foot (the climb is strenuous), is the **Jagdschloss Schachen** (☎ **08821/2996**), a hunting lodge built by Ludwig II, the "dream king," in 1871. The exterior of the lodge resembles a Swiss chalet, but the king insisted on an elaborately fanciful Moorish-style interior. The only way to see the lodge is by guided tour (in German only), given at 11 a.m., 1 p.m., 2 p.m., and 3 p.m. from early June to early October. Admission is €2.50 ($3.10) for adults, free for children younger than 14. You need about four hours to get there and back. The tourist office in Garmisch-Partenkirchen (see "Finding information" earlier in this section) can supply further details.

Ascending the Zugspitze

For a spectacular view of the Bavarian and the Tyrolean (Austrian) Alps, you can go all the way to the summit of the **Zugspitze,** Germany's tallest mountain (2,960m/9,720 ft.). You can choose between two different ways to reach the Zugspitze from the center of Garmisch, both involving a ride on a cog railway and a cable car:

> ✔ The first way begins with a trip on the **Zugspitzbahn** (cog railway), which departs from the back of Garmisch's main railway station daily every hour from 8:35 a.m. to 2:35 p.m. The train travels uphill, past giant boulders and rushing streams, to the *Zugspitzplatte,* a high

plateau with sweeping views. At the Zugspitzplatte, you transfer onto a cable car, the **Gletscherbahn,** for a four-minute ride uphill to the *Zugspitzgipfel* (summit), where you find extraordinary panoramas, a cafe and restaurant, a gift shop, and many alpine trails. Total travel time to the top is about 55 minutes.

✔ The second way to get to the summit of the Zugspitze is to take the **Zugspitzbahn** for a shorter trip, disembarking 14km (9 miles) southwest of Garmisch at the lower station of the **Eibsee Sielbahn** (Eibsee Cable Car). The stop is next to an alpine lake and clearly marked. From here, the cable car carries you to the Zugspitzgipfel. The entire trip takes about 40 minutes. The Eibsee Sielbahn makes runs every half hour from 8:30 a.m. to 4:30 p.m. (5:30 p.m. in July and August).

A round-trip ticket enables you to ascend one way and descend the other for the widest range of spectacular views. The round-trip fare is €43 ($54) for adults, €29.50 ($37) for youths 16 and 17, and €25 ($31) for children ages 6 to 15. A family ticket for two adults and one child costs €96 ($120). For more information, contact the **Bayerische Zugspitzbahn,** Olympiastrasse 27, Garmisch-Partenkirchen (☎ **08821/ 797-900**).

Discovering the local nightlife

From mid-May through September, Bavarian folk music and dancing take place every Saturday night in the **Bayernhalle,** Brauhausstrasse 19. During the same season, the **Garmisch park bandstand** plays host to classical concerts Saturday through Thursday. On Friday, these concerts move to the **Partenkirchen bandstand.** Check with the local tourist office (see "Finding information" earlier in this section) for details about these programs. The twin towns also play host to a five-day **Richard Strauss Festival** in June; the composer lived in Garmisch from 1908 until 1949.

A side trip to Schloss Linderhof: Ludwig's little Versailles

A scenic drive through the Emmertal, a valley flanked by 1,500m to 1,800m (5,000- to 6,000-foot) peaks, takes you to Schloss Linderhof (☎ **08822/ 92030;** www.linderhof.de), the most elaborate of King Ludwig II's fairy-tale palaces. Linderhof is open year-round and makes a wonderful day trip from Munich or Garmisch-Partenkirchen. (See "The Romantic Road" map earlier in this chapter.)

Getting there

If you're **driving** from Munich, take the Munich–Garmisch autobahn (A95) south, turning west on B23 about 5km (3 miles) toward Ettal, and then drive for 13km (8 miles) on the signposted road, passing the hamlet of Graswang on the way.

Oberammergau: Woodcarvers and Passion Plays

An alpine village located 20km (12 miles) north of Garmisch-Partenkirchen, Oberammergau has been famous for its woodcarvers and *Hinterglas* artists since the 15th century. *Hinterglas* (behind glass) painting, an art form unique to Bavaria, Croatia, and parts of Austria, is painting done directly on glass, and in reverse. Every ten years, a crowd from around the world converges on Oberammergau to see the **Passionspiele** (Passion Play).

Competition is fierce for sales of local woodcarvings made in hamlets and farmhouses throughout the region. Most of the carvings are of religious scenes, but you also find drinking or hunting scenes, animals, and folkloric figures. Know before you buy that even some of the most expensive "handmade" pieces may have been carved by machine prior to being finished off by hand. If you're looking for authentic woodcarvings, the following stores are reliable:

- ✔ **Holzschnitzerei Franz Barthels,** Schnitzlergasse 4 (☎ **08822/4271**), sells a wide range of carvings, everything from small figures of saints for €54 ($67) to jumping jacks with movable legs for €36 ($45).

- ✔ **Tony Baur,** Dorfstrasse 27 (☎ **08822/821**), has the most-sophisticated inventory of woodcarvings crafted from maple, pine, and linden. Prices start around €11 ($14) and go up to €5,110 ($6,387).

Actors first performed the famous Passion Play in Oberammergau in 1634 when the town's citizens took a vow to give thanks for being spared from the plague. Locals have performed the 5½-hour, 16-act drama depicting Christ's journey to the Cross every decade since 1680 (the last was in 2000, the next will be in 2010). The cast for this religious epic numbers in the hundreds. Actors must be natives of or have lived in the town for at least 20 years. Performances take place in the **Passionspiel Theater,** Passionswiese 1 (☎ **08822/92310**).

A shuttle bus runs back and forth between Garmisch-Partenkirchen and Oberammergau daily. If you're coming by **car** from Garmisch-Partenkirchen, take E533 north and turn west onto B23 at Oberau.

Exploring Schloss Linderhof

In 1869, King Ludwig II decided to redesign this former royal hunting lodge to resemble the Petit Trianon at Versailles. The rustic lodge was transformed into a small, dazzling-white chateau overloaded with statues and decorations derived from many different periods and countries. The ornate exterior is actually restrained when compared with the interior, which is a riot of neo-rococo flashiness, glittering with gold leaf, mirrors, and crystal chandeliers. For all its ostentation, Linderhof is not without charm, thanks in large part to the beauty of its natural setting in the Ammerberge range and its formal French gardens.

Linderhof is an extremely popular tourist attraction, so arrive early or you may have a long wait. You can see the palace only by guided tour; tours in English are available throughout the day. Your ticket has a specific entry time. A sign at the front of the palace tells you what group is currently being admitted. When your time arrives, feed your ticket through the electronic turnstile to gain entrance. A guide will meet your group outside the castle.

The park contains several small, fanciful buildings, including the **Grotte** (Grotto), inspired by the famous Blue Grotto at Capri. Built of artificial rock, with stalagmites and stalactites dividing the cavelike room into three chambers, the grotto contains an artificial lake fed by an artificial waterfall and a stage hung with a backdrop scene of the first act of Wagner's opera *Tannhäuser*. The original colored-light effects still illuminate the room. On the lake, which had artificial waves, Ludwig kept two swans and a gilded, swan-shaped boat, in which he was rowed about the lake.

The palace and grounds are open April through September daily from 9 a.m. to 6 p.m.; October through March, the Grotto and other park buildings close, but the castle is open daily from 10 a.m. to 4 p.m. Admission in the summer is €7 ($8.75) for adults, €6 ($7.50) for seniors older than 65 and students. Winter admission is €6 ($7.50) for adults, €5 ($6.25) for students and seniors. The parking fee is €2 ($2.50).

Chapter 17

The Bodensee and the Black Forest: Scenic Southwest Delights

In This Chapter

▶ Enjoying the Bodensee, Germany's largest lake
▶ Discovering the island city of Lindau
▶ Exploring the Black Forest
▶ Bathing in Baden-Baden
▶ Wandering through the medieval town of Freiburg

Southwestern Germany is an area rich in scenic splendor. In this corner of the country, you find the Bodensee, one of the great lakes of Europe, and the legendary Black Forest. (See the "The Bodensee [Lake Constance]" map in this chapter.) Atmospheric old towns such as Freiburg share the forest setting with glamorous resorts like Baden-Baden, while towns on the lake bask in an almost Mediterranean balminess. Vineyards and fruit orchards thrive in the region's mild, sunny climate.

The Bodensee (Lake Constance)

What is the proper name, you ask: the Bodensee or Lake Constance? Both names are correct. In Germany, this 74km-long (46-mile) lake in the foothills of the Alps (elevation 395m/1,300 ft.) is called the Bodensee. In Switzerland and Austria, the countries that share its 258km (160 miles) of shoreline, it's called Lake Constance.

The Bodensee is Germany's largest and Central Europe's third-largest lake. The widest point is almost 14km (9 miles) across. Visitors to the Bodensee enjoy the warm climate and stunning scenery. On the north (German) shore, vineyards slope down to crowded marinas, and charming old towns bask in the golden sun. Looking south across the lake, you see the towering, snow-capped Alps. Fierce winds from the mountains

The Bodensee (Lake Constance)

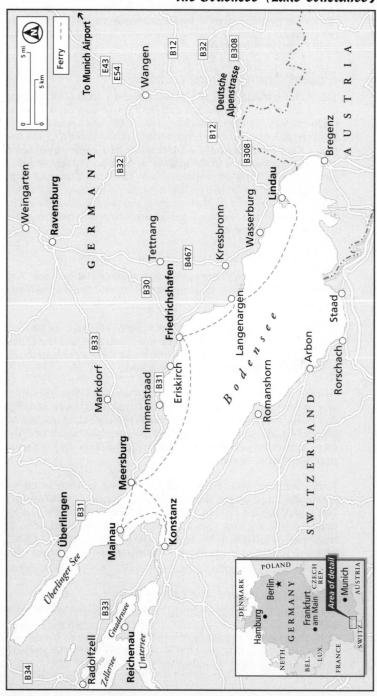

occasionally whip up the waters of the Bodensee, but for the most part the lake is placid. You even find subtropical vegetation growing in sheltered gardens. Lindau, a lovely island city on the northeastern shore, makes a good place to stay.

Lindau: Sunny island charmer

The historic island-town of Lindau, located 179km (111 miles) southwest of Munich at the northeastern corner of the Bodensee, was founded in the ninth century, and for hundreds of years the town was a center of trade between Bavaria, Italy, and Switzerland. The Altstadt, or old town, occupies a small island in the lake (accessible by a causeway); the newer part of Lindau spreads out to the mainland. A town of pretty, flower-bedecked squares and a harbor-side promenade, Lindau is a popular tourist destination that feels a bit like an Italian resort. (See the "Lindau" map in this chapter.) A profusion of gardens gives the town a quasi-Mediterranean air. So many historic buildings line its narrow streets that the entire town is a protected landmark.

Getting to Lindau

Lindau is one of the Bodensee's major transportation hubs. A road bridge and a causeway for walkers and trains connect the town to the mainland.

By **train,** you can get direct connections to Lindau from Munich, Basel, Prague, and Zurich. Lindau is on a major rail line, and the train station is right in the Altstadt across from the harbor. For information and train schedules, call **German Rail** at ☎ **11861.**

By **car** from Munich, take the A96 Autobahn and then B31 into Lindau. If you're driving from Füssen, follow B310 and B308 west, turning south on B12 (Kemptenstrasse). After you cross the causeway, park in one of the large car parks outside the Altstadt, because you won't be able to drive into the historic center. Day and overnight tickets for car parks can be purchased from ticket machines.

From Lindau, you can travel by **boat** to towns in Austria and Switzerland and to Konstanz on the western side of the lake. Several ferries per day link Konstanz with Lindau, stopping at Meersburg and Mainau; the entire trip takes three hours. Check with the tourist office in Lindau or contact **Bodensee-Schiffsbetriebe,** Schützingerweg 2, Lindau (☎ **08382/2754-810;** www.bsb-online.com), and Hafenstrasse 6, Konstanz (☎ **07531/3640-398**).

Finding information and taking a tour

The **Lindau Tourist Information Office,** Ludwigstrasse 68 (☎ **08382/260-030;** www.lindau-tourismus.de), across from the train station, is open Monday through Friday 9 a.m. to 1 p.m. and 2 to 6 p.m., and Saturday and Sunday from 10 a.m. to 2 p.m. (Apr–Oct); winter hours are Monday through Friday 9 a.m. to noon and 2 to 5 p.m.

Lindau

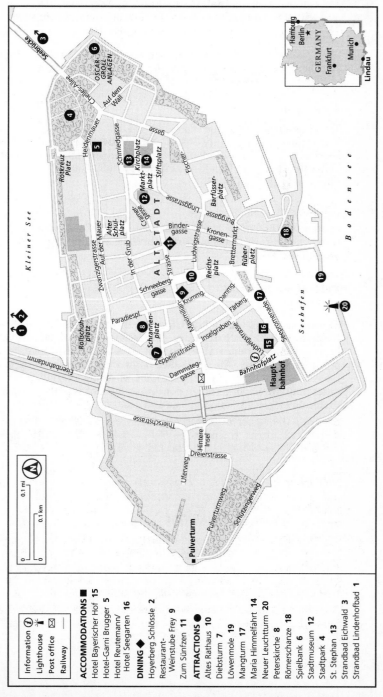

Information ⓘ
Lighthouse ⌖
Post office ⊠
Railway ──────

ACCOMMODATIONS ■
Hotel Bayerischer Hof **15**
Hotel-Garni Brugger **5**
Hotel Reutemann/
Hotel Seegarten **16**

DINING ◆
Hoyerberg Schlössle **2**
Restaurant-
Weinstube Frey **9**
Zum Sünfzen **11**

ATTRACTIONS ●
Altes Rathaus **10**
Diebsturm **7**
Löwenmole **19**
Mangturm **17**
Maria Himmelfahrt **14**
Neuer Leuchtturm **20**
Peterskirche **8**
Römerschanze **18**
Spielbank **6**
Stadtmuseum **12**
Stadtpark **4**
St. Stephan **13**
Strandbad Eichwald **3**
Strandbad Lindenhofbad **1**

You can join a guided **walking tour** on Monday (in English) or Tuesday and Friday mornings (in German) at 10 a.m. from April through October. The group meets in front of the tourist office; the cost is €4 ($5).

For information on **boat trips** around the Bodensee, contact **Bodensee-Schiffsbetriebe** (☎ 08382/2754810). Its harbor-side kiosk has excursion information and timetables.

Getting around Lindau

The charming Altstadt, the island part of Lindau, is flat and easily walkable. The Lindau Stadtbus (City Bus; ☎ 08382/704-242) provides half-hourly service to all parts of Lindau daily from early morning until 10:40 p.m. If you want a taxi, call **Taxi-Ring-Zentrale** (☎ 0800-6006-6666) or **Lindauer Funk-Taxi** (☎ 08382/4455).

Staying in Lindau

See also the listing for **Hotel Reutemann/Hotel Seegarten** ($$–$$$$), which includes the adjacent **Hotel Bayerischer Hof** ($$$–$$$$), in Chapter 22.

Hotel-Garni Brugger
$ Altstadt

This welcoming 23-room hotel, located at the end of the causeway, is the best affordable choice in Lindau. The rooms are up-to-date and furnished in a functional, comfortable, modern style with lots of light. Some open onto a rear balcony. The small, tiled bathrooms have showers (two rooms have tubs and showers). Larger rooms with small sitting areas are in an older building (a glass-roofed conservatory connects the two). The location is an easy walk from the lake and casino.

See map p. 309. Bei der Heidenmauer 11, 88131 Lindau. ☎ *08382/93410. Fax: 08382/4133.* www.hotel-garni-brugger.de. *Rack rates: €86–€92 ($107–$115) double. Rates include continental breakfast. AE, DC, MC, V.*

Dining in Lindau

Hoyerberg Schlössle
$$$$ Mainland   CONTINENTAL

The Hoyerberg Schlössle, located on the mainland about a 15-minute drive from the Altstadt, has few rivals on the Bodensee. You can dine inside or out, with a view of the mountains and lake. Menu offerings vary seasonally but may typically include cream of scampi soup, local perch stuffed with herbs, and saddle of venison with flour dumplings and French beans. Meals here are a memorable experience. The adjoining cafe is more informal.

See map p. 309. Hoyerbergstrasse 64, at Lindau-Aeschach. (From the causeway, take Langenweg and Friedrichshafener Strasse northwest to Hoyerbergstrasse.) ☎ *08382/25295. Reservations required in the restaurant; not required in the cafe. Main courses: €22–€35 ($27–$44). Fixed-price menus: €62–€79 ($77–$98). AE, DC, MC, V. Open: Restaurant Tues–Sun noon to 2 p.m. and 6–10 p.m.; cafe Tues–Sat 2 –4:30 p.m. Closed Jan 15–Feb 28.*

Restaurant-Weinstube Frey
$ Altstadt   GERMAN

The oldest *Stubl* (drinking and dining room) on Maximilianstrasse, Frey's has outdoor tables on the pedestrian street and a small second-floor restaurant with a beamed ceiling and pleasantly old-fashioned ambience. You may want to sample the local Meersburger wines as you dine on chicken breast with raspberry sauce, beef stroganoff, trout baked in a potato crust, or spinach *Spätzle* (a potato-based pasta) baked with cheese and ham. The restaurant can get smoky.

See map p. 309. Maximilianstrasse 15. ☎ *08382/5278. Main courses: €8–€16 ($10–$20). No credit cards. Open: Daily 11 a.m.–2:30 p.m. and 5–11:30 p.m.*

Zum Sünfzen
$–$$ Altstadt   GERMAN/BAVARIAN

This old restaurant at the east end of Maximilianstrasse serves good, dependable food at reasonable prices. Dishes range from schnitzels (breaded veal cutlets), pepper steaks, and roast pork with homemade spätzle to filet of venison. Fresh fish from the Bodensee is a specialty.

See map p. 309. Maximilianstrasse 1. ☎ *08382/5865. Reservations recommended. Main dishes: €10–€20 ($12–$25). AE, DC, MC, V. Open: Daily 10:30 a.m.–11 p.m.*

Exploring Lindau

Lindau is best enjoyed by simply taking a couple of hours to stroll around the **Altstadt.** (See the "Lindau" map in this chapter.) Located almost directly across from the main train station, the town's famous harbor, completed in 1856, is the most attractive on the whole of the Bodensee. Rising from the promenade at the edge of the harbor is the 13th-century tower called the **Mangturm;** the name derives from the laundry, or "mangle house," that once stood beside the tower. Flanking the harbor entrance is the 19th-century **Neuer Leuchtturm** (lighthouse) and the **Löwenmole,** a pillar with a sculpted lion (the symbol of Bavaria) looking out over the lake. You can climb up the narrow spiral staircase of the lighthouse (open daily 9:30 a.m.–5 p.m.; admission €1.60/$2) for a panoramic vista of the Swiss and Austrian Alps across the water. At night, thousands of lights create a magical atmosphere around the harbor.

Located just north of Maximilianstrasse, Lindau's main pedestrian-only thoroughfare, the **Diebsturm** (Thieves' Tower), is the city's most famous landmark. Built around 1370 at the most westerly point of the old town wall, this round tower with projecting upper turrets and oriel windows once served as the town jail (hence its name). The tower is not open to the public. Standing beside the Diebsturm on Schrannenplatz is Lindau's oldest building, the **Peterskirche** (St. Peter's Church; open daily 9 a.m.– 5 p.m.). A rectangular building with a flat wooden ceiling and a tall, square tower, the church was built around A.D. 1000. The interior walls have late-15th-century frescoes by Hans Holbein the Elder. In 1928, the church became a war memorial for the fallen soldiers of World War I (WWI).

Return to Maximilianstrasse and follow the street eastward to the **Altes Rathaus** (Old Town Hall), erected in 1422 and notable for its grandly painted façade of a princely procession. The building's stepped gables are typical of the 15th-century Gothic style, but in the 16th century the building received a Renaissance facelift. Successive eras saw the additions of other architectural styles. The interior, once used as a council hall, houses the centuries-old town library (not open to the general public).

Continuing east on Maximilianstrasse and Cramergasse brings you to the **Marktplatz** (Market Square) with a pretty, flower-bedecked fountain in the center. In a stately, 18th-century baroque town house called the Haus zum Cavazzen, you find the **Stadtmuseum** (Town Museum; ☎ 08382/944-073). The museum contains a large collection of furniture (ranging from Gothic to Art Nouveau), silverware, glassware, tin and ceramic objects, and historical toys, paintings, and sculptures. A special attraction is the collection of mechanical musical instruments, including barrel organs, orchestral instruments, and mechanical pianos. The museum is open April through September Tuesday to Friday from 11 a.m. to 5 p.m., Saturday from 2 to 5 p.m., and Sunday from 11 a.m. to 5 p.m. Admission is €2.50 ($3.10).

On the east side of Marktplatz stand side-by-side Lutheran and Catholic churches. **St. Stephan,** the Lutheran church on the left, has a barrel-vaulted ceiling and a fairly bare interior. **Maria Himmelfahrt** (Church of the Ascension), the Catholic church on the right, is full of baroque decoration and has a frescoed ceiling. The churches generally are open from 8 a.m. to 5 p.m.

Continuing east from Marktplatz on Schmiedgasse, you come to the waterside **Stadtpark** (City Park) with its modern **Spielbank** (casino).

Enjoying lakeside activities

For as little as €9 ($11) you can rent a bike (*Fahrrad,* pronounced *fa*-rahd) and go cycling along the shores of the Bodensee. The bike-rental office, **Fahrrad-Station-Lindau** (☎ 08382/21261), in the train station, is open Monday through Friday from 9 a.m. to 1 p.m. and from 2 to 6 p.m., and Saturday from 9:30 a.m. to 7 p.m. **Lindenhofpark,** on the mainland, is the most scenic area for biking.

Three lakeside beaches (a beach is a *Strandbad,* pronounced *strahnd-*
bod) are open in summer Monday through Friday from 10:30 a.m. to
7:30 p.m. and Saturday and Sunday from 10 a.m. to 8 p.m. The biggest
beach is **Strandbad Eichwald** (☎ **08283/5539**), with a grassy lakeside
area and three heated swimming pools. The location is about a ½-hour
walk east along Uferweg, on the mainland, or take bus No. 1 or No. 2 to
Anheggerstrasse, then bus No. 3 to Karmelbuckel. Admission to the beach
is €2.55 ($3.20) for adults, €1.55 ($1.90) for children. **Römerschanze**
(☎ **08283/6830**), a smaller beach popular with families, is located next
to Lindau harbor in the Altstadt; this beach charges the same rates
as the beach at Eichwald. The third beach, **Strandbad Lindenhofbad**
(☎ **08283/6637**), is located in Lindenhof Park on the mainland, west of
the causeway. To reach it, take bus No. 1 or No. 2 to Anheggerstrasse,
then bus No. 4 to Alwind. Admission is €2.05 ($2.60) for adults and €1.30
($1.60) for children.

Taking a turn at the tables

At Lindau's glitzy new **Spielbank** (*shpeel*-bank; casino), Oskar-Groll-
Anlage 6 (☎ **08382/27740**), you can play slot machines from noon to
2 a.m. and blackjack and roulette from 3 p.m. to 2 a.m. Admission is
€2.55 ($3.20), and a passport is required as proof of age. Appropriate
attire is a cut above casual: Men should wear a jacket and tie, and
women, something dressy.

Mainau: A day trip from Lindau

The island of Mainau, famed for its subtropical gardens, makes for a
pleasant day trip from Lindau. (See "The Schwarzwald [Black Forest]"
map in this chapter.) If you're driving through this part of southern
Germany, you may want to stop at Mainau on your way to or from
Freiburg in the Black Forest (see "Freiburg: Little brooks and lots of
books" later in this chapter).

Getting to Mainau

Bodensee-Schiffsbetriebe, Schützingerweg 2, Lindau (☎ **08382/2754-
810;** www.bsb-online.com), provides daily passenger service by **boat**
between Lindau, Mainau, and Konstanz, the largest city on the Bodensee.
A one-way fare from Lindau to Mainau is €9.80 ($12). You can also drive
west from Lindau to Meersburg, on the lake's north shore, and catch a
car-ferry to Mainau. The cost is €3 ($3.75) for adults and €1.50 ($1.90)
for children. Car fees range from €4.65 to €9.30 ($5.80 to $12), depending
on the size of your car. Generally, from 8:30 a.m. to 11 p.m., two ferries
per hour make the 4.2km (2½-mile) crossing (one per hour through the
night) to Konstanz; not all of them stop at Mainau, so check before
boarding. Service is less frequent on Saturdays, Sundays, and holidays.
Contact **Autofähre Konstanz-Meersburg** (☎ **07531/803-666**) for information and schedules.

If you're **driving,** you can park and leave your car in Meersburg, hop on the ferry, and easily walk through Mainau. This is the best (and only) way to see Mainau, because cars are restricted on the island.

Visiting the island of Mainau

The semitropical island of Mainau, where palms and orange trees grow and fragrant flowers bloom year-round, lies 6km (4 miles) north of Konstanz, in an arm of the Bodensee known as the Überlingersee. The **baroque castle** that forms the centerpiece of the island once was a residence of the Knights of the Teutonic Order. In 1853, Grand Duke Friedrich I of Baden purchased the island as a summer residence. A passionate plant lover, he laid the foundations for the **Arboretum,** the **Rose Garden,** and the **Orangery,** gardens that his great-grandchild, Count Lennart Bernadotte, the current owner of this 110-acre botanical wonderland, would later develop. Palms, citrus and fruit trees, orchids, azaleas, rhododendrons, tens of thousands of tulips in the spring, and roses in the summer fill the gardens. Butterflies from throughout the world flit and flutter through the **Butterfly House.** The island has a Mediterranean luxuriance that invites leisurely strolling.

The island's gardens are open daily year-round. From October 20 through March 25, hours are 9 a.m. to 6 p.m. From April 1 through October 21, hours are 7 a.m. to 8 p.m. Summer admission is €11 ($14) for adults, €9.60 ($12) for seniors older than 65, €5.40 ($6.75) for students, €3 ($3.75) for children, €21 ($26) for family (parents and children up to 15). Admission during the rest of the year is €5.50 ($6.90) for adults and free for children up to age 15. Admission includes the gardens, the Butterfly House, the Palm House, and an exhibition on Lake Constance in the castle.

From April through mid-October, several places on the island are open daily for dining or a quick snack. The island's culinary highpoint is the **Schwedenschenke** (☎ 07531/303-156; open 11 a.m. to 10 p.m.), which features seasonal specialties such as asparagus in the spring, chanterelle mushrooms in late summer, and game dishes in the fall. Casual dining options include the Butterfly Bistro (open 10 a.m.–8 p.m.) and the Castle Café (open 11 a.m.–6 p.m.)

For more information, call ☎ 07531/3030. Give yourself at least two hours to explore and enjoy the island.

The Schwarzwald (Black Forest)

Travelers to the Schwarzwald (*schvahrtz*-vald), or Black Forest, come to two cities in particular: Baden-Baden, a spa resort with thermal waters and an elegant casino, and the medieval university town of Freiburg. (See the "The Schwarzwald [Black Forest]" map in this chapter.) For the Germans themselves, however, the mountainous, legend-filled forest is a favorite place to spend holidays outdoors, amid nature. Villages with half-timbered buildings, hiking trails, and pretty spots where stressed-out city dwellers take *die Kur* (the cure) at health resorts fill the pine- and

The Schwarzwald (Black Forest)

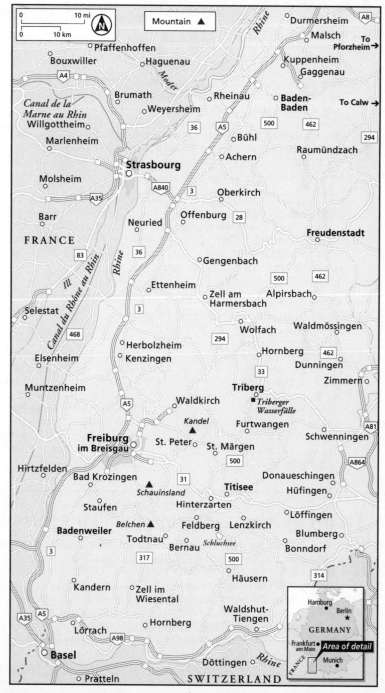

spruce-filled forest, which dominates the southwestern corner of Germany. The Black Forest, about 145km (90 miles) long and 40km (25 miles) wide, runs parallel to the Rhine, which serves as a boundary with Switzerland to the south and France to the west. The Bodensee (Lake Constance) adjoins the forest to the east.

Visitors with limited time generally skip the area's cure and sports aspects and focus instead on the scenic pleasures of the Schwarzwald, long associated with legends, fairy tales, and cuckoo clocks.

The name "Black Forest" is a translation of the Latin *Silva Nigra,* the name given to the forest by Romans some 2,000 years ago. Why did they call it that? Because from a distance the dark green pine and fir trees look black.

You can explore the Black Forest in many ways. You can easily reach Baden-Baden and Freiburg, the two towns I recommend as overnights, by train. Having a car opens up more of the countryside. One of the most popular auto trips is from Baden-Baden to Freudenstadt on the **Schwarzwald Hochstrasse** (Black Forest High Road; B500), which runs almost the entire length of the forest.

Baden-Baden: Germany's premier spa town

Baden-Baden is one of the world's most famous spa resorts. The thermal springs bubbling up from beneath the town have been healing aches and pains for more than 2,000 years. The composition of the slightly radioactive mineral water is almost the same today as when the Romans built the first bath complexes here in the third century. Even the Roman emperor Caracalla traveled to this part of the Black Forest to get some relief from his arthritis. In the 19th century, European nobility and clients such as Queen Victoria and Kaiser Wilhelm I rediscovered Baden-Baden's waters, and Napoléon III gave the town a glamorous new aristocratic cachet. The personalities of the day — artists like Berlioz, Brahms, and Dostoyevsky — also helped to make Baden-Baden the most elegant and sophisticated playground in Germany.

From cake to sausage: Black Forest treats

Maybe you've heard of that famous thick, chocolatey cake flavored with cherry preserves and called *Schwarzwälder Kirschtorte* (Black Forest Cherry Cake). The famous cake is one of the specialties of a region that's something of a culinary crossroads. The forest's proximity to France and Switzerland has influenced the cooking you find in many Black Forest restaurants. If you want to sample other regional specialties, look for *Zwetchgentorte* (plum pastry), *Zwiebelkuchen* (onion tart), *Schwarzwald Schinken* (Black Forest smoked ham), meat and fowl dishes with creamy sauces, and wild game such as venison and boar. Most restaurants make their own *Hauswurst* (sausage) and guard the recipe.

Baden-Baden

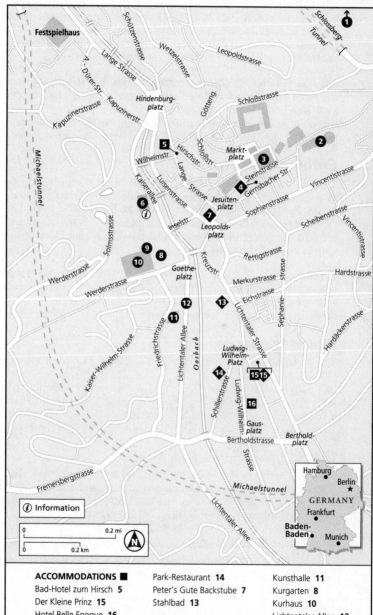

ACCOMMODATIONS ■
Bad-Hotel zum Hirsch **5**
Der Kleine Prinz **15**
Hotel Belle Epoque **16**

DINING ◆
Der Kleine Prinz **15**
Münchner Löwenbräu **4**

Park-Restaurant **14**
Peter's Gute Backstube **7**
Stahlbad **13**

ATTRACTIONS ●
Altes Schloss **1**
Caracalla-Therme **2**
Friedrichsbad **3**

Kunsthalle **11**
Kurgarten **8**
Kurhaus **10**
Lichtentaler Allee **12**
Spielbank **9**
Trinkhalle **6**

Baden-Baden still evokes that aura of 19th-century privilege. The town has the most up-to-date spa facilities in Germany, and people still flock here to soak and be healed of various ailments and to try their luck in the famous casino. If you're not into a health regimen or interested in gambling, you may find Baden-Baden a bit boring-boring.

Located 174km (108 miles) south of Frankfurt in the northern portion of the Black Forest, Baden-Baden attracts many sports and outdoor enthusiasts, who come to hike, golf, play tennis, and ride horses. The horseracing season at nearby **Iffezheim,** one of *the* summer sporting events in Europe, takes place in August. (See the "Baden-Baden" map in this chapter.)

Getting to Baden-Baden

You can easily reach Baden-Baden by **train** from anywhere in Germany. Trip time from Munich is about four hours; from Frankfurt, about three hours. For train information, call **German Rail** at ☎ **11861.** The Bahnhof (railway station) is at Baden-Oos, about 5km (3 miles) north of town. To get into the center of town, you take bus No. 201 or a taxi, always available in front of the station.

For those with a **car,** the A5 Autobahn between Basel and Frankfurt runs north–south through the entire region, and the A8 Autobahn runs east–west, connecting Baden-Baden to Munich. The drive south from Frankfurt takes about two hours; from Munich, about four hours.

Finding information

The **Tourist Information Office** in the Trinkhalle, Kaiser Allee 3 (☎ **07221/275-200;** www.baden-baden.com), is open daily from 9 a.m. to 7 p.m. It has a complete schedule of events and information on town and regional attractions. If you're driving into town, you can easily access a second tourist office outside the center, on Schwarzwaldstrasse 52 (same phone, same hours). Both offices offer a free hotel-booking service.

Getting around Baden-Baden

After you arrive in Baden-Baden, you can walk everywhere. Bus No. 201, which runs at ten-minute intervals, connects the railway station to most of the sites in town. A one-way fare is €1.80 ($2.25); purchase tickets from the driver or from ticket machines at bus stops.

Staying in Baden-Baden

See also Chapter 22 for descriptions of the outstanding **Der Kleine Prinz** ($$$–$$$$) and **Hotel Belle Epoque** ($$$–$$$$).

Bad-Hotel zum Hirsch
$$–$$$

Several buildings in the heart of the Old Town were joined to make this tranquil, old-fashioned hotel. The 59 large, old-fashioned rooms are individually furnished with 19th-century antiques. Many of them have balconies and piped-in thermal water. You find an on-site sauna and water-cure facility.

See map p. 317. Hirschstrasse 1, 76530 Baden-Baden. ☎ 800/223-5652 in the U.S. and Canada or 07221/9390. Fax: 07221/38148. Bus: 201. Rack rates: €138–€150 ($172–$187) double. Rates include buffet breakfast. AE, DC, DISC, MC, V.

Dining in Baden-Baden

Der Kleine Prinz
$$$ FRENCH/REGIONAL

The restaurant in the hotel Der Kleine Prinz ("The Little Prince") is one of the finest in the entire region, and a meal in the intimate dining room served by the highly polished but friendly staff is a memorable experience. Everything is homemade from the best and freshest local ingredients, and menu offerings change daily. Try one of the tasting menus. You can begin with assorted appetizers, move on to goose-liver parfait with mushroom salad, followed by a fish soup with cheese dumplings and leg of venison with cranberry sauce, and finish with fresh strawberries and homemade ice cream.

See map p. 317. In the hotel Der Kleine Prinz, Lichtentaler Strasse 36. ☎ 07221/3464. Bus: 201. Main courses: €15–€28 ($19–$35). Tasting menus: €52–€70 ($65–$87). AE, DC, MC, V. Open: Daily noon to 2 p.m., 7–10 p.m.

Münchner Löwenbräu
$–$$ GERMAN/BAVARIAN

This restaurant serves simple, affordable, and well-prepared food in two settings: on a romantic terrace beneath linden trees or in an indoor dining room with curved, glass walls. Many kinds of German sausage are on the menu with Bavarian specialties and a wide selection of cheeses. Regional devotees order pork knuckles fresh from the grill. For dessert, try the apple fritters. The restaurant also has a popular beer garden.

See map p. 317. Gernsbacher Strasse 9 (in the Altstadt). ☎ 07221/22311. Bus: 201. Main courses: €6–€16 ($7.50–$20). AE, DC, V. Open: Daily 10 a.m.–11:30 p.m.

Park-Restaurant
$$$$ INTERNATIONAL/RHINELAND

This fancy, high-priced restaurant in the glamorous Brenner's Park Hotel is one of the renowned hotel dining rooms of Europe. The emphasis is on French (Alsatian) dishes, along with regional Rhine Valley foods. Specialties include sauteed goose liver, roast saddle of venison or lamb, and grilled lobster and fish. For dessert, try an ice-cream soufflé.

See map p. 317. In Brenner's Park Hotel, Schillerstrasse 4. ☎ 07221/900-890. Bus: 201. Reservations required. Main courses: €29–€32 ($35–$40). AE, DC, MC, V. Open: Wed–Mon 7–9:30 p.m.

Peter's Gute Backstube
$ PIZZA/LIGHT MEALS

Restaurants in Baden-Baden tend to be pricey, so it's good to know about this inexpensive cafe on busy Leopoldsplatz. Duck in here for a breakfast of eggs and ham, a slice of pizza, or a lunch-time sandwich. I also recommend stopping for a slice of afternoon *Kuchen* (cake); the coffee (all you can drink for €1.75/$2.10) is very good. Pete's can't be beat for cheap, quickly served food, although the atmosphere is like a fast-food restaurant.

See map p. 317. Sophienstrasse 10–12. ☎ 07221/392-817. Bus: 201. Breakfast €5–7 ($6.25–$8.75); Sandwiches: €3 ($3.75). No credit cards. Open: Mon–Fri 6:30 a.m.–7 p.m., Sat 6:30 a.m.–6 p.m., Sun 8 a.m.–7 p.m.

Stahlbad
$$$–$$$$ CONTINENTAL

In the center of town, this elegant restaurant with a garden terrace is a tranquil and charming place to dine. The atmosphere and décor, including prints, copper vessels, antique pewter plates, mugs, and engravings, evoke a tavern. Continental specialties include pepper steak and seasonal venison steak, fresh fish, warm goose liver with Calvados sauce, and lobster salad.

See map p. 317. Augustaplatz 2. ☎ 07221/24569. Bus: 201. Reservations required. Main courses: €18–€30 ($22–$37). AE, DC, MC, V. Open: Tues–Sun noon to 2 p.m. and 6–10 p.m.

Exploring Baden-Baden

When it comes to tourist destinations, Baden-Baden isn't a demanding town, with major museums and important historic sights that you must see. (See the "Baden-Baden" map in this chapter.) The pace is relaxed, and the streets are geared toward pleasurable strolls and upscale shopping. I recommend that you visit one of the bath complexes (see "Bathing in Baden-Baden" later in this chapter) and then spend a couple of hours wandering through the Altstadt.

The **City-Bahn** (☎ 07221/991-998; www.citybahn.de) is a sightseeing train that makes stops at all of Baden-Baden's major attractions. The train runs daily from 9:30 a.m. to about 5 p.m., making stops at the Kurhaus, Lichtentaler Allee, the Caracalla Baths, and other spots. Tickets cost €4.50 ($5.60) for adults and €2.50 ($3.10) for children 5 to 15. English commentary is available on a headset.

The time-honored center of activity is **Lichtentaler Allee,** an elegant park promenade lined with rhododendrons, azaleas, roses, and ornamental trees set along the bank of the narrow Oosbach River (called the Oos; pronounced *ohs*). At the north end of the promenade are the formally landscaped grounds of the **Kurgarten** and the neoclassical **Kurhaus,** one of the town's most important buildings. Originally, the building was a "Promenade House," where the rich and prominent came to see and be seen. In the 1820s, the Kurhaus was turned into a "Conversation House," a place for more-formal gatherings and events. The site has remained the hub of Baden-Baden's social scene ever since, used for receptions and galas. The Kurhaus does not, as you may think, contain spa facilities; the right wing of the building is Baden-Baden's casino (see the next paragraph), and the left wing houses a large, lavish restaurant with a terrace overlooking the gardens with their shop-lined colonnades, concert shell, and gas lights lit and extinguished by hand every day.

Marlene Dietrich, the glamorous film star, once remarked, "The most beautiful casino in the whole world is in Baden-Baden — and I have seen them all." You can see for yourself by visiting the famous Baden-Baden **Spielbank** (Casino), Kaiserallee 1 (☎ **07221/21060**), Germany's oldest casino, in operation for more than 200 years. (The Russian writer Dostoyevsky wrote *The Gambler* based on his disastrous experience at the tables here.) This casino is definitely not the kind of glitzy, informal, slot-machine-haven you find in Las Vegas. The various casino rooms were designed in the style of an elegant French château. Men must wear jackets and ties; women, classy eveningwear. Guests can play French and American roulette, baccarat, blackjack, poker, and other games. Minimum bets are €5 ($6.25). Maximum bets are €10,000. To enter the casino, you must possess a valid passport and be at least 21 years old. The casino is open for gambling daily from 2 p.m. to 2 a.m. (until 3 a.m. Fri–Sat). Admission is €3 ($3.75). You find slot machines, a very recent addition, in the vaulted cellars of the Kurhaus in attractive new rooms, which also contain roulette, poker, blackjack, and bingo machines.

 If you don't want to gamble, you can take a guided tour of the historic gaming rooms daily, every 30 minutes, between 9:30 a.m. and noon. (Oct–Mar 10 a.m. to noon). The tour costs €4 ($5). Arrange in advance for tours in English.

In the Kurhaus gardens, you also find the **Trinkhalle** (Pump Room), Kaiserallee 3 (☎ **07221/275-200**), a large hall built in the 1840s, surrounded by an open walkway and decorated with frescoes depicting Black Forest legends. The building, where guests once sipped the salty, slightly radioactive waters of Baden-Baden, now is used as the main tourist office (see "Finding information" earlier in this section about Baden-Baden).

The **Kunsthalle** (State Art Gallery), Lichtentaler Allee 8a (☎ **07221/ 23250**), completed in 1909, showcases visiting contemporary art exhibits. A new wing, opened in 2004, houses an impressive collection of modern paintings and sculptures bequeathed by Baden-Baden collector Frieder Burda. The gallery is open Tuesday through Sunday from 11 a.m. to 6 p.m. (Wed until 8 p.m.). Admission is €5 ($6.25) for adults and €3 ($3.75) for students.

The **Altes Schloss** (Old Palace), a ruined castle originally called Hochbaden (High Baden), is located on a hillside above town. From the 11th to the 15th centuries, Hochbaden was the seat of the margraves of Baden. You get a nice view of the town and the Black Forest from this fortresslike structure. Admission is free.

Bathing in Baden-Baden

Getting into hot water is what Baden-Baden is all about. At the **Caracalla-Therme** (Caracalla Baths), Römerplatz 1 (☎ **07221/275-940**), you decide on your own bath regimen. The slightly radioactive water, rich in sodium chloride, bubbles up from artesian wells at a temperature of about 160°F (70°C). Bathers usually begin in cooler pools, working up to the warm water. The baths also have a sauna area. You must wear bathing suits in the pools, but the scene is *au naturel* in the saunas. Medicinal treatment includes mud baths, massages, and whirlpools. The facility has a bar and a cafeteria. Admission is €12 ($15) for two hours. The baths are open daily from 8 a.m. to 10 p.m.

Friedrichsbad, Römerplatz 1 (☎ **07221/275-920**), dates back to 1877 and follows an ancient Roman-Irish bath method. The complete bath program, which takes about three hours, involves a shower, two saunas, a brush massage, thermal steam baths, and three freshwater baths ranging from warm to 60 °F (15 °C), followed by a 30-minute period of rest and relaxation. After experiencing the Friedrichsbad, you better understand what Mark Twain meant when he said, "Here at Baden-Baden's Friedrichsbad you lose track of time in 10 minutes and track of the world in 20." Admission is €21 ($26) for three hours without massage, €29 ($36) with soap-brush massage (3½ hours). The baths are open Monday through Saturday from 9 a.m. to 10 p.m. and Sunday from noon to 8 p.m. (last admission is two hours before closing). *Note:* Clothes may not be worn in the Friedrichsbad, and women and men share the pools.

Shopping in Baden-Baden

Sophienstrasse and **Gernsbacher Strasse,** lined with some of the most expensive boutiques in Germany, are part of a flower-flanked pedestrian zone. This is where you buy those elegant duds required to enter the casino. The women's wear available at **Escada Boutique,** Sophienstrasse 18 (☎ **07221/390-448**), is created by one of Germany's most emulated designers. Another shop, **Münchner Moden,** Lichtentalerstrasse 13 (☎ **07221/31090**), carries women's designs in loden-colored wool during autumn and winter, and offers Austrian and Bavarian silks, linens, and cottons during warmer months. The best men's store, **Herrenkommode,** Sophienstrasse 16 (☎ **07221/29292**), is a bit more international, focusing on designers Giorgio Armani and Renee Lazard.

Leather goods by Gold Pfiel and other manufacturers are sold at **Inka,** Sophienstrasse 26 (☎ **07221/23955**), where the inventory includes luggage, wallets, and handbags. Cuckoo clocks, puppets, and other locally produced items can be found at **Boulevard,** Lichtentaler Strasse 21 (☎ **07221/24495**). **Schwarzwald Bienen-Honig-Haus,** Langestrasse 38 (☎ **07221/31453**), carries beeswax- and honey-based products such as candles, cosmetics, candies, schnapps, and wine, plus many varieties of bottled honey.

Discovering the performing arts in Baden-Baden

Baden-Baden's 2,500-seat **Festspielhaus** (Festival Hall), Beim Alten Bahnhof 2 (☎ **07221/301-3101**), opened in 1998. The building is the second-largest opera and concert hall in Europe. The hall presents classical music concerts, operas, and ballets throughout the year.

Freiburg: Little brooks and lots of books

With a population of about 200,000 residents (and an additional 30,000 students), Freiburg is the largest city in the Schwarzwald and considered to be its capital. Only 111km (69 miles) southwest of Baden-Baden, this picturesque city with its medieval Altstadt, nestles in a plain below high mountain peaks. The town is called Freiburg im (in) Breisgau to distinguish it from other German and Swiss Freiburgs. Breisgau, now part of the German state of Baden-Württemberg but once part of the Roman Empire, is a historical region stretching from the Rhine to the Black Forest.

Although surrounded by alpine scenery, Freiburg enjoys the benefits of warm air currents that come up from the Mediterranean through Burgundy. In the summer, the days can get very hot, but a cool mountain breeze called the *Höllentaler* flows down into the town like clockwork twice every night between 7 and 7:30 and 9 and 9:30 p.m., cooling things down. The Altstadt's splashing fountains and shallow, fast-flowing streams called *Bächle* (little brooks) that run alongside the streets in stone-lined channels are ancient cooling systems. Freiburg bursts with springtime blooms while snow still covers the surrounding peaks, and in autumn, the smell of new wine fills the narrow streets even as snow is already falling on those nearby summits.

Wine? Yes, surrounding the city are 1,600 acres of vineyards, more than you find near any other city in Germany. And winegrowing always requires celebrations. In Freiburg, on the last weekend in June, a four-day public wine-tasting festival takes place in the Münsterplatz, the square outside Freiburg's magnificent Gothic cathedral.

 Festivals are a year-round part of life in Freiburg. Their pre-Lenten carnival called *Fasnet* is one of the best in Germany, with bonfires and parades. The May *Frühlingsmess* (Spring Fair) and October *Herbstmesse* (Autumn Fair) both last ten days. *Weinkost* is a long wine-tasting event in mid-August. And in June, the city plays host to the two-week-long *Zeltmusik festival* (Tent Music Festival), with performances in giant outdoor tents.

If you're traveling in the Black Forest, Freiburg makes for an atmospheric overnight stay. Although the town was heavily damaged during World War II (WWII), including by a bombing in error by the German Luftwaffe, Freiburg's medieval charm has been preserved. Wandering through its ancient streets is a pleasure at any time of year, and exploring the sights in the surrounding Schwarzwald is easy and fun. The large student presence adds a lively, youthful edge to the old city. (See the "Freiburg" map in this chapter.)

Getting to Freiburg

Frequent **trains** connect Freiburg to Baden-Baden and other cities throughout Germany and Europe. The train trip from Frankfurt takes about two hours; from Hamburg, about eight hours. For train information, call German Rail at ☎ **11861.**

For those coming by **car,** the A5 Autobahn runs north and south through the Black Forest, providing access to Freiburg. If you're driving from the Bodensee (Lake Constance), take B31 west.

Finding information

The **Tourist Information Office,** Rotteckring 14 (☎ **0761/388-1880;** www.freiburg.de), is open June through September, Monday through Friday 10 a.m. to 8 p.m., Saturday 10 a.m. to 5:30 p.m., Sunday 10 a.m. to noon; October through May, Monday to Friday 10 a.m. to 6 p.m., Saturday 10 a.m. to 2 p.m., Sunday 10 a.m. to noon.

Getting around Freiburg

The Altstadt, where you find all the major attractions, is easily walkable. **RVF** (☎ **0761/207-280**) operates the city's bus and tram system. A one-way fare costs €1.90 ($2.40); a day ticket costs €4.70 ($5.90). **Plus-Punkt,** Salzstrasse 3 (☎ **0761/451-1500**) in the Altstadt, has schedules and information, and sells passes. The office is open Monday through Friday from 8 a.m. to 7 p.m. and Saturday from 8 a.m. to 2 p.m.

Staying in Freiburg

Rappen
$-$$ Altstadt

The best rooms in this charming, low-key, 20-room inn have smack-dab views of Freiburg's mighty cathedral, located right outside. Rooms are generally on the small side and simply but comfortably furnished. The units with private bathrooms have showers. You find plenty of activity right outside the hotel on Münsterplatz, site of a big weekday outdoor market.

See map p. 325. Münsterplatz 13, 79098 Freiburg. ☎ *0761/31353. Fax: 0761/382-252. www.hotelrappen.de. Rack rates: €110 ($137) double with bath, €70 ($87) double without bath. Rates include buffet breakfast. AE, DC, MC, V. All trams stop just behind the hotel.*

Zum Roten Bären
$$-$$$ Altstadt

Zum Roten Bären, which means "At the Red Bear," is the oldest inn in Germany, with a pretty painted façade and a list of innkeepers that goes back to the 14th century. This wonderfully atmospheric and unpretentious inn

Freiburg

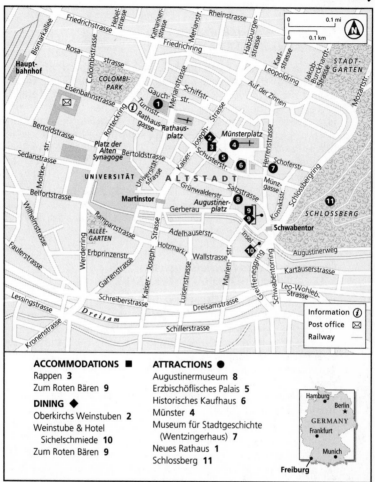

ACCOMMODATIONS ■
Rappen **3**
Zum Roten Bären **9**

DINING ◆
Oberkirchs Weinstuben **2**
Weinstube & Hotel
  Sichelschmiede **10**
Zum Roten Bären **9**

ATTRACTIONS ●
Augustinermuseum **8**
Erzbischöflisches Palais **5**
Historisches Kaufhaus **6**
Münster **4**
Museum für Stadtgeschichte
  (Wentzingerhaus) **7**
Neues Rathaus **1**
Schlossberg **11**

has only 25 rooms and one of the best restaurants in Freiburg for traditional Black Forest fare and regional wines from the nearby Kaiserstühl vineyards (see the next section about "Dining in Freiburg"). Rooms in the older section have more charm; those in the modern wing have little balconies overlooking leafy gardens and red-tiled rooftops. Standing just outside the hotel is one of Freiburg's medieval gateways, and the surrounding neighborhood is wonderfully picturesque.

See map p. 325. Oberlinden 12, 79098 Freiburg. ☎ *0761/387-870.* www.roter-baeren.de. *Rack rates: €138–€148 ($172–$185) double. Rates include breakfast. AE, DC, MC, V.*

Dining in Freiburg

Oberkirchs Weinstuben
$-$$ **Altstadt** **GERMAN**

This historic wine tavern on Freiburg's busy Münsterplatz, or Cathedral Square, provides good regional cooking and comfortable rooms. You can dine in the *Weinstube* (wine tavern) with its ceiling-high ceramic stove or at a table on the square. This place serves hearty portions of good, old-fashioned food: tasty soups (bean, pea, or vegetable), meat dishes (veal schnitzel, pork filets in morel cream sauce), poultry, and seasonal dishes like pheasant. Above the Weinstube, 25 rooms all have private bathrooms or showers. Doubles range from €126 to €147 ($157 to $184), including continental breakfast.

See map p. 325. Münsterplatz 22, 79098 Freiburg. ☎ *0761/202-6868. Fax: 0761/202-6869. Reservations recommended. Main courses: €11–€23 ($14–$29). Fixed-price menus: €16–€19 ($20–$24). AE, MC, V. Open: Mon–Sat noon to 2 p.m. and 6:30–9:15 p.m. Closed Jan. Tram: 1, 4, or 5.*

Weinstube & Hotel Sichelschmiede
$-$$ **Altstadt** **REGIONAL/INTERNATIONAL**

For outdoor summer dining, this *Weinstube* is the most picturesque and romantic spot in Freiburg. The tavern sits on a small square flanked by a rushing *Bächle* (little brook) and horsechestnut trees. The good food arrives in extremely large portions. The chef's daily recommendation may be cream of tomato soup, a salad with smoked lox, or tagliatelle with shrimps. This place is a good one for trying *Zwiebel* (onion) dishes, a specialty of the region. *Zwiebelschmelze* is a spinach-and-vegetable-filled ravioli covered with sauteed onions. A simpler *Vesperkarte* (late-evening menu) is available from 10 p.m. to midnight.

See map p. 325. MapInsel 1. ☎ *0761/35037. Main courses: €8–€15 ($10–$19). MC, V. Open: daily noon to midnight. Tram: 1.*

Zum Roten Bären
$$-$$$ **Altstadt** **GERMAN/REGIONAL**

The "Red Bear" has one of the best kitchens in Freiburg and one of the most authentically atmospheric dining rooms, where you can sample seasonal dishes, such as *Spargel* (white asparagus), available in May and June. The *Spargelpfannkuchen* is asparagus served with a special pancake, cooked ham, and Hollandaise sauce. A young Rivaner wine, grown on the nearby Kaiserstühl vineyards, is a light, fruity accompaniment. The menu presents a full array of wonderfully prepared dishes using local ingredients.

See map p. 325. In the hotel Zum Roten Bären, Oberlinden 12 (just inside the Schwabentor). ☎ *0761/387-870. Main courses: €11–€20 ($14–$25). Fixed-price menus: €30 ($38), €40 ($50). AE, DC, MC, V. Open: Mon–Sat noon to 3 p.m. and 6:30–11:30 p.m. Tram: 1.*

Exploring Freiburg

Most of what you want to see is in the **Altstadt,** an area bounded by the Hauptbahnhof (main train station) on the west side of the inner city, the Dreisam river on the south, and a wooded hill called the Schlossberg on the east. This part of town is medieval Freiburg at its most appealing. Give yourself at least two hours to stroll and poke around. (See the "Freiburg" map in this chapter.)

All visitors eventually congregate in the **Münsterplatz** (Cathedral Square), site of Freiburg's rose-colored **Münster** (Cathedral; ☎ **0761/202-790;** Tram: 4, 5, or 6), one of Germany's masterpieces of Gothic architecture. The cathedral was begun in 1200 in the Romanesque style, but by the time the structure was completed in 1620, Gothic elements had been incorporated into the design. Its West Tower, a magnificent openwork spire atop an open octagonal belfry, is one of the most beautiful in Germany. Gargoyles peer down from the tower's roof, one of them with its backside turned toward the archbishop's house across the square, supposedly a sign of the architect's contempt for the city fathers. The cathedral contains some superb stained-glass windows; the earliest, dating from the 13th century, are in the south chancel. Admission to the cathedral is free. The building is open Monday through Saturday from 10 a.m. to 6 p.m. and Sunday 1 to 6 p.m.

 For a wonderful view of Freiburg and the distant mountains, you can climb to the top of the Münster's famous West Tower. From April through October, the tower is open Monday through Saturday from 9:30 a.m. to 5 p.m., Sunday from 1 to 5 p.m.; November through March, closed Monday.

A trio of historic buildings stands along the south side of Münsterplatz, across from the cathedral. The mid-18th-century **Erzbischöfliches Palais** (Archbishop's Palace) has a pale-yellow façade and an ornate wrought-iron balcony. The oxblood-colored **Historisches Kaufhaus** (Historical Department Store), a Gothic emporium with protruding, pointed-roof watchtowers and a 16th-century gallery decorated with the statues of four Habsburg emperors, is still used as the town's official reception hall. The third building to the left of the Historisches Kaufhaus is the Baroque **Wentzingerhaus,** built in 1761 for a local painter and sculptor and now home to the **Museum für Stadtgeschichte** (Town History Museum; ☎ **0761/201-2515**), open Tuesday through Sunday from 10 a.m. to 5 p.m.; admission is €2 ($2.50).

Chestnut trees and a fountain add to the charm of **Rathausplatz,** another busy square just west of the cathedral. On the west side of the square is Freiburg's **Neues Rathaus** (New Town Hall), comprised of two highly decorated 16th-century merchants' houses connected by an arcade.

The Bächle of Freiburg

To help the town stay cool in the hot summer sun, Freiburg has many lovely old fountains and a unique system of streams called *Bächle* (little brooks) that date back to the 12th century. The brooks channel water from the Dreisam River through the old university town. They were first devised to keep the city clean and to help fight fires. You can see the Bächle running alongside many Altstadt streets. According to local folklore, if you step in a Bächle, you must marry a person from Frieburg.

East of the university you find the **Martinstor** (St. Martin's Gate), one of two surviving gates from the Middle Ages, when Freiburg was a walled city. The **Schwabentor** (Swabian Gate), the other city gate, dates from around 1200 and stands on the southeast edge of the Altstadt, near the Schlossberg. Paintings on the tower include one of St. George, the city's patron saint. The neighborhood around the Schwabentor is called the **Insel** (Island) because rushing streams, called Bächle, surround it. The Insel is the most picturesque quarter in Freiburg, with narrow cobblestone streets and restored houses once used by fishermen and tanneries. A 14th-century Augustinian monastery with a yellow baroque front houses the **Augustinermuseum** (Augustinian Friars Museum), Augustinerplatz (☎ 0761/201-2531), the chief attraction in the Insel Quarter. Inside you find a collection of religious art spanning more than 1,000 years. Admission to the museum is €2 ($2.50) for adults, €1 ($1.25) for students, free for children 17 and younger. The museum is open Tuesday through Sunday from 10 a.m. to 5 p.m.

From the Schwabentor, a pathway climbs up the **Schlossberg,** a hill that provides good views of the cathedral. You can also ascend the Schlossberg by cable car (☎ 0761/39855) from the Stadtgarten (City Gardens). The cable car operates June through September from 10 a.m. to 7 p.m., October through January from 11:30 a.m. to 6 p.m. The round-trip fare is €3 ($3.75).

Driving through the Upper Black Forest

From Freiburg, you can make an easy 145km (90-mile) circuit through a scenic part of the Black Forest and be back in time for dinner. Along the way, you pass some of the forest's highest peaks and two of its most beautiful lakes. (See "The Schwarzwald [Black Forest]" map in this chapter.)

From Freiburg, head south on Kaiser-Joseph-Strasse to Günterstal and follow the narrow, twisting road to **Schauinsland.** From the parking lot, you can climb 91 steps to an observation tower for a panoramic view toward the Feldberg, a nearby peak. The area also has easy hiking trails.

Continue south to the hamlet of **Todtnau,** where you find a 1.6km-long (1-mile) footpath to an impressive series of waterfalls. (You need about an hour to get to the falls and back.) From Todtnau, pick up B317 west to Utzenfeld and follow the narrow road northwest to the **Belchen,** a famous mile-high peak. A new, enclosed gondola, the **Belchen Seilbahn,** Belchenstrasse 13 (☎ **07673/888-280**), takes you to the peak for one of the most spectacular views in the Schwarzwald. From the grassy summit you can see the Feldberg and other nearby mountains, green hillside pastures, tile roofs in small villages, and the vast Rhine plain to the west. Give yourself about 90 minutes for the gondola ride and a stroll on the summit. The round-trip costs €5 ($6.25) for adults, €4 ($5) for children.

From the Belchen, backtrack to Utzenfeld and follow B317 east to Feldberg, where another enclosed gondola, the **Feldbergbahn** (☎ **07655/8019**), takes visitors to the 1,450m (4,750-ft.) summit of a peak called **Seebuck.** The round-trip takes about an hour, and on a clear day, you can see the highest peaks of the Alps to the south. The round-trip ride costs €6 ($7.50) for adults, €4 ($5) for children.

Continue on B317 east and turn south on B500 to **Schluchsee,** one of the loveliest of the Black Forest lakes. From Schluchsee, head back north along B500 to **Titisee,** another popular Black Forest lake. From Titisee, you can return to Freiburg by heading west along B31.

Discovering nightlife in Freiburg

The **Konzerthaus** (Concert House) plays host to a variety of events, ranging from classical music to theater to pop concerts. In June, huge tents house the annual **Zeltmusik festival** (Tent Music Festival), which emphasizes jazz but includes other musical styles. Summer also brings a series of chamber-music concerts to the **Historisches Kaufhaus,** in Münsterplatz, and a program of organ recitals in the **Münster,** Freiburg's cathedral (described earlier). Information about all venues and events, including program schedules and ticket sales, is available from the Tourist Information Office (see "Finding information" earlier in this section about Freiburg).

With some 25,000 university students, the city also has a thriving bar and club scene. Two clubs in one, **Crash,** Schnewlinstrasse 3 (☎ **0761/32475;** open Wed–Sat 10 p.m.–3:30 a.m.; Tram: 1, 4, or 5), serves drinks and plays background punk, house, and funk; in the basement, **Drifler's Club** (no phone; open Thurs–Sat midnight to 4 a.m.) plays house and techno for dancers. Neither club charges a cover.

Hausbrauerei Feierling, Gerberau 46 (☎ **0761/26678;** Tram: 1 or 2), a brewpub with a popular beer garden across the street, is open daily from 11 a.m. to midnight.

Time out: Buying a Black Forest cuckoo clock

Since 1667, when the first wooden clock was made in Waldau, clocks have been produced in the Black Forest. As early as 1840, Black Forest clocks were being shipped to China, Russia, Turkey, England, and America.

If you're looking for a traditional timepiece to take home from the Black Forest, **Triberg,** 48km (30 miles) northeast of Freiburg on B33, is a good place to go. In addition to cuckoo clocks, shops also sell woodcarvings, music boxes, and other traditional crafts. (*Note:* Triberg can be jammed with cuckoo-clock shoppers in the summer.)

You may also want to visit the **Haus der 1000 Uhren** (House of 1,000 Clocks), An der Bundesstrasse 33, Triberg-Gemmelsbach (☎ **07722/96300**), located on B33 between Triberg and Hornberg. You can't miss the shop: A giant cuckoo clock and waterwheel are in front. Josef Weisser, a painter of clock faces, launched the business in 1824; his great-great-grandson is the current owner. The shop is open Monday through Saturday from 9 a.m. to 5 p.m. The shop ships to the United States and Canada and takes American Express, Diners Club, MasterCard, and Visa.

Clock watchers with time on their hands may want to drive the **Deutsche Uhrenstrasse** (German Clock Road; www.deutsche-uhrenstrasse.de). Triberg is one of the stops on this 320km (200-mile) scenic route through the Black Forest from Villingen-Schwenningen to Bad Duerrheim. Along the way, you find all kinds of museums and sights related to clocks. One of the most interesting museums on the route is the **Deutsches Uhrenmuseum** (German Clock Museum), Robert-Gerwig-Platz 1, Furtwangen (☎ **07723/920-117**). In addition to the world's largest collection of Black Forest clocks, the museum has timepieces from all around the world and from all epochs. The museum is open daily April through October from 9 a.m. to 6 p.m., and November through March from 10 a.m. to 5 p.m. Admission is €3 ($3.75) for adults, €2 ($2.50) for students.

Chapter 18

Heidelberg, Stuttgart, and Nuremberg: Castles and Kaisers

· ·

In This Chapter

▶ Visiting romantic Heidelberg

▶ Discovering the cultural delights of Stuttgart

▶ Exploring historic Nuremberg

· ·

1 devote this chapter to three special cities in central Germany. **Heidelberg,** located on the Neckar River in the state of Baden-Württemberg, is one of Germany's most romantic cities. **Nuremberg,** or Nürnberg as it's known in German, is a historic and very attractive city in the state of Bavaria. Both are castle-crowned cities worth visiting for a day or two. **Stuttgart,** the cultural center of this region, can easily be visited as a side trip from Heidelberg.

Heidelberg: Romance on the River

Heidelberg, on the Neckar River, 88km (55 miles) south of Frankfurt, is renowned for its castle and its university. (See the "Heidelberg" map in this chapter.) According to a song from the operetta *The Student Prince,* which is set in Heidelberg, summertime in Heidelberg is a time for music and romance. Today, summer is also a time when droves of visitors from around the globe invade this beautiful city. Many Americans know Heidelberg because of the nearby U.S. Army base.

Heidelberg is one of the few German cities that was not leveled by air raids in World War II (WWII), so you still can see original buildings from the Middle Ages, Renaissance, baroque, and neoclassical eras. This architecture is certainly a major part of Heidelberg's appeal. But some of its legendary romantic allure stems from what was basically a 19th-century public-relations campaign. The looming ruins of the ancient castle, the old lanes and squares, the leafy hills and woodlands beside the Neckar, and the youthful student population all had great appeal to the German Romantics. The great writer Goethe and many other poets, painters, and musicians "discovered" Heidelberg in the early 19th century. They praised the town in their writings and immortalized it in their music and paintings. The town came to symbolize Old World German Romanticism at its most picturesque.

Getting there

Heidelberg is easily accessible by train from all major cities in Germany and Europe. The train trip to Heidelberg's Hauptbahnhof (main train station) is only one hour from Frankfurt and about three hours from Nuremberg. For train schedules and information, call **Deutsche Bahn** ☎ **11861.**

Finding information

The **Tourist Information Office,** Willy-Brandt-Plaza 1(☎ **06221/19433;** www.heidelberg.de), outside the main train station, is open Monday through Saturday from 9 a.m. to 7 p.m. and Sunday from 10 a.m. to 6 p.m. (closed Sun from Nov–Mar). The office has maps and brochures.

The **Heidelberg Card,** good for two days and available for €12 ($15) from the Tourist Information Office and at many hotels, provides admission to Heidelberg Castle and discounts on attractions, walking and boat tours, and unlimited use of public transportation.

Taking a guided tour

A two-hour **guided walking tour** of the city (in German) departs from the Lion's Fountain on Universitätsplatz at 10:30 a.m. daily from April through October, and only on Saturday from November through March. Between April and October, a walking tour in English departs from the same place Thursday through Sunday at 10:30 a.m. The cost is €6 ($7.50) for adults, €4 ($5) for students and children. Purchase your ticket from the Tourist Information Office at the train station.

From April through October, **guided bus tours** of the city (in German and English), including the castle, depart from Universitätsplatz on Thursday and Friday at 2:30 p.m., Saturday at 10:30 a.m. and 2:30 p.m., and Sunday and holidays at 10:30 a.m.; November through March the tour takes place only on Saturday at 2:30 p.m. The cost is €12 ($15) for adults, €9 ($11) for students and children. Purchase tickets at the Tourist Information Office at the train station.

From Easter through October, **Rhein-Neckar-Fahrgastschiffahrt** (☎ **06221/20181;** www.rnf-schifffahrt.de) offers daily **guided boat tours** (commentary in German and English) on the Neckar River between Heidelberg and Neckarsteinach. The round-trip tour lasts about three hours and costs €9.50 ($12) for adults, €5.50 ($7) for children. Boats depart from the landing stage near the Stadthalle, between the Theodor-Heuss-Brücke (bridge) and the Alte Brücke (Old Bridge).

Heidelberg

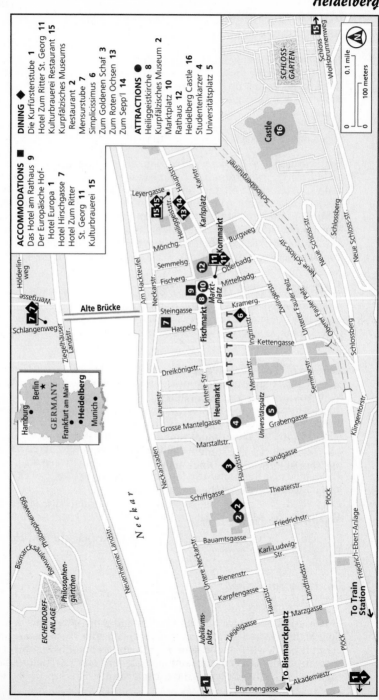

ACCOMMODATIONS ■
Das Hotel am Rathaus **9**
Der Europäische Hof-
Hotel Europa **1**
Hotel Hirschgasse **7**
Hotel Zum Ritter
St. Georg **11**
Kulturbrauerei **15**

DINING ◆
Die Kurfürstenstube **1**
Hotel Zum Ritter St. Georg **11**
Kulturbrauerei Restaurant **15**
Kurpfälzisches Museums
Restaurant **2**
Mensurstube **7**
Simplicissimus **6**
Zum Goldenen Schaf **3**
Zum Roten Ochsen **13**
Zum Sepp'l **14**

ATTRACTIONS ●
Heiliggeistkirche **8**
Kurpfälzisches Museum **2**
Marktplatz **10**
Rathaus **12**
Heidelberg Castle **16**
Studentenkarzer **4**
Universitätsplatz **5**

Orienting yourself

Your first glimpse of "romantic old Heidelberg" as you emerge from the Hauptbahnhof on the west side of town may be disappointing. The city, like many in Germany and throughout Europe, has a modern and a historic face, and the modern one is what you encounter first. Modern Heidelberg centers on **Bismarckplatz** (streetcar lines 1 and 2 run there from the train station), an area of tall buildings and shopping plazas. The **Altstadt** (Old Town), to the east, is where you want to focus your sightseeing activities. The Altstadt is a long wedge of slate-roofed buildings along the Neckar River, beneath Heidelberg's *Schloss* (castle).

Hauptstrasse, a wide, busy pedestrian street with narrow medieval lanes on both sides, runs from Bismarckplatz into the compact Altstadt. The main squares in the Altstadt are **Universitätsplatz,** a focal point for famed Heidelberg University; **Fischmarkt,** dominated by the Heiliggeistkirche (Church of the Holy Spirit); the **Marktplatz,** or Market Square; and the **Kornmarkt.** The Schloss crowns a hill to the south, above the Altstadt. Across the Neckar River is the **Philosophenweg** (Philosopher's Way), a popular walking trail; a zoo; and a botanical garden.

Getting around Heidelberg

After you arrive in the Altstadt you can walk everywhere. However, the Altstadt is about a half-hour's walk from the train station, so I recommend that you take a streetcar or bus to Bismarckplatz or Universitätsplatz to begin your explorations.

Heidelberg is crisscrossed with a network of streetcars and buses operated by the local transportation department, **HSB** (☎ **06221/513-2000**). Many bus and streetcar lines intersect at Bismarckplatz in the town center. Buses 41 and 42 travel between the railway station and Universitätsplatz on the west side of the Altstadt. A single fare on the bus or tram costs €1.90 ($2.40); a 24-hour pass, valid for up to five persons traveling within a group, costs €8 ($10). A **Bergbahn** (funicular; ☎ **06221/22796**) runs from Kornmarkt, in the Altstadt, up to the castle, between 9 a.m. and 7:40 p.m. daily; the round-trip fare is €3 ($3.75) for adults, €2 ($2.50) for children and students.

Staying in Heidelberg

See also the listing for the outstanding **Der Europäische Hof-Hotel Europa** ($$$$) in Chapter 22.

Das Hotel am Rathaus
$–$$ Altstadt

This hotel is one of Heidelberg's nicest and most affordable. It's located right in the heart of the city on the Marktplatz. The 17 rooms are small but very pleasant, with simple modern furnishings and tiled bathrooms with showers. Some larger rooms are suitable for families. The one potential drawback: The hotel doesn't have an elevator.

See map p. 333. Heiliggeiststrasse 1, 69117 Heidelberg. ☎ 06221/14730. Fax: 06221/ 147-337. www.hotels-in-heidelberg.de. Bus: 11 to Rathaus/Kornmarkt (then a 4-minute walk north on Oberbadgasse to Heiliggeiststrasse on the east side of Marktplatz). Rack rates: €99–€154 ($124–$193) double. Rates include breakfast buffet. AE, DC, MC, V.

Hotel Hirschgasse
$$$–$$$$ North side of the river

Nestled on the hillside of a historic lane adjoining the famous Philosophenweg on the north side of the Neckar, this historic hotel enjoys a tranquil and romantic setting. The hotel dates from 1472 and has lodged such impressive figures as Mark Twain and Bismarck. The 20 rooms are all sumptuously comfortable suites decorated with Laura Ashley fabrics, and all come equipped with shower-tub-whirlpool combinations in the bathrooms. The **Mensurstube** restaurant is one of the most historically atmospheric spots in town (see the "Dining in Heidelberg" section, next). The Altstadt is a ten-minute walk from the hotel.

See map p. 333. Hirschgasse 3, 69100 Heidelberg. ☎ 06221/4540. Fax: 06221/454-111. www.hirschgasse.de. Bus: 34 from Bismarckplatz to Hirschgasse stop. Rack rates: €150–€335 ($188–$419) double. AE, DC, MC, V.

Hotel Zum Ritter St. Georg
$$$–$$$$ Altstadt

Located right on the Marktplatz on Hauptstrasse, the main street in the Altstadt, the Zum Ritter St. Georg is a well-preserved rarity from the German Renaissance. Built in 1592 as the home of a cloth merchant, the hotel is among Heidelberg's sightseeing attractions thanks to its highly decorated, gabled façade. The hotel doesn't have public lounges. Many of the 40 rooms are modest in size, but the beds are comfortable. Most of the rooms contain tiled bathrooms with shower-tub combinations. Although they have Romantic Altstadt views, the front rooms also can be noisy because of neighboring cafes and restaurants. The dining room specializes in duck breast and venison.

See map p. 333. Hauptstrasse 178, 69117 Heidelberg. ☎ 06221/1350. Fax: 06221/135-230. www.ritter-heidelberg.de. Bus: 11 to Rathaus/Kornmarkt (then a 3-minute walk north on Oberbadgasse to Marktplatz). Rack rates: €141–€240 ($176–$300) double. Rates include buffet breakfast. AE, DC, MC, V.

Kulturbrauerei
$$ Altstadt

This small (21 rooms), hip, brand-new hotel, just a couple of minutes' walk from the river, is connected to a microbrewery. The hotel has a cool, minimalist style. The medium-size rooms have light-colored hardwood floors and are furnished with comfortable beds and large wooden cupboards. Bathrooms are adequately roomy with tub-shower combinations (four rooms have showers only). Unfortunately, the hotel doesn't have air-conditioning, and courtyard-facing rooms can be noisy in the summer, when tables are set up in the microbrewery's beer garden. If you don't stay here, you may want to dine at the on-site restaurant (see the "Dining in Heidelberg" section, next).

See map p. 333. Leyergasse 6, 69117 Heidelberg. ☎ 06221/90000. Fax: 06221/900-099. www.heidelberger-kulturbrauerei.de. Bus: 11 or 33 to Neckarmünzplatz (then a 3-minute walk south on Leyergasse). Rack rates: €116–€135 ($134–$169) double. AE, MC, V.

Dining in Heidelberg

Die Kurfürstenstube
$$$$ Altstadt FRENCH

The best dining spot in Heidelberg is the wood-paneled Die Kurfürstenstube in the deluxe Der Europäische Hof-Hotel Europa. The menu is in English, but the cuisine is mainly French, with fixed-price and à la carte meals. The restaurant uses only the highest-quality seasonal ingredients. Look for culinary delights such as cream of watercress soup with poached quail egg and summer truffles in tempura, carpaccio of scallops and Scottish wild salmon with mushrooms in raspberry vinaigrette, veal with stuffed pumpkins, and filet of turbot with celery on saffron foam with coriander tortellini. The dessert menu is equally scrumptious, and the wine list is the most impressive in town.

See map p. 333. In Der Europäische Hof-Hotel Europa, Friedrich-Ebert-Anlage 1. ☎ 06221/5150. Streetcar: 1 or 2 to Bismarckplatz (then a 3-minute walk south to Friedrich-Ebert-Anlage). Reservations required. Main courses: €25–€30 ($31–$37). Fixed-price menus: €60–€72 ($75–$90). AE, DC, MC, V. Open: Daily noon to 2:30 p.m. and 6:30–11:30 p.m.

Hotel Zum Ritter St. Georg
$$ Altstadt GERMAN/INTERNATIONAL

At this restaurant, located in one of Heidelberg's most famous Renaissance buildings, you can dine in the large Rittersaal (Knights' Hall) or the smaller Councilors' Chamber. The house specialty is saddle of venison for two (in season). Locals flock here when this dish is on the menu. A good beginning may be the snail soup with herbs or tomato soup with whipped cream. Other menu offerings include staples such as pork loin with sauerkraut or roast salmon in a basil-cream sauce. If you like beer, try the Dortmunder Actien-Brauerei. A children's menu includes dishes such as *Wiener Würstchen* (small Vienna-style sausages).

See map p. 333. Hauptstrasse 178. ☎ 06221/1350. Bus: 11 to Rathaus/Kornmarkt (then a 3-minute walk north on Oberbadgasse to Marktplatz). Reservations recommended. Main courses: €10–€15 ($12–$19). Fixed-price menus: €20–€35 ($25–$44). AE, DC, MC, V. Open: Daily noon to 2 p.m. and 6–10 p.m.

Kulturbrauerei Restaurant
$ **Altstadt GERMAN/REGIONAL**

Part of a microbrewery and hotel complex (see the previous "Staying in Heidelberg" section), this large, popular restaurant formerly was a dance hall. You can eat on the balcony or, in summer, in the beer garden. Come here when you're in the mood for hearty portions of traditional German food washed down by one of the homemade Scheffel's beers. You can order salads, seasonal specialties (herring, pork stomach, spareribs), dishes from the grill (bratwursts, pork filet with mushrooms, roast fish), or vegetarian meals.

See map p. 333. Leyergasse 6. ☎ *06221/90000. Bus: 11 or 33 to Neckarmünzplatz (then a 3-minute walk south on Leyergasse). Main courses: €9–€19 ($11–$24). MC, V. Open: Daily 11 a.m.–11 p.m.*

Kurpfälzisches Museums Restaurant
$$ **Altstadt GERMAN/INTERNATIONAL**

On a warm summer's day or evening, nothing is more enjoyable or romantic than dining in the museum's garden courtyard with its splashing fountain. The restaurant also has a pleasant dining room. Fresh fish dishes may include zander with lemon cream, swordfish with a pepper crust, or tuna fish with tomatoes, olives, and herbs. You can also get meat dishes: a good rib-eye steak, lamb with rosemary, or pork medallions in a pepper-cream sauce with homemade *Spätzle* (a potato-based pasta). For dessert, try the mocha and Grand Marnier parfait with fruit sauce.

See map p. 333. Hauptstrasse 97. ☎ *06221/24050. Streetcar: 1 or 2 to Bismarckplatz (then a 5-minute walk east on Haupstrasse). Reservations recommended for dinner. Main courses: €13–€20 ($16–$25). MC, V. Open: Daily 10 a.m. to midnight.*

Mensurstube
$$–$$$ **North Bank GERMAN/REGIONAL**

No other place in Heidelberg captures bygone days quite like this rustic and cozy spot in the ancient Hotel Hirschgasse, where swords hang from the ceiling and you sit at 200-year-old tables. The limited menu wisely sticks to traditional dishes made with fresh ingredients. Potato soup is a good starter, followed by homemade noodles, oxtail, or lamb shank. The menu often includes *Rinderfilet* (filet of beef) served with bone marrow and a red-wine sauce. Almost everything is best accompanied by Pils beer on tap.

See map p. 333. In the Hotel Hirschgasse, Hirschgasse 3. ☎ *06221/4540. Bus: 34 (from Bismarckplatz to Hirschgasse stop). Reservations recommended. Main courses €15–€20 ($19–$25). AE, DC, MC, V. Open: Daily noon to 2 p.m. and 6–10 p.m.*

Simplicissimus
$$$–$$$$ Altstadt   FRENCH

This elegant gourmet restaurant in the Altstadt is known for its *cuisine moderne*. The menu changes often but may include lamb with a red wine and onion purée, fresh mushrooms in cream sauce with homemade noodles, duck breast with asparagus, or crayfish with fresh melon and herb-flavored cream sauce. Service is friendly, and the wine list is good.

See map p. 333. Ingrimstrasse 16. ☎ 06221/183-336. Bus: 11, 12, 33, 35, or 41. Reservations required. Main courses: €19–€45 ($24–$56). Fixed-price menu: €34–€85 ($42–$106). AE, MC, V. Open: Wed–Mon 6 p.m. to midnight. Closed 2 weeks in Mar and Aug.

Zum Goldenen Schaf
$$ Altstadt   GERMAN/REGIONAL

Located on Hauptstrasse, the main street in the Altstadt, this historic pub-restaurant offers a menu emphasizing regional dishes from Swabia and the Pfalz. You may want to try the *Kringelbratwurst* (roast sausage with sauerkraut and mashed potatoes) or Swabian sauerbraten (marinated beef with red cabbage and noodles). Portions are hearty and very filling, but try to save room for warm apple strudel with vanilla ice cream and whipped cream.

See map p. 333. Hauptstrasse 115. ☎ 06221/20879. Streetcar: 1 or 2 to Bismarckplatz (then a 5-minute walk east on Haupstrasse). Main courses: €8–€18 ($10–$22). AE, DC, MC, V. Open: Mon–Fri noon to 1 a.m., Sat–Sun 11 a.m.–1 a.m.

Exploring Heidelberg

Heidelberg is a wonderfully pleasant town to explore, and wandering through the old lanes and squares of the Altstadt is as essential a part of any tour as visiting the tourist attractions. The town has few must-see attractions, and for many visitors there is only one: the famous *Schloss* that looks down on the Altstadt.

Visiting the top attraction

Heidelberg Castle

Most visitors reach the huge red-sandstone *Schloss* (castle) on foot, or by taking a two-minute cable-car ride from Kornmarkt (see "Getting around Heidelberg" earlier in this chapter). Walking is the most rewarding approach because of the constantly changing views of the town and surrounding countryside. The easiest and most gradual path begins at the Klingentor; you also find a shorter, steeper path up Burgweg from Kornmarkt.

Set amidst woodlands and terraced gardens, the enormous ruins of the castle are undeniably picturesque. Even in its deteriorated state, it is one of the finest Gothic-Renaissance castles in Germany, and one of the most famous historic monuments in Europe. Plan to spend about two hours here.

Entering at the main gate, you first come upon the **Pulverturm** (Gun Tower) and a terrace with views of Heidelberg and the Neckar Valley. The **Elizabethentor** (Elizabeth's Gate), erected by Friedrich V in 1615 for his teenage wife (Elizabeth Stuart, daughter of the English king James I) leads to the bridge crossing the former moat.

Along the north side of the courtyard stretches the **Friedrichsbau** (palace of Friedrich IV), erected from 1601 to 1607 and less damaged than other parts of the castle. Its restored rooms can be seen on guided tours. The palace's terrace offers a magnificent view of Heidelberg and the Neckar Valley. At the west end of the terrace, in the 16th-century cellars of the castle, sits the **Grosse Fass** (Great Cask). This enormous wine barrel, the largest in the world, was built in 1751 and once held more than 208,000 liters (55,000 gallons) of wine.

To the east, connecting the palace of Friedrich IV to the **Ottheinrichsbau** (palace of Ottheinrich), is the shell of the **Spiegelbau** (Hall of Mirrors building), constructed in 1549. Housed within Ottheinrich's palace is the **Apothekenmuseum** (Pharmacy Museum; ☎ **06221/25880**), re-creating a baroque- and rococo-era chemist's shop with utensils and laboratory equipment from the 17th and 18th centuries. The museum is open daily from 10 a.m. to 5 p.m.; your castle entrance ticket includes admission.

The **Hortus Palatinus** (Castle Gardens) originally were created in the 17th century. In the southeast corner, you find the remains of a grotto and a sandstone sculpture of Father Rhine.

Schlossberg. ☎ *06221/538-431. Admission: Castle grounds: free; entrance courtyard, Pharmacy Museum, and Great Cask: €2.50 ($3.10) adults, €1.30 ($1.60) children. Tours: Frequent 1-hour guided tours of the castle in English, €3 ($3.75) adults, €1.50 ($1.90) children. Audio tours: €3 ($3.75). Open: Daily 8 a.m.–5:30 p.m.*

The history of Heidelberg Castle

An elevated fortress rose above Heidelberg as early as 1225, but the castle as it stands today was built in two main phases. During the first phase, between about 1400 and 1544, fortifications and living quarters were constructed. The second phase, from 1549 to 1620, saw the transition from Gothic to Renaissance styles as various prince electors of the Palatinate added to the building. The castle was the residence of the prince electors for centuries until French troops sacked and destroyed it in the late 17th century. After it was rebuilt, the castle was struck by lightning. In the 19th century, the ruins of the castle became a symbol for the German Romantics and a mecca for tourists from around the world.

Touring the Altstadt

Marktplatz (Market Square) is the main square in the Altstadt. On market days (Wed and Sat), stalls of fresh flowers, fish, vegetables, cheese, meat, and baked goods fill the square. The **Rathaus** (Town Hall), on the east side of the square, is an early-18th-century building reconstructed in 1908 following a fire.

The late-Gothic **Heiliggeistkirche** (Church of the Holy Ghost; no phone; open daily 8 a.m.–5 p.m.), built around 1400, dominates the west end of Marktplatz. For nearly 300 years, the church was the burial place of the Palatinate electors. In 1706, a wall was erected to divide the church between Roman Catholics and Protestants. The wall has since been removed and the church restored to its original plan.

The highly decorated Renaissance mansion, now the **Hotel Zum Ritter St. Georg** (see "Staying in Heidelberg" earlier in this chapter), stands on the south side of Marktplatz. A Huguenot cloth merchant who emigrated from France to Heidelberg erected the building in 1592. The hotel is named for the statue of the *Ritter* (knight) at the top.

A five-minute walk west from the Marktplatz on Hauptstasse and south one block on Grabengasse brings you to **Universitätsplatz** (University Square). On the northeastern side is the Alte Universität (Old University), a building from the 18th century, and at the south end of the square is the Neue Universität (New University), completed in 1932. Heidelberg University, founded in 1386, is the oldest in Germany.

A few steps past the Old University, you find the **Studentenkarzer** (Students' Prison), Augustinerstrasse 2 (☎ 06221/543-554), where from 1778 to 1914 generations of students were incarcerated in cramped cells for minor offenses. Graffiti and drawings, including portraits and silhouettes, cover the walls and even the ceilings. Admission is €2.50 ($3.10) for adults, €2 ($2.50) for students and children 14 and younger. The prison is open April through September, Tuesday through Saturday from 10 a.m. to 6 p.m., October through March, Tuesday through Friday from 10 a.m. to 4 p.m.

A two-minute walk west on Hauptstrasse from Universitätsplatz brings you to the **Kurpfälzisches Museum** (Museum of the Palatinate), Hauptstrasse 97 (☎ 06221/583-402). Housed in a baroque palace, Heidelberg's most noteworthy museum contains a large collection of regional painting and sculpture from the 15th to the 19th centuries. The one masterpiece on display is Tilman Riemenschneider's 1509 wooden altarpiece showing Christ and the Apostles. You can also see an archaeological collection with a cast of the jawbone of the 600,000-year-old Heidelberg Man *(Homo heidelbergensis),* discovered in the vicinity nearly 100 years ago, and a section on the history of the Palatinate. Give yourself about 45 minutes to browse through the various exhibits. The museum restaurant (see "Dining in Heidelberg" earlier in this chapter) is a good choice for lunch or dinner. Admission to the museum is €2.50

($3.10) for adults, €1.50 ($1.90) for students and children 17 and younger. The museum is open Tuesday through Sunday from 10 a.m. to 6 p.m. (Wed until 8 p.m.).

Shopping in Heidelberg

The main shopping street is the traffic-free **Hauptstrasse.** A lively **outdoor market** is open on Wednesday and Saturday at the Marktplatz. Some noteworthy shops include:

- ✔ **Altstadt-Galerie Stefan,** UntereStrasse 18 (☎ 06221/28737), sells charming original engravings for as little as €10 ($12).

- ✔ **Black Forest Shop,** Hauptstrasse 215 (☎ 06221/619-983), near Karlsplatz, sells Hummel figurines, cuckoo clocks, and beer steins.

- ✔ **Gätschenberger,** Hauptstrasse 42 (☎ 06221/14480), is known for its array of fine linens and embroideries for bed, bathroom, and table.

- ✔ **Kinderwaren Troll,** Plöck 71 (☎ 06221/893-6677), is a children's clothing and toy store with handcrafted puppets, dolls, and wooden blocks and figures.

- ✔ **Michael Kienscherff,** Hauptstrasse 177 (☎ 06221/24255; Tram: 1 or 5), offers a wide assortment of handicrafts from across Germany: music boxes, nativity scenes, nutcrackers, and glass and crystal ornaments.

Living it up after dark in Heidelberg

The large student population keeps Heidelberg humming after dark. Early evenings often start in the bars along Hauptstrasse; late nights get rolling in clubs around Marktplatz.

The performing arts

The main performance stage is **Theater der Stadt,** Friedrichsstrasse 5 (☎ 06221/583-502; Bus: 41 or 42), where nightly entertainment includes plays, opera, and dance productions. For five weeks beginning in late July, the **Schlossfest-Spiele** festival brings opera, classical music, jazz, and theater to venues around the area, including Heidelberg Castle. Contact ☎ 06274/58352 for tickets.

Historic taverns

Heidelberg's most famous and revered student tavern, **Zum Roten Ochsen** (Red Ox Inn), Hauptstrasse 217 (☎ 06221/20977), opened in 1703. Revelers sit at long oak tables arranged in horseshoe fashion around a pianist. As the evening progresses, the songs become louder and louder. A mug of beer costs €2.40 ($3) and up. Meals go for €10 to €18 ($12 to $22). The tavern is open April through October on Monday through Saturday from 11:30 a.m. to 2 p.m. and 5 p.m. to midnight; November through March hours are 5 p.m. to midnight.

Next door is **Zum Sepp'l,** Hauptstrasse 213 (☎ **06221/23085**), filled with photographs and memorabilia. The building dates from 1634. Meals cost €8 to €13 ($10 to $16). A mug of beer goes for €2.95 ($3.70). A pianist performs nightly. It's open Monday through Friday from 5:30 p.m. to midnight, Saturday and Sunday from noon to 2:30 p.m. and 5:30 p.m. to midnight.

A Side Trip to Stuttgart

Located in the Neckar Valley, 115km (71 miles) southeast of Heidelberg, Stuttgart is the capital of the federal state of Baden-Württemberg, but most of the people who live here still call the area *Swabia*. For more than a century Stuttgart has been a center of German industry, yet it remains surprisingly verdant (green), nestled in gently rolling hills with woods and vineyards reaching right down into the city. As a cultural center, Stuttgart has no equal in southwestern Germany. Visitors come from across the region to enjoy the city's museums and performing arts. Stuttgart makes for a great day trip from Heidelberg. (See the "Stuttgart" map in this chapter.)

A visit to Stuttgart can be even more enjoyable when you time your trip to coincide with one of the city's major festivals. All of them take place right in the center of town on Marktplatz and Schillerplatz. At the **Stuttgart Wine Festival** in late August, wine lovers converge to taste a selection of more than 350 Württemberg wines and sample regional food specialties. The 16-day **Stuttgart Beer Festival,** the second largest in Germany after Munich's Oktoberfest, begins in late September with a grand procession of horse-drawn beer wagons and people in traditional costumes. Dating back to 1818, the beer festival features food, rides, and tents for some 20,000-beer drinkers. Starting in late November, Stuttgart plays host to a lively **Christmas Market (Weihnachtsmarkt)**, one of the oldest and largest in Europe, with about 230 decorated stalls selling gifts, mulled wine, and cinnamon waffles. For dates and more information, visit the city's Web site at www.stuttgart-tourist.de.

Getting to Stuttgart

By **train,** trip time from Heidelberg is only 40 minutes. For train schedules and information, call **Deutsche Bahn (☎ 11861).** Access by car is via the A8 Autobahn east and west or the A81 north and south. **Stuttgart Airport (☎ 0711/948-3388),** located 13km (8 miles) south of the city, serves as a major gateway to southern Germany. From the airport's Terminal 1, you can take the S2 or S3 S-Bahn directly to the main train station in central Stuttgart for €2.60 ($3.25).

Finding information & taking a tour

Located opposite the main train station, the **I-Punkt Tourist Information Office,** Königstrasse 1A (☎ 0711/222-8259; www.stuttgart-tourist.de), is open Monday to Friday 9 a.m. to 8 p.m., Saturday 9 a.m. to 6 p.m., and Sunday 11 a.m. to 6 p.m. (November through April, 1 to 6 p.m.).

Stuttgart

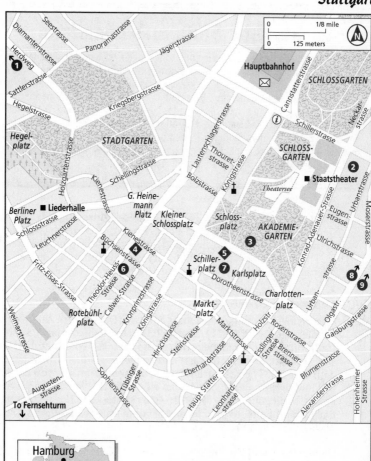

ATTRACTIONS ●

Altes Schloss and Württembergisches
  Landesmuseum **7**
Mercedes-Benz Museum **9**
Neue Galerie **6**
Neues Schloss **3**
Staatsgalerie **2**
Weissenhofsiedlung **1**
Wilhelma **8**

DINING ◆

Alte Kanzlei **5**
Café Königsbau **4**

Church ⊥
Information ⓘ
Post Office ✉

Swabia: Stuttgart's homeland

Swabia (*Schwaben* in German) is the name for a medieval duchy now contained within the federal state of Baden-Württemberg in southwestern Germany. The name comes from *Suevi*, the original inhabitants, who were conquered by the Franks in the 5th century A.D. With Stuttgart as its capital, Swabia has been a leader of German industry for decades, but the region also is renowned for its scenic countryside. To the north, the **Schwäbische Wald** (Swabian forest) stretches to the **Schwäbische Alb**, a wedge of limestone upland south of Stuttgart. Forests sweep south to the Bodensee, also part of Swabia, and west to the Danube River. The smaller Neckar River flows past Heidelberg and Stuttgart through a vineyard-covered valley.

The tourist office offers a 2½-hour **guided sightseeing bus tour** (in German and English) daily at 1 p.m. from April through October, and in March on Fridays, Saturdays, and Sundays at 1:30 p.m. The cost is €17 ($21) per person. Ninety-minute city walking tours (in German only) are offered on Saturday year-round at 10 a.m. for €6 ($7.50).

Dining in Stuttgart

Occupying a section of the Altes Schloss (Old Castle), **Alte Kanzlei,** Schillerplatz 5A (☎ 0711/29-44-57; U-Bahn: Schlossplatz), specializes in traditional Swabian dishes such as *Maultaschen* (pasta stuffed with ham, egg, spinach, or other fillings) and *Zwiebelrostbraten* (roast beef topped with onions). The restaurant has a cafe section where you can get breakfast and lighter meals, or you can sit out on the terrace and have an ice cream. Main courses go for €9 to €16 ($11 to $20). The restaurant is open daily from 11 a.m. to 11 p.m. and accepts American Express, Diners Club, MasterCard, and Visa.

Coffee, cake, and light meals are served at **Café Königsbau**, Königstrasse 28 (☎ 0711/290-787), an old-fashioned *Konditorei* (pastry shop) located in the colonnade of the Königsbau next to the new art museum. The cafe is open Monday through Friday 9 a.m. to 7 p.m., Saturday 9 a.m. to 8 p.m., and Sunday 11 a.m. to 6 p.m.

Exploring Stuttgart

From the train station you can reach all the major attractions in the Altstadt on foot. (See the "Stuttgart" map in this chapter.) The Mercedes Museum and some other sights require the use of public transportation or a taxi. Stuttgart has a comprehensive S-Bahn system that links up with the U-Bahn (subway). Fares are based on zones; a one-way ticket costs €1.60 ($2) for one zone. A **one-day ticket (Einzel Tageskarte)** costs €4.90 ($6.10) for two zones. Purchase tickets from the automated machines in U-Bahn stations or from the bus driver. For information, call the city's transportation authority **VVS** (☎ 0711/66060).

Stuttgart U-Bahn and S-Bahn

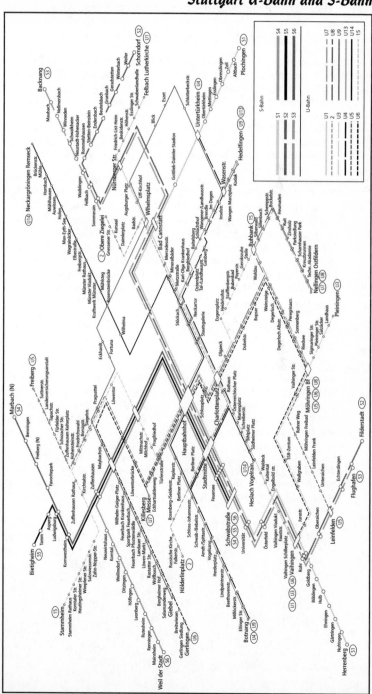

Altes Schloss and Württembergisches Landesmuseum (Old Castle and State Museum of Württemberg), Schillerplatz 6 (☎ 0711/279-3400; U-Bahn: Schlossplatz), is one of Stuttgart's oldest standing structures, first built as a moated castle in the 14th century and later redone in Renaissance style. Rebuilt after WWII, the castle now houses a state museum tracing the art and culture of Swabia and Württemberg from the Stone Age to the present. You'll see prehistoric stone sculptures, the Württemberg crown jewels (in the royal vault), a large collection of Swabian sculptures, and treasures found in the tomb of a Celtic prince (circa A.D. 530). You can see the highlights in an hour or so. Admission is €2.60 ($3.25) for adults, €1.50 ($1.90) for students. The museum is open Tuesday 10 a.m. to 1 p.m. and Wednesday through Sunday 10 a.m. to 5 p.m.

It's worth a trip to Stuttgart just to see the **Neue Galerie (New Stuttgart Art Gallery)**, Schlossplatz (☎ 0711/216-2188; U-Bahn: Schlossplatz), scheduled to open in spring 2005. Designed by Berlin architects Hascher and Jehle, the museum is a filigree glass cube surrounding a rough-hewn limestone inner core. The new gallery houses the city's collection of 19th- and 20th-century works by artists from southern Germany; the paintings by Otto Dix are particularly compelling. The top floor, a cafe open to the public daily until 1 a.m., provides a fabulous panoramic view of Stuttgart and its surrounding hills. Hours of operation and admission prices were not available for *Germany For Dummies,* 2nd Edition, but like the old gallery it replaces, the new gallery probably will be open Tuesday through Sunday 11 a.m. to 6 p.m., with the hours extended on Wednesday until 8 p.m.

A must for anyone who has an interest in cars, vintage or otherwise, the **Mercedes-Benz Museum,** Mercedesstrasse 137, Stuttgart-Cannstatt (☎ 0711/172-2578), honors the invention of the motorcar by Carl Benz and Gottlieb Daimler. Nearly 75 historical vehicles are shown, including the first motorcycle (built in 1885) and the first Mercedes (1902). Give yourself at least an hour here; you'll enjoy every minute. The museum is free, and you can get a free audio guide in English. To reach the museum, take S-Bahn line S1 to Gottlieb-Daimler-Stadion, then follow signs to DaimlerChrysler Werk, Untertürkheim Tor 1 (about a ten-minute walk); from there, a free shuttle bus takes you to the museum, open Tuesday through Sunday from 9 a.m. to 5 p.m.

The **Staatsgalerie (State Art Gallery),** Konrad-Adenauer-Strasse 30–32 (☎ 0711/470-400; U-Bahn: Staatsgalerie), the city's finest art museum, exhibits works spanning some 550 years. Highlights include Giovanni Bellini's *The Mourning of Christ,* Hans Memlings's *Bathsheba at her Bath,* and Rembrandt's *St. Paul in Prison.* The "New State Gallery," designed by the British architect James Stirling and completed in 1984, is considered an icon of postmodern architecture. In this section, you find the 19th- and 20th-century collection, with works of the German Expressionists Ernst Kirchner, Ernst Barlach, and Max Beckmann, in addition to representatives of the Bauhaus school and Blue Rider group, such as Paul Klee and Lyonel Feininger. Some famous examples of European art from the late

19th and early 20th centuries also are exhibited, including works by Modigliani, Picasso, and Monet. Art lovers will want to give themselves a couple of hours here. The museum is open Tuesday through Sunday 10 a.m. to 6 p.m. (Thursday until 9 p.m.). Admission is €4.50 ($5.60) for adults, free for children 13 and younger; free on Wednesday.

Home to more than 9,000 animals and plants from around the world, **Wilhelma,** Neckartalstrasse, Bad-Cannstatt (☎ **0711/54020**), is the largest zoo and botanical garden in Europe. The park was laid out in 1848 and contains a collection of historical buildings in the Moorish style. The animal houses and greenhouses are open year-round from 8:15 a.m. to 5 p.m. (November through February until 4 p.m.); admission is €9 ($11) adults, €4.50 ($6) children younger than 17. To get there, take U-Bahn line 14 to the Wilhelma stop.

Stuttgart performing arts

Even if you're staying in Heidelberg, Stuttgart is so close (only 40 minutes by train) that you may want to consider spending an evening there at the ballet, opera, or concert hall. Listings of the various cultural events and tickets are available from the tourist office (see above). The magazine *Lift,* available at newsstands, lists all the happenings around Stuttgart. **Staatstheater** (State Theater), Oberer Schlossgarten (☎ **0711/20-20-90;** S-Bahn: Hauptbahnhof), is home to the highly regarded **Stuttgart Ballet** and the **Staatsoper** (State Opera). Classical and other concerts are given in the **Liederhalle,** Schloss-Strasse (☎ **0711/2167110;** U-Bahn: Liederhalle/ Berlinerplatz), home to the Stuttgarter Philharmoniker and the Radio Symphony Orchestra. Tickets for all concerts are on sale at the tourist information office.

Classics of modernist architecture

Architecture buffs will want to pay a visit to **Weissenhofsiedlung (Weissenhof Estate),** a housing estate built for a building exhibition in 1927. Walking through the estate you see houses created by architects such as Ludwig Mies van der Rohe (Am Weissenhof 14–29), Le Corbusier (Rathenaustrasse 1–3), and Hans Scharoun (Hölzweg 1). Many of the existing houses represent the functional style that was being promoted by the Bauhaus school of art and design. Displays in the small **Architektur-Galerie,** Am Weissenhof 30 (☎ **0711/257-1434;** www.weissenhofgalerie.de), provide information about the project and the architects involved; the gallery is open Tuesday through Saturday 2 to 6 p.m. and Sunday noon to 5 p.m.); walking tours are available on Saturdays at 11 a.m. To reach the Weissenhof Estate, take a taxi or the U-Bahn line 7 to the Killesberg-Messe stop and walk northeast around the Messe into the residential neighborhood. For a private architectural tour by an English-speaking city guide/taxi driver, call Anselm Vogt-Moykopf at ☎ **0172/740-1138** (www.stadtrundfahrt-stuttgart.de).

Shopping in Stuttgart

You'll find department stores and boutiques lining **Königstrasse,** right outside the main train station. But for a special shopping experience, head to the **Markthalle (Market Hall),** Dorotheenstrasse 4 (U-Bahn: Schlossplatz), an Art Nouveau building dating from 1914 and full of stalls selling local and foreign delicacies.

Serious shoppers, take note: **Metzingen,** a small town 35km (21 miles) south of Stuttgart and easily accessible by train, is the home of Germany's best and most numerous **factory-outlet stores.** On and around **Kanalstrasse,** you find a selection of international designer outlets selling clothing, shoes, sports equipment, tableware, and more.

Nuremberg: Renaissance and Rebirth

Nuremberg (or Nürnberg in German) is located in Bavaria, 148km (92 miles) northwest of Munich. (See the "Nuremberg" map in this chapter.) This strikingly attractive and lively city has about half a million residents. Spending a day or more exploring its streets, churches, historic buildings, and museums definitely is worth it.

"Nourenberc," as the city originally was known, dates back to about 1050. In 300 years, the city grew from a fortress and military base in eastern Franconia (a medieval duchy of south-central Germany) to a virtually self-governing Free Imperial City *(Freie Reichsstadt).* From 1356 onward, each newly elected emperor of the Holy Roman Empire had to convene his first *Reichstag,* or meeting with the princes of the empire, in Nuremberg. The city's role as capital of the empire, and its location at the crossroads of major trade routes, made it one of the wealthiest and most important cities in medieval Germany. During the 15th and 16th centuries, a cultural flowering made Nuremberg the center of the German Renaissance.

But the city fell into decline until, under Hitler, Nuremberg made its second, and most infamous, mark on German history. To Hitler, the city's architecture and previous role in the Holy Roman Empire represented the quintessence of Germany. After he seized power in 1933, Hitler made Nuremberg the Nazi party's permanent convention and rally site. As a result, no other German city, with the exceptions of Dresden and Berlin, suffered such wartime devastation. After the war, the Nazi war crimes trials were held here, convened by the International Military Tribunal.

In the postwar years, many of Nuremberg's most important buildings, including some of the finest Gothic and Renaissance churches in Germany, were restored or reconstructed in the Altstadt, the historic center. Nearly every German city has a restored Altstadt, but few have been reborn with the kind of evocative grace and charm of Nuremberg. As you wander through the streets of this ancient capital of the Holy Roman Empire, you find reminders of Nuremberg's brightest period.

Nuremberg

ACCOMMODATIONS ■
Burghotel Stammhaus **6**
Dürer-Hotel **4**
Hotel-Weinhaus
  Steichele **17**
Le Meridien Grand
  Hotel Nürnberg **20**

DINING ◆
Bratwurst-Häusle **12**
Essigbrätlein **7**
Goldenes Posthorn **10**
Heilig-Geist-Spital **16**
Kettensteg **5**

ATTRACTIONS ●
Albrecht-Dürer-Haus **3**
Altes Rathaus **13**
Dokumentationszentrum
  Reichsparteitagsgelände **21**
Frauenkirche **15**
Germanisches
  Nationalmuseum **18**
Hauptmarkt **14**
Kaiserburg **2**
Schöner Brunnen **11**

Schwurgerichtssaal 600 **1**
Spielzeugmuseum **8**
St.-Lorenz-
  Kirche **19**
St.-Sebaldus-
  Kirche **9**

Church ╪
Information ⓘ
Railway ——

Getting there

You can easily reach Nuremberg **by train** from anywhere in Germany or
Europe. Travel time from Frankfurt is about two hours; from Munich, one
hour 40 minutes; from Berlin, less than five hours. For information and
schedules, call **Deutsche Bahn** (☎ **11861**). The city's **Hauptbahnhof** is
within walking distance of all the major attractions.

For those traveling **by plane,** connections are available to Nuremberg's
small airport, **Flughafen Nürnberg** (☎ **0911/93700**), 6km (4 miles) north
of the city center, from major German and European cities.

By car from Munich, take the A9 Autobahn north; from Frankfurt, head southeast along the A3 Autobahn; and from Berlin, take the A9 Autobahn south.

Finding information and taking a tour

The **Tourist Information** office, opposite the train station at Königstrasse 93 (☎ **0911/233-6132**; www.nuernberg.de), is open Monday through Saturday from 9 a.m. to 7 p.m. An additional branch at Hauptmarkt 18 (☎ **0911/233-6135**) is open Monday through Saturday from 9 a.m. to 6 p.m. and Sunday (May–Sept only) from 10 a.m. to 1 p.m. and 2 to 4 p.m.

A guided 2½-hour **walking tour** of the city center in English departs daily (May–Oct and Nov 30–Jan 6) at 1 p.m. from the Tourist Information office at the Hauptmarkt. The tour includes a visit to the Kaiserburg (Imperial Castle). The cost is €7.50 ($9.40), children younger than 14 free, plus admission to the castle. Buy your tickets from the Tourist Information office or from the guide.

From April through October and on weekends in November and March, a small sightseeing train operated by **Nürnberger Altstadtrundfahrten** (☎ **0911/421-919**) runs through the Altstadt, passing all the major sights on a 40-minute tour with commentary in German (English translations available). The train departs from the fountain in the Hauptmarkt in front of the tourist office several times a day from 10:30 a.m. to 4 p.m. Cost is €4 ($5) for adults, €2 ($2.50) for children.

Orienting yourself

Nearly all that is of interest to the visitor is found in Nuremberg's **Altstadt,** one of the most successfully restored historic city centers in Germany. Roughly oval in shape, the entire Altstadt lies within a double wall of medieval fortifications, parts of which still remain and have rampart walks and gateway towers.

The **Hauptbahnhof** lies on the southern perimeter of the Altstadt; crowning the northern periphery is the **Kaiserburg,** the old imperial castle. The small, picturesque **Pegnitz River** bisects the Altstadt. You find historic sights both north and south of the river. To the north lies the **Hauptmarkt,** the city's main market square.

Getting around Nuremberg

Nuremberg's Altstadt is almost entirely closed to traffic. Although the Altstadt is larger than the historic centers in many other German cities, all of its sights are easily accessible on foot. In 30 minutes, you can walk from the Hauptbahnhof to the Kaiserburg through the heart of the city's medieval core and past most of the historic monuments. Walking in the Altstadt is easier than using public transportation.

Nuremberg's transportation system consists of a **U-Bahn** (subway), **trams,** and **buses.** Fares are based on zones. The easiest way to use the system is to buy a **TagesTicket** (day ticket) for €3.60 ($4.50); tickets purchased on Saturday also are good all day Sunday. Buy your tickets from the machines in the U-Bahn stations. For more information, call the city's transportation authority, **VGN** (☎ 0911/270-750). For a **taxi,** call ☎ 0911/19410.

Staying in Nuremberg

Like other German cities, Nuremberg has its fair share of overnight accommodations. See Chapter 22 for a listing of **Le Meridien Grand Hotel Nürnberg** ($$$–$$$$).

Burghotel Stammhaus
$ Altstadt

This reliable, 46-room hotel provides good, solid comfort in a great Altstadt location for a reasonable price. Bedrooms are compact and nicely furnished. The functional bathrooms are tiled and come with shower units. The hotel is below the castle walls in one of the most historic parts of the old city, next to Albrecht Dürer's house (see the "Exploring Nuremberg" section later in this chapter).

See map p. 349. Lammsgasse 3, 90403 Nürnberg. ☎ *0911/20-30-40. Fax: 0911/226-503.* www.burghotel-stamm.de. *Tram: Tiergärtnertor (then a 5-minute walk south on Albrecht-Dürer-Strasse to Lammsgasse). Rack rates: €75–€99 ($94–$124) double. Rates include continental breakfast. AE, DC, MC, V.*

Dürer-Hotel
$$–$$$ Altstadt

The 107-room Dürer stands beside the birthplace of its namesake, alongside the castle wall, and close to all the major sightseeing attractions in the Altstadt. The ambience throughout is modern and pleasant. Medium-size rooms done in pastel colors open onto the street or a back garden. The smallish tiled baths have showers (some have tub-shower combinations). You can enjoy your breakfast, the only meal served, in a pretty room off the lobby.

See map p. 349. Neutormauer 32, 90403 Nürnberg. ☎ *0911/214-6650. Fax: 0911/2146-65555.* www.duererhotel-nuernberg.de. *Tram: Tiergärtnertor (then a 5-minute walk southwest along the city wall). Rack rates: €125–€180 ($156–$225) double; special weekend and summer rates. Rates include buffet breakfast. AE, DC, MC, V.*

Hotel Weinhaus Steichele
$–$$ Altstadt

Despite renovations in 1998, this small, charming hotel from 1860 still retains its old-fashioned allure. The location is a tranquil street near Jacobsplatz, not far from the train station. The building is a beautiful stone structure with a sloping roofline. A modern annex next door blends harmoniously with the older building. The 58 rooms, decorated in a rustic Bavarian style, each have a small shower-only bathroom. The Weinhaus is noted for its excellent kitchen and selection of wines from its own vineyards in Baden and Rheinpfalz.

See map p. 349. Knorrstrasse 2–8, 90402 Nürnberg. ☎ **0911/202-280.** *Fax: 0911/221-914.* www.steichele.de. *U-Bahn: Weisser Turm (then a 3-minute walk south on Knorrstrasse). Rack rates: €75–€130 ($94–$162) double. Rates include buffet breakfast. AE, DC, MC, V.*

Dining in Nuremberg

Nuremberg is in a region called Franconia, known for its hearty and relatively uncomplicated cuisine. The city is famous for its finger-size *Rostbratwürste* made of pork and various spices and then broiled on a charcoal grill. You may hear the sausage seller in an open booth on the street shouting, "*Eins, zwei, drei* . . ." (one, two, three . . .) and so on. The hungry consumer shouts back the number of bratwursts he or she desires. The locals consider fewer than six bratwursts a snack; people typically consume up to 14 for lunch. Your bratwursts may come with sauerkraut or rye bread with very hot mustard. Seasonal game and fish dishes also are staples in restaurants serving Franconian fare.

Bratwurst-Häusle
$ FRANCONIAN

The Bratwurst Häusle is the most famous bratwurst house in the city, located opposite the Rathaus and close to the church of St. Sebald. In winter, the open grill in the rustic, wood-paneled dining room warms you; in summer, you can dine on a leafy outdoor terrace. Come to sample original *Nürnberger Rostbratwurste* (6, 8, 10, or 12 pieces), served on pewter plates. You can also get them to go *(zum mitnehmen).* A good beer to go with your wursts is Lederer Pils, a beer brewed locally since 1468.

See map p. 349. Rathausplatz 1. ☎ **0911/227-695.** *U-Bahn: Lorenzkirche (then a 5-minute walk north on Königsttrasse to Rathausplatz). Main courses: €5.50–€10 ($6.90–$12). AE, MC, V. Open: Mon–Sat 10 a.m.–10:30 p.m.*

Essigbrätlein
$$$$ FRANCONIAN/CONTINENTAL

The city's most ancient restaurant, dating from 1550, originally was a meeting place of wine merchants. Its upscale Franconian and Continental cuisine is inventive and refreshing, with many nouvelle recipes. Look for an ever-changing menu based on seasonal availability. The traditional specialty is roast loin of beef marinated in vinegar (what the name of the restaurant means in German).

See map p. 349. Weinmarkt 3. ☎ **0911/225-131.** *Bus: 36 to Hauptmarkt (then a 5-minute walk north on Winklerstrasse to Weinmarkt). Reservations required. Main courses: €20–€27 ($25–$34). Fixed-price meals: €38–€42 ($47–$52) lunch, €65–€79 ($81–$99) dinner. AE, DC, MC, V. Open: Tues–Fri noon to 1:30 p.m.; Tues–Sat 7–9:30 p.m. Closed Jan 1–15 and 2 weeks in Aug (dates vary).*

Goldenes Posthorn
$$–$$$ FRANCONIAN

No other restaurant in Nuremberg can match the antique atmosphere of the Goldenes Posthorn, which claims to be in the oldest house in Germany. Among its mementos is a drinking glass reputedly used by Albrecht Dürer. The restaurant's Franconian cuisine features such old-fashioned but satisfying dishes as quail stuffed with goose liver and nuts, venison in red wine with plums, fresh carp (in winter), and wurst with a mixture of onions and vinegar. The restaurant has a fine wine list, including vintages that date back to 1889.

See map p. 349. Glöckleingasse 2. ☎ *0911/225-153. Bus: 36 to Burgstrasse (then a 2-minute walk south to Glöckleingasse). Reservations required. Main courses: €7–€20 ($8.75–$25). Fixed-price meals: €17 ($21) lunch, €20–€42 ($25–$52) dinner. AE, DC, MC, V. Open: Mon–Sat noon to 2:30 p.m. and 6–11:30 p.m.*

Heilig-Geist-Spital
$ FRANCONIAN

Nuremberg's largest historical wine house, in business for 650 years, spans the Pegnitz River and is an atmospheric spot to dine. The main dishes are typical Franconian fare, hearty and filling. Carp is a specialty, and so are pork knuckle and sauerbraten. In season, you can order leg of venison with noodles and berries. The wine list is abundant and excellent, with more than 100 vintages.

See map p. 349. Spitalgasse 16. ☎ *0911/221-761. Bus: 46 or 47 to Spitalgasse. Main courses: €10–€14 ($12–$17). AE, DC, MC, V. Open: Daily 11 a.m. to midnight.*

Kettensteg
$ FRANCONIAN/INTERNATIONAL

This restaurant, bar, and beer garden beside the river in a romantic corner of the Altstadt is a real scene on warm evenings, when the tables fill up fast and everyone stays late, talking and drinking and eating under the trees. The menu is limited to just a few dishes, such as curried chicken on rice, Wiener schnitzel with french fries, and bratwursts. Vegetarians can choose from vegetable lasagne or various salads. Kettensteg is a nice place to relax and have a good time.

See map p. 349. Maxplatz 35. ☎ *0911/221-081. Bus: 36 to Maxplatz. Main courses: €8–€13 ($10–$16). No credit cards. Open: Summer 11 a.m.–11 p.m., winter 11 a.m.–2:30 p.m. and 6–11:30 p.m.*

Exploring Nuremberg

You need at least one full day to explore the main attractions of Nuremberg, nearly all of which are found in the Altstadt. Most of the historic core is for pedestrians only, so walking is a pleasure.

Albrecht-Dürer-Haus (Albrecht Dürer House)

Albrecht Dürer, one of the great German artists of the Renaissance, lived in this house from 1509 to 1528. Built in 1420, it's the only completely preserved Gothic house left in Nuremberg. Typical of the well-to-do burghers' houses of the 15th century, the structure has a first floor of sandstone surmounted by two half-timbered stories and a gabled roof. Exhibits inside the house are devoted to Dürer's life and works. Furnishings in many of the rooms are important historical pieces, original etchings and woodcuts, and copies of Dürer's paintings.

See map p. 349. Albrecht-Dürer-Strasse 39. ☎ 0911/231-2568. Tram: Tiergärtnertor (then a 3-minute walk south on Albrecht-Dürer-Strasse). Admission: €5 ($6.25) adults, €2.50 ($3.10) students and children ages 6 through 15; tours €2.50 ($3.10). Open: Mon (July–Sept only) 10 a.m.–5 p.m., Tues–Sun 10 a.m.–5 p.m. (Thurs until 8 p.m.). Tours: Guided tours in English Sat 2 p.m.

Germanisches Nationalmuseum (German National Museum)

Germany's largest and most important museum of German art and culture is the one must-see museum in Nuremberg. The collection covers the entire spectrum of German craftsmanship and fine arts from their beginnings to the present day. The prehistoric and early historical sections contain finds from the Stone Age and from the burial sites of the Merovingians (a Frankish dynasty ruling from about A.D. 500 to 750). The extensive painting and sculpture sections include works by Renaissance greats Albrecht Dürer and Veit Stoss, a sculptor and woodcarver known for his "nervous" angular forms and realism. The world's first globe, created by Martin Behaim, is on display, as is a self-portrait by Rembrandt. Everyday life in Germany through the ages is documented with domestic furnishings, folk objects, dollhouses, historic musical instruments, weapons, and the healing arts. This is an exhaustive and exhausting place, and you need to give yourself at least two hours.

See map p. 349. Kartäusergasse 1. ☎ 0911/13310. U-Bahn: Opernhaus (then a 3-minute walk north on Kartäusergasse). Admission: €4 ($5) adults, €3 ($3.75) children and students. Open: Tues–Sun 10 a.m.–5 p.m. (Wed until 9 p.m.).

Hauptmarkt (Main Market Square)

The cobblestoned Hauptmarkt, just north of the Pegnitz River at the northern end of Königstrasse, is Nuremberg's geographic and symbolic heart. Filled with stalls selling fresh flowers, fruits, and vegetables, the Hauptmarkt is the most colorful square in the city. In the northwest corner stands the **Schöner Brunnen** (Beautiful Fountain), an 18m-high (60-ft.) pyramid-shaped stone fountain from 1396. The 14th-century **Frauenkirche** (Church of Our Lady; ☎ 0911/206-560; open Mon–Sat 9 a.m. to 6 p.m., Sun 12:30 to 6 p.m.), on the eastern edge of the square, has on its façade a gilded 16th-century mechanical clock called the *Männleinlaufen* (a hard-to-translate word meaning "little men running"); every day at noon, figures of the seven electors appear and pay homage to Emperor Karl IV. The oldest part of the **Altes Rathaus** (Old Town Hall), on Rathausplatz just off the market square, dates from 1340; a later section, completed in 1622, marks the architectural transition from Renaissance to baroque style.

Kaiserburg (Imperial Castle)

The Kaiserburg, looming above the city from its hilltop at the northern edge of the Altstadt, was the official residence of the German kings and emperors from 1050 to 1571. The oldest portion, the 11th-century **Fünfeckturm** (Pentagonal Tower), has been in ruins since a fire destroyed it in 1420. Watchmen and guards used the ramparts with their parapet walks and secret passages to protect the kings and emperors, who lived in the inner core of the castle complex. Most of the buildings were constructed during the 12th century. With their heavy oak beams and painted ceilings, the great **Rittersaal** (Knights' Hall) on the ground floor and the **Kaisersaal** (Imperial Hall) on the second floor look much as they did when King Frederick III rebuilt them in the 15th century. The rooms are decorated with period Gothic furnishings.

The council of Nuremberg erected another set of buildings in the 14th and 15th centuries when its responsibilities expanded to include the protection of the emperor. The new buildings include the **Kaiserstallung** (Emperor's Stables), now a youth hostel; the massive bastions of the fortress; the **Tiefer Brunnen** (Deep Well); and the castle gardens. A fine view of the roofs and towers of Nuremberg can be seen from its terraces. Allot at least an hour to explore the various nooks and crannies of the castle.

Judgment at Nuremberg

If you're interested in a famous landmark of World War II (WWII), visit the **Schwurgerichtssaal 600** (International Military Tribunal), Fürther Strasse 110 (☎ 0911/ 231-5421; U-Bahn: Bärenschanze), where the Nuremberg Trials took place. Here, in room 600, a specially remodeled courtroom, 21 of the surviving leaders of the Third Reich stood trial in November 1945 for crimes against humanity. Afterward, ten were hanged. The building still serves as a courthouse, so tours (in German only) are available only on Saturday and Sunday from 1 to 4 p.m. Admission is €2 ($2.50).

In November 2001, the huge Congress Hall designed by Hitler's architect, Albert Speer, reopened as the new **Dokumentationszentrum Reichsparteitagsgelände** (Documentation Center Nazi Party Rally Grounds). A glass corridor now pierces Speer's Congress Hall, which is larger than the Colosseum in Rome. The corridor houses an exhibition that chronicles the ruthless misuse of power under National Socialism. The center is open Monday through Friday 9 a.m. to 6 p.m., Saturday and Sunday 10 a.m. to 6 p.m.; the €5 ($6.25) admission includes an audio guide. To reach the center, take Tram 9 or 6, or Bus 36, 55, or 65 to the "Docu-Zentrum" stop.

The **Kaiserburg Museum** (☎ 0911/2009540) contains antique weaponry, armor, and paintings, and explains the history of the castle.

See map p. 349. Burgstrasse. ☎ 0911/225-726. Tram: Tiergärtnertor (then a 10-minute walk north following signs). Admission: €5 ($6.25) adults, €4 ($5) students; free for children 16 and younger. Open: Apr–Sept daily 9 a.m.–6 p.m.; Oct–Mar daily 10 a.m.– 4 p.m.

Spielzeugmuseum (Toy Museum)

Nuremberg is a major toy center, and toys, both hand- and machine-made, fill all three floors of this museum. Some date from medieval times. Exhibits include a large collection of dolls and old dollhouses, optical toys (such as peep shows, magic lanterns, and stereoscopes), and model railways and other miniature vehicles. Objects on the top floor illustrate the history of toys since 1945, including Barbie dolls and LEGO blocks. Kids can play with toys, draw, or do crafts in a supervised playroom. You don't have to be a kid, though, to enjoy this acclaimed museum. Give yourself at least an hour, more if you have kids in tow.

See map p. 349. Karlstrasse 13–15. ☎ 0911/231-3164. Bus: 36 to Hauptmarkt (then a 3-minute walk west on Augustinerstrasse and north on Karlstrasse). Admission: €5 ($6.25) adults, €2.50 ($3.10) students and children. Open: Tues–Fri 10 a.m.–5 p.m., Sat–Sun 10 a.m.–6 p.m.

St.-Lorenz-Kirche (Church of St. Lawrence)

The largest and most beautiful Gothic church in Nuremberg rises above Lorenzerplatz. The St.-Lorenze-Kirche was begun in 1270 and took more than 200 years to complete. Twin towers flank the west portal with its sculptures depicting the theme of redemption, from Adam and Eve through the Last Judgment. Inside, soaring pillars adorned with expressive Gothic sculptures line the nave, and a magnificent stained-glass rosette window glows above the organ at the west end. The church contains two more remarkable works: *The Angelic Salutation* (1519), carved in linden wood by Veit Stoss, hangs over the entrance to the choir, and, to the left of the altar, a stone tabernacle by Adam Krafft (1496) presents likenesses of the sculptor and two apprentices.

See map p. 349. Lorenzer Platz 10. ☎ 0911/209-287. U-Bahn: Lorenzkirche (the church is on the square as you exit). Admission: Free. Open: Mon–Sat 9 a.m.–5 p.m., Sun 1–4 p.m.

St.-Sebaldus-Kirche

Consecrated in 1273, this church dedicated to Nuremberg's patron saint represents the stylistic transition from late Romanesque to early Gothic styles. The nave and west choir are Romanesque; the larger east choir, consecrated in 1379, is Gothic. Between the two east pillars is a 16th-century Crucifixion group dominated by a life-size Crucifix by Veit Stoss.

See map p. 349. Sebalderplatz. ☎ 0911/214-2516. U-Bahn: Lorenzkirche (the church is on the square as you exit the station). Admission: Free. Open: Mar–May daily 9:30 a.m.– 6 p.m.; June–Oct daily 9:30 a.m.–8 p.m.; Nov–Feb daily 9 a.m.–4 p.m.

Shopping in Nuremberg

Located across from the railway station, the **Handwerkerhof** (Craftsmen's Courtyard; U-Bahn: Hauptbahnhof) is an enclave of half-timbered shops and stalls where artisans create and sell a wide range of handicrafts (along with touristy souvenirs). The shops are open weekdays (and Sunday in December) from 10 a.m. to 6:30 p.m., and Saturday from 10 a.m. to 4 p.m.

Hofman, Rathausplatz 7 (☎ **0911/204-848;** Bus: 36), sells painted tin figures of soldiers and Christmas decorations. **Steiff Galerie,** Kaiserstrasse 1–9 (☎ **0911/235-5075;** U-Bahn: Lorenzerkirche), has classic and collectible Steiff bears for €90 to €140 ($112 to $175).

From Advent Sunday to December 24, Nuremberg's Hauptmarkt becomes the setting for the **Christkindlmarkt,** the oldest Christmas fair in Germany, held here for some 400 years. The Christmas fair transforms Hauptmarkt into a small town of wood-and-cloth stalls selling tree ornaments, handicrafts, candies, fruitcakes, *Lebkuchen* (see the sidebar "Love that *Lebkuchen*"), tinsel, and *Glühwein* (hot red wine spiced with cloves and cinnamon). Performances by singers and musicians, and theater, dance, and puppet groups occur daily. The square is especially beautiful at night, when all the surrounding buildings are floodlit.

Living it up after dark in Nuremberg

The **Städtische Bühnen** (State Theaters), Richard-Wagner-Platz 2–10 (☎ **0911/231-3808;** U-Bahn: Opernhaus), is a theater complex offering productions of drama (in the Schauspielhaus) and opera (in the Opernhaus). Tickets range from €8 to €50 ($10 to $63).

An artists' hangout, **Triebhaus,** Karl-Griolenberger-Strasse 28 (☎ **0911/223-041;** U-Bahn: Weisser Turm), opens early for big breakfasts (served all day) that run from €4 to €18 ($5 to $22) and offers soup, salad, and sandwich specials from €4.50 to €6 ($5.60 to $7.50) until 10:30 p.m. The cafe is open Monday through Friday from 8 a.m. to 1 a.m. and Saturday and Sunday from 9 a.m. to 1 a.m.

Love that *Lebkuchen*

Lebkuchen (*layb*-koo-kin) is to Nuremberg what marzipan is to Lübeck. The city's been the capital of Lebkuchen since the early 15th century. These delicious honey-and-spice cakes evolved into their round shape in Nuremberg. While jealously guarding their recipes, many places make and sell Lebkuchen in several different forms. **Lebkuchen Frauenholz,** Bergstrasse 1 (☎ **0911/243-464;** U-Bahn: Lorenzkirche), sells Lebkuchen packed in containers that look like half-timbered German houses. Many consider **Lebkuchen Schmidt,** Zollhausstrasse 30 (☎ **0911/89660;** www.lebkuchen-schmidt.com), to be the best Lebkuchen store in Nuremberg. Lebkuchen makes a great, inexpensive gift.

Café Ruhestörung, Tetzelgasse 21 (☎ 0911/221-921; U-Bahn: Lorenzkirche), has a pleasant patio where you can order a drink or a sandwich. Sandwiches and light meals cost €4.50 to €7 ($5.60 to $8.75). The cafe is open Monday through Friday from 7:30 a.m. to 1 a.m. and Saturday and Sunday from 9:30 a.m. to 1 a.m.

Chapter 19

Cologne and the Romance of the Rhine

In This Chapter

▶ Discovering the Rhineside city of Cologne
▶ Enjoying a boat trip on the Rhine
▶ Exploring the warm wine country of the Rheingau
▶ Taking in the scenery of the lovely Mosel Valley

*T*he Rhine (spelled *Rhein* in German) is one of the world's great rivers. Some 1,320km (820 miles) long, the river originates in south-eastern Switzerland, flows through the Bodensee (Lake Constance; see Chapter 17), and forms Germany's southwestern boundary as it contin-ues west, north, and northwest to the North Sea.

Through the centuries, the Rhine has inspired many legends, the most famous being the one attached to a high rock called the Lorelei (also spelled *Loreley*) towering above the town of St. Goarshausen. Lorelei, so the story goes, was a beautiful young woman who threw herself into the Rhine in despair over a faithless lover. Transformed into a siren, she sat on the rock combing her long, blonde hair and taking out her revenge by luring fishermen and ship captains to their destruction. The Rhine also is at the musical heart of Richard Wagner's four-opera cycle *Der Ring des Nibelungen.*

For about two centuries now, the mighty Rhine has attracted visitors from around the world, who come to enjoy the romantic scenery of hilltop castles, medieval towns, and vineyard-covered slopes. The **Rhineland,** the area along the river's west bank, encompasses roughly 23,000 sq. km (9,000 square miles) and is a treasure trove for tourists. (See the "The Rhineland" map in this chapter.)

In this chapter, I give most of the coverage to **Cologne,** the Rhineland's largest and most important city. Sitting right on the river, this city makes a wonderful headquarters for exploring the Rhineland. From Cologne, you can drive into the **Rheingau,** a lovely winegrowing section of the Rhine Valley from Koblenz south to Alsace. And although not as grand and

The Rhineland

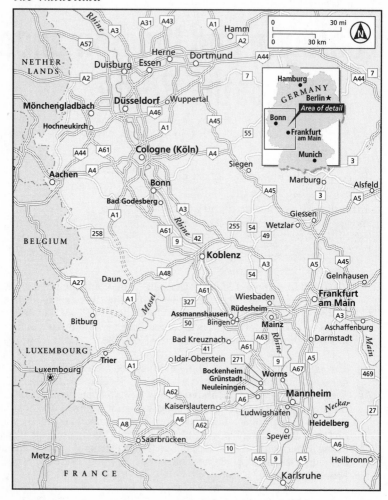

legend-filled as the Rhine, the **Mosel Valley,** covered with meticulously tended vineyards, is also worth exploring. I describe the highlights of all these side trips later in this chapter.

Cologne: Pleasures beside the Rhine

Visitors to this lively metropolis on the Rhine, Germany's fourth-largest and oldest city, are immediately struck by Cologne's cheek-by-jowl juxtaposition of the very old with the very new. You can see Roman ruins in an underground parking garage, a dizzyingly ornate Gothic cathedral

Cologne

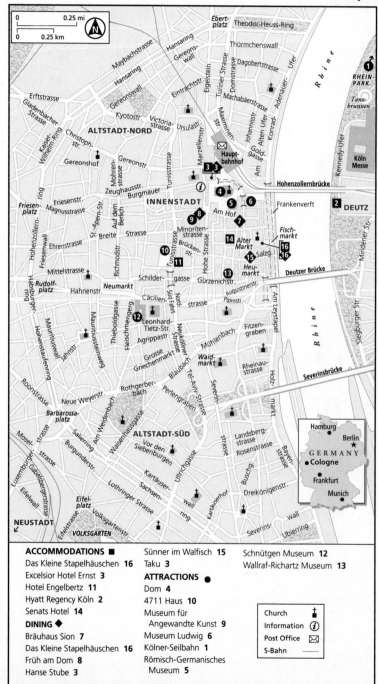

ACCOMMODATIONS ■
Das Kleine Stapelhäuschen **16**
Excelsior Hotel Ernst **3**
Hotel Engelbertz **11**
Hyatt Regency Köln **2**
Senats Hotel **14**

DINING ◆
Bräuhaus Sion **7**
Das Kleine Stapelhäuschen **16**
Früh am Dom **8**
Hanse Stube **3**

Sünner im Walfisch **15**
Taku **3**

ATTRACTIONS ●
Dom **4**
4711 Haus **10**
Museum für
  Angewandte Kunst **9**
Museum Ludwig **6**
Kölner-Seilbahn **1**
Römisch-Germanisches
  Museum **5**

Schnütgen Museum **12**
Wallraf-Richartz Museum **13**

Church	†
Information	ⓘ
Post Office	✉
S-Bahn	——

beside a modern museum complex, and a humble Romanesque church wedged in among luxury shops built in the booming 1980s. On a ten-minute walk in Cologne, you can traverse 2,000 years of history.

Cologne — spelled "Köln" in Germany and pronounced *koeln* — is far more than a city with Germany's largest cathedral, although the cathedral is, of course, what initially draws most visitors. The range of its museums, the buildings that house them, and the quality of their collections make Cologne one of the outstanding museum cities of Germany. Music, regardless of whether a symphony concert in the modern philharmonic hall, an opera at the highly regarded opera house, or a boisterous outdoor concert in the Rheinpark, is likewise a vital component of life here. The city also is famous as the birthplace of eau de Cologne, also called toilet water.

Cologne traces its beginnings to 38 B.C., when Roman legions set up camp here. As early as A.D. 50, the emperor Claudius gave the city municipal rights as capital of a Roman province. In addition to its substantial Roman legacy, the city boasts 12 major Romanesque churches. Older than the cathedral, the churches drew medieval pilgrims from all across Europe to "Holy Cologne," one of the most important pilgrimage cities in medieval Christendom.

The Kölner themselves are refreshingly relaxed and down-to-earth in how they enjoy their city. Every year they welcome millions of visitors, many of whom come to attend the giant international trade fairs held in the Köln *Messe,* or trade-fair grounds. Ancient traditions are annually renewed in the city's raucous pre–Lenten Carnival (called *Fasching*), a time of masked balls, parades, and general delirium. When the weather turns warm, visitors and citizens alike stroll along the Rhine promenades and flock to outdoor taverns and restaurants to enjoy the pleasures of a *Kölsch,* Cologne's unique and delicious beer, and a substantial meal of typical Rhineland cuisine.

Getting there

Cologne is one of the major cities in western Germany, and getting there is easy by train, car, or plane.

By plane

Cologne's airport, **Konrad-Adenauer-Flughafen Köln/Bonn** (☎ **02203/ 40-40-01;** www.airport-cgn.de), is located 14km (9 miles) southeast of the city. Direct flights arrive from most major European cities. The fastest and simplest way to get into the city is by taking a **StartBahn** (☎ **11861**) train from the new airport train station directly to the Cologne main train station. It runs from 5 a.m. to nearly 2 a.m. The trip takes 20 minutes; the fare is €5 ($6.25). A **taxi** from the airport to the city center costs about €25 ($31).

By train

Cologne is a major rail hub, so reaching the city from anywhere in Germany or the rest of Europe is easy. Frequent daily trains arrive from Berlin (trip time: 5½ hours), Frankfurt (trip time: 2½ hours), and Hamburg (trip time: 4½ hours). The Cologne Hauptbahnhof is in the heart of the city, next to the cathedral. For train information and schedules, call **German Rail** at ☎ **11861.**

By car

Cologne is easily reached from major German cities. The **A3** Autobahn connects the city to the north and south, while the **A4** Autobahn travels east and west.

Finding information

The **Köln Tourismus Office,** Unter Fettenhennen 19 (☎ **0221/221-30400;** www.koeln.de; U-Bahn: Hauptbahnhof), is located just a few steps from the cathedral. The office has city maps, a room-rental service (€3/$3.75), and information on city attractions. The office is open Monday through Saturday from 9 a.m. to 9 p.m. (until 10 p.m. July through September) and Sunday 10 a.m. to 6 p.m.

Getting oriented

The major sights of Cologne, including the mighty cathedral and the most important museums, are located in the **Altstadt** (Old Town), the restored and much altered medieval core of the city. The Altstadt spreads in a semicircle west from the Rhine to a ring road that follows the line of the 12th-century city walls (demolished, except for three gateways, in the 19th century). (See the "Cologne" map in this chapter.) The center of the Altstadt is the **Innenstadt** (Inner City), the historical heart of Cologne, where the Romans built their first walled colony.

The ring road and a greenbelt in the southwest (the location of the university) girdle **Neustadt,** the "new" part of town dating from the 19th century. The area across the river, on the Rhine's east bank, is called **Deutz.** Besides providing the best views of the cathedral-dominated Cologne skyline, Deutz is where you find the **Köln Messe** (trade-fair grounds) and the **Rhinepark.** The city's early industrial plants were concentrated in Deutz, and many of them are still there.

Getting around

The compact and pedestrian-friendly Altstadt, where you find the cathedral and most of the major attractions, is easily explored on foot. The city also has an excellent **bus, tram, U-Bahn** (subway), and **S-Bahn** (light-rail) system. A **CityTicket,** good for a single one-way fare within the inner city is €1.60 ($2) for adults, €.85 ($1.10) for children. A day ticket, the **TagesTicket,** costs €4.30 ($5.40) and enables you to travel

Cologne U-Bahn and S-Bahn

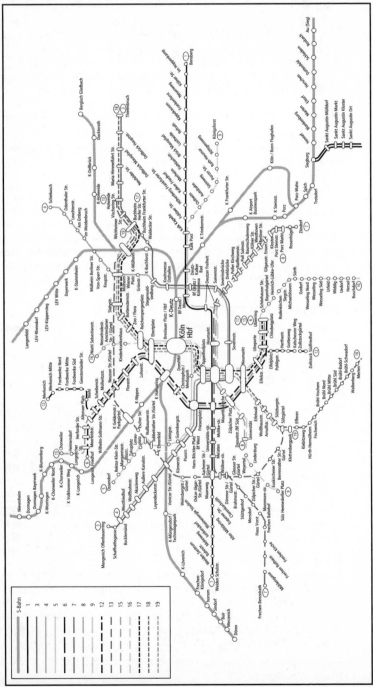

Celebrating carnival in Cologne

Cologne's Carnival, the city's "fifth season," is one of the most eagerly anticipated events in Germany. The season officially lasts from New Year's Eve to Ash Wednesday. The city buzzes with masked balls, parades, and general delirium. Natives call this citywide celebration *Fasteleer* or *Fastelovend*.

---

throughout the city's transportation network. A day ticket, which is good for up to five people traveling together, costs €6.50 ($8.10). Purchase tickets from the automated machines (labeled *Fahrscheine*), from bus drivers, or at the stations. Be sure to validate your ticket; validation machines are in stations and on buses. For information about public transportation, call VRS at ☎ **01803/504-030.**

Taxi meters start at €2 ($2.50), plus €1 ($1.25) if you hail it from the street; the fare rises €1.25 ($1.60) per kilometer for rides between 6 a.m. and 10 p.m., and €1.35 ($1.70) per kilometer for rides between 10 p.m. and 6 a.m. To order a taxi, call **Taxi-Ruf** at ☎ **0221/19410.**

Staying in Cologne

Also see Chapter 22 for details on Cologne's premier hotel, **Excelsior Hotel Ernst** ($$$$).

Das Kleine Stapelhäuschen
$–$$ Altstadt

The two town houses that make up this hotel stand on a corner of a historic square, right on the Rhine in the busiest section of the Altstadt. From the wine restaurant on the ground floor (see "Dining in Cologne" later in this chapter), you climb up a curving, wooden staircase (or take the elevator) to your room. The 31 rooms are fairly basic but comfortable and not lacking in a kind of old-fashioned charm; some rooms have beamed ceilings. Ten units come with a small, tiled bathroom with shower.

See map p. 361. Fischmarkt 1–3, 50667 Köln. ☎ *0221/272-7777. Fax: 0221/257-4232.* www.koeln-altstadt.de/stapelhaeuschen. *U-Bahn: Heumarkt (then a 5-minute walk north on Buttermarkt to Fishmarkt). Rack rates: €64–€85 ($80–$106) double without bathroom; €90–€141 ($112–$176) double with bathroom. Rates include buffet breakfast.*

Hotel Engelbertz
$ Altstadt

This modest, family-run hotel is in a central location close to everything in the Altstadt. The hotel has 40 rooms, all with small bathrooms that have a tub or shower. The decoration throughout is light, cheery, and modern.

See map p. 361. Obenmarspforten 1–3, 50667 Köln. ☎ **0221/257-8994**. Fax: 0221/ 257-8924. www.hotel-engelbertz.de. U-Bahn: Heumarkt (then a 5-minute walk west on Gürzenichstrasse, north on Hohe Strasse, and east on Obenmarspforten). Rack rates: €96 ($120) double. Rate includes breakfast. AE, MC, V.

Hyatt Regency Köln
$$–$$$$ Deutz

Located in Deutz, a five-minute walk across the Rhine from the train station, this modern full-service hotel features a dramatic lobby with a waterfall and a glamorous overall ambience. The 305 rooms are comfortably large and stylishly furnished. Many have views of the Rhine and the cathedral on the other side. Bathrooms have deep tubs with showers. The Hyatt has fine restaurants and a fitness center with a pool, sauna, and steam room. The staff can arrange baby-sitting.

See map p. 361. Kennedy-ufer 2A, 50679 Köln-Deutz. ☎ **0180/523-1234** or 0221/ 828-1234. Fax: 0221/828-1370. www.cologne.regency.hyatt.de. U-Bahn: Hauptbahnhof (then a 5-minute walk across the bridge). Rack rates: €125–€340 ($156–$425) double. AE, DC, MC, V.

Senats Hotel
$$–$$$$ Altstadt

This small, stylish hotel with its bright-yellow lobby is located in the heart of the Altstadt. The furnishings in the 59 rooms have a comfortable, modern style. Bathrooms are on the small side but vary according to the room. The hotel has a nice ambience throughout.

See map p. 361. Unter Goldschmied 9–17, 50667 Köln. ☎ **0221/20620**. Fax: 0221/ 206-2200. www.senats-hotel.de. U-Bahn: Hauptbahnhof (then a 5-minute walk across Roncalliplatz and south on Unter Goldschmied). Rack rates: €115–€245 ($144–$306). Rate includes buffet breakfast. AE, MC, V.

Dining in Cologne

Although several highly rated restaurants have established themselves here in recent years, Cologne is not a city particularly known for its gourmet dining. Rather, it's a place for conversation and drinking, generally over enormous portions of typical Rhineland fare in crowded restaurants that are *gemütlich* (cozy) rather than elegant.

To eat and drink as the Kölner do, visit one of the city's old tavern-restaurants (see listings for Früh am Dom and Bräuhaus Sion, later in this section). Local dishes at these and other nongourmet restaurants generally include *Halver Hahn* (a rye bread roll with Dutch cheese), *Tatar* (finely minced raw beef mixed with egg yolk, onions, and spices and served on bread or a roll), *Kölsch Kaviar* (smoked blood sausage served with raw onion rings), *Matjesfilet mit grünen Bohnen* (pickled white herring served with green butter beans and potatoes), *Hämchen* (cured

---

Kölsch: Cologne's beer of choice

Even if you don't like beer, you'll probably like *Kölsch (koehlsch),* a dry, delicious, top-fermented beer that's brewed only in Cologne. Kölsch has an alcohol content of about 3 percent (most other types of German beer have an alcohol content ranging from 4 to 6 percent). If you go to any of the taverns in town, you can order a Kölsch from one of the blue-aproned waiters, called a *Köbes.* The waiters always serve the beer in a tall, thin glass, called a *Stangen,* which they bring to your table in a special carrier called a *Kölschkranz.* Expect to pay about €1.35 ($1.70) for a small glass of Kölsch on tap.

---

pork knuckle cooked in vegetable broth), *Himmel und Äd* (apples and potatoes boiled and mashed together and served with fried blood sausage), and *Speckpfannekuchen* (pancakes fried in smoked bacon fat).

Bräuhaus Sion
$$ Altstadt KÖLNER/GERMAN

If you want a traditional local Bräuhaus where the beer is good, the wood paneling a little smoky with time and frequent polishing, and the food portions inexpensive and generous, Sion is the place. The main courses are traditional and filling Rhineland fare, such as *Riesenhämchen* (boiled pigs' knuckles) with sauerkraut, *Bockwurst* (sausage) with potato salad, or sauerbraten (pot- or oven-roasted marinated beef) with an almond-raisin sauce.

See map p. 361. Unter Taschenmacher 5. ☎ 0221/257-8540. U-Bahn: Heumarkt (then a 5-minute walk north along the Rhine promenade, west on Mühlengasse, and north on Unter Taschenmacher). Main courses €8–€16 ($10–$20). No credit cards. Open: Daily 11 a.m.–11 p.m.

Das Kleine Stapelhäuschen
$–$$ Altstadt GERMAN

This popular wine restaurant (and hotel, see "Staying in Cologne" earlier in this chapter) opens onto the old fish-market square and the Rhine, just a few minutes' walk from the cathedral. Although the wine is the main reason for coming (the local Rhine wines are that special), the cuisine also is very good. You may start with escargots, marinated herring, or stuffed mushrooms. Fish main courses include roasted perch-pike on lentils with balsamic vinegar and salmon poached in Rhine wine. A Rhineland meat specialty is sauerbraten with almonds, raisins, and potato dumplings. The menu also includes vegetarian and pasta dishes.

See map p. 361. Fischmarkt 1–3. ☎ 0221/272-7777. U-Bahn: Heumarkt (then a 5-minute walk north on Buttermarkt to Fishmarkt). Reservations recommended. Main courses: €8.50–€20 ($11–$25). AE, MC, V. Open: Daily noon to 11:30 p.m. Closed Dec 22–Jan 10.

Früh am Dom
$$ Altstadt KÖLNER/GERMAN

This *Bräuhaus* is the best all-around for atmosphere, economy, and hearty portions. You can eat in the upstairs or downstairs dining rooms (upstairs, on the ground floor, is better), with a different German specialty offered every day of the week. The menu is in English. A favorite dish is *Hämchen,* a Cologne specialty of smoked pork knuckle served with sauerkraut and potato purée. Other specialties include *Sauerkrautsuppe* (sauerkraut soup) and *Kölsch Kaviar* (blood sausage with onion rings). Früh-Kölsch, the tavern's beer on tap, has a 1,000-year-old brewing tradition. In summer, this tavern also has a beer garden.

See map p. 361. Am Hof 12–14. ☎ *0221/261-3250. U-Bahn: Hauptbahnhof (then a 5-minute walk south past the cathedral and across Roncalliplatz to Am Hof). Main courses: €9.25–€19 ($11–$24). No credit cards. Open: 8 a.m. to midnight.*

Hanse Stube
$$$–$$$$ Altstadt FRENCH

One of Cologne's top gourmet restaurants, Hanse Stube offers excellent cuisine and service in quiet, elegant surroundings. The menu changes daily but may include salmon with herb sour cream and avocado sherbet or cream of leek soup with crab for starters. Tasty main courses include stuffed kohlrabi with truffle, iced melon risotto with shrimp skewer, and leg of venison with a cognac-thyme sauce. For dessert, how about strawberries with cappuccino-chocolate sauce? The wine list is exemplary.

See map p. 361. In the Excelsior Hotel Ernst, Domplatz. ☎ *0221/270-3402. U-Bahn: Hauptbahnhof (then a 2-minute walk west on Trankgasse). Reservations recommended. Main courses: €14–€30 ($17–$37). Fixed-price menus: €50–€75 ($62–$94). Fixed-price business lunch: €29–€34 ($36–$42). AE, DC, MC, V. Open: Daily noon to 2:30 p.m. and 6:30–10:30 p.m.*

Sünner im Walfisch
$–$$ Altstadt GERMAN/FRENCH

This Brauhaus, on a narrow street set back from the Rhine, is a good choice for atmospheric dining. A step-gabled inn with a black-and-white timbered façade, it dates from 1626. The restaurant serves many Rhineland specialties and dishes influenced by French cuisine. You may try the pork cutlet with fried onions and crispy roast potatoes or the land-and-sea platter with roast beef and several kinds of fish.

See map p. 361. Salzgasse 13. ☎ *0221/257-7879. U-Bahn: Heumarkt (then a 3-minute walk west on Salzgasse). Reservations recommended. Main courses: €10–€16 ($12–$19). AE, DC, MC, V. Open: Mon–Thurs 5 p.m. to midnight, Fri 3 p.m. to midnight, Sat–Sun 11 a.m. to midnight.*

Taku
$$$–$$$$ **Altstadt   JAPANESE/ASIAN**

When it comes to fine dining, the Excelsior Hotel Ernst has no equal in Cologne. Taku, the hotel's Asian restaurant, is a serenely comfortable spot to enjoy sea-fresh sushi and sashimi or more ambitious dishes such as venison with bok choi and black pepper sauce or filet of parrotfish with spinach and lemongrass sauce. The food is memorable, the service superb. The striking design includes a serpentine fish tank built into the floor.

See map p. 361. In the Excelsior Hotel Ernst, Domplatz. ☎ *0221/270-3910. U-Bahn: Hauptbahnhof (then a 2-minute walk west on Trankgasse). Reservations recommended for dinner. Main courses: €22–€29 ($27–$36). Fixed-price menus: €15–€29 ($19–$36). AE, DC, MC, V. Open: Daily noon to 2:30 p.m. and 6–10 p.m.*

Exploring Cologne

You find the cathedral and all the major museums in the **Innenstadt,** the roughly half-square-mile area of the original Roman colony. After a day of sightseeing, round off your visit with an evening stroll along the Rhine promenade in Deutz.

The Cologne **Welcome Card,** available from the tourist office, is good for travel on all forms of public transportation and gets you into most museums for free or at a reduced cost. A one-day card costs €9 ($11), a two-day card costs €14 ($17), and a one-day family/group card good for two adults and two children or three adults costs €18 ($22).

Dom (Cathedral)

Considering how much time passed during the building of this gigantic edifice, the largest cathedral in northern Europe, it's a wonder that the Gothic façade is stylistically coherent. More than 600 years elapsed from the laying of the cornerstone in 1248 to the placement of the last finial (a decorative element) on the south tower in 1880. Upon completion, the Cologne cathedral was the tallest building in the world, its twin filigreed spires rising to a height of 157m (515 ft.). Overwhelming is the simplest way to describe it.

The **Dreikönigschrein** (Shrine of the Three Magi), housed in a glass case at the end of the choir, is the cathedral's major treasure. The giant reliquary is a masterpiece of goldsmith work dating from the end of the 12th century. The **choir,** which can be visited only on guided tours, is the most important part of the cathedral. Consecrated in 1322, the choir contains original, richly carved oak stalls, screen paintings, and a series of statues made in the cathedral workshop between 1270 and 1290. The famous **Three Kings windows** in the clerestory (the area above the nave) were installed in the early 14th century. In addition to some magnificent Renaissance-era stained-glass windows in the north aisle, the cathedral really has only two other must-see treasures. The **Gero Cross,** hanging in a chapel on the north side of the choir, is a rare monumental sculpture carved in Cologne in the late 10th century and reputedly the oldest-existing large-scale crucifix in the Western world. On the south side of the choir is Stephan Lochner's altarpiece, *Adoration of the Magi,* created around 1445. The painting is a masterpiece of the Cologne school — Italian in format, Flemish in the precision of its execution.

The cathedral's **Schatzkammer** (Treasury) is rather disappointing, and you aren't missing much if you skip it. If, on the other hand, you're in reasonably good shape, you can climb the 509 stairs of the 14th-century south tower (entry through the Portal of Saint Peter) for an inspiring view of the city and the Rhine.

You can make a circuit of the interior in about half an hour; the guided tours last one hour.

See map p. 361. Domkloster. ☎ *0221/9258-4730. U-Bahn: Hauptbahnhof (you see the cathedral as you come out of the train station). Admission: Cathedral free; treasury and tower combined €5 ($6.25) adults, €2.50 ($3.10) children and students; tower alone €2 ($2.50) adults, €1 ($1.25) children and students. Open: Cathedral daily 6:00 a.m.–7:30 p.m.; tower daily 9 a.m.–5 p.m. (winter until dusk); treasury daily 10 a.m.–6 p.m. Tours: English-language tours Mon–Sat 11 a.m. and 12:30, 2, and 3:30 p.m., Sun 2 and 3:30 p.m.; tour cost: €4 ($5) adults, €2 ($2.50) children and students.*

Kölner Seilbahn (Cologne Cable Car)

You get the best panoramic view of the city of Cologne by taking the Kölner Seilbahn, the first and only cable car system in Europe designed to span a major river. In operation since 1957, the enclosed gondolas cross the river beside the Zoobrücke (Zoo Bridge) between the Rheinpark in Deutz and the zoo. You get a great view of the cathedral and the river traffic along the Rhine. The trip takes about 15 minutes each way.

See map p. 361. Riehler Strasse 180. ☎ *0221/547-4184. U-Bahn: Zoo/Flora (then a 2-minute walk south to the departure point on the west side of the river). Open: Apr–Oct daily 10 a.m.–6 p.m. Admission: Round-trip ticket €5.50 ($6.90) adults, €3 ($3.75) children.*

Museum für Angewandte Kunst (Museum of Applied Art)

The treasures on display in this museum include furniture, home décor, and handicrafts from the Middle Ages to the present day. The Art Nouveau room is particularly impressive. On the ground floor and mezzanine, the exhibits, exclusively from the 20th century, include rooms and furniture by Finnish architect Alvar Aalto, German architect Mies van der Rohe, and the American designer Charles Eames, among others. Give yourself about an hour to see everything.

See map p. 361. An der Rechtsschule. ☎ *0221/221-23860. U-Bahn: Hauptbahnhof (then a 5-minute walk south past the Dom on Unter Fettenhenn to An der Rechtsschule). Admission: €4.20 ($5.25) adults, €2.10 ($2.60) children 6–12. Open: Tues–Sun 11 a.m.–5 p.m.; Wed 11 a.m.–8 p.m.*

Museum Ludwig

This museum, dedicated to 20th-century and contemporary art, opened in 1986. Exhibits represent nearly every major artist and art movement of the 20th century. The **Agfa-Foto-Historama,** a museum within the museum, is devoted to the history of photography. Give yourself at least an hour, more if you love modern art.

See map p. 361. Bischofsgartenstrasse 1. ☎ *0221/221-22379. U-Bahn: Hauptbahnhof (then a 5-minute walk south past the cathedral and east on Roncalliplatz). Admission: €5.80 ($7.25) adults, €3.30 ($4.10) children and students. Open: Tues 10 a.m.–8 p.m., Wed–Fri 10 a.m.–6 p.m., Sat–Sun 11 a.m.–6 p.m.*

 ## Römisch-Germanisches Museum (Roman-Germanic Museum)

Cologne's history, and the fabric of the city today, is inextricably bound with the history of Rome — a legacy that is documented in this fascinating museum. Before you enter, look at the section of the **Roman North Gate** preserved on Domplatz in front of the cathedral; on the right side of the museum is **Hafenstrasse,** a street paved with its original stones, which once ran down to the Roman harbor. Portions of an original **Roman wall** still stand beneath Domplatz in the underground parking lot.

The Roman-Germanic museum was built around the magnificent **Dionysius mosaic,** produced in a Rhineland workshop in the third century and discovered in 1941 by workers digging an air-raid shelter. Towering over the mosaic, which extols the joys of good living, is the **tomb of Lucius Poblicius,** constructed around A.D. 40 for a Roman officer; it is the largest antique tomb ever found north of the Alps.

The exhibits explore themes or types: religious life, trade and industry, the cult of the dead, and so on. The museum covers the period that extends from the Stone Age to the period of Charlemagne (ninth century). On the second floor, you can see a superlative collection of Roman glassware and a world-renowned collection of Roman jewelry. On the lowest level, devoted to the daily life of the Romans, you find an ancient black-and-white mosaic floor covered with swastikas. Centuries before the symbol became ominously identified with the atrocities of the Third Reich, the swastika — probably Indian in origin — was a symbol of good luck and happiness, and was known in Latin as the *crux gamata.* You need at least an hour to browse through the entire museum.

See map p. 361. Roncalliplatz 4. ☎ *0221/221-22304. U-Bahn: Hauptbahnhof (then a 3-minute walk south past the cathedral to Roncalliplatz). Admission: €4.20 ($5.25) adults, €2.10 ($2.60) children. Open: Tues–Sun 10 a.m.–5 p.m.*

Schnütgen Museum

The Romanesque church of St. Cäcilien (St. Cecilia, patron saint of music) houses one of Cologne's finest art collections. Try not to miss this small, splendid sampling of sacred art from the early Middle Ages to the baroque. The relics, reliquaries, crucifixes, and sculpture on display give you an idea

---

The Roman city of Colonia

By 50 B.C., Julius Caesar had extended the borders of the Roman Empire as far as the Rhine and established an alliance with the Germanic Ubii tribe on the site of present-day Cologne. The area became a military garrison with an imperial shrine and eventually was granted rights as a Roman city called Colonia Claudia Ara Agrippinensium (CCAA) in A.D. 50. Cologne's Roman period lasted until A.D. 401, when the Roman legions were recalled from the Rhine frontier.

---

of the artistic blessings bestowed upon "Holy Cologne." Outside, around the back, a skeleton has been spray-painted on the walled-in western portal of the church. Called simply *Tod* (Death), this oddly engaging work is by the Zürich graffiti artist Harald Nägele.

See map p. 361. Cäcilienstrasse 29. ☎ 0221/221-22310. U-Bahn: Neumarkt (then a 5-minute walk west on Pipinstrasse, which becomes Cäcilienstrasse). Admission: €3.20 ($4) adults, €1.90 ($2.40) children. Open: Tues–Fri 10 a.m.–5 p.m., Sat–Sun 11 a.m.–5 p.m.

Wallraf-Richartz Museum

The Wallraf-Richartz Museum is one of the country's greatest repositories of art from the Middle Ages to the late 19th century. Opened in 1861, the museum also is one of Germany's oldest. In 2000, the museum moved to a new building designed by Cologne architect Oswald Mathias Ungers. The new museum nicely shows off the art but somehow feels like an office building from the 1950s.

On the first floor, you find an outstanding collection of paintings by the medieval Cologne school (most done between 1330 and 1550). Many of the paintings and altarpieces depict legends from the lives of martyred saints who became identified with the "Holy Cologne" of the Middle Ages — St. Ursula in particular. The Renaissance section includes works by Albrecht Dürer and Lucas Cranach. A memorable collection of 17th-century Dutch and Flemish paintings holds pride of place on the second floor. Here you find Rubens's *Self-Portrait Amidst the Circle of Friends from Mantua* and an enigmatic self-portrait by Rembrandt. In addition to important French and Spanish works, the museum boasts a rich collection of 19th-century paintings, with major pieces by the German Romantic painter Caspar David Friedrich, Gustave Courbet, Edvard Munch, Auguste Renoir, and Vincent van Gogh, among scores of others. Give yourself about two hours if you want to browse through all the galleries.

See map p. 361. Martinstrasse 39. ☎ 0221/221-21119. U-Bahn: Heumarkt (then a 3-minute walk north on Unter Käster to Martinstrasse). Admission: €5.80 ($7.25) adults, €3.30 ($4.10) students and children. Open: Tues 10 a.m.–8 p.m., Wed–Fri 10 a.m.–6 p.m., Sat–Sun 11 a.m.–6 p.m.

Shopping in Cologne

The first *Füssgänger* (pedestrians-only) shopping zones in Germany originated in Cologne and present a seemingly endless and interconnected conglomeration of shops and shopping arcades.

Hohe Strasse, the main north–south street in Roman times, is now Cologne's busiest commercial drag, jammed every day except Sunday with shoppers, musicians, organ grinders, snack shops, fruit sellers, and endless stores. On Hohe Strasse and its surrounding streets, you find all the major international designer-clothing boutiques; stores selling silver, fine jewelry, and perfumeries; and the big department stores. **Schildergasse** is where you find international men's fashions, fine leather bags and purses, and French, German, and Italian designer shoes.

Three specialty shops worth knowing about: **Schirmbusch,** Ehrenstrasse 104, carries a huge selection of umbrellas; **Walter König's Postkartenlade,** Breite Strasse 93, stocks a large selection of art postcards and greeting cards; and **Filz Gnoss,** Apostelnstrasse 21 (☎ **0221/257-0108**), sells unusually decorated and comfortable felt slippers and those enormous *Überpantoffeln* you slip over your shoes and slide around in when touring German palaces.

Discovering nightlife in Cologne

One of Germany's major cultural centers, Cologne offers a variety of fine arts and nightlife options. To find out what's going on in the city, pick up a copy of *Monats Vorschau* (€1.20/$1.50) at newsstands). You can purchase tickets at a venue's box office *(Kasse)* or at **Köln-Ticket,** Roncalliplatz 4, next to the cathedral (☎ **0221/2801;** U-Bahn: Hauptbahnhof).

Dance clubs

E-Werk, Schanzenstrasse 28 (☎ **0221/962-790;** U-Bahn: Keupstrasse), is a combination disco–concert hall housed within a former electrical

Cologne from Cologne: No. 4711

Any kind of toilet water is now called *eau de Cologne,* or simply "cologne," but *Echt Kölnisch Wasser* (the original eau de Cologne) remains the official designation of origin for the distinctive toilet waters created in the city of Cologne. **4711 Haus,** Glockengasse 4711 (☎ **0221/925-0450;** U-Bahn: Neumarkt), sells the orange-and-lavender scented water first developed in Cologne in 1709 by Italian chemist Giovanni Maria Farina. The Mühlens family, another early producer of Kölnisch Wasser, also lived and worked in this house at number 4711. The street number eventually became the trademark name for their product. You can buy 4711 cologne in all sizes and shapes, as soap, and even as premoistened towelettes. The smallest bottle costs about €4 ($5).

power plant. Recorded music alternates with live acts. E-Werk is open every Friday and Saturday night at 10 p.m.

Live bands and DJs play for dancers at **MTC,** Zulpicher Strasse 10 (☎ **0221/170-2764;** U-Bahn: Zulpicherplatz), open from 10 p.m. to 3 a.m. with a €4 to €10 ($5 to $12) cover.

Gay and lesbian bars

Chains, Stephansstrasse 4 (☎ **0221/238-730;** U-Bahn: Neumarkt), a gay bar in the Marienplatz area, is open from 10 p.m. to 2 or 3 a.m.

The most sophisticated rendezvous for gays and lesbians in Cologne is **Gloria,** Apostelnstrasse 11 (☎ **0221/254-433;** U-Bahn: Neumarkt), open Sunday to Thursday from 9 a.m. to 1 a.m., Friday and Saturday from 9 a.m. to 3 a.m.

Quo Vadis Pub, a good gay bar for men and women, is near Marienplatz at Pipinstrasse 7 (☎ **0221/258-1414;** U-Bahn: Heumarkt). The bar is open daily from noon to midnight during the week and from 11 a.m. to 1 a.m. on the weekend.

Jazz clubs

Klimperkasten (also known as **Papa Joe's Biersalon**), Alter Markt 50–52 (☎ **0221/258-2132;** U-Bahn: Hauptbahnhof), is a small and intimate jazz and piano bar with live music every night beginning around 8 p.m.

Papa Joe's Jazzlokal, Buttermarkt 37 (☎ **0221/257-7931;** U-Bahn: Heumarkt), is best on Sunday, when the music begins at 3:30 p.m. and lasts until 1 a.m. The club is also open for live jazz Monday to Saturday from 7 p.m. to 2 a.m. The club doesn't charge a cover.

The performing arts

The **Kölner Philharmonie** concert hall, Bischofsgartenstrasse 1 (☎ 0221/ **2801;** www.koelner-philharmonie.de; U-Bahn: Hauptbahnhof), completed in the late 1980s, is the home of two fine orchestras: the **Gürzenich Kölner Philharmoniker** and the **Westdeutscher Rundfunk Orchestra** (West German Radio Orchestra). The hall also presents pop and jazz programs. Ticket prices vary, anywhere from €8 to €125 ($10 to $156), according to the event.

Oper der Stadt Köln (Cologne Opera), Offenbachplatz (☎ **0221/2212-8400;** www.buehnenkoeln.de; U-Bahn: Neumarkt), is the Rhineland's leading opera house. Dance programs also take place here. Tickets range from €11 to €66 ($14 to $82).

The **Schauspielhaus,** Offenbachplatz (☎ **0221/8400;** U-Bahn: Neumarkt), is the site of three theaters, each with its own performances and schedules.

Cruises along the Rhine

Cologne is a major embarkation point for Rhine cruises. Even if you don't have time for a long Rhine cruise, you can enjoy a trip on the river aboard one of the many local boats.

KD (Köln–Düsseldorfer Deutsche Rheinschiffahrt), Frankenwerft 15 (☎ **0221/208-8318**; www.k-d.com), offers boat tours of the Rhine from Cologne. The KD ticket booth and boarding point is right on the river, a short walk south from the cathedral.

The one-hour **Panorama Rundfahrt** (round-trip) is a pleasant way to see the stretch of Rhine immediately around Cologne. The tour departs daily at 10:30 a.m., noon, 1:45 p.m., and 6:15 p.m. The cost is €6 ($7.50). A daily **Nachmittags** (afternoon) cruise with *Kaffee und Kuchen* (coffee and cake) leaves at 3:30 p.m. and returns at 5:45 p.m.; the cost is €9.20 ($11). Prerecorded commentary in English plays on both of these sightseeing cruises.

If you want to see the most scenic stretch of the Rhine, with the legendary Lorelei rock and many hilltop castles, take one of KD's **daylong cruises between Mainz and Koblenz,** departing Mainz daily at 8:45 a.m. and 9:45 a.m. and returning at 7:20 p.m. and 8:20 p.m. The round-trip cost is €46 ($57).

For more information on Rhine river cruises, contact **Viking KD River Cruises of Europe,** represented in North America by JFO Cruise Service, 2500 Westchester Ave., Purchase, NY 10577 (☎ **800/346-6525**), or visit the company's Web site at www.rivercruises.com.

Taverns

Päffgen Bräuhaus, Friesenstrasse 64–66 (☎ **0221/135-461**; U-Bahn: Friesenplatz), a 110-year-old tavern, serves its Kölsch brand of beer, along with regional cuisine. Seating is available indoors and out. The tavern is open daily from 10 a.m. to midnight.

Altstadt Päffgen, Heumarkt 62 (☎ **0221/257-7765**; U-Bahn: Heumarkt), also serves the local beer, *Kölsch,* with German dishes. The tavern is open Tuesday to Sunday from noon to midnight.

The Mosel Valley: Great Wines, Beautiful Scenery

The Mosel Valley, southwest of Cologne, is a scenic winegrowing region like the nearby Rheingau (see the "Sampling the wines of Rheingau" sidebar in this chapter). Winding through the steep slopes of the Eifel and Hunsruck hills in the German state of Rheinland-Palatinate, the Mosel Valley follows

The Mosel Valley

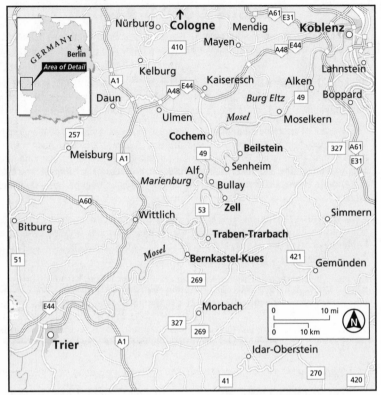

the course of the Mosel River (spelled *Moselle* in English) for more than 160km (100 miles) between **Trier** and **Koblenz,** where the waters flow into the Rhine. (See the "The Mosel Valley" map in this chapter.)

The valley encompasses thousands of acres of vineyards, a full 10 percent of the national total. Its beautiful scenery, fine wine, Roman ruins, medieval castles, and riverside towns with cobbled streets and half-timbered houses make the Mosel Valley a prime area for exploration.

Touring the valley by boat or car

If you're headquartering in Cologne and want to enjoy a **boat cruise** down the Mosel River, the easiest way is to take a train to Koblenz. From there, a boat operated by **KD** (☎ **0221/20881;** www.k-d.de) sails down the Mosel to Cochem, 51km (32 miles) southwest of Koblenz. From late April to late October, boats depart daily from Koblenz at 9:45 a.m. and arrive in Cochem at 3 p.m. A return boat departs at 3:40 p.m., arriving in Koblenz at 8 p.m. The round-trip fare is €22 ($27).

The **A49** Autobahn runs between Koblenz and Trier; the prettier **A53** runs alongside the Mosel between Zell and Schweich.

Stopping in Cochem

About halfway down the Mosel River from Koblenz is Cochem, a medieval riverside town surrounded by vineyards. Cochem is a popular spot for wine tastings and festivals. The **Tourist Information office,** Endertplatz 1 (☎ **0267/60040;** www.cochem.de), is open November through March, Monday through Friday 9 a.m. to 1 p.m. and 2 p.m. to 5 p.m.; April through October, Monday through Thursday 9 a.m. to 5 p.m. and Friday 9 a.m. to 6 p.m. The office also is open Saturday from May through August (9 a.m.– 5 p.m.), and Sunday in July and August (9 a.m. to noon).

If you're driving through the Mosel Valley, Cochem is your best choice for an overnight stopover between Koblenz and Trier, and you can also reach Cochem by train from either of those cities.

Mosel-Wein-Woche (Mosel Wine Week), celebrating the region's wines with tasting booths and a street fair, begins the first week of June. The similar **Weinfest** takes place the last weekend of August. For information, contact the Cochem Tourist Information office.

Cochem's biggest attraction is **Reichsburg Cochem** (☎ **02671/255**), a restored 11th-century castle at the top of the hill behind the town. The castle, the most famous and photographed sight along the Mosel River, is open daily mid-March to November 9 a.m. to 6 p.m. Admission is €4 ($5) for adults and €2 ($2.50) for children and students.

Sampling the wines of Rheingau

The Rhine Valley from Koblenz south to Alsace, with its almond, cherry, fig, and other fruit trees and its sheltered sunny slopes covered with vineyards, is like a northern extension of Italy. This part of the Rhineland not only turns out fine wines, but has been fundamentally formed by the culture of wine, as reflected in its economy, traditions, and festivals.

The **Rheingau wine district** (see map p. 360) follows a 45km (27-mile) stretch of the Rhine west of Wiesbaden to the attractive Rhineside town of **Bingen.** Vineyards have produced wine here since Roman times. The wind-sheltered southern slopes of the Taunus range, on the river's northern bank, get plenty of sunshine and comparatively little rain, conditions the Romans recognized as perfect for grape-growing. The Rheingau wine grapes produce a delicately fruity wine with a full aroma. Eighty percent of this wine comes from the Riesling grape, and wine fans consider Rheingau Rieslings to be among the best white wines made anywhere.

If you take a Rhine cruise between Koblenz and Mainz (see the "Cruises along the Rhine" sidebar in this chapter), you sail through this scenic winegrowing region. If you're driving, the **B42** highway runs beside the river between **Boppard** and **Eltville,** the Rheingau's unofficial capital.

Both a hotel and a wine restaurant, **Alte Thorschenke,** Brückenstrasse 3, 56812 Cochem (☎ **02671/7059;** Fax: 02671/4202), is one of the oldest and best-known establishments along the Mosel. The half-timbered structure, originally built in 1332, added a modern wing and became a hotel in 1960. A creaking wooden staircase (you can also take the elevator) leads to most of the 35 rooms. A few of the rooms have four-poster beds; all contain shower-tub combinations. Rack rates range from €110 to €120 ($137 to $150) for a double, buffet breakfast included. All major credit cards are accepted. The hotel is closed from January 5 to March 15.

For a fine meal, drive to Enterttal, 1.6km (1 mile) northwest of Cochem, and dine at **Weissmühle im Enterttal,** Endertstrasse 1 (☎ **02671/8955**). Try the trademark dish of fresh trout stuffed with herbs, baked, and kept warm at your table with a hot stone. Main courses range from €15 to €27 ($19 to $34). Diners Club, MasterCard, and Visa are accepted. The restaurant is open daily from noon to 2 p.m. and 6 to 9 p.m.

Chapter 20

Frankfurt am Main: Apple Wine and Euros

*L*ocated on the River Main, and sometimes called "Mainhattan," because of its skyscraper-studded skyline, Frankfurt is Germany's fifth-largest city. Because the Frankfurt airport serves as the country's main international hub, many travelers get their first introduction to Germany in this city. (See the "Frankfurt am Main" map in this chapter.)

Frankfurt has been a major banking city since the Rothschilds opened their first bank here more than 200 years ago. Today, Frankfurt is not only the financial center of Germany but also of the entire European Union (EU), home of the Bundesbank, Germany's central bank, and the Central Bank of the EU. At last count, 438 banks maintained headquarters here, a fact that helps account for all those designer skyscrapers (more than in any other German city, and including the tallest building in Europe). The huge € symbol that stands on Willy-Brandt-Platz in front of the new opera house can be regarded as the city's logo.

Frankfurt definitely focuses on business. Millions of visitors descend on the city during its trade shows in spring and autumn. The best known is the International Book Fair, the most important meeting place in the world for the acquisition and sale of book rights and translations.

Leveled during Allied bombing raids in World War II (WWII), a small portion of Frankfurt's Altstadt (Old Town) was lovingly rebuilt. But Frankfurt is first and foremost a modern, cosmopolitan city. Besides being a much-visited business center, the city is a tourist destination with fine museums and art collections, a rich cultural life, great shopping, and a lively nightlife. A very strong American presence exists in this city on the Main. Nearly 40,000 American soldiers were stationed in Frankfurt until 1990.

Frankfurt am Main

GERMANY

Hamburg Berlin ★

● Frankfurt
   am Main

Munich ●

MIQ./ADICKESALLEE

Adickes Allee

Miquel allee

Eysseneckstrettenstr.

Cron...

Hansa Allee

Bremer Strasse

Holzhausenstr.

HOLZHAUSENSTRASSE

Wolfgangstr.

Baustrasse

GRÜNEBURGWEG

GRÜNEBURG
PARK

Grüneburgweg

Fürsten-
bergerstr.   **4**   str.

Wolfgang-

Grüneburgweg

Siesmayer str.

Feldburgstr.

Freidburgstr.

WESTEND

Staufenstr.

Gärtnerweg

Rothschild's
Park

Anl.

ESCHENHEIMER
TOR

5

Bockenheimer

6

Miquel allee

Franz Rücker allee

Falkstrasse

Leipziger Str.

Bockenheimer Landstrasse

1

3

University

Senckenberganlage

Schumannstr.

Beethovenstr.

2

Mendelsonstr.

Arndtstr.

Lindenstr.

Guiollett str.

TAUNUSANLAGE

Hochstr.

Alte Oper ■

Gr. Bockenheimerstr.

Börse ■

An der Zei

HAUPTWACHE

Hauptwache

7   Junghof Str.

Neue Mainzer

Goethe-
platz   **8**

9   Berliner Str

9   Braubach

Willy-Brandt-
Platz

10

11

12

THEATERPLATZ

MESSE

Güterplatz

Westendstrasse

HAUPTBAHNHOF

Taunus str.

Kaiserstr.

(i)

Munchener   Str.

MUSEUMS
UFER

Untermainbr.

Schweizer Pl.

17

16

Leuschner Str.

Untermain Kai

M a i n

SCHWEIZERPLATZ

GUTLEUTVIERTEL

Schaumainkai

15

Oppenheimer

Gutleut strasse

Friedensbrücke

Kennedy allee

14

Mainzer Land str.

13

(i)   Information

──────   S-Bahn

(U)   U-Bahn
       Station

0   1/8 mile

0   125 meters

(N)

Güterbahnhof

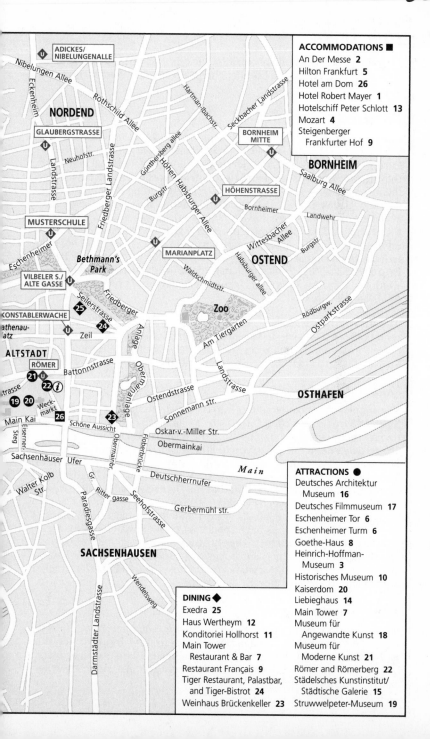

ADICKES/
NIBELUNGENALLE

Nibelungen Allee

Eckenheim

Rothschild Allee

Hartman-Ibachstr.

Seckbacher Landstrasse

NORDEND

GLAUBERGSTRASSE

Neuhofstr.

Landstrasse

Friedberger Landstrasse

Guntherberg allee

Höhen

Habsburger Allee

Burgstr.

BORNHEIM
MITTE

BORNHEIM

Saalburg Allee

HÖHENSTRASSE

Bornheimer

Landwehr

MUSTERSCHULE

Eschenheimer

Wittesbacher
Allee

Burgstr.

MARIANPLATZ

Habsburger allee

OSTEND

*Bethmann's
Park*

Waldschmidtstr.

VILBELER S./
ALTE GASSE

Seilerstrasse

Friedberger

KONSTABLERWACHE

Rödburgw.

Rödbw.

Ostparkstrasse

athenau-
atz

Zeil

Zoo

Am Tiergarten

ALTSTADT

RÖMER

Battonnstrasse

Obermainanlage

Ostendstrasse

Landstrasse

OSTHAFEN

strasse

Weck-
markt

Sonnemann str.

Main Kai

Schöne Aussicht

Oskar-v.-Miller Str.

Obermainkai

Eisernersteg

Sachsenhäuser Ufer

Obermainbr.

Floberbrücke

Main

Walter Kolb
Str.

Deutschherrnufer

Paradiesgasse

Gr. Ritter gasse

Seehofstrasse

Gerbermühl str.

SACHSENHAUSEN

Wendelsweg

Darmstädter Landstrasse

ACCOMMODATIONS ■
An Der Messe **2**
Hilton Frankfurt **5**
Hotel am Dom **26**
Hotel Robert Mayer **1**
Hotelschiff Peter Schlott **13**
Mozart **4**
Steigenberger
  Frankfurter Hof **9**

DINING ◆
Exedra **25**
Haus Wertheym **12**
Konditoriei Hollhorst **11**
Main Tower
  Restaurant & Bar **7**
Restaurant Français **9**
Tiger Restaurant, Palastbar,
  and Tiger-Bistrot **24**
Weinhaus Brückenkeller **23**

ATTRACTIONS ●
Deutsches Architektur
  Museum **16**
Deutsches Filmmuseum **17**
Eschenheimer Tor **6**
Eschenheimer Turm **6**
Goethe-Haus **8**
Heinrich-Hoffman-
  Museum **3**
Historisches Museum **10**
Kaiserdom **20**
Liebieghaus **14**
Main Tower **7**
Museum für
  Angewandte Kunst **18**
Museum für
  Moderne Kunst **21**
Römer and Römerberg **22**
Städelsches Kunstinstitut/
  Städtische Galerie **15**
Struwwelpeter-Museum **19**

Getting There

All roads, rail lines, and air corridors lead to Frankfurt. If you fly into Germany from outside of Europe, chances are you'll land at the city's airport.

By plane

The city's airport, **Flughafen Frankfurt/Main** (☎ **069/6901;** www. frankfurt-airport.de), lies 11km (7 miles) from the city center. Europe's busiest airport and Germany's major international gateway, this airport serves more than 110 countries worldwide, with direct flights from many U.S. and Canadian cities, including Atlanta, Boston, Chicago, Dallas, Denver, Detroit, Miami, Montreal, Newark, New York, Philadelphia, Pittsburgh, Portland (Oregon), Toronto, and Washington, D.C. Terminal 1 handles most European flights; Terminal 2 handles international flights. A people-mover system (called Sky Line) links the two airport terminals, in which you find many banks (Commerz Bank, Dresdner Bank, SEB Bank, and Finanz Bank) with currency exchange windows. Privately operated currency exchanges (Travelex is one) and ATMs are also there.

The airport has two railway stations, a bus terminal, and several car-rental offices. The long-distance **AIRail Terminal** links the airport to cities throughout Germany and neighboring countries. Regional and local trains operate from the **Regional Station** directly below Terminal 1.

Taking the train into the city

The simplest method for getting into the city from the airport is by **train.** **S8** and **S9** trains (direction Offenbach or Hanau) to Frankfurt's city center depart about every ten minutes from the regional train station, platform 1. These two S-Bahn lines take you to Frankfurt's Hauptbahnhof (main railway station) in about ten minutes. A one-way ticket costs €4.85 ($6.10). Tickets are available from the RMV ticket machines (with English translations) at the regional station and at the **Deutsche Bahn (DB) Travel Center**, Terminal 1, Level 0 (☎ **069/691-844**), open daily from 6 a.m. to 11:30 p.m. (RMV are the initials of the public transportation authority.) The RMV ticket machines have special fast-selection buttons for the S-Bahn journey to Frankfurt. They are marked: *Einzelfahrt Frankfurt* (single ticket to Frankfurt) and *Tageskarte Frankfurt inkl. Flughafen* (a reduced-price one-day transportation ticket within Frankfurt, including the trip from the airport).

Hopping a bus into the city

If you want to travel to the city center by bus, you have many options from which to choose. You find bus stops in front of Terminal 1 on the arrivals level and in front of Terminal 2 on Level 2. Some airlines offer special bus-shuttle services to Frankfurt from the airport; check when you purchase your ticket.

Catching a cab into the city

A taxi ride from the airport to the city center costs about €20 ($25) and takes about 20 minutes. Taxis are available in front of the terminals.

By train

Frankfurt's **Hauptbahnhof** is the busiest train station in Europe, with connections to all major German and European cities. **Tourist Information Hauptbahnhof,** opposite the main entrance (☎ **069/2123-8800**), is open Monday to Friday from 8 a.m. to 9 p.m., and Saturday and Sunday from 9 a.m. to 6 p.m. You find currency exchange windows and bank ATMs in the station. For travel information, including schedules and fares, call **Deutsche Bahn** (☎ **11861**).

By car

The A3 and A5 autobahns intersect near Frankfurt's airport. The **A3** comes in from the Netherlands, Cologne, and Bonn and continues east and south to Würzburg, Nürnberg, and Munich. The **A5** comes from the northeast (Hannover) and continues south to Heidelberg and Basel, Switzerland. From the west, the **A60** connects with the **A66,** which leads to Frankfurt.

Finding Information After You Arrive

You find tourist information in two locations:

✔ **Tourist Information Hauptbahnhof,** opposite the main entrance of the train station (☎ **069/2123-8800;** www.frankfurt-tourismus. de), is open Monday to Friday 8 a.m. to 9 p.m., Saturday and Sunday 9 a.m. to 6 p.m. This office offers a hotel-booking service for €2.50 ($3.10).

✔ **Tourist Information Römer,** Römerberg 27 (☎ **069/2123-8800**), in the Altstadt, is open Monday to Friday from 9:30 a.m. to 5:30 p.m., Saturday and Sunday from 10 a.m. to 4 p.m.

Orienting Yourself in Frankfurt

The **Main River** divides Frankfurt. You find most of the historic sights and several museums in the **Altstadt** on the north bank. Concentrated in the **city center** around the Altstadt are hotels, restaurants, and nightlife. The Altstadt contains an even older section referred to as the **Innenstadt,** or Inner City. The exclusive **Westend** district, west of the Altstadt, is a residential and embassy quarter. It was the only part of Frankfurt that was not destroyed during the WWII Allied bombing of the city. The huge, modern Frankfurt **Messe** (trade-fair convention center) is considered part of the Westend.

The **Hauptbahnhof** is located at the western edge of the city center. As you walk out of the station, Baselerstrasse is on your right and heads south toward the Main River. You have a choice of streets heading east to the Altstadt: Münchner Strasse leads directly into **Theaterplatz,** with its opera house; Taunusstrasse goes to three of the major Altstadt squares in the southern part of the city (**Goetheplatz, Rathenauplatz,** and the **Hauptwache.**

Museumsufer, the embankment along the river's south side, is the site of many prominent museums, some of them housed in former riverside villas. **Sachsenhausen,** a district on the south side of the river, is a popular entertainment quarter filled with Frankfurt's famous apple-wine taverns.

Getting around Frankfurt

After you arrive in the Altstadt, you can easily get everywhere, including the Museumsufer on the opposite bank of the river, on foot. For longer distances, you can take the U-Bahn (subway), a tram, or a bus.

Using public transportation

A network of modern subways *(U-Bahn),* trams *(Strassenbahn),* and buses, administered by the **RMV (Rhein-Main Verkehrsverbund; ☎ 069/ 19449;** www.vgf-ffm.de), links Frankfurt. All forms of public transportation can be used interchangeably at a single price based on fare zones. Tickets are good for one hour on routes going in the same direction. Purchase your tickets *(Fahrscheine)* at ticket counters or from the coin-operated machines found in U-Bahn stations and next to tram and bus stops. The ticket machines have user screens in English to guide you through the process. A one-way single ticket *(Einzelfahrkarte)* within the city center costs €1.30 ($1.60) for adults, €0.80 ($1) for children.

 Buy your ticket before you board the U-Bahn or a tram in Frankfurt (on a bus you can buy a ticket from the driver). If you're caught traveling without the proper ticket, you may be fined €30 ($37) on the spot.

 Two special tickets help you save money on public transportation in Frankfurt:

 ✔ A **24-hour ticket** *(Tageskarte),* good for unlimited travel inside Frankfurt's central zone, costs €3.80 ($4.75) for adults and €2.30 ($2.90) for children. You can buy this ticket from the ticket machines.

 ✔ The **Frankfurt Card,** available at the city's tourist offices, allows unlimited travel anywhere within the greater Frankfurt area, transport on the airport shuttle bus, a reduction on the tourist offices' sightseeing tour (see "Seeing Frankfurt by Guided Tour" later in this chapter), and half-price admission to many of the city's museums. The cost is €7.80 ($9.75) for a one-day card and €12 ($14) for a two-day card.

Frankfurt U-Bahn and S-Bahn

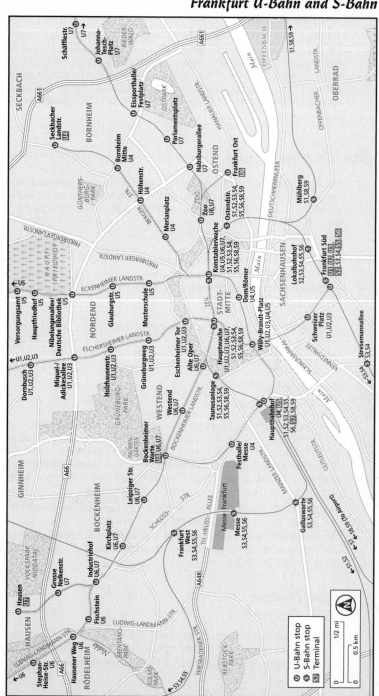

Taking a taxi

To call a taxi, dial ☎ **069/230-001.** You don't have to pay a surcharge for calling a cab. You can also get a cab at one of the city's clearly designated taxi stands, or by hailing one on the street (the car's roof light will be illuminated if it's available). Taxis charge by the trip and by the carload, without extra surcharges for luggage. The initial charge is €2 ($2.50); each kilometer costs €1.40 to €1.50 ($1.75 to $1.90), depending on the time of day.

Staying in Style

During busy trade fairs, finding a room in Frankfurt can be difficult. I recommend that you book your hotel in advance. If you arrive without a room, the tourist office in the main train station can help find you a room for a €2.50 ($3.10) fee. You can book a room for free by calling ☎ **069/ 2123-0808** or by visiting the Web site www.frankfurt-tourismus.de.

Frankfurt is one of two German cities (Munich is the other) with lots of air-hotel packages available from major airlines. You can save a bundle by booking one of these packages. See Chapter 6 for more information on packages to Germany.

Because Frankfurt is such a business-oriented city, hotels tend to be more expensive than elsewhere in Germany. Rates generally go up during the trade fairs. Many hotels offer lower weekend rates.

An Der Messe
$$$–$$$$ **Westend**

This quiet, 46-room charmer is a ten-minute walk from the train station, the banking district, and the fairgrounds. Rooms are comfortably large and stylishly furnished, each with a different theme or motif (Asian, Art Nouveau, French Provincial, and more). The large bathrooms have tub-shower combos. Rooms in the back, some with balconies, look out onto leafy gardens. The hotel can arrange baby-sitting.

See map p. 380. Westendstrasse 104, 60325 Frankfurt am Main. ☎ *800/221-6509 in the U.S. or 069/747-979. Fax: 069/748-349.* www.hotel-an-der-messe.de. *U-Bahn: Bockenheimer Warte (then a 5-minute walk south on Senckenberganlage and east on Westendstrasse). Rack rates: €149–€310 ($186–$387) double. Rates include breakfast. AE, DC, MC, V.*

Hilton Frankfurt
$$$$ **City Center**

With a soaring 12-story atrium and vast expanses of glass, this is one of Frankfurt's newest (the facility opened in 1998) and most modern hotels. A sense of hip, high-design theatricality prevails in the 342 bedrooms.

Prices vary according to size, view, and degree of luxury. Rooms overlooking the hotel's central atrium are the least expensive. The hotel has a health club and a pool, a bonus for most kids. The staff can also arrange baby-sitting.

See map p. 380. Hochstrasse 4, 60313 Frankfurt am Main. ☎ *800/445-8667 in the U.S. or 069/1338-000. Fax: 069/1338-1338.* www.frankfurt.hilton.com. *U-Bahn: Eschenheimer Tor (then a 3-minute walk west on Hochstrasse). Rack rates: €229–€400 ($286–$500) double. AE, DC, MC, V.*

Hotel am Dom
$$–$$$ Altstadt

You couldn't ask for a more central location: This small, appealing, family-owned hotel sits directly beside the cathedral in the heart of the Altstadt. In terms of style, a simple, European minimalism prevails in the lobby and 31 guest rooms. Bathrooms are nice but on the small side, with either a shower or a tub. Many opera singers stay here when they're in town. Breakfast is the only meal served; museums are at the doorstep.

See map p. 380. Kannengiessergasse 3, 60311 Frankfurt am Main. ☎ *069/138-1030. Fax: 069/28-32-37.* www.hotelamdom.de. *U-Bahn: Römer (then a 2-minute walk to the street behind the cathedral). Rack rates: €110–€170 ($137–$212) double. Rates include breakfast. AE, MC, V.*

Hotel Robert Mayer
$$–$$$$ Westend

This artfully decorated hotel is within walking distance of Frankfurt's trade-fair complex. The building dates from 1905, but the rooms were completely redone in 1994, when 11 artists were hired to lend their individual visions to each of the 11 bedrooms. One room design was inspired by Frank Lloyd Wright, another looks Italian postmodern with pop art. All the rooms are comfortable. Many restaurants are nearby.

See map p. 380. Robert-Mayer-Strasse 44, 60486 Frankfurt am Main. ☎ *069/970-9100. Fax: 069/9709-1010.* www.art-hotel-robert-mayer.de. *U-Bahn: Bockenheimer Warte (then a 10-minute walk south of Senckenberganlage and west on Robert-Mayer-Strasse). Rack rates: €129–€200 ($161–$250) double. Rates include breakfast. AE, DC, MC, V.*

Hotelschiff Peter Schlott
$ Höchst

Permanently moored at the Frankfurt suburb of Höchst, this 1950s riverboat has 19 small but evocative rooms. All of them have washbasins, ten have tiny showers, but none have private toilets. Everything is cabin-size and very basic (just a cut above a hostel), and mattresses are a bit thin, but if you love boats you'll enjoy hearing the waters of the Main lapping beneath your porthole. The ship's narrow and steep staircases are not easy to navigate if you have lots of luggage or difficulties walking.

See map p. 380. Mainberg, 65929 Frankfurt-Höchst. ☎ **069/300-4643.** *Fax: 069/307-671.* www.hotel-schiff-schlott.de. *S-Bahn: Höchst (then a 10-minute walk south on Königsleiter Strasse to Mainberg on the river). Rack rates: €60–€71 ($75–$89) double without shower; €80–€85 ($100–$106) double with shower. Rates include breakfast. AE, DC, MC, V.*

Mozart
$$–$$$$ Westend

Many consider this to be the best small hotel in Frankfurt. The location is a few blocks east of the Palmengarten and south of the university, right off the busy Fürstenbergerstrasse. The 35 rooms, each with a shower-only bathroom, are small but comfortable. The breakfast room, with its crystal chandeliers and Louis XV–style chairs, looks like an 18th-century salon. The staff is polite and helpful.

See map p. 380. Parkstrasse 17, 60322 Frankfurt am Main. ☎ **069/156-8060.** *Fax: 069/ 156-8061.* www.hotelmozart.de. *U-Bahn: Holzhausenstrasse (then a 10-minute walk south on Landstrasse and west on Fürstenbergerstrasse to Parkstrasse). Rack rates: €105–€185 ($131–$231) double. AE, DC, MC, V. Closed Dec 24–Jan 1.*

Steigenberger Frankfurter Hof
$$$$ City Center

The most prestigious hotel in Frankfurt, the Steigenberger Frankfurter Hof boasts excellent service and a historic setting that's central to everything in town. The five-story, 332-room flagship of Germany's elegant Steigenberger hotel chain was established in 1872. Public areas are plushly elegant. In the older part of the hotel, light floods the large, high-ceilinged bedrooms, all gracefully furnished, some with fine antiques. Rooms in the newer wing have a blander look. Bathrooms are large, luxurious, and completely up-to-date, with tub-shower combinations. Amenities include an on-site business center and a health club with sauna. The staff can arrange baby-sitting.

See map p. 380. Am Kaiserplatz, 60311 Frankfurt am Main. ☎ **800/223-5652** *in the U.S. and Canada, or 069/21502. Fax: 069/215-900.* www.frankfurter-hof. steigenberger.de. *U-Bahn: Willy-Brandt-Platz (take Willy-Brandt-Platz exit; the hotel is a 1-minute walk north on Friedenstrasse). Rack rates: €445–€495 ($556–$619) double; Fri–Sun €139–€175 ($174–$224) double. AE, DC, MC, V.*

Dining Out

In recent years Frankfurt has become, along with Berlin and Munich, one of Germany's great dining capitals, with restaurants that offer an array of richly varied cuisines. The *Apfelwein* (*ep*-ful-vine; apple wine) taverns in Sachsenhausen (see the nearby "Sachsenhausen and the apple-wine taverns" sidebar), on the south bank of the Main, tend to serve traditional Hessian dishes such as *Rippchen mit Kraut* (pickled pork chops with sauerkraut), *Haspel* (pigs' knuckles), and *Handkäs mit Musik* (strong,

Frankfurter versus hot dog

In Sachsenhausen and taverns around the city, you find real *Frankfurters,* smoked sausages made from pork and spices. The oldest-known recipe dates from 1487. The local product has been labeled "genuine Frankfurt sausage" since about 1900 to distinguish it from the American hot dog (hot dogs are for sale in Frankfurt, too, but always under the name "hot dog"). Unlike the hot dog, Frankfurters are long, skinny, and always served in pairs; like all German sausages, they contain no fillers.

smelly cheese with vinegar, oil, and chopped onions; not for the faint of heart or recommended for honeymooners). One dish unique to Frankfurt is *grüne Sosse,* a green sauce made from seven herbs and other seasonings, chopped hard-boiled eggs, and sour cream, usually served with boiled eggs, boiled beef *(Tafelspitz),* or poached fish.

Exedra
$–$$ City Center   GREEK/MACEDONIAN

Behind an ornate 19th-century façade is one of the best Greek restaurants in Frankfurt. This large and fairly plain *taverna,* with big windows overlooking the street, serves as a cafe-bar in the early mornings. All the menu offerings are reliably good. The grilled lamb with feta cheese sauce and grilled sweet peppers and the pan-fried veal with white wine and lemon sauce are both excellent.

See map p. 380. Heiligkreuzgasse 29. ☎ 069/287-397. U-Bahn: Konstablerwache (then a 5-minute walk east on Zeil and north on Kapperfeldstrasse to Heiligkreuzgass). Reservations recommended. Main courses: €11–€19 ($14–$24). AE, DC, MC, V. Open: Mon–Thurs 9 a.m.–1 a.m., Fri 9 a.m.–2 a.m., Sat 4 p.m.–2 a.m, Sun 4 p.m.–1 a.m.

Haus Wertheym
$–$$ Altstadt   GERMAN/HESSIAN

Wertheym operates three old-fashioned, atmospheric (and sometimes smoky) restaurants: Restaurant Haus Wertheym, a half-timbered house on a cobblestone street just west of the Römer; Historix (Saalgasse 19; ☎ 069/29-44-00), an apple wine tavern right across from it; and Römer-Bembel, a larger tavern with outdoor tables right on Römer square (☎ 069/28-83-83). Wood paneling and antique accessories decorate the interiors of all three, and the waiters can be brusque when the places are busy. The menus favor traditional dishes such as Frankfurter sausages, pork *schnitzels* (breaded cutlets), *Frankfurter Hacksteak* (chopped steak), and a good *Tafelspitz* (boiled beef) that comes with the restaurant's trademark green sauce.

See map p. 380. Fahrtor 1. ☎ 069/28-14-32. U-Bahn: Römer (then a 3-minute walk west to Fahrtor). Main courses: €6–€18 ($7.50–$22). No credit cards. Open: daily 11 a.m.–11 p.m.

Main Tower Restaurant & Bar
$$$$ City Center   INTERNATIONAL

The 53rd floor of Frankfurt's second-tallest skyscraper is the setting for this classy restaurant with views that extend for miles. The cuisine is fresh and reliable, with menus divided into traditional and "new" dishes. You may choose from main courses, such as braised veal with shrimp, capers and lime, or saddle of suckling pig. Fish dishes may include saltwater mackerel with melon risotto or pike-perch ravioli with cooked eel and celery cream.

See map p. 380. Neue Mainzer Strasse 52–58. ☎ 069/3650-4777. U-Bahn: Willy-Brandt-Platz (then a 5-minute walk north on Neue Mainzer Strasse). Reservations recommended. Main courses: €20–€27 ($25–$34). Fixed-price dinners: €55–€85 ($69–$106). AE, DC, MC, V. Open: Sun, Tues–Thurs 5:30 p.m.–1 a.m., Fri–Sat 5:30 p.m.–2 a.m.

Restaurant Français
$$$$ City Center   FRENCH

This dressy, upscale restaurant (jackets and ties for men) occupies two stately blue-and-gold dining rooms in the Steigenberger Frankfurter Hof, Frankfurt's most prestigious hotel. The imaginative French cuisine is beautifully prepared and presented. Appetizers may include a goose-liver terrine with an orange compote, beetroot tart with caviar, or quail consommé with truffle-stuffed tortellini. For the main course, you may find saltwater crayfish served with a vegetable couscous or suckling pig served with stuffed vegetables, caramelized garlic, and purple mustard sauce.

See map p. 380. In the Steigenberger Frankfurter Hof, Am Kaiserplatz. ☎ 069/21502. U-Bahn: Willy-Brandt-Platz (take the Willy-Brandt-Platz exit; the hotel is a 1-minute walk north on Friedenstrasse). Reservations required. Main courses: €28–€34 ($35–$42). AE, DC, MC, V. Open: Tues–Sat 6:30–11:30 p.m.

Tiger Restaurant, Palastbar, and Tiger-Bistrot
$$$$ City Center   MEDITERRANEAN/INTERNATIONAL

Come to these three places if you want to check out "the scene" (and be seen). The gourmet Tiger Restaurant, in a basement-level dining room adjacent to the Tigerpalast, a famous cabaret theater, earned a Michelin star in 1997. High-powered politicians and celebrities come to dine on seasonal Mediterranean cuisine. Expect to find dishes such as crayfish tartar with almonds and caviar, beef carpaccio with arugula polenta, roast lobster tail on basmati rice with curry sauce, and for vegetarians, chocolate canneloni with hibiscus cream and raspberry-balsamic ice cream. Meals in the Palastbar and the Tiger-Bistrot, which opened in 2001, are less elaborate and cheaper.

See map p. 380. Heiligkreuzgasse 16–20. ☎ 069/9200-2250. U-Bahn: Konstablerwache (then a 5-minute walk east on Zeil and north on Kapperfeldstrasse to Heiligkreuzgasse). Reservations required. Main courses: Tiger Restaurant €20–€32 ($25–$40); Palastbar and Tiger-Bistrot €20–€24 ($25–$30). Fixed-price menus: Tiger

Restaurant €62–€90 ($77–$112); Palastbar and Tiger-Bistrot €30–€46 ($37–$57). AE, MC, V. Open: Tiger Restaurant Tues–Sun 5 p.m.–2 a.m.; Palastbar Tues–Sun 5 p.m.– 3 a.m.; Tiger-Bistrot Tues–Sat 5 p.m.–1 a.m.

Weinhaus Brückenkeller
$$$$ Altstadt   GERMAN/INTERNATIONAL

Located in the heart of the Altstadt, this leading restaurant harks back to the 19th century, both in food and tavernlike décor. A typical meal may begin with cream of sorrel soup or goose liver with green beans, followed by a tender saddle of venison or lamb. The *Tafelspitz* (boiled beef) is the best in town. For dessert, try the soufflé of strawberries with vanilla sauce. You can choose from an excellent assortment of German wines.

See map p. 380. Schützenstrasse 6. ☎ *069/298-0070. U-Bahn: Römer (then a 10-minute walk east on Mainkai and Schöne Aussicht and north on Schützenstrasse). Reservations required. Main courses: €28–€38 ($35–$47). AE, DC, MC, V. Open: Mon–Sat 6 p.m. to midnight. Closed Dec 20–Jan 8.*

Sightseeing in Frankfurt

You can explore Frankfurt's compact Altstadt and Innenstadt on foot. Nearly all the main sights lie within the boundaries of the old town walls (which today form a stretch of narrow parkland around the Altstadt) or are just across the river along the **Museumsufer** (Museum Embankment).

Allow about a half-day to explore the attractions of the Altstadt, specifi- cally the **Römerberg,** the historic core of the old city; the **Kaiserdom;** and the **Goethe House,** birthplace of Germany's greatest writer. At the northern edge of the Altstadt is the city's most important square, called **An der Hauptwache,** named for the old guardhouse *(Hauptwache)* that stands upon it. Give yourself another half or full day to visit the muse- ums on the south bank of the river. The **Städelsches Kunstinstitut** gallery (called "the Städel" for short) is the most important of the seven museums on the Museumsufer.

Walking through the city

Many visitors to Frankfurt are in the city for only one day before head- ing off to other German destinations. If you want to see the city on foot, take advantage of the vast network of *Fussgängerzonen* (pedestrian streets) for sightseeing and shopping. For a general walking tour, start at the **Alte Oper** (U-Bahn: Alte Oper), stroll east along Grosse Bockenheimer Strasse (better known as Fressgass', or Gluttony Lane, because food stores and restaurants line the street), and continue to **An der Hauptwache,** Frankfurt's Times Square. Northwest of the Hauptwache is the **Börse,** Frankfurt's stock exchange. A block to the north of Hauptwache, at the end of Grosse Eschenheimer Strasse, stands the **Eschenheimer Turm,** a restored medieval tower, and the **Eschenheimer Tor,** a medieval gateway. Running east from An der

Hauptwache is the broad **Zeil,** the busiest shopping street in Germany. South of An der Hauptwache, via Liebfrauenstrasse and Neue Kräme, the **Römerberg** and the **Kaiserdom** form the heart of the **Altstadt.** From there, Limpurgergasse leads to the river and the iron footbridge called the **Eisener Steg,** which crosses to the **Museumsufer** along the south bank of the Main. From the footbridge and the south bank, you have the best views of Frankfurt. Farther south, beyond Gartenstrasse, lies the picturesque district of **Sachsenhausen,** famed for its apple-wine taverns.

Discovering the top attractions from A to Z

Deutsches Architektur Museum (German Architecture Museum)
Museumsufer

This museum is for those with an interest in architecture or urban planning. On display is a collection of 19th- and 20th-century architectural plans and models, examples of international modern architecture, and a series of exhibits showing how human dwellings have evolved over time in different parts of the world. A pair of 19th-century villas house the museum, designed by Oswald Matthias Ungers. The museum has a very good gift shop.

See map p. 380. Schaumainkai 43. ☎ 069/2123-8844. U-Bahn: Schweizer Platz (then a 5-minute walk north on Schweizer and west on Schaumainkai). Admission: €6 ($7.50) adults, €3 ($3.75) students and children. Open: Tues–Sun 10 a.m.–5 p.m. (Wed until 8 p.m.).

Deutsches Filmmuseum (German Film Museum)
Museumsufer

Deutsches Filmmusum is one of the two top film museums in Germany; the other is in Berlin. The first-floor galleries chronicle the history of the German and European filmmaking industry with examples of moviemaking equipment and models illustrating how special effects are shot. Old German films play continuously on the second floor. If you have an interest in film, you can easily spend an hour or more here.

See map p. 380. Schaumainkai 41. ☎ 069/2123-8830. U-Bahn: Schweizer Platz (then a 5-minute walk north on Schweizer and west on Schaumainkai). Admission: €2.50 ($3.10) adults, €1.30 ($1.60) students and children. Open: Tues, Thurs, Fri, Sun 10 a.m.– 5 p.m., Wed 10 a.m.–8 p.m., Sat 2–8 p.m.

Goethe-Haus (Goethe House)
City Center

Johann Wolfgang von Goethe (1749 to 1832), Germany's greatest writer, was born in this spacious, light-filled house and lived here until 1765, when he moved to Weimar (see Chapter 14). Reconstructed after wartime damage, the ochre-colored house still manages to convey the feeling of a prosperous, tranquil homelife in bygone days. The interior decoration reflects the baroque, rococo, and neoclassical styles of the 18th century.

Paintings of friends and family adorn the walls. The room where Goethe wrote is on the second floor; the room next door displays one of his most cherished childhood possessions, a puppet theater. Annexed to the house is the modern, glass-fronted **Goethe-Museum.** Of interest to Goethe specialists, the museum contains a library of books, manuscripts, graphic artworks, and paintings associated with Goethe and his works. To see the house and museum, give yourself about half an hour.

See map p. 380. Grosser Hirschgraben 23–25. ☎ *069/138-800. U-/S-Bahn: Hauptwache (then a 5-minute walk west). Admission: €5 ($6.25) adults, €1.50 ($1.90) students, €1 ($1.25) children. Open: Daily 10 a.m.–5:30 p.m. (Sat until 6 p.m).*

Historisches Museum (Historical Museum)
Altstadt

The exhibits in this large, drab-looking museum at the south end of the Römerberg showcase the history and culture of Frankfurt from its earliest settlement to the present day. Collections include examples of gold and silver plateware and jewelry; pottery and porcelain; and paintings, lithographs, and photographs. On the first floor, have a look at the models of the Altstadt at various periods of its development (Middle Ages, end of WWII, present day). As you can see from the models, when Allied bombs fell on Frankfurt in 1944, one of Europe's largest medieval cityscapes was completely wiped out. The amount of time you spend here depends on your interest level; you can browse through in half an hour.

See map p. 380. Saalgasse 19. ☎ *069/2123-5599. U-Bahn: Römer (the museum is at the west end of the square). Admission: €4 ($5) adults, €2 ($2.50) children 6–18. Open: Tues, Thurs, Fri, Sun 10 a.m.–5 p.m., Wed 10 a.m.–8 p.m., Sat 1–5 p.m.*

Kaiserdom (Cathedral)
Altstadt

The famous dome-topped West tower of the Kaiserdom (also known as **Bartholomäus-Dom**/Cathedral of St. Bartholomew) dominates the Altstadt. The highly ornamented tower dates from the 15th century and is built of red sandstone. Construction on the cathedral began in the 13th century and went on to the 15th, but the structure wasn't entirely completed until 1877. The church gained cathedral status in the 14th century when it

Stopping for coffee and pastry

For a quick and inexpensive cup of coffee and an excellent piece of pastry, duck into **Konditoriei Hollhorst,** Fahntor 1 (☎ 069/282-769; U-Bahn: Römer), a small bakery directly across from the Historisches Museum. A coffee and a delicious *Apfelhörnchen* (a pastry with apple filling) cost about €3.25 ($4.10). The Konditorei is open Tuesday through Saturday from 10:30 a.m. to 6 p.m. and Sunday from noon to 6 p.m.

became the site of the election of the emperors (called *Kaisers* in Germany) of the Holy Roman Empire. Later, between 1562 and 1792, the Kaisers also were crowned here, so the church became known as the Kaiserdom. Previous coronations had taken place in Aachen Cathedral.

Destroyed by Allied bombs in 1944, the cathedral was rebuilt in 1953. The layout is a fairly simple Gothic hall-church with three naves and a transept. The **Dom Museum** (☎ 069/1337-6186), in the church's 19th-century cloister, exhibits coronation robes of the imperial electors. The oldest vestments date from the 1400s. You can see everything in and around the cathedral and museum in about a half-hour.

See map p. 380. Domplatz. ☎ 069/2970-3236. U-Bahn: Römer (then a 2-minute walk east). Admission: Church free, Dom Museum €2 ($2.50) adults, €1 ($1.25) children. Open: Church daily 9 a.m. to noon and 2–6 p.m.; Dom Museum, Tues–Fri 10 a.m.–5 p.m., Sat–Sun 11 a.m.–5 p.m.

Liebieghaus (Liebieg Sculpture Museum)
Museumsufer

Housed in a late-19th-century villa, this sculpture museum includes statuary from ancient Egypt, Greece, and Rome, and from medieval and Renaissance Europe. You can see several noteworthy pieces from antiquity. In the medieval section, look for the 11th-century carving of the *Virgin and Child* created in Trier, Tilman Riemenschneider's expressive *Madonna*, Andrea della Robbia's altarpiece of the Assumption, and the 16th-century *Black Venus with Mirror*. Give yourself about an hour to see the major works.

See map p. 380. Schaumainkai 71. ☎ 069/2123-8617. U-Bahn: Schweizer Platz (then a 10-minute walk north on Schweizer and west on Schaumainkai). Admission: €4 ($5) adults, €2.50 ($3.10) seniors, students, and children. Open: Tues–Sun 10 a.m.–5 p.m. (Wed until 8 p.m.).

Main Tower
City Center

The outdoor observation deck on the 56th floor of this gleaming, cylindrical tower provides a spectacular panorama of Frankfurt and the entire region. Kids of all ages enjoy the heights and views. You find the Main Tower Restaurant & Bar on the 53rd floor (see the listing in the "Dining Out" section earlier in this chapter).

See map p. 380. Neue Mainzer Strasse 52–58. ☎ 069/3650-4777. U-Bahn: Willy-Brandt-Platz (then a 5-minute walk north on Neue Mainzer Strasse). Admission: €4.50 ($5.60), €12 ($15) family (2 adults/2 children). Open: Daily 10 a.m.–9 p.m. (until 7 p.m. in winter).

Museum für Angewandte Kunst (Museum of Applied Arts)
Museumsufer

Two buildings — one an early-19th-century villa, the other a 1985 structure designed by architect Richard Meier — house this enormous collection of

European, Asian, and Islamic objects. The museum has outstanding collections of glassware (including 15th-century Venetian pieces), German rococo furnishings, and porcelain. An overall view takes about an hour. *See map p. 380. Schaumainkai 17.* ☎ *069/2123-4037. U-Bahn: Römer (then a 5-minute walk south across the Eisener-Stieg footbridge to Schaumainkai). Admission: €5 ($6.25) adults, €2.50 ($3.10) students and children older than 5: Tues–Sun 10 a.m.–5 p.m. (Wed until 9 p.m.).*

Museum für Moderne Kunst (Museum of Modern Art)
Altstadt

Located one block north of the cathdral in the Altstadt, this museum opened in 1991 in a postmodern building designed by Austrian architect Hans Hollein. The massive triangular structure has projecting and receding window openings. Exhibitions include major artists since the 1950s, such as Americans Roy Liechtenstein, Claes Oldenburg, Andy Warhol, and George Segal, all from the New York School. Works by modern German artists also are on view. You can see the works in about an hour. A cafe-restaurant is on the premises. *See map p. 380. Domstrasse 10.* ☎ *069/2123-0447. U-Bahn: Römer (then a 3-minute walk east across Domplatz and north on Domstrasse). Admission: €6 ($7.50) adults, €3 ($3.75) students: Tues–Sun 10 a.m.–5 p.m. (Wed until 8 p.m.).*

Römer and Römerberg
Altstadt

The Altstadt centers around three Gothic buildings with stepped gables, known collectively as the **Römer.** These houses, just west of the cathedral, originally were built between 1288 and 1305 and then bought by the city a century later for use as the Rathaus (Town Hall). After his coronation in the Kaiserdom, a new emperor and his entourage paraded westward to the Römer for a banquet. In the **Kaisersaal** (Imperial Hall; ☎ **069/2123-4814**), on the second floor of the center house, you can see romanticized images of 52 emperors sculpted in the 19th century to celebrate the thousand-year history of the Holy Roman Empire. The hall is open daily 10 a.m. to 1 p.m. and 2 to 5 p.m. Admission is €1.50 ($1.90).

Medieval city officials and their families watched plays and tournaments from a specially built gallery on the **Nikolaikirche** (St. Nicholas Church), the small chapel in front of the city hall. The chapel has a 35-bell carillon that plays at 9:05 a.m., 12:05 p.m., and 5:05 p.m. **Römerplatz**, the square in front of the Römer, is one of Frankfurt's most popular spots, with a series of rebuilt half-timbered buildings housing cafes and restaurants.

The elaborate façade of the Römer, with its ornate balcony and statues of emperors, overlooks the **Römerberg** (Roman Hill). As early as the Stone Age, people occupied this high ground that was later settled by the Romans. After Germanic tribes conquered the Romans, the settlement fell into ruins and was forgotten until construction workers in the 20th century stumbled across its remains. *See map p. 380. U-Bahn: Römer.*

Struwwelpeter (a.k.a. Shockheaded Peter)

He's a memory now, but up until World War II (WWII), the image of Struwwelpeter, with his enormous shock of hair and Edward Scissorhands–length fingernails, was ingrained in the nightmares of every German child and many children throughout the world. Published in 1844, Struwwelpeter was the creation of Heinrich Hoffman (1809 to 1894), a Frankfurt physician who wrote gruesomely moralistic children's stories. Struwwelpeter's grotesque hair and fingernails were the result of his bad-boy behavior. The illustrated story became one of the most popular "children's books" in Germany and was translated into 14 languages (in England, Struwwelpeter became "Shockheaded Peter").

The entertaining **Struwwelpeter-Museum,** Schirn, Römerberg, Bendergass 1 (☎ **069/ 281-333**), displays original sketches and illustrations with copies of the book (and its classic image of Struwwelpeter) from many different countries. Admission is free; the museum, located alongside the Schirn Gallery, is open Tuesday to Sunday 11 a.m. to 5 p.m. Struwwelpeter fans also can visit the **Heinrich-Hoffman-Museum,** Schubertstrasse 20 (☎ **069/747-969;** U-Bahn: Westend), the home of Struwwelpeter's creator.

Städelsches Kunstinstitut/Städische Galerie (Städel Art Institute/ Städel Gallery)
Museumsufer

Frankfurt's most important art gallery contains a fine collection of European paintings. The first floor features French Impressionists such as Renoir and Monet, along with German painters of the 19th and 20th centuries, including Tischbein's famous *Portrait of Goethe in the Campagna in Italy.* If you're short on time, the second floor displays an outstanding collection of Flemish primitives, 17th-century Dutch artists, and 16th-century German masters, such as Dürer, Grünewald, and Memling. One of the most impressive paintings is Jan van Eyck's *Madonna* (1433). A large altarpiece and an impish nude Venus represent the work of Lucas Cranach. In the Department of Modern Art hang works by Francis Bacon, Dubuffet, Tapies, and Yves Klein. To get a good sense of what's on display, you need at least two hours.

See map p. 380. Schaumainkai 63. ☎ 069/605-0980. U-Bahn: Schweizer Platz (then a 5-minute walk north on Schweizer and west on Schaumainkai). Admission: €6 ($7.50) adults, €5 ($6.25) children 9–16, €10 ($12) family ticket. Open: Tues, Fri, Sun 10 a.m.–5 p.m., Wed–Thurs 10 a.m.–9 p.m.

Seeing Frankfurt by Guided Tour

A very good way to see Frankfurt, especially when your time is limited, is by the daily, guided tour offered by the city's tourist offices. The 2½-hour bus tour, in English, picks up passengers at 2 p.m. from Touristinfo Römer

(Römerberg 27, in the Altstadt; ☎ **069/2123-8800**) and at 2:15 p.m. from Touristinfo Hauptbahnhof (opposite the main entrance of the train station; ☎ **069/2123-8800**). From April through October, an additional tour leaves from the Römer at 10 a.m. and from the train station at 10:15 a.m. The tour covers the entire city and includes a trip to the Goethe House and, in the summer, the top of the Main Tower, Frankfurt's tallest skyscraper. The cost is €25 ($31) for adults, €20 ($25) for students, and €10 ($12) for children ages 6 to 10. Buy tickets at the tourist offices.

Shopping for Local Treasures

Frankfurt has several shopping areas. On the **Zeil,** a pedestrian zone between the Hauptwache and Konstablerwache, you find department stores, clothing shops, shoe stores, record stores — in short, just about everything. Shoppers generally pack the Zeil, reputedly the busiest shopping street in Germany. The **Hauptwache,** in the center of Frankfurt, has two shopping areas, one above and one below ground. **Schillerstrasse,** another pedestrian zone, lies between Hauptwache and Eschenheimer Turm, near the stock exchange. Walking from Schillerstrasse northeast toward Eschenheimer Tor, you pass many elegant boutiques and specialty shops. Southwest of the Hauptwache is **Goethestrasse,** with exclusive stores evocative of Paris or Milan.

Shops are generally open Monday through Friday from 9 a.m. to 6:30 p.m. and Saturday from 9 a.m. to 2 p.m. (until 4 or 6 p.m. on the first Saturday of the month).

Department stores

Hertie, Zeil 90 (☎ **069/929-050;** U-Bahn: Hauptwache), a Frankfurt shopping tradition, carries clothes and shoes for every budget, has a toy department, and operates a food hall in the basement. **Kaufhof,** Zeil 116–123 (☎ **069/21910;** U-Bahn: Hauptwache), Hertie's main competitor, stocks just about everything on its seven floors: porcelain, clothes, jewelry, glassware, gifts, and gadgets. The top-floor restaurant has panoramic views of Frankfurt.

Porcelain

Höchster Porzellan Manufaktur, Am Kornmarkt/Berliner Strasse 60 (☎ **069/295-299;** U-Bahn: Römer), contains one of Germany's largest inventories of Höchst porcelain, called "white gold" and manufactured for the past 250 years. You can buy a beautiful white porcelain vase for as little as €18 ($22).

Sachsenhausen and the apple-wine taverns

Sachsenhausen, the district south of the River Main, has long been known for its taverns where *Apfelwein* (ep-ful-vine; apple wine), not beer, is the special drink. At an apple-wine tavern, everyone sits together at long wooden tables and, sooner or later, the singing starts.

Apfelwein, pronounced *ebb*-el-vye, in the local dialect, is a dry, alcoholic, 12-proof apple cider. The wine always is poured from a blue-and-gray stoneware jug into glasses embossed with a diamond-shaped pattern. The first sip may pucker your whole body and convince you that you're drinking vinegar. If drinking straight Apfelwein is too much for you, try a *Sauergespritzt* (sour spritzer), a mixture of Apfelwein and plain mineral water, or a *Süssgespritzt* (sweet spritzer), Apfelwein mixed with lemonade-flavored mineral water.

Although available year-round, Apfelwein also comes in seasonal versions. *Süsser* (sweet), sold in the autumn, is the dark, cloudy product of the first pressing of the apple harvest. When the wine starts to ferment it's called *Rauscher,* which means it's darker and more acidic. You're supposed to drink Süsser and Rauscher straight, not mixed.

The Apfelwein taverns in Sachsenhausen display a pine wreath outside when a new barrel has arrived. The taverns usually serve traditional meals, and hard rolls, salted bread sticks, and pretzels for nibbling are on the tables, too. What you eat, including the snacks, goes on your tab. The following is a list of a few traditional Apfelwein taverns in Sachsenhasen; all of them are *Gartenlokale,* meaning they move their tables outside in good weather:

✔ **Zum Eichkatzerl,** Greieichstrasse 29 (☎ **069/617-480**), open Thursday to Tuesday from 3 p.m. to midnight.

✔ **Fichtekränzi,** Wallstrasse 5 (☎ **069/612-778**), open Monday to Saturday from 5 p.m. to midnight.

✔ **Zum Gemalten Haus,** Schweizer Strasse 67 (☎ **069/614-559**), open Wednesday to Sunday from 10 a.m. to midnight; closed mid-June to the end of July.

On Saturdays, Sundays, and holiday afternoons throughout the year, you can hop on the "**Ebbelwei-Express**" (☎ **069/2132-2425**), an old, colorfully painted trolley, and ride all through Frankfurt and over to the apple-wine taverns in Sachsenhausen. The entire route takes about an hour and costs €5 ($6.25) for adults and €2.50 ($3.10) for children up to 14. The fare includes a bottle of apple wine (or apple juice). You can buy tickets from the conductor. You can catch the trolley at Römer, Konstablerwache, or the main train station; service starts about 1:30 p.m. and ends about 5 p.m.

Discovering Nightlife in Frankfurt

For details about what's happening in Frankfurt, pick up *Journal Frankfurt* at newsstands throughout the city. *Fritz* and *Strandgut,* both free and available at the tourist office, also have listings.

To purchase tickets for major cultural events, go to the venue box office or to the **Touristinfo** office at the main train station or in the Römer. The department store **Hertie,** Zeil 90 (☎ **069/294-848;** U-Bahn: Hauptwache), also has a theater ticket office.

One of the best ways to spend an evening in Frankfurt is at one of the apple-wine taverns in Sachsenhausen (see the "Sachsenhausen and the apple-wine taverns" sidebar in this chapter).

Raising the curtain on the performing arts

When the **Alte Oper** (Old Opera House), Opernplatz (☎ **069/134-0400;** www.alteoper.de; U-Bahn: Alte Oper), opened in 1880, critics hailed the building as one of the most beautiful theaters in Europe. Destroyed in WWII, the Alte Oper didn't reopen until 1981. Today the theater, with its golden-red mahogany interior and superb acoustics, is the site of frequent symphonic and choral concerts, but opera is not performed here.

English Theater, Kaiserstrasse 52 (☎ **069/2423-1620;** www.english-theatre.org; U-Bahn: Hauptbahnhof), presents English-language musicals, comedies, dramas, and thrillers from September to July. Tickets range from €19 to €39 ($24 to $49).

Oper Frankfurt/Ballet Frankfurt, Willy-Brandt-Platz (☎ **069/134-0400;** www.oper-frankfurt.de; U-Bahn: Willy-Brandt-Platz), is Frankfurt's premier showcase for world-class opera and ballet. Ticket prices range from €10 to €110 ($12 to $137).

Theater der Stadt Frankfurt, Untermainanlage 11 (☎ **069/2123-7999;** U-Bahn: Willy-Brandt-Platz), has three stages. One belongs to the **Frankfurt Municipal Opera,** the other two present dramas. A variety theater, **Kunstlerhaus Mouson Turm,** Waldschmidtstrasse 4 (☎ **069/4058-9520;** kuenstlerhaus-mousonturm.de; U-/S-Bahn: Merianplatz), hosts plays, classical music concerts, and dance programs almost every night of the week. Tickets run €10 to €26 ($12 to $32).

Having fun at a cabaret

Tigerpalast, Heiligkreuzgasse 16–20 (☎ **069/289-691;** www.tigerpalast. de; U-Bahn: Konstablerwache), is the most famous cabaret in Frankfurt. Shows take place in a small theater, where guests sit at tiny tables to see about eight different acts per show. Each show lasts two hours with breaks for drinks (€10/$12) and snacks. You don't need to know German to enjoy the show, which is excellent family-style entertainment. (The cabaret acts are not raunchy or suggestive, but more like circus entertainment.) Tickets are €48 ($59), half-price for children younger than 12. Three recommended restaurants are part of this cabaret (see the Tiger-Restaurant, Palastbar, and Tiger-Bistrot listing in "Dining Out" earlier in this chapter).

Checking out bars and clubs

If you're going to paint the town red, be aware that porno movies, sex shows, sex shops, and discos teeming with prostitutes line several blocks in front of the main train station. This area can be dangerous at night, so don't go there alone. If you're looking for a night out, you find plenty of clubs, discos, bars, and cafes across the Main River in the **Sachsenhausen** district. Most gay bars and clubs are located in a small area between Bleichstrasse and Zeil.

Bars and cafes

Café Karin, Grosser Hirschgraben 28 (☎ **069/295-217;** U-Bahn: Hauptwache), is a relaxing, unpretentious cafe with art-filled walls, old wooden tables, daily newspapers, and cafe food. The cafe is open Monday to Thursday from 9 a.m. to 1 a.m., Friday and Saturday from 9 a.m. to 2 a.m., and Sunday from 10 a.m. to 7 p.m.

Café Laumer, Bockenheimer Landstrasse 67 (☎ **069/727-912;** U-Bahn: Westend), a classic German *Kaffeehaus* with a large garden, serves some of the best pastries in town. The cafe is open Monday to Saturday from 7:30 a.m. to 7 p.m., Sunday from 10 a.m. to 7 p.m.

Café-Restaurant in der Schirn (Schirn Café), Römerberg 6A (☎ **069/291-732;** U-Bahn: Römer), in the heart of the Altstadt, is a stylish steel, glass, and granite see-and-be-seen cafe-bar-restaurant designed by Philippe Starck. Tables spill out onto the pavement in summer. The restaurant is open Tuesday to Friday from noon to 3 p.m. and 6 to 10:30 p.m., Saturday and Sunday from noon to 10:30 p.m. The bar is open Tuesday to Sunday from noon to midnight.

Luna, Stiftstrasse 6 (☎ **069/294-774;** U-Bahn: Hauptwache), is a hip bar that's always packed with young professionals. The bartenders serve all manner of cocktails, including grasshoppers, juleps, champagne fizzes, and tropical coladas. The bar is open Sunday to Thursday from 7 p.m. to 2 a.m., Friday and Saturday from 7 p.m. to 3 a.m.

Nightclubs

Cooky's, Am Salzhaus 4 (☎ **069/287-662;** U-Bahn: Hauptwache), plays a mix of hip-hop and house music. Cover is €6 to €8 ($7.50 to $10), depending on the night. Hours are Tuesday, Thursday, and Sunday from 11 p.m. to 4 a.m., Friday and Saturday from 10 p.m. to 6 a.m.

Nachtleben, Kurt-Schumacher-Strasse 50 (☎ **069/20650;** U-Bahn: Konstablerwache), has a cafe-bar upstairs and a disco downstairs that plays hip-hop, funk, soul, and house. Cover for the disco is €4 to €10 ($5 to $12). Hours are Monday through Wednesday from 11:30 a.m. to 2 a.m, Thursday through Saturday from 11:30 a.m. to 4 a.m., Sunday 7 p.m. to 2 a.m.

Gay and lesbian clubs

Blue Angel, Bronnerstrasse 17 (☎ 069/282-772; U-Bahn: Konstabler-wache), is a mixed dance club where the scene heats up after midnight. Cover is €5 to €8. Hours are daily from 9 p.m. to 1 a.m.

Harvey's Cafe Bar, Bornheimer Landstrasse 64 (☎ 069/497-303; U-Bahn: Hauptwache), is a popular indoor/outdoor bistro that occasionally features live disco bands on the weekend. The bar is open daily from 10 a.m. to 1 a.m. (until 2 a.m. Friday and Saturday).

La Gata, Seehofstrasse 3 (☎ 069/614-581; U-Bahn: Südbahnhof), the most upfront lesbian bar in Frankfurt, looks like an English pub and serves soups and snacks. The bar is open daily from 9 p.m. to 1 a.m.

Fast Facts: Frankfurt

American Express

Located at Kaiserstrasse 8 (☎ 069/21050; U-Bahn: Hauptwache), the American Express office is open Monday through Friday from 9:30 a.m. to 6 p.m., Saturday from 10 a.m. to 2:30 p.m.

ATMS

You find ATM machines all across Frankfurt — this is a banking city, after all.

Bookstores

The best English-language bookstore is British Bookshop, Börsenstrasse 17 (☎ 069/280-492; U-Bahn: Hauptwache). Hours are Monday through Friday from 9:30 a.m. to 7 p.m. and Saturday from 9:30 a.m. to 4 p.m.

Consulates

The U.S. Consulate is at Siesmayerstrasse 21 (☎ 069/75350; U-Bahn: Westend). The British Consulate is at Bockenheimer Landstrasse 42 (☎ 069/170-0020; U-Bahn: Bockenheimer Warte).

Country Code and City Code

The country code for Germany is **49.** The city code for Frankfurt is **069.**

Currency Exchange

The Reise-Bank kiosk (☎ 069/2427-8591; U-Bahn: Hauptbahnhof) in the main train station is open daily from 7:30 a.m. to 10 p.m.

Dentists and Doctors

For an English-speaking doctor or dentist in an emergency, call ☎ 069/19292. Call ☎ 069/11500 for emergency dental service.

Emergencies

Dial ☎ **110** for the police; ☎ **112** for a fire, first aid, and ambulance.

Internet Access

CyberRyder, Tongegasse 31 (☎ 069/9139-6754; www.cyberyder.de; U-Bahn: Hauptwache), is open Monday through Thursday from 9 a.m. to 11 p.m., Friday and Saturday from 9 a.m. to midnight, and Sunday from 11 a.m. to 11 p.m.

Pharmacies

In Germany, a drugstore is an *Apotheke* (ah-po-*tay*-kuh). For information about pharmacies open near you, call (☎ 069/ 11500).

Post Office

The post office at the main train station (☎ 069/242-4270; U-Bahn: Hauptbahnhof) is open Monday through Friday from 6:30 a.m. to 9 p.m., Saturday from 8 a.m. to 6 p.m., and Sunday and holidays from 11 a.m. to 6 p.m.

Restrooms

You find many well-kept public facilities in central Frankfurt, especially in the Altstadt.

A restroom is called a *Toilette* (toy-*let*-uh) and often is labeled "WC," with either "F" (for *Frauen,* women) or "H" (for *Herren,* men).

Safety

Frankfurt is a relatively safe city, but you need to stay away from the area around the main train station at night.

Web Sites

The Tourist Information office Web site, www.frankfurt.de, is good for general information. You find more specific information at www.frankfurt-tourismus.de.

Part V
The Part of Tens

The 5th Wave   By Rich Tennant

"I think we're getting close to Cologne."

In this part . . .

This part is full of extraspecial hints, helpers, and recommendations. First off, in Chapter 21, I give you ten German lessons, providing useful words and phrases in ten different categories. Then, in Chapter 22, I give you my list of ten personally recommended hotels — so if you want to travel really well in Germany and you have deep pockets, you know right where to go. In Chapter 23, I help you to focus your sightseeing by giving you quick summaries of what I regard as the ten best museums in Germany. In Chapter 24, you find out what distinguishes one type of German wine from another.

Chapter 21

Ten *(Zehn)* German Lessons

In This Chapter

▶ Getting to know the basics: Days, numbers, time, and more

▶ Traveling from place to place: Directions and transportation

▶ Finding the fun: Entertainment and attractions

Maybe you're going to take some German lessons or listen to a German tape before you fly off to Deutschland. But maybe you're not — in which case, this chapter is especially for you. This chapter presents ten basic categories — from travel to entertainment — and gives you a few basic words or phrases (and their pronunciations) in each one. Turn to this handy glossary if you're wondering how to say something *auf Deutsch* (owf *doytsch;* in German). For food and restaurant words, see the Cheat Sheet in the front of the book.

 Bear in mind that you encounter different regional pronunciations and dialects throughout Germany.

Basic Words and Phrases

Yes = Ja (yaw). **No** = Nein (nine). **Please** = Bitte (*bit*-tuh). **Thank you** = Danke (*donk*-uh). **Good morning** = Guten morgen (*goo*-ten *mor*-gun). **Good evening** = Guten abend (*goo*-ten *ah*-bent). **How are you?** = Wie geht es dir (vee *gate* ess dear)? **How much does it cost?** = Wie kostet es (vee *cost*-tet ess)? **Women** = Damen (*dom*-in). **Married woman** = Frau (frow). **Girl or unmarried woman** = Fräulein (*froy*-line). **Men** = Herren (*hair*-en). **Man** = Herr (hair). **Boy** = Knabe (kuh-*nob*-buh). **Parents** = Eltern (*el*-turn). **Children** = Kinder (*kin*-dur). **Family** = Familie (fuh-*me*-lee-uh).

Accommodations

Do you have a room available? = Haben Sie ein Zimmer frei (*hob*-ben zee ein *tsim*-mer fry)? **Hotel** = Hotel (ho-*tel*). **Guesthouse** = Gasthof (*gahst*-hofe) or Gasthaus (*gahst*-house). **B&B** = Pension (pen-see-*own*). **Room** = Zimmer (*tsim*-mer). **Room number** = Zimmer nummer (*tsim*-mer noomer). **Double room** = Doppelzimmer (*dop*-pel-tsim-mer). **Single room** = Einzelzimmer (*ine*-zul-tsim-mer). **Bed** = Bett (bet). **Double bed** =

Doppelbett (*dop*-pel-bett). **Single bed** = Einzelbett (*ine*-zul-bett). **Bathtub** = Bad (bod). **Shower** = Dusche (*doo*-sha). **Toilet** = Toilette (toy-*let*-tuh). **Stairs** = Treppe (*trep*-puh). **Elevator** = Fahrstuhl (*far*-shtool). **Towel** = Handtuch (*hond*-tuke). **Pillow** = Kopfkissen (*kopf*-kis-sen). **Soap** = Seife (*sigh*-fuh). **Water** = Wasser (*vahs*-ser). **Hot** = heiss (hise). **Cold** = kalt (kahlt). **Breakfast** = Frühstück (*froo*-shtook). **Breakfast buffet** = Frühstücksbuffet (*froo*-shtooks-boo-fay).

Colors

Black = Schwarz (shvartz). **Blue** = blau (blau). **Green** = grün (groon). **Orange** = orange (oh-*rahnj*-ah). **Pink** = rosa (*ro*-sa). **Purple** = purpur (pur-*pur*). **Red** = rot (rote). **Yellow** = gelb (gelb). **White** = weiss (vise).

Days of the Week

Monday = Montag (*moan*-tog). **Tuesday** = Dienstag (*deens*-tog). **Wednesday** = Mittwoch (*mitt*-voch). **Thursday** = Donnerstag (*doe*-ners-tog). **Friday** = Freitag (*fry*-tog). **Saturday** = Samstag (*zoms*-tog) or Sonnabend (*sone*-uh-bent). **Sunday** = Sonntag (*zone*-tog).

Directions

Street = Strasse (*shtraw*-suh) or Weg (vegg). **Where is . . . ?** = Wo ist . . . (*voe ist . . .*)? **Left** = links (lynx). **Right** = rechts (rexts). **Straight ahead** = geradeaus (guh-*rod*-duh-owse). **East** = Ost (oast). **West** = West (vest). **North** = Nord (nord). **South** = Süd (sued). **Meter** = Meter (*may*-ter). **Kilometer** = Kilometer (*kill*-oh-may-ter). **Open** = offnen (*ofe*-nin). **Closed** = geschlossen (*guh*-shlosn).

Entertainment and Attractions

Ticket = Karte (*car*-tuh). **Box office** = Kasse (*kah*-suh). **Evening box office** (usually open 1 hour before performance) = Abendkasse (*ah*-bent-kah-suh). **Opening hours** = Öffnüngszeiten (*ohff*-noongs-sight-en). **Closed** = geschlossen (guh-*schloss*-en). **Museum** = Museum (moo-*zay*-ume). **Opera** = Oper (*oh*-per). **Concert** = Konzert (cone-*sert*). **Theater** (building) = Schauspielhaus (*shau*-shpeel-house). **Movies/cinema** = Kino (*keen*-oh). **Do you have tickets for this evening?** = Haben Sie Karten für heute abend (hob-ben zee *car*-ten fear hoy-tuh *ah*-bent)?

Numbers

1 = eins (einz). 2 = zwei (zvy). 3 = drei (dry). 4 = vier (fear). 5 = fünf (foonf). 6 = sechs (zex). 7 = sieben (*zee*-ben). 8 = acht (okt). 9 = neun (noyn). 10 = zehn (tzane).

11 = elf (elf). 12 = zwölf (tzwelf). 13 = dreizehn (*dry*-tsane). 14 = vierzehn (*fear*-tsane). 15 = fünfzehn (*foonf*-tsane). 16 = sechszehn (*zek*-tsane). 17 = siebzehn (*tseeb*-tsane). 18 = achtzehn (*ok*-tsane). 19 = neunzehn (*noine*-tsane). 20 = zwanzig (*tswan*-tsig). 21 = einundzwanzig (*ein*-oont-tswan-tsig). 22 = zweiundzwanzig (*zvy*-oont-tswan-tsig) and so on.

30 = dreizig (*dry*-tsig). 40 = vierzig (*fear*-tsig). 50 = fünfzig (*foonf*-tsig). 60 = sechszig (*zek*-tsig). 70 = siebzig (*zeeb*-tsig). 80 = achtzig (*ok*-tsig). 90 = neunzig (*noine*-tsig). 100 = hundert (*whon*-dert).

Seasons and Elements

Spring = Frühling (*froo*-ling). **Summer** = Sommer (*zoam*-er). **Autumn** = Herbst (erbst). **Winter** = Winter (*vin*-ter). **Rain** = Regen (*ray*-gun). **Snow** = Schnee (schnay). **Sun** = Sonne (*zone*-uh).

Time

Time = Zeit (zite). **What time is it?** = Welche Zeit ist es (vell-tcha *zite* ist es)? **Clock/watch** = Uhr (uer). **Hour** = Stunde (*shtoon*-duh). **Minute** = Minute (min-*ooh*-tuh). **Morning** = Morgen (*mor*-gun). **Afternoon** = Nachmittag (*nock*-mit-tog). **Evening** = Abend (*ah*-bent). **Midnight** = Mitternacht (*mit*-ter-knockt). **Day** = Tag (tog). **Night** = Nacht (knocked). **Early** = Früh (fhree). **Late** = Spät (shpate).

Transportation

Ticket = Fahrkarte (*far*-car-tuh). **One-way ticket** = Einzelfahrkarte (*ine*-sell-far-car-tuh). **Round trip** = Hin und zürück (hin und zoo-*rook*). **Reservation** = Resevierung (res-uh-*veer*-oong). **Seat** = Platz (plotz). **Arrival** = Ankunft (*on*-koonft). **Departure** = Abfahrt (*ob*-fart). **Transfer** = umsteigen (*oom*-shty-gun). **Get in/all aboard** = einsteigen (*ine*-shty-gun). **Get out** = aussteigen (*owsh*-shty-gun). **Window** = Fenster (*fen*-ster). **Door** = Tür (tooer). **Train** = Bahn (bon). **Train station** = Bahnhof (*bon*-hofe). **Main train station** = Hauptbahnhof (*howpt*-bon-hofe). **Track** = Gleis (glice). **Train car** = Wagen (*vog*-gin). **Restaurant car** = Speisewagen (*shpeye*-suh-vog-gin). **Airplane** = Flugmaschine (*floog*-ma-sheen-uh). **Airport** = Flughafen (*floog*-hof-fen). **Streetcar** = Strassenbahn (*shtraw*-sen-bon). **Bus** = Bus (boose) or Autobus (*ow*-to-boos). **Car** = Auto (*ought*-toe) or Wagen (*vog*-gen).

Warning Signs

This extra section alerts you to words and phrases that you may hear or read while traveling.

Achtung! (Ach-*toong*) = Attention! **Vorsicht!** (*for*-zicht) = Careful! **Vorsicht Stufe!** (*for*-zicht *shtoo*-fuh) = Careful, stairs! **Vorsicht frisch gebohnert!** (*for*-zicht frish guh-*bone*-ert) = Careful, freshly waxed floor! **Nicht hinauslehnen!** (nicked hin-*aus*-lay-nen) = Don't lean out! (or, don't lean against!) **Bitte nichts behühren!** (*bit*-tuh nichts buh-*roo*-en) = Please don't touch! **Nicht gestattet!** (nicked guh-*shtat*-et) = Not allowed! **Nicht aus dem Gras betreten!** (nicked aus dame *grahss* buh-*tray*-ten) = Don't walk on the grass!

Chapter 22

Ten of the Best German Hotels

---

*E*very hotel that I recommend in this guidebook is a good one, and you can stay at any one of them in comfort. However, for those who want to stay at Germany's *finest* hotels, I compiled a list of my favorites in this chapter. (In some of the descriptions, I also mention some equally worthy sister hotels.) Each one of these places offers something extra in terms of service, comfort, and aesthetics. At these hotels you find the highest standards of German hotel-keeping — and those standards are very high indeed. All of the listed hotels are kid-friendly.

Der Europäische Hof-Hotel Europa, Heidelberg

The impeccable, family-run Der Europäische Hof-Hotel Europa, Friedrich-Ebert-Anlage 1, 69117 Heidelberg ($$$$; ☎ 800-223-4541 in the U.S. and Canada, or 06221/5150; www.europaeischerhof.com), is the best hotel in Heidelberg and the only five-star hotel in the Rhine-Neckar region. Built in 1865 and carefully expanded over the decades, the property has a kind of glamorous elegance that few hotels can match. The large, traditionally furnished rooms have luxuriously appointed bathrooms. The new pool and sauna area is beautifully designed. The hotel's restaurant, **Die Kurfürstenstube,** is the top gourmet restaurant in Heidelberg. Those in charge have thoughtfully taken care of every detail in this service-oriented hotel. See the "Heidelberg" map on p. 333 for the hotel's location.

Der Kleine Prinz, Baden-Baden

In 2002, the readers of *Condé Nast Traveler* voted the family-owned and -operated Der Kleine Prinz, Lichtentaler Strasse 36, 76530 Baden-Baden ($$$–$$$$; ☎ 07221/346-600; www.derkleineprinz.de), the best hotel in Germany. Named for the children's book character created by Antoine de Saint-Exupery, Der Kleine Prinz (The Little Prince) resides in two turn-of-the-century mansions. Each of the large, high-ceilinged rooms is furnished differently, with hand-chosen furniture and accessories. Der Kleine Prinz is one of only two hotels in Baden-Baden to have air-conditioning. Personalized service is the hotel's strong point. The rates include a superlative breakfast buffet and afternoon high tea. Free Internet use is another amenity. The owners recently opened their second property, the **Hotel Belle Epoque** ($$$–$$$$; ☎ 07221/300-660; www.hotel-belle-epoque.de), just a block away. The same impeccably high standards prevail in this small, sumptuous hotel created from a villa built in 1870. See the "Baden-Baden" map on p. 317 for each hotel's location.

Excelsior Hotel Ernst, Cologne

Walk out of the train station in Cologne and you stare up, mesmerized, at the enormous cathedral, one of the architectural wonders of Europe. You can see the cathedral from some of the rooms in the grand Excelsior Hotel Ernst, Trankgasse 1–5, 50667 Cologne ($$$$; ☎ 0221/2701; www.excelsiorhotelernst.de), founded in 1863. The exterior looks a bit unassuming (it's a protected building, so the façade can't be altered), but walk inside and you'll be bowled over by the sheer luxury of the place. The lobby and public areas are gleaming and elegant with marble floors and beautiful finishes. Guest rooms are spacious and beautifully appointed, with very large and fully equipped bathrooms (among the best in Germany). The hotel's small fitness center has a whirlpool and steam room, and guests have free access to a business center with computers and high-speed Internet service. The **Hanse Stube** restaurant is one of Cologne's top gourmet restaurants, and **Taku** is one of Germany's preeminent Japanese restaurants. Hotel Excelsior Ernst really stands out for its incredibly friendly and helpful staff. They make you feel most welcome, without a hint of snobbery. See the "Cologne" map on p. 361 for the hotel's location.

Hotel Adlon Kempinski, Berlin

The old Adlon, across from the Brandenburg Gate, was the most famous and glamorous hotel in prewar Berlin. The new Hotel Adlon Kempinski, Unter den Linden 77, 10117 Berlin ($$$$; ☎ 800-426-3135 in the U.S. or 030/22610; www.hotel-adlon.de), built on part of the original site and completed in 1997, recaptures the Art Deco glory of the original. Everything about this property is five-star deluxe, and staying here truly is an experience. The 337 rooms are sumptuously decorated and have large bathrooms with double sinks, soaker tubs, and separate showers. The spa area, with a large pool, saunas, and steam rooms, is wonderfully elegant. This is a pampering hotel where every detail relating to the guest's comfort is taken care of. Service is top-notch, and baby-sitting can be arranged. See the "Berlin Mitte" map on p. 129 for the hotel's location.

Hotel Brandenburger Hof, Berlin

The beautifully appointed, 86-room Hotel Brandenburger Hof, Eislebener Strasse 14, 10789 Berlin ($$$$; ☎ 030/214-050; www.brandenburger-hof.com), offers superior service, an on-site spa, and one of the top restaurants in Berlin. Centrally located in western Berlin, this Relais & Châteaux hotel is close to the Ku-Damm and the main train station, Bahnhof Zoologischer Garten. Located in a building erected at the start of the 20th century, the guest rooms are unusually large for Berlin and furnished in an elegant Bauhaus style found in no other German hotel. Bathrooms have wood and granite finishes. You can enjoy the sumptuous breakfast buffet, included in the price of the room, in a glass-walled conservatory built around a Japanese garden. The hotel's gourmet restaurant, **Die Quadriga** (named for the four-horse chariot atop the Brandenburg Gate), earned a Michelin star. See the "Western Berlin Accommodations and Dining" map on p. 126 for the hotel's location.

Hotel Eisenhut, Rothenburg

For sheer historical panache, no other city along the Romantic Road can match Rothenburg. Hotel Eisenhut, Herrngasse 3–7, 91541 Rothenburg ($$–$$$$; ☎ 09861/70545; www.eisenhut.com), is Rothenburg's only luxury-oriented hotel. It has a charming, old-fashioned ambience, the largest bedrooms and bathrooms in town, a fine-dining restaurant, and a central location right across the street from bustling Marktplatz. The hotel is comprised of three interconnected medieval houses with a fourth house, the most atmospheric of them all, across the street. All 78 rooms differ in size and layout, and they're all decorated differently, in a wide range of styles. If you want a historical, service-minded hotel in Rothenburg, this is it. The hotel is closed in January and February. See the "Rothenburg ob der Tauber" map on p. 287 for the hotel's location.

Hotel Reutemann/Hotel Seegarten, Lindau

One of the nicest places to stay on the Bodensee is the upscale lakeside Hotel Reutemann/Hotel Seegarten, Seepromenade, 88131 Lindau ($$–$$$$; ☎ 08382/9150; www.bayerischerhof-lindau.de), two connected buildings with 64 rooms between them, located right on the harbor promenade. The Reutemann has large rooms and bathrooms with showers and big tubs. The Seegarten has flower-filled balconies and spacious rooms, some with lake views. The décor is modern in both. More luxurious is the adjacent **Hotel Bayerischer Hof** ($$$–$$$$), part of the same management. All three buildings share a lakefront garden with sunbathing areas, outdoor pool, fitness center, and sauna. The room rate includes a lovely breakfast buffet. Children younger than 10 stay free, and baby-sitting can be arranged. You can drive to these hotels and park in the underground garage. See the "Lindau" map on p. 309 for each hotel's location.

Kempinski Hotel Atlantic Hamburg

Movie stars, politicians, and royalty stay at Kempinski Hotel Atlantic Hamburg, An der Alster 72–79, 20099 Hamburg ($$$$; ☎ 800-426-3135 or ☎ 040/28880; www.kempinski.atlantic.de), with good reason, because the hotel is the finest in northern Germany. Situated across from Alster Lake, this hotel was one of the few buildings to escape wartime destruction. Age is a real asset for this grande dame because hotels nowadays simply don't have rooms (or hallways) as generously proportioned as the ones here, with high ceilings and spacious bathrooms. Everything is posh but comfortable. Amenities include an on-site pool and sauna and beautiful public spaces. You can even make a grand entrance down the staircase into the lobby. See the "Hamburg" map on p. 176 for the hotel's location.

Kempinski Hotel Vier Jahreszeiten München

Along chic Maximilianstrasse, tucked beneath a porte-cochere, you find the entrance of the grand Kempinski Hotel Vier Jahreszeiten München, Maximilianstrasse 17, 80539 Munich ($$$$; ☎ 800-426-3135 in the U.S. or 089/21250; www.kempinski-vierjahreszeiten.de). Founded in 1858, the Vier Jahreszeiten (Four Seasons) exudes a subdued, old-fashioned self-assurance in keeping with its history as the hotel of choice for royalty and celebs. The large rooms are richly appointed and technologically up-to-date. Bathrooms are roomy. Amenities include an on-site health club with pool. The hotel is just a few minutes' walk from the Residenz and the National Theater. See the "Central Munich Accommodations and Dining" map on p. 250 for the hotel's location.

Le Meridien Grand Hotel Nürnberg

At one time, you could find hotels like Le Meridien Grand Hotel Nürnberg, Bahnhofstrasse 1–3, 90402 Nuremberg ($$$–$$$$; ☎ 800-543-4300 in the U.S. or 0911/23220; www.grand-hotel.de), all across Europe. They were always the largest and most glamorous places to stay. Built before World War I, this grand hotel escaped destruction in World War II and consequently still retains much of its unique Art Nouveau atmosphere and detailing. Le Meridien recently acquired the hotel and has spruced up the property even more. The guest rooms, the largest in Nuremberg (some with an entrance vestibule), have roomy, marble-clad bathrooms. See the "Nuremberg" map on p. 349 for this hotel's location.

Chapter 23

Ten Great German Museums

*G*ermany is full of museums — more museums on every subject, in fact, than you can ever hope to visit. In this chapter, I assemble a list of my top recommendations. You often need to know German to enjoy the text-heavy exhibits in many German museums, but displays in these places let you enjoy art and objects without language barriers. You find addresses, opening times, and admission prices in the cited chapters.

Albertinum, Dresden

Through the centuries, German rulers accrued vast collections of art treasures. Today these collections form the basis of museums throughout Germany. One of the greatest is the Albertinum in Dresden, which holds the dazzling cache assembled by Albert, a Saxon king, between 1884 and 1887. The **Gemäldegalerie Neue Meister** (New Masters Gallery), which takes up two floors of the Albertinum, concentrates on works by German artists, starting with the great 19th-century Romantic artist Caspar David Friedrich and going up to the brilliant Expressionist works of Dresden-born Otto Dix (1891 to 1969). *Note:* The legendary **Grünes Gewölbe** (Green Vaults) containing 18th-century treasures — including rococo chests, ivory carvings, gold jewelry, bronze statuettes, intricately designed mirrors, and priceless porcelain — moved from the Albertinum to the Residenzschloss in 2004. See Chapter 14.

Alte Pinakothek, Munich

Masterpieces by the greatest European artists of the 14th through the 18th centuries are on display in this magnificent museum. The paintings were collected over the centuries by Bavaria's ruling family, the Wittelsbachs, and first put on public display in 1836. You can see works by famous 15th-century Flemish and German artists Rogier van der Weyden, Hans Memling, Lucas Cranach the Elder, and the Brueghel family. Seek out the self-portrait by Germany's greatest artist of the Renaissance, Albrecht Dürer, who lived and worked in Nuremberg. Dürer was the first artist to paint a self-portrait; he did three, and this museum has one of the most striking, painted when Dürer was 28 years old. Works by the 15th- and 16th-century Italian painters Botticelli, Raphael, and Leonardo da Vinci hang in the galleries, and you can see more Rubens than in any other museum in Europe. See Chapter 15.

Deutsches Museum, Munich

You won't find any paintings or porcelain in this massive museum of science and technology. You can see the first electric locomotive (1879), the first electric dynamo (1866), the first automobile (1886), the first diesel engine (1897), and the laboratory bench at which the atom was first split (1938). The automobile department contains a shining collection of luxury Daimlers, Opels, and Bugattis. The Aeronautics section displays a biplane flown by the Wright brothers in 1908 and the first airliner (1919). See Chapter 15.

Gemäldegalerie, Berlin

Berlin's famous painting gallery moved to this new building in 1998. Inside, you encounter one of Germany's greatest collections of European painting, including outstanding examples of medieval German and Dutch art and Italian masterpieces by Raphael, Bronzino, Veronese, Titian, Tintoretto, and Giorgione. The collection of 17th-century Dutch painting includes one of the largest collections of Rembrandts. See Chapter 12.

Germanisches Nationalmuseum, Nuremberg

The collections in this enormous museum present an extraordinary compendium of German art and culture through the centuries. The painting section showcases works by the great Renaissance painter Albrecht Dürer, who lived and worked in Nuremberg, and Hans Holbein, whose painting of Martin Luther is one of the highlights of the collection. The sculpture collection contains superlative pieces by Veit Stoss and Tilman Riemenschneider, artists known for their expressive realism. The world's oldest surviving globe, created in 1493, is on display. The collection of musical instruments is amazing — but so is almost everything in this varied and wide-ranging museum. Domestic furnishings, folk objects, clothes, interiors, and dollhouses document everyday life in Germany through the ages. See Chapter 18.

Jüdisches Museum, Berlin

American architect Daniel Libeskind designed the Jewish Museum, Berlin's newest and most talked about museum. The building is a piece of architectural art as important as the museum's collections. Inside, Libeskind created "psychological spaces" that evoke an uneasy sense of imbalance, imprisonment, and loss as you walk through them. The collections celebrate all aspects of Jewish life in Germany throughout the centuries, following a chronological pathway that is periodically interrupted by powerful memorial spaces. See Chapter 12.

Mercedes-Benz Museum, Stuttgart

This highly enjoyable museum, a must for anyone who has an interest in cars, vintage or otherwise, honors the invention of the motorcar by Carl Benz and Gottlieb Daimler. On display in chronological order are nearly 75 historical vehicles, including the first motorcycle (built in 1885) and the first Mercedes (1902). The vehicles from the 1930s are especially splendid. The racecars date from 1899 onward, and include the Blitzen-Benz, the Silver Arrow, the Sauber Mercedes, and the 300 SL Gullwing. (The museum glosses over the war years, during which Mercedes-Benz built tanks and trucks for the Third Reich.) See Chapter 18.

Pergamon Museum, Berlin

This giant old museum is the best reason to visit Museum Island in eastern Berlin. Created in 1930, the museum looks rather cold and forbidding, but an amazing collection of ancient Greek, Roman, and Babylonian buildings fills the space. What everyone goes to this museum to see is the Pergamon Altar, part of the enormous Temple of Zeus and Athena excavated in Pergamon, Turkey, and brought to Berlin in the 19th century. The temple, dating from 180 to 160 B.C., was considered one of the wonders of the ancient world. Other major architectural treasures include the two-storied Market Gate of Miletus, a Roman building façade from around A.D. 165; the Processional Way of Babylon with the Ishtar Gate, dating from 580 B.C.; and the throne room of Nebuchadnezzar. See Chapter 12.

Staatsgalerie, Stuttgart

Stuttgart's finest art museum exhibits works spanning some 550 years. Highlights among the oldest works include Giovanni Bellini's *The Mourning of Christ,* Hans Memlings's *Bathsheba at her Bath,* and Rembrandt's *St. Paul in Prison.* The **Neues Staatsgalerie** (New State Gallery), designed by the British architect James Stirling and completed in 1984, is an icon of post-modern architecture. In this wing of the museum, you find the 19th- and 20th-century collection, with works by the German Expressionists Ernst Kirchner, Ernst Barlach, and Max Beckmann, and representatives of the Bauhaus school and Blue Rider group, such as Paul Klee and Lyonel Feininger. You also find famous examples of European art from the late 19th and early 20th centuries, including works by Modigliani, Picasso, and Monet. Art and architecture lovers will also want to visit Stuttgart's beautiful **Neue Galerie,** which opened in 2005. See Chapter 18.

Zwinger, Dresden

The Zwinger is a magnificent baroque palace housing a stunning collection of museums, the most important being the **Gemäldegalerie Alte Meister** (Old Masters Gallery), one of the best galleries of European painting in the world. You can see Raphael's famous *Sistine Madonna* and my personal favorite, Giorgione's *Sleeping Venus.* But take your pick: Well-known works by Titian, Correggio, Vermeer, Dürer, Rubens, and Rembrandt adorn the walls. Noteworthy, too, are a series of detailed townscapes of Dresden painted in the mid-18th century by Canaletto, so true-to-life that they were used as reference works during the post–World War II reconstruction of the city. Other museums in the Zwinger include the **Porzellansammlung** (Porcelain Collection), with Japanese, Chinese, and Meissen porcelain from the 18th and 19th centuries, and the intriguing **Mathematische-Physikalischer Salon** (Salon of Mathematics and Physics), which displays clocks and scientific instruments of the 16th to 19th centuries. See Chapter 14.

Chapter 24

Ten Things to Know about German Wine

*W*ine has been part of German life and culture ever since the Romans began tending vineyards some 2,000 years ago. The most famous vineyards are found in the western and southwestern parts of the country, in the Rhine Valley and along the Mosel River (see Chapter 19). The German practice of harvesting grapes at various stages of ripeness (selective harvest) determines the official quality category that is indicated on the label. Under the German wine law, there are two categories of quality — *Tafelwein* and *Qualitätswein.*

Tafelwein

Tafelwein (*taf*-fel vine; table wine) is made from normally ripe grapes. If you want a simple, inexpensive German table wine, you have two choices: *Deutscher Tafelwein* and *Deutscher Landwein.*

Deutscher Tafelwein

Deutscher Tafelwein (doy-tcher-*toff*-el-vine; German table wine) is a simple table wine made from normally ripe grapes. It's meant for everyday enjoyment and primarily consumed where it's grown in Germany. Deutscher Tafelwein comes from one of five broad Tafelwein regions.

Deutscher Landwein

Deutscher Landwein (doy-tcher-*lahnd*-vine; special table wine) is a hearty, fresh regional wine with more body and character than Tafelwein because the grapes must be riper at harvest. Dry or semidry, Landwein comes from and is named after one of 19 Landwein regions.

If the word "Deutsch" is missing on the label of a bottle of Tafelwein or Landwein, then it is not made solely of German grapes, but rather a foreign wine that may or may not have been blended with German wine. It is likely to have been bottled but not grown in Germany.

Qualitätswein

Made from ripe, very ripe, or overripe grapes, *Qualitätswein* (qwal-ee-*tates*-vine; quality wine) is divided into two types: *Qualitätswein mit Prädikat* (see *"Prädikatswein"* next) and **Qualitätswein bestimmter Anbaugebiete (QbA)**. If you see "QbA" on the label, it means the wine comes from one of the 13 specified winegrowing regions and is made from approved grape varieties that have ripened sufficiently to assure that the wine will have the style and traditional taste of its region. Light, refreshing, and fruity, these wines are meant to be consumed while young, for everyday enjoyment or with meals.

Prädikatswein

Qualitätswein mit Prädikat (QmP) includes all the finest wines of Germany. Referred to as *Prädikatswein* (*pray*-dee-cots-vine), each of these wines carries one of six special attributes *(Prädikat)* on its label. Those six attributes are Kabinett, Spätlese, Auslese, Beerenauslese, Eiswein, and Trockenbeerenauslese. Each type is explained in the sections that follow in ascending order of ripeness. The degree of *ripeness* represents the natural sugar content of the grape juice at harvest.

Kabinett

Kabinett (cob-ee-*net*) wines are fine, usually naturally light, and made of fully ripened grapes, the lightest of the Prädikat wines generally showing the lowest alcoholic strength.

Spätlese

Spätlese (*spate*-lay-zuh) literally means "late harvest." These superior quality wines are made from grapes harvested after the normal harvest. Spätlese wines are more intense in flavor and concentration, but not necessarily sweet. They go well with richer, more flavorful foods, or can be drunk by themselves.

Auslese

Auslese (*aus*-lay-zuh) is the harvest of select very ripe bunches. These wines are noble, intense in bouquet and taste, and usually (but not always) sweet.

Beerenauslese

Beerenauslese (*beer*-en-aus-lay-zuh) is the harvest of individually selected, overripe berries *(Beeren)* with a high sugar content. These are rich, sweet dessert wines.

Eiswein

Eiswein (*ice*-vine), or "ice wine," is made from grapes harvested and pressed while frozen to concentrate sugar and acidity. Of Beerenauslese intensity, Eiswein is truly unique, with a remarkable concentration of fruity acidity and sweetness.

Trockenbeerenauslese

Trockenbeerenauslese (*trock*-en-beer-en-*aus*-lay-zuh) is made from individually selected overripe berries dried up almost to raisins. Such wines are rich, sweet and honeylike.

Appendix

Quick Concierge

Fast Facts

American Express

You find American Express offices in cities throughout Germany, including Berlin, Bremen, Cologne, Dresden, Frankfurt am Main, Hamburg, Heidelberg, Leipzig, Munich, Nuremberg, and Stuttgart. Access addresses for American Express offices in Germany at www.americanexpress.com.

ATMs

In German cities, you can easily find 24-hour ATMs in airports, train stations, and outside banks. You can get cash 24 hours a day using your bank card or an international credit card. *Cirrus* (☎ 800-424-7787; www.mastercard.com) and *Plus* (☎ 800-843-7587; www.visa.com/atms) are the most popular networks; check the back of your ATM card to see which network your bank belongs to. The networks' toll-free numbers and Web sites give you locations of ATMs where you can withdraw money in Germany.

Business Hours

Most banks are open Monday through Friday from 8:30 a.m. to 1 p.m. and 2:30 to 4 p.m. (to 5:30 p.m. on Thursday). Money exchanges at airports and border-crossing points are generally open daily from 6 a.m. to 10 p.m. Exchanges at border railroad stations stay open for arrivals of all international trains.

Most businesses are open Monday through Friday from 9 a.m. to 5 p.m. and on Saturday from 9 a.m. to 1 p.m. Store hours can vary from town to town, but shops generally are open Monday through Friday from 9 or 10 a.m. to 6 or 6:30 p.m. (to 8:30 p.m. on Thursday). Saturday hours generally are from 9 a.m. to 1 or 2 p.m., except on the first Saturday of the month, when stores may remain open until 4 p.m. Bakeries and florist shops sometimes are open on Sunday mornings. On the four Saturdays prior to Christmas, shops throughout Germany are open until 6 p.m.

Credit Cards

You can use American Express, Diners Club, MasterCard, and Visa throughout Germany. Smaller pensions (B&Bs) and restaurants may not accept credit cards. If your credit card is lost or stolen, you can call the following numbers in Germany: American Express ☎ 954-503-8850 (collect); Diners Club ☎ 702-797-5532 (collect); MasterCard ☎ 0800/819-1040 (toll-free); Visa ☎ 0800/811-8440 (toll-free) or 417-581-9994 (collect).

Currency Exchange

You find currency exchanges, called *bureaux de change* or *Geldwechsel,* in airports, railway stations, post offices, and many banks. Currency exchange is discussed in Chapter 5.

Customs

Entering Germany: You can bring in gifts duty-free up to a total value of €175 ($219). The following items are permitted into Germany duty-free from non-EU

(European Union) countries: 200 cigarettes; 1 liter of liquor above 44 proof, or 2 liters of liquor less than 44 proof, or 2 liters of wine; 50 grams of perfume and 0.25 liters of eau de cologne; 500 grams of coffee; and 100 grams of tea.

Returning to Australia: The duty-free allowance in Australia is A$400 or, for those younger than 18, A$200. Adult citizens can bring in 250 cigarettes or 250 grams of loose tobacco, and 1.125 liters of alcohol. For more information, contact Australian Customs Services, GPO Box 8, Sydney NSW 2001 (☎ 02/6275-6666 in Australia), or go to www.customs.gov.au.

Returning to Canada: For a clear summary of Canadian rules, write for the booklet "I Declare," issued by the Canada Customs and Revenue Agency (☎ 800-461-9999 in Canada; www.ccra-adrc.gc.ca). Canada allows its citizens a C$750 duty-free exemption, which, for adults, includes 200 cigarettes, 2.2 pounds of tobacco, 1.5 liters of liquor, and 50 cigars. In addition, you can mail gifts to Canada from abroad at the rate of C$60 a day, provided that gifts are unsolicited and don't contain alcohol or tobacco (write on the package "Unsolicited gift, less than $0 value"). *Note:* The C$750 exemption can be used only once a year and only after an absence of seven days.

Returning to New Zealand: The duty-free allowance for New Zealand is NZ$700. Citizens older than 17 can bring in 200 cigarettes, or 50 cigars, or 250 grams of tobacco (or a mixture of all three if their combined weight doesn't exceed 250 grams) plus 4.5 liters of wine and beer, or 1.125 liters of liquor. Most questions are answered in a free pamphlet, available at New Zealand consulates and Customs offices, called "New Zealand Customs Guide for Travellers, Notice No. 4." For more information, contact New Zealand Customs, 50 Anzac Ave., P.O. Box 29, Auckland (☎ 09/359-6655; www.customs.govt.nz).

Returning to the United Kingdom and Ireland: Citizens of the United Kingdom and Ireland who are returning from a European Union (EU) country go through a separate Customs exit (called the "Blue Exit") especially for EU travelers. In essence, there is no limit on what you can bring back from an EU country, as long as the items are for personal use (this includes gifts) and you have already paid the necessary duty and tax. However, customs law sets out guidance levels of 3,200 cigarettes, 200 cigars, 3 kilogram smoking tobacco, 10 liters of spirits, 90 liters of wine (of this not more than 60 liters can be sparkling wine), and 110 liters of beer. If you bring in more than these levels, you may be asked to prove that the goods are for your own use. For more information, contact HM Customs & Excise, Passenger Enquiry Point, 2nd Floor Wayfarer House, Great South West Road, Feltham, Middlesex, TW14 8NP (☎ 0181/910-3744; www.open.gov.uk).

Returning to the United States: Returning U.S. citizens can bring back $800 worth of merchandise duty-free. A flat rate of 10 percent duty is levied on the next $1,000 worth of purchases. You cannot bring fresh foodstuffs into the United States, only tinned foods and packaged foods. You can mail gifts back to people in the United States duty-free if the value of the entire gift package does not exceed $200. For more information, contact the U.S. Customs Service, 1300 Pennsylvania Ave., NW, Washington, DC 20229 (☎ 877-287-8867), and request the free pamphlet "Know Before You Go," also available on the Web at www.customs.ustreas.gov.

Drugstores

Pharmaceuticals are sold at a pharmacy, called an *Apotheke* (ah-po-*tay*-kuh). For cosmetics, go to a *Drogerie*. German pharmacies are open regular business hours. They take turns staying open nights, on Sunday, and on holidays, and each *Apotheke* posts a list of those that are open off-hours.

Electricity

The electricity is 220 volts (50 Hz). For any U.S. appliances, you need a transformer and a converter plug with two round prongs for German sockets.

Embassies

All embassies and consulates are located in Berlin, Germany's capital.

Australia: The embassy is at Friedrichstrasse 200 (☎ 030/880-0880; U-Bahn: Uhlandstrasse), open Monday through Friday from 9 a.m. to noon.

Canada: The embassy is at Friedrichstrasse 95 (☎ 030/203-120; U-Bahn: Friedrichstrasse), open Monday through Friday from 9 a.m. to noon.

Ireland: The embassy is at Friedrichstrasse 200 (☎ 030/220-720; U-Bahn: Uhlandstrasse), open Monday through Friday from 9:30 a.m. to noon and 2:30 to 3:45 p.m.

New Zealand: The embassy is at Friedrichstrasse 60 (☎ 030/206-210; U-Bahn: Friedrichstrasse), open Monday through Friday from 9 a.m. to 1 p.m. and 2 to 5:30 p.m.

South Africa: The embassy is at Friedrichstrasse 60 (☎ 030/220-730; U-Bahn: Friedrichstrasse), open Monday through Friday from 9 a.m. to noon.

United Kingdom: The embassy is at Under den Linden 32–34 (☎ 030/201-840; U-Bahn: Under den Linden), open Monday through Friday from 9 a.m. to 4 p.m.

United States: The embassy is at Clayallee 170 (☎ 030/832-9233; U-Bahn: Dahlem-Dorf), open Monday through Friday from 8:30 a.m. to noon.

Emergencies

Throughout Germany, the emergency number for police is ☎ **110**; for fire or to call an ambulance, dial ☎ **112**.

Holidays

See Chapter 3 for a list of public holidays in Germany.

Information

See "Where to Get More Information," later in this appendix, to find out where to get visitor information before you leave home.

Internet Access and Cybercafes

You find cybercafes in all of the larger cities in Germany; for locations, ask at the local tourist office or your hotel.

Liquor Laws

Officially, you must be 18 to consume any kind of alcoholic beverage in Germany. Bars and cafes may request proof of age. Local authorities treat drinking while driving as a very serious offense.

Medical Assistance

Most major hotels have a physician on staff or on call. If you can't get hold of a doctor and the situation is life-threatening, dial the emergency service, ☎ **112**, which is open day and night. Medical and hospital services aren't free, so be sure that you have appropriate insurance coverage before you travel. See Chapter 10 for more information on general medical matters in Germany.

Newspapers/Magazines

In Germany, you find daily editions of *the International Herald Tribune* and an international edition of *USA Today.* Many newsstands carry *Time* magazine.

Police

The German word for police is Polizei (po-lit-*sigh*). Throughout the country, dial ☎ 110 for emergencies.

Post Offices

The words *Deutsche Post* identify a post office. Post offices are open from 8 a.m. to 6 p.m. Monday through Friday, 8 a.m. to noon on Saturday. In larger cities, the post office in the main train station may be open longer hours. Street mailboxes are yellow. To find international rates and services from Germany, check out the Web site for Deutsche Post, www.deutschepost.de.

Restrooms

Use the word *Toilette* (twah-*leh*-teh). A Women's Toilette is usually marked with an "F" for *Frauen,* and a men's Toilette with an "H" for *Herren.* Restrooms in train stations sometimes require a €0.20 coin to enter. Many restrooms have an attendant who expects a small tip (never more than €0.50); the attendant in a men's Toilette may be female.

Safety

Germany is generally a safe country in which to travel, with the usual caveats to use common sense and be aware of your surroundings. At night, avoid areas around the large railway stations in Frankfurt, Munich, Berlin, and Hamburg.

Taxes

Germany imposes a *Mehrwertsteuer* (MWST), or value-added tax (VAT), of 16 percent on most goods and services. The prices of restaurants and hotels include

VAT. Stores that display a TAX FREE SHOPPING sign can issue you a Global Refund Cheque at the time of purchase. See Chapter 5 for details on how to obtain your refund.

Telephone

The country code for Germany is **49**. To call Germany from the U.S., dial the international access code 011, then 49, then the city code, then the regular phone number, which may have from four to nine digits. *The phone numbers listed in this book are to be used within Germany; when calling from abroad, omit the initial 0 in the city code.*

Local and long-distance calls may be placed from post offices and coin-operated public telephone booths, though coin-operated devices are increasingly rare. The unit charge is €.15. Most phones in Germany now require a *Telefonkarte* (telephone card), available at post offices and newsstands in increments of €5, €10, and €20 ($6.25, $13, $25). Telephone calls made through hotel switchboards cost significantly more than the regular charge at a pay phone or post office. To make an international call from a public phone, look for a phone marked INLANDS UND AUSLANDSGESPRÄCHE; most have instructions in English.

To call the United States or Canada from Germany, dial 01, followed by the country code (1), then the area code, and then the number. Alternatively, you can dial the various telecommunication companies in the States for cheaper rates. From Germany, the access numbers are ☎ 0800/225-5288 for AT&T and ☎ 0800/888-8000 for MCI.

Time Zone

Germany operates on central European time (CET), which means that the country is six hours ahead of eastern time in the United States and one hour ahead of Greenwich mean time (GMT). Summer daylight saving time begins in April and ends in

September — there's a slight difference in the dates from year to year — so there may be a period in early spring and in the fall when there's a seven-hour difference between eastern time and CET. Always check if you're traveling during these periods, especially if you need to catch a plane.

Tipping

If a restaurant bill says *Bedienung,* it means a service charge has already been added, so just round yours up to the nearest euro. If not, add 5 to 10 percent, depending on your satisfaction. Round up to the nearest euro for taxis. Bellhops get €1/$1.25 per bag, as does the doorperson at a hotel, restaurant, or nightclub. The room-cleaning staff gets a small tip in Germany, as do concierges who perform special favors such as obtaining theater or opera tickets. Tip hairdressers or barbers 5 to 10 percent.

Water

Tap water is safe to drink in all German towns and cities, but bottled drinking water is a way of life. Restaurants do not freely offer water with your meal. You order *Sprudelwasser* (*shprew*-dil-vos-er; water with gas) or *Still* (shtill; noncarbonated water).

Weights and Measures

Germany uses the metric system. Heights are given in centimeters (cm) and meters (m), distances in kilometers (km), and weights in grams (g) or kilograms (kg). Temperature is measured in degrees Celsius (0°C = 32°F). To translate Celsius into Fahrenheit, multiply the number by 1.8 and add 32.

Toll-Free Numbers and Web Sites

Major airlines serving Germany

Aer Lingus
☎ 800-474-7424
☎ 01/886-8888 (Ireland)
www.aerlingus.com

American Airlines
☎ 800-443-7300
www.aa.com

British Airways
☎ 800-247-9297
☎ 0345/222-111 (U.K.)
www.british-airways.com

British Midland
☎ 0345/554-554 (U.K.)
www.flybmi.com

Continental Airlines
☎ 800-231-0856
www.continental.com

Delta Air Lines
☎ 800-241-4141
www.delta.com

Lufthansa
☎ 800-645-3880
www.lufthansa-usa.com

Northwest Airlines
☎ 800-225-2525
www.nwa.com

Qantas
☎ 800-227-4500
☎ 008/112-121 (Australia)
www.qantas.com

United Airlines
☎ 800-538-2929
www.united.com

Major car-rental agencies operating in Germany

Alamo
☎ 800-462-5266
☎ 0800/272-200 (U.K.)
www.alamo.com

Auto Europe
☎ 800-223-5555
☎ 207/842-2222 (Australia)
☎ 0800/169-6417 (U.K.)
www.autoeurope.com

Avis
☎ 800-331-1212
☎ 136-333 (Australia)
☎ 0870/606-0100 (U.K.)
www.avis.com

Budget
☎ 800-527-0700
☎ 800/472-3325 (Europe)
www.budget.com

Hertz
☎ 800-654-3001
☎ 800/263-0600 (Canada)
☎ 01805/333-535 (Germany)
www.hertz.com

National
☎ 800-227-7368
☎ 800/227-3876 (Europe and Australia)
☎ 0990/565-656 (U.K.)
www.nationalcar.com

RailEurope
☎ 888/382-7245
☎ 800/361-7245 (Canada)
www.raileurope.com

Major hotel chains in Germany

Best Western Hotels
☎ 800-937-8376 (ask for "International")
www.bestwestern.com

Hilton International
☎ 800-445-8667
www.hilton.com

Hyatt
☎ 800-233-1234
www.hyatt.com

Inter-Continental Hotels & Resorts
☎ 800-327-0200
www.intercontinental.com

Kempinski Hotels & Resorts
☎ 800-426-3135
www.kempinski.com

Le Meridien Hotels & Resorts
☎ 800-225-5843
www.meridien.com

Radisson SAS Hotels & Resorts
☎ 800-333-3333
www.radissonsas.com

Sheraton
☎ 800-325-3535
www.sheraton.com

Steigenberger Hotels & Resorts
☎ 800/223-5652
www.steigenberger.de

Where to Get More Information

For more information on Germany, you can contact the following **German National Tourist Board** offices:

✔ **In Germany:** The German National Tourist Board headquarters is at Beethovenstrasse 69, 60325 Frankfurt am Main (☎ **069/ 2123-8800**). The general Web site is www.germany-tourism.de.

✔ **In Australia:** P.O. Box 1461, Sydney NSW 2001 (☎ **02/8296-0487**; fax: 02/8296-0487).

✔ **In Canada:** 480 University Ave., Suite 1410, Toronto, ON M5G
1V2 (☎ 416/968-1685; fax: 416/968-0562).

✔ **In South Africa:** C/O Lufthansa German Airlines, P.O. Box 412246,
Craighall 2024, Johannesburg (☎ **011/325-1927;** fax 011/325-
0867).

✔ **In the United Kingdom:** P.O. Box 2695, London W1A 3TN
(☎ **020/7317-0908;** fax: 020/7317-0917).

✔ **In the United States:** 122 E. 42nd St., 52nd Floor, New York, NY
10168-0072 (☎ **212-661-7200;** fax: 212-661-7174); P.O. Box 59594,
Chicago, IL 60659-9594 (☎ **312-644-0723;** fax: 312-644-0724).

Contacting regional tourist boards

For specific information on a particular region, contact regional tourist
boards or check their Web sites. *Note:* The Web sites of some regional
offices may be in German only.

Northern Germany

✔ Hamburg: **Hamburg Tourist Board,** P.O. Box 102249, 20015
Hamburg (☎ **040/3005-1300;** www.hamburg-tourism.de).

✔ Schleswig-Holstein: **Tourismus Agentur Schleswig-Holstein,**
Walkendamm 17, 24103 Kiel (☎ **01805/600-604;** www.sht.de).

Eastern Germany

✔ Brandenburg: **MB Tourismus Marketing Brandenburg,** Am
Neuen Markt 1, 14467 Potsdam (☎ **0331/200-4747;** www.
reiseland-brandenburg.de).

✔ Thuringia: **Service Center Thüringer Tourismus,** Postfach 219,
99005 Erfurt (☎ **0361/37420;** www.thueringen-tourismus.de).

✔ Saxony: **Tourismus Marketing Gesellschaft Sachsen,** Bautzener
Strasse 45–47, 01099 Dresden (☎ **0351/491-700;** www.sachsen-
tour.de).

Southern Germany

✔ Bavaria: **Bayern Tourismus Marketing,** Leopoldstrasse 146,
80804 München (☎ **089/212-3970;** www.btl.de).

✔ Bodensee (Lake Constance): **Internationale Bodensee-
Tourismus,** Insel Mainau, 78465 Konstanz (☎ **07531/90940;**
www.bodensee-tourismus.de).

Western and central Germany

✔ Baden-Württemberg: **Tourismus-Marketing Baden-Württemberg,**
Esslinger Strasse 8, 70182 Stuttgart (☎ **0711/238-580;** www.
tourismus-baden-wuerttemberg.de).

- North Rhine–Westphalia: **Nordrhein-Westfalen Tourismus,** Worringer Strasse 22, 50668 Köln (☎ **0221/179-450;** www. nrw-tourismus.de).

- Rhineland-Palatinate: **Rheinland-Pfalz Tourismus,** Pottfach 200563, 56005 Koblenz (☎ **0261/915-200;** www.rlp-info.de).

Surfing the Net

Throughout this guide, I mention various Web sites. In this section, I point you toward the best of them.

Tourist info on all of Germany

For general information on all of Germany, try these sites for starters:

- www.germany-tourism.de: The Web page for the German National Tourist Board in Germany offers useful information on all aspects of German life, travel, and culture.

- www.visits-to-germany.com: This site is another useful version of the German National Tourist Board's general Web site.

- www.yahoo.com: Type in "Germany" in Yahoo's search engine and call up Yahoo's Germany Visitor Guide with the latest news, a photo gallery, and special offers.

General info on specific cities

The following tourist information center Web sites provide directories of hotels, restaurants, attractions, and events in specific cities throughout Germany (not all sites have information in English):

- **Baden-Baden:** www.baden-baden.com

- **Berlin:** www.berlin.de

- **Bremen:** www.bremen-tourism.de

- **Cologne:** www.koeln.de

- **Dresden:** www.dresden.de

- **Frankfurt:** www.frankfurt-tourismus.de

- **Freiburg im Breisgau:** www.freiburg.de

- **Füssen:** www.fuessen.de

- **Garmisch-Partenkirchen:** www.garmisch-partenkirchen.de

- **Hamburg:** www.hamburg-tourism.de

- **Heidelberg:** www.cvb-heidelberg.de

- **Leipzig:** www.leipzig.de

- **Lindau:** www.lindau-tourismus.de

- **Lübeck:** www.luebeck-tourismus.de
- **Munich:** www.munich.de
- **Nuremberg:** www.nuernberg.de
- **Rothenburg ob der Tauber:** www.rothenburg.de
- **Stuttgart:** www.stuttgart-tourist.de
- **Weimar:** www.weimar.de

Index

• *I* •

USINESS, CAREERS & PERSONAL FINANCE

Grant Writing
DUMMIES
A Reference for the Rest of Us!

0-7645-5307-0

Home Buying
DUMMIES
A Reference for the Rest of Us!

0-7645-5331-3 *†

Also available:
- Accounting For Dummies †
  0-7645-5314-3
- Business Plans Kit For Dummies †
  0-7645-5365-8
- Cover Letters For Dummies
  0-7645-5224-4
- Frugal Living For Dummies
  0-7645-5403-4
- Leadership For Dummies
  0-7645-5176-0
- Managing For Dummies
  0-7645-1771-6

- Marketing For Dummies
  0-7645-5600-2
- Personal Finance For Dummies *
  0-7645-2590-5
- Project Management
  For Dummies
  0-7645-5283-X
- Resumes For Dummies †
  0-7645-5471-9
- Selling For Dummies
  0-7645-5363-1
- Small Business Kit For Dummies *†
  0-7645-5093-4

OME & BUSINESS COMPUTER BASICS

Windows XP
DUMMIES
A Reference for the Rest of Us!

0-7645-4074-2

Excel 2003
DUMMIES

0-7645-3758-X

Also available:
- ACT! 6 For Dummies
  0-7645-2645-6
- iLife '04 All-in-One Desk Reference
  For Dummies
  0-7645-7347-0
- iPAQ For Dummies
  0-7645-6769-1
- Mac OS X Panther Timesaving
  Techniques For Dummies
  0-7645-5812-9
- Macs For Dummies
  0-7645-5656-8
- Microsoft Money 2004 For Dummies
  0-7645-4195-1

- Office 2003 All-in-One Desk
  Reference For Dummies
  0-7645-3883-7
- Outlook 2003 For Dummies
  0-7645-3759-8
- PCs For Dummies
  0-7645-4074-2
- TiVo For Dummies
  0-7645-6923-6
- Upgrading and Fixing PCs
  For Dummies
  0-7645-1665-5
- Windows XP Timesaving
  Techniques For Dummies
  0-7645-3748-2

OOD, HOME, GARDEN, HOBBIES, MUSIC & PETS

Feng Shui
DUMMIES
A Reference for the Rest of Us!

0-7645-5295-3

Poker
DUMMIES
A Reference for the Rest of Us!

0-7645-5232-5

Also available:
- Bass Guitar For Dummies
  0-7645-2487-9
- Diabetes Cookbook For Dummies
  0-7645-5230-9
- Gardening For Dummies *
  0-7645-5130-2
- Guitar For Dummies
  0-7645-5106-X
- Holiday Decorating For Dummies
  0-7645-2570-0
- Home Improvement All-in-One
  For Dummies
  0-7645-5680-0

- Knitting For Dummies
  0-7645-5395-X
- Piano For Dummies
  0-7645-5105-1
- Puppies For Dummies
  0-7645-5255-4
- Scrapbooking For Dummies
  0-7645-7208-3
- Senior Dogs For Dummies
  0-7645-5818-8
- Singing For Dummies
  0-7645-2475-5
- 30-Minute Meals For Dummies
  0-7645-2589-1

NTERNET & DIGITAL MEDIA

Digital Photography
DUMMIES
A Reference for the Rest of Us!

0-7645-1664-7

Starting an eBay Business
DUMMIES
A Reference for the Rest of Us!

0-7645-6924-4

Also available:
- 2005 Online Shopping Directory
  For Dummies
  0-7645-7495-7
- CD & DVD Recording For Dummies
  0-7645-5956-7
- eBay For Dummies
  0-7645-5654-1
- Fighting Spam For Dummies
  0-7645-5965-6
- Genealogy Online For Dummies
  0-7645-5964-8
- Google For Dummies
  0-7645-4420-9

- Home Recording For Musicians
  For Dummies
  0-7645-1634-5
- The Internet For Dummies
  0-7645-4173-0
- iPod & iTunes For Dummies
  0-7645-7772-7
- Preventing Identity Theft
  For Dummies
  0-7645-7336-5
- Pro Tools All-in-One Desk
  Reference For Dummies
  0-7645-5714-9
- Roxio Easy Media Creator
  For Dummies
  0-7645-7131-1

Separate Canadian edition also available
Separate U.K. edition also available

Available wherever books are sold. For more information or to order direct: U.S. customers visit www.dummies.com or call 1-877-762-2974. U.K. customers visit www.wileyeurope.com or call 0800 243407. Canadian customers visit www.wiley.ca or call 1-800-567-4797.

SPORTS, FITNESS, PARENTING, RELIGION & SPIRITUALITY

0-7645-5146-9

0-7645-5418-2

Also available:
- Adoption For Dummies
  0-7645-5488-3
- Basketball For Dummies
  0-7645-5248-1
- The Bible For Dummies
  0-7645-5296-1
- Buddhism For Dummies
  0-7645-5359-3
- Catholicism For Dummies
  0-7645-5391-7
- Hockey For Dummies
  0-7645-5228-7

- Judaism For Dummies
  0-7645-5299-6
- Martial Arts For Dummies
  0-7645-5358-5
- Pilates For Dummies
  0-7645-5397-6
- Religion For Dummies
  0-7645-5264-3
- Teaching Kids to Read
  For Dummies
  0-7645-4043-2
- Weight Training For Dummies
  0-7645-5168-X
- Yoga For Dummies
  0-7645-5117-5

TRAVEL

0-7645-5438-7

0-7645-5453-0

Also available:
- Alaska For Dummies
  0-7645-1761-9
- Arizona For Dummies
  0-7645-6938-4
- Cancún and the Yucatán
  For Dummies
  0-7645-2437-2
- Cruise Vacations For Dummies
  0-7645-6941-4
- Europe For Dummies
  0-7645-5456-5
- Ireland For Dummies
  0-7645-5455-7

- Las Vegas For Dummies
  0-7645-5448-4
- London For Dummies
  0-7645-4277-X
- New York City For Dummies
  0-7645-6945-7
- Paris For Dummies
  0-7645-5494-8
- RV Vacations For Dummies
  0-7645-5443-3
- Walt Disney World & Orlando
  For Dummies
  0-7645-6943-0

GRAPHICS, DESIGN & WEB DEVELOPMENT

0-7645-4345-8

0-7645-5589-8

Also available:
- Adobe Acrobat 6 PDF
  For Dummies
  0-7645-3760-1
- Building a Web Site For Dummies
  0-7645-7144-3
- Dreamweaver MX 2004
  For Dummies
  0-7645-4342-3
- FrontPage 2003 For Dummies
  0-7645-3882-9
- HTML 4 For Dummies
  0-7645-1995-6
- Illustrator CS For Dummies
  0-7645-4084-X

- Macromedia Flash MX 2004
  For Dummies
  0-7645-4358-X
- Photoshop 7 All-in-One Desk
  Reference For Dummies
  0-7645-1667-1
- Photoshop CS Timesaving
  Techniques For Dummies
  0-7645-6782-9
- PHP 5 For Dummies
  0-7645-4166-8
- PowerPoint 2003 For Dummies
  0-7645-3908-6
- QuarkXPress 6 For Dummies
  0-7645-2593-X

NETWORKING, SECURITY, PROGRAMMING & DATABASES

0-7645-6852-3

0-7645-5784-X

Also available:
- A+ Certification For Dummies
  0-7645-4187-0
- Access 2003 All-in-One Desk
  Reference For Dummies
  0-7645-3988-4
- Beginning Programming
  For Dummies
  0-7645-4997-9
- C For Dummies
  0-7645-7068-4
- Firewalls For Dummies
  0-7645-4048-3
- Home Networking For Dummies
  0-7645-42796

- Network Security For Dummies
  0-7645-1679-5
- Networking For Dummies
  0-7645-1677-9
- TCP/IP For Dummies
  0-7645-1760-0
- VBA For Dummies
  0-7645-3989-2
- Wireless All In-One Desk Referen
  For Dummies
  0-7645-7496-5
- Wireless Home Networking
  For Dummies
  0-7645-3910-8

EALTH & SELF-HELP

7645-6820-5 *†   0-7645-2566-2

Also available:

- Alzheimer's For Dummies
  0-7645-3899-3
- Asthma For Dummies
  0-7645-4233-8
- Controlling Cholesterol For Dummies
  0-7645-5440-9
- Depression For Dummies
  0-7645-3900-0
- Dieting For Dummies
  0-7645-4149-8
- Fertility For Dummies
  0-7645-2549-2

- Fibromyalgia For Dummies
  0-7645-5441-7
- Improving Your Memory For Dummies
  0-7645-5435-2
- Pregnancy For Dummies †
  0-7645-4483-7
- Quitting Smoking For Dummies
  0-7645-2629-4
- Relationships For Dummies
  0-7645-5384-4
- Thyroid For Dummies
  0-7645-5385-2

DUCATION, HISTORY, REFERENCE & TEST PREPARATION

0-7645-5194-9   0-7645-4186-2

Also available:

- Algebra For Dummies
  0-7645-5325-9
- British History For Dummies
  0-7645-7021-8
- Calculus For Dummies
  0-7645-2498-4
- English Grammar For Dummies
  0-7645-5322-4
- Forensics For Dummies
  0-7645-5580-4
- The GMAT For Dummies
  0-7645-5251-1
- Inglés Para Dummies
  0-7645-5427-1

- Italian For Dummies
  0-7645-5196-5
- Latin For Dummies
  0-7645-5431-X
- Lewis & Clark For Dummies
  0-7645-2545-X
- Research Papers For Dummies
  0-7645-5426-3
- The SAT I For Dummies
  0-7645-7193-1
- Science Fair Projects For Dummies
  0-7645-5460-3
- U.S. History For Dummies
  0-7645-5249-X

Get smart @ dummies.com®

- **Find a full list of Dummies titles**
- **Look into loads of FREE on-site articles**
- **Sign up for FREE eTips e-mailed to you weekly**
- **See what other products carry the Dummies name**
- **Shop directly from the Dummies bookstore**
- **Enter to win new prizes every month!**

† Separate Canadian edition also available
* Separate U.K. edition also available

Available wherever books are sold. For more information or to order direct: U.S. customers visit www.dummies.com or call 1-877-762-2974.
U.K. customers visit www.wileyeurope.com or call 0800 243407. Canadian customers visit www.wiley.ca or call 1-800-567-4797.

Do More with Dummies
Products for the Rest of Us!

From hobbies to health,
discover a wide
variety of fun products

DVDs/Videos • Music CDs • Games
Consumer Electronics • Software
Craft Kits • Culinary Kits • and More!

Check out the Dummies Specialty Shop at
www.dummies.com for more information!